In this volume leading scholars look at the heritage and impact of the important work done by the Stockholm School from the 1920s to the present. The first part of *The Stockholm School of Economics Revisited* covers the early years and is followed by an extensive review of the approaches to economics adopted by the school. A number of contributors investigate the Stockholm School's relation to and impact on their own work, the work of other economists, and the approaches pursued by other schools. A final roundtable discussion delves into the question "What remains of the Stockholm School?" A readable collection for anyone interested in economic history, history of economic thought, or the ideas lying behind Swedish economic policy.

Historical Perspectives on Modern Economics

The Stockholm School
of Economics Revisited

Historical Perspectives on Modern Economics

General Editor: Professor Craufurd D. Goodwin, Duke University

This series contains original works that challenge and enlighten historians of economics. For the profession as a whole it promotes better understanding of the origin and content of modern economics.

Other books in the series
William J. Barber: *From new era to New Deal: Herbert Hoover, the economists, and American economic policy, 1921–1933*
Kim, Kyun: *Equilibrium business cycle theory in historical perspective*
Gerard M. Koot: *English historical economics, 1870–1926: The rise of economic history and neomercantilism*
Don Lavoie: *Rivalry and central planning: The Socialist calculation debate reconsidered*
Takashi Negishi: *Economic theories in a non-Walrasian tradition*
E. Roy Weintraub: *General equilibrium analysis: Studies in appraisal*

The Stockholm School
of Economics Revisited

Edited by
Lars Jonung
Handelshögskolan i Stockholm

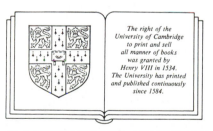

The right of the
University of Cambridge
to print and sell
all manner of books
was granted by
Henry VIII in 1534.
The University has printed
and published continuously
since 1584.

CAMBRIDGE UNIVERSITY PRESS
Cambridge
New York   Port Chester
Melbourne   Sydney

Published by the Press Syndicate of the University of Cambridge
The Pitt Building, Trumpington Street, Cambridge CB2 1RP
40 West 20th Street, New York, NY 10011, USA
10 Stamford Road, Oakleigh, Melbourne 3166, Australia

First published 1991

Printed in the United States of America

Library of Congress Cataloging-in-Publication Data

The Stockholm School of Economics Revisited / edited by Lars Jonung.
     p.   cm. – (Historical perspectives on modern economics)
  Papers from a conference held Aug. 31–Sept. 1, 1987 outside
Stockholm, Sweden.
  Includes bibliographical references.
  ISBN 0-521-39127-X (hardcover)
   1. Economics – Sweden – History – Congresses. 2. Economics – Study
and teaching (Higher) – Sweden – History – Congresses.
3. Handelshögskolan i Stockholm – History – Congresses. I. Jonung,
Lars. II. Series.
HB116.5.A2S76   1991
330.15 – dc20   90-38355
                                                                  CIP

British Library Cataloguing in Publication available

ISBN 0–521–39127–X   hardback

To the memory of
ERIK LUNDBERG

Contents

Preface

"1937 was a great year for Swedish economics. Erik Lundberg defended his dissertation and Bertil Ohlin made the Stockholm School or Swedish School of economics of the 1930s known internationally through two articles in *Economic Journal*." This view was put to me by Kumara Velupillai in the fall of 1986. He continued along the following lines: "The anniversary is coming up next year. Why don't you Swedes celebrate the Stockholm School?" That question was the beginning of this volume.

Actually, Swedes had not celebrated the Swedish School before. There had been no "20, 25, 30, or 40 years after." The Swedish economics profession has paid surprisingly little attention to its roots. The Stockholm School was no exception to this neglect, although it marks the heyday of Swedish economics. Neither before nor since did the work of Swedish economists attract such international interest. Moreover, there were still a few survivors and close followers of the School who most likely had interesting stories to tell.

The grand old man of Swedish economics, Erik Lundberg, gave me his moral support to organize a conference on "The Stockholm School After 50 Years." The Marianne and Marcus Wallenberg Foundation generously provided the financial support for the conference that took place at Grand Hotel Saltsjöbaden outside Stockholm on August 31–September 1, 1987.

Erik Lundberg was full of ideas and in spite of his failing health was always ready to comment in his frank and ironic way on my suggestions. The conference was intended to celebrate Erik Lundberg's role as the leading surviving member of the School as well. Erik, however, firmly insisted that the conference should focus on the whole School, downplaying his own contributions.

Erik was surprised that I was interested in organizing a conference on the Stockholm School. I did not come from Stockholm but from Lund,

a place of learning not particularly impressed by the Stockholm economists as a consequence of Johan Åkerman's influence (see the contribution by Jan Petersson), although both Erik Lindahl and Bertil Ohlin
began their studies of economics in Lund and Knut Wicksell, the intellectual father of the Stockholm School, was professor in Lund from
1901 to 1916.

Moreover Erik and I had been debating the role of monetary and fiscal factors in Swedish macroeconomic developments in the 1930s. Erik
held a strongly Stockholm School or Keynesian view, a belief shaped by
his experience during the 1930s. I had argued, contrary to Erik's view,
that monetary factors and monetary policy played a much more important role than envisaged by the fiscal activists of the Stockholm School.
Erik gave me a free hand on whom to invite as long as I did not turn to
any extreme monetarists.

I am indebted to many for their help and support. Axel Leijonhufvud
was my generous host in Los Angeles for two days in May 1987, discussing in detail the organization of the conference. Kumara Velupillai
continued to give me valuable advice. He and Axel took a very active
part in bringing Sir John Hicks to Stockholm. Björn Hansson,
Rolf G. H. Henriksson, Don Patinkin, and many others helped me with
the program. The practical arrangements were skillfully handled by Klas
Fregert, who served as conference secretary and also prepared the dra-
matis personae and the bibliography on the Stockholm School in this
volume.

The Skandinaviska Enskilda Banken showed a great interest in the
arrangements and treated the conference participants to a splendid dinner in Erik Lundberg's honor, celebrating his long service as a scientific
advisor to the Bank. Olle Lindgren was most helpful in having Erik
Lundberg's contribution translated and made available for the conference. (This contribution will appear in the companion volume *The
Stockholm School of Economics Remembered.*)

In the long process of editing the conference papers, I was advised and
helped by Hans Brems, Björn Hansson, Mats Persson, Claes-Henric
Siven, Björn Thalberg, Eskil Wadensjö, Lars Werin, and many others.
Axel Leijonhufvud gave me valuable guidance concerning the style and
contents of the introduction. Alan Harkess improved the English of all
contributions written by non-English authors with great patience and
skill. I am also indebted to the Department of Economics at the University of Lund and at the Stockholm School of Economics for generous
support. The Bertil Ohlin fund of the Royal Academy gave financial
support for the publication of this volume, which was given the title *The
Stockholm School of Economics Revisited.*

As Erik Lundberg suffered from terminal cancer, he could not attend the conference. He sent a few words of welcome to the participants in the spirit typical of him:

> I am surprised and very much impressed by the number and quality of the papers presented. Do remember, however, that there is also a need for not so good papers – even in some sense bad papers – in order to realize the outstanding qualities of the really good ones. We need valleys in order to perceive mountains. The organization committee has even succeeded – as far as I can judge – in fulfilling this aim. There are therefore also on this score the best preconditions for a successful conference.

As his home was a couple of minutes' walk from the Saltsjöbaden conference site, Erik Lundberg was able to see some of his old friends attending the conference briefly in his home. Shortly after the conference, Erik told a visiting fellow economist: "I am so happy. I have heard my obituary and now I can die." He passed away on September 15, 1987, less than three weeks after the conference.

Erik was both proud of being regarded as a member of the Stockholm School and critical of the idea of such a school. He once told me, probably jokingly – but you could never tell – that there had never been a Stockholm School and that he suspected that the conference would reveal this fact. I insisted that he was wrong and that the conference would clearly prove that there was such a school and that it was worthy of a conference. It is my hope that this volume supports my prediction *ex post*.

Lund and Stockholm
December 1989

Lars Jonung

Contributors

Jens Christopher Andvig
Norwegian Institute of International
  Affairs
Oslo, Norway

William J. Baumol
Princeton University
Princeton, New Jersey, and
New York University
New York, New York, USA

Claes Berg
Department of Economics
University of Stockholm
Stockholm, Sweden

Hans Brems
University of Illinois at Urbana-
  Champaign
Urbana, Illinois, USA

Benny Carlson
Department of Economic History
University of Lund
Lund, Sweden

Gustav Cederwall
(former Governor of a Province)
Stockholm, Sweden

Robert Clower
Department of Economics
University of South Carolina
Columbia, South Carolina, USA

Earlene Craver
Department of Economics,
University of California, Los Angeles
Los Angeles, California, USA

Karl O. Faxén
Docent, SAF,
Stockholm, Sweden

Klas Fregert
Department of Economics
University of Lund
Lund, Sweden

Bo Gustafsson
Department of Economic History
University of Uppsala
Uppsala, Sweden

Björn Hansson,
Department of Economics
University of Lund
Lund, Sweden

Rolf G. H. Henriksson
Department of Economics
University of Stockholm
Stockholm, Sweden

Sir John Hicks
(deceased in May 1989)
formerly of All Souls College
Oxford, Great Britain

Lars Jonung
Department of Economics
Stockholm School of Economics
Stockholm, Sweden

David Laidler
Department of Economics
University of Western Ontario
London, Ontario, Canada

Axel Leijonhufvud
Department of Economics
University of California, Los Angeles
Los Angeles, California, USA

Assar Lindbeck
Institute for International Economic
  Studies
University of Stockholm
Stockholm, Sweden

Bengt Metelius
Docent
formerly at University of Stockholm
Stockholm, Sweden

Johan Myhrman
Department of Economics
Stockholm School of Economics
Stockholm, Sweden

Don Patinkin
The Hebrew University of Jerusalem
Jerusalem, Israel

Mats Persson
Institute for International Economic
  Studies
University of Stockholm
Stockholm, Sweden

Jan Petersson
Department of Social Work
University of Lund
Lund, Sweden

Paul A. Samuelson
Department of Economics
Massachusetts Institute of
  Technology
Cambridge, Massachusetts, USA

Nadim Shehadi
Centre for Lebanese Studies
Oxford, Great Britain

Claes-Henric Siven
Department of Economics
University of Stockholm
Stockholm, Sweden

Lars E. O. Svensson
Institute for International Economic
  Studies
University of Stockholm
Stockholm, Sweden

Otto Steiger
Department of Economics
University of Bremen
Bremen, Germany

Björn Thalberg
Department of Economics
University of Lund
Lund, Sweden

Brinley Thomas
Department of Economics
University of California
Berkeley, California, USA

Kumaraswamy Velupillai
Department of Economics
University of Copenhagen
Copenhagen, Denmark

Eskil Wadensjö
SOFI, University of Stockholm
Stockholm, Sweden

Lars Werin
Department of Economics
University of Stockholm
Stockholm, Sweden

Dramatis personae at the end of 1937

KLAS FREGERT

In alphabetical order. Numbers in brackets refer to biographical sources listed in the References (with author of article in parentheses in some cases).

Gustaf Johan *Åkerman.* Age 51. From 1931 Professor of economics and sociology at the University of Gothenburg. Received his Ph.D. at the faculty of law at the University of Lund in 1923 for the dissertation *Realkapital und Kapitalzins* (I–II, 1923–1924), which won high acclaim from Knut Wicksell. Published 1931 *Om den industriella rationaliseringen och dess verkningar särskilt beträffande arbetarsysselsättningen* (On industrial rationalization and its effects especially on labor employment) on behalf of the Committee on Unemployment. [1 (K. Velupillai), 3]

Johan Henrik *Åkerman.* Age 49. Associate Professor of economics at the University of Lund since 1932. Brother of Gustaf Åkerman. Received his Ph.D. in economics at the University of Lund in 1928 with the dissertation *Om det ekonomiska livets rytmik* (On the rythm of economic life), an econometric study of the relation between seasonal, business cycle, and secular changes. Stressed the institutional and political factors governing economic change. Wrote extensively on methodology. Critical of the Stockholm School. [1 (K. Velupillai), 3]

Gösta Adolfsson *Bagge.* Age 55. From 1921 Professor at the University of Stockholm in economics and social policy. Director of The Institute for Social Sciences at the University of Stockholm, which he founded 1920. Leader of the Conservative party since 1935. Received his Ph.D. in 1917 for his dissertation *Arbetslönens reglering genom sammanslutningar* (Wage determination through organizations). Editor of the conservative journal *Svensk Tidskrift* (1911–18 coeditor with Eli Hecksher). Member of the Committee on Unemployment (Arbetslöshetskommissionen) for which he wrote the report *Orsaker till arbetslöshet* (Causes of unemployment), 1931. Chief author of *Wages in Sweden 1860–1930* (1936), with Erik Lundberg and Ingvar Svennilson as coauthors. [3, 4]

xvii

Gustav Karl *Cassel.* Age 71. Professor Emeritus at the University of Stockholm since 1933. Received his Ph.D. degree in mathematics in 1895 in Uppsala. Made extended trips to Germany and Great Britain 1898–1902 to study economics. Published an article in 1899, "Grundrisse einer elementaren Preislehre," that contained many of the elements in his synthesis of general equilibrium theory, later presented in his textbook *Theoretische Socialökonomie* (finished 1914, published 1918, English edition 1923, Japanese edition 1926, French edition 1927, Swedish edition 1934). Professor of economics in 1904 at the University of Stockholm. Served as an expert on many government committees on banking, taxation, government budget systems, and railway rates. Became internationally known as a leading expert on monetary relations. Published and lectured widely on monetary issues from the beginning of World War I, both in Sweden and internationally. Presented the purchasing power parity theory of exchange rates in articles in *Economic Journal* 1916–18. Influential in Sweden through his columns in *Svenska Dagbladet,* which he started to write 1897; he had published about 1,300 columns by 1937. The columns became progressively more critical of state interventionism, the welfare state, and trade unions. Considered an inspiring teacher by his pupils – among them Bertil Ohlin and Gunnar Myrdal, although they parted from him on both theoretical and political grounds. [1 (B. Gustafsson), 2 (B. Ohlin)]

David Davidson. Age 83. Professor Emeritus at the University of Uppsala. Studied law at the University of Uppsala and received his Ph.D. in 1878. Associate Professor in financial law (*finansrätt*) 1879 and Professor 1889. Editor of *Ekonomisk Tidskrift,* which he founded in 1899. Grand old man of Swedish economics, influenced by the classical English economists, especially Ricardo. Published all of his work in Swedish; mainly on taxation and monetary matters. Served as a member on various government committees. Advocated that prices move in inverse proportion to productivity, an idea later taken up by Erik Lindahl, though from a different perspective. [1 (C. G. Uhr), 2 (B. Ohlin)]

Ragnar Anton Kittil *Frisch.* Age 42. Professor of economics at the University of Oslo. Received his Ph.D. degree there in 1926 in mathematical statistics. Associate Professor 1926 and Professor 1931. Cofounder of the Econometric Society and chief editor of *Econometrica* since 1933. Head of the newly started Institute of Economics in Oslo since 1932. Worked in many areas of economics. Proponent of the use of mathematics and statistics in economics. Presented one of the first dynamic macromodels, where he introduced the distinction macro(dynamics)/micro(dynamics) (See his Propagation problems and impulse problems in dynamic economics (1933)). [1 (P. Nörregaard Rasmussen)]

Dag Hjalmar Agne Carl *Hammarskjöld.* Age 32. Under Secretary of the Treasury since 1936 in the Social Democratic government that came to power in 1933. Advisor to the Riksbank since 1935. Received his Ph.D. degree in economics in 1934 at the University of Stockholm for the 1933 dissertation *Konjunkturspridningen* (The dispersion of the business cycle), which was published as a report to the Committee on Unemployment where he was the secretary

1932–34 (assistant secretary 1928–32). The dissertation contained sequence analyses of the business cycle. [1 (B. Hansson), 2]

Eli Filip *Heckscher.* Age 58. Professor at Handelshögskolan where he was appointed to a personal research chair in economic history in 1929. Received his Ph.D. in economics at the University of Uppsala in 1907 for a dissertation on the importance of railways for the economic development of Sweden. Professor of economics (with statistics) at the Stockholm School of Economics and Business Administration in 1909. Member of several government committees, among them the first Committee on Unemployment (1926–8). Pioneer in the use of economic theory and statistics in the study of economic history; his most well known work is *Merkantilismen* (1931, English edition 1935). Gave the impetus to the Heckscher-Ohlin theorem, later formulated by Ohlin. Politically, initially a conservative but changed his outlook to liberalism (European style) during World War I. Wrote numerous articles in *Dagens Nyheter* against state interventionism and stressed the importance of monetary stability. [1 (C. G. Uhr), 2 (B. Ohlin)]

Alf Hilding *Johansson.* Age 36. Associate Professor at the University of Stockholm since 1934. Received his Ph.D. in 1934 at the University of Stockholm for the dissertation *Löneutvecklingen och arbetslösheten* (Wage movements and unemployment), published as a report to the Committee on Unemployment. Principal teacher of economics at Stockholms Högskola. Close connections with the labor movement. [3]

Erik Robert *Lindahl.* Age 46. Professor at the University of Gothenburg. Received his Ph.D. at the faculty of law at the University of Lund in 1919 with the dissertation *Die Gerechtigkeit der Besteuerung* (part of it translated in *Classics in Public Finance,* Musgrave and Peacock, eds., 1958). Various teaching positions until he received a full professorship at the University of Gothenburg in 1932. [His career was not "comet-like" (Lundberg) and he was advised by Heckscher to become a lawyer.] Published in the areas of public finance, monetary theory, price theory, and empirical national income research (*National Income of Sweden,* 1936). Member of government committees on taxation. Adviser to the Riksbank in 1931 and later to the Treasury (1937) on the design of countercyclical policy, as well as an adviser to the League of Nations (1936). Formulated the idea of intertemporal equilibrium and later the idea of temporary equilibrium, which stressed the sequential character of an economy; a cornerstone in the Stockholm School analysis. These ideas were developed in the context of monetary theory and policy. Proposed the inverse productivity rule of the price level for monetary policy, as Davidson had done earlier, but on stabilization grounds. He also stressed the role of expectations, announcements, and credibility in the conduct of monetary policy. For these reasons he advocated an independent central bank, free of political pressures. Influenced Myrdal and Ohlin as well as being influenced by them, though the latter were occasionally his rivals. [1 (O. Steiger), 2 (E. Lundberg)]

Erik Filip *Lundberg.* Age 30. Director of the newly started National Institute of Economic Research (Konjunkturinstitutet). Studied at American universities as Rockefeller fellow 1931–3. Worked at the Riksbank (1934–5, and as adviser to Iceland's commission for the planned economy 1935. Ph.D. in 1937 in economics at the University of Stockholm with the dissertation *Studies in the Theory of Economic Expansion* where he presented numerical sequences of multiplier-accelerator schemes as well as inventory cycles. Contributor to the study *Wages in Sweden 1860–1930* (1936), together with Bagge and Svennilson. [1 (A. Lindbeck), 3]

Gunnar Karl *Myrdal.* Age 39. Professor of economics at the University of Stockholm on Cassel's chair since 1933. Received a Dr. of Law in 1927 at the University of Stockholm under Cassel with the dissertation *Prisbildningsproblemet och föränderligheten* (The problem of price formation and change) where he explicitly considered expectations and uncertainty. These ideas were expanded into a macroeconomic context in his article *Der Gleichgewichtsbegriff als Instrument der geldtheoretischen Analyse* (expanded into a book in 1939, *Monetary Equilibrium*) where he introduced the concepts of *ex ante* and *ex post*. Professor at Institut Universitaire des Hautes Etudes Internationales in Geneva 1931–3. Published in 1934 *Finanspolitikens ekonomiska verkningar* (The economic effects of fiscal policy) as an expert to the Committee on Unemployment where he advocated balancing the budget over the business cycle, not year by year, as a stabilization device. Social Democratic member of Parliament since 1935. Published books and articles on economic and social policy aimed at the general public with strong interventionist tendencies. [1 (P. Streeten), 3]

Bertil Gotthard *Ohlin.* Age 38. Professor of economics at the Stockholm School of Economics and Business Administration since 1929. Leader of the Liberal Party's youth organization (Folkpartiet) since 1934. Some of his university studies were conducted abroad at Grenoble, Oxford, and Harvard. Received his Ph.D. under Cassel at the University of Stockholm in 1924 with *Handelns teori* (The theory of trade), published in an extended English version in 1933 as *International and Interregional Trade,* where he set out the Hecksher-Ohlin theorem (a term introduced by Stolper and Samuelson, 1941). Professor at the University of Copenhagen 1924 (in competition with Erik Lindahl). Presented a macroeconomic sequence analysis with Keynesian features (the multiplier) as well as the accelerator in a report published by the Committee on Unemployment in 1934, *Penningpolitik, offentliga arbeten, subventioner och tullar som medel mot arbetslösheten. Bidrag till expansionens teori* (Monetary policy, public works, subsidies and tariffs as means against unemployment. Contributions to the theory of expansion). Advocated deficit-financed public investment projects to combat unemployment, selected not to crowd out private investment. These ideas were particularly inspired by Lindahl and Myrdal; in two articles in *Economic Journal* (1937), he dubbed their thinking "the Stockholm School of economics," Also active in the daily press as a "social liberal" where he accepted stabilization policy within the confines of the market economy. Internationally recognized in his exchange with Keynes on the transfer problem in 1929. [1 (H. Brems), 3]

Ingvar Sven *Svennilson.* Age 29. Doctoral student at the University of Stockholm working on his thesis *Ekonomisk planering.* Collaborator with Gösta Bagge and Erik Lundberg on *Wages in Sweden 1860–1936* (1936) at the Institute for Social Sciences. [1 (B. Hansson), 3]

Ernst Johannes *Wigforss.* Age 56. Secretary of the Treasury in the Social Democratic government; a position he had held 1925–6, 1932–June 1936, and then from September 1936. Leading socialist ideologue with Fabian leanings. Proponent of countercyclical fiscal policy inspired by the English Liberals and the younger generation of Swedish economists. Avid student of economics. Ph.D. in 1914 in Nordic languages at the University of Lund with a dissertation on the dialects of Halland (province in Southern Sweden). Social Democratic member of parliament since 1919. [3]

References

1 *The New Palgrave: A Dictionary of Economics.* London: The Macmillan Press Limited, 1987.
2 *Svenskt biografiskt lexikon.* Stockholm: Albert Bonniers förlag, 1918–87. Various volumes.
3 *Svenska män och kvinnor. Biografisk uppslagsbok.* Stockholm: Albert Bonniers förlag, 1942–55. Various volumes.
4 *Svensk uppslagsbok.* Second revised edition. Malmö: Förlagshuset Norden AB, 1947–55.

Introduction and summary

LARS JONUNG

1   The foundations of Swedish economics

Sweden has produced two generations of outstanding economists. The first generation, which included David Davidson, Knut Wicksell, Gustav Cassel, and Eli Heckscher, were the founders of economics as an independent academic discipline in Sweden.[1] These men made economics a well-known and respected subject in the eyes of the public, thus paving the way for the second generation that emerged in the 1920s and 1930s. This second generation attracted worldwide attention and became known as the Stockholm School.

Davidson (1854–1942) was appointed professor at Uppsala in 1889, a chair that he held until 1921. In 1899 he founded *Ekonomisk Tidskrift,* the first scientific journal in economics in Sweden, and remained its sole editor until 1939 when he retired at the age of eighty-five. Under Davidson's editorship, *Ekonomisk Tidskrift* became established as an important forum for the emerging economics profession, with Wicksell, Cassel, and Heckscher as early major contributors. Here Davidson himself published a large number of articles and comments on current economic events, particularly dealing with monetary issues and problems of taxation.

In the late 1870s a young man presented a public talk in Uppsala, in which he argued that the major social ills in Swedish society were due to overpopulation. His message immediately became a source of immense public debate and criticism. One of his critics was David Davidson, who suggested that the speaker, Knut Wicksell (1851–1926), lacked a knowledge of economics. Inspired by this critique, driven by a strong desire to improve social conditions, supported by generous grants, and determinedly helped by the woman with whom he had entered a contract of cohabitation, Knut Wicksell eventually started to study economics.

1

In the 1890s he published a number of books, *Über Wert, Kapital und Rente, Finanztheoretische Untersuchungen,* and *Geldzins und Güterpreise* – a remarkable achievement considering his age and late entry into the field. In 1901 he managed to obtain a temporary position as Professor of Economics at the University of Lund, and in 1904 he was appointed full professor in spite of strong resistance from conservative groups. At roughly the same time he got his permanent chair, Wicksell summarized his work in brilliant fashion in the two volumes of his *Lectures.*

Knut Wicksell was competing for the chair in Lund in 1901 with a young economist who had a degree in mathematics, Gustav Cassel (1866–1944). Around the turn of the century Cassel had published only a few articles in *Zeitschrift für die Gesamte Staatswissenschaft* and a book in English, *The Nature and Necessity of Interest.* He became the first Professor of Economics in 1904 at the Stockholms Högskola, which was transformed into the University of Stockholm in 1960. His major work was *Theoretische Sozialökonomie* written prior to World War I but not published until 1918 in German, in 1923 in English, and later in various translations. In the 1910s and 1920s he turned to monetary issues and became a leading international authority on monetary economics, perhaps the best-known economist on the international scene in the 1920s.

In 1909 a young *docent* in history and former assistant to Gustav Cassell, Eli Heckscher (1879–1952), was appointed to the chair in economics at the newly founded Handelshögskolan in Stockholm. Although he was trained as an historian, after his appointment he turned to the study of economics, in particular to the work of English economists, and acquired a thorough knowledge of economics. He founded the subject of economic history in Sweden, becoming the first holder of a chair in this discipline in 1929. He is best known for his monumental work on the mercantilist system, and his contribution to the theory of international trade, "Utrikeshandelns verkan på inkomstfördelningen," published in *Ekonomisk Tidskrift* in 1919, is known today as the origin of the Heckscher-Ohlin theorem.

These four men – Cassel, Davidson, Heckscher, and Wicksell – established economics as an academic discipline in Sweden and raised Swedish economics to a high international standard. In 1910 they held four of the five chairs in economics that existed in the country at that time[2] (Table 1). Wicksell, Cassel, and Heckscher also exerted a profound influence on the public standing of their discipline. Davidson played a less prominent role in this context, although his position as founder and edi-

Table 1. *Holders of chairs in economics in Sweden, 1889–1950*

Uppsala		Lund	
1. 1889–1919	David Davidson	1901–16	Knut Wicksell
1921–41	Fritz Brock	1919–39	Emil Sommarin
1942–	Erik Lindahl	1939–42	Erik Lindahl
2. 1948–	Tord Palander	1943–	Johan Åkerman

Gothenburg		Stockholm	
University of Gothenburg		University of Stockholm	
1903–29	Gustaf Steffen	1. 1904–33	Gustav Cassel
1931–	Gustav Åkerman	1934–50	Gunnar Myrdal
		2. 1921–49	Gösta Bagge
Handelshögskolan		1949–51	Kjeld Philip
1923–32	Gunnar Silverstolpe	3. 1946–	Erik Lundberg
1932–39	Erik Lindahl	4. 1947–	Ingvar Svennilson
1941–48	Tord Palander		
1949–	Ivar Sundbom	Handelshögskolan	
		1. 1909–29	Eli Heckscher[a]
		1929–	Bertil Ohlin
		2. 1927–46	Sven Brisman
		1947–	Torsten Gårdlund
		3. 1940–	Arthur Montgomery

[a]Eli Heckscher obtained a personal chair in economic history in 1929.

tor of *Ekonomisk Tidskrift* and as a close friend to Knut Wicksell was important.

Wicksell, Cassel, and Heckscher had much in common besides being brilliant scholars. First of all, they were all active in public debate, serving as journalists-lecturers-debaters-opinion makers and as members of parliamentary committees. Wicksell had supported himself as a free-lance journalist early in his life, and after he got his chair, he continued to publish articles in newspapers all over Sweden (about 400 articles altogether). Cassel was also a prolific writer, publishing 1,506 articles in *Svenska Dagbladet* between 1903 and 1944, and Heckscher was the author of about 300 articles in *Dagens Nyheter*. All three also lectured in economics for public audiences. Wicksell generally spoke to labor groups, and Cassel talked to chambers of commerce and similar gatherings. Cassel was even assigned to teach economics at the Court.

Heckscher went on the air expounding economics in a series of radio programs, speaking with precision and clarity without manuscript. All contributed frequently to that Swedish institution, the SOU (*statens offentliga utredningar,* literally the government's public investigations); that is, they took part in a number of government committees on various issues, often concerning taxation and monetary policy but also on subjects like tariffs, regulation of monopolies and government agencies and so on. They also all served as advisors in various capacities in the Riksbank and to governments. In short, they made economics publicly known and respected. Rarely have economics and economists had stronger standing than in Sweden.

A second common feature of the three was their political outlook, all being liberals of various leanings. Wicksell was the radical liberal opposed to the church, royalty, marriage, and the military. He was always ready to shock the public with his stance on practically every public issue. Cassel started out as fairly radical but became more conservative with age. Heckscher moved in the opposite direction. In his early years, he was a strong conservative. After studying economics and acting as a government advisor, he experienced an economic-political crisis of faith during World War I, emerging as a staunch proponent of classical liberalism. None of them were influenced by Marxism, a view that they strongly rejected. Their liberal stand was formed during the era of the classical gold standard, ending in 1914. This was a period of rapid economic growth for Sweden, combined with considerable macroeconomic stability.

A third common feature was that they all remained in academia rather than entering political careers. None of them tried to become a member of the parliament or gain a political position in the government. Wicksell's radical views could not possibly have fit into party politics. The conservative party once asked Cassel to run for parliament, but the party leader would not agree to his demand that he be allowed to run as an independent and remain independent in the Riksdag.

In the 1920s and 1930s the second outstanding generation of economists gradually entered onto the stage. The best-known members of the new generation were Erik Lindahl, Erik Lundberg, Gunnar Myrdal, Bertil Ohlin, and Ingvar Svennilson. They were initially inspired by the older generation (Lindahl by Wicksell's work on public finance and monetary economics, Ohlin by Heckscher and Cassel, Myrdal by Cassel and by Wicksell's monetary studies), and they extended the research of their elders in important ways in the 1920s. Dag Hammarskjöld, Alf Johansson, and Karin Kock were also members of this generation.

The new generation had much in common with the old. They were

Per cent

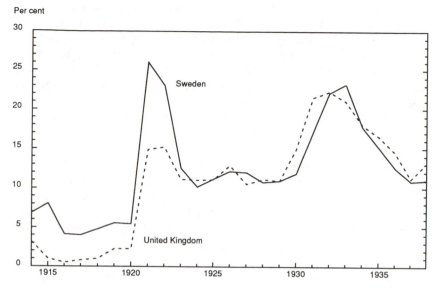

Figure 1. Unemployment in Sweden (solid line) and the United Kingdom (dashed line), 1914–38.

articulate and took part in public debate, writing in newspapers and journals and publishing popular books. Myrdal and Ohlin became even better known to the public than Wicksell and Cassel. Like their predecessors, they worked on government committees, and some of them became consultants to the Riksbank and the government.

However, on a number of issues they were opposed to the prevailing orthodoxy. First of all, the older generation was preoccupied by value theory and monetary economics in a traditional sense, that is, assuming full employment. The sharp rise in unemployment in Sweden in the 1920s and 1930s (see Figure 1) became the major challenge for the younger economists. Believing that the old theories did not provide an answer, they developed new theories to account for unemployment and to explain business cycles in the 1930s. Later Lindahl introduced the term macroeconomics for their field of study.

A second difference was that the new generation favored state intervention and active countercyclical policies and emphasized fiscal measures, whereas the older generation saw price stabilization as the main goal of monetary policy. Ohlin suggested in 1931 that the budget should not be balanced on an annual basis but over the business cycle. At an early stage he proposed that the level of employment should be stabilized. Myrdal contributed a report to the 1933 budget presented by the new Social Democratic government that had come to power in 1932, providing a theoretical rationale for an active countercyclical fiscal policy. In essence, the new generation was proposing Keynesian policies before Keynes and "functional finance" before Lerner. It displayed a leftist leaning in its political outlook compared to the older generation, and some of the young economists like Myrdal and Kock became Social Democrats in the 1930s.

The older and younger generations clashed in the 1930s. Cassel and Heckscher remained extremely critical of the new economics.[3] For various reasons they rejected the new theories as well as the policy conclusions associated with these theories, stemming domestically from the work of the younger economists and internationally from Keynes's *General Theory*. Cassel argued that the Great Depression of the 1930s was due to restrictive American monetary policy, which should be counteracted by expansionary monetary measures, not by fiscal measures and government intervention.[4] Heckscher was of the opinion that once the principle of the balanced budget had been rejected, governments would underbalance the budget during recessions but be unwilling or unable to overbalance it during booms. Heckscher and Cassel were strongly opposed to the central planning and socialism that attracted the younger economists, in particular Myrdal. The divergent views between the older and younger generations developed into a rift that was never bridged.

Another difference concerned political involvement. The new generation of economists became more actively engaged in party politics and in the conduct of economic policies, whereas the older generation had generally refrained from supporting any specific party. Myrdal became a member of the Social Democratic party and later of parliament and eventually of the cabinet. Ohlin was head of the youth organization of the Liberal Party and was elected to parliament in the 1930s, emerging as party leader in the 1940s, and for a short time was a member of the cabinet. Lundberg was appointed as the first head of the Konjunkturinstitut in 1937 and remained in close contact with policymakers during the 1940s and 1950s. Dag Hammarskjöld started to work in the Riksbank and became under-secretary in the ministry of finance, chairman of the board of the Riksbank, member of the cabinet, and secretary general of the United Nations in the 1950s.[5] Karin Kock, who worked with Myrdal on Sweden's monetary policy in the early 1930s, became the first woman cabinet member in the late 1940s.

After World War II the new generation's views on economic policies – later combined with the import of Keynesian doctrines – dominated Swedish economic research and economic policy. Their approach became an important element of the Swedish model, stressing full employment and a highly active role for the government in economic affairs.[6]

There was initially no name for this younger generation of economists. In response to the publication of the *General Theory*, Bertil Ohlin published two articles in *Economic Journal* in 1937 introducing the Stockholm School to an international audience and arguing that the Swedes had developed ideas similar to those of Keynes at an earlier stage. The term Stockholm or Swedish School quickly became accepted, although Ohlin's colleagues in Sweden were a bit perplexed; they had not viewed themselves as members of any school, in the case of Gunnar Myrdal not of the same school as Bertil Ohlin at least.[7]

In the late 1930s, the Stockholm School was regarded as a promising approach to macroeconomics, and it was considered a serious challenge to the Keynesian approach before the complete success of the latter after World War II. The Stockholm School reached fifty years of age in 1987. To celebrate this anniversary, a two-day conference was arranged in Saltsjöbaden in early September 1987. The contributions of this conference are arranged here in three parts: the roots of the School, the approach of the School, and the impact of the School. The final part presents the round-table discussion that concluded the conference.[8]

2   The roots of the Stockholm School

The roots of the Stockholm School are primarily domestic ones. The School traces its evolution to three main sources. The first is the work in economics of the older generation, in particular the monetary economics of Knut Wicksell and the Walrasian price theory of Gustav Cassel. Wicksell's cumulative process and the dynamic approach it represented served as a major source of inspiration for the younger generation, in particular for Gunnar Myrdal, Erik Lindahl, and Bertil Ohlin. The second source was the huge national income project organized by Gösta Bagge (generously financed by the Rockefeller Foundation for more than a decade), and involving Erik Lindahl, Erik Lundberg, Karin Kock, Gunnar Myrdal, and others. At a very early stage their work gave Sweden a complete set of national income statistics. The third source was the Committee of Unemployment set up in 1927, which published its final report in 1935. Dag Hammarskjöld was one of the main secretaries, and Bertil Ohlin was an expert on the committee and was responsible for a major report.

The 1920s and 1930s provided an extremely fertile ground for research in economics in Sweden. The younger economists began their work with the advantage of being inspired by an older generation headed by well-established economists. They extended their work in the 1920s into the fields of public finance, monetary economics, international and interregional trade, expectations, and intertemporal pricing. In the late 1920s and early 1930s, the high and persistent rate of unemployment that arose after World War I was a problem of the utmost social importance that had to be resolved by new theories, and this problem became the major challenge for the younger economists. They were given ample opportunities to carry out research as members of various projects and committees. They had the attention of leading politicians and the public, and sometimes they worked in cooperation with policy makers and were actually able to see some of their proposals put into action.

The sources of the Stockholm School are considered in three contributions. In Chapter 1 Rolf Henriksson provides us with the history of the Political Economy Club during the years 1917–51. His account amounts to a short history of the School. The Club served as an important meeting place for economists in the Stockholm area. Here they discussed theoretical issues as well as current policy problems and met with invited foreign guests, the "high point in the history of the Club" being the talk by Keynes in 1936.

When Knut Wicksell retired in 1916 from his chair at the University of Lund in southern Sweden, he and Anna Bugge wanted to return to their beloved Stockholm. (This radical couple never felt completely at home in the small town of Lund and had most of their friends in Stockholm.) Inspired by a proposal from Anna, Eli Heckscher organized the Political Economy Club to serve as a meeting place for senior economists in Stockholm. In the years to come, it served largely as a graduate seminar. In the 1920s Knut Wicksell, David Davidson, Eli Heckscher, Gustav Åkerman, Erik Lindahl, and Bertil Ohlin were among the main speakers at Club meetings. Wicksell was an ardent attendant, debating in fifty-three of the fifty-six meetings prior to his death in 1926, passing on, according to Henriksson, "the oral tradition of Wicksell." However, the Club did not gather all economists. Cassel stayed away after 1919, Gösta Bagge was not a frequent visitor, and Bertil Ohlin was professor in Copenhagen from 1924 to 1929 before returning to Stockholm to the chair at the Handelshögskolan vacated by Eli Heckscher, who moved over to a personal chair in economic history.

The Club witnessed the ideological revolt of the young economists in 1928. Gunnar Myrdal, supported by Alf Johansson, attacked the liberal views of Eli Heckscher in a lecture on utilitarianism. The theoretical revolt was triggered a few years later at the onset of the depression of the 1930s. Following Sweden's departure from the gold standard in September 1931, at Heckscher's suggestion the economists were planning a stabilization program. The younger and older economists basically shared the same views. Nevertheless, Heckscher and Myrdal eventually published their own books. The probable explanation was that Heckscher found Myrdal leaning too far toward interventionism. Both books attracted considerable public interest. The younger group of economists had now begun to be drawn into policy debate and policy advice, a process that accelerated in the 1930s.

Under Ohlin's chairmanship in the 1930s, the Club meetings dealt with issues that arose as a result of theoretical work on unemployment and business cycles as well as with current topics. Practically all of the members of the Stockholm School appeared as principal speakers, among them Lundberg, Svennilson, Myrdal, Lindahl, Johansson, Hammarskjöld, and Ohlin. The Minister of Finance, Ernst Wigforss, and the Head of the Riksbank, Ivar Rooth, were also allowed to attend the Club. Ohlin made the Club a forum for invited foreign guests, including John Maynard Keynes, Oskar Morgenstern, Jan Tinbergen, and John and Ursula Hicks.

In Chapter 2 Earlene Craver tells the story of Gösta Bagge's efforts to launch a major research program in the social sciences in Stockholm. Several of the members of the Stockholm School worked within the national income project launched in the mid-1920s by Bagge, who was Professor of Economics and Social Policy at the University of Stockholm. This project, generously funded by the Laura Spelman Rockefeller Memorial during the years 1926–1940, should be viewed as one of the sources of the Stockholm School.

In the fall of 1924, Gösta Bagge arrived at the Rockefeller Foundation in New York proposing funding for social research at the School of Social Work that he had headed in Stockholm since 1917. He was fortunate. The Rockefeller Memorial was in the process of launching a major program of support for research in the social sciences in the United States and Europe. The London School of Economics became one of the major beneficiaries, and in due time, the Rockefeller foundation gave a five-year grant for a study of wages in Sweden. Gösta Bagge brought Erik Lindahl, Gunnar Myrdal, and Alf Johansson into the project. Later Erik Lundberg and Karin Kock also became involved in Bagge's program. Bagge, who was the first Swedish economist to study in the United States, was also instrumental in obtaining Rockefeller fellowships for Swedish social scientists. Gunnar and Alva Myrdal, Erik Lundberg, Sune Carlson, and Tord Palander studied in the United States in the interwar period, thereby exposing Swedish economics to American influences.

The whole project, which received its final grant in 1936, produced a number of monographs that were eventually published in the Stockholm Economic Studies series. Bagge met with a series of difficulties in completing the project, problems that he tried to hide from the Americans in order not to threaten the flow of funding. His main disappointment was Erik Lindahl, who was absorbed by theoretical issues and fell seriously behind schedule in delivering his work on the construction of national income data. Besides, Lindahl's divorce and remarriage upset the Victorian Bagge. After a few years, Bagge and Lindahl were not on speaking terms, and eventually Bagge had to dismiss him from the project. Myrdal too turned out to be attracted by other pursuits such as working on various reports for the government, drifting into public debate, and traveling to the United States.

How did the national income project influence Swedish economics? The project brought together a group of economists working on common problems and allowed them to study economics without experiencing financial pressure.[9] However, one cannot discern any major impact on the theoretical approach of the School. This may be partially explained by the rift that gradually developed between the young economists and Gösta Bagge. Bagge was an institutionalist, interested in micro-issues and active in the Conservative party. The young economists were skeptical of his approach, nicknaming it Baggology. Instead their more radical political outlook and the unemployment of the depression led them to an examination of theoretical issues in macroeconomics. The rich set of data on prices, wages, and incomes that was collected and constructed could have set them off also in other fruitful directions but did not.

Another undertaking that played a crucial role in forming the approach of the Stockholm School was the Committee on Unemployment, active in the period 1927–34. In Chapter 3 Eskil Wadensjö highlights the work of the economists within the Committee by examining its archives. It is quite surprising that this has not been done previously considering the central importance assigned the Committee in Swedish economy history and economic thought.

The Committee was set up in 1927 with Heckscher as the driving force. Its initial aim was to investigate the causes of the high and permanent unemployment of the 1920s (see Figure 1). Later, as the depression of the 1930s led to rising unemployment in Sweden, an examination of cyclical unemployment also became part of the investigation. The Committee was made up of six members including Gösta Bagge and Ernst Wigforss, secretaries, and various experts. Over the years a number of economists served as experts producing memoranda, some of them later published as supplements to the two final reports of the

Committee. The first report, dealing with the causes of permanent unemployment, was published in 1931, and the final one, dealing with measures against permanent as well as cyclical unemployment, was published in 1935.

Several prominent members of the Stockholm School were involved with the Committee: Dag Hammarskjöld served as secretary and was in charge of drafting the final report, Alf Johansson wrote one of the supplements, Erik Lindahl authored five memoranda, Karin Kock wrote one memorandum, Gunnar Myrdal wrote one memorandum and one supplement, Bertil Ohlin wrote five memoranda and one supplement, and Ingvar Svennilson was also among the experts. The Committee produced altogether about 140 memoranda. The memoranda and supplements by the experts and the secretaries were used in the preparation of the final reports. As a rule, these were prone to compromise, being more careful and balanced in their conclusions than the material from which they were drawn.

Wadensjö examines in detail the contributions of Ernst Wigforss and Bertil Ohlin. Wigforss, member of parliament for the Social Democratic party and a non-economist trained as a linguist, showed great interest in the work of the Committee. He produced three memoranda on unemployment and business cycle theories before he became Minister of Finance in 1932 and was responsible for the "crisis" program of 1933. He won the respect of the younger generation of economists while being the object of strong criticism by the older generation, that is, by Cassel and Heckscher.

Starting from Ohlin's work for the Committee, Wadensjö traces the development of Ohlin's views on stabilization policy: his support of public works early in 1930, his critical attitude towards the "Vienna School" (that is, the Austrian approach) as represented by the work of Johan Åkerman, his support for a norm of employment stabilization in 1932 (at a time when the majority of Swedish economists were proposing price level stabilization), and his early use of the multiplier to estimate the effects of public work programs. These last calculations met with harsh criticism from Hammarskjöld, which caused Ohlin to delete them in his supplement on monetary policy published in 1934.

The Committee became a central meeting place for economists and politicians interested in the causes and cures of unemployment. Here some of the most important contributions of the Stockholm School were drafted, scrutinized, and redrafted. The Committee worked in a quite scholarly manner, serving as an advanced workshop in macroeconomics. Once the Committee had been dissolved, the Stockholm economists were unable to find a suitable alternative forum but became absorbed in various government activities and dispersed throughout the academic landscape.

3   The approach of the Stockholm School

The Stockholm School did not coalesce around one commonly accepted model. The unifying feature was rather the study of change, that is, dynamic processes. The individual members of the School developed different approaches, starting with Myrdal's dissertation of 1927, *Prisbildningsproblemet och föränderligheten* (Price Formation in a Changing World), followed by contributions by Lindahl, Hammarskjöld, Johansson, Lundberg, and Svennilson. The Swedes wanted to replace prevaling timeless static equilibrium theory by introducing anticipations, risk, and uncertainty. From this followed the conceptual devices of the Stockholm School: plan, period, and expectations, and the key concepts *ex ante–ex post,* stressing the difference between expected and realized outcomes. Erik Lindahl also wanted to build macroeconomic theory on firm microeconomic foundations.

Struggling with these problems, they did not apply formal techniques but relied instead on verbal reasoning. Accordingly their analysis often became vague and unclear. Ohlin, Johansson, and Lundberg relied most strongly on "process" analysis or sequence analysis, a method that properly should be translated as the case-study approach. They also developed different constructions to analyze dynamics. Hence it is better to talk about the approach rather than the model of the Stockholm School.

The School is commonly associated with the development of macroeconomics because Ohlin, in his 1937 articles in *Economic Journal,* made the Swedish School internationally known as an alternative to Keynes's analysis in his *General Theory.* However, the Stockholm School began as an attempt to develop a dynamic microeconomic theory of individual firm behavior in the late 1920s prior to the *General Theory.* The microeconomics of the School and the discussion of the bridge between micro- and macroeconomics have been overshadowed by the "perennial" comparison between Keynesianism and the Stockholm School, the anticipations issue.[10] Besides, in the 1930s, the microeconomic contributions of the Swedes were available only in Swedish.

Eleven contributions examine and interpret the theoretical approach of the Stockholm School. In Chapter 4 Claes-Henric Siven traces the development of the microeconomics of the Stockholm School by examining Myrdal's and Svennilson's dissertations of 1927 and 1938, respectively, and then describes the bridge between microeconomics and macroeconomics that Erik Lindahl outlined. Myrdal set out to give Cassel's static price theory based on Walrasian general equilibrium a dynamic form by introducing uncertainty, risk, and anticipations and discussing intertemporal planning under uncertainty. Expected future events immediately influence the present behavior of individual firms. The adjustment will not be complete, however, as a result of inertia or "gaps" in the pricing of firms.[11] According to Myrdal, the difference between anticipated and realized outcomes forced firms to make new adjustments. However, he did not specify any explicit adjustment mechanism.

A decade later Svennilson extended the work of Myrdal in his dissertation *Ekonomisk planering* (Economic Planning). He made it both more consistent and formal, using a probability analysis of expectations, and worked out a number of intertemporal connections between short-run and long-run decisions. Svennilson's dissertation did not have an impact on the work of the Stockholm School, with the possible major exception of Bent Hansen's dissertation of 1951. According to Siven the reason may be that Svennilson's approach "amounted to a series of conceptual exercises" that did not give rise to any behavioral equations.

On the basis of the concept of plan-period-expectations, Erik Lindahl designed a research strategy for constructing macroeconomics on the foundations of the microeconomic theory of planning. However, he did not succeed for various reasons. He was unable to develop a systematic theory of how the disequilibrium created by the difference between *ex ante* and *ex post* outcomes caused revisions in the behavior of individual firms or households. Nor did he develop a theory of the interaction between decision units under such a disequilibrium. Although the Stockholm School stressed expectations, it did not construct a formal systematic model of expectations similar to present-day theories of adaptive and rational expectations. Rather, Lindahl held a vision of a bridge between micro- and macrotheory that was unmanageable by available mathematical and statistical techniques. This contributed to the gap between the microeconomics of the School and the macroeconomics based on the case-study approach that Ohlin and Lundberg adopted when analyzing macroeconomic processes.

Inspired by his teachers Lundberg and Svennilson, Karl-Olof Faxén developed the microeconomics of the Stockholm School in his dissertation *Monetary and Fiscal Policy under Uncertainty,* published in 1957. He analyzed stabilization policies under imperfect competition with reference to a game theoretic approach. Returning to this work thirty years later, in Chapter 5 Faxén wonders whether the sequence analysis of the School can be given a firm microeconomic foundation.

A main problem of the period-plan-expectations approach was to show how expectations about future developments as well as their revisions influence present behavior and decisions. The Swedes used three approaches according to Faxén. First, Ohlin simply relied on "verbal reasoning." Second, Lundberg worked with ad hoc reaction functions, although he did not believe them to be stable over time. He wanted to analyze a number of possible sequences deemed interesting, that is, fairly close to reality, while remaining skeptical of their predictive power. Third, Lindahl and Svennilson started from the assumption of optimizing behavior by individual households and firms. However, they failed to show how each decision unit revised its probability distributions pertaining to future states using new information emerging at the end of the period or how the individual decision units interacted. To remedy these shortcomings, Faxén applied the game theory of von Neumann and Morgenstern. Nash equilibria and adjustment paths with two players were studied in order to facilitate the analysis. Today, Faxén would rather have used less restrictive assumptions. Nevertheless, he is not optimistic about the prospect for using game theory to develop manageable dynamic models in the spirit of the Stockholm School since such models tend to give rise to extremely complicated structures.

In Chapter 6 Lars Werin stresses the distinction between the early microeconomic research and the later macroeconomic work of the Swedes. In his opinion one should speak of two separate Stockholm Schools. The first one developed price theory and general equilibrium analysis in the 1920s, the second one macroeconomics in the 1930s. Major attention has been paid to the second School while the first has generally been neglected, but Werin suggests strong reasons why the achievements of the first should be ranked higher than those of the second.

The first School started from the Walrasian system in its simplified Cassel version, extending it in three important ways. Ohlin included international and interregional trade in his dissertation of 1924, followed by his extensive monograph in English in 1933. Myrdal incorporated expectations and intertemporal allocation decisions in his dissertation of 1927, and Lindahl brought capital into a Walrasian framework in his long article of 1929, first available in English in 1939 in his *Studies*. Lindahl's dissertation of 1919 introduced public goods and taxation into price theory, albeit in a partial, not general, equilibrium setting. Furthermore, Lindahl's work on the aims and means of monetary policy published in 1924 and 1929 should be included in the work of the first School.

These accomplishments, achieved between 1919 and 1933, are viewed by Werin as belonging to the Walras-Arrow-Debreu tradition.

They extend the original Walras system to encompass international and interregional trade, expectations, intertemporal decisions, capital, taxes, and public expenditure. In retrospect, this Walrasian research program, inspired by Cassel rather than by Wicksell, had considerable impact. It also provided important stepping stones for the macroeconomics of the School for the simple reason that the very same Casselians of the 1920s turned to the study of unemployment in the 1930s and thus to dynamic macroeconomics as a result of the Great Depression. They all became prominent members of the second Stockholm School, deserting the Cassel heritage by adopting Wicksellian clothes.

Why has the brilliant work of the first School been assigned such a secondary role? Werin provides some tentative answers. A major reason is probably that the issue of unemployment and business cycles rose to the top of the research agenda in the 1930s and forced the Swedes to abandon the Cassel price system, which was basically a full employment model. Once work was under way on the new approaches, they had an interest in distinguishing them from previous work, disassociating themselves from the vestiges of the conservative Cassel. Most likely they also had political reasons for doing so. The young economists became more radical in the 1930s while Cassel and Heckscher stubbornly defended their orthodox approach to economics and politics.

Turning from the microeconomics to the macroeconomics of the Stockholm School, Erik Lundberg's dissertation *Studies in the Theory of Economic Expansion,* published in 1937, stands out as the main contribution to Stockholm sequence analysis. Lundberg constructed a number of illustrative numerical calculations to study macroeconomic processes step-by-step. These calculations did not result in analytical solutions since Lundberg wanted to study the process per se, rejecting the idea of an equilibrium towards which the economic system converged.

In Chapter 7 William Baumol examines Lundberg's approach to dynamics, emphasizing the difference between post–World War II business cycle theories based on equilibrium (linear) theory generating analytical solutions as opposed to Lundberg's experiments with various parameter values to construct different time paths. There is a trade-off between these two approaches in Baumol's opinion, that is, "between the abstraction . . . that the more formal procedures engender" and "the insights offered by the painstaking calculations that are vital for Lundberg's numerical time paths."

Starting from a general difference equation, Baumol presents the merits of the Lundbergian method, showing how it can be used to examine nonlinear models with the assistance of any personal computer – a technnology not available to Lundberg. Commonly, economists have been preoccupied with linear dynamic models because these give rise to manageable analytical solutions. However, the assumption of linearity may turn out to be a straitjacket, a disadvantage, when applied to phenomena that are not inherently linear in character.

In two recent major fields of research where the assumption of linearity is not fruitful, economists are now returning to techniques similar in spirit to that of Lundberg. The first field is the study of evolutionary processes where the equilibrium may change over time. Here the focus is on the process per se, not on the final solution – as in Lundberg's work. The second field is chaos theory. Baumol sets up a simple nonlinear model showing extreme sensitivity to minor changes in parameter values, arguing that the complexity of such models induces research along the lines developed by Lundberg, that is, the use of step-by-step techniques. Actually Baumol's calculations are similar to Lundberg's; they both show how small changes in initial conditions in a system that depends on parameters may create widely different time paths of the variable studied.

Joseph Schumpeter once argued that Erik Lundberg's thesis of 1937 displayed "the micro- and macrodynamic roots of current Keynesianism much better than Keynes did himself." Starting from this judgment, in Chapter 8 Claes Berg sets out to answer the question What is the unique message in Lundberg's *Studies* not found in Keynes's *General Theory?* Berg first traces Lundberg's inspiration to Wicksell, Hayek, and Keynes and to other Stockholm economists. In Chapter IX, the central chapter in the *Studies,* Lundberg considers five groups of case studies of sequence analysis, each case built upon its own assumptions. All runs are theoretical experiments with no attempt at a portrayal of actual events. The purpose of these sequential exercises is to examine whether an economic system as modeled during a period of expansion will continue on such a path or be halted and reversed by itself. Lundberg does not derive a general solution for these sequences, but is interested in the evolution over time of the economy, not in the characteristics of any final equilibrium or in the existence of such an equilibrium.

Berg uses a computer to recalculate in detail Lundberg's sequences. In this way, he is able to pursue Lundberg's work along its own lines and to reconsider Lundberg's conclusions, an exercise that has not been previously carried out. In the first of the five groups of sequences in Chapter IX, Lundberg's system of difference equations with constant investment represents, at the limit, the standard Keynesian multiplier. The second family of sequences dealing with investment in working capital illustrates the first numerical illustration of the multiplier-accelerator principle. In the third and fourth groups of sequences, investment in residential housing (fixed capital) and the role of a variable rate of interest are considered. Berg extends Lundberg's calculations and evaluates their strength and weaknesses. Finally, in Chapter IX, Lundberg analyzes economic growth in the spirit of Cassel's "uniformly progressing economy." Here Berg first demonstrates that the Domar model and then the Harrod model are implied in Lundberg's exercises.

Berg concludes that Lundberg's *Studies* contain a much richer menu of dynamic analysis – including the simple multiplier, the multiplier-accelerator model, and the Harrod-Domar growth model – than Keynes's *General Theory,* thus supporting Schumpeter's claim. However, the complexity of Lundberg's many sequences and iterations and his failure to find a general form for his system of equations prevented his work from having a strong impact on the profession.

In Chapter 9 Hans Brems makes an attempt to express the dynamics of the Stockholm School mathematically. He offers two intersecting classifications of dynamics. The first is between equilibrium dynamics where expectations come true and disequilibrium dynamics where expectations are not fulfilled. The Wicksell tradition developed by Lindahl, Lundberg, and Ohlin belongs to the latter category. The second is between continuous dynamics represented by differential equations that use periods of vanishing lengths and discontinuous dynamics that adopt difference equations using finite-length periods. Here the Swedes fall into the latter category.

Brems focuses on the multiplier-accelerator interaction of Ohlin and Lundberg. He compares Ohlin's verbal models of the early 1930s with those of Keynes's *General Theory,* and concludes that Ohlin had the "richer" model. The operational simplicity of Keynes, however, did carry the day. Similarly, as Claes Berg also points out, the case studies of Lundberg's dissertation did not offer an analytical solution to his system. An analytical solution was first presented by Paul Samuelson in his celebrated 1939 article on the multiplier-accelerator interaction.

Next, Brems moves from discontinuous into continuous disequilibrium dynamics, demonstrating how the Lundberg-Samuelson problem can be solved equally well by differential equations. Brems suggests that the use of continuously distributed lags may give a more real-life flavor to the analysis. Equilibrium dynamics are shown to be a special case of such continuously distributed lags. Cassel's growth theory would be an example. Summing up, Brems argues that the "lasting contribution of the Stockholm School was its early insistence on the use of lags."

The publication of Keynes's *General Theory* inspired Ohlin to publish a lengthy response in the *Economic Journal,* comparing the approach of

Keynes with that of the Stockholm economists. Ohlin was critical of Keynes for a number of reasons, in particular he rejected Keynes reliance on equilibrium analysis while stressing the Stockholm approach based on sequence analysis. Ohlin's article marked the beginning of a prolonged debate about the relationship between the Stockholm School and Keynes. Did the work of the Swedes anticipate the *General Theory?* In Chapter 10 Robert Clower joins this discussion, starting from Patinkin's by now commonly accepted interpretation of the "central message" of the *General Theory* as a theory of effective demand with output as equilibrating aggregate demand and aggregate supply. According to Patinkin's view the Stockholm economists clearly did not anticipate the *General Theory.* Clower presents, however, an interpretation that he considers closer to the spirit of the *General Theory* than Patinkin's, thus arriving at a more positive verdict on Ohlin's analysis of Keynes.

Inspired by Ohlin's review of Keynes's major work, Clower develops a Marshallian model of effective demand built upon the distinction between two types of markets, one with "thick" trading and the other with "thin" trading. In thick markets with many traders and frequent transactions, individual producers can rapidly adjust output to aggregate demand. In thin markets, on the other hand, output is demand-determined in the short run; shifts in aggregate demand cause output and prices to move, whereas only output shifts in an equilibrating way in thick markets. According to Clower, the thick market model is the proper representation of Keynes's central message while Patinkin has based his argument on the thin market version.

In the Ohlin-Keynes debate, Clower tends to side with Ohlin, stating that Ohlin had a grasp of the *General Theory* "perhaps better than its author," but Clower's main conclusion is that *"The analytical substance of Keynes's* General Theory *and of the "Stockholm Theory" is already contained in earlier work by Marshall and Wicksell"* (Clower's italics). Finally, he conjectures that the most important chapter in the Ohlin-Keynes debate has not been written. The process analysis of the Swedes may be a promising route in the future.

The quantity theory of money provided the basis for the monetary analysis of both Wicksell and Cassel. Both of them made important theoretical contributions to the field: Wicksell introduced a modern banking system in his cumulative process, and Cassel developed the purchasing power parity theory. During and after World War I, both published an impressive number of popular articles on monetary issues in the spirit of the quantity theory. However, the next generation, that is, the Stockholm School, deserted the quantity theory.

Why were the Stockholm economists so critical of the quantity theory? In Chapter 11 Johan Myhrman answers this question by examining the views of Lindahl, Myrdal, and Ohlin. Of all the Stockholm economists, Lindahl remained closest to Wicksell throughout his life as a proponent of a monetary norm. He strongly emphasized the role of expectations, maintaining that the central bank ought to use measures such as public announcements to set expectations at their correct level. In his monetary analysis, Myrdal concentrated on theoretical issues, ignoring policy considerations. In a series of contributions in the 1930s and 1940s, Ohlin founded the Stockholm oral tradition that money did not matter.

The common theme for all of the Stockholm economists was the view that the money stock determined neither the price level nor the level of output (money was "passive"). Consequently, they had no interest in further analysis of the money supply and money demand. Their reliance on the case-study method led them to conclude that a number of other developments could affect prices and output and that money had no major role to play. This was particularly the case with Ohlin.

Macroeconomics as a separate field of study traces its roots to the 1930s. At least three competing strands of macroeconomic thinking were developed in that decade in Europe: the Austrian business cycle theory of Hayek and Robbins in Vienna and in London at London School of Economics, the work of the Swedes centered in Stockholm, and the contributions by Keynes and his associates in Cambridge. In those days it was not obvious which of these schools would carry the future, if any of them. The first postwar decades witnessed the rapid success of the Keynesian approach and the demise of the Vienna and Stockholm schools, both schools being relegated to the periphery of economics, often viewed as "failures" with few followers and not taken seriously.

In Chapter 12 David Laidler examines the nature of these failures and the causes of the wide divergency between the Austrian and the Stockholm schools, where the Swedes rapidly moved towards a Keynesian position, even before the *General Theory,* and the Austrians remained strongly anti-Keynesian. This is a remarkable development in Laidler's opinion since the Swedes and the Austrians started from the common heritage of Wicksell's cumulative process and the concept of monetary equilibrium; furthermore, both wanted to explain the same problem, namely, the cycle and cyclical unemployment.

Hayek stressed the role of the rate of interest in coordinating intertemporal choices, focusing on the nonneutral effects of monetary changes. These effects lead sooner or later to a crisis. Policy measures could only postpone the inevitable course of events. As existing monetary systems based on deposit banking could not guarantee the establishment of monetary equilibrium – where the rate of interest equated savings and investments – the existence of trade cycles had to be accepted as a fact of life.

The Swedes started from the same Wicksell-Böhm-Bawerk foundation but took a different route according to Laidler, downplaying the Austrian idea of a technically determined natural rate of interest unaffected by monetary developments. Instead the Swedes stressed the role of subjective expectations, which could change for a variety of reasons. Monetary equilibrium now had to encompass expectations as well, allowing an infinite number of possible sequences depending on how expectations evolved over time. The Swedes did not develop a theory of expectations, although they discussed perfect foresight as an extreme and unrealistic case. The result was a dynamic open-ended approach to macroeconomic issues without any formal solutions, lacking in Laidler's word "a core model." The policy pessimism of the Austrians contrasts to the policy optimism of the Swedes, who saw the opportunity to influence expectations as part of an expansionary policy.

Turning to his second issue, the divergent fates of the two schools, Laidler argues that many of the main elements of the Stockholm School were absorbed into mainstream Keynesian economics – of which the *General Theory* is one part. Accordingly, the Stockholm School is not a "failure." On the other hand, the Austrian business cycle theory of Hayek appeared quite unsuccesful until recently when some of its basic ideas have returned, reincarnated in the shape of the New-Classical macroeconomics of Lucas, Sargent, Wallace, and others. As their work of the 1980s closely resembles Hayek's approach of the 1930s, Laidler suggests that the term neo-Austrians should replace the term neo-Classicals. If it turns out that the research agenda of the neo-Austrians dominates future macroeconomic work, rather than the Stockholm and Cambridge schools, the latter two will become the failures of the future. Laidler adds a final line of caution borrowed from Sir Dennis Robertson: Perhaps economics moves in circles; if so, the failure or success for any school of thought becomes a matter of dates of reference.

What are the roots of the Stockholm School? Earlier we have traced them to the work of Wicksell and Cassel. In Chapter 13 Kumaraswamy Velupillai provides an even broader perspective, boldly proposing that the macroeconomics of the Stockholm School is founded on and inspired by political arithmetic. In his opinion, Davidson, Wicksell, Cassel, Lindahl, Ohlin, and Myrdal were working in the tradition of political arithmetic, "the art of reasoning by figures upon things relating to government" once founded by Petty, and added monetary economics, public finance, business cycle theory, justice, dynamics, and rationality to form what eventually emerged as the field of macroeconomics in the 1930s.

Velupillai adduces a good deal of evidence in support of his interpretation. Wicksell's and Lindahl's research on the theory of taxation and justice was followed by work on the concepts of income and wealth, and on national accounting. The debate among the Swedes on the proper norm of monetary policy, starting with the exchange between Wicksell and Davidson at the turn of the century and lasting at least until the mid-1940s, was another main line of thought. Wicksell's cumulative process and Cassel's "uniformly progressive economy" are elements in the development of dynamics.

Finally, Velupillai compares the microeconomic framework of the rational expectations theory to the macroeconomics of the Swedes on a number of issues, such as credibility, neutrality, and expectations. He concludes that the Swedish tradition in economics and political arithmetic can challenge the claim of the adherents to the rational expectations theory that their approach is the only one suitable for the analysis of macroeconomic problems.

The period 1927–1937 is commonly regarded as the heyday, the founding years, of the Stockholm School. During these years, the major works of the School were forthcoming. World War II marks the beginning of the end. After the war, Stockholm School tradition was still pursued within Sweden, but foreign influence was gradually getting stronger, "diluting" the original domestic approach.

Starting from the classification of the dynamic methods of Myrdal, Lindahl, and Lundberg in 1927–37 in his doctoral thesis,[12] in Chapter 14 Björn Hansson examines the post–World War II contributions to the dynamic analysis of the School. First, he considers Erik Lindahl's critical review of Keynes's *General Theory* published in the early 1950s, basically demonstrating that Lindahl held to his earlier views and did not accept Keynes's approach. Next, Björn Hansson shows how Bent Hansen's dissertation of 1951, *A Study in the Theory of Inflation,* merges the Stockholm tradition with Hicks's work, being more mathematical in form than previous Stockholm School contributions.

In the early 1950s the econometric representation of the Stockholm School approach was discussed. This was actually the only instance when the empirical implications of the work of the School were seriously considered. Herman Wold, influenced by the dynamics of the Stockholm School, argued that econometric research should be based on recursive (unidirectional) models, as opposed to Trygve Haavelmo's stress on interdependent (simultaneous) models. Ragnar Bentzel and Bent Hansen joined the debate, proposing that under certain circumstances, the Stockholm School approach suggests that "basic" models containing only recursive systems can be constructed. However, because of statistical considerations, for example, lack of data on expectations, econometricians will have to work with simultaneous models.

In his summary, Björn Hansson suggests that the Stockholm School made important contributions to the development of dynamic method, some of which were actually incorporated in the Keynesian approach: In being absorbed by the Keynesian revolution, the Stockholm School has wrongfully been regarded as a failure.

4   The impact of the Stockholm School

What was the impact of the Stockholm School on economics? Five contributions suggest an answer to this question. As the connection between Erik Lindahl and Sir John Hicks is often cited in the literature on the Stockholm School, Sir John Hicks's account of the Swedish influence on *Value and Capital* is presented first (Chapter 15). Hicks's original encounter with Swedish economics was through Wicksell's *Lectures* in the German translation. His *Theory of Wages* was influenced by it, and Hicks notes that he corrected the translation of *Lectures I* into English.

Reviewing Myrdal's article in German – the same article that later became *Monetary Equilibrium* – Hicks found the discussion of dynamics of interest. Myrdal was relying on a Swedish debate that Hicks was unable to acquaint himself with because of the language barrier. As the name of Lindahl was commonly cited, Hicks thought of writing to Lindahl. At that time, however, Lindahl turned up at the London School of Economics (LSE) looking for help with the translation of his work and John Hicks suggested a lady specializing in public finance, Ursula Webb, later to be his wife. She accepted, and as a result Lindahl's *Essay in the Theory of Money and Capital* was published in 1939, the same year as *Value and Capital*.[13] Hicks discusses the connection between these two books, concluding that Lindahl's dynamics was a source of inspiration for his construction of temporary equilibrium theory. This was in his opinion a "theory of the start." Since then he has been looking for a theory of behavior over the whole period, that is, a "theory of the finish," without reaching an acceptable solution. He also notes that Lindahl's concept of income has been fruitful both in *Value and Capital* and in his later writings.

In Chapter 16 Nadim Shehadi describes how Swedish contributions played a role in the "battle of ideas" taking place at the LSE in the 1930s. This battle started when young Lionel Robbins became professor in 1929. He set out to build a program of theoretical economics by bringing Friedrich von Hayek to London in order to break away from the LSE tradition of historically oriented inductive economics. The LSE had been founded in opposition to the theoretical economics of Marshall's Cambridge. They were soon surrounded by a group of brilliant young Hayekian followers including Hicks, Kaldor, and Lerner.

An early connection between the LSE and Sweden is the fact that Hayek unintentionally laid the basis for Gunnar Myrdal's international fame. In the early 1930s, the Wicksellian-Austrian roots of Lindahl's work induced Hayek to ask Lindahl to contribute to a volume that Hayek was editing. Lindahl declined and suggested Myrdal as a replacement. In this way Hayek published in German the contribution by Myrdal that was later translated as *Monetary Equilibrium.*

Brinley Thomas formed the main bridge between the Stockholm School and the LSE. He spent a year in Sweden, learned Swedish, and returned to the LSE to publish his *Monetary Policy and Crises* strongly inspired by Lindahl and Myrdal. In this work he favored an expansionary stabilization program along Swedish lines while rejecting a Hayekian interpretation of the depression. His lectures inspired G. L. S. Shackle to desert the Austrian approach and merge Swedish and Keynesian ideas into his *Expectations, Investment and Income.*

Hayek and Robbins were successful in establishing theoretical economics at the LSE. However, they eventually faced the formidable challenge of Keynes's *General Theory,* which they tried in vain to prevent from infiltrating the department at the LSE. Converts were not promoted and felt induced to leave the LSE; Hicks went to Cambridge, Lerner went to the United States, Thomas turned to economic growth and demography, and Kaldor left to work with Myrdal in Geneva. Eventually Robbins himself accepted Keynesianism. This success of Keynesianism was facilitated by the ideas from Stockholm that reached London through Thomas.[14]

Initially Paul Samuelson, the author of Chapter 17, was invited to contribute a paper on the impact of the Stockholm School on non–Swedish economics. Adopting an American perspective, he summarizes this influence in a few points. In short: Lundberg's *Studies* of 1937 and Ohlin's *Economic Journal* articles of 1937 were read; Lindahl's work was not well known; Myrdal's *Monetary Equilibrium* was something of a disappointment when it appeared in English in 1939; and after World War II, the promising young Swedish economists were absorbed into extramural activities, turning their backs on serious academic work; they were critical of new developments in mathematics and econometrics, and this made Swedish economics "regress towards the mean."

As such a paper would be "embarrasingly short" – clearly Samuelson is of the opinion that the Stockholm School has not had any major influence on economics outside Sweden – he instead broadens his perspective to consider the development of macroeconomics in the 1930s. First, he looks upon Ohlin's claim that Wicksell's *Interest and Prices* contains the foundation for a theory of aggregate output. Samuelson stresses that Wicksell was working within the Quantity Theory tradition assuming full employment and consequently that Ohlin was wrong in suggesting that Wicksell departed from this assumption. Next, Samuelson focuses on the central message of the Keynesian revolution, that is, the multiplier doctrine, and traces its roots to the pre–*General Theory* work of, among others, Richard Kahn and J. M. Clark.

Considering the anticipations issue, Samuelson agrees with Patinkin's view that the Swedes did not develop a theory of effective demand based on a formal model. (See, however, Wadensjö's discussion of the hitherto unexplored archives of the Committee on Unemployment which show that Ohlin worked explicitly with multiplier analysis.) However, according to Samuelson, this type of formal macromodel was not required for the Swedes to recommend expansionary policy measures in the early 1930s. Policy advice in a Keynesian spirit was forthcoming from leading academic economists before the *General Theory*. Samuelson concludes that the Stockholm School has passed into history because the School lacked a manageable formal model.

In Norway Ragnar Frisch founded a strong and lasting tradition in economics. According to Jens Christopher Andvig, the author of Chapter 18, the "Oslo School" did not find much inspiration in the Stockholm School, although the Swedes and Frisch had a lot in common. They both started from Wicksell; they aimed at a dynamic macrotheory and rejected the statics of the *General Theory*. However, the Swedish route toward dynamics differed from Frisch's. He constructed mathematical models of business cycles whereas the Swedes relied on verbal reasoning that allowed an infinite number of outcomes to emerge.

Andvig displays the difference between Frisch and the Swedes by studying the 1934–5 lecture notes on monetary economics in which Frisch examined Lindahl's *Penningpolitikens medel* and Myrdal's article of 1932 in Swedish on monetary equilibrium. Frisch was critical of Lindahl's research methodology, saying that it gave rise to complex indeterminate models in which basically anything could happen. Frisch was also skeptical of the attempt by Lindahl and Myrdal to find microeconomic roots for their discussion as well as of the stress that they gave to expectations. Instead, Frisch wanted to rely on determinate macromodels without any explicit microeconomic foundations. In his opinion, Lindahl and, in particular, Myrdal were too "ambitious" and made things too complicated.

Frisch's approach turned out to be the successful one. Economics, he felt, should be a rigorous science similar to the natural sciences, one that made use of mathematical models and econometrics. This program is the main reason the Frisch school in Oslo survived longer as an active center of research than did the Stockholm School.

The Stockholm School did not have a major impact on economics outside Sweden, and even inside Sweden it had problems in establishing a firm footing. One reason was that the academic base in Sweden was fairly limited (see Table 1). This prevented the members of the School from obtaining chairs when they were most actively engaged in research. Some chairs were also held by professors who were indifferent to or even critical of the School, most notably Johan Åkerman, professor in Lund from 1943 to 1961 and highly successful as an adviser to doctoral students. Consequently, Lund was the alma mater of many of the economists who obtained chairs in the 1960s and 1970s. Myrdal and Ohlin on the other hand did not advise any doctoral students who subsequently became professors.[15]

In Chapter 19 Jan Petersson describes Johan Åkerman's critique of the Stockholm School in the 1950s. Åkerman was an institutionalist with a strong interest in methodology and in empirical work on business cycles and structural changes. He originated the literature on the political business cycle. The interaction between different social groups was an important determinant of the business cycle according to Åkerman, and thus there could be no general theory of the cycle independent of the existing social structure. Any general theory was doomed to become quickly outmoded.

Åkerman raised three major objections to the Stockholm School. First, he criticized Lindahl's attempt to build a general theory and then study special cases of it. Second, the School did not solve the aggregation problem adequately. Finally, the School lacked a realistic theory of expectations. Åkerman was involved in lively exchanges on these issues in the 1950s with Harald Dickson, Ragnar Bentzel, and Bent Hansen, who defended the approach of the Stockholm School, but Lindahl did not take part himself. This discussion, which did not reach a synthesis, marks the end of the Stockholm School as a subject of current interest and controversy within the Swedish economic profession.

5   The decline of the Stockholm School

The Stockholm School and Keynesian macroeconomics were both founded in the 1930s. The new generation of Swedish economists of that decade were optimistic. They believed that they were laying a theoretical basis for macroeconomics, and in particular for an expansionary eco-

Table 2. *Number of references to the Stockholm School and to Keynes's* General Theory, *1972–85*

Period	The Stockholm School[a]	General Theory
1972–75	13	163
1976–80	33	386
1981–85	21	481
Total	67	1,030

[a]The Stockholm School is represented by the writings of Erik Lindahl, Erik Lundberg, Gunnar Myrdal, and Bertil Ohlin relevant to the School.
Source: Social Citation Index, 1972–85.

nomic policy that could help bring the economy out of depression. The younger economists in Sweden seemed to have a promising future in the mid-1930s. They were closely involved in policy advice and policy making and their views received attention. Because Sweden did not suffer as badly in the worldwide depression as several other countries, notably the United States, Swedish monetary as well as fiscal policies attracted considerable positive interest from abroad. Thus, the new breed of Swedish economists, the Stockholm School, appeared successful by most standards. Their optimism and pride is apparent from the memoirs of Ohlin (1972, 1975) dealing with the 1930s, from Lundberg's (1957, 1983) accounts of his experience of the 1930s, and from Myrdal's (1982) reminiscences.

The publication in 1936 of Keynes's *General Theory* did not have much initial impact on Swedish economic thought. Representatives of the older generation of economists were openly critical. The new generation, represented by Myrdal and Ohlin, was not impressed. They viewed Keynes's approach as too static and inferior to their dynamic approach. During the fifty years after Ohlin's introduction of the Stockholm School to English-speaking readers Keynes and Keynesianism have dominated the field of macroeconomics. The Stockholm School is primarily dealt with in the history of economic theory, and, of course, English not Swedish is the language of macroeconomics.

Tables 2 and 3 quantify this state of affairs in a simple manner. Table 2 shows the number of references to the Stockholm School and to Keynes's *General Theory* during the period 1972–85. Table 3 displays the number of articles on the Stockholm School and on Keynes from 1925 to 1985. Here the Stockholm School is represented by the writings

Table 3. *Number of articles on the Stockholm School and on Keynes, 1925–85*

Period	The Stockholm School	Keynes
1925–39	2	0
1940–49	2	42
1950–59	3	33
1960–69	2	65
1970–79	14	214
1980–85	6	93
Total	29	447

Source: Index of Economic Articles, 1925–79, *Journal of Economic Literature,* 1980–85.

of Lindahl, Lundberg, Myrdal, and Ohlin dealing with macroeconomics or monetary economics. The two tables demonstrate the overwhelming dominance of the *General Theory.*

What are the reasons for the demise of the once so promising Swedish approach to macroeconomics? What happened to the Stockholm School during the past 50 years? An answer to these questions can be provided by drawing together some of the threads from the above discussion and adding some additional ones.[16]

Publication lag in English

Although the Swedes had carried out a number of studies with a very strong Keynesian flavor, they made the fundamental mistake of not publishing their work in English prior to the publication of the *General Theory* in January 1936. Most likely, the *General Theory* would not have appeared so revolutionary if some of its basic ideas had already been known to English-speaking readers. Support for this view can be found in Hansen's (1981, p. 258) account of Myrdal's and Ohlin's work prior to the *General Theory.*

> No one who has studied Myrdal's and Ohlin's monographs, presented as Supplements 5 and 7 to the Main Report II of the Committee on Unemployment (1934) can possibly deny that these two authors, as early as 1933–34, had a fairly good understanding of the mechanisms of that kind of macroeconomic process which we know under the name of multiplier process and which conventionally is associated with Keynes' *General Theory.* Definitional subtleties apart, it is also unde-

niable that both Myrdal and Ohlin discussed such a macro process in terms of national income aggregates with functional forms very similar, if not identical, to those employed by Keynes two years later in the *General Theory*. To that extent, Myrdal and Ohlin did indeed anticipate Keynes' *General Theory*. And their understanding of the importance for multiplier processes of reaction speeds and lag structures and of leakages related to import and tax payments was certainly more advanced than the *General Theory*.

Both Myrdal and Ohlin consider and lament the fact they they did not publish their work in English at an early stage. Ohlin tried to engage Brinley Thomas in 1934 to translate into English his report for the Committee on Unemployment published in the spring of 1934. Ohlin was planning to publish the report the subsequent year, that is, a year before the *General Theory*. However, Brinley Thomas was unable to carry out the translation at the time. Ohlin gave the Finlay lectures in Dublin in 1934. These lectures were published three years later in *Economic Journal* with the title "The Stockholm Theory of Saving and Investment." By that time, Ohlin had added some qualifications and "a comparison with and a critique of Keynes' recently published *General Theory*" (see Ohlin, 1975, p. 168).[17] Ohlin considers what would have happened if he had published his work earlier:

> I thought that it was a bit distressing that I was not ready to publish the Dublin lectures before Keynes book was out. Otherwise, economists around the world who found Keynes' presentation sensational could not have avoided noticing the very large similarities concerning the theoretical foundation and the *policy conclusions* [Ohlin's italics]. But such a reaction was perhaps at least partly a result of vanity from the Stockholm School and from my side, because it is uncertain how much faster these ideas would have made an international breakthrough by an earlier publication.

Myrdal (1982) spends a whole section explaining his "inåtvändhet" in the 1930s, that is, his propensity to publish only in Swedish.[18]

> I wrote in Swedish for Swedes and to some extent for Scandinavians, and was not particularly concerned that my thoughts did not reach an international audience. . . . I remember that I received an invitation from the International Labor Bureau to publish in their journal a translated version of my appendix to the Social Democratic government budget that was presented in January 1933. However, I declined the invitation on the grounds that I was fully preoccupied with work in Sweden and did not wish to have the trouble of proofreading a translation. For similar reasons, I declined to accept Heckscher's generous offer to arrange for the translation of my doctoral dissertation from 1927.

Myrdal had some of his work published in German in the 1930s thanks to translations carried out by a German friend, Gerhard Mackenroth, who was an unpaid *Privatdozent* in Halle. Incidentally, Mackenroth, struggling with the translation of Myrdal's Swedish article on monetary equilibrium, suggested the use of terms *ex ante* and *ex post.*

Later, after the publication of *General Theory,* some of the work of the Stockholm School became available in English. In 1937 Erik Lundberg wrote his dissertation in English, and Lindahl and Myrdal published major contributions in English immediately before World War II. However, at that time, the Keynesian revolution had started to have an impact in the academic world and the work by the Swedes, coming in the wake of the *General Theory,* did not attract much interest.

It is tempting to conclude that the Swedes by publishing in their native language prevented an international breakthrough for their ideas prior to the publication of the *General Theory.* If their theories had been available earlier, they would have established a stronger claim to being in the forefront, improving the chances of attracting students and followers.

The methodology of the Swedes

The Swedes aimed at analyzing behavioral sequences, with an emphasis on the discrepancies between expectations and outcomes. For a number of reasons this approach turned out, however, to be less successful than the Keynesian approach.

Expectations played an important role in this framework. However, the Swedes did not develop an explicit theory of the formation of expectations. Instead they ended up with very "open" and indeterminate systems where "anything could happen" (see Hansen, 1981, p. 274). The analysis of economic processes tended to develop into "verbal story-telling" where there was no end to the story, that is, no equilibrium solution to the system, as expectations and thus behavior and attitudes were subject to continuous revisions and changes as new outcomes and developments were recorded. This approach was associated with a disbelief in stable relationships between economic aggregates. Consequently, the Swedes were skeptical of constant multipliers, stable propensities to consume or save, and so forth. This was in particular the case with Lundberg and Ohlin. As emphasized by Siven (1985), Lundberg's 1937 dissertation is a prime example of this critical attitude toward economic analysis based on formal models. Specifically, Lundberg was skeptical of Keynes's use of equilibrium analysis or multiplier analysis. In his opinion, this approach was too static.

Lundberg's dissertation deals with intellectual experiments that do not require data from the "real world." Later, when turning to empirical work on the Swedish economy, he maintained a hostile attitude toward using a general or formal approach such as the Keynesian or the monetarist ones. Here (see Lundberg, 1957, and 1983) the stress is on describing processes in the "open" Stockholm School manner using data in a verbal fashion to illustrate the argument. According to Lundberg, the "real world" is characterized by so much instability that it is hardly fruitful to use formal econometric tests of various hypotheses. Actually, the case-study approach combined with this dynamic method threatened to put the Swedes into a defeatist atheoretical position that denies or downplays the merit of formal analysis.

The strength of the Keynesian approach, as it developed from Hicks's 1937 contribution, is apparent from a comparison with the Swedish School. The Keynesian model was constructed as a static equilibrium model with no explicit role for time, revisions of plans, and so forth, as in the Stockholm approach. This model has the advantage of tractability. As the economic profession during the post–World War II period turned to a greater use of mathematics, research based on the Keynesian model became more attractive.

The Keynesian model had the additional advantage of providing straightforward policy recommendations, most notably, the unemployment of the 1930s should be reduced by an expansionary fiscal policy that would raise domestic aggregate demand. The Swedish economists suggested the same remedy but anchored it in a more complex approach to macroeconomics. The Swedes were in favor of an expansionary fiscal policy, in particular in the 1930s, but were unable to support it by a formal model. The openness of the Swedish approach also meant that the Swedes did not have a unifying model to rally around. They were thus not able to develop as coherent a school as the Keynesians did. Instead, there was a tendency among them to develop their own taxonomies. This was in particular the case with Svennilson and Lindahl.

Disinterest in empirical work

The Swedes showed surprisingly little interest in empirical testing of their theories. There are at least three reasons for this lack of interest. First of all, the lack of a formal analysis prevented the development and design of econometric tests. The case-study view proved again to act as a brake on the School. Second, there were no data available to them on the central building blocks of their approach. Most important, they did not have any measures of the plans and expectations of decision makers, nor did they make any serious attempt to obtain any such data. Neither did they empirically analyze the length of the period proper to their period analysis. Third and finally, as pointed out earlier, the "parameter pessimism," that is, the disbelief in stable behavioral relationships, made the Swedes simply disinterested in empirical work.

The Swedish National Institute of Economic Research was founded in 1937 with Lundberg as its first director. The institute collected data and published empirical studies, but it did not develop into a research center adopting econometric techniques. Attempts were made by Lundberg in the late 1930s to start econometric studies, but these plans were interrupted by World War II. Later they were unsuccessful for various reasons. Instead, the Stockholm nontechnical methodology permeated the activities of the institute from the post–World War II period until the 1980s. In contrast, the key concepts of the Keynesian model were easy to operationalize. As soon as data became available, Keynesian models became the vehicles of the rapidly growing branch of econometrics. The Swedes fell behind in this development.

Narrow academic base and extramural activities

Another reason the Stockholm School disappeared was that already in the 1930s most of the Stockholm School economists stopped developing the theoretical tradition of the Swedish approach. There were several reasons associated with this early disappearance.

First of all, almost all of the young economists were attracted into other careers or fields of work. Myrdal left the study of macroeconomics around 1934 when he became involved in the population question. He returned briefly to monetary economics in connection with the translation and publication of *Monetary Equilibrium* in 1939. In the 1940s he published *An American Dilemma*. He was a minister in the Social Democratic government, worked for the United Nations, and later turned to development issues.[19] Ohlin gradually became involved in Swedish politics, became the leader of the Liberal Party, and did not return to academic work until late in his life, when he revived his interest in Swedish economic thought. He maintained, however, his chair in Stockholm until 1965 while he was a politician.

Other members of the School also left for nonacademic careers. Hammarskjöld was working for the Riksbank already in the 1930s. Johansson became involved in the Swedish housing program. Lundberg and Svennilson established distinguished academic careers but did not develop the theory of the School any further. Their students such as Ingvar Ohlson, Bengt Metelius, Lars Lindberger, Karl-Olof Faxén,

Rudolf Meidner, and Gösta Rehn did graduate work in macroeconomics, but with the exception of Faxén did not pursue theoretical problems in depth. Svennilson turned to studies of industrial economics and economic growth. Both he and Lundberg were also engaged in nonacademic work. Lindahl was the major exception to this pattern. He eventually became a professor in Uppsala after holding a chair in Gothenburg and Lund. His most famous student, Bent Hansen, continued to work in the Swedish tradition.

The main reason for this exodus of young talent was the incentive structure of the Swedish system of higher education. Generally, a department of economics consisted of one or two professors and one or a few associated professors with the title *docent*. Young graduates, even if they were bright, had little chance of staying on at the university after finishing their doctoral thesis. In the 1930s, economics was taught at five institutions: Uppsala, Lund, Gothenburg, Stockholm, and Handelshögskolan in Stockholm (see Table 1). It was difficult for such a small set of universities to maintain an independent line of thought in macroeconomics. Besides, the ideas of the Stockholm School did not catch on at all the Swedish universities. In Lund, as discussed by Jan Petersson, Johan Åkerman was openly hostile to the ideas emanating from the capital. He became the leading Swedish critic of the Stockholm School.[20]

Disregard of graduate students

The members of the Stockholm School did not attract students and followers who could carry on the tradition. Rather, they adhered to the Swedish tradition in economics of regarding graduate students as something of a nuisance. Graduate students were supposed to find a thesis topic by themselves, to pursue their work independently, and eventually to emerge with an original and independent piece of work. Neither Ohlin nor Myrdal actively advised any doctoral students that later became professors in the Swedish system. Their many activities outside academia did not leave them much time or energy for students, nor for teaching or academic work.[21] Lundberg had a tendency to intimidate students and was known for his sarcastic critique at seminars.[22] Myrdal was too obsessed by himself to serve as an effective graduate advisor. Here too, Lindahl was something of an exception.[23]

Moreover, the Stockholm School did not produce a textbook version of its approach to pass on the School to new generations of students, which would have improved the prospects for survival. In Stockholm the reading list for undergraduate courses included for a long time Lundberg's book from 1953 as the main text, partly translated as Lundberg (1957), although Keynesian textbooks dominated the reading lists at least from the 1960s onwards. Lundberg's book was too demanding for students and teachers compared to standard textbooks.[24]

The Swedish economics profession became rapidly Keynesian after World War II. The Anglo-American ideas were not largely at variance with Swedish economic thought, and this affinity certainly contributed to this transition.

Considering the small size of the Swedish economics profession and the adverse incentive structure of the Swedish system of higher education, perhaps the proper question to ask is the opposite one: How was it possible that a group of economists could develop such a promising approach within such a short period of time as was done in Sweden in the 1930s? The appearance of the Stockholm School is perhaps more of a riddle than its disappearance.

6   What remains of the Stockholm School?

What remains of the Stockholm School today when the School celebrates its first half century? This question, touched upon in several of the contributions mentioned here, was posed to the panel at the final session. The answers varied.

The first two discussants consider the relationship between the Stockholm School and Keynesianism. Assar Lindbeck stresses the difference between the Stockholm School of "Keynesian-oriented macroeconomics" and other contributions by Swedish economists in the interwar period. As a consequence of all the effort that went into a comparison of the Stockholm School with Keynes to decide whether the Swedes anticipated the *General Theory,* the lasting contributions of the School in other fields have been neglected, such as Lindahl's work on public finance and on monetary norms, Ohlin's contributions to international trade, Myrdal's *An American Dilemma,* and Svennilson's analysis of economic growth. Lindbeck also refutes two myths: first, that the Swedes anticipated the *General Theory* and, second, that an expansionary fiscal policy pulled Sweden out of the depression in the 1930s.

According to Don Patinkin, the "central message" of the Stockholm School, that is, its focus upon the role of expectations in a dynamic context, is "an essential part of present-day macroeconomics." This absorption into the modern framework is so complete that it erased the original Swedish character of the contribution. If the Swedes had presented a formal theory of the generation of expectations that was subject to empirical testing, they could have had a greater impact on the profession.

The next two panel discussants contrast the Stockholm School with post–Keynesian macroeconomics. David Laidler starts from two issues: the problem of measuring capital (the aggregate production function) and the theory of rational expectations. He refutes the claim of the real business cycle theorists, as well of the adherents of the rational expectations school, of constructing a macrotheory from firm microfoundations. This claim is not well substantiated, although the mathematical dress of these two theories attracts present-day economists. Laidler wonders if business cycle theory has actually proceeded much further since the contributions of the Stockholm School.

Kumaraswamy Velupillai pleads for the wholesale translation into English of the work of Swedish economists such as the exchange between Wicksell and Davidson on the proper norms for monetary policy and the dissertations of Myrdal, Hammarskjöld, Svennilson, and Åkerman. Once this is done, Velupillai predicts that the "topicality, freshness and depth, in relation to modern macro" will be found striking. Because the old Swedes tackled the same issues as the Lucasians, who claim to hold the ground of modern macroeconomics, there could be a fruitful confrontation.

In the closing comment, Axel Leijonhufvud proposes that the work of the Stockholm School, or for that matter of any school in the history of economics, should not be read solely from the vantage point of what constitutes present mainstream orthodoxy. We should not look upon the Swedish contributions of the interwar period through the Keynesian glasses of the post–World War II period. As an example he brings out Lindahl's monetary work, which today appears "tremendously modern in the light of the rational expectations theory." Striking an optimistic tone, Leijonhufvud hints that there is more to be found in the work of the Swedish economists active in the interwar period if we put it in proper perspective.

To sum up the conference in a brief way, at the age of fifty the Stockholm School has not survived as a continuous "live" tradition of research either in Sweden or elsewhere. However, elements of the School have been absorbed in mainstream economics and continue to have an influence. There is also more work to be done on the School to get a complete and balanced picture of its achievements.

Notes

1 Economics was introduced as an academic subject at an early stage in Sweden. Inspired by developments in Germany, a chair was established in Uppsala in 1741 and another in Lund in 1750. Economics remained, however,

a subject combined with law and biology (botany) during most of the eighteenth and nineteenth centuries. See Sandelin (1990) for an account of early economics in Sweden.

2 A fifth chair, established in 1903 in Gothenburg, was in economics and sociology and was held by Gustaf Steffen from 1903 to 1929. Steffen, however, was primarily interested in economic history and sociology. He was also involved in politics, becoming a member of parliament for the Social Democratic party (from which he was later excluded on the grounds of right wing tendencies). He had no lasting impact on mainstream Swedish economics.

3 See Carlson (1988) for a discussion of Cassel's and Heckscher's response to the new economics.

4 Cassel was a strong proponent of monetary (monetarist) interpretations of the causes and cures of the Great Depression. See Jonung (1979).

5 Gustav Cassel noted in a speech on his seventieth birthday in 1936 that he had remained "unpolitical" *(opolitisk)* while all of his students were members of the parliament: Nils Wohlin for the Farmer's party, Gunnar Myrdal for the Social Democratic party, Bertil Ohlin for the Liberals, and Gösta Bagge for the Conservatives (see Myrdal, 1972b, p. 271). Cassel argued that this proved that he was a man of great tolerance to his pupils. Cassel's tolerance stands in contrast to the attitude of Wicksell, who advocated strongly that his students should adopt a Malthusian approach and maintain a critical attitude toward socialism (i.e., Marxism).

6 See, for example, Lundberg (1985).

7 There was a group of economists "in between" the founding fathers and the Stockholm School economists encompassing Gösta Bagge, Sven Brisman, Fritz Brock, Gunnar Silverstolpe, and Emil Sommarin. With the exception of Gösta Bagge, they did not have lasting influence on Swedish economics. See Jonung (1989).

8 The Stockholm School attracted considerable interest among Swedish economists witnessing the reception of Landgren's (1960) dissertation on the new economics in Sweden 1927–1939 and the subsequent debate. The contributions to this debate are all in Swedish, however.

9 See for example Myrdal (1982) translated in Jonung (1990).

10 On the anticipations issue, see Patinkin (1982, Chap. 2).

11 Myrdal thus did not develop an early perfect foresight version of the rational expectations theory.

12 See Hansson (1982).

13 See also Petersson (1987) for a discussion of the relationship between Lindahl and Hicks.

14 See Thomas's memories from Stockholm and the LSE in Jonung (1990).

15 On this point see Jonung (1989).

16 This section builds upon Jonung (1986). See also Siven (1985) and Petersson (1987) on the decline of the Stockholm School.

17 See also Ohlin's contribution in Jonung (1990).

18 See Myrdal's recollections of the Stockholm School in Jonung (1990).

19 Myrdal did not stop using the methodology of the Stockholm School.

Rather, he applied it to other issues than monetary and macroeconomic ones. *An American Dilemma* and *Asian Drama* are verbal accounts, which can be viewed as based on an "open" sequence analysis. Actually, it is my opinion that he continued working within the Swedish approach, reached an atheoretical position, and eventually turned into an institutionalist. See also Myrdal (1972a).

20 The Swedish ideas were not spread by emigration of members of the School similar to the emigration of Central European economists to the United States.

21 The oral tradition tells about Ohlin's examining students in taxis on the way to the parliament. On this point see also Carlson's recollections of Ohlin in Jonung (1990). According to personal communication with Staffan Burenstam-Linder, Ohlin's lectures on current economic problems at Handelshögskolan in the 1950s dealt with cyclical developments in the 1930s.

22 The oral tradition is full of stories of Lundberg's skeptical attitude toward theory. A typical Lundberg statement, still cited now and then: "before the seminar we were confused, and now after the seminar, we are still confused, but at a higher level." Once the author, who is not a student of Lundberg, asked him why he was so critical. He answered something like this: "I once tried to be nice throughout a whole seminar, I almost managed but at the end I had to say something. And that's it."

23 Bent Hansen recollects that he first went to Stockholm in the 1940s. There he found that the teachers, including Lundberg and Svennilson, often came late, if at all, to their lectures and left early for other committments. Hansen decided to leave for Lindahl in Uppsala (personal communication with Bent Hansen).

24 One participant at the Saltsjöbaden conference, Ingemar Ståhl – who started his studies in economics in Stockholm with a set of teachers consisting of Lundberg, Myrdal, Svennilson, and Östlind – succinctly summarized the decline of the Stockholm School as follows: "A school with no teachers, no students and no textbook will not survive for long."

References

Carlson, Benny (1988), *Staten som monster. Gustav Cassels och Eli Heckschers syn på statens roll och tillväxt.* Lund: Studentlitteratur.

Hansen, Bent (1981), "Unemployment, Keynes, and the Stockholm School," *History of Political Economy,* 13, 256–77.

Hansson, Björn (1982), *The Stockholm School and the Development of the Dynamic Method.* London: Croom Helm.

Jonung, Lars (1979), "Knut Wicksell's Norm of Price Stabilization and Swedish Monetary Policy in the 1930s," *Journal of Monetary Economics,* 5, 459–96.

  (1986), "The Stockholm School after 50 Years. An Attempt of Appraisal," mimeo, invited paper for the AEA meeting in New Orleans, December 1986.

(1989), "Economics the Swedish Way 1889–1989," mimeo, report prepared or the HSFR evaluation of economics in Sweden.

Jonung, Lars, ed. (1990), "The Stockholm School of Economics Remembered," in preparation.

Landgren, Karl-Gustav (1960), *Den 'nya ekonomien' i Sverige: J. M. Keynes, E. Wigforss, B. Ohlin och utvecklingen 1927–1939* (The new economics in Sweden: J. M. Keynes, E. Wigforss, B. Ohlin and the development 1927–1939). Stockholm: Almqvist & Wiksell.

Lundberg, Erik (1957), *Business Cycles and Economic Policy.* London: Allen & Unwin.

(1983), *Ekonomiska kriser förr och nu* (Economic crises in the past and present). Stockholm: SNS.

(1985), "The Rise and Fall of the Swedish Model," *Journal of Economic Literature,* 23, 1–36.

Myrdal, Gunnar (1972a), "Response to Introduction," *American Economic Review,* 62, 456–62.

(1972b), *Vetenskap och politik i nationalekonomin.* Stockholm: Rabén och Sjögren.

(1982), *Hur styrs landet?* (How is Sweden governed?). Borås: Rabén och Sjögren.

Ohlin, Bertil (1972), *Bertil Ohlins memoarer: Ung man blir politiker* (Bertil Ohlin's memoirs: A young man becomes a politician). Stockholm: Bonniers.

(1975), *Bertil Ohlins memoarer: 1940–1951. Socialistisk skördetid kom bort* (Bertil Ohlin's memoirs 1940–1951. How Socialism's harvest time vanished). Stockholm: Bonniers.

Patinkin, Don (1982), *Anticipations of the General Theory? And Other Essays on Keynes.* Chicago: University of Chicago Press.

Petersson, Jan (1987), *Erik Lindahl och Stockholmsskolans dynamiska metod* (Erik Lindahl and the Dynamic Method of the Stockholm School), dissertation, Lund University.

Sandelin, Bo, ed. (1990), *The History of Swedish Economic Thought.* London: Routledge.

Siven, Claes-Henric (1985), "The End of the Stockholm School," *Scandinavian Journal of Economics,* 4, 577–93.

PART I

The roots

CHAPTER 1

The Political Economy Club and the Stockholm School, 1917–1951[1]

ROLF G. H. HENRIKSSON

On October 1, 1936, the Stockholm economists hosted a very distinguished guest, John Maynard Keynes. Homeward bound from a visit to the Soviet Union, Keynes appeared at the Political Economy Club. The minutes, as recorded by Ingvar Svennilson, report:

> 1. At the invitation of the club, Mr. J. M. Keynes lectured at the Institute of Social Science on the subject "My grounds for departure from orthodox economic traditions." The lecture was arranged with support from J. H. Palme's fund for economic education and economic research. Some 100 persons attended the lecture.
>
> 2. Following the lecture, the club arranged a dinner at the student union building. In addition to Mr. and Mrs. Keynes, the dinner was attended by: the chairman Professor Ohlin, Miss Kock, Messrs. Björk, Böök, Cederwall, Dahlgren, Hammarskjöld, Helger, Johansson, Lagercrantz (guest), Lundberg, Myrdal, Rothlieb, Rooth, Suoviranta (Finland, guest) and Wigforss, as well as the undersigned. After dinner there was a discussion that continued until midnight.

The general content of Keynes's lecture is known.[2] In accounting for the reasons he departed from the classical tradition, Keynes evidently expounded on the theory of the rate of interest developed in his *General Theory* (Keynes, 1936). The audience's reception was perhaps not the one Keynes expected. In his memoirs Bertil Ohlin relates with amicable irony that Keynes, in his efforts to clarify what was new and central in his book, surprised the listeners by stressing features that few readers would have considered particularly innovative (Ohlin, 1975, p. 110). In greeting Keynes's presentation, Ohlin is also reported to have told Keynes with facetious malice that the Stockholm School economists had read his *General Theory* "with the joy of recognition."[3] Gunnar Myrdal reports how "one after another" of the younger Swedish economists "stood up and accused Keynes of being too classical." At first Keynes was amused, but as the call went down the row he betrayed an increasing degree of irritation. Erik Lundberg, Ingvar Svennilson, and others "were stealing his show."[4] The terse statement of the minutes leaves room for imaginative hypotheses about the course of the discussion, but the fact that the debate lasted until midnight indicates that the disagreements on what had been accomplished in the *General Theory* remained unresolved.

Keynes's visit may be considered the high point in the history of the Political Economy Club. However, as the following inquiry into the annals of the Club indicates, there were many other interesting events. Although the minutes preserved for the period 1917–51 do not present the content of the lectures or the discussions, a certain amount of reconstruction of what occurred has nevertheless been possible by use of additional source materials. In this way, a picture has been obtained of the main features of the Club's history, yielding an opportunity also to elucidate the life cycle of the Stockholm School and describe the interactions of the leading members. The Club was a major component in the institutional base of the Stockholm School and performed an important "hub-of-the-wheel" function in the emergence and evolution of both its research program and its policy stance. Even the eventual eclipse of the School can to some extent be explained by the changing role of the Club beginning in the late 1930s.

1   Foundation of the Club

The Club's beginnings: In 1916 Knut Wicksell retired from his chair at Lund. His wife Anna Bugge Wicksell, who often arranged the practical details of her husband's social relationships, contacted Eli F. Heckscher at the Business College (usually referred to today as the Stockholm School of Economics) in Stockholm. She asked him whether something could be arranged when Knut returned to Stockholm in order that he could continue to devote his energies to economic research. Her request was well received, and Heckscher took the initiative for creating an economic club that would provide Wicksell with a forum for his ideas and at the same time would stimulate economic research and debate in Stockholm. At that time, there was a relatively large number of economists in the Swedish capital, but there was no professional forum for the exchange of ideas. The meetings of the venerable Swedish Economic Society, started in 1877, were primarily devoted to discussion of economic policy questions where politicians were still predominant. Nor was there any formal graduate training in political economy. The curriculum of the Business College, where Heckscher had held a chair in economics since 1909, was admittedly well developed and included not only lectures but also seminars and colloquiums in economics. However, they were naturally constrained to suit the needs of business students. Gustav Cassel's teaching at the University of Stockholm comprised mainly lectures, with little organized seminar activity. The instruction given at the Institute of Social Science that he established in 1903 primarily filled the needs of law students (Henriksson, 1989).

The minutes from the first Club meeting in January 1917 report that the declared purpose of the club was "to bring together those who devoted themselves to scientific work in the area of political economy for a private exchange of ideas about scientific problems." An invitation to attend the first meeting was sent to some twenty persons, of whom slightly more than half attended. In addition to Wicksell and Heckscher, David Davidson and Cassel were also present. Wicksell was elected chairman, and the secretarial duties fell upon Fabian von Kock. It was also decided that unanimous approval would be required for the election of new members and that meetings would be held on the third Friday of every month. Heckscher then delivered a lecture on the import of securities into Sweden during the war. It was followed by a discussion in which all the professors present participated. As will be seen, it was unique to have them all gathered and on speaking terms with one another.

The Club's proceedings: The forms for the Club's proceedings adopted at the first meeting were maintained for quite some time. During the first five-year period, the Club met in quite frugal settings on the premises of the Business College. Thereafter it became increasingly common to hold the meetings at the home of one of the members. Wicksell was never host, but Heckscher and Sven Brisman, who in 1917 was appointed to the second chair in economics at the Business College, often served the Club in that way. This meeting tradition continued even after the death of Wicksell in 1926 and into the 1930s. After Heckscher left Club activities in 1932 and a younger circle under Ohlin's leadership assumed responsibility, the Club often met in Ohlin's home but also occasionally at the home of Gunnar Myrdal and other club members.

The development of the Club is summarized graphically in Figure 1.1. The club officials are presented at the top of the figure. There were six chairmen and five secretaries during the period 1917–51. Wicksell was chairman for the first five years, followed by Heckscher for a little more than three years, whereupon Brisman held the post until Ohlin assumed the chair in 1932. Despite his short period of formal chairmanship,

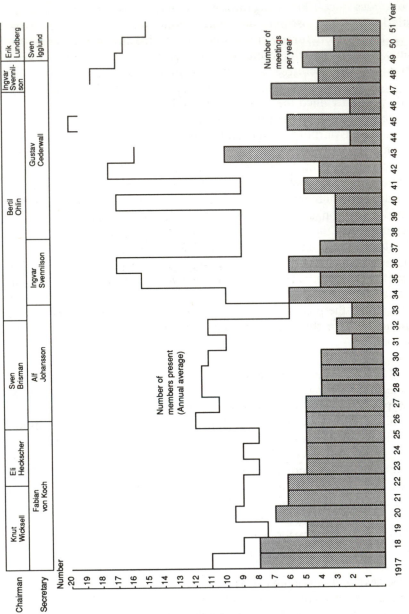

Figure 1. The Political Economy Club, 1917–51.

Heckscher shaped Club activities for its first eighteen years. This period in the Club's history is therefore termed *the Heckscher era*. The subsequent *Ohlin era* also lasted eighteen years. In the last phase of the Club records, Svennilson was chairman for a short period before the final chairmanship was passed on to Lundberg.

The curve describing attendance at club meetings and the bar diagram describing the number of meetings per year speak for themselves. For the following discussion, however, one should note the low frequency of meetings during the depression years 1931–33, which also represented a transition period between the Heckscher and Ohlin eras. The relatively high attendance toward the end of the 1920s and the rise during the first Ohlin years should also be noted. The first period was the important preparatory period for the Stockholm School, and the second period represented its heyday.

2   The Heckscher era, 1917–32

The Wicksell period, 1917–26

If the general purpose of the Club was to bring together all those in the Stockholm area who devoted themselves to scientific work in economics, it was never completely fulfilled. The Club lost its character as a general meeting place for the leading economists in Stockholm as early as at the beginning of the Heckscher era. Thus Davidson, who lived in Uppsala, was able to participate in the meetings only sporadically. However, what most seriously limited the Club's function was the withdrawal of Cassel from its meetings. He was invited to speak at the Club's second meeting but had to decline because of illness. His attendance then fell rapidly, and finally in 1919 he attended only one meeting. On this last occasion, he presented a summary of the contents of his recently published work *Theoretische Sozialökonomie* (Cassel, 1918). It is well known that the relationship between Heckscher and Cassel was not the best. Moreover, Cassel was also very sensitive to criticisms from Davidson and Wicksell. It is possible that when presenting his book at the Club, Cassel received too many of the negative criticisms that Wicksell (1919) published in his famous review later that year. Following this meeting, Cassel did not reappear at the club for more than two decades.

Another prominent member of the club who failed to play the role one might have expected was Gösta Bagge. Through his early studies both in history and economics, Bagge had become a close collaborator of Heckscher's. He was admitted to the Club in its first year, 1917, after a dissertation on wage formation (Bagge, 1917), which immediately gained him an appointment as *docent* (associate professor) at the University of Stockholm. In 1921 he was appointed to its second chair in economics, which was set up in that year. The reason his role in the Club became somewhat restricted appears to have been that he could not cope with the radical and somewhat anarchistic leaning of Wicksell. They were worlds apart ideologically. However, the infrequent presence of Bagge continued even after the demise of Wicksell and was no doubt due to his many other activities, some of which were an important part of the "institutional base" of the Stockholm School. In 1917 Bagge set up Sweden's first organized lower-level seminar (a so-called proseminar) in economics at the Institute of Social Science, and in 1922 he established its licentiat seminar, the country's first modern graduate-level seminar in the field (Henriksson 1979b, 1989). He was also the one who arranged the important financial support of the Rockefeller Foundation for the development of social science, particularly economic, research and teaching at the University of Stockholm from the mid-1920s through the interwar period (Andreen and Boalt, 1987; Craver, this volume). He also played an important role in the famous 1927 Unemployment Committee (Carlson 1982; Wadensjö, this volume). Many of these developments will be touched upon further below.

The discussions in the Club: Despite a rather strong presence of economic historians, the Club's debates during the Wicksell period were primarily devoted to theoretical questions or at least dealt with principal aspects of some contemporary economic policy problem. The period prior to Wicksell's death was an innovative period for economic policy measures, and there was a strong need for a theoretical treatment of these questions.

One of the most interesting participants was Gustaf Åkerman, who made important contributions to capital theory (Åkerman, 1923). He became a member of the Club in 1923 and lectured there several times in the 1920s. But he was not a permanent resident of the Stockholm area and was therefore only a marginal contributor to the continuous proceedings of the Club. His 1923 lecture dealt with the issue of inventories in price adjustments. In 1926 he lectured on the wage question, to which he returned in 1927 when he discussed the connection between high wages and unemployment. This was an early airing of the views he was to work out as a member of the aforementioned 1927 Unemployment Committee (Åkerman, 1931).

Erik Lindahl, elected a member in 1922, began to be a regular participant in the meetings only in 1924 when he was brought to the University of Stockholm by Bagge. In 1924 he published the first volume of his seminal two-volume treatise on monetary policy (Lindahl, 1924). In a 1925 lecture on the means of stabilizing the price level, he revealed that he had begun work on the second volume, which, however, did not appear until 1929 (Lindahl, 1930; Hansen, 1981).

Several lectures by Wicksell, Heckscher, and Davidson also dealt with monetary policy problems. Early in 1920 Heckscher discussed the effect of a too low rate of interest. He had in the preceding months started a campaign in the newspapers against the central bank and exhorted the public to present their holdings of bank notes for redemption in gold, which the law entitled them to do. This soon forced the central bank to raise its rate of interest to protect its gold reserve, making Heckscher a national public figure (Henriksson, 1979b).

A particularly important and intensely discussed monetary problem was the issue of the foreign exchange rate. Davidson discussed this question in a Nordic perspective in September 1920. Wicksell addressed himself to the currency issue in 1921 when Sweden had embarked on a policy of realignment with the gold standard at the prewar par, thereby inducing a violent deflation. Together Heckscher and Wicksell analyzed the German currency situation in 1922.

When the realignment had been reached, monetary discussions turned in a more theoretical direction as evinced by a lecture by Davidson in April 1924 on "The Price Level and the Value of Money." Policy debates continued but were now turned toward trade and unemployment problems. Heckscher raised the tariff issue in 1924 when the result of his protracted work with the Tariff Commission was presented. He was a staunch free trader, and he may not have liked the lecture Ohlin gave the year after on the use of tariffs to counter unemployment. In this lecture, Ohlin may have announced the so-called Stolper-Samuelson theorem, which he stated in the Brentano Festschrift the same year. This lecture also foreshadowed Ohlin's later contribution to the 1927 Unemployment Committee (Ohlin, 1925, 1927).

Ohlin was the foremost of the younger members of the Club. Already in 1919 his lecture on "Commodity Shortages and the Price Level" had attracted great interest. In a letter to Heckscher, who had not been present, Brisman reports that Ohlin astounded the audience. Brisman himself was quite active on the theoretical front. He was the Club member who in particular addressed himself to business cycle problems.

Staging the Wicksellian oral tradition: Any comment on the theoretical discussions held by the Club must, of course, cover the role of Wicksell more closely. As noted above he was a frequent speaker, and more significantly he was present and participated in discussions at fifty-three of the fifty-six meetings of the Club that took place before he died (Gårdlund, 1956). Always doubting the validity and value of his own work, Wicksell repeatedly came back to various issues on which he had been working, particularly in his monetary theory. The members in the Club therefore had many opportunities to share in the various revisions and second thoughts Wicksell had about his own work. As noted earlier he also sometimes gave his views on the work of others. In this way, Wicksell may be said to have exerted an influence on the Stockholm economists through what we shall refer to as *the oral tradition* of Wicksell.

This oral tradition was probably most important in monetary theory. It is well known that in his later years Wicksell expressed quite severe criticism of his own earlier work in the quantity theory tradition. Whether Wicksell actually recanted the quantity theory has, however, been disputed by Lindahl, the closest Swedish follower of Wicksell in monetary theory (Lindahl, 1951).

The post–Wicksell period, 1926–32

After Wicksell's death in 1926, a considerable rejuvenation in Club membership occurred as a large number of younger economists were elected members. One of these was Karin Kock, who was to have the distinction of being the most prominent woman in the Stockholm group. She presented her licenciate degree thesis dealing with capital movements in 1925 and completed her doctor's degree in 1929 with a dissertation on the rate of interest (Kock, 1929). Her dissertation was the first work of a member of the younger Stockholm group to be published in English.

The renewal that took place in the Club is particularly associated with the entry of Myrdal in 1926. He became the dynamic element in a rebellion against the elders related below. Together with the earlier members Lindahl and Johansson, he formed a closely knit troika that in several ways was also effective outside the Club. All three were put in charge of various investigations in Bagge's Rockefeller project. They were also colleagues as teachers at the Institute of Social Science. These common dealings held them together for almost a five-year period before Myrdal left for his long sojourn abroad in 1929–31.

It should be noted that Ohlin was not a member of this group. Although he gave a number of lectures at the Club in the latter half of the 1920s, his continuous participation in the Club's debates was hindered for five years following his appointment in 1924 as a professor at Copenhagen University, a position he had won in competition with Lindahl and Åkerman. But as we shall see, Ohlin was not totally out of the picture.

The younger economists' revolt: The first reported confrontation between the younger economists on the one side and Heckscher, together with the other elders in the Political Economy Club, on the other, took place in 1928. It most likely had its origins in Keynes's (1926) pamphlet *The End of Laissez Faire.* This work induced Johansson to urge Myrdal to write a similar work. Both were under the influence of Max Weber and the Swedish moral philosopher Axel Hägerström and were critical of the scientific outlook of the elder Swedish economists, who drew no demarcation line between ideology and science. The younger economists reacted against the use of economic theory in legitimizing liberal economic policy standpoints.

Partly as a result of Johansson's exhortation, in 1930 Myrdal published his *Vetenskap och Politik i Nationalekonomin* (The Political Element in the Development of Economic Theory) (Myrdal, 1930). Myrdal accomplished the first stage of his work in a series of lectures on the history of economic thought in the spring of 1928. When he presented some material for this lecture series to the Club in early 1928, a clear conflict developed between Myrdal and Heckscher. In his 1930 review of Myrdal's book, Brisman (1930) relates:

> One day about two years ago, a remarkable meeting was held at our political economy discussion club in Stockholm. Here we elder economists had gone for years, basking in our own splendidness, full of an unfeigned mutual admiration, convinced that we had finally found the only True and Correct economic viewpoint. And then came Gunnar Myrdal, who was a young docent at that time, about whom I knew little more than that he had defended a brilliant dissertation. Figuratively speaking, he turned all of us upside-down. His presentation was one long glowing sermon from the mount against everything we had considered most valuable in our economic education. And it was apparent that he had a group of enthusiastic followers among the even younger, who were indignant over the writings of Cassel, Heckscher and myself. All our old and beloved concepts, especially "maximum welfare," and "efficiency," not to mention "population optimum" and "the economic correct distribution of productive forces," "national income," "price level" and much more – all these were blown away like straw in the wind, until we didn't know if we stood on our heads or on our feet.

What had happened on this occasion can be symbolically described as the declaration of independence of the younger generation of Swedish economists from the older generation. To be sure, Lindahl and Myrdal had earlier been so outspoken in Bagge's graduate seminar that Bagge was eventually forced to ask them to refrain from attending. However, it was Heckscher who represented the great parricidal challenge. It should also be mentioned as quite notable that Bagge actually joined the "young Turks" on the above occasion. Bagge's position on many economic policy questions was such that he hardly deserved the sobriquet of "our Swedish Pigou."

It should further be noted that Ohlin, even though he was not physically present and was not a member of the troika, nevertheless indirectly supported the emancipation that was taking place. He had already achieved an early, purely intellectual independence from Heckscher in 1924 when he earned his doctorate on a dissertation in which he presented his contribution to the Heckscher-Ohlin theory (Ohlin, 1924). After his arrival in Copenhagen, Ohlin furthermore began to display a strong sympathy for Keynes's criticism of those liberal doctrines that Heckscher had so strongly defended (Ohlin, 1972). Yet, as late as 1929, Heckscher chose Ohlin as his self-evident successor when he left his chair in economics for a personal research chair in economic history. An open schism betwen them did not appear until Ohlin had succeeded Heckscher (Henriksson, 1979b).

It is interesting to note the position held by Johansson in the above-mentioned revolt. As the protégé of Heckscher, Johansson was "a child of sorrows." There were close personal ties between Johansson and Heckscher. Johansson was even living in with the Heckscher family and was treated as a son in the house. However, Heckscher would never disown a man because he was an intellectual opponent, rather the contrary. What disappointed Heckscher most was probably Johansson's rather slow progress in his dissertation work and his (at that time) somewhat bohemian lifestyle.

It appears that Dag Hammarskjöld also belonged to the opposition group in 1928. After his first economic studies under Fritz Brock at Uppsala, he studied with Keynes at Cambridge in the autumn of 1927 and returned with a licentiate thesis on utilitarianism. It was a subject that fitted well with Myrdal's emancipation lecture, which also dealt with utilitarianism.

It should be added that this declaration of independence of the younger economists did not include the Stockholm School's youngest generation. Tord Palander, Lundberg, and Svennilson were only at the "proseminar" stage in their studies at this point in time. They were not elected to Club membership until after the emancipation year – Palander in 1930, Lundberg in 1931, and Svennilson in 1933.

The emergence of "the dynamic approach": As was made clear above, the 1928 revolt was mainly ideological and not a matter of any developed theoretical position. Although the seminal ideas had been sown already, they had not yet generated any new methodological position. To the extent that the younger generation at this time was thinking along dynamic rather than static lines, there was no reason for the older generation to feel set aside. Discussions about problems of economic dynamics had already taken place in the Club in the early 1920s among the old members. Heckscher had himself lectured on the subject in 1922 when he first developed his ideas about the role of fixed capital. Issues of capital theory were as much the heart and blood of the old members as of the younger generation. Myrdal's basic ideas about the role of expectations presented in his dissertation (1927) could not have been controversial to anyone who had participated in the war and postwar debates on price level changes where the Wicksellian model was frequently applied. Lindahl's main thinking in macrotheory, which developed particularly from 1922–23 onwards, started from Wicksell and Davidson and did not strike anyone as particularly original. Discussions about the use of the rate of interest as a means for stabilizing the value of money were certainly not alien to the older members. Ohlin's thinking along his later macrotheoretical lines had been new in its embryonic 1919 form, but these ideas had later been accepted by many older members, particularly by Brisman.

Yet although the above-mentioned meeting of the Club closed with the confirmation that everyone was basically in agreement on issues of theory, the rupture in the Club could not be healed. Myrdal had shown the other members of the younger generation that they were no longer bound by their elders' thinking. They were free to cast out or retain whatever they pleased in the intellectual baggage they had inherited. The event in January 1928 thus was an important emancipation for the thinking of the younger members, and their various seminal ideas could from then on be more easily brought together in an endogenous process of cross-breeding. The years 1928–30 were a period that saw the birth of the *dynamic method* that was to be the new methodological position associated with the Stockholm School (Hansson, 1982).

All this was mainly the contribution of Lindahl, who had pushed ahead in monetary theory even before the demise of Wicksell. But he undoubtedly received an important stimulus from Myrdal's (1927) microtheoretical dissertation. He served as its official discussant, although he had also read the early drafts (Lindhal, 1929). Myrdal provided him with an important new point of departure. Although expectations had been explicitly dealt with in the many earlier applications of the Wicksellian model, Myrdal's particular approach brought the intertemporal dimension of market equilibration to the fore in a new way. This was decisive for the development of Lindahl's thinking during the following two years when he tried to bring the Wicksellian synthesis of the Austrian and Lausanne schools within the confines of the Marshallian short run. Presenting "the intertemporal tussle" along the later Arrow-Debreu line, he was apparently unaware of Hayek's (1928) contribution, however, and his ideas on the sequence approach appear also to be entirely his own. They must be seen as the logical outcome of introducing uncertainty into the intertemporal general equilibrium framework. Once the sequence idea is conceived, the various ensuing concepts such as the notions of temporary equilibrium and disequilibrium seem to follow naturally.

With the publication of Lindahl's (1930) *Penningpolitikens Medel* (The Means of Monetary Policy), the basic research program of the Stockholm School may be said to have been launched. Here the dynamic method, although not yet formally worked out as an endogenous sequence method, is applied to the central issues of macroeconomics within the frame of reference of the Wicksellian model. Here we also find the embryo of the Lindahl income concept. The seminal quality of this work by Lindahl, where among other things the word *macro* is used perhaps for the first time, does not mean, however, that Lindahl was alone among the Stockholm School members in developing the more substantive macro ideas associated with the school. On these Ohlin had also made important progress. He revealed a clear analytical grasp of the Keynesian income adjustment mechanism in the transfer debate with Keynes in the *Economic Journal* in 1929 (Ohlin, 1929). He had already in early 1928 sent off the manuscript of his Harvard treatise on international trade theory (Ohlin, 1933c), where one finds his well-developed insights into the role of income adjustments richly demonstrated not only in the context of balance of payment theory. There is furthermore little doubt that Ohlin arrived at these insights independent of Lindahl. As noted earlier, Ohlin had a legacy in monetary theory dating back to his early work in 1919–21. But he was not merely thinking along Wicksellian lines. His ideas also sprang from trying to deal with issues of structural change and variations in employment within the framework of trade theory where the Marshallian short run also claimed attention.

Having set things going, Myrdal appears to have been little involved in the continued development before 1930, although it should be recognized that his excursion into the history of ideas in his 1930 contribution contains many openings for subsequent conceptual developments. He was also quite close to Lindahl as the latter struggled with the definitional and statistical difficulties of measuring national income, which he had first presented in the 1927 Unemployment Committee but then continued as his major task under Bagge in the Rockefeller project (Lindahl, 1927). Since they were both specialists on taxation, they naturally had a common theoretical vantage point when dealing with the macroissues posed within the frame of reference of the Wicksellian model. However, Myrdal did not focus on these issues in the same way and to the same extent that Lindahl had done before 1930. When Lindahl completed his manuscript in the fall of 1929, Myrdal had already left for the United States. Assisting Lindahl at the time and reading his manuscripts were instead two younger members of the School, Lundberg and Palander. Their assistance to Lindahl even went so far as writing some of his footnotes. It has not been possible to find out whether the two younger members of the school wrote the footnote that was later pointed to as Lindahl's key anticipation of Keynes's *General Theory* (Henriksson, 1987a).

However, these Keynesian features were not the dominant macrotheoretical developments in the early thinking of the Stockholm School. By 1929 Lindahl had worked out a neo-Wicksellian analysis that was strikingly close to that offered by the pre-Keynesian Keynes in the *Treatise on Money* that appeared a year later (Keynes, 1930). Indeed, if the Stockholm School in any way anticipated Keynes, it was not only the *General Theory* (Keynes, 1936) that was anticipated but also the *Treatise*. This explains why the *General Theory* was so eagerly awaited and also why they became so disappointed with it.

In all these developments the Club no doubt played an important role. It is true that Ohlin was present only once during the two-year period. However, on that occasion in October 1928, he lectured on capital movements, and both Myrdal and Lindahl were present. It is not very likely that he did that without touching upon the income adjustment mechanism, dealing explicitly with situations of unused resources. Lindahl was present at every meeting during the two-year period as was Myrdal up until his departure for his study period abroad in the second half of 1929. But the cross-fertilization of ideas also occurred in their work on the Rockefeller project – at least at the level of logistical fraternization – and as teaching colleagues at the Institute of Social Science.

As previously mentioned, even the youngest generation represented by Lundberg took its first steps in 1930. Lundberg assisted Lindahl, but of course the net gainer in this collaboration was Lundberg himself. In 1930 he published his licentiate thesis in the *Ekonomisk Tidskrift* wherein the embryo of his 1937 dissertation, the peak performance of the Stockholm School according to many, can be found (Lundberg, 1930, 1937).[5] However, in that embryo of his work one may also note the influence of ideas that were to be not only peripheral but even opposed to the Stockholm School. This influence emanated from, among others, Johan Åkerman, the younger brother of the aforementioned Gustaf Åkerman.

Åkerman, who was a graduate of the Business College in Stockholm like Ohlin and Johansson, had after a sojourn in the United States in the early 1920s introduced the Persons business forecasting method in Sweden (Henriksson, 1987b, 1987c). In 1928 he had presented a dissertation on the problems of the business cycle, a study read by Wicksell in an early version (Åkerman, 1928). He made his first appearance as a speaker in October 1929 when he lectured on the state of the international economy. He was at that time head of the private business cycle forecasting service set up by the Federation of Swedish Industries. Åkerman had quite successfully predicted the coming of the depression, which was quite an achievement since generally most business forecasts had failed, especially the Persons method used at Harvard.

However, all these developments could not have converged on a school without a catalyzing agent. The catalyst was the depression, which in the fall of 1931 set off a chain of events within the Club that brought developments to a head.

The catalyzing phase: The onset of the depression was brought to a climax in September 1931 when Sweden suspended the gold standard. The increasing unemployment and the currency crisis during the autumn of that year generated a new set of policy issues that intensely engaged all Swedish economists. The leading names were drawn into the policy-making process as internal advisors and consultants, and they also generally exerted a strong influence on public opinion through the media (Henriksson, 1979a; Jonung, 1979). But their response to the situation by no means formed a united front.

One of the main deviators was Johan Åkerman. His thinking on the policy issues emerging in the fall of 1931 was more akin to that of Hayek and classical economists, who advocated wage cuts to restore profitability as a cure to the unemployment problem. To neutralize the influence of Åkerman and other divergent views and to impress their own views on the policy makers in an efficient way, the leading members of the Club took an initiative that turned out to be decisive for the subsequent debate. At a Club meeting at the end of October 1931, one month after the dramatic suspension of the gold standard, Karin Kock presented a lecture on the exchange crisis. The meeting was well attended by the younger members, except for "the deviate" Johan Åkerman, and the old generation was represented by Heckscher and Brisman. A proposal was made by Heckscher that the economists should issue a public statement presenting their unanimous viewpoint in order to facilitate the efforts of the country's economic policy leadership to gain control over the crisis situation. Myrdal was assigned to produce a draft statement that would then be considered by the leading group of economists.

As the group gathered some weeks later to discuss Myrdal's draft proposal, there was a surprisingly strong consensus on what we today would call the stabilization policy goals. The level of employment was to be protected as far as possible while maintaining the value of money. In the absence of Johan Åkerman, there was furthermore no strong disagreement on the choice of policy instruments. There was, in fact, a notable agreement between the older generation led by Heckscher and the younger generation led by Ohlin and Myrdal about the possibilities of influencing the employment situation through statements and measures that operated via the formation of expectations. Yet the attempt to produce a unified guide to action failed. What seemingly prevented Heckscher in particular from accepting Myrdal's draft proposal was the practical design of the price stabilization goals. Heckscher wanted above all to stabilize the wholesale price level whereas Myrdal and the younger group wanted to stabilize the price level of consumption goods. The cause of the failure thus appears to have been that Heckscher's proposal had a slightly deflationary bias and that of the younger group a slightly inflationary bias. However, the real rift was probably a deeper one. Myrdal's draft proposal suggested too many regulatory and directly interventionist measures that were alien to the liberal vision of Heckscher, who sensed that by signing the draft he would endorse a policy that in practice would turn out to be a step toward central planning. Although the stabilization issue was the primary concern in the autumn of 1931, these crisis months witnessed the start of a protracted and fierce battle between Myrdal and Heckscher on the issue of the free market system versus central planning.

As a result of this failure, Heckscher wrote his own draft and published it within a month (Heckscher, 1931). Myrdal, who clearly felt outflanked by Heckscher's hastily published book, was soon after able to get his own manuscript published together with Kock's lecture (Myrdal, 1931). These publications attracted great attention. The fact that two books were published rather than one seems not to have detracted from the influence that the economists exerted over the making of policy. Rather, the contrary seems to have been the case. The public at large and politicians in general did not perceive any great difference betwen the books. What aroused opinion in favor of both was their lucid exposition and analysis of the situation and its background and their rich agendas for action. Many of the subsequent policy measures that were to attract so much international attention were presented, albeit in an embryonic form.

However, the policy importance of the Club meetings in the fall of 1931 is not limited to the influence of these publications. The discussions in the Club also dealt with important policy issues that were never the subject of much open debate. One of these was a proposal for setting up an institute especially devoted to alerting the authorities to short-run developments in the state of the economy. It was discussed as part of a larger proposal to set up an economic advisory council patterned on a similar body set up in 1930 in Britain. The advisory council proposal was never followed up, although Hammarskjöld was undoubtedly influenced by the different views put forth by Heckscher, Myrdal, and Ohlin on the issue of the institute. As secretary of the 1927 Unemployment Committee (a position to which he was appointed in 1930 at the age of twenty-five), he made this his own pet project in the committee and pushed it all the way through to the creation in 1937 of the National Institute of Economic Research with Lundberg as director (Henriksson, 1987b).

From the point of view of the development of the Stockholm School, however, the main significance of the events in the Club in the fall of 1931 was that it brought the younger generation in touch with policy issues. Although many of them had long participated in public discussion, this was their real debut as unofficial advisors. In the early phase of the crisis, the proceedings tended to be dominated by the older generation of economists, including not only Cassel and even Davidson but also Heckscher as its most energetic and active representative. The meetings of the Club during the later phase of the crisis opened the door for the younger generation to the internal policy-making process. The most important role played by the crossing of swords in the club that autumn was the influence it exerted on the reinitiated work within the 1927 Unemployment Committee. During that autumn the committee decided to go ahead with a series of studies that some years later resulted in innovative reports by Johansson, Ohlin, Myrdal, and Hammarskjöld (Landgren, 1957, Uhr, 1977).

It should be noted, however, that the very youngest group of the later Stockholm School was not yet admitted to the tables of power and influence. They were still absorbed in their theoretical studies. Palander had devoted considerable attention to monetary theory but was at that time on his way toward a contribution to location theory following up a research line of Ohlin's in regional economics. Svennilson, heavily engaged in Bagge's Rockefeller work on the project dealing with the history of wages and the labor market in Sweden, was turning his theoretical attention toward microtheoretical issues of the firm and the demand for labor leading up to his later dissertation. Lundberg had at that time completed his part of the same project in the Rockefeller studies and had left for a protracted study period as a Rockefeller fellow in the United States. This youngest generation therefore was never very involved, practically or theoretically, in the depression economics. Instead their interests were more directed toward the budding issues of microeconomics and in the case of Lundberg toward the general problems of the business cycle (Lundberg, 1987).

3   The Ohlin era, 1932–47

The transition period, 1932–3

The year 1932 was an important transition point in the history of the Club. Ohlin succeeded Brisman, who had held the chairmanship since 1926, and Heckscher's collaboration in the activities of the Club ended. This changing of the guard may to some extent have been the result of the cleavage that had developed between the older and the younger members of the club in the preceding years, but it was mainly a natural event. Ohlin had returned to Stockholm from Copenhagen and succeeded Heckscher in the economics chair at the Business College. Heckscher's retreat from the Club had furthermore less to do with the growing tension between Ohlin and himself mentioned earlier than with Heckscher's increasing commitment to the field of economic history (Henriksson, 1979b).

During the transition period 1931–3, the activities of the Club remained at a fairly low level, although this had little to do with the transition per se. The depression turned the interests of the economists toward current problems. Several meetings were therefore devoted mainly to discussions of the economic policy issues of the day. Brisman himself lectured in early 1931 on the international price decline, and the previously discussed meetings in the fall of 1931 also testify to the fact that the interests of the economists that year were strongly diverted from theory. Furthermore the major shift in the social function of the Club that occurred during the Ohlin era away from the seminar style toward a more social gathering with invited guest speakers is already noticeable in this transition period.

However, the major reason for the low level of activity in the Club during the transition years appears to have been that the depression generated so many government activities and inquiries calling for the assistance of the economists that they had little time left for Club meetings. This absorption of the economists by the government became particularly pronounced in the fall of 1931 when the 1927 Unemployment Committee started its second round of investigations. This work occupied much of the time of Hammarskjöld, Johansson, Myrdal, and Ohlin for the next two years, 1932 and 1933. Lindahl, eventually overburdened by assignments to such an extent that in 1933 Bagge was forced to dismiss him from his responsibilities in the Rockefeller project, was in 1931 put to work by the Central Bank on the construction of a price index while at the same time after many years of frustrated attempts he finally obtained a chair in economics and moved residence to Gothenburg.

Only one of the known meetings of the Club in 1932 was devoted to a theoretical topic. Furthermore, the speaker on that occasion was not a professional economist, but Ernst Wigforss, who was to become the minister of finance in the Social Democratic government that took office after the election in the autumn of that year. As the public finance expert of the Social Democrats, during the 1920s he had followed the debates of the economists not only in Sweden but also abroad, particularly the discussion in England. He had also kept up with the theoretical developments in the field. As a leading member of the 1927 Unemployment Committee, he wrote several interesting reports of which one stands out as perhaps the earliest discovery of what is today referred to as the Phillips curve (Wigforss, 1929).[6] The economists' respect and esteem for Wigforss as a theoretician was formally acknowledged at the aforementioned meeting by his admission to Club membership. This was the first exception to the rule that only professional economists were admitted to membership. A second exception was made some years later when the governor of the Central Bank, Ivar Rooth, was also admitted.

In his lecture on "Depression and Thrift," Wigforss displayed his already well-developed (what we would today call Keynesian) insights to a large audience. Among those present at the meeting were all the contributors to the second round of the Unemployment Committee except Ohlin. They undoubtedly welcomed the opportunity to exchange views on issues central to their assignments at an early stage. The committee work was mainly carried out as commissioned reports, and there were long periods of little current discussion within the committee. As secretary, Hammarskjöld acted as a clearing agent, but he could of course not act as a substitute for direct contacts between committee members. As the reports were submitted to Hammarskjöld, he sent them out for review by outside experts. However, Ohlin's manuscript was also reviewed internally by, among others, Bagge, who still held a central position in the committee. As a result Hammarskjöld, adding criticism of his own, had to ask Ohlin to rework the report, which delayed publication of Ohlin (1934). This is probably the origin of the somewhat aloof relationship between Ohlin and Hammarskjöld noticeable throughout their later careers.

The fact that the various reports were not typical committee compromise products naturally adds to their value as evidence of where the author stood and his accomplishments as a scientist. However, seen from the committee's point of view, the reports no doubt could have profited from some rounds of internal discussions and hearings. It fell on Hammarskjöld as the secretary of the committee to carry out the task of synthesizing the various contributions into a final report. However, he did not do that entirely alone. The chairman Gunnar Huss and other older members, especially Bagge, undoubtedly played some role in shaping the final compromise report. Bagge had worked out a plan for a final report as early as 1930. As the first among the Stockholm economists to make his entry into active politics as a member of parliament in 1932, he was naturally anxious to keep an eye on how the committee work was summed up. Furthermore, the first draft of the final report was subjected to a thorough discussion during a concentrated work period with the various members and staff assembled. A similar discussion took place upon the completion of the second draft before the publication of the final report. Although Hammarskjöld wrote most of the text, many of his own ideas were suppressed, especially in the second draft and in the final report. One should therefore be careful before attributing all the views and achievements in the final report to Hammarskjöld or to him alone.

The intense work on their assignments in the Unemployment Committee, especially during the second half of 1932 but also continuing into 1933, undoubtedly goes a long way to explain why there were so few meetings in the Club. However, substitute forms of communication proliferated. Ohlin in particular tried to engage the others in a more joint work effort by circulating memos and writing letters. And of course there was also the telephone. It is hard to conceive that this medium was not used by those who wanted to give Ohlin their views on his memos, for example, the one he wrote for the Unemployment Commmittee on the Austrian school (Ohlin, 1933a).

The heyday of the Stockholm School

With Ohlin as chairman and Svennilson as the new secretary (after Johansson), it was not long before the activities of the Club were revitalized. In March 1933 at the first meeting of the Club after the election of Ohlin as chairman, Ohlin himself lectured on a "prae [sic]-Wicksellian" monetary theory. This presentation was a sequel to the well-known paper Ohlin had circulated among Club members in the autumn of 1932 and then published in the *Ekonomisk Tidskrift* in 1933 (Ohlin, 1933b, 1981). Ohlin had in that paper worked out his own approach to monetary theory in response to what he referred to as the neo-Wicksellian thinking of Lindahl and Myrdal. The paper was also an offshoot from his work in the Unemployment Committee. In the spring of 1933, Ohlin completed the draft of his committee report that was to appear in a revised form in the following year as Ohlin (1934). Myrdal and Johansson, who were also completing their drafts at that time, were present at the Club meeting, and they undoubtedly had much to say on the theoretical issues raised by Ohlin. They were all informed about the evolving international debate on these issues. The controversy between Hayek and Keynes in particular, and in Sweden the sharpened criticism especially from Johan Åkerman, forced them to articulate their own thinking. In these endeavors, Ohlin was the one who was most active in trying to demonstrate how the thinking among the Stockholm economists could be considered an approach different from that of the Vienna School but close to that of the Cambridge School. He actually referred to "the Cambridge-Stockholm School" at that time. But the theoretical divergences between the members of the group made it difficult for them to see that what they had in common might be considered "a third school."

Furthermore, they were divided by increasing rivalry and ideological dissension. Alf Johansson had followed Myrdal in moving toward a socialist position, preventing them both from rallying behind Ohlin. The election of Ohlin as chairman of the Club should not be interpreted as evidence that he was the leader of the Stockholm group. The other members somehow looked upon Ohlin as a newcomer to a discussion that they had been carrying on for years.

Ohlin's presentation in the spring of 1933 marks him, however, as the coming entrepreneur of the conception of a Swedish school. He was the one in the group who had been most exposed to the thinking abroad and had participated most actively in international debates. This enabled him at an early stage to view the Swedish discussions from the outside. He had already in 1925, in the Brentano paper mentioned earlier, identified what he referred to as a particularly Swedish brand of economic science. Although Ohlin's position as a spokesman for the Stockholm group was never accepted by all the other members, they were, as we shall see below, soon to accept his view that they had an approach in common and to bow to the international profile that was being imposed on them.

One of the Club's most intensive years of theoretical debate was 1934. Lundberg had returned from his two-year study period in the United States, and in January he presented his impressions from that sojourn. Later in the spring, he presented his first models in his coming dissertation in a lecture entitled "Some Theoretical Questions Concerning the Relationship between Investment Time, Circulation Velocity and Purchasing Power." Club attendance was unusually large on that occasion, and the minutes relate that "the discussion was lively," which was usually the case when Lundberg was involved. Lindahl, Myrdal, Kock, and Hammarskjöld all participated in the discussion as well as Ohlin. Lundberg reports in his memoris that Ohlin was a severe critic at that time, and one may infer that this criticism had a major influence on Lundberg, who was then in a very formative phase of his dissertation work (Lundberg, 1987). Perhaps some of the notable strengths and weaknesses of the dissertation were a result of the influence of Ohlin.

In November, Lindahl presented his famous "A Note on the Dynamic Pricing Problem" (Steiger, 1971). He had previously circulated this paper among a wide circle of economists in Sweden and abroad. It attracted great attention at the London School of Economics, but the Cambridge reaction was more subdued. Keynes replied later that year that "your way of dealing with time leads to undue complications and will be very difficult either to apply or to generalize about" (Moggridge, 1979). Thus, Lindahl and the other Club members were informed early about Keynes's new attitude toward sequence analysis, and this undoubtedly raised even further their expectations of the book they so eagerly awaited. The reaction of Lindahl's Swedish colleagues was much more favorable. Ohlin even produced an appreciative counternote and showed how his approach related to Lindahl's.

Wigforss attended this meeting, revealing his continued great interest in economic theory. His presence shows that despite the strong orientation toward theory in this period, there was still much attention to policy issues. In this vein, the Club listened to Hammarskjöld in 1935 lecturing on the state of the currency problem and in early 1936 heard Lundberg report on his experience as consultant to the Economic Planning Commission on Iceland during the second half of 1935 (Lundberg, 1987). But some members such as Johansson and Lindahl were again so absorbed in government inquiries that they had little time left for the Club.

Foreign guest appearances: In 1934 the Club began to pursue in earnest its role as host for foreign guest lecturers, which then increasingly became its primary function in the research community of economists in Stockholm. During the Heckscher era, foreign visitors were rather uncommon at the Club meetings, and except for the Norwegian Ragnar Frisch, who actually lectured in the Club in 1928, they were mainly listeners to the discussions. The record mentions only one non-Scandinavian, Gerhard Mackenroth from Germany, who attended the Frisch lecture.

There were three types of foreign guests. The first type was a small but notable group that made its way to Stockholm attracted by the growing international stature of Swedish economics. They wanted to learn at the source what the Swedish economists had achieved. Early in 1934, Brinley Thomas addressed the Club on the subject of "Some Remarks on the Swedish Crisis Literature." Dispatched from the London School of Economics, he came to spend about six months in Sweden and in that brief time learned the language so well that he was able to summarize the Swedish research situation and its background in an excellent book (Thomas, 1936); which appeared in early 1936. Even before then Thomas had presented the Swedish ideas to the English-speaking world through a lecture series at the London School of Economics in the fall of 1934.[7] These lectures coincided with John Hicks's *Economica* review of Myrdal's 1933 contribution to monetary theory that aided in seducing George Schackle into a lifelong devotion to the Myrdal approach. They also made the London School a springboard for the dissemination of the Swedish ideas across the Atlantic through various American students in residence at the London School at that time (Hart, 1951).

In early 1936, the Club was visited by a Dutch economist, Johan Koopmans, who lectured on "Various Notions of Monetary Equilibrium," a theme clearly related to Myrdal's neo-Wicksellian contribution just mentioned. Koopmans had contributed a paper on the neutrality of money in the volume edited by Hayek (1933), in which Myrdal's important contribution to monetary equilibrium theory appeared in German. This was where the German translator, the aforementioned Mackenroth, introduced the passwords of the Stockholm School, *ex ante* and *ex post,* as convenient substitutes for some of Myrdal's verbal equilibristics in the Swedish text (Myrdal, 1933). Generally, rigor and comprehension are lost in translation, but in the case of the Swedish authors, sometimes the opposite occurred.

The relatively unknown Polish economist Michal Kalecki attended Koopman's lecture. He had contacted Myrdal and traveled to Sweden on a Rockefeller grant. Kalecki never made a presentation at the Club, but he was an active participant in the licentiate seminar at Stockholm University (from 1931 led mainly by Myrdal, who in 1933 took over the chair held by Cassel after Cassel benignly retired upon Myrdal's own request). However, Kalecki broke off his Swedish visit in early 1936 after reading Keynes's *General Theory* and moved the remainder of his grant-financed activities to England. His stay in Sweden was too brief to exert any influence on the Swedes, and according to Lundberg he was not a very sociable person anyhow. He quite obviously abandoned Stockholm for pastures that looked greener to him (Feiwel, 1975; Lundberg, 1987).

The second group consisted of refugees, mainly Jewish, who left the German sphere of Europe after Hitler's "Machtübernahme" in 1933. One of them was the mathematician Willy Feller, who eventually moved to the United States, where various universities could better take advantage of his talents. In Stockholm he collaborated with the Harald Cramér group of mathematicial statisticians in their research in actuarial and probability theory, but he also associated with Lundberg and Svennilson, whom he inspired and helped in their theoretical work (Lundberg, 1987).

The third and most prominent group of visiting foreign economists were those who had been extended a special invitation. In 1935 the Club received a grant from the J. H. Palme Fund, where Heckscher acted as the principal administrator in the distribution of funds (Henriksson, 1979b). The Club was thereby given the opportunity to invite foreign guest lecturers. In April 1936 Frisch visited the Club. Among the leading non-Swedish economists he was the one best qualified to follow and understand the development of the new thinking in Sweden, not only through the entry offered by the Norwegian language but also because of his thorough familiarity with Wicksell's writings (Andvig, 1985 and this volume). Frisch's two-day lectures in the Club dealt with "The Swedish Approach to Monetary Theory and the Choice of Time Periods in Monetary Analysis." It may be recalled that Lundberg had treated this subject two years earlier.

It can be noted that in his lecture Frisch used the expression "the Swedish approach." This confirms that the notion of a Swedish school had become accepted in the neighboring countries. Even the Swedes themselves had swung around so that, as noted in the introduction, Keynes faced a rather united front in his meeting with the Swedes in the autumn of 1936. The Swedes would, however, use the term Swedish school only grudingly in discussions with foreigners since the school could by no means cover all Swedish economists. For this reason the term "the Stockholm School," allegedly first used by Johan Åkerman in his criticism of the new approach, was a convenient label when Ohlin (1937) delivered his grand presentation of the school in the *Economic Journal.*

Developments after the Keynes visit

As noted in the introduction, the Palme grant financed Keynes's visit, and additional funds in 1937 made possible visits by, among others, Oskar Morgenstern and Jan Tinbergen. Both lectured on current issues in business cycle theory. At that time, Morgenstern was still director of the Austrian Institute for Business Cycle Research, which was later placed under the supervision of the Institute for Business Cycle Research in Berlin. Tinbergen was in charge of the corresponding Dutch institute. Bringing these leading representatives of business cycle research to Stockholm naturally engaged Lundberg, who in 1937 became the director of the Swedish business cycle research institute, the National Institute of Economic Research, a position he held for eighteen years. The meeting with Tinbergen was particularly important, since it established a contact with the Dutch institute that turned out to be of some importance for the development of the Swedish institute. Tinbergen's lecture to the Club was also notable because both Heckscher and Cassel attended the subsequent dinner.

The foreign guest lecturers in 1938 and 1939 received less attention from Club members. However, the appearance of Mr. and Mrs. Hicks attracted quite a large audience when they visited in May 1939. Ursula Hicks lectured for two days on public finance. Her husband gave a lecture on the first day on "Risk Factors and Interest Rates." On the second day he lectured on "The Logical Foundations of Welfare Economics," which appeared later that year as a well-known paper in the *Economic Journal* (Hicks, 1939).

Toward the end of the 1930s, there were so many visiting guest lecturers that there was little room for Swedish presentations. However, two younger members of the Stockholm School made their debut as speakers in the Club in this period. In November 1938 Palander spoke on "Conceptions of Competitive Behavior of Firms in Oligopolistic Situations," showing that the interests of the Stockholm economists were not limited to monetary and macrotheoretical problems but included microtheoretical questions as well. The second younger Swedish speaker was the then former secretary of the Club, Svennilson. He had followed up the microtheoretical work of Myrdal of 1927 in a dissertation On

Economic Planning (Svennilson, 1938). In his dissertation he demonstrated how the sequence approach could be applied in the theory of the firm. Palander, who served as the main discussant, criticized it with acerbity, which may have been one of the reasons this profoundly innovative work did not at that time receive the esteem it was later shown to be due.

The Club's increasingly predominant function as host for renowned foreign economists naturally contributed an important stimulus to economic thinking and research in Stockholm, although the "crowding-out effect" of the host function meant that the community of professional economists in Stockholm lost an important forum for internal dialogues. However, compensating institutional developments occurred. The setting up of the National Institute for Economic Research was of course an important event (Henriksson, 1987d). Another important development was the extended and differentiated seminar developments and activities in the Institute of Social Science at the University of Stockholm. These activities were often led by Johansson, Kock, and other members at the Institute. Myrdal and Bagge, the professors in charge, were often off on long leaves of absence to cater to their political duties or undertake other mostly government assignments (Henriksson, 1989).

A third development concerned the *Ekonomisk Tidskrift,* Davidson's creation of 1898, which had been an ailing institution for Swedish economists at least since the death of Wicksell. It was rejuvenated in 1938 when Davidson was bought out from his editorship (Henriksson, 1979b). Under the new editors, Lundberg and Svennilson, the journal entered into a period of renewed expansion with a book review section as an important feature. The fact that no formal book reviews were presented in *Ekonomisk Tidskrift* during the heyday of the Stockholm School helps to explain certain weaknesses in the development of the School. This situation of course made the meetings of the Political Economy Club even more important.

A Nordic tradition asserted: A most significant development during the post-*General Theory* period, which compensated for the failure of the Club to serve as a meeting place for scientific discussions, was the growing institutionalization of the contacts between the professional economists in the various Nordic countries. Following an old tradition from the nineteenth century, Nordic economic meetings were held regularly, but they were dominated by current economic policy issues and did not allow the small number of professional economists to make themselves heard. Noting that the needs of economic science were not adequately served by these meetings, which furthermore took place too seldom, Frisch took an important initiative during the Nordic Economic Meeting in Oslo in June 1935. At a luncheon to which he had invited the leading economists from each of the Nordic states, he presented a proposal that regular annual meetings between the professional Nordic economists should be arranged. The luncheon group agreed with Frisch and decided that a meeting should be arranged in August of every year at a place located equidistantly from the capitals of the different countries, except for Helsinki. Such a location was found at Marstrand in the vicinity of Gothenburg, where the first meeting occurred in August 1936. These meetings have been called the Marstrand meetings, although not all of them have been located there.

All these good developments were interrupted by the war, but most of them could be resumed when the war was over. There is good reason to talk about, if not a Nordic school in economics, at least a Nordic tradition in the field. This broader identity perhaps has more of a standing in the outside world than the national ones of the individual countries. Of course, the interwar ideas of the Stockholm School was disseminated to all Nordic countries, but the most important integrating factor was probably the broader heritage of Wicksell.

The war period, 1940–47

The final years of the 1930s marked the end of the role of the Political Economy Club as an important part of the institutional base of the Stockholm School, and the war years saw a decline in the School itself. The ideas of the Stockholm School were, however, to some extent preserved in Uppsala where Lindahl and later also Palander obtained chairs and where important contributions were made by Bent Hansen, Ragnar Bentzel, and Herman Wold. Paradoxically, the continued criticism by Johan Åkerman in Lund also kept the issues alive through a protracted rear guard discussion with Harald Dickson and others into the 1950s (Petersson, 1987, this volume; Hansson, this volume). Some theoretical work along the Stockholm School line continued even in Stockholm, especially at the National Institute of Economic Research, which (having been closed during the first war years) resumed work in 1943 (Henriksson, 1987d). Under the continued directorship of Lundberg it addressed itself particularly to the new macroissues arising with the inflationary gap problems during the war (Berg, 1987). But few of these new theoretical issues were taken up for discussion in the Club. In March 1942 Ohlin lectured on the Stockholm School position on the quantity theory (Ohlin, 1943). However, this was almost the only offshoot in the Club of the continued theoretical discussion in the Stockholm School tradition. Current developments totally dominated the meetings during the war.

4   Epilogue

After the war the Political Economy Club resumed its main role as host to visiting foreign economists. In 1948 the membership listened to Lawrence Klein on economic research, and in 1949, to Joan Robinson on monopoly theory and to Alvin Hansen on business cycle theory and growth theory. In 1950 Tjalling Koopmans lectured on transportation and localization theory, and Tryggve Haavelmo spoke on the relationship between static and dynamic market theory. The fastest rising star in those days, Paul Samuelson, was also a guest, although this is not mentioned in the minutes.[8] The Swedish contribution in these lectures remained small, even in this new phase. The only Swedish lecturer, Ingvar Ohlsson, spoke in 1948 on the Swedish national budget.

An important meeting took place under the chairmanship of Lundberg in early 1951 with Heckscher as the guest of honor. Heckscher, who had started the Political Economy Club to provide Wicksell an opportunity for creative emeritus life was himself now emeritus and chairman of an Economic History Club that had been created to offer him the same retirement life. He had now been invited together with the Economic History Club and his successor Ernst Söderlund to participate in a discussion of Dahmén's trail-blazing dissertation, a work in the tradition of Johan Åkerman and Joseph Schumpeter (Dahmén, 1950). In the work of Dahmén, Heckscher saw the promise that economics and history could still meet in a fruitful way (Henriksson, 1979b). Even Lundberg was enthusiastic about Dahmén's attempt to bring economic theory and economic history closer together. While Heckscher made "a plea for theory in economic history," Lundberg's plea was for history in economic theory.[9]

The Club's last lecture noted in the minutes was given by Dennis Robertson on October 1, 1951. He spoke on the subject Keynes had touched on in his lecture fifteen years earlier on precisely that day, namely, the rate of interest. An old intellectual tie existed between the Stockholm economists and Robertson on this controversial issue since both disputed Keynes's theory of interest and also had the sequence approach in common. The division between Robertson and Keynes in the 1930s was equally as serious as that between Keynes and the Stockholm School; however, Keynes's controversy with the Swedes was probably a less personal one. The Swedes had paid tribute to Keynes before the war by awarding him the foremost decoration the Swedish Academy of Science could offer before the days of Nobel Prize, its gold medal in economics. They also decided before the war, supported by Ohlin, to have the *General Theory* (Keynes, 1936) translated into Swedish. This work, led by Palander and carried out by Leif Björk, was not completed until the end of the war, however, and Keynes probably never saw the result (Keynes, 1945). But even so, the leading Swedish economists, although accepting Keynesian policy measures, which were after all also the measures advocated by the Stockholm School tradition, held onto a rather non-Keynesian line in theory. There was some original work done along the lines of the Stockholm School even in the 1950s (Hansen, 1951, 1955, Metelius, 1955, Faxén, 1957).[10] But eventually even the Swedes had to bear the Keynesian cross constructed by Samuelson (1947).

5   Summary

This chapter has been an attempt at assessing the importance of the Political Economy Club for the development of the Stockholm School. The results may be summed up with reference to a three-phase life-cycle view of the School.

First, the Club was important for the creation of the Stockholm School. The Club brought Wicksell into personal contact with Stockholm economists and created an important "oral" link in the transfer of the Wicksellian legacy to the next generation. The Club then played an equally significant role after Wicksell's death, when it became the stage for the younger generation's emancipation from the influence of their elders. The emancipation process began with the ideological confrontation in 1928, which released a process of theoretical advance. This was soon directed to macroeconomic theory, anticipating, but eventually also surpassing, Keynes through the catalytic debate beginning in the fall of 1931. Without the Club, this emancipation process would probably have been much more difficult and perhaps incomplete, and the development of the new theoretical ideas might have been delayed or even aborted.

Second, the club was a vital factor underlying the contributions of the Stockholm School during its heyday coinciding with the first phase of the Ohlin era in the Club's history. Although the ideas of the Stockholm School were often developed in other contexts, such as in the Unemployment Committee or at the licentiate seminar at Stockholm University, much of the important dialogue and the mutual criticism occurred within the Club's circle. It brought together economists who would not otherwise have met so often because of personal animosity or for other reasons.

Third, having noted the Club's importance for the creation and flowering of the Stockholm School, it is natural to ask what role the club played in the School's subsequent development. To the extent that this later development can be considered a period of decline, one can readily point to the Club's increasing role as a host institution for foreign visitors. This may have enriched and stimulated the Swedish discussion in its earlier phase, when the Swedish economists, especially Ohlin but even Lindahl, were spurred by the scientific competition that arose between the Vienna School and the Cambridge School. But after the Keynesian year of 1936, it is possible that the visits of foreigners contributed to a stifling of the Swedish debate by denying it its most important forum.

In conclusion, it should be noted that the Club's importance cannot be assessed only from the perspective of the history of economic thought. In the broader perspective of economic history, the Club's role in the economic policy debate is probably equally interesting. Economists from politically divergent camps were often brought together in the Club. Even when consensus was not reached, they nonetheless sharpened and developed the arguments that they would present to a larger public. The Club thereby strengthened those features that from an international point of view appeared particularly unique and perhaps as worthy of attention as the theoretical contributions of the Swedish economists, namely, the great influence of Swedish economics on economic debate and economic policy within Sweden.

Notes

1 I am very grateful to Sven Igglund who permitted me to use the minutes of the club and to Bengt Metelius who first stimulated this inquiry and then offered comments on the draft, and as well to the one-time secretary of the club, Gustav Cederwall, who supplied me with much information and also offered important comments on the draft. I would like to thank Erik Dahmén who supplied me with further source material from the Club and Per G. Andreen for aiding my research on Gösta Bagge by supplying me with important archival material complementing my own excerpts from the deposits in the Swedish National Archives from the 1927 Unemployment Committee and the local Swedish Social Science Board for the Rockefeller Foundation. I have incurred debts to the late Pierre Guinchard and Gunnar Myrdal and especially to the late Erik Lundberg, who read an early draft. I want to express my gratitude to Leif Björk. Claes-Henric Siven has offered encouragement. Editorial assistance has been given by the editors of *Ekon-*

omisk Debatt, Christina Jonung and Ann-Charlotte Ståhlberg. Comments by Charles P. Kindleberger, Joel Mokyr, and Paul A. Samuelson on a more extensive manuscript (Henriksson, 1989) have also benefited this presentation. Lars Jonung has shown great patience in accepting an overdue final version. I acknowledge with gratitude typing help from Karin Norberg and Bo Kåwe and translation assistance from Steven Wentworth and Bill Wright. Research expenses have been covered by the Swedish Academy of Science and by the Jacob Wallenberg Fund. Space considerations have prevented any extensive footnoting. A more complete documentation will be made available in a forthcoming study.

2 Moggridge has published Keynes's lecture notes, which give the main points of the lecturer's introduction. He reports that the title of the lecture was "Further Reflections on Liquidity Preference." The lecture was later published in a revised version in A. D. Gayer (ed.) *The Lessons of Monetary Experience: Essays in Honour of Irving Fisher* (1937) under the title "The Theory of the Rate of Interest" (see Moggridge, 1973). I have also had available a newspaper report about Keynes's lecture written by Cederwall.

3 The quote is from an interview with Leif Björk in 1983.

4 Interview with Gunnar Myrdal, January 30, 1980.

5 This paper has been translated and will appear in Lundberg (1990).

6 This report is discussed by Wadensjö in Chapter 3.

7 Interview with Brinley Thomas at the History of Economics Society meeting in Charlottesville, Virginia, in 1983. See also Thomas (1987).

8 Letter from Paul Samuelson, June 9, 1988. Samuelson was even "sounded out" for a Swedish chair in economics.

9 Interview with Erik Lundberg published in Henriksson (1987d).

10 There are traces of this tradition even in Lindbeck (1963).

References

Åkerman, Gustaf (1923, 1924), *Realkapital und Kapitalzins I und II.* Stockholm: Centraltryckeriet.

 (1931), *Om den industriella rationaliseringen och dess verkningar.* SOU 1931:42, Stockholm.

Åkerman, Johan (1928), *Om det ekonomiska livets rytmik.* Stockholm: Nordiska Bokhandeln.

Andreen, Per G., and Gunnar Boalt. (1987), *Bagge får tacka Rockefeller.* Rapport i Socialt arbete Nr. 30, Socialhögskolan, Stockholms Universitet, Stockholm.

Andvig, Jens C. (1985), *Ragnar Frisch and the Great Depression.* Oslo: Norsk Utenrikspolitisk Institutt.

Bagge, Gösta (1917), *Arbetslönens reglering genom sammanslutningar.* Stockholm: AB Nordiska Bokhandeln.

Bagge, Gösta, Erik Lundberg, and Ingvar Svennilson (1933, 1935), *Wages in Sweden. 1860–1930. Vol. I and II.* Stockholm Economic Studies. No. 3a and 3b. London: P. S. King & Son Ltd.

Berg, Claes (1987), "Utvecklingen av de svenska bidragen till inflationsgapsan-
   alysen," in Rolf G. H. Henriksson, ed., *Konjunkturinstitutet under Erik
   Lundbergs tid.* Stockholm: Konjunkturinstitutet, pp. 153–70.
Brisman, Sven (1930), "De unga nationalekonomernas revolt," *Göteborgs Han-
   dels- och Sjöfarts Tidning,* 5 December.
Carlson, Benny (1982), *Bagge, Lindahl och nationalinkomsten. Om "National
   Income of Sweden 1861–1930,"* Meddelande Ekonomisk-Historiska Insti-
   tutionen, No. 27, Lunds Universitet, Lund.
Cassel, Gustav (1918), *Theoretische Sozialökonomie.* Leipzig: C. F. Wintersche
   Verlagshandlung.
Dahmén, Erik (1950), *Svensk industriell företagarverksamhet,* Band 1 och 2.
   Industriens Utredningsinstitut. Uppsala: Almqvist & Wiksell.
Faxén, Karl-Olof (1957), *Monetary and Fiscal Policy under Uncertainty.* Stock-
   holm Economic Studies. New Series I. Almqvist & Wiksell, Uppsala.
Feiwel, George R. (1975), *The Intellectual Capital of Michal Kalecki.* Knoxville:
   The University of Tennessee Press.
Gårdlund, Torsten (1956), *Knut Wickselll. Rebell i det nya riket.* Stockholm:
   Bonniers.
Hansen, Bent (1951), *Studies in the Theory of Inflation.* London: George Allen
   & Unwin Ltd.
   (1955), *Finanspolitikens ekonomiska teori.* SOU 1955:25. Uppsala.
   (1981), "Unemployment, Keynes, and the Stockholm School," *History of
   Political Economy* (Summer), 13, 256–76
Hansson, Björn A. (1982), *The Stockholm School and the Development of
   Dynamic Method.* London: Croom Helm Ltd.
Hart, Alfred G. (1951), *Anticipations, Uncertainty and Dynamic Planning.* New
   York: Augustus M. Kelley, Inc.
Hayek, Friedrich A. (1928), "Das internationale Gleichgewichtssystem der
   Preise und die Bewegungen des 'Geldwertes,'" *Weltwirtschaftliches Archiv,*
   28, 33–76.
   (ed.), (1933), *Beiträge zur Geldtheorie.* Vienna: Verlag von Julius Springer.
Heckscher, Eli F. (1924), "Intermittent fria nyttigheter," *Ekonomisk Tidskrift,*
   26, 41–54.
   (1931), *Sveriges penningpolitik. Orientering och förslag.* Stockholm: P. A.
   Norstedt & Söners Förlag.
Henriksson, Rolf G. H. (1979a), "Swedish Economists and the Fall of the Gold
   Standard in 1931," unpublished paper.
   (1979b), "Eli F. Heckscher och svensk nationalekonomi," *Ekonomisk Debatt,*
   7, 510–20.
   (1987a), "Towards the Accelerator-Multiplier Prototype," Paper presented at
   the History of Economics Society Conference in Boston, June 19–22.
   (1987b), Konjunkturinstitutsidén och konjunkturbevakning före Konjunkturinstitutet," in Rolf G. H. Henriksson, ed., *Konjunkturinstitutet under
   Erik Lundbergs tid.* Stockholm: Konjunkturinstitutet, pp. 1–10.
   (1987c), "Konjunkturbevakning före Konjunkturinstitutet," unpublished
   draft.

(ed.), (1987d), *Konjunkturinstitutet under Erik Lundbergs tid.* Stockholm: Konjunkturinstitutet.

(1989), "The Institutional Base of the Stockholm School; The Political Economy Club 1917–51," *History of Economics Society Bulletin,* vol. 11, Spring, 59–97.

Hicks, John (1939), "The Foundations of Welfare Economics", *Economic Journal,* 49, 696–712.

Jonung, Lars (1979), "Cassel, Davidson and Heckscher on Swedish Monetary Policy: a Confidential Report to the Riksbank in 1931," *Economy and History,* 22, 85–101.

Keynes, John M. (1926), *The End of Laissez Faire.* London: The Hogarth Press.

(1930), *A Treatise on Money. Vol. I. The Pure Theory of Money. Vol. II. The Applied Theory of Money.* London: Macmillan.

(1936), *The General Theory of Employment Interest and Money.* London: Macmillan.

(1945), *Sysselsättningsproblemet. Allmän teori för produktion, ränta och pengar.* Stockholm: Tidens Förlag.

Kock, Karin (1929), *A Study of Interest Rates,* Stockholm Economic Studies, No. 1. London: P.S. King & Son, Ltd.

Landgren, Karl-Gustav (1957), *Economics in Modern Sweden.* Washington, D.C.: Library of Congress.

Lindahl, Erik (1924), *Penningpolitikens mål.* Lund: C. W. K. Gleerup.

(1927), PM No. 9, 41:1–2. 1927 års Arbetslöshetsutredning, Riksarkivet, Stockholm.

(1929), "Dynamic Pricing" [review of Myrdal (1927)], *Economic Journal,* 39, 89–91.

(1930), *Penningpolitikens medel.* Lund: C. W. K. Gleerup.

(1951), "Till hundraårsminnet av Knut Wicksells födelse," *Ekonomisk Tidskrift,* 53, 197–243.

Lindbeck, Assar (1963), *A Study in Monetary Analysis,* Stockholm Economic Studies. New Series III. Stockholm: Almqvist & Wiksell.

Lundberg, Erik (1930), "Om begreppet ekonomisk jämvikt," *Ekonomisk Tidskrift,* 32, 133–60.

(1937), *Studies in the Theory of Economic Expansion,* Stockholm Economic Studies, No. 6. P.S. London: King & Son Ltd.

(1987), "Som stockholmsekonom och konjunkturforskare på 30-Talet," in Rolf G. H. Henriksson, ed., *Konjunkturinstitutet under Erik Lundbergs Tid.* Stockholm: Konjunkturinstitutet, pp. 141–52.

(1990), *Studies in Economic Instability and Change.* With editorial assistance of Rolf G. H. Henriksson. Stockholm: SNS.

Metelius, Bengt (1955), *Utlandstransaktionerna och den svenska ekonomin.* SOU, 1955:13, Stockholm.

Moggridge, Donald (1973), *Collected Writings of John Maynard Keynes,* Vol. 14, "The General Theory and After"; Part II: "Defense and Development." London: Macmillan, Cambridge University Press.

(1979), *Collected Writings of John Maynard Keynes,* Vol. 29, "The General Theory and After, a supplement." London: Macmillan, Cambridge University Press.

Myrdal, Gunnar (1927), *Prisbildningsproblemet och föränderligheten.* Uppsala: Almqvist & Wiksell.

(1930), *Vetenskap och politik i nationalekonomin.* Stockholm: Norstedt & Söner.

(1931), *Sveriges väg genom penningkrisen.* Stockholm: Natur och Kultur.

(1933), "Der Gleichgewichtsbegriff als Instrument der geldtheoretischen Analyse," in Friedrich A. Hayek, ed., *Beiträge zur Geldtheorie.* Vienna: Verlag von Julius Springer, pp. 361–487

Ohlin, Bertil (1921), "Något om prisstegring, inflation och valutapolitik," *Ekonomisk Tidskrift,* 23, 55–69.

(1924), *Handelns Teori.* Stockholm: Centraltryckeriet.

(1925), "Strömungen in der schwedischen Nationalökonomie," Festgabe für Lujo Brentano. *Die Wirtschaftswissenschaft nach dem Kriege. Zweiter Band: Der Stand der Forschung.* Munich and Leipzig: Verlag von Duncker & Humblot, 79–95.

(1927), "Tendencies in Swedish Economics," *Journal of Political Economy,* 35, 343–63.

(1929), "The Reparation Problem: A Discussion: I. Transfer Difficulties, Real and Imagined" and "Mr. Keynes' Views on the Transfer Problem: II, A Rejoinder," *Economic Journal,* 39, 172–82 and 400–4.

(1933a), Bilaga 4b till Betänkande II, 1933. 1927 års Arbetslöshetsutrednings arkiv. Stockholm: Riksarkivet.

(1933b), "Till frågan om penningteorins uppläggning," *Ekonomisk Tidskrift,* 35, 45–81.

(1933c), *Interregional and International Trade.* Cambridge, Mass.: Harvard University Press.

(1934), *Penningpolitik, offentliga arbeten, subventioner och tullar som medel mot arbetslöshet.* Stockholm: P. A. Norstedt & Söner.

(1937), "Some Notes on the Stockholm Theory of Savings and Investment I and II," *Economic Journal,* 47, 53–69 and 221–40.

(1943), "Stockholmsskolan kontra kvantitetsteorin," *Ekonomisk Tidskrift,* 45, 27–46.

(1972), *Bertil Ohlins memoarer: Ung man blir politiker.* Stockholm: Bonniers.

(1975), *Bertil Ohlins memoarer: Socialistisk skördetid kom bort.* Stockholm: Bonniers.

(1981), "Stockholm and Cambridge: Four Papers on the Monetary and Employment Theory of the 1930's" edited with introduction and comments by Otto Steiger. *History of Political Economy* (Summer), 13, 189–255.

Petersson, Jan (1987), *Erik Lindahl och Stockholmsskolans dynamiska metod.* Lund Economic Studies 39, Lund.

Samuelson, Paul A. (1947), *Economics. An Introductory Analysis.* New York: McGraw Hill.

Siven, Claes-Henric (1985), "The End of the Stockholm School," *Scandinavian Journal of Economics,* 87, 577–93.

Steiger, Otto (1971), *Studien zur Entstehung der Neuen Wirtschaftslehre in Schweden – Eine Anti-Kritik.* Berlin: Duncker & Humblot.

Svennilson, Ingvar (1938), *Ekonomisk planering.* Uppsala: Almqvist & Wiksell.

Thomas, Brinley (1936), *Monetary Policy and Crises.* London: George Routledge and Sons, Ltd.

(1987), "Some Reminiscenses of the Stockholm School and the LSE," paper presented to the Conference on the Stocholm School after 50 years, Saltsjöbaden, August 31 and September 1, 1987 (to appear in Lars Jonung, ed., *The Stockholm School of Economics Remembered,* in preparation).

Uhr, Carl G. (1977), "Economists and Policymaking 1930–1936: Sweden's Experience," *History of Political Economy* (Spring) 9, 89–121.

Wicksell, Knut (1919), "Professor Cassels nationalekonomiska system," *Ekonomisk Tidskrift,* 21, 195–226.

(1925), "Valutaspörsmålet i de skandinaviska länderna," *Ekonomisk Tidskrift,* 27, 205–22.

Wigforss, Ernst (1929), P.M. No. 84., 1927 års arbetslöshetsutrednings arkiv, Riksarkivet, Stockholm.

Comment

GUSTAV CEDERWALL

As one of the survivors from the Economics Department of Stockholm University from the 1930s, I would like to supplement the paper by Rolf Henriksson about the Political Economy Club with some remarks based on my recollections and experiences.

First let me introduce myself. I started my studies at Stockholm University in 1931, where my introduction to economics was handled by Alf Johansson. I passed my first examination in the subject for Gösta Bagge in 1934 and my advanced examination later in the 1930s for Johansson. I listened to Gustav Cassel's lectures in his last year and to the lectures given by Gunnar Myrdal, who spoke vividly about the problems that preoccupied him at that time, namely, business cycles and public finance. In the corridors and at advanced seminars, I met Erik Lindahl, Karin Kock, and Dag Hammarskjöld. As fellow students, I also met Erik Lundberg and Ingvar Svennilson, who were a few years ahead of me.

In 1936 I was appointed secretary of a committee that was investigat-

ing the problems of monopolies in Swedish industry with Bertil Ohlin as chairman. In due course this led to a number of other assignments that finally made me give up the academic for an administrative career. I have given a somewhat fuller account of the environment at Stockholm University in the 1930s and my own adventures in the forthcoming volume *The Stockholm School of Economics Remembered* (edited by Lars Jonung).

Leaving aside an extremely dull elementary introduction, I was brought up as an economist on two works: Wicksell's *Lectures* and Myrdal's *Vetenskap och Politik (The Political Element in the Development of Economic Theory)*. Henriksson has recorded the reaction of the older school of economists to the Myrdal revolution. Brought up in the new school, I became and have remained skeptical of the classics. I share to some extent what has been called Myrdal's contempt for the marginal utility theory, and my doubts have focused especially on all loose concepts of welfare. The study of Wicksell and Myrdal concentrated interest on dynamic developments. General equilibrium theory, showing what would happen in the long run, was pushed aside with the remark that in the long run we are dead – a slogan we got from Keynes. From Wicksell and Myrdal, we learned that deviation from equilibrium did not necessarily give rise to an adjustment back toward balance but could result in a cumulative movement. The economic system could exhibit a tendency to become subject to cyclical variations. Erik Lundberg, who spent his whole life as an economist in the study of economic instability, used to talk about the rocking-horse.

I was elected member of the Political Economy Club in the mid-1930s and I served as its secretary, as well as secretary of the venerable Economic Society, during the second half of the 1930s and most of the 1940s. The peak event in the history of the Political Economy Club was certainly a visit by Keynes in 1936 as described by Henriksson. (Of the eighteen persons who took part in the dinner for Keynes on that occasion, only three were still alive at the time of the conference: Erik Lundberg, Leif Björk, and myself. After the conference, Erik Lundberg died in September 1987.) I was asked by the news agency for the Swedish dailies to report on the public lecture given by Keynes on "My Grounds for Departure from Orthodox Economic Tradition." The summary I made must have been written in a great hurry in the short interval between the lecture and the dinner. Among my old papers, I have found a copy of my report.

I have a vivid recollection of the discussion at the dinner, which went on until midnight. I can confirm the description given by Myrdal, who has called Keynes's ideas "unnecessarily original" and for those brought up in the Wicksellian tradition, not in any sense a revolutionary break-through. I can also confirm Ohlin's remark in his 1937 articles in the *Economic Journal.* Perhaps it should be stressed that the lively discussion in England of Keynes' *General Theory* had by this time not yet reached Stockholm. This included the basic reviews, among them Hick's famous *Keynes and the Classics.*

It was certainly a remarkable event when the great prophet came to Stockholm pretending that he had seen a new light only to be taken down by the Swedish youngsters – Myrdal and Ohlin were around thirty-five, Hammarskjöld thirty, Lundberg and Svennilson under thirty – who told him that he was rather old-fashioned, that the Swedish economists had gone much further, and that his, Keynes's, very method, the equilibrium method, was unsuitable for the treatment of dynamic problems. To listen to that debate was certainly an unforgettable experience for a young man. I was myself only twenty-three.

As secretary of the Club as well as of the Economic Society, it was my duty to act as a sort of guide to visiting economists. Henriksson has mentioned a number of names. I could add quite a few. From the 1930s I remember, next to Keynes, the visit in 1939 of Mr. and Mrs. Hicks. I also have a recollection of having seen Schumpeter and Haberler before the war. The Economic Society had T. E. Gregory and Lionel Robbins as guests in 1935 and 1936. After the war there was a stream of visitors. I have noted Hayek in 1946, Dick Stone in 1947, Geoffrey Crowther, editor of the *Economist,* in 1949, followed by Alvin Hansen, John Jewkes, and D. H. Robertson. Milton Friedman came in 1954 and R. F. Harrod in 1957. They did not all speak at the Political Economy Club, the subject of Henriksson's report. Some were invited to appear before the Economic Society. But they all came to Stockholm, which was, for a time, a kind of Mecca for economists.

In conclusion, I would wish to associate myself with Henriksson's final conclusion. The economists in Stockholm did not deal only with economic theory. They were all interested and deeply involved in actual economic policy. They were dealing with applied economics. Their theories were rather by-products of these other interests. This largely applies to the debates in the Political Economy Club. It also applies in my view to what has been called the Stockholm School.

All this must of course be seen against the background of the economic crisis in the 1930s. It was a period when there was a lively discussion – not only among economists – about changes in exchange rates, the causes of the depression and its development, and methods to improve the economic situation and to counteract unemployment.

Henriksson has dealt with the Political Economy Club and referred to the divergent views held by economists in connection with monetary policy in the period after Sweden left the gold standard in 1931. Wadensjö provides some glimpses of work of the unemployment committee. There was certainly a highly intensive debate going on in other places. Ohlin wrote a great number of articles in Handelsbanken's *Index* and in the *Stockholmstidningen* and other periodicals. The Economic Society had a great debate on public works and the underbalancing of the budget as a means of combatting unemployment in 1932, introduced by Lindahl. Wigforss, who was minister of finance at that time, presented the budget proposals to the Society and debated with conservative opponents. Especially his presentation of a new policy in 1933 marks a new epoch.

I would like to stress therefore that, apart from the theoretical works referred to by most of the authors of the papers presented at this conference, there is also important literature available on policy formation. It is to be found in a wide range of articles and speeches, as well as in official publications. Committee reports from the 1930s onwards include a good deal of the economic research carried out in Sweden, both empirical and to some extent theoretical. This should not be overlooked.

In this "grand debate," almost the entire new generation of economists stood up as standard-bearers for expansionism and planning. For myself and I think for my generation, the Stockholm school embodied this whole concept of expansionism. We had a sense of living at a time when economists saw a new light, a feeling wonderfully described by Lundberg. I think that this commonly held attitude by economists dealing with actual and administrative problems is at the center of what I would like to call the Stockholm School.

CHAPTER 2

Gösta Bagge, the Rockefeller Foundation, and empirical social science research in Sweden, 1924–1940[1]

EARLENE CRAVER

When large philanthropic foundations came into being in the United States at the turn of the century, the sheer magnitude of their financial resources gave them the ability to shape the direction of research in those fields they chose to support. Some observers have gone so far as to suggest that these foundations have been the "gatekeepers" of contemporary American "intellectual life" (Coser, 1965). One need not go that far to recognize that the development of the social sciences in the period between the wars owed much to Rockefeller Foundation money. It has been estimated that approximately 95 percent of the total funds expended on the social sciences by American foundations during this period came from the Laura Spelman Rockefeller Memorial and its successor, the Social Science Division of the Rockefeller Foundation. As an American, I am pleased to participate in this conference by telling the story of the ways in which an American foundation contributed to the development of the social and economic sciences in Sweden.

In September 1924, Gösta Bagge, Professor of Economics and Social Politics at the University of Stockholm *(Stockholms Högskola),* arrived at the offices of the Laura Spelman Rockefeller Memorial at 61 Broadway in New York City armed with a formal letter of introduction dated September 16 from John M. Glenn of the Russell Sage Foundation. Bagge's purpose in approaching the American foundation, Glenn explained, was to find support for a school for social workers that he had "inaugurated and was carrying on under very great difficulties" in Stockholm.[2] Although Bagge had been directed to the Memorial, he scarcely could have known when he arrived at the foundation's offices on that day in September how well his proposal fit into the plans of the Memorial's young director, Beardsley Ruml.

Ruml, who later became dean of social sciences at the University of Chicago and served on the National Resources Planning Board in the Roosevelt administration, was then just twenty-eight years old. Two years earlier he had been appointed director of the Laura Spelman Rockefeller Memorial, a foundation generously endowed in 1918 by John D. Rockefeller in memory of his late wife. Blessed with an unusually persuasive personality, Ruml convinced trustees of the Memorial that the foundation should be transformed from an organization principally devoted to charitable relief to one engaged in the financing of basic social science research. Ruml himself had been trained in the social sciences. He held a doctorate from the University of Chicago in experimental psychology and, during the war, had helped develop one of the first occupational tests in the United States. As a consequence, he placed great emphasis on inductive methods of research. Universities were hampered in doing this kind of work, he thought, by the inadequacy of their financial resources and by the heavy demands on academic social scientists for teaching and publication.

> As a result production from the universities is largely deductive and speculative, on the basis of second-hand observations, documentary evidence and anecdotal material. It is small wonder that the social engineer finds his social science abstract and remote, of little help to him in the solution of his problems.[3]

In Ruml's view, the Memorial could best assist in the development of research in the social sciences by providing funds for equipment, books, and statistical and clerical assistance and by providing fellowships to emancipate a future generation of teachers from "the traditional conceptual thinking and *a priori* generalizations of the present generation of teachers."[4]

The Ruml Memorandum approved by the trustees in October 1922 started the foundation on a new course. The Memorial supported social science research at a number of major university centers in the United States and was one of the major contributors to the National Bureau of Economic Research. Not content to limit the foundation's efforts to America, Ruml boldly set forth to see what the Memorial could do to encourage the development of a more "realistic" social science in Europe as well. The problem lay in finding the right persons in the right institutional setting. In England, the London School of Economics (LSE) became a major beneficiary of Rockefeller support in Europe in the 1920s because its commitment to an interdisciplinary, and empirically based social science fit the objectives of the Memorial. Sir William Beveridge, director of LSE, became one of the foundation's most valued informal advisers. Ruml was less encouraged by reports he received on the state of the social sciences on the continent (Craver, 1986). For this reason, he was especially interested in what his Swedish visitor had to say.

Bagge, it turned out, was not a stranger to America. He had studied at Johns Hopkins in 1904–5, had returned a few years later to do research on the Swedish emigration, and was currently in the United States on a Swedish-American foundation fellowship with the intention of visiting at Stanford and Harvard. A student of Gustav Cassel, Bagge had completed his doctoral thesis in 1917 with a study of *The Determination of Wages through Collective Bargaining (Arbetslönens reglering genom sammanslutningar)*. But like others of his generation and social background, he also felt called to government service. Since 1913, he had been a member of the Stockholm City Council. In 1921, he was named to the chair in Economics and Social Politics newly created and endowed by Centralförbundet för Socialt Arbete (The Swedish National Association for Social Work) on the condition that its holder direct a proposed school to train those seeking a career in social work and municipal administration (Andreen and Boalt, 1987; Carlson, 1982).

In that same year, the School for Social and Municipal Work (Institutet för Socialpolitisk och Kommunal Utbildning och Forskning) was established. Although trustees of the school had hoped that the school would become something more than a teaching institution, Bagge told Ruml, the Swedish depression had made it difficult to raise funds from either private or public sources. As a consequence, the institute's staff consisted of part-time, though well-qualified, teachers and its student body of part-time students largely drawn from the ranks of municipal program administrators. Bagge insisted that the Institute could be turned into an important center for research if it were given adequate resources. During the last few decades, the Scandinavian countries "have been very proficient in practical social development," he explained. Yet,

> [T]here is in fact no institution in Scandinavia today where scientific social research is being carried out on a systematic plan. Occasionally a professor of economics might make an investigation of that kind a part of his work, but he has many other fields to cover and the curricula of the general universities do not afford opportunity for work of this kind.[5]

Sweden was "an ideal laboratory for scientific social research" in his view. It had long runs of historical data, extensive in their coverage, of excellent quality, and based on a homogeneous population.[6] If "scientific social investigations could be carried on . . . in a more systematic way and the results published in English," he said, these studies surely would be of general interest. For example, using Swedish data, researchers might investigate the results of wartime unemployment relief, or the consequences of recent revisions in Swedish child welfare legislation, or the effects of unionization and the eight-hour workday on the level of wages. In short, as one Rockefeller official later described it, Bagge painted the picture of Sweden as an "Eldorado" of social research. In the last year, the institute had an operating budget of just 45,730 kronor. In order to mine these rich resources the Swedish professor argued that he needed about 50,000 additional kronor to give research fellowships and statistical assistance to three or four students who would work under his direction on these projects.[7]

As Bagge sketched out his proposal, answering questions posed by Ruml and the Memorial's president, Colonel Arthur Woods, who was also present during the September 19 meeting, Ruml scribbled facts and figures on scratch paper noting that Stockholm was a "considerable city" and the "best place in Scandinavia." At some point it must have become apparent to Bagge that the interview was going well because he was asked to submit a formal memorandum summarizing his request.

The next day he dashed off a six-page memorandum to Ruml with an anxious cover letter clarifying "one point" that had come up during the previous day's discussions.[8]

> Mr. Woods asked me if it was of any importance to me to have this work started in the very near future. I answered him that it was not – and of course it was not in a way. But I have been thinking of it since I left you and it is rather important for me to be not too much delayed in starting this work. I am now forty-two years old and this kind of work – organizing a new department – certainly does require a certain amount of activity and enthusiasm for the work. If I have to wait several years I will be an older man and not have so many years of usefulness before me. That is the reason why I would be very glad to start this as soon as possible if the whole plan can be realized.

For his part, Ruml set about making inquiries regarding the Swedish professor. On September 26, he wrote William Beveridge in London asking him what he knew about Bagge and the Stockholm School, adding that he had met Bagge in New York and was "pleasantly impressed."[9] Beveridge replied on October 14 that he did not know of him but that Bagge's colleague, Professor Gustav Cassel, would know, and he offered to make the inquiry should Ruml wish. Ruml so wished and asked that Beveridge do it discreetly without mentioning the Memorial.[10] On November 21 Beveridge forwarded Cassel's reply written a week earlier. The letter did not fail to reveal the conservative attitudes of the renowned economist. The Stockholm School of Social and Municipal Work, Cassel wrote Beveridge, had been founded

> in order to fill up the former lack of economic education of those who had to take care, in the democratic society of ours, of local government and of social work generally, and also of those who are engaged as servants in such works. The institution is not connected with the University, but the leader of the school, Professor Bagge, is my colleague at the University and is an economist of high standing. The school is not what we should regard of a University standard, but I have reason to believe that the economic education of the school is good as far as it goes.
>
> My objection to the school is that there is rather too much instruction given in all sorts of practical details. That is not my idea of a liberal education which I think should concentrate itself upon forming the habit of scientific thinking. Of course this is my private view and I am convinced that the work of the school is quite reliable. The school has without doubt a good public estimation."[11]

Far from discouraged by Cassel's description, Ruml added Stockholm to his European travel agenda, arriving there with his wife in late May of 1925. He met with Cassel and Bagge, the two economics professors of Stockholms Högskola, and he probably met with other members of the humanities faculty or university administration as well.[12] In any case, on June 30, 1925, a formal proposal signed by the Rector, Ivar Bendixen, and Gösta Bagge was submitted to the trustees of the Memorial.

Interestingly enough, the formal request asked that money be appropriated to Stockholms Högskolas Socialvetenskapliga Institut (Institute of Social Science) rather than to the School for Social and Municipal Work as Bagge originally had hoped and had led Ruml to believe. The law faculty, in particular, appears to have balked at the notion of bringing within the university this new school whose students, like those of the New School for Social Research in New York in its early days, were largely part-timers recruited from the ranks of secondary school teachers and municipal administrators.[13]

The proposal, however, was Bagge's, and though the proposal did not directly state it, his 1917 book on the regulation of wages was expected to provide the framework for the first set of empirical investigations on the level of wages between 1913 and 1923. There were sound, scientific reasons for choosing this time span, the proposal said. Because this period was characterized by "extraordinary changes in the general price-level and other violent forces," effects that in "peaceful and normal times are almost imperceptible" would become "large enough to be made objects of observation." The social scientists could look at such questions as the impact of labor organizations on the economy or the consequences of applying the "living wage" principle that paid married men with families at a higher rate than those who were single. With this inductive work "we will thus have left the old method of studying the wages [*sic*] question as determined by one or two factors from which all the wage problems are deduced, a method which obviously is too abstract to give the knowledge we really want concerning this important field of social science." In order to begin these studies, the proposal requested an appropriation of 50,000 kronor ($13,500) per year for five years. With this money, the Institute expected to give three or four fellowships and provide clerical assistance for the project.[14] (To give a context to this request, income for the "university as a whole" in 1925 was reported to the Rockefeller Foundation as being 267,052 kronor).[15] Bagge would be in charge of planning the actual research program subject to approval of the humanities faculty of which he was soon to be named dean.

After several months of anxious waiting, Bagge was notified on November 11 that the Memorial had made an appropriation of $15,000 per year for five years beginning January 1, 1926.[16] Although this research grant of $75,000 pales in comparison to the $1,145,000 given to LSE for building, library development, and research, it was otherwise one of the largest institutional grants to a European university before 1930. (Cambridge would receive $150,000 to establish a chair in political science, and the Institute for International Studies in Geneva was appropriated $100,000.) It was, therefore, a strong vote of confidence in Stockholms Högskola and in Bagge, who also became the Swedish adviser to the Memorial on the selection of social science fellows chosen to study abroad (Bulmer and Bulmer, 1981; Craver, 1986.)

Buoyed by the unexpected generosity of the American foundation, Bagge began the studies with docent Erik Lindahl as the senior research fellow assisted by Gunnar Myrdal, Master of Law, Gösta Bergstad, Master of Arts and Law, and amanuensis Alf Johansson. For his part in directing the project, Lindahl would receive an annual fellowship of 8,000 kronor; the others, 6,000 each. Bagge, whose professorial salary was 8,500 kronor, does not appear to have taken a salary or fee (nor did he as director of the Institute for Social and Municipal Work in its earliest years) (Andreen and Boalt, 1987).

Before the infusion of Rockefeller money, the Institute of Social Science had been little more than a shell consisting of a small one-room library open just two times a week for one-half hour. It now became a center of activity. While junior members of the team compiled data on wages in various industries and the agricultural sector, Lindahl first focused on finding the "normal wage" before the perturbations of World War I. By 1927, having discovered the set of raw statistical data since 1913 complete, he split the project further and focused his attention on constructing one of the earliest national income accounts based on a long time series.[17] But the task he had set for himself was difficult because it involved a series of conceptual decisions, and the work, in a day before computers or electric self-correcting typewriters, was tedious. Although the investigations regarding the costs of living in Sweden 1830–1914 were completed, translated, and set in type in 1929, and a preliminary survey of internal migration between the years 1895 and 1927, conducted under Myrdal's leadership, was completed by 1929, other parts of the project – in particular, the investigation regarding national income and production, which went far beyond anything Bagge originally had envisaged – was long delayed. This proved embarrassing to Bagge in further dealings with Rockefeller representatives especially since an early and, as it turned out, unfortunate decision had been made to publish the volumes in translation simultaneously. Some of the internal problems surrounding the project have been told from the Swedish side (Carlson, 1982). The archives of the Rockefeller Foundation help to give us a fuller picture of the original goals of the project's directors and the constraints they faced.

Ruml had believed that Stockholm would become a center of social science research in Scandinavia and, therefore, had decided that it should be one of the major institutional centers in Europe supported by the Rockefeller Foundation. His successors after 1929 in the Social Science Division of the restructured Rockefeller Foundation also continued to give Stockholm high marks. John Van Sickle, a Harvard-trained economist who monitored social science programs in Europe from the Foundation's Paris office for the new director of the Social Sciences in New York, Edmund Day, visited Stockholm on January 5, 1930 not long after taking on his new job. He was met by Bagge at the station, treated to lunch at Den Gyllene Freden, and entertained by Bagge and his family at a black tie dinner attended by Professor Gustav Cassel, Bertil Ohlin, two former Rockefeller fellows, Karl Petander and John Lindberg, Per Jakobsen, and Bagge's brother, Dr. Algot Bagge, a justice on the High Court. In the course of this visit, Bagge approached the Foundation regarding money for building construction, showing Van Sickle the site made available to Stockholms Högskola by the City of Stockholm.[18] One year later, when Van Sickle, accompanied by the head of the foundation's Paris office, Selskar Gunn, visited Stockholm again, Bagge raised this question more directly. He pointed out the advantages of bringing the disparate elements of the social sciences (including his School for Social Work that still was not an official part of the university) together in the same building and asked that the Rockefeller Foundation help by contributing approximately 70 percent of the total cost. Although Gunn warned him that the Rockefeller Foundation was presently "not disposed to aid building programs" and Bagge, in return, promised to approach the Swedish "match-king [Ivar] Krüger about the matter,"[19] in fact, Gunn and the Paris office gave a positive recommendation to Day in New York. During that same visit, Bagge reassured his visitors that the studies begun under the five-year grant from the Memorial were nearing completion. However, in discussing the nature of further research grants from the Rockefeller Foundation, Van Sickle noted that Bagge was "emphatic . . . that he does not want funds which must be used regardless of availability of interested scientific workers. He admits that under [the] recent . . . grant he had to keep a man at a part of the project submitted in connection with that grant despite the man's interest in a more theoretical problem."[20]

In fact, there were more internal problems with the project than Bagge wished the American to know. While it was true that Lindahl had carried on his theoretical work during the period of the grant, publishing several works on monetary theory and policy in 1929 (Lindahl (1929a, 1929b, 1929c, 1929d), Bagge's original agreement with Lindahl must have envisaged that. Nonetheless, Bagge grew impatient with Lindahl's delay in completing his part of the series.

Earlier accounts have emphasized the intellectual differences between the two men, but recent evidence has thrown light on the purely personal nature of the rift that developed in 1929 over Lindahl's marital infidelity. Bagge's letters to Myrdal in 1929–30 reveal a Victorian sense of propriety that went beyond modern notions of decency as he attempted to assert his authority over Lindahl to prevent a marital separation and divorce (or, at least, delay any action until Lindahl's connection with the Institute had ended). Although Bagge, in effect, broke with Lindahl when such efforts failed,[21] he carefully hid from visiting representatives of the rich American foundation the deep feelings of personal animosity he held toward Lindahl. Van Sickle, who often recorded such confidences in his official diary, apparently was not told of the marital scandal.

From the start, one of Bagge's primary goals had been to put the Institute for Social Work on a sound financial and academic footing. But the research money he received from the Memorial had instead gone to the Institute of Social Science, and five years later the Institute for Social and Municipal Work remained in a precarious position. Bagge, however, had not lost sight of his goal. Despite the fact that the research studies were not yet complete, he approached the American foundation once more. By dangling before local funding sources the probability that the Rockefeller Foundation would contribute the bulk of the costs for a social science building to house both institutes and a library, he managed to gather funds from various Swedish sources. In return, he held before Rockefeller Foundation officials the promises from Swedish sources in order to reassure them that the Foundation's "seed money" would encourage rather than supplant local funding. And this time he was successful (Andreen and Boalt, 1987).

On April 15, 1931, trustees of the Rockefeller Foundation voted to give "$100,000 or as much thereof as may be necessary" to the University of Stockholm for the construction of a social science building. (The exchange rate was 3.74 kronor to one U.S. dollar.) In addition, the foundation agreed to continue its research support with a five-year grant of $30,000 beginning September 1, 1931, and ending August 31, 1936. One year later, the three-story building at 61 Odengatan was inaugurated. In keeping with the practice of the American foundation, there would be no plaque commemorating its contribution.

With the construction of the social science building, Bagge had brought the Institute for Social Work into closer physical association with Stockholms Högskola since it occupied the ground floor. The top floor was composed of offices and seminar rooms for the social science faculty, and the middle floor consisted of a working library and research facilities. This had all been done for less than $100,000, and $12,193 of the building grant was allowed to lapse in a demonstration of Scandinavian prudence that the Rockefeller Foundation, after its experiences elsewhere, could not help but admire.[22]

This would not be the last of Bagge's requests, however. Where he once had approached the American foundation with trepidation, he now showed increasing boldness. On May 13, 1932, Gunn wrote Day in New York about a new request from the Swedish professor concerning Gunnar Myrdal. Myrdal, who had been given a Rockefeller Foundation fellowship in 1929–30, had been working with William Rappard in Geneva for some time, "but always in anticipation of returning to Stockholm," Gunn explained.[23]

> Bagge now writes us that recently he had an interview with Professor Cassel with regard to the time when Cassel will vacate his chair. As a result of this conversation Cassel has consented to give up his chair in September 1933 on condition that Myrdal be taken care of during the next year. Myrdal is the real candidate for this chair. The only other person in Sweden who might be seriously considered is Ohlin, but

> Ohlin has definitely decided not to present his candidacy. Myrdal will have a docent fellowship of 7000 crowns, and, in addition, will have a revenue of 4000 crowns from other sources. If we could add 4000 crowns for one year only, it would make it possible to hold Myrdal in Stockholm until he can take over Cassel's chair.

In confidential conversations with the Paris office, Rappard had agreed to let Myrdal out of his commitment to a third year in Geneva, Gunn reported, continuing, "Of course, it is a matter of great satisfaction to us that one of our returned fellows should be considered as a successor to Cassel." One month later, the grant-in-aid was approved. After all, one of the goals of the Rockefeller Foundation was to see their fellows return home to train others.

There was another side to Bagge's request, however. The preliminary study of internal migration with which Myrdal had been associated had been expanded, and Bagge was anxious to have someone competent in charge. It appears that he suggested that the Rockefeller Foundation help by bringing over Dorothy Swaine Thomas, a sociologist with strong demographic skills who was then at Yale. Gunn suggested that by "giving this grant to Myrdal, the work on Swedish migrations can go ahead as the Institute still has fluid funds of ours at its disposal. Under the circumstances, delay on our part in reaching a final decision on the Thomas Plan need not cause any undue complications."[24]

The Foundation had a more difficult time deciding whether to contribute toward the development of a working social science library. While the Memorial, under Ruml's leadership, had contributed to library development programs, largely financing the creation of the splendid economics library in Kiel, for example, the Social Science division under Day's administration had not continued this policy. Bagge, who probably had learned of the Memorial's earlier grants, had cautiously broached the topic with Van Sickle in Paris in October of 1931 even before the new building was complete. He explained that he thought a good working library in the social sciences would require about 40,000 volumes of which just 10,000 currently were available in the general university holdings. The contributions he expected from the city council would cover the cost of hiring a librarian, and the interest on the endowment would enable them to add to a basic collection but would not be sufficient to cover the costs of establishing a solid social science collection. He estimated the cost for building a good working library would be about $75,000, Van Sickle reported to Gunn and Day.[25] Although Bagge did not make headway with the Rockefeller Foundation at that time, a year later, when the building was near completion, Bagge formally requested that the $12,000 saved on construc-

tion costs be used for the library instead.[26] Since the director of the
Social Science Division, Edmund Day, objected to handling the matter
in that way, officers of the Foundation kicked around the notion of making an outright library grant. There was just the little problem of the
research series that had never appeared! On February 15, 1933, Van
Sickle, having spent three days in Stockholm, wrote Day.

> I feel some hesitation about making recommendations regarding the
> library. This hesitation is due in part to the poor progress Bagge has
> made with the research program which we have been supporting since
> the beginning of 1926. For the last three or four years Bagge has
> reported that publication would begin within the next few months. Yet,
> to date, not a thing has been published. This delay has been primarily
> due to an error in judgment – that is to the decision not to begin pub-
> lication until all parts of the program were completed. It was thought
> that the essential unity of the program made this course desirable. The
> result has been that all have had to wait upon the slowest man – Lin-
> dahl. Lindahl has now accepted a professorship at Göteborg and Bagge
> is having difficulty in getting him to complete his part of the program.
> Bagge is very much chagrined at the lack of progress and has intro-
> duced administrative modifications that should bring better results in
> the future.[27]

Van Sickle explained that a Social Science Research Board had been set
up and that investigators would be required to report to it three times a
year.[28] He went on to say that he had seen the page proofs of a number
of the studies that had been completed and that he had no doubt that
the results would soon appear. One reason for the slow progress, he
explained, was the "many claims upon the time of the Stockholm
group." For example, Bagge had just directed an enormous study for the
government on the unemployment situation, and Myrdal had drafted a
long report for the government on housing reform and another on the
budget situation.

> Despite the disappointingly slow progress my confidence in the excel-
> lence of the Stockholm group is not diminished. They are well trained,
> thorough and enthusiastic. Despite differences in social attitudes that
> would split a German faculty wide open, they work together smoothly
> and cordially.

Van Sickle and the Rockefeller Foundation had a good deal of experience with the kind of bitter animosities that characterized German and
Austrian universities, often frustrating the Foundation in its efforts to
bring about an atmosphere of scientific cooperation. They were, therefore, struck all the more by the ability of the Swedes, whose political

opinions ranged from the conservative Bagge to the social democratic Myrdal, to work together.

Van Sickle did not know the whole story, of course. Beyond strained personal relations between Bagge and Lindahl, there were other elements of discord: Myrdal's lack of interest in these empirical studies, for example, and generational differences in methodological approach. Where Bagge's approach was microtheoretic and institutionalist, Lindahl, Myrdal, and their younger collaborators were interested in macroeconomics questions. Erik Lundberg, who was first recruited to the project in 1928, knew little about the origin of these empirical studies. But as he saw it,

> Bagge was not a leader in the work. He may have been the primary initiator but after that he lost interest. He was in that unemployment study and that took his time and he didn't guide our work in any way. Bagge did not work well with Lindahl and it was worse still with Myrdal. Bagge, of course, was a microeconomist (we called it Baggology) and we younger economists were in opposition to him. The driving force, instead, weas Lindahl. He guided the work and he lived with us in it. Lindahl was conceptually and logically interested in the development of national income.[29]

Although Van Sickle did not know of these frictions, he was sufficiently distressed by the slow progress on the project to request a full report. He sent a part of the material received from Bagge on to New York, explaining that, in his opinion, the report and its methodological appendices "constitute rather convincing evidence that the research of the Stockholm group is exceptionally thorough and original from the point of view of methodology" and that he suspected they would "attract wide attention."[30] Once again, directors of the Rockefeller Foundation expressed their confidence in the work of the Stockholm research group by approving an annual library grant to the Institute of Social Science that would run to 1937 and total $22,000 and an additional research grant for three years totaling $9,000. In a separate action, the Foundation also agreed to pay $3,750 in 1934–5 for Dorothy Thomas to come over on loan from Yale for part of a year to help establish a program in sociology and to assist in the migration studies that were still under the directorship of Myrdal, even though he was by then deeply involved in government work and politics.

But the days of big expenditures in the social sciences were coming to an end. In 1933 the Foundation, which had contributed much to the rebuilding of the sciences and social sciences in Germany, found itself instead the principal American foundation involved in the effort to rescue German scholars. At the same time, the yield on its endowment began to show the adverse effects of the Great Depression. Faced with diminishing resources, trustees of the Foundation felt compelled to reassess their priorities. Moved by the human consequences of unemployment and the gathering clouds on the international horizon, Foundation officials began to look for projects promising more immediate practical results. In 1934 Van Sickle was called back to New York to head programs in "social security," a term that in the language of the time meant economic security or full employment policy. While officers in New York prepared a report redefining Foundation policy, Van Sickle's replacement in Paris, Tracy Kittredge, continued his traditional rounds, arriving in Stockholm in October where he met with the Board of the Institute of Social Sciences and certain members of the research staff.

Kittredge reported to New York that, at last, publication had begun on the research projects supported by the foundation. However, Bagge and Myrdal, in lengthy discussions, had spelled out the problems created for the Institute by demands on their time by governmental commissions and political parties.

> There appears to be no possibility at present of the creation of any new professorships or docentships. Docent Hammarskjöld and Erik Lundberg (former S[ocial] S[cience] Fellow) have been employed by the Bank of Sweden to organize an economic research division and hence appear lost to the Institute. Bagge had hoped to associate them both with the future research program. He realizes keenly the potential possibilities for intensive research work in Stockholm. He feels however that the greatest need at the present time is to have two or three additional full time research directors to take charge of programs in the field of social history, economic statistics, and industrial and agricultural problems. With the uncertainty of academic appointments in Sweden Bagge feels that the only real solution would be to have new professorships created, to which could be invited men who could also become research directors at the institute. They would also provide graduate seminars, in which advanced students, from Sweden, from other Scandinavian countries and from abroad, could receive methodological training and adequate supervision of their independent research. Bagge would like for example to offer a chair in Social History (similar to Tawney's in London) to Prof. Arthur Montgomery; a chair in Economic Statistics to Docent Hammarskjöld and possibly a third chair in Industrial Economics to Docent Johansson. He would like also to have two or three places as Senior Research Assistants with Docents' rank and pay for young economists like Erik Lundberg, Svenn[ilson] and Dr. Karin Kock. Bagge feels that only some such additions to the staff would permit the Institute to attain [its] maximum possibilities.[31]

Although a chair was being created in political science that would doubt-less go to Herbert Tingsten, the Institute wanted help in keeping on Dor-othy Thomas until a chair in sociology also was established. Although Kittredge reacted favorably to these hints, saying in his report that, in his opinion, Stockholm's importance had increased with the "disap-pearance of an objective social science in Germany," he was not in a position to act. As he was writing his report, a decision was being taken in New York to phase out programs of institutional support.

In January 1935 Bagge and Myrdal were informed that, henceforth, the Rockefeller Foundation would support projects in three areas: pub-lic administration, relations between governments, and economic sta-bility. Officers of the Foundation were certain that the work of the Stockholm group fit into the new projected emphasis on business cycle research.[32] To their surprise, the Swedes simply were not interested. Bagge and Myrdal both emphasized that their difficulty was not in find-ing funds for immediate, practical studies but in finding "enough finan-cial help for the purely scientific research work in the social sciences" and enough general resources in the university to train a younger gen-eration of social scientists.[33] In fact, they explained, the Swedish govern-ment was in the process of creating and financing a new institute to con-duct business cycle research and other economic studies of immediate concern to the government. What Sweden and Stockholm needed was help in financing basic research and deepening and broadening their research programs.

Ironically, the same set of conditions that had pressed Swedish econ-omists into government service, directing unemployment studies and offering expert advice, had its counterpart in the United States. Trustees of the Rockefeller Foundation – well-connected men, belonging to the old East Coast "Establishment" – were themselves concerned with mar-shaling the diminishing resources of the Foundation, turning it toward research that bore more directly on the human condition. The bounding optimism that had stood behind the Memorial's lavish expenditures on institutional programs and basic research in the 1920s had been sup-planted in the 1930s by a more pessimistic view, a more urgent desire for scientific studies leading to pragmatic action. To soften the blow, a tapering grant to the Institute of Social Science totaling $20,000 was made in 1936 that would end Rockefeller institutional research support by August 1940.

This was not quite the end, however. The human migration studies dragged on, frustrating still another researcher, Dorothy Thomas, who found that she was devoting more of her time to research on the project, still nominally under the direction of Myrdal, than to teaching, as few students were interested since it was not a regular part of the curriculum. Sydnor Walker, who had risen to temporary leadership of the social science division of the Foundation, was annoyed by this revelation since she felt that the foundation had continued to provide for Thomas's presence in Stockholm to the tune of $7,500 in order to help establish an instructional program in concrete sociological studies.[34] In 1937 Myrdal requested an additional appropriation of $10,000 to help get the migration studies into print. With a mixture of irritation and relief, Foundation officials approved this request, and during World War II, the last set of research studies first financed by the Rockefeller Foundation in the 1920s went into print.[35]

In all, since the days of the Memorial, the Rockefeller Foundation had given over $250,000 to support research in the social sciences in Stockholm. Rockefeller fellowships, largely reflecting the interests of Gösta Bagge, went in disproportionate numbers to those associated with the Institute of Social Science and Institute for Social Work: Gunnar Myrdal (and his wife Alva) received fellowships in 1929–30, Erik Lundberg in 1931–3, Sune Carlson in 1934–6, Herbert Tingsten in 1934–5, and Tord Palander in 1935–7. Yet, as Andreen and Boalt (1987) acknowledge, the American foundation has hardly been given its due.

Bagge, too, had played a primary role in fostering the development of the social sciences in Stockholm. With Rockefeller Foundation help, he had seen to the construction of a social science building, the establishment of a social science library, the creation of research fellowships, and the publication of economic studies that were the first of their kind in their use of long series of empirical data. These were major accomplishments. Yet, he has been given little credit for this work. Why? As the personal correspondence of the principal players in the story of this period comes into the public domain, I believe historians will be better able to answer this question. In the meantime, I would like to offer some tentative explanations.

Perhaps Bagge merely suffered the fate of many a college rector or university president who discovers toward the end of his career that his preoccupation with the finances involved in building up a program or a school has lost him the intellectual respect of his younger colleagues who know little and care even less about the institution's past. But I think there are other reasons as well. Bagge's social attitudes, political opinions, and theoretical approach to economics had been formed before World War I. As the years passed, he fell more and more out-of-step with the younger generation of economists. And Bagge himself felt it. In 1938 Selskar Gunn, head of the Paris office of the Rockefeller Foundation, wrote to Sydnor Walker in New York that he found his interview

with Bagge in Stockholm on November 4 "eminently discouraging."
Bagge had painted a "blue picture" of work at the Institute for Social
Sciences.

> He stated bluntly that with Myrdal and himself away from the Institute
> the situation was unsatisfactory. He did not seem to think much of the
> substitute teachers who have taken the place of Myrdal and himself.
> He said that no research work was being carried on, nor did he see any
> reason why there should be research work at the present time, as the
> people in charge were not capable. . . . He further stated that there did
> not seem to be any good young men coming along in the S[ocial]
> S[ciences] and that the prospects were dismal.[36]

Bagge's gloomy view extended to Swedish politics, although "this is to a
large extent due to his political affiliation," the American concluded. In
Bagge's view the coalition between the social democrats and agricultural
party led to government programs that "approached totalitarianism,"
Gunn continued. "He stated that people were afraid to risk capital and
that no new industrial enterprises were being developed."

Glimmers of Bagge's old enthusiasm showed through only when he
spoke to Gunn of the School of Social Work. On this one count, he felt
secure in having accomplished something worthwhile.

Notes

Much of the information in this chapter is from the documents in the Rockefeller Archive Center (RAC). In the notes that follow, LSRM designates the
Laura Spelman Rockefeller Memorial Series III and RF designates the Rockefeller Foundation, Archive Group 1.1.

1 I wish to thank Bengt Metelius, Rolf Henriksson, Benny Carlson, and Eskil
   Wadensjö for their comments, Axel Leijonhufvud for his help in translation, and the archivists of the Rockefeller Archive Center for their usual
   efficiency.
2 Letter, September 16, 1924 (LSRM).
3 Cited in Bulmer and Bulmer (1981), p. 363.
4 Report, Lawrence Frank, "The Status of Social Science in the United
   States," 1923 (LSRM).
5 Memorandum, Gösta Bagge, submitted with letter dated September 20,
   1924 (LSRM).
6 In the 1920s, before regression analysis had been widely adopted in economics as the techniques for dealing with heterogeneity, Bagge's comments on
   the relative homogeneity of the Swedish data would have been seen as a
   strong argument. For a succinct statement of the problem see the review by
   Carl Christ [*Journal of Economic Literature,* 35:4 December 1987, pp.
   1859–60] of the excellent book by Stephen M. Stigler, *The History of Sta-*

tistics: The Measurement of Uncertainty before 1990 (Cambridge, Mass.: Harvard University Press, 1986).

7 Formal proposal submitted June 30, 1925 (LSRM); also, memorandum submitted September 20, 1924.

8 Letter with memorandum, September 20, 1924 (LSRM).

9 Letter from Ruml to Beveridge, September 26, 1924 (LSRM).

10 Letter from Beveridge to Ruml, October 14, 1924; reply from Ruml to Beveridge October 24, 1924. While waiting for Cassel's reply, Ruml also inquired of Henry Goddard Leach of *The Forum,* Park Avenue, New York City, October 28, 1924 (LSRM).

11 From retyped copy of handwritten letter from Cassel to Beveridge, November 14, 1924 (LSRM).

12 Cassel (1941), p. 99.; also, letter from Bagge to Ruml, June 30, 1925 (LSRM).

13 Correspondence Bagge-Ruml, especially Bagge letter of October 16, 1925 (LSRM); also Andreen and Boalt (1987), pp. 36–8. The undated memorandum of Ruml's interview with Bagge states that there were sixty students with no formal requirements for admission. Although eighteen students were qualified to enter the university, nineteen were graduates of a girls' secondary school, eight had completed the commercial school (Handelsinstitut), five had graduated from normal schools, seven had some secondary education, and twenty had work experience. (The numbers do not quite add up, but these were doubtless approximations.) These students were, in the words of the memorandum, "municipal secretaries, controllers, Poor Law administration, unmarried mothers, housing inspectors, factory inspectors, national social insurance, labor exchange, welfare workers in factories, secondary teachers of social science."

14 Formal proposal, June 30, 1925 (LSRM).

15 From statement of budget attached to report of June 11, 1927 (LSRM).

16 Bagge's letters to Ruml that summer and fall reveal his state of mind. Proposal approved by Trustees, November 5, 1925 (LSRM).

17 Colin Clark (British) and Simon Kuznets (Russian-born American) are generally credited with pioneering this field (Clark, 1932, 1937; Kuznets, 1934, 1937, 1941).

18 Entry of January 5, 1930 in official diary of John Van Sickle (RAC).

19 Entry of January 6, 1931, ibid.

20 Ibid.

21 The personal aspect of their differences is only now beginning to come to light. I wish to thank Kumaraswamy Velupillai for first alerting me to Bagge's treatment of Lindahl and Eskil Wadensjö for providing me with extracts from the letters of Bagge to Myrdal that show how anxious Bagge was, after the breakdown of their personal relations, to be "rid of him" so he "wouldn't have to see him in Stockholm" (Myrdal archive, Arbetarrörelsens arkiv, Stockholm).

22 Approved dockets and summary to 1938 (RF).

23 Gunn to Day, May 13, 1932 (RF); grant in aid approved June 24.

24 Ibid.
25 July 15, 1931 entry, Van Sickle diary (RAC); also a letter of October 6, 1931 (RF). Bagge said his idea also had the support of the famed Chicago sociologist W. I. Thomas and of Ruml, then dean at the University of Chicago. Van Sickle said, "Ruml told him that if it were not for the library situation, he would like to send Chicago graduates to Sweden to work."
26 Bagge to Van Sickle, August 12, 1932 (RF).
27 Van Sickle to Day, February 15, 1933 (RF).
28 Formed in 1931 partly as an administrative means of resolving problems between Bagge and Lindahl on completion of the project, the Board in 1933 consisted of Bagge, Chairman; Myrdal, Secretary and Research Director; Olof Kinberg, Criminology; Eli Heckscher, Economic History; and Harald Cramer, Statistics. In 1934 it was broadened to include Nils Herlitz in Political Science, Arthur Montgomery in Economic History, and docent K. A. Edin.
29 Quoted in Carlson (1982), p. 20; also see Jonung (1987).
30 Van Sickle to Day, March 7, 1933 (RF).
31 Tracy Kittredge to Sydnor Walker, October 29, 1934 (RF).
32 Kittredge told the home office that, in his opinion, there was no country where so close a relation between research and application existed as in Sweden, report of January 18, 1935 (RF).
33 Report by Myrdal to Kittredge, March 28, 1935 (RF). Same opinion expressed by Bagge in report of conversation in September 1935 between Bagge and Walker in Geneva.
34 See Walker's notation on Kittredge's letter dated May 15, 1936 (RF).
35 Well, this was still not quite the end. Like the earlier national income studies, the human migration studies dragged on, with Myrdal so busy and inattentive to administrative details that Thomas grew exceedingly annoyed. In March 1940, Thomas wrote Walker from the University of California–Berkeley that she was worried about Myrdal attending to the matter of getting money released to Macmillan for final publication of the manuscript. He had asked her not to bother Bagge, but she was worried since "there is a good deal of wishful thinking in his makeup." On May 4, she wrote again saying that she had not been able to get hold of Myrdal and he apparently had gone back to Sweden. "I am terribly provoked about the thing," she confessed. "I don't know whether you know the details of how the Swedish collaborators* messed up everything in connection with this whole study for the past five years, and how difficult it was to get anything finally done," adding beside an asterisk at the bottom of the page in pen, "Not Bagge, however. He has been even more provoked than I seem to be about the whole thing." Walker managed to calm her down, explaining that upon hearing of the German invasion of Norway Gunnar had left with the family "in a highly emotional state". Correspondence, March-April-May 1940 (RF).
36 Gunn to Walker, November 16, 1938 (RF).

References

Andreen, Per G., and Gunnar Boalt (1987), *Bagge får tacka Rockefeller,* Stockholms Universitet, Socialhögskolan: Rapport i Socialt Arbete 30.

Bulmer, Martin, and Joan Bulmer (1981), "Philanthropy and Social Science in the 1920's: Beardsley Ruml and the Laura Spelman Rockefeller Memorial, 1922–29," *Minerva,* Autumn, 19.

Carlson, Benny (1982), *Bagge, Lindahl och nationalinkomsten.* Lund: Lunds Universitet Ekonomisk-historiska institutionen, no. 27.

Cassel, Gustav (1941), *I förnuftets tjänt,* vol. II. Stockholm: Bokförlaget Natur och Kultur.

Clark, Colin G. (1932), *The National Income, 1924–31.* London: Macmillan.

(1937), *National Income and Outlay.* London: Macmillan.

Coser, Lewis (1965), "Foundations as Gatekeepers of Contemporary Intellectual Life," in Lewis Coser, ed., *Men of Ideas.* New York: Free Press, pp. 337–48.

Craver, Earlene (1986), "Patronage and the Directions of Research in Economics: The Rockefeller Foundation in Europe, 1924–1938," *Minerva* (Summer-Autumn), 24, 205–22.

Jonung, Lars (1987), "Intervju med Gunnar Myrdal," *Ekonomisk Debatt* (April), 15; 327–9.

Kuznets, Simon, *National Income, 1929–1932.* Washington, D.C.: Government Printing Office.

(1937), *National Income and Capital Formation.* New York: National Bureau of Economic Research.

(1941), *National Income and Its Composition, 1919–1938,* 2 vols. New York: National Bureau of Economic Research.

Lindahl, Erik (1929a), "Prisbildningsproblements uppläggning från kapitalteoretisk synpunkt", *Ekonomisk Tidskrift,* 31, 31–81.

(1929b), *Penningpolitikens mål,* 2nd edition. Lund: Gleerup.

(1929c), *Penningpolitikens medel.* Lund: Gleerup.

(1929d), *Om förhållandet mellan penningmängd och prisnivån.* Uppsala: Lundequistska and Almqvist and Wiksell.

Comment

BENNY CARLSON

I found it most interesting to hear the story of the Rockefeller money and Gösta Bagge's project told from the depth of the American archives. It would be possible to discuss a whole range of questions concerning the possible purposes and consequences of the project, which started in

1926 and soon developed into investigations on the cost of living, wages, and national income within a long-run perspective (1830/60–1930). I will touch on this range of questions very briefly.

Gösta Bagge not only obtained money but also inspiration from the United States. He was inspired by the institutionalists, and his main purpose at the outset was to study the impact of institutional factors – employers' associations, trade unions, collective contracts – on wages; the interest in these matters also grew with the permanently high levels of unemployment in the 1920s. In a broader sense Bagge's purpose was to conduct empirical research in order to make it possible to verify and develop economic theory.

At the beginning of the 1920s the institutionalists in the United States started investigating the growth of American national income and then moved on to wages. However, for Bagge's project in Sweden it was the other way around. It started with wages and continued with national income.

Erik Lindahl, who soon became the driving force behind the project, started the national income investigation in 1927. The possible objectives and implications of this work are, in my view, of considerable interest if one wishes to detect connections between Bagge's project and the development of economics in Sweden.

This investigation could easily be linked with the interest in economic growth, an area focused upon by Gustav Cassel and brought to the fore by the rapid industrial growth in the 1920s, and in structural change and business cycles, areas subsequently developed by members of Bagge's team, Ingvar Svennilson and Erik Lundberg. The investigation has also, needless to say, come to play an important role in economic history.

I would at this point, however, like to concentrate on the issue of interest to this conference: the possible connection between Bagge's project and the emergence of the Stockholm School.

The mere fact that five out of seven members of what came to be called the Stockholm School were engaged in Bagge's project – namely, Erik Lindahl, Gunnar Myrdal, Erik Lundberg, Alf Johansson, and Ingvar Svennilson – is quite remarkable. (Bertil Ohlin and Dag Hammarskjöld did not take part in it.) That these persons were brought under one roof, erected on a foundation of Rockefeller dollars, and that these same persons some years later came to be regarded as a "school" may, however, not mean much more than that the number of young and promising economists in Sweden was limited. The situation was the same regarding the Committee on Unemployment where six out of seven members of the Stockholm School were engaged (all but Lundberg). One may in this context note that Bagge's project fed the committee with statistical information.

The fact that most participants in the project, except Bagge, had a Wicksellian macroeconomic outlook and that Lindahl, often regarded as the pioneer of the Stockholm School, played a crucial role in the project also seems to point in a certain direction. There are, however, some witnesses who can be called to support or contradict this rather loose evidence.

Karl-Gustav Landgren (1957, p. 11) wrote: "Just after the middle of the 1920's a team of investigators began to meet together in Stockholm, and from these beginnings the so called Stockholm School emerged." The same author, in his famous dissertation on the "new economics" in Sweden (Landgren, 1960, p. 224), did *not* elaborate this position. He only quoted Alf Johansson, who said that Bagge's project "did not lead to a teamwork of such a kind, that it resulted in a Stockholm School."

Ingvar Svennilson (1949) expressed the same view when he wrote about "the new economic theories that at the end of the 1920's and the beginning of the 1930's, that is parallel to the inductive research work but apparently without any major direct influence from it, were developed within the circle of economists, who during these years were more or less tied to the university of Stockholm."

Gunnar Myrdal, in an interview in January 1982, tended to regard the whole project as a flop: "It was Bagge's project and it stands rather isolated in the development of economics in Sweden. Many of us earned a living by working with these books, but I don't think they played any essential role." However, Myrdal at the same time said that he was never especially interested in "that devilry."

In another interview in February 1982, Erik Lundberg expressed his surprise about the way the theoretical and empirical worlds lived side by side: "I am surprised that, in spite of these studies, so little quantification emerged from the Stockholm School. Ohlin, Myrdal and Lindahl used almost nothing from these investigations. It was particularly remarkable that Lindahl in the early 1930's made so little use of the statistics that were brought forward."

We can consequently conclude that four of the five members of the Stockholm School who were engaged in Bagge's project did not perceive any direct link between the project and the School. However, the only man who could have given a definite answer on this link is Lindahl, and unfortunately he has not done so. It is possible, I suppose, that a close study of Lindahl's development of the national income concept in this project in relation to the development of his general economic thinking might provide some kind of "Lindahl answer."

I would like to conclude by speculating – from some of the information in Earlene Craver's paper – about the possible *negative* influence of the Rockefeller donations on the development of the Stockholm School.

The Swedish economists in the 1930s were so involved in different projects that they could hardly absorb any more donations. There was a lack of men, not of funds. The Rockefeller money was, so to say, partly responsible for a situation where Stockholm economists had too many irons in the fire. (That was, of course, due in turn to the "small" academic system.) Lindahl especially, the "slowest man" in the team, was put under great pressure. As long as his part of the work was not completed, Bagge had problems raising fresh money. This may very well have meant that Lindahl was hampered or at least delayed in his theoretical work.

References

Carlson, Benny (1982), "Bagge, Lindahl och nationalinkomsten," *Meddelande från Ekonomisk-historiska institutionen,* Lunds Universitet, no. 27.

Landgren, Karl-Gustav (1957), *Economics in Modern Sweden.* Washington, D.C.: Library of Congress.

Landgren, Karl-Gustav (1960), *Den "nya ekonomien" i Sverige.* Stockholm: Almqvist & Wiksell.

Svennilson, Ingvar (1949), "Nationalekonomi," *Stockholms högskola under Sven Tunbergs rektorat.* Stockholm: Minnesskrift.

Comment

BENGT METELIUS

The main thrust of this conference is directed toward the theoretical and methodological achievements of the Stockholm School of Economics. But we must not forget that most of its members were well versed in empirical, fact-finding economics. And several of them took a very active part in shaping actual economic policy.

Earlene Craver has thrown light on the crucial rôle Gösta Bagge played in initiating and finding finance for the long-term "Stockholm Economic Studies." Here Gunnar Myrdal studied the development of the cost of living in Sweden 1830–1930. Gösta Bagge, Erik Lundberg, and Ingvar Svennilson investigated wages from 1860 to 1930. Erik Lindahl, Einar Dahlgren, and Karin Kock prepared two massive volumes about the national income in Sweden 1861–1930.

One of the off-shoots of the Unemployment Committee was the Konjunkturinstitut (The Swedish Economic Research Institute). Dag Hammarskjöld, Undersecretary of the Treasury in 1936, was instrumental in realizing the project. And Erik Lundberg was head of the Institute until 1955.

Another important feature of the life and work of the Stockholm School economists was their heavy involvement in politics and the day-to-day running of economic policy. Bagge became leader of the Conservative Party and was a member of the coalition Cabinet during the war years. Bertil Ohlin became leader of the Liberal Party and served – like Myrdal – for a period, albeit short, as Minister of Trade. Even more important, however, was the fact that Ernst Wigforss, who was Secretary of the Treasury from 1932 to 1949, had very close ties with the Stockholm School. As Rolf Henriksson has indicated, he belonged to the Political Economy Club and could in a way be regarded as an honorary member of the School. Hammarskjöld was his Undersecretary for ten years, and Lindahl, Lundberg, and Svennilson worked on numerous occasions as advisers to the Ministry of Finance and the Riksbank.

One sometimes hears the view expressed that the Stockholm School ended with the doctoral theses of Lundberg and Svennilson. I do not share this view. The School lived on in practical economic policy, in the business cycle analysis of the Konjunkturinstitut, and in the long-term studies of the Institute of Industrial Research (IUI) under Svennilson's leadership. And in the theoretical works by pupils of the original members, such as Ragnar Bentzel, Karl-Olof Faxén, and Bent Hansen.

CHAPTER 3

The Committee on Unemployment and the Stockholm School[1]

ESKIL WADENSJÖ

The Committee on Unemployment was instrumental in creating the great interest in business cycle theory and monetary and fiscal policy in Sweden in the 1930s. The Committee (1927–35) engaged many economists, several of whom – Dag Hammarskjöld, Alf Johansson, Karin Kock, Erik Lindahl, Gunnar Myrdal, Bertil Ohlin, and Ingvar Svennilson – are today considered members of the Stockholm School. Thus the Committee played a crucial role in the development of the Stockholm School. Some of the most important works of the early Stockholm School were published as supplements to the reports of the Committee.

The purpose of this contribution is to examine one of the settings in which the Stockholm School developed and to present new information on the development of some of the ideas of the Stockholm School by using unpublished and previously nonutilized material from the Committee.[2] The contributions to the Committee by Ernst Wigforss and Bertil Ohlin and the treatment of public works are chosen as examples.

The Committee on Unemployment

The Committee on Unemployment was appointed in April 1927, several years before the depression of the 1930s. The starting point was thus not the mass unemployment of the 1930s but the considerably lower unemployment rate of the second half of the 1920s.

The impetus for appointing a committee came from another committee – the Unemployment Committee of 1926 (1926 års Arbetslöshetssakkunniga) – which dealth with unemployment insurance and measures for helping the unemployed. This committee proposed (and the government also accepted) that the new committee should investigate "the nature and causes of unemployment." The main argument in support of the new committee was that in spite of a period of prosperity

103

(as in 1927), unemployment was still much higher than before World War I. Youth unemployment was a particular source of concern.

Eli Heckscher, one of the members of the Unemployment Committee of 1926, was, in his own words, the driving force behind the initiation of the new committee. "If any specific person can be said to have taken the initiative for this new committee [the Committee on Unemployment], it was probably me, and I have high expectations regarding their work."[3] Heckscher was especially pleased that Gösta Bagge, professor at Stockholms Högskola (now the University of Stockholm) and a specialist in labor economics, was appointed as one of the members of the committee. Gunnar Huss, head of the National Social Welfare Board, was named chairman. The other members were Elis Boseaus, Conrad Carlesson, Ernst Wigforss, and Anders Örne. Four of the six members of the Committee were nonsocialists. Bagge was a member of the Conservative Party (later its chairman), Carlesson and Huss were members of the Liberal Party, and Boseaus was an industrialist.

Wigforss and Örne, on the other hand, were both members of the Riksdag for the Social Democratic party. Wigforss had previously been Minister of Finance and would take on that post again when the Social Democratic Party formed its government after the election in September 1932. Wigforss, who was later to become the politician most strongly associated with the new economic policy of the 1930s, was an advocate of an active economic policy. Örne was his direct opposite in the Social Democratic Party and the most consistent advocate of a non-interventionist policy.[4] The majority of the Committee was firmly market-oriented, and wage reductions were the expected recommendation from the Committee.

A Swedish governmental committee is traditionally assisted in its work by secretaries and experts. Sven Skogh was the First Secretary from March 1928, and Dag Hammarskjöld, Assistant Secretary from August 1930, replaced Skogh in April 1932 when Skogh got a position in the Unemployment Commission (the authority in charge of the measures for the unemployed). Skogh and Hammarskjöld were both economists, and among the many experts engaged by the Committee were several other economists.

Work in the Committee was intense. The minutes of the Committee meetings for the period March 1928 to April 1932 show that the Committee had 150 days of meetings during this period. Bagge, Huss, and Wigforss had the highest rate of attendance. Bagge was absent only two days, and Huss and Wigforss attended every day when meetings were held. Örne was present much less frequently than the other members of the Committee. In a short note to the first report, he stated that he had taken little part in the work of the Committee due to other assignments (Arbetslöshetsutredningens Betänkande I, 1931, p. 504).

According to the directives to the Committee, a first report dealing with the current unemployment situation was expected to be completed by 1927. Thereafter the Committee would continue with analyses of the causes of unemployment and the effects of various measures to reduce it.

Two volumes of statistical information on the current unemployment situation based on labor union statistics and an unemployment census made by the Committee were published in 1928 and 1930, respectively. However, the first report of the Committee was delayed and not published until 1931. It contained an extensive account of the size and structure of unemployment in the 1920s and also an analysis of the causes of noncyclical unemployment (called "permanent" unemployment). Three separately published supplements to the report by Bagge (1931), Huss (1931), and Gustaf Åkerman (1931) dealt with various aspects of the causes of unemployment. Only a fraction of the material produced by the Committee was published. In total, 102 memoranda were completed in the period before the publication of the first report. Some of them, however, were preparations for the second report, which was to deal with measures to reduce the "permanent" unemployment.

The first report dealt with the causes of noncyclical unemployment. However, studies on the causes of cyclical unemployment were then demanded. The further work of the Committee was therefore devoted both to the study of business cycle theory and to the effects of measures against "permanent" as well as cyclical unemployment. In the period up to the completion of the second report, several new studies were initiated by the Committee, among them the four later well-known supplements to the final report written by Dag Hammarskjöld (1933a), Alf Johansson (1934), Gunnar Myrdal (1934), and Bertil Ohlin (1934). In this period, approximately thirty-five unpublished memoranda were also prepared.

The composition of the Committee changed during the preparation of the second report. Ernst Wigforss left when he was appointed Minister of Finance in September 1932 and was replaced by Frans Severin. Severin's views on unemployment were well known. He had commented on the first report of the Committee on Unemployment earlier in the same year in two articles in *Fackföreningsrörelsen* (see Severin, 1932). He accepted its conclusion that some of the unemployment in 1925–9 might be explained by too high wages. However, he was strongly against wage reduction as a measure against cyclical unemployment and argued in favor of public investments. Anders Örne was succeeded in

April 1932 by Richard Lindström. Severin and Lindström were both Social Democratic members of the Riksdag. Lindström resigned from the Committee two weeks before the second report was finalized in November 1934 and thus did not sign the report.

The economists and the Committee on Unemployment

The Committee engaged many economists, most of them as experts for specific studies. Gösta Bagge and Dag Hammarskjöld were two economists who had administrative positions in the Committee.

Gösta Bagge, professor at Stockholms Högskola (University of Stockholm) and head of the Social Science Institute there, played an important part in the Committee. He was a member from its inception to its end, (seven and one-half years), and was, as mentioned earlier, one of its most active members. He wrote one of the supplements to the first report and took a large part in the writing of the two reports. Many of the economists who were engaged as experts by the Committee, for example, Johansson, Lindahl, Myrdal, and Svennilson, worked at the Social Science Institute and were probably recruited by Bagge, as was Ohlin, at that time a professor in Copenhagen.[5]

Hammarskjöld, assistant secretary from August 1930 and the Committee's only secretary from April 1932, contributed to the writing of both the first and second reports, especially the second. He was also the author (under his own name) of a memorandum on unemployment in England and English unemployment policy (Hammarskjöld, 1930) as well as one of the four supplements to the second report, *Business Cycles* (Hammarskjöld (1933a). This supplement was included in the plans of the Committee from September 1931.

Lindahl was commissioned by the Committee as early as 1927 to make studies for the first report. He wrote four memoranda on the development of national income, prices, and productivity in Sweden. In practice the memoranda were a part of the project that Bagge led at the Social Science Institute financed by grants from the Rockefeller Foundation (up to 1929 the Laura Spelman Rockefeller Memorial).[6] Several years later the results were published in *Stockholm Economic Studies* (Lindahl, Dahlgren, and Kock, 1937). Lindahl was later engaged by the Committee to comment on Myrdal's supplement (Lindahl, 1934).[7] From this memorandum, it is evident that Lindahl was even more in favor of deficit spending than the proposals presented in Myrdal's report.

Gustaf Åkerman and Johan Åkerman were both engaged by the Committee in 1928. Gustaf Åkerman prepared a study on the effects of industrial rationalization (G. Åkerman, 1931) and Johan Åkerman, one on the postwar business cycle in Sweden (J. Åkerman, 1929). Gustaf Åkerman's study was published as a supplement to the first report. Johan Åkerman's study, however, was never published (Bagge's dislike of the study may be one factor behind that).[8]

Through Bagge's initiative Bertil Ohlin was recruited in April 1929 for a study of the effects of tariffs on unemployment. He delivered a seventy-six–page memorandum in January 1930 dealing with the effects on unemployment not only of tariffs but also of public works (Ohlin, 1930). The memorandum is skeptical of tariffs and public works as measures against noncyclical unemployment but in favor of the same as measures against cyclical unemployment. Ohlin's study on tariffs (and public works) was planned to be published as a supplement to the first report, but the assignment was instead expanded to include monetary policy.

Ohlin's first memorandum on monetary policy and unemployment was submitted in April 1931 (Ohlin, 1931). The study was expanded gradually and resulted eventually in the well-known *Monetary Policy, Public Works, Subsidies and Tariff Policy as Remedies for Unemployment* (Ohlin, 1934). Between the two memoranda from 1930 and 1931 and the published version of the supplement in 1934, Ohlin wrote a number of other memoranda. One of them was the preliminary version of the theoretical part of the supplement, which in a revised version appeared in *Ekonomisk Tidskrift*. It has been previously commented on by Otto Steiger.[9] There is also a short memorandum (thirteen pages) on the norm for monetary policy and a memorandum containing a long, critical presentation of the Austrian business cycle school. These memoranda and various versions of the supplement make it easier to date Ohlin's theoretical development. We will return to his contributions later.

Gunnar Myrdal was engaged by the Committee in October 1931 after he had presented a short memorandum on the effects of the tax system on unemployment (Myrdal, 1931a). His appointment as an expert was not uncontroversial, however. Hammarskjöld describes the situation in a letter to Myrdal in the autumn of 1931:

> We haven't yet been able to get exact information about your assignment due to nervousness on the part of the Ministry of Finance. Bergendal, an extremely capable and decent fellow, is a die-hard liberal and has therefore reacted strongly against not only your assignment (not to mention your memorandum), but also against the entire disposition of the next report (the underlying intent of which he has seen

through without difficulty). In the meantime, Huss has asked me to tell you that the matter is settled between himself and Sam Larsson, but that the formalities would be postponed for the time being, since due to the reasons I've mentioned, there is no sense in trying to force the matter in the Ministry of Finance until things have calmed down and become more reasonable there. Therefore, the delay of the Cabinet decision should not worry you, it's just one of the small mysteries of the Swedish administration.[10]

The formal decision to engage Myrdal was made in March 1932 by Samuel Larsson, the Minister of Social Affairs. On the same occasion Alf Johansson and Bertil Ohlin were engaged by the Committee to write supplements to the final report. The real decisions were in all three cases made earlier.

Myrdal's work resulted in his supplement to the second report. One by-product was his appendix to the government's budget proposal in 1933 (Myrdal, 1933).

Of the other Stockholm School economists, Alf Johansson was asked in December 1931 to make a study of changes in wages and unemployment. It resulted in his supplement to the final report (Johansson, 1934). Karin Kock wrote a memorandum on capital formation in Sweden for the First Report, and Ingvar Svennilson assisted Dag Hammarskjöld in his work on the Second Report. Svennilson also wrote a five-article overview of the Report for LO's journal *Fackföreningsrörelsen* (Svennilson, 1935).[11]

A list of the contributions to the Committee by economists whom we now include among the Stockholm School economists is given in Table 1.

The reports of the Committee

The work of the Committee was organized around the preparation of the two reports. The other studies (including the supplements) were means for achieving better reports. Three of the Committee members, Bagge, Huss, and Wigforss, took an active part in the work on the first report. Bagge (1931) as well as Huss (1931) wrote supplements for it. Bagge's supplement, which was essentially completed by 1928 (Bagge, 1928), was the more important of the two. It served as the point of departure for the chapter that led to the most conflict in the Committee during the period of the first report: the chapter on the causes of unemployment.

The first five versions of the chapter (written by the secretaries of the Committee) closely followed Bagge's supplement. Bagge's approach was

Table 1. *List of memoranda and supplements of the Stockholm School economists to the Committee on Unemployment*

Dag Hammarskjöld

1. "PM angående arbetslösheten i England" (Memorandum on the issue of unemployment in England), 67 pages, October 24, 1930
2. *Konjunkturspridningen. En teoretisk och historisk undersökning* (Business cycles. A theoretical and historical study), Supplement 4 to the Reports of the Committee, 266 pages, SOU, 1933:29
3. "PM till professor Ohlins bilaga" (Memorandum to Professor Ohlin's supplement), 16 pages, August 16, 1933

Karin Kock

1. "PM angående kapitalbildningen i Sverige åren 1924–1929" (Memorandum regarding capital formation in Sweden 1924–1929), 10 pages, October 20, 1930
2. *Undersökning rörande kapitalbildningen i Sverige åren 1924–1929. Tabellbilaga D* (revised version of 1). (Study regarding capital formation in Sweden 1924–1929), pp. 542–8 in SOU, 1931:20

Alf Johansson

1. "PM rörande frågeställning och disposition för behandling av löneförändringars verkan på arbetslösheten" (Memorandum regarding the framing of the problem and the design of a study on the effects on unemployment of wage changes), 14 pages, no date, 1931(?)
2. "Löneutvecklingen och 'strukturarbetslösheten'" (Wage formation and "structural unemployment"), 31 pages, no date, 1932(?)
3. *Löneutvecklingen och arbetslösheten* (Wage formation and unemployment), Supplement 6 to the Reports of the Committee, 162 pages, SOU, 1934:2

Erik Lindahl

1. "PM angående uppskattningen av Sveriges nationalinkomst" (Memorandum on the estimation of the Swedish national income), 10 pages, April 27, 1927
2. "PM angående Sveriges nationalinkomst enligt skattestatistiken" (Memorandum on the Swedish national income according to tax-based statistics), 11 pages, December 8, 1927
3. "PM angående Sveriges nationalinkomst enligt produktionsstatistiken" (Memorandum on the Swedish national income according to the statistics on production), 26 pages, December 10, 1927
4. "Industrins produktionskostnader 1913–1926" (The industrial production costs 1913–1926), 25 pages, February 9, 1929
5. "PM angående Gunnar Myrdal: finanspolitikens ekonomiska verkningar" (Memorandum on Gunnar Myrdal: The economic effects of fiscal policy), 24 pages, April 27, 1934

Gunnar Myrdal

1. "PM angående en undersökning av det svenska skattesystemet från synpunkten av dess verkningar" (Memorandum on an investigation of the effects of the Swedish tax system), 7 pages, October 24, 1931
2. *Finanspolitikens ekonomiska verkningar* (The economic effects of fiscal policy), Supplement 5 to the Reports of the Committee, 279 pages, SOU, 1934:1

Table 1. *(cont.)*

Bertil Ohlin

1. "Tullar som medel mot arbetslöshet" (Tariffs as a remedy for unemployment), 76 pages, January 13, 1930
2. "PM rörande penningpolitiska åtgärder mot arbetslöshet" (Memorandum on monetary policy against unemployment), 12 pages, April 16, 1931
3. "PM rörande den konjunkturpolitiska diskussionen med särskild hänsyn till kostnadssänknings- och konsumtioninskränkningsteorin" (Memorandum on the debate on business cycle theory with special regard to cost-reduction and consumption-reduction theories), 50 pages, December 21, 1932
4. "PM rörande penningpolitik och arbetslöshet" (Memorandum on monetary policy and unemployment), 13 pages, no date (1932)
5. "Till penningteorins centralproblem" (On the central problem of monetary theory), 49 pages, no date (1932)
6. *Penningpolitik, offentliga arbeten, subventioner och tullar som medel mot arbetslöshet* (Monetary policy, public works, subsidies and tariff policy as remedies for unemployment), Supplement 7 to the Reports of the Committee, 176 pages, SOU, 1934:12

Note: A total of about 150 memoranda and supplements were published. Included here are only those by Stockholm School economists and not those by, for example, Gösta Bagge, Ernst Wigforss, Gustaf Åkerman, or Johan Åkerman.

a Marshallian analysis of the labor market. Using the concepts of demand price and supply price, he analyzed the occurrence of noncyclical unemployment. In this type of framework high wages are always the cause of unemployment. A sufficiently low wage would always eliminate unemployment. However, Bagge did not regard wage raises as the main factor behind unemployment. According to him, differences between the demand and supply prices of labor were usually caused by changes in the size and structure of the demand or the supply of labor. Even if unemployment had been caused by a wage raise, Bagge emphasized that a wage reduction was not necessarily the best antidote. (The study of measures against unemployment was to be the main object of the second report.)

Bagge was cautious and avoided policy conclusions in his analysis. Wigforss, however, was critical. After the fifth version of the chapter on the causes of unemployment (written by Dag Hammarskjöld), Wigforss himself wrote a sixth version, which differs from the earlier versions in two particular respects.

First, Wigforss stressed that wages are set by the market and not by individual workers (an unemployed person cannot get a job by suggesting a wage below the market rate). Second, Wigforss underlined that to be able to assess the effects of a wage reduction, it is not enough to study the labor market; studies of other markets and the interrelations between the different parts of the economy are necessary. According to Wigforss, Bagge's analysis was too partial to be sufficient for an assessment of the relation between wage changes and unemployment.

Most of the changes Wigforss made were retained in the seventh version (prepared by Hammarskjöld) and in the chapter that was printed subsequently. Wigforss, however, was not quite content and drafted a separate comment *(särskilt yttrande)* to be published in the first report. He withdrew it later and added instead a short note *(anteckning)* to the report:

> Mr. Wigforss wishes to record that certain aspects of the presentation of the problem of the causes of unemployment are such as would incline him to make certain objections which, however, may be better presented when the Committee, in connection with the discussion of measures against unemployment, once again and in more definite terms deals with the problem of the causes of unemployment. (Arbetslöshetsutredningens Betänkande I, 1931, p. 504).

As a reaction to comments in the newspapers on the first report, Wigforss decided to publish parts of his criticism of the Committee. He did so as an unsigned comment in the Social Democratic periodical *Tiden* (Wigforss, 1931b).

The first report had lost some of its immediate interest when it was published. The labor market situation had deteriorated drastically in 1931. The report was concerned with unemployment in a period of prosperity, but the public debate now dealt with unemployment on a higher level and of a different character. The depression had reached Sweden. The first report (dated June 11, 1931) and also the preparations for the next report originated while Sweden was on a gold standard. Sweden, however, left the gold standard on September 27, 1931, and the Swedish krona was substantially depreciated. The number of available economic measures against unemployment was enlarged.

The work on the second report – on measures against unemployment – was begun long before the publication of the first one. Bagge presented an outline of the disposition of the second report as early as 1929 and in October of the same year, a proposal for special studies for "book II." The disposition as well as the plan for special studies was revised on several occasions.

The documents of the Committee on Unemployment reveal that three persons were the main authors of the second report: the Secretary of the Committee, Dag Hammarskjöld; the Chairman, Gunnar Huss; and Gösta Bagge. Hammarskjöld wrote the main theoretical parts of the report and Bagge the chapter on public works. Wigforss's successor, Frans Severin, made several long, critical comments to the various versions and an extensive separate comment to the final report (*Arbetslöshetsutredningens Betänkande II,* 1935, pp. 293–338). In that comment, referring to Myrdal's supplement, he advocated more deficit financing and more public works but also regulation of foreign trade and the building sector.

The second and final report of the Committee was published in 1935. Like the first one, this report was written in a very cautious manner, and just as was the case for the first report, it was superseded by political and economic developments. The political debate and the declared policy were both more interventionist than the report, but the Committee was nevertheless very influential in a more indirect way. By involving many economists and politicians in its work, it initiated research on monetary and fiscal theory among economists. At the same time as they wrote memoranda and supplements for the Committee, they published books and articles in journals and newspapers on the same issues. In this way, the Committee on Unemployment affected the theoretical development of macroeconomics and economic policy in Sweden.

Wigforss: "Prices, Monetary Policy and Unemployment"

Most of the economists of the Stockholm School took part in the work of the Committee on Unemployment, as did Ernst Wigforss. Wigforss, more than any other politician, has been connected with the introduction of the new economic policy in Sweden. As mentioned earlier, he took an active part in the Committee's work and wrote among other things three memoranda, all very different from one another. The first one was a detailed comparison of unemployment in Gothenburg according to the unemployment census and to union statistics (Wigforss, 1928a). His second memorandum dealt with the relation between the public sector and employment (Wigforss, 1928b). It consisted of two parts, one mainly a statistical description of the development of the public sector in the 1920s and the other more analytical. Only the descriptive part was included in the first report (it constitutes Chapter XII). The most interesting of the three memoranda is an original survey of business cycle theory (Wigforss, 1929). Besides Swedish economists such as Cassel, Davidson, and Wicksell, Wigforss builds on the work of British and American economists such as Fisher, Hawtrey, Mitchell, and Pigou.

This third memorandum is of interest because it shows how early the ideas that later were connected with the Stockholm School were discussed, even among noneconomists. Wigforss surveyed the literature on the relationship beween inflation and unemployment and also presented new empirical information for Sweden (and the United States as a comparison). The growth of unemployment (inverted rate) and inflation are compared in charts. Wigforss found that the best adjustment of the two curves was achieved when inflation was lagged one quarter; that is, higher unemployment was combined with lower inflation a quarter later. "The start of a change in the industrial activity" (p. 14) would therefore not start with prices. According to Wigforss price changes were important, however, for the subsequent development of the business cycle.

> The economic debate has lately made it increasingly obvious that we have to make a clear distinction between the effects of price reductions and price raises in "the long run" and under "normal conditions" – what that actually means – and their effects in a period of "crisis" or "prosperity." The standard price formation analysis is based, as we know, on the argument that every change in the "equilibrium position" set forces in motion, which strive to stop the change and restore equilibrium. . . .
> It is this automatic price mechanism which is put out of order during periods of crisis. Falling prices fail to stimulate an increase in demand. On the contrary, the price decrease encourages the belief that prices will be even lower later on, demand decreases further which gives rise to an even larger fall in prices. On the supply side, there are effects in the same direction. In anticipation of further price decreases, less is produced. Unemployment increases, workers' incomes decline, consumption decreases, and prices are forced down even more. (Wigforss, 1929, pp. 20–1)

Wigforss described a business cycle in which the downturn started with increased unemployment, which gave rise to a cumulative process if the disturbance was considerable. With this type of business cycle theory, wage decreases would not be the preferred policy. It is not difficult to understand with this knowledge of Wigforss's view of the business cycle that he could easily comprehend and make use of the theories of the Stockholm School and Keynes. If we compare Wigforss's memorandum with earlier studies by the Stockholm School economists, it is probably closest to Ohlin's *Saet Produktionen i Gang* (Ohlin, 1927b). Ohlin emphasized in this study that wage reductions influence expectations and lead to less investment and thereby to a worsening of a downturn of the business cycle. Wigforss's study is, however, the more elaborate one.

Bertil Ohlin and the Committee on Unemployment

Bertil Ohlin was one of the Stockholm School economists most actively engaged in work for the Committee on Unemployment. Already when the Unemployment Committee of 1926 in February 1927 proposed the founding of a new committee on the Causes of Unemployment he wrote an article strongly supporting the proposal (Ohlin, 1927a). Two years later he was himself commissioned to write a report to the Committee.

Ohlin's supplement to the second report has been praised. However, within the Committee, this study was not uncontroversial. As already pointed out, Ohlin started his work on the effects of tariffs and public works on unemployment as early as 1929. His study was gradually extended. In the late spring of 1933, he presented the first full-length version of his book for the Committee and received a very critical sixteen-page examination in return (dated August 16, 1933). Huss has signed the critical assessment, but it was quite obvious that it was written by Hammarskjöld (1933b). Besides the criticism of the concepts in the theoretical part of the study that Ohlin mentions in his memoirs, the examination contained many other critical remarks.[12] The criticism was divided into six general admonitions and nine special problems. Ohlin was criticized, for example, for drawing his own political conclusions from his analysis (a privilege open to the Committee, rather than to the writers of the supplement) and for dealing with material that was the subject of other reports. Hammarskjöld was also critical of the multiplier effect calculated by Ohlin. It was labeled unrealistic. This criticism explains why a lot of the material in the memoranda was not included in the published version of Ohlin's book. The presentation of these memoranda throws light on Ohlin's theoretical development. A few issues will be addressed below.

Public Works

A subject dealt with in earlier studies of the Stockholm School is Ohlin's advocacy of public works and tariffs as measures against unemployment. From the documents of the Committee, it is evident that he did so as early as January 1930 (Ohlin, 1930). He was, however, in favor only of those measures against cyclical unemployment, not against "permanent" (frictional, structural) unemployment.

Austrian versus Anglo-Saxon business cycle theories

Two interrelated issues in the history of the Stockholm School are when the Stockholm School was first considered a school and what the relationship between the Stockholm School and British economists was. A memorandum written in the autumn of 1932 is of interest in this context.[13] At a conference held that year, Ohlin had debated monetary policy and theory with Johan Åkerman, whose business cycle theory was close to that of the Austrians. This was one of several exchanges of views on business cycle theory between Ohlin and Åkerman.[14] After that debate, Ohlin wrote a fifty-page critical analysis of what he called the Vienna School for the Committee on Unemployment.

Ohlin argued that it was possible to divide business cycle theorists into two main groups, one English

> represented by authors as Keynes, Robertson and Hawtrey. Most American and Scandinavian economists largely adopt the same line. In decided opposition to this group of economists, who recommend price increases and public works, there are a few French economists and the so-called Vienna School, which has lately also won followers in London. This school includes Mieses, Hayek, Harberler, Strigl, Robbins, Benham and probably also Gregory. (Ohlin, 1932b, p. 2)

Ohlin also included Johan Åkerman in this Vienna School.[15] He emphasized that it was important for the Committee to take a standpoint on which theoretical school they would rely on:

> Since the memoranda, prepared by Myrdal, Johansson, Hammarskjöld, and myself will be closely associated with it [the Anglo-Saxon School], it appears to be of some importance that the Committee in its assessment of the views presented in these memoranda should also have access to an account of the opposite point of view. If the Committee should concur with [the Vienna School], it follows that all these memoranda cannot provide a basis for the Committee's standpoint in public works, wage policy, monetary policy and fiscal policy. I will give such an account below. (Ohlin, 1932b, p. 3)

It is evident that Ohlin meant that the authors of the four supplements had the same basic theoretical view and belonged to the same theoretical school. However, Ohlin's colleagues in the Stockholm School were not necessarily of the same opinion.[16] It is also evident that in 1932, Ohlin did not see the Stockholm economists and Keynes as two separate schools. On the contrary, he stressed that the Swedish economists (with the exception of Johan Åkerman) belonged to the same tradition as most British economists.

Employment norms

Wicksell's norm for monetary policy was price stabilization. Leading Swedish economists – Cassel, Davidson, and Lindahl – held this view in the 1930s (Jonung, 1979). Ohlin, however, had not adopted price stabilization as the norm for monetary policy in his analysis. In an early document, probably written in 1932, he declared that "the norm for monetary policy, on which the following study is based, is another, that is: the minimization of unemployment" (Ohlin, 1932c p. 2). The discussion of the choice of norm for the monetary policy is not included in his supplement to the Committee, however.

Multiplier effects

As previously mentioned, in earlier versions of the supplement, Ohlin calculated the multipler effect of public works. It is derived as a sum of a geometric series; that is, Ohlin calculates the static multiplier effect. The calculation was much criticized by Hammarskjöld (1933b) but is still in the printer's proof of December 2, 1933. In the published version, however, the calculation is deleted.[17]

The Committee on Unemployment on public works

Public works played a vital part in the new economic policy of the 1930s and was also a controversial political issue. However, it was not a matter of much conflict within the Committee.

The Committee made a proposal in favor of countercyclical public works in its second report. Public works, however, should not be employed to counteract noncyclical unemployment. This is hardly surprising considering the composition of the Committee. The two leading non-Social Democratic members of the Committee had argued in favor of countercyclical variations of public works long before the appointment of the Committee. Huss proposed countercyclical public works against unemployment as early as 1908. The works should be ordinary works at the going wage rate for the job but undertaken earlier than otherwise would have been the case.[18]

> It should be emphasized that in the creation of jobs one should, if possible, arrange so-called extra work, that is, work that would be done in any event but not at just that point in time. From both a theoretical and practical point of view, both the municipalities and the unemployed themselves should see that the work carried out is unequivocally useful to society and worthwhile in itself. It therefore follows as a consequence that this work is paid at the going rate, to the extent that these laborers are as qualified as the average laborers in their field. (Huss, 1908, p. 33)

Bagge (1925, pp. 519–20) argued in the same way in favor of counter-cyclical public works in 1925:

> The core of the matter is ... a redistribution in time of production which is considered necessary and unavoidable *in toto*, but which can be shifted from a period of full employment to a period of recession. The question is, if it isn't more suitable to place this production in the latter part of the economic cycle than in the former. This should also, in many cases, be (more) in the direct economic interests of both the municipalities and the state, since apparently both production and loans are cheaper during a depression than to forge ahead during an economic boom, thereby also causing incalculable damage to society.

Compared to most nonsocialists, Huss and Bagge were both interventionists.

In several memoranda and supplements, arguments favoring public works to counteract cyclical unemployment were put forward. As is evident from the above, Ohlin came out in favor of public works in times of deflation in his first memorandum for the Committee (Ohlin, 1930).[19] Hammarskjöld prepared a memorandum on English unemployment and unemployment policy in the same year, 1930. Among other things, he provided an account of the Liberal Party's 1929 proposals on economic policy. In that connection, Hammarskjöld argued for counter-cyclical public works but was highly skeptical of public works as a means against noncyclical unemployment. Both Myrdal (1934) and Ohlin (1934) advocated public works to diminish unemployment in their supplements to the second report.

Only three dissenting voices can be found among the Committee's members and economic experts. Anders Örne opposed public works as a means to eliminate unemployment.[20] However, he left the Committee long before the completion of the second report. On the other hand, Severin and Lindahl wanted more public works than did the majority of the Committee. In his separate comment to the final report, Severin advocated more lenient rules for public works. More important, he wanted governmental control of the building sector. According to Severin, the governmental sector was too small to enable significant variations in public works. The regulation of the building sector would make possible considerably more variation in public works.

The argument that public works could also serve as a measure to diminish noncyclical unemployment was put forward by Lindahl in his comment to the Committee on Myrdal's supplement (Lindahl, 1934). The public works could be financed by deficit spending. According to Lindahl, a budget deficit may not be used to counteract cyclical unemployment only but also against noncyclical unemployment in periods of prosperity.[21]

Conclusions

The Committee on Unemployment engaged several economists, especially from the younger generation. In this way, it contributed to the interest taken by numerous Swedish economists in monetary and fiscal theory and policy. The Committee did not direct the economists to write in a specific theoretical tradition and did not give them too narrowly defined problems. In supplements and especially in memoranda, the authors were able to write relatively freely. On the other hand, they had to be prepared to meet harsh criticism, and the Committee's own reports were cautious products characterized by compromise.

From the memoranda and earlier versions of the supplements, it is possible to more accurately date the development of the ideas of the Stockholm School. I want to stress two conclusions: First, the chief architect of the new economic policy in Sweden, Ernst Wigforss, also took an active part in the development of the theoretical analysis. Second, Ohlin was in favor of a Keynesian policy (public works, tariffs) as early as 1930. In 1933 he used the multiplier to analyze the effects of public works. He also based his analysis of economic policy on the norm of employment stabilization as early as 1932.

A governmental investigation was a flexible form of organization that made it economically feasible for many researchers to work with the same problem at the same time. The universities were not equally flexible. But the fact that the research was conducted on behalf of a governmental investigation may also help explain why most of the economists of the Stockholm School did not continue research in the same area. Most of the economists did not have tenured positions at the universities and continued on to new assignments and posts in the governmental sector. For others, political interests took an increasing part of their time. Three of them, Bagge, Myrdal, and Ohlin, became members of the Riksdag and were, along with Hammarskjöld, periodically members of the government. The organizational form of the research – a government investigation – was simultaneously a factor behind the rise of the Stockholm School and its failure to create a tradition of its own.

Notes

1 I have benefited from many comments on earlier versions. I especially want to thank Bo Gustafsson and Otto Steiger. Alan Harkess has translated most of the quotations.

2 All material from a governmental committee is filed in Riksarkivet (the National Archives). The file for the Committee on Unemployment contains letters, many unpublished memoranda, minutes from meetings, and so forth. This material has not been used by Landgren or Steiger, for example.

3 Heckscher in the Proceedings of Nationalekonomiska Föreningen 1928, p. 118. The meeting was on the report of the Unemployment Committee of 1926.

4 As an illustration, see the debate between Myrdal (1931b) and Örne (1931) in *Tiden*. See also Landgren (1960), pp. 158–9.

5 See the letter from Bagge to Ohlin dated February 15, 1929, Kungliga Biblioteket (The Royal Library).

6 Andreen and Boalt (1987) give a detailed and lively account of the organization of the project funded by the Rockefeller grant. See also the contribution of Earlene Craver in this volume.

7 Lindahl's memorandum was later published in a revised version in *Ekonomisk Tidskirft* (Lindahl, 1935).

8 In a letter to Myrdal dated August 18, 1929, Bagge writes: "What I have seen of Johan Åkerman's work for the Committee on Unemployment makes me hesitate to entrust new assignments to him" (Arbetarrörelsens Arkiv). In a letter to Ohlin from August 3, 1929, he states: "Johan Åkerman's [study] was useless for our purposes" (Kungliga Biblioteket).

9 See Ohlin (1932d, 1933, 1978). Steiger's comments and analysis of the development of Ohlin's article are in Steiger (1971, 1978).

10 Arbetarrörelsens Arkiv. Sam(uel) Larsson was the Minister of Social Affairs and Bergendal was Undersecretary of the Ministry of Finance.

11 When writing the articles Svennilson asked Hammarskjöld for advice and comments. See letter from Svennilson to Hammarskjöld of February 15, 1935 (Committee on Unemployment; Riksarkivet).

12 Not until December 1934 did Ohlin respond to the criticism. He did so indirectly by way of a letter to Lindahl (December 7, 1934; Kungliga Biblioteket), with copies to members of the Political Economy Club including Hammarskjöld. Hammarskjöld responded to the critism in a letter of December 22, 1934 (Committee on Unemployment; Riksarkivet). Ohlin answered by sending a letter to the Committee on Unemployment (January 25, 1935; Committee on Unemployment; Riksarkivet).

13 A letter from Ohlin to Huss of January 10, 1933 (Committee on Unemployment; Riksarkivet) makes it possible to date the memorandum to December 21, 1932.

14 See *Industriförbundets Meddelanden* (1932) and also Ohlin (1932e) and Åkerman (1932a, 1932b).

15 Åkerman's conclusions on the debate of the two schools are summarized in Åkerman (1933).

16 In the earlier mentioned letter to Huss of January 10, 1933, Ohlin complained about Bagge's and Hammarskjöld's critical views of his memorandum. Ohlin mentioned two possible responses, either an enlargement of the treatment of the two Schools to 500–600 pages or a shortening. He followed

the second line. Part of the discussion on the two schools, however, was published in *Weltwirtschaftliches Archiv* (Ohlin, 1932b). In this letter he also stresses that an article published in *Index* (Ohlin 1932a) is a first version of part of his supplement. The article is a summary of "The Newmarch Lectures" Ohlin gave at London University in May 1932.

17 Ohlin wrote a three-article review of the Second Report of the Committee on Unemployment in *Stockholmstidningen* (Ohlin (1935a, 1935b, 1935c). In the first of the articles (Ohlin, 1935a), he critized the Committee for not taking into account that the public works could lead to an expansion of private production. The Committee had not "utilized the new ground gained by economic science."

18 Huss's study is one of the three sources that are mentioned in the report by the parliamentary committee that dealt with a Social Democratic motion for countercyclical public works in 1912. See Steiger (1971, p. 110).

19 See also Ohlin's review of "Can Lloyd George Do It?" in *Stockholmstidningen* in May 1929 (Ohlin, 1929).

20 See, for example, his sharp criticism of public works as a measure against cyclical unemployment in Örne (1933). One of the members of the Committee, Lindström, criticized Örne for his statement in an editorial in *Ny Tid.*

21 This idea is developed in Lindahl (1944).

References

Andreen, Per G., and Gunnar Boalt (1987), *Bagge får tacka Rockefeller* (Bagge and the Rockefeller Foundation). Rapport i Socialt Arbete No. 30, Stockholms Universitet, Socialhögskolan.

Arbetslöshetsutredningens Betänkande I (1931), *Arbetslöshetens omfattning, karaktär och orsaker* (The extent, character and causes of unemployment). Statens Offentliga Utredningar (SOU), 1931:20.

Arbetslöshetsutredningens Betänkande II (1935), *Åtgärder mot arbetslöshet* (Policies for dealing with unemployment). SOU, 1935:6.

Bagge, Gösta (1925), "Produktionens reglering som medel mot arbetslöshet" (The regulation of production as a remedy against unemployment). *Svensk Tidskrift*, 15, 513–23.

    (1928), "PM angående arbetslöshetsproblemet ur teoretiska synpunkter" (Memorandum on theoretical aspects of the unemployment problem). Arbetslöshetsutredningen PM no. 60.

    (1931), *Orsaker till arbetslöshet* (Causes of unemployment). Arbetslöshetsutredningens Betänkande I Bilagor, Band I. SOU, 1931:21.

Direktiv för Arbetslöshetsutredningen (Terms of reference for the Committee on Unemployment). *Post och Inrikestidningar*, March 12, 1927.

Hammarskjöld, Dag (1930), "PM angående arbetslöshetsfrågan i England" (Memorandum on the issue of unemployment in England). Arbetslöshetsutredningens PM no. 97, October 1930.

(1933a), *Konjunkturspridningen. En teoretisk och historisk undersökning* (Business cycles. A theoretical and historical study). Bilaga 4 till Arbetslöshetsutredningens Betänkanden. SOU, 1933:29.

(1933b), "PM till professor Ohlins bilaga" (Memorandum to Professor Ohlin's supplement). Arbetslöshetsutredningen, August 16, 1933.

Huss, Gunnar (1908), "Promemoria angående arbetslösheten i Sverige hösten 1908 samt kommunala åtgärder i anledning av arbetslöshet" (Memorandum on unemployment autumn 1908 in Sweden and municipal measures due to unemployment). Meddelande från Kungl. Civildepartementet. Stockholm.

(1931), *PM angående arbetsmarknaden och de faktorer som bestämma dess utveckling* (Memorandum on the labor market and factors determining its development). Arbetslöshetsutredningens Betänkande I, Bilagor, Band I. SOU, 1931:21.

Industriförbundets Meddelanden (1932), "Sveriges industri och världskrisen. Diskussion vid Sveriges Industriförbunds årsmöte den 19 april 1932" (Swedish industry and the world economic crisis. Debate at Annual Meeting of the Federation of Swedish Industries; participating, among others, Bertil Ohlin and Johan Åkerman), No. 2, pp. 66–101.

Johansson, Alf (1934), *Löneutvecklingen och arbetslösheten* (Wage formation and unemployment). Bilaga 6 till Arbetslöshetsutredningens Betänkanden. SOU 1934:2.

Jonung, Lars (1979), "Knut Wicksell's Norm of Price Stabilization and Swedish Monetary Policy in the 1930's." *Journal of Monetary Economics,* 5, 459–96.

Landgren, Karl-Gustav (1960), *Den 'nya ekonomien' i Sverige. J. M. Keynes, E. Wigforss, B. Ohlin och utvecklingen 1927–39* (The 'new economics' in Sweden: J. M. Keynes, E. Wigforss, B. Ohlin and the development 1927–39). Stockholm: Almqvist & Wiksell.

Lindahl, Erik (1934), "PM angående Gunnar Myrdal: finanspolitikens ekonomiska verkningar" (Memorandum on Gunnar Myrdal: The economic effects of fiscal policy). Arbetslöshetsutredningen, April 27, 1934.

(1935), "Arbetslöshet och finanspolitik" (Unemployment and fiscal policy). *Ekonomisk Tidskrift,* 37, 1–36.

(1944), "Teorin för den offentliga skuldsättningen" (The theory of public debt), *Studier i ekonomi och historia* tillägnade Eli F. Hecksher. Uppsala.

Lindahl, Erik, Einar Dahlgren, and Karin Kock (1937), *National Income of Sweden 1861–1930,* 2 vols. Stockholm Economic Studies. London: P. S. King & Son.

Myrdal, Gunnar (1931a), "PM angående en undersökning av det svenska skattesystemet från synpunkten av dess verkningar" (Memorandum on an investigation of the effects of the Swedish tax system). Arbetslöshetsutredningens PM no. 104, October 24, 1931.

(1931b), "Den svenska penningkrisen" (The Swedish monetary crisis), "Svar på anmärkningarna" (Rejoinder to the comments), "Slutreplik" (Last rejoinder). *Tiden,* 23, 521–42; 591–9; 607–12.

(1933), *Konjunkturer och offentlig hushållning* (Business Cycles and Public Finance). Stockholm.

(1934), *Finanspolitikens ekonomiska verkningar* (The economic effects of fiscal policy). Bilaga 5 till Arbetslöshetsutredningens Betänkanden. SOU 1934:1.

Ohlin, Bertil (1927a) "Böra arbetslöshetens orsaker undersökas?" (Should the causes of unemployment be investigated?) *Stockholmstidningen,* February 27.

(1927b), *Saet Produktionen i Gang* (Start up production again). Copenhagen: Aschehoug.

(1929), "Valet och arbetslösheten i England" (The election and unemployment in England), *Stockholmstidningen,* May 26.

(1930), "Tullar som medel mot arbetslöshet" (Tariffs as a remedy for unemployment). Arbetslöshetsutredningens PM no. 93, January 13, 1930.

(1931), "PM rörande penningpolitiska åtgärder mot arbetslöshet" (Memorandum on monetary policy against unemployment). Arbetslöshetsutredningens PM no. 101.

(1932a), "Nu eller aldrig" (Now or never), *Index,* 7, 123–53.

(1932b), "PM rörande den konjunkturpolitiska diskussionen med särskild hänsyn till kostnadssänknings- och konsumtionsinskränkningsteorin" (Memorandum on the debate on business cycle theory with special regard to the cost reduction or consumption reduction theory). Bilaga 4b till Betänkande II, Arbetslöshetsutredningen, December 21.

(1932c), "PM rörande penningpolitik och arbetslöshet" (Memorandum on monetary policy and unemployment). Arbetslöshetsutredningen, no date.

(1932d), "Till penningteorins centralproblem" (On the central problem of monetary theory). PM, Arbetslöshetsutredningen, no date.

(1932e), "Prisstegringens problem. Replik till fil.dr. Johan Åkerman" (The problem of the rise of prices. Rejoinder to Dr. J. Åkerman), *Det Ekonomiska Läget,* No. 4.

(1932f), "Ungelöste Probleme der gegenwärtigen Krises" *Weltwirtschaftliches Archiv,* 36, no. 2, 1–23.

(1933), "Till frågan om penningteorins uppläggning," (translated as Ohlin, 1978). *Ekonomisk Tidskrift,* 35, 45–81.

(1934), *Penningpolitik, offentliga arbeten, subventioner och tullar som medel mot arbetslöshet* (Monetary policy, public works, subsidies and tariff policy as remedies for unemployment). Bilaga 7 till Arbetslöshetsutredningens Betänkanden. SOU, 1934:12.

(1935a), "Hur arbetslöshet botas och förebyggas" (How unemployment is remedied and prevented) *Stockholmstidningen,* March 13.

(1935b) "Socialdemokratisk arbetslöshetspolitik" (Social Democratic unemployment policy), *Stockholmstidningen,* March 16.

(1935c) "Sveriges sysselsättningsproblem" (Sweden's problem of unemployment), *Stockholmstidningen,* March 19.

(1978), "On the Formulation of Monetary Theory," *History of Political Economy,* 10, 353–88.

Severin, Frans (1932), "Lönesänkningarna och depressionen" (Wage reductions and the depression), *Fackföreningsrörelsen,* Vol. XII, Part I, pp. 626–30 and 646–52.

Sociala Meddelanden (1927), "Utredning om arbetslöshetens karaktär och orsaker" (Committee on the characteristics and causes of unemployment), No. 3.

Steiger, Otto (1971), *Studier zur Entstehung der Neuen Wirtschaftslehre in Schweden.* Berlin: Duncker & Humblot.

(1978), "Substantive Changes in the Final Version of Ohlin's 1933 Paper," *History of Political Economy,* 10, 389–97.

Svennilson, Ingvar (1935), "Den stora arbetslöshetsutredningen" (The great Committee on Unemployment) *Fackföreningsrörelsen,* Vol XV, pp. 247–51, 311–18, 343–50, 396–401.

Wigforss, Ernst (1928a), "PM angående undersökning av siffrorna för arbetslöshetsräkningen i Göteborg jämförda med fackföreningarnas uppgifter" (Memorandum on a comparison of the unemployment census and unemployment according to the unions for Gothenburg). Arbetslöshetsutredningens PM no. 61, January 27, 1928.

(1928b), "Förändringar i den offentliga hushållningen sedan tiden före kriget" (Changes in the public sector since the period before the war). Arbetslöshetsutredningens PM no. 81, March 1, 1928.

(1929), "Prisnivå, penningpolitik och arbetslöshet" (Prices, monetary policy and unemployment). Arbetslöshetsutredningens PM no. 84, May 22, 1929.

(1931a), "Utkast till särskilt yttrande till Arbetslöshetsutredningens första betänkande" (Draft to separate comment to the First Report of the Committee on Unemployment). Arbetslöshetsutredningen, June 1931.

(1931b), En utredning om arbetslöshetens orsaker. Reflexioner till ett kommittébetänkande (An investigation on the causes of unemployment. Some comments on a report by a governmental committee). *Tiden* 23, 457–68.

Åkerman, Gustaf (1931), *Om den industriella rationaliseringen och dess verkningar* (Industrial rationalization and its effects). Bilaga 3 till Arbetslöshetsutredningens Betänkande I, SOU, 1931:42.

Åkerman, Johan (1929), "De ekonomiska konjunkturerna i Sverige efter kriget" (Business cycles in Sweden in the post-war period). Arbetslöshetsutredningens PM no. 78, February 1, 1929.

(1932a), "Prisstegringens problem" (The problem of the rise in prices). *Det Ekonomiska Läget,* No. 3, pp. 1–34.

(1932b), "Prisstegringens problem. Svar till prof. Bertil Ohlin," *Det Ekonomiska Läget,* No. 4, pp. 33–50.

(1933), "Saving in the Depression," *Economic Essays in Honour of Gustav Cassel.* London: Allen & Unwin.

Örne, Anders (1931), "Några anmärkningar till Gunnar Myrdals artikel om den svenska penningkrisen" (Some comments to Gunnar Myrdal's article on the Swedish monetary crisis). "Gensvar" (Rejoinder). *Tiden,* 23, 585–90, 600–6.

(1933), "'Liberal' eller 'socialistisk' nationalekonomi" (Liberal or socialist economics), *Ny Tid,* February 17 and 18, 1933.

Comment

BO GUSTAFSSON

Wadensjö's paper is an important contribution to our understanding of how the notions of the Stockholm School arose with special regard to the interplay between economic theory and politics. His findings seem to reinforce the conclusions previously reached by Karl-Gustav Landgren in his book on the rise of the new economics in Sweden from 1927 to 1939 published in 1960, namely, that the chief architect of the new economic policy and, in fact, the most consistent advocate of the new theoretical insights was Ernst Wigforss; and that the only academic economist who at an early stage succeeded in liberating himself from the preconceptions of the old theory was Bertil Ohlin. Ohlin was actually the only member of the Stockholm economists who came close to a theory of output as a whole. One point of considerable interest in Wadensjö's paper is his discovery that Ohlin, under pressure from Hammarskjöld and others, published a somewhat emasculated version of his theory in his supplement to the report from the Committee on Unemployment. Wadensjö's concluding reflections on the considerable dependence of the Stockholm economists upon governmental assignment (e.g., the Committee on Unemployment) for developing their theoretical work raises interesting questions that are worthy of further consideration.

As Wadensjö rightly emphasizes, the Committee on Unemployment (1927–35) was sidetracked by political events, primarily by the advent of the new Social Democratic government after the 1932 election, but also by rapid theoretical developments nationally as well as internationally. Like its predecessor (the 1926 Unemployment Committee), the 1928 Committee on Unemployment appointed by the moderately liberal Ekman government was largely created to give the impression that the government cared about unemployment without really doing anything about it. The most visible expression of the continuity in aims and thinking is the fact that Heckscher was succeeded by his close comrade-in-arms Gösta Bagge with Gunnar Huss, head of the National Social Welfare Board, as his aide. They were both backed up by Elis Bosaeus and A. O. C. Carleson, who represented the business community. Carleson was also a liberal member of parliament. Faced with this majority, the advanced political and theoretical views of the Social Democrat Ernst Wigforss were unable to make any headway. As Wadensjö notes, Ernst Wigforss's colleague Anders Örne was "a consistent advocate of a non-interventionistic policy".

When the Social Democrats took over government power in 1933 and embarked upon expansionist unemployment and fiscal policies, the Committee was pushed aside. The majority members of the Committee, however, were still able to use it as a platform for a rearguard action against interventionism. They could not decide upon the content of the supplements written by nonmembers, even if, as Wadensjö notes, they made use of their right (and duty) to offer criticism. In writing the reports, however, the Committee majority could decide upon its own formulations. This was a power of which it made some use.

I have the impression that Wadensjö somewhat underestimates the conservatism of the reports. Let me elaborate on this point. The first report, published in 1931, was mainly descriptive. When summarily discussing the causes of unemployment at the end of the report, attention is drawn to several factors, for example, substitution of labor for capital and demographic change. However, there is no doubt that the Committee assigned the most important role to the wage level per se (see SOU, 1931:20, pp. 497–8 and 501–2). The substitution of labor for capital was also affected by an excessively high wage level. It did not occur to the Committee that the labor-saving investments of the 1920s (the so-called rationalization movement) might have been a technological imperative irrespective of the wage level (at least within wide margins). Alf Johansson, however, pointed out in his supplement that the mechanization of industry in Germany had been as rapid as in Sweden, although wages had increased less and interest rates were higher. The explanation was that the productivity increases made possible by mechanization were so large that they remained profitable even at considerably lower wage rates (Alf Johansson, *Löneutvecklingen och arbetslösheten*, 1934, pp. 24–5).

The second part of the report discussed the problem of how unemployment should be fought. It was introduced by a theoretical discussion of the causes of unemployment, which ultimately landed in an Austrian position à la Hayek. It was stressed that a "lack of unemployment opportunities, as well as unused capacity as a whole, is explained by the scarcity of different productive means, as well as by their quality in relationship to the effective monetary demand for goods and services for final consumption and by the stickiness of certain prices" (p. 13). The discontinuity of capital formation during the business cycle was not mainly caused by variations in demand but by "the discontinuity of technical change" (p. 36). The report was very skeptical toward the use of fiscal policy as an instrument against unemployment and emphasized strongly that "monetary policy [is] the most important instrument when attempts are made to mitigate the fluctuations of the business cycle" (p. 257).

Public investments were only "a valuable complement to monetary policy in specific situations," for example, in case of "a very severe depression" (p. 268). Public investments were also characterized as belonging to the sphere of theoretical possibilities (p. 269). In the discussion of public investments as an instrument against unemployment, the report put forward so many reservations that one receives the impression that the committee really did not advocate them. Public investments were difficult to select, difficult to plan, and difficult to finance. If, in spite of all these difficulties, they were used, they might become too large (Chapter XIX). No wonder that Severin (who took Wigforss's place on the Committee after he became Minister of Finance) in his personal statement for the report found that the many reservations of the Committee "could be interpreted as a clear although not expressive dissuasion" from public investments in depressions (p. 323). In conclusion, Severin regretted that the Committee had nothing but wage cuts as an antidote against permanent unemployment (p. 296).

In his condensed analysis of Bagge's supplement to the report, "Causes of Unemployment" (SOU, 1931:21), Wadensjö suggests that for Bagge "wage rises are not the main factor behind unemployment" (p. 7). According to Bagge it is evident that unemployment is caused by a too high general *level* of wages. "The wage," Bagge emphasized, "is always 'too high' at unemployment in the sense, that the supply price is higher than the demand price for a certain quantity of labour power. This applies to all different 'kinds of unemployment.' In this sense, as was emphasized before, all kinds of unemployment have fundamentally the same character. This applies even where the mix of factors that *together* determine the difference between the supply and the demand price for labour power, varies from situation to situation or from different points of view" (p. 16). According to Bagge, the demand price for labor usually varied, for example, during the course of the business cycle, while the supply price was sticky, owing to the wage policy of the trade unions. Hence, in a fundamental sense, unemployment *was* conditioned by the existence and the policy of the trade unions (pp. 14–15). In the absence of trade unions and collective bargaining, the supply price of labor would have adapted to the vagaries of the demand price and no unemployment would have ensued. This, I think, was Bagge's fundamental view of the unemployment problem.

In fact, Bagge considered that conditions in output markets were quite irrelevant for the unemployment problem. Few of the orthodox economists were so consistent as Bagge in upholding Say's law. "Total national income," he said, "must always in some way or another, as already pointed out, be used for expenses and thus give rise to demand for means of production" (p. 42). If the public sector uses its purchasing power for current expenses, "total saving in society will decrease and thus also the demand for labour power" (p. 45). "An increase of demand in one industry because of enlarged orders etc from the public sector implies decreases in other industries" (p. 70). And to leave no doubt about his position, Bagge squarely states: "Savings are only expenses, i.e. utilization of the incomes of a certain kind. Capital formation implies a reduction of the current consumption of the savers and the investment of their 'waiting' in an increased quantity of real capital" (p. 48). With these views it is quite clear that Bagge could not agree to any kind of expansionism without committing intellectual hara-kiri.

Only Ohlin's supplement, "Monetary Policy, Public Works, Subsidies and Tariff Policy as Remedies for Unemployment" with the significant subtitle "A Contribution to the Theory of Expansion" (1934) made a clear and decisive break with the ruling orthodoxy. Wadensjö has shown how Ohlin was forced to delete calculations of multiplier effects from his book. Nevertheless, its main character was preserved. This and only this work can legitimately be regarded as a really new macroeconomic theory, on a par with Keynes's forthcoming *General Theory* in content, if not in sophistication. This has already been demonstrated by Landgren in his book. A stable price level was no longer regarded as the overriding goal for economic policy. National income and employment are treated as variables and functions of the demand for consumption and investment goods, and full employment is the really relevant target for economic policy. Increased saving is a function of increased income that is effected by increasing investment, which also leads to increasing consumption. In the event of unemployment, wage cuts would not increase saving and income but would lower both national income and saving and investment. The multiplier is there and so is the accelerator. The interest rate is not the equilibrium price of saving and investment but reflects the demand and supply of loanable funds. In a truly dynamic paragraph, Ohlin even suggests that wage increases probably increase the profitability of capital in industry through the economies of scale effected at higher levels of output.

Why wasn't this promising approach toward a new macroeconomics followed up in the subsequent development of the Stockholm School? Part of the answer should probably, as Wadensjö suggests, be sought in the specific social and political conditions of Sweden in the 1930s. There was a social demand for "new economists," and Swedish social scientists were then as now much more involved in policy problems than their colleagues in other countries. However, this is only part of the answer. Keynes was also heavily involved in politics. I think that Wadensjö touches on an important aspect of the problem when he points out the conditions for research created by governmental investigations. But I do think that the crux is not "the flexible form of organization" but rather the fact that the Committee work made a concentration of intellectual efforts possible. A parallel is the results from the concerted efforts of Lindahl, Myrdal, Lundberg, and Svennilson in the economic-historical work on national income, wages, and prices financed by the Rockefeller Foundation. In a small country like Sweden, small and isolated intellectual efforts usually give rise to small and isolated results. However, when it is possible to rally several scholars in a more or less united attack on a common problem by providing an intellectually stimulating basic unit, creative work may ensue.

When the Stockholm economists took up new assignments and posts in different areas of social practice (Myrdal and Ohlin became deeply involved in politics, Lindahl became an advisor to Wigforss, Johansson became a public servant, and Lundberg became head of the newly founded Konjunkturinstitutet), there was less time for purely theoretical work and still less time for purely theoretical communication. Maybe the outcome would have been different if there had been more tenured positions at the universities. Nevertheless, I suspect that even then the temptations to practice rather than to develop the new economics would have been too strong. On the one hand, the number of Swedish economists was fairly limited. Moreover, they were usually dispersed. On the other hand, they were provided with ample opportunities to apply their new theories at an early stage. Both of these factors tended to inhibit theoretical development.

Comment

OTTO STEIGER

As one of the authors who in recent decades have discussed, in their work on macroeconomic theory and policy in Sweden at the time of the Great Depression, the relation of the Stockholm School to the Swedish Committee on Unemployment – most notably Landgren (1960), Steiger (1971, 1976, 1978b), Uhr (1977), and Ohlin (1981) – I am impressed by the richness of the unpublished and, with two exceptions,[1] hitherto unknown material from the Committee discovered by Eskil Wadensjö. It goes without saying that Wadensjö is able to offer only an outline of these new sources in his presentation. In spite of some more detailed information on the contributions of Ernst Wigforss and Bertil Ohlin, this new material allows only tentative conclusions to be drawn on how our view of the Stockholm School ought to be revised. For a fuller acount, we have to wait for Wadensjö's forthcoming edition of the Committee's unpublished memoranda.[2]

Unfortunately, in his contribution Wadensjö does not provide an account of the earlier debate on the origin, ideas, and development of the Stockholm School as well as its importance for Swedish policy on reducing cyclical fluctuations by credit-financed public works vis-à-vis the role of Ernst Wigforss, the Social Democratic politician and Minister of Finance after the change of government in the autumn of 1932. I think that some information on this controversy is necessary for a better understanding of how "the Committee on Unemployment affected the theoretical development of macroeconomics and economic policy in Sweden" (Wadensjö's words) because the debate was focused not only on the genesis of the advocacy of public works but also on the macrotheoretical underpinnings of such a policy (see the extensive review of the debate by Carlson, 1988, pp. 369–95). This type of discussion is, however, not taken up by Wadensjö.

The debate about the genesis of macroeconomic theory and policy in Sweden in the 1930s started with Karl-Gustav Landgren (1960), who made two assertions: (i) The alleged influence of the Stockholm School on Swedish unemployment policy was unimportant, for the influential forces consisted rather of the ideas of English liberals of the 1920s, with John Maynard Keynes as their intellectual spearhead. These ideas were introduced in Sweden by Wigforss. (ii) The Stockholm School was an *ex post* construction by Ohlin (1937), who did not understand the extent of the fundamental discrepancy between his aggregate demand/supply approach (Ohlin, 1933), where he had anticipated Keynes (1936), and the savings/investment approach of Erik Lindahl (1929) and Gunnar Myrdal (1932).

In opposition to Landgren's views I developed the following theses (Steiger, 1971): (i) While I agreed with him about Wigforss's central role in the new economic policy in Sweden, I modified his assertion about Wigforss's intellectual roots by showing that the latter's advocacy of public works can be traced back to the efforts of Social Democrats in the Swedish parliament in 1912. These were renewed toward the end of the 1920s and then not only reformulated by Wigforss, under the influence of the English liberals, but also given a theoretical foundation (Wigforss, 1931) that was essentially in harmony with the views expressed by the Stockholm School. (ii) Contrary to Landgren, I showed that there was no fundamental discrepancy but a continuous development in the macroeconomic analysis of the early Stockholm School – that is, Lindahl, Myrdal, and Ohlin – and the employment policy based on it that supported Wigforss's proposals. The central idea that I identified in the writings of Lindahl (1929, 1932, 1934b, 1935), Myrdal (1932, 1933, 1934), and Ohlin (1932c, 1933, 1934a)[3] was the fundamental insight that saving is not only an action undertaken by individuals but also an outcome of the economy as a whole, that is, that the equality of savings and investment is brought about by changes in aggregate income. It was this understanding that led the early Stockholm economists to the consideration of a systematic use of variations in the relation between public expenditure and taxes, that is, the budget balance, as a means to stabilize the level of aggregate output and employment. (iii) Already before Keynes's *General Theory,* and not as late as 1937, Ohlin (1934b) regarded the authors of this macroeconomic approach as forming a special "school" – a view that, as I tried to explain in a later paper (Steiger, 1976), Ohlin developed in response to Dag Hammarskjöld's critical memorandum (1933) discussed by Wadensjö.

How does the new material from the Committee on Unemployment change our picture of the Stockholm School as it has emerged in the debate presented above? First of all, Wadensjö gives further evidence in support of my thesis that the Stockholm School was not an *ex post* construction by Ohlin. The latter's memorandum on the Vienna School (Ohlin, 1932a), however, modifies my thesis. In this memorandum, in contrast to his letter to Lindahl (1934b) – where he demonstrated the considerable similarities between only Lindahl's, Myrdal's, and his own macroeconomic approaches – Ohlin also included Hammarskjöld and Alf Johansson in the same theoretical school, which is in accordance with his definition of the Stockholm School in 1937. Ohlin's neglect of Lindahl in 1932 (Ohlin, 1932a) has to be explained by the fact that Lindahl's memorandum was first written in 1934, while Ohlin's later concentration on the early Stockholm School (Ohlin, 1934b) has to be interpreted only as a direct result of Hammarskjöld's attack in 1933.

Wadensjö's contribution also provides further evidence in support of both Landgren's and my thesis that the policy of public works was not invented by the Stockholm School. By referring to the nonsocialists Gunnar Huss (1908) and Gösta Bagge (1925) as advocates of such a policy, however, Wadensjö only emphasizes what has been proved already (see Steiger, 1978b, p. 437, and in greater detail Schulz, 1987) by historians of economic thought, namely, that long before Keynes and the

Stockholm School, economists as well as politicians, bankers, unionists, and other "cranks" all over the world had argued for countercyclical public works. These policy conclusions were, however, at their best – as Wadensjö's quotations from Huss and Bagge exemplify – based on the common sense reasoning that public works that would be carried out in any event should be redistributed from boom to recession, thereby taking advantage of the lower costs in the latter part of the cycle. Such recommendations not only lacked a theoretical underpinning but were also inconsistent with the premises of their proponents' macroeconomic theory, as Wadensjö ought to have stressed more explicitly with respect to Bagge (1931).

On the other hand, Wadensjö indicates that Wigforss's (1929) proposals did not lack a theoretical foundation because he was able to show why the price mechanism did not work during a depression. Wigforss's thesis that falling wages and prices, instead of stimulating an aggregate demand, are likely to have the opposite effect by creating expectations of further price decreases should have been completed with a reference to the more elaborate reasoning in his main theoretical treatise (Wigforss, 1931, pp. 45–51, 77), where the increase in the real burden of business debt associated with general deflation was seen as the decisive case against downward wage and price flexibility. This can be regarded as a clear anticipation of Keynes's central argument against wage reductions in the *General Theory* (Chapter 19)[4] – an anticipation that was also far superior to the discussion on the subject by the Stockholm School, for example, Ohlin (1933, pp. 368–9), who only considered the unfavorable effects on consumption demand. It would also have been possible to provide further documentation on the progress that Wigforss had made in macrotheory at an early stage of the Great Depression. For instance, in his discussion of savings and investment (Wigforss, 1931, pp. 52–60) he explicitly rejected the equilibrating role of the rate of interest and showed, furthermore, that it is not the scarcity of savings but the high elasticity of the preference for holding money at low rates of interest that hinders investment (pp. 59–60). Since this reasoning can be regarded, too, as an anticipation of the *General Theory,* which the Stockholm School at best hinted at (e.g., Ohlin, 1934a, p. 42), I think that Wadensjö understates Wigforss's originality by crediting him with only "that he could easily comprehend and make use of the theories of the Stockholm School and Keynes."[5]

The fact that the Stockholm School neither invented the policy of public works nor was first in Sweden to provide it with a macrotheoretical foundation does not mean, however, that its contributions were relatively unimportant in comparison with those of Wigforss. In particular, the analysis by Lindahl, Myrdal, and Ohlin of changes in aggregate output and the equilibrating role of these variations with respect to savings and investment, in which they anticipated many of the central ideas of the *General Theory*,[6] seems to be far superior to Wigforss's treatment of these relations. Wigforss still adhered to the Wicksellian view that savings were implicitly equivalent to the provision of finance by emphasizing that during a depression, unused savings or hoardings formed the basis of an increase in output by loan-financed public works (Wigforss, 1931, pp. 54–60, 114–18). On the other hand, the early Stockholm economists showed, in accordance with Keynes, that the proposed public works, in the same way as private investment, were not only financed independently of savings but, on the contrary, generated the necessary savings by creating an expansion of aggregate income.

In his review of Ohlin's unpublished memoranda, Wadensjö ought to have pointed out that the former's advocacy of public works was firmly based on this fundamental macrotheoretical insight (Ohlin, 1930, pp. 50–66). Ohlin showed that a rise in aggregate output and a decrease in unemployment caused by an increase in investment through public works "increases savings by increasing incomes" (p. 65). Moreover, he had criticized the Vienna School (Ohlin, 1932a, pp. 37–38, 42, 48) for neglecting changes in aggregate output. Ohlin's insights were in fact a precondition for his extensive discussion of the multiplier developed in the earlier versions, however, deleted in the published version of his supplement to the Committee on Unemployment (1934a).[7] A greater emphasis on Ohlin's macrotheoretical underpinnings of the policy of public works would also have revealed how "the Committee on Unemployment affected the theoretical development" (Wadensjö's words) of the Stockholm School, namely, by stimulating its members to direct their analysis to changes in output and (un)employment, and not only to changes in the price level, which had been the main object in the early writings of Lindahl (1929) and Myrdal (1932), who first in their contributions to the Committee (Lindahl, 1932; Myrdal, 1933)[8] analyzed public works in the same manner as Ohlin had done in 1930.[9]

The conclusion to be drawn from Ohlin's unpublished memoranda is, therefore, not only that "Ohlin was in favor of a Keynesian policy . . . as early as 1930" (Wadensjö's words) but that he already at this date had succeeded in giving a theoretical foundation to such a policy.[10] Furthermore, his early macroeconomic underpinning allows not only for a revision of my earlier thesis about a continuous development in the theoretical writings of Lindahl, Myrdal, and Ohlin, but also for a solution of the "very difficult" puzzle to find out who was first [in the Stockholm School] to expound these ideas" (Hansson, 1982, p. 184) of the equilibrating mechanism of changes in total output. From the new material of the Committee on Unemployment, it becomes clear that Ohlin has to be regarded as a forerunner with respect to the analysis of these variations.

Notes

1 The exceptions are Ohlin (1932d) and Hammarskjöld (1933). The former memorandum has been commented on by Steiger (1971, pp. 191–2; 1976, pp. 353–4; 1978a, passim), the latter by Ohlin (1972, p. 171), Steiger (1976, p. 362), and Hansson (1982, p. 188); see also note 2.

2 This edition would benefit from a detailed comparison between the unpublished memoranda and their already published parts, which I sometimes miss in Wadensjö's paper. Two examples: (i) Most of Lindahl's comment (1934a) on Myrdahl's supplement (1934) was published in Lindahl (1935), where also his advocacy that "a budget deficit may not be used to counteract cyclical unemployment only but also against noncyclical unemployment" (Wadensjö's words) can be found (Lindahl, 1935, pp. 3–7). (ii) Larger parts of Ohlin's memorandum (1932a) on the Vienna School were published in Ohlin (1932b), which also contains (p. 3) his main criticism against the Austrian economists discussed below: their neglect of changes in aggregate output.

3 However, it has to be emphasized that Ohlin already hinted at this idea in a 1929 review of the proposals of the English liberals (Steiger, 1971, pp. 187–8, and 1976, pp. 349–50). For the recognition that Ohlin, in face of his first memorandum to the Committee on Unemployment (1930), has to be regarded as a forerunner with respect to the analysis of changes in aggregate output, see my discussion below.

4 It might be emphasized that his important insight of the "self-defeating way to achieve equilibrium at full employment" by wage and price flexibility has been entirely lost in the dominating interpretations of the *General Theory* that instead have "ticketed Keynes as the theorist of sticky-price macroeconomics" (Hahn and Solow, 1986, p. 5).

5 A similiar understatement holds true for the characterization by one of the contributors to this Conference, namely, that "the testimony of Ernst Wigforss . . . that he was little affected by Sweden's domestic economists . . . is standard drill" that we, therefore, should not "make too much of" (Samuelson, this volume).

6 It has to be emphasized, however, that they never succeeded in formulating an approach that is akin to Keynes's principle of effective demand determining the equilibrium level of (un)employment; see Hansen (1981, passim), Hansson (1982, pp. 73–81, 140–52, 182–93), and Patinkin (1982, passim).

7 In this connection it deserves mention that Myrdal, who wrote the theoretical outline to Wigforss's budget proposal in 1933 (personal communication with the author), in his supplement to this budget (1933, but actually written already in 1932) also had commented on the multiplier extensively and,

among other things, produced an early formulation of the balanced-budget multiplier (Myrdal, pp. 33–4; see also Steiger, 1971, p. 184).

8 Lindahl's contribution was a lecture given at the proceedings of the Swedish *Nationalekonomiska Föreningen* in November 1932, which, however, can be regarded as a preliminary version of his views on public works developed in his comment (Lindahl, 1934a) on Myrdal's (1934) supplement to the Committee on Unemployment. In preparing his lecture, Lindahl had studied a draft of Myrdal (1933) (see Hansson, 1982, p. 184), the enlarged version of which would become Myrdal (1934).

9 The fact of this foundation of the policy of public works in the writings of Lindahl, Myrdal, and Ohlin for the Committee on Unemployment, to which the unpublished memoranda give further evidence, also contradicts the view of one of the contributors to this Conference, namely, that these early Stockholm economists only "advocated public works and fiscal stimulation to combat unemployment" because in their contributions no case can be identified where "variations in output take the place of variations in prices" (Myhrman, this volume). Myhrman's conclusion results from his neglect of Lindahl (1932, 1935), Myrdal (1933, 1934), and Ohlin (1934a, Chapter V), which contains his most advanced analysis of public works.

10 A closer look at Ohlin's unpublished memoranda reveals, however, that his discussion of the price mechanism during a depression (1930, pp. 64–6, 1932a, pp. 44–6) is less elaborate than that of Wigforss indicated above, discussing only the unfavorable effects of wage reductions on consumption demand and still adhering to the "classical" idea that the rate of interest should be regarded as an equilibrator of savings and investment, at least in the long run.

References

Bagge, G. (1925), "Produktionens reglering som medel mot arbetslöshet" (The regulation of output as means against unemployment). *Svensk Tidskrift* 15, 513–23.

(1931), *Orsaker till arbetslöshet* (Causes of unemployment). Bilaga 1 till Arbetslöshetsutredningens Betänkanden I. Stockholm: Statens Offentliga Utredningar (SOU), 1931:21, band I, 1–127.

Carlson, B. (1988), *Staten som monster. Gustav Cassels och Eli Heckschers syn på statens roll och tillväxt* (The state as monster. G. Cassel's and E. F. Heckscher's view on the role and growth of the state (with a summary in English). Lund: Studentlitteratur.

Hahn, F. H., and R. M. Solow (1986), "Is Wage Flexibility a Good Thing?" in W. Beckerman, ed., *Wage Rigidity and Unemployment*. London: Duckworth, 1–19.

Hammarskjöld, D. (1933), *P(ro) M(emoria) till professor Ohlins bilaga* (Memorandum on Prof. Ohlin's supplement). Stockholm: Arbetslöshetsutredningen, August 16, 1933 (ms.).

Hansen, B. (1981), "Unemployment, Keynes and the Stockholm School," *History of Political Economy* 13 (2, Summer), 256–77.

Hansson, B. A. (1982), *The Stockholm School and the Development of Dynamic Method.* London: Croom Helm.

Huss, G. (1908). *Promemoria angående arbetslösheten i Sverige hösten 1908 samt kommunala åtgärder i anledning av arbetslöshet* (Memorandum on unemployment in Sweden autumn 1908 as well as on municipal measures against unemployment). Stockholm: Meddelande från Kungl. Civildepartementet.

Keynes, J. M. (1936), *The General Theory of Employment, Interest and Money.* London: Macmillan.

Landgren, K. -G. (1960), *Den 'nya ekonomien' i Sverige. J. M. Keynes, E. Wigforss, B. Ohlin och utvecklingen 1927–39* (The 'new economics' in Sweden. J. M. Keynes, E. Wigforss, B. Ohlin and the development 1927–39) (with a summary in English). Stockholm and Uppsala: Almqvist & Wiksell.

Lindahl, E. (1929), *Penningpolitikens medel* (The means of monetary policy). Lund/Malmö: Gleerup/Försökringsaktiebolaget. Enlarged 2nd Ed. 1930; abr. transl. as "The Rate of Interest and the Price Level," in E. Lindahl, *Studies in the Theory of Money and Capital,* London: George Allen & Unwin, 1939, pp. 139–260.

(1932), "Offentliga arbeten i depressionstider" (Public works in times of depression). *Nationalekonomiska Föreningens Förhandlingar,* November 25, pp. 127–37, 163–4.

(1934a), *P(ro) M(emoria) angående Gunnar Myrdal: Finanspolitikens ekonomiska verkningar* (Memorandum on G. Myrdal: The economic effects of fiscal policy). Stockholm: Arbetslöshetsutredningen, April 27 (ms.).

(1934b), "A Note on the Dynamic Pricing Problem" (mimeo), Gothenburg, October 13; corr. version published in Steiger (1971), pp. 204–11.

(1935), "Arbetslöshet och Finanspolitik" (Unemployment and fiscal policy). *Ekonomisk Tidskrift* 37 (1–2), 1–36; abr. transl. as "The Problem of Balancing the Budget," in Lindahl (1939), pp. 351–77.

Myrdal, G. (1932), "Om penningteoretisk jämvikt. En studie över den 'normala räntan' i Wicksells penninglära" (On monetary equilibrium. A study on the "normal rate of interest" in Wicksell's monetary doctrine). *Ekonomisk Tidskrift* 33 (5–6), 1931 (printed July 1932), 191–302; rev. transl. as "Der Gleichgewichtsbegriff als Instrument der geldtheoretischen Analyse," in F. A. Hayek, ed., *Beiträge zur Geldtheorie,* Vienna: Julius Springer, 1933, pp. 361–487; further rev. transl. as *Monetary Equilibrium,* London: William Hodge, 1939.

(1933), *Konjunktur och offentlig hushållning. En utredning* (The business cycle and public finance. An expert report). Stockholm: Kooperativa Förbundet.

(1934), *Finanspolitikens ekonomiska verkningar* (The economic effects of fiscal policy). Bilaga 5 till Arbetslöshetsutredningens Betänkanden II. Stockholm: SOU, 1934:1.

Ohlin, B. (1929), "Lloyd George och arbetslösheten" (Lloyd George and unemployment). *Stockholms-Tidningen,* April 18, p. 11.

(1930), *Tullar som medel mot arbetslöshet* (Tariffs as means against unemployment). Stockholm: Arbetslöshetsutredningens P(ro)M(emoria) no. 93, January 13 (quoted from draft of E. Wadensjö's forthcoming edition).

(1932a), *P(ro) M(emoria) rörande den konjunkturpolitiska diskussionen, med särskild hänsyn till kostnadssänknings- och konsumtionsinskränkningsteorien* (Memorandum on the debate on cyclical policy with special regard to the cost cutting and consumption reduction theory). Bilaga 4b till Betänkanden II. Stockholm: Arbetslöshetsutredningen, December 21 (quoted from draft of E. Wadensjö's forthcoming edition).

(1932b), "Ungelöste Probleme der gegenwärtigen Krisis," *Weltwirtschaftliches Archiv,* 36 (II/1, July), 1–23.

(1932c), "Prisstegringens problem. Replik till fil. dr. Johan Åkerman" (The problem of raising prices. Rejoinder to Dr. J. Åkerman"). *Det Ekonomiska Läget,* No. 4 (August), pp. 21–32.

(1932d), *Till penningteoriens centralproblem* (On the central problems of monetary theory). P(ro) M(emoria), Stockholm: Arbetslöshetsutredningen, no date (ms., draft of Ohlin, 1933).

(1933), "Till frågan om penningteoriens uppläggning." *Ekonomisk Tidskrift* 35 (2), 45–81; quoted from and transl. as "On the Formulation of Monetary Theory," *History of Political Economy* 10 (3, Fall), 1978, 353–88.

(1934a), *Penningpolitik, offentliga arbeten, subventioner och tullar som medel mot arbetslöshet. Bidrag till expansionens teori* (Monetary policy, public works, subsidies and tariffs as means against unemployment. A contribution to the theory of expansion). Bilaga 7 till Arbetslöshetsutredningens Betänkanden II, Stockholm: SOU 1934:12.

(1934b), Open letter to Erik Lindahl, Stockholm, December 7 (mimeo) German transl. in Steiger (1971), pp. 214–16; extensive excerpts in Steiger (1976), pp. 360–1.

(1937), "Some Notes on the Stockholm Theory of Savings and Investment I–II," *The Economic Journal* 47 (185/186, March/June), 53–69 (I), 221–40 (II).

(1972), *Bertil Ohlins memoarer. Ung man blir politiker* (B. Ohlin's memoirs. A young man becomes a politician). Stockholm: Bonniers.

(1981), "Stockholm and Cambridge: Four Papers on the Monetary and Employment Theory of the 1930s," posthumously edited by O. Steiger, *History of Political Economy* 13 (2/Summer), 189–255.

Patinkin, D. (1982), "Anticipations of the General Theory? The Stockholm School," in D. Patinkin, *Anticipations of the General Theory? And Other Essays on Keynes,* Chicago: Chicago University Press, pp. 36–57.

Schulz, F. (1987), *Zur Dogmengeschichte der funktionalen Finanzwirtschaftslehre. Eine literaturgeschichtliche Untersuchung zur Entstehung der "functional finance" vom Merkantilismus bis zur "neuen Wirtschaftslehre."* Berlin: Duncker & Humblot.

Steiger, O. (1971), *Studien zur Entstehung der Neuen Wirtschaftslehre in Schweden. Eine Anti-Kritik.* Berlin: Duncker & Humblot.

(1976), "Bertil Ohlin and the Origins of the Keynesian Revolution," *History of Political Economy* 8 (3, Fall), 341–66.

(1978a), "Substantive Changes in the Final Version of Ohlin's 1933 Paper". *History of Political Economy* 10 (3, Fall), 389–97.

(1978b), "Prelude to the Theory of a Monetary Economy: Origins and Significance of Ohlin's 1933 Approach to Monetary Theory," *History of Political Economy* 10 (3, Fall), 420–46.

Uhr, C. G. (1977), "Economists and Policymaking 1930–1936: Sweden's Experience," *History of Political Economy* 9 (1, Spring), 89–121.

Wigforss, E. (1929). *Prisnivå, penningpolitik och arbetslöshet* (The price level, monetary policy and unemployment). Stockholm: Arbetslöshetsutredningens p(ro)m(emoria) no. 84, July 20 (quoted from E. Wadensjö's forthcoming edition).

(1931). *Den ekonomiska krisen* (The economic crisis). Stockholm: Tidens Förlag.

PART II

The approach of the Stockholm School

CHAPTER 4

Expectation and plan: The microeconomics of the Stockholm School

CLAES-HENRIC SIVEN[1]

The Stockholm School had its roots in Knut Wicksell's (1898) macroeconomic analysis of the cumulative process and Gunnar Myrdal's (1927) attempt to extend neoclassical microeconomics (in Gustav Cassel's version) to cover nonstationary phenomena. Both Wicksell's analysis of price level changes and Myrdal's of firm planning in a changing and uncertain environment were attempts to study processes for which comparative statics was an insufficient analytical tool.

The macro- and the microeconomic lines were connected in the twin concepts *ex ante* and *ex post*.[2] Starting from the expectations for the future *(ex ante),* individual firms and households plan their actions for the coming period. The values of the expectation variables registered at the end of the period *(ex post)* will, however, differ from the expectations held at the beginning of the period. This may result from a lack of coordination between the plans of individual agents or from unexpected external events. The discrepancy between expectations *ex ante* and outcomes *ex post* will initiate revisions of both expectations and plans for the coming period. The unexpected – the gap between expectations *ex ante* and outcomes *ex post* – is thus one of the factors that drives the system in the period analysis of the Stockholm School (see Lindahl, 1939).[3] The stress on analyzing gaps between plans and expectations on one hand and outcomes on the other reflected the dissociation from equilibrium theory that was a characteristic feature of the Stockholm School. This was both a strength and a weakness: a strength in the sense that new territory, the problem of change, was covered; and a weakness since equilibrium analysis was deserted as a method, but essentially without replacing it with other analytical instruments.

Ever since the Stockholm School was introduced to the international public by Bertil Ohlin (1937), it has mainly been perceived as a macroeconomic school contemporary (and competitive) to that of Keynes. This perception has, for good reasons, dominated the scientific discussion about the Stockholm School.[4] As a consequence of this concentration on the macroeconomics of the Stockholm School, the following perspectives were ignored. First, the conception of the world as uncertain, changing, and not amenable to interpretation by equilibrium analysis can, through Myrdal (1927), be traced back to the international discussion about profits as a reflection of the unanticipated and about the closely related problem of entrepreneurship. Second, there was a clear relationship between the microeconomics of the Stockholm School, characterized by analysis of the plans and expectations of individual firms and households, and its macroeconomics. In other words, the macroeconomics of the Stockholm School can partly be explained by its microeconomic "foundations."[5]

Here I will discuss the following questions:

What did the microeconomic theory of plans and expectations of the Stockholm School look like?
Which were the main intellectual sources of the Stockholm School analysis of the effects of gaps between outcomes and expectations?
What problems and possibilities were connected with the microeconomics of the Stockholm School as a basis for its macroeconomics?

To answer these questions, I will partly follow a chronological order. Thus I first present what I believe to be an important source of inspiration for the interest of the Stockholm School in the problem of uncertainty: Knight's investigation of the entrepreneurial role, which was, in its turn, preceded by Schumpeter's analysis of the innovation process. In the second section, I consider the two central microeconomic works of the Stockholm School: Myrdal's dissertation *Price Formation and Change* from 1927 and Svennilson's dissertation *Economic Planning* from 1938. In the third section, I discuss the development of the microeconomics of the Stockholm School from a more systematic point of view. The fourth section contains an evaluation of the connection between the microeconomics and the macroeconomics of the Stockholm School based on Lindahl's (1939) program for period analysis. The fifth section summarizes the discussion.

1   The background

Joseph Schumpeter

In *Lectures,* Wicksell (1906) discussed the origin of profits. Under "full" (perfect) competition, factors of production were remunerated according to their marginal productivity. Under constant returns to scale, remunerations would then be equal to the value of production. Profits (defined economically, not according to accounting definitions) could then be due either to disequilibrium or to imperfect competition. These aspects were combined by Schumpeter (1912, 1934) in his theory of economic development.

There are no profits and the rate of interest is equal to zero when the circular flow is characterized by stationary equilibrium. The repetition of the state period by period makes creative behavior unnecessary. All decisions are made according to mechanical rules. The stationary equilibrium of the circular flow is, however, broken by the introduction of new goods and new methods of production; new markets are opened, new raw materials are used, and new types of organization appear. Innovations constitute a disturbance mechanism that destroys equilibrium. Entrepreneurs not only recognize the new possibilities, they also take advantage of them. When other agents act by routine, the role of entrepreneurship implies abandoning the routine.

Since an innovation implies that revenues are larger than costs, profits will appear during the innovation process. During this process, firms will price their products monopolistically until competitors are able to imitate the product or method of production or are able to enter the new market. Schumpeter thus explained profits in terms of monopoly. However, monopolies were transient, arising as a result of the disequilibrium caused by innovations at the original relative prices of the circular flow. He emphasized the role of the entrepreneur, placing it within the broad context of economic growth and the business cycle.

Frank Knight

Schumpeter's theory essentially concerns the effects of, not the analysis of, entrepreneurial behavior. The latter was to be an important task for Frank Knight, who wanted to describe the entrepreneurial role. Profits are closely connected to the genuine uncertainty that is connected with almost all enterprise.[6]

According to Knight there are three types of situations with incomplete information: (1) A priori probabilities. These are logical probabilities that are based on equivalent and mutually exclusive events. (2) Statistical probabilities (frequency probabilities). (3) Estimates. He characterized these in the following way: "The distinction here is that there is *no valid basis of any kind* for classifying instances. This form of probability is involved in the greatest logical difficulties of all, and no very satisfying discussion of it can be given, but its distinction from the other types must be emphasized and some of its complicated relations indicated" (Knight, 1921, p. 225). Knight stressed, however, that the line of demarcation between probability situations of types 2 and 3 is not very sharp. Nothing is absolutely unique.

Knight considered business to be mainly characterized by the third type of probability situation. This type of uncertainty has at the same time been neglected by economists. On the other hand, the uncertainty or risk that we can estimate may often be eliminated by the law of large numbers (diversification of the portfolio, insurance, et cetera). It is through the third type of probability – uncertainty – that profits emerge.[7]

According to Knight, there are several reasons for uncertainty. The entrepreneur has first of all an incomplete knowledge of the external environment of the firm. He does not know how much he will be able to sell; alternatively the price of the product will be unknown. He will also be uncertain about the amount that competitors will supply as well as about the preferences and purchasing power of consumers.

The greatest uncertainty regarding the external environment concerns economic development itself, particularly improvements in knowledge. A new invention cannot be described before it is made. New products create changes in demand and supply that will affect the market situation for old goods and services and factors of production. This implies that investment activity is closely connected to entrepreneurship since investments will yield returns in a more or less distant future. This is the foremost form of evaluation under uncertainty.

Nor has the entrepreneur complete knowledge of and control over the internal environment of the firm. Especially for large firms the complexity of control makes delegation necessary. The most important decision-making problem confronting the entrepreneur concerns persons rather than facts. But could not (assuming risk aversion) uncertainty and thus profits/losses be eliminated via diversification and insurance? Knight thought that two circumstances hinder this: the impossibility of measuring risks and moral hazard.

To sum up, while Schumpeter examined the macroeconomic effects of entrepreneurial activity, Knight studied the microeconomics of entrepreneurial behavior. But Knight went further, discussing how the institutional characteristics of the economy are affected by the prevalence of risk and the desire to avoid it.

2   Myrdal and Svennilson on the planning process

Myrdal's price formation and change

The aim of Myrdal's dissertation was to "a certain extent embody the factor of change in price theory, that is liberate it from the static assumption" (Myrdal, 1927, p. 4). This approach was a generalization of his teacher Gustav Cassel's analysis of an economy in general equilibrium used to cover the problem of economic transformation. In this approach he was greatly (but not uncritically) inspired by Frank Knight. Myrdal's most important contribution was his investigation of when uncertainty is important for profits and his further examination of intertemporal planning under uncertainty.

Myrdal stressed that *a change* in the capital value of the firm constitutes profits or losses caused by the price change. Monopoly profits are not included in Myrdal's definition of profits. They are instead capitalized in the capital value of the firm. Knight had earlier hinted at this in his discussion of the capitalization of the returns from innovations.

Changes that are subject to certainty do not give rise to profits. This was also pointed out by Knight in a polemical exchange with Clark in 1914. New information thus creates profits for those who have access to it and are able to use it. Comparison can also be made with Schumpeter's analysis of innovation profits, where the existence of differential information is a central ingredient.

Myrdal defined in a somewhat unorthodox fashion the economic risk as the mathematical product of the value of a possible revenue or cost and its probability. The risk of an entrepreneur is the mathematical expectation of profits. According to Myrdal (1927, pp. 16–17), economic risk is due to four interacting causes: (1) Production is time consuming. (2) Changes are possible during the production process. (3) These changes are not predicted with complete certainty but may be expected as more or less probable. (4) Adjustment to changes takes time.

According to Myrdal, a rational risk perception is "objective." This does not imply that the entrepreneur has perfect information but that he has a correct apprehension of his own ignorance. The risk is a function of the entrepreneur's relative ignorance of the future. If experience and judgment are given, we can talk about objectively correct perceptions of the future (this has some similarity to rational expectations; see Myrdal, 1927, p. 98). However, Myrdal did not talk about knowledge of the behavior equations of other agents.[8] Myrdal (1927, p. 101) also pointed out that risk perceptions are most often irrational: ". . . a too large trust, a too low recognition of risks may be a normal human trait."

The choice of different actions by the entrepreneur is, however, not only determined by the (subjectively recognized) expected outcome. Myrdal also introduced a valuation coefficient which reflects the risk attitude. Myrdal talked about different factors that would make the risk coefficient larger than unity (i.e., there is risk aversion), one of which is the law of decreasing utility (i.e., marginal utility). Myrdal also referred to Bernoulli. Myrdal criticized Knight's view that the condition for a risk to be insurable is that it should be possible to measure. The reason ordinary business risks are not insurable is not the absence of measurability but a combination of non-independence and moral hazard (personal risks according to Myrdal's terminology). Conversely it is possible (cf. mutual insurance companies) to insure risks that are not measurable. Risk (in contrast to uncertainty) is neither a necessary nor a sufficient condition for insurability. The skillfulness of the entrepreneur is tested in situations where risks cannot be eliminated by for example, insurance.

In the second section of his dissertation, "The Problem of Profits," Myrdal tried to explain the connection between pricing at different points of time. The connecting link is people's expectations about the future. He thus presented a theory of intertemporal planning and expectations of the individual firm, not an aggregate theory explaining the emergence of profits.

Since expectations about the future are affected by different events, the potential equilibrium price (or the "normal" price according to Myrdal's terminology) will change. Future changes will affect pricing as soon as they are anticipated. At the same time, however, there is inertia in price adjustment to changes in supply and demand conditions. Myrdal referred to

> the time momentum of pricing inertia, the lagged character of the actual movement of pricing towards its changing equilibrium. . . . The inertia of the actual change reactions of pricing will cause what aptly has been called "gaps" in pricing – that is from our point of view: the possibility that new investments will be associated with expectations of revenues that are supernormally large in comparison to expectations of costs. This is due to actual pricing lagging after its natural equilibrium.[9] (Myrdal, 1927, p. 121)

Myrdal stressed frequently that the discrepancy between expectation and outcome (compare *ex ante–ex post*) constitutes the dynamic element of pricing:

> Revenues and costs of a firm may be looked upon from two different points of view . . . – expectations and results – . . . Pricing is only explained under the condition of "the principle of costs." The thereby postulated coincidence between the cost and price of each product will however only be maintained under the assumption, that all acting individuals have a certain and complete knowledge of the future. . . . In a state of risk, the principle of costs will be lacking. . . . The time momentum within the relative economic inertia has namely prevented a complete adjustment to past changes. . . . [There] arise as a result of the different circumstances certain differences in the calculations of invest-

ments. In a certain sense, one could summarize all these dynamic elements of pricing in the term "profits." (Myrdal, 1927, pp. 117–18)

Svennilson's economic planning

A problem with Myrdal's dissertation (and with Knight's) is the unsystematic presentation. Sometimes the same problem reappears in many places in the book. It is often not clear whether Myrdal is talking about market solutions or merely about the adjustment of the individual firm to the market. There is a plethora of interesting observations, but it is not always easy to see their relation to the main argument.

In a way, Svennilson's dissertation from 1938 may be looked upon as a reaction to this older form of presentation. In essence, Svennilson built on and further developed Myrdal's analysis of intertemporal planning under risk for the individual firm. But Svennilson's presentation is much more logical and systematically worked through.

When Svennilson wrote his *Economic Planning,* period analysis had been introduced, among others by Lindahl (1930).[10] One of the aims of his dissertation was to investigate the microeconomic foundations of the theory of time demanding economic processes of the Stockholm School and to give this investigation a quantitative specification.

Svennilson (1938, p. 39) discussed the possibility of analyzing expectations in terms of probabilities. He first asked himself whether this is necessary:

> The valuation of uncertain returns may be assumed to be determined by different circumstances, that occur, when the individual decides to act in a certain way. These circumstances must namely be assumed to determine the expectations of the individual. By this the probability problem would be completely eliminated. In order to reach a unified theory of economic planning it seems suitable, however, as a link between the valuation of final possible returns and the actual circumstances of the scheme of interpretation, to insert one of the latter conditioned judgements about *the degree of certainty.*

Svennilson was of the opinion that the difference between the short and the long run is partly that constraints are stricter in the short run, partly that uncertainty is greater as to events in the more distant future. He spoke about systems of restrictions in different time perspectives.

Svennilson discussed the preference system as a starting point for microeconomic analysis. Cassel (1932) dissociated himself from utility theory as being unnecessary while Myrdal (1930) stressed that it gave rise to an ideological and therefore unscientific bias. Wicksell and Lindahl in his dissertation on just taxation (Lindahl, 1919), on the other hand, were using marginal utility in their analysis. Svennilson, however, thought that it is not necessary to assume a conscious calculation of the effects of action. In the analysis one could instead start from the assumption that agents act *as if* they maximized a goal function.

In an interesting footnote, Svennilson (1938, pp. 17–18) commented on Myrdal's discussion of whether the actions of entrepreneurs could be described in that way. In his dissertation *Price Formation and Change* Myrdal thought that behavior could be described as "goal rational," but in *Monetary Equilibrium* (the German version) he abandoned this type of reasoning. Svennilson commented on this in the following way: "Such restless depreciation of the theory of value is, as I can understand, only possible, if one in the same way as within static price theory abstracts from the time and risk dimension of expectations."

Svennilson discussed the characteristics of preferences under risk, stating that expectations of returns must be determined both as to the time when they occur and as to the probability of the event. The value should thus be a function of three arguments: the sum, the point of time, and the probability.

Svennilson (1938, p. 57) referred to the Hicks-Allen theory of ordinal utilities, but he did not say anything about the possibility of quantifying utilities (cf. his discussion on p. 41 on the possibility of quantifying probabilities if one assumes that something is equally, less, or more probable, and the sum is continuously varied). He also discussed the utility of a risky alternative in comparison to the riskless alternative. If the value of the riskless one is equal to the mathematical expectation of the outcome, there is risk neutrality (Svennilson did not use this terminology but spoke about neutral risk valuation) and the valuation coefficient v is equal to unity (cf. also Myrdal).

When Svennilson formally analyzed utility, he started by adding marginal sums of money with different probabilities [for example see his formula (5) on p. 64 or the more general formula (11) on p. 66}. As an example, consider the utility of the "expectational complex": (a) to obtain with certainty at least ten dollars, (b) to obtain a further ninety dollars subject to the probability of 2/3, and (c) to obtain on top of that an additional sum of twenty dollars at a probability of 1/3. This could be written in the following way:

$$1 \cdot 10 \cdot v(10,1) + 2/3 \cdot 90 \cdot v(90,2/3) + 1/3 \cdot 20 \cdot v(20,1/3)$$

where v denotes the valuation coefficient as a function of the amount of the added sum and the probability of the addition. The probabilities have thus been cumulated whereas the monetary sums are represented by the marginal additions.

We can rewrite the expression as:

$$1/3 \cdot 10 \cdot v(10,1) + 1/3 \cdot [10 \cdot v(10,1) + 90 \cdot v(90,2/3)]$$
$$+ 1/3 \cdot [10 \cdot v(10,1) + 90 \cdot v(90,2/3) + 20 \cdot v(20,1/3)]$$

This is equal to the mathematical expectation of utility[11] if there is risk neutrality. Since the risk valuation coefficients are functions of probabilities, one would think that Svennilson's formula contains von Neumann-Morgenstern's mathematical expectation of utility as a special case. At the same time, however, the first argument contains only monetary *additions,* not the *original* sum of money. To calculate the mathematical expectation of utility, we have to take utility as a function of the *final* sum (original + addition) of money at different states of the world (and then multiply the utilities with the respective probabilities, and sum). This means that it is not possible to derive the von Neumann-Morgenstern maximization of utility as a special case of Svennilson's formulas. To do so, it would be necessary that in addition the initial sum of money was included as an argument of v.[12] Svennilson (1938, p. 70) consequently wrote that this is a

> simple special case of the general case, where the risk free value is determined as a function of the whole form of the expectational complex. The risk free value can then be expressed as a functional.

An important problem for Svennilson was whether long-run planning is of relevance for short-run behavior. Why must short-time action be placed in an intertemporal context? He gave some reasons that this is the case. First, the planner must be interested in future developments. Second, the actions of today must influence future action possibilities and/or future outcomes.[13]

In Chapter 7, Svennilson (1938) considered intertemporal planning under risk. In principle, the outcome of planning is described by the maximization of an object function subject to constraints. However, the description is relatively abstract and without concrete examples. An important question is whether Svennilson used a technique of planning similar to dynamic planning. He wrote (Svennilson, 1938, pp. 138–9):

> The alternatives of action are attached to different development alternatives. This attachment may be expressed by different *reaction functions,* that describe the planned values of the parameters of action as unique functions of the events, that determine the expectations of the

> future development. . . . [T]he planned reaction is not only determined by realized expectations but also by the thereby combined actions.

Section II:2 (Svennilson, 1938, pp. 141–2) contains a discussion in principle of intertemporal planning under risk. On the other hand, Bellman's principle of optimality is not involved, with the result that no explicit account is taken of dynamic programming.[14]

This is an important section since it throws light on the *ex ante* and *ex post* view of the Stockholm School. It is not always meaningful to discriminate between expected (= *ex ante*) and realized (= *ex post*) values since under risk many outcomes with various probabilities are conceivable. If an outcome was expected, even if the *ex ante* probability of its occurrence was less than unity, could one then speak about a discrepancy between what was expected and the final outcome?[15]

Svennilson's achievement was to systematically analyze how the outcome should form the starting point, not for plan revisions but for reactions conditioned on the observed development. But these conditional reactions are already planned in advance as a result of the optimal intertemporal plan. On the other hand, Svennilson did not analyze the interactions between the plan revisions of the different agents, nor did he discuss the rationing effects emanating from price and wage stickiness.

Although Svennilson discussed the significance of constraints and also treated imperfect competition, he did not analyze the behavior of the firm under disequilibrium conditions. Much of what Svennilson wrote about liquidity planning is, as far as I can see, based on assumptions of the existence of risk and the nonexistence of perfect competition. For example, the price obtained may depend on the length of the time that one tries to sell the good.[16]

To sum up, Svennilson's dissertation consists to a considerable extent of a series of conceptual exercises. However, his discussion is much more advanced than that of his predecessors. He also influenced to a considerable extent Bent Hansen's *The Economic Theory of Fiscal Policy*.[17] The dissertation is also partly an answer to a number of questions produced by the Stockholm School. How are plans formulated? What happens under uncertainty? Is it possible to use the *ex ante* and *ex post* concepts when expectations are not subjectively certain? Svennilson seems to have been well versed in (at the time) modern mathematical statistics. At the same time, the conclusions are rather vague. In spite of the fact that the analysis of the capitalist firm in the last three chapters of the dissertation contains many interesting observations, a common consistent idea is lacking.

3   **The microeconomics of intertemporal planning under uncertainty**

The environment

An important motive for the microanalyses of Myrdal and Svennilson was to break with classical microeconomics based on stationary equilibrium and complete information. They had, of course, many predecessors. In this paper, I have pointed specifically to Schumpeter and Knight. Schumpeter is cited only by Svennilson (1938, pp. 26, 76), although Knight is the more important for both of them.

Schumpeter described the entrepreneur as the agent who actively breaks the stationary equilibrium of the circular flow. However, he did not provide any detailed analysis of the environment in which the entrepreneur operated. Knight was to give much attention to this question, as well as to the reactions of the entrepreneur to uncertainty. His account provides a genuine feeling of the daily worries of management.

Myrdal essentially started from the environment depicted by Knight. Possible additions were the stress on expectations about the future and the discussion of disequilibrium, "gaps in pricing." In Svennilson's case it was not so much the question of describing the environment in a different way, but rather the need to make the description more systematic, mainly through the introduction of period analysis in the microeconomics of individual firm behavior.

Is there equilibrium? Myrdal spoke about the "time momentum of pricing." By this he evidently meant that, owing to price stickiness, there is no continuous temporary equilibrium. The price system will also depart from what would be "natural" (by this Myrdal possibly meant that average cost is equal to price). Not even Svennilson has a clear discussion on this point. However, he did speak about the different restrictions that the firm has to consider. It could naturally be a question of the production capacity of the firm. But it could also (without explicitly being mentioned) have to do with different sorts of rationing restrictions.

It is interesting to observe that there is no explanation of the prevalence of risk/uncertainty in Myrdal's or Svennilson's accounts. Uncertainty is exogenously given. But what mechanism generates uncertainty? For Schumpeter, uncertainty was produced by the innovation process, which was in its turn unexplained. In a corresponding way, Knight looked upon uncertainty as a "natural" ingredient of business life.

Perception of the environment

How do agents perceive their environment? Is it possible to describe their knowledge using probabilities? Let me start with a quotation from Knight (1921, pp. 201–2):

> We *perceive* the world before we react to it, and we react not to what we perceive, but always to what we *infer*. The universal form of conscious behavior is thus action designed to change a future situation inferred from a present one. . . . We do not perceive the present as it is and in its totality, nor do we infer the future from the present with any degree of dependability, nor yet do we accurately know the consequences of our own actions. In addition, there is a fourth source of error to be taken into account, for we do not execute actions in the precise form in which they are imaged and willed.

Knight consequently thought that probability calculus was not a good instrument for describing the expectations of the entrepreneurs. Since it is impossible to provide a probability measure for a considerable part of the uncertainty that is connected to business life, one should talk about uncertainty instead of risk. One reason may be that it is not even possible to perceive that some things may actually happen, far less attach a probability to them. Another difficulty with the probability calculus is that "the unique" makes it an inadequate instrument.

Myrdal stressed that even if perception of probability was often vague, in most cases it did not have to be exact. Both Myrdal and Svennilson were more optimistic than Knight concerning the possibility of analyzing the problem of choice in situations where it was impossible to attach probabilities to future events. Myrdal further made the important distinction between objective (the empirically "true" conditional probabilities, given the information of the entrepreneur) and subjective (perceived) probabilities (see Myrdal, 1927, p. 98). Perception of probability is rational if objective and subjective probabilities coincide. This is a clear parallel to rational expectations. It should be stressed, however, that in the latter case, it is also a matter of evaluating the reaction functions of other agents (individually or as aggregates). This is something that Myrdal did not discuss.

Myrdal spoke about frequency probabilities, but also stated that these will be influenced by the level of knowledge prevailing in the firm. One interpretation of this is that it is a question of *conditional* frequency probabilities. Svennilson (1938, p. 41) evidently had conditional probabilities in mind when he wrote:

> The practical probability judgement must instead imply, abstracting from certain properties of the individual events, that this will be

assigned to a set of equal events, on which a certain theoretical probability scheme is said to approximately be applicable. Certain data are available at the time of decision-making. The probability judgement indicates the frequency of an event with the properties in question in the hypothetical set, that would arise, if the same data were at hand at the time of judgement in a series of cases.

Preference theory

The point of starting from preference theory is that this places a certain (but rather limited) restraint on the behavior of the studied agent in different environments. Through analyzing (probabilistic) expectations one could also connect the objective reality known by the "observing economist," on one hand, and that perceived and acted upon by the agent, on the other hand. With given preferences, a changed behavior could be due either to a changed environment or to changed knowledge about the environment. A change in behavior from one period to the next could be determined as a part of the intertemporal plan but could also be caused by a change of the (perceived) environment. If in particular expectations are probabilistic, a certain event will have a double effect: on one hand, one of the possible cases has been realized, which implies that the probabilities of future events that are conditional on the presently observed event have changed; on the other (if the probability distribution is not subjectively certain) the agent will revise its probability judgment, for example, via Bayes's law.

How did the different authors look upon prefence theory? Knight assumed the firm to behave as if it maximized the mathematical expectation of profits, with due regard to uncertainty. At the same time Knight stated that behavior cannot be described as a conscious maximization. On page 211 (Knight, 1921) he states that the mental processes, which our behavior is based on, are wrapped in mystery. Contrary to formal deduction, our decisions are based on judgment, common sense, or intuition. We conclude on the basis of our complete past experience.

Myrdal was more explicit. He thought that it was possible to depict the behavior of the firm as based on maximization of the (adjusted) capital value. In the case of risk neutrality, the capital value should not be adjusted. If there was risk aversion, the monetary value of the different outcomes should be multiplied by an adjustment coefficient greater than one.[18]

Myrdal was in principle against the preference theory of his time, that is, marginal utility theory. While Myrdal's teacher Gustav Cassel's foremost argument against marginal utility theory was that it was unnecessary (it is possible to start directly from the behavior equations), Myrdal thought that it would introduce an ideological bias into the analysis (see Myrdal, 1930).

Svennilson built on Myrdal's analysis but was, in contrast, positive toward preference theory. This, as well as the fact that Svennilson worked with formal probability arguments, may have to do with the technical-systematic approach that he chose. Formal analysis thus had methodological consequences. But Svennilson's approach may also have been influenced by the Hicks-Allen reformulation of preference theory in the beginning of the 1930s. However, he was not aware of the requirements of measurability of utility under risk.

Intertemporal analysis

In principle, both Knight and Myrdal have an intertemporal analysis of the planning of the firm. Svennilson extended the analysis to explicitly consider several periods. For Svennilson it was important to make clear *why* the analysis had to be intertemporal. The paradoxical question was to what extent the future would influence the present. Intertemporal analysis is not very interesting if there is no essential difference between the future and the present. This in turn implies that there is a connection between the problem of change and intertemporal analysis. It would, however, be only the first period that would be of direct interest since future action would depend on the chain of events that would develop in the future. Nevertheless, Svennilson showed how in principle it would be possible to extend his analysis to generalize period analysis.

The great vision

According to Schumpeter, innovations are motivated by potential profits at the original relative prices. When, as a result of the innovation process and the attached investments, the production system has been changed, the price system will no longer correspond to the new potential equilibrium. Estimates of costs and revenues become more difficult to make, uncertainty grows, interest rates increase, and we enter a depression. But the role of the depression is to restore equilibrium. The structual problems that emerged as a consequence of the original growth shock have to be eliminated, and this will take place during the depression, which thus has an important role to play as a phase of consolidation. When the consolidation period is over, profits and losses are eliminated, goods prices have decreased, real incomes have increased, and the fruits of the innovations have been redistributed from the innovators to the whole population. The new equilibrium also implies that there is less uncertainty and the apropriate initial conditions for the next expansion period are at hand.

Schumpeter's account can, however, be characterized as a vision rather than as a systematic analysis of the business cycle built on microeconomics. The accounts of Knight, Myrdal, and Svennilson implied great advances when it comes to the analysis of the firm. Why then was the microeconomics of the Stockholm School not to form a good basis for its macroeconomic sequence analyses?

4   From micro to macro[19]

When Erik Lindahl described how the process analysis ought to be constructed, he talked about two building blocks: (a) the general theory of planning, and (b) the general theory of development.[20] In Patinkin's (1956) terminology we could talk about individual experiments and market experiments.

The general theory of planning

Lindahl stressed that planning presupposes a prognosis about the future (cf. Knight). Expectations are mostly "many-valued." But how could it then happen that agents are subjected to surprises? There is no discussion of this in Lindahl's account (compare also Lindahl, 1939, p. 44). Neither acting nor planning takes place in continuous time. This is due to the imperfection of the human brain. Time should be divided into periods.[21] Some changes of behavior are partly planned as a consequence of earlier plans while others are a consequence of new plans [see Lindahl's (1939) discussion on pp. 47–8]. The first part of Lindahl's research program for process analysis, "the general theory of planning," was partly worked out in Svennilson's dissertation. What about the second part, "the general theory of development"?

The general theory of development

Lindahl (1939, pp. 37–8) discussed how he thought that the theory of development (macroeconomics) should be built on the foundation of the theory of planning:

> If we know (1) the *plans* of the economic subjects concerned at the initial point of time, if we further know (2) how these individuals are

likely to *change their plans* in the future under different assumptions, and if we have (3) enough knowledge of *external conditions* to be able to make definite statements with regard to future changes in plans, and the results of the actions undertaken then it should be possible to provide a theoretical construction of the developments that will be the outcome of the initial position.

Starting from the plans and external conditions valid at the initial point of time, we have first to deduce the development that will be the result of these data for a certain period forward during which no relevant changes in the plans are assumed to occur. Next we have to investigate how far the development during the first period – involving as it must various surprises for the economic subjects – will force them to revise their plans of action for the future, the principles for such a revision being assumed to be included in the data of the problem.

According to Lindahl, the problem of pricing should be analyzed so that prices are assumed to be set at the beginning of a time period and there is not necessarily equilibrium between supply and demand during the period. The price will be changed in the beginning of the next period in accordance with the developments that take place during the preceding period (how expectations are affected and how the situation of the sellers has developed, for example, with respect to the amount of stocks).

Lindahl had in fact made an outline of how general dynamic analysis should be developed. But the Stockholm School did not succeed at the microlevel to analyze the disequilibrium caused by a lack of coordination between the plans of agents. There was no analysis of how this would affect pricing. The inflation theories of Lindahl (1930) and Myrdal (1931) did not build on an explicit analysis of the effects of disequilibrium. In this perspective, it may be said that the contribution of the Stockholm School was not dynamic macroeconomics but rather the study of dynamic planning problems under uncertainty.

Lindahl (1939) started his discussion of the construction of sequence analysis by discussing economic theories of different generality. He thought that economic theory does not have a value of its own but should form the basis for analyzing concrete problems. This could either be an analysis of past events or a basis for predictions. The analysis does not need to be specialized on concrete problems, however:

> If we use comparatively abstract terms which will cover many cases, the theory expounded becomes more generally important than if it is based on more concrete terms having reference to particular cases. (Lindahl, 1939, pp. 25–6)

In its way, this is a defense for the often quite abstract arguments in Svennilson's dissertation. Note also that it is an argument against Ohlin and his casuistics.[22]

There is a peculiar contrast within the Stockholm School. On one hand, attention was concentrated on the particular, the study of concrete processes (see Ohlin, 1937). On the other hand, the lack of systematic analysis implied that there was not a good theoretical basis for further applications. The analysis of the Stockholm School formed a sort of art that was difficult to replicate. The Keynesian analysis was much easier both to apply and to generalize for others. This may be due to the fact that Keynes actually worked with behavioral equations of a simple sort and that he had studied comparative statics (although not formally).[23]

Would it then have been possible on the basis of Svennilson's dissertation to further develop the period analysis of the Stockholm School? I think so. But it would have been much easier if the analysis in Svennilson's dissertation had been more concrete. Note also that pure technical-mathematical and statistical problems put a limit on what it was possible to achieve at that time.

The reason the microeconomics of the Stockholm School did not form a suitable foundation for its macroeconomics was possibly that it did not encompass any *behavioral equations*. Those who developed the macroeconomic models of the Stockholm School, and who analyzed virtual business cycles, had accordingly no theoretical foundation (built on preference theory) on which to base their analysis.

The task of constructing relevant microeconomic foundations for the general theory of development was extremely difficult. It was not only a question of formulating an intertemporal theory of individual firm and household planning under uncertainty. In addition, the problem of disequilibrium interaction between individual agents had to be faced.

One example of problems that have to be recognized is that behavior equations derived in ordinary microeconomics are defined only for equilibrium situations (see Haavelmo, 1958). This means that disequilibrium behavior has to be explicitly modeled. This was done by Barro and Grossman (1971, 1976), using ordinary neoclassical procedures, when they succeeded in deriving firm and household behavior under disequilibrium (for example, under Keynesian underemployment). The trick was to further constrain the choice sets of the agents by introducing rationing restrictions that were generated by the lack of equilibrium. Their analysis was, however, set in a Keynesian context and consequently much less involved than that of the Stockholm School.

Another example of problems that have to be tackled in such an analysis is that the market form will generally change as a consequence of disequilibrium. Arrow (1959) sketched the outcome of disequilibrium in a market that would in equilibrium be perfectly competitive as degenerating into a changing set of bilateral monopolies.[24] This means that, at least for disequilibrium situations, game theory might be the adequate analytical tool (see Faxén's contribution in this volume). There would then be an additional source of uncertainty, game uncertainty, to take into consideration. The problem would even be further complicated by the intertemporal link between market forms in different time periods.

Considering the difficulties of implementing Lindahl's program, it is no paradox that there arose a wide gap between the microeconomics of the Stockholm School built on general arguments and its applied macroeconomics.[25]

5   The microeconomics of the Stockholm School

In his presentation of the Stockholm School in *Economic Journal,* Bertil Ohlin (1937) said that Swedish development of employment theory was based on two influences: Knut Wicksell's (1898) cumulative process and Gunnar Myrdal's (1927) analysis of anticipations. The interest in studying processes over time came from Wicksell. This was to be further developed by Erik Lindahl (1930, 1939) into time period analysis.

The period analysis presupposed an analysis of the plans and expectations of the individual agents. One important reason for the process to continue endogenously was that plans and expectations formulated by the individual agents at the beginning of the period would not be fulfilled. This would in its turn lead to revisions of plans and expectations and therefore to new behavior in the coming period. The macroeconomics of the Stockholm School was founded on microeconomic considerations, even if these were not always explicit.

The goal of Myrdal's dissertation was to reach a more realistic description of the functioning of the market mechanism than that of his teacher Gustav Cassel (based on general equilibrium theory). Myrdal was inter alia influenced by Frank Knight's analysis of the activities of the entrepreneur in an environment that, contrary to the Cassel case, could be described by risk and uncertainty. In his analysis, Myrdal left Cassel's abstract general but idealized analysis in favor of an investigation of the problem of change.

From one point of view, the combination of Cassel and Knight implied the same type of analysis as that of Schumpeter. Schumpeter started from general equilibrium (Cassel) but then investigated how general equilibrium will be broken by innovations. The actions of the entrepreneurs (Knight) was of central importance. As a matter of fact, Knight's analysis was inspired by that of Schumpeter. Consequently, Myrdal was at least indirectly influenced by Schumpeter.

Myrdal's analysis was also microeconomic in the sense that he concentrated his attention on the plans and expectations of the individual agents. These were defined for several periods. The agents were also assumed to be aware of their imperfect knowledge of the future, and this would (via risk aversion) affect their behavior.

The Wicksell and Myrdal roots of the Stockholm School converged in Myrdal's (1931) article in *Ekonomisk Tidskrift*. This article was basically a further development of Lindahl's (1930) analysis of Wicksell's cumulative process in terms of period analysis. Myrdal added to Lindahl's analysis by introducing more explicitly the plans and expectations of the individual agents. However, the notions of *ex ante* and *ex post* were not introduced until the German translation of Myrdal's article.

Even if the duality of expectations and outcomes was of central importance for the development of employment theory by the Swedish economists at the beginning of the 1930s, this did not imply that their macroeconomics was founded on microeconomics. It is true that Gunnar Myrdal discussed the intertemporal planning of the firm under uncertainty. He even discussed a disequilibrium case ("gaps in pricing"). But his discussion was verbal and vague. Even if his book was inspiring with its many new ideas, it was difficult to build macroeconomics on that basis.

It was this theoretical imperfection that Ingvar Svennilson (1938) tried to overcome by his statistical-mathematical analysis of the planning of the firm. He did not construct microeconomic foundations for the employment theory of the Stockholm School. His ambitions were instead to study what consequences the time period analysis of the Stockholm School would have for the theory of the firm: What was going on behind the time processes presented by the Swedish economists? In the preface of his book Svennilson also added that ". . . the theory of total developments presupposes a certain awareness of the minute structure of the system."

By the time Svennilson wrote his dissertation, the analysis of consumer behavior based on ordinal utility theory of Hicks and Allen had appeared. Svennilson described the planning of the firm in terms of the maximization of an intertemporal utility function subject to constraints. Even if Svennilson's discussion was much more systematic and clear than that of Myrdal, he did not go all the way through; his analysis did not result in any behavioral equations. His main interest was instead to discuss how to model the planning problem of the firm.

Svennilson modeled expectations as explicitly probabilistic. This meant that in addition to all of the analytical advantages, there was a conceptual disadvantage: How was it possible to speak about the tension between expectations and outcomes as a transmitter of the endogenous movement of the economic system when expectations were multivalued and plans were of an alternative nature? The answer was partially that the simple interpretation of *ex ante* and *ex post* had to be abandoned. But the paradox was that it was in this simple conceptual form that the Stockholm School had at least a partial international breakthrough.

More fundamental was the fact that Svennilson's microeconomic analysis of intertemporal planning under risk did not result in an investigation of what would happen if plans were not fulfilled as a result of rationing constraints or, alternatively, of how the agents took rationing constraints into consideration. This meant that the microeconomics of the Stockholm School did not form a suitable basis for their macroeconomic analyis of time demanding adjustment processes under disequilibrium.

Svennilson's work could, however, have formed a starting point for further developments of sequence analysis. His book fitted well into the research program of the Stockholm School as it was formulated by Lindahl (1939). In the introductory chapter of *Money and Capital,* Lindahl provided an outline of how general dynamic theory should be constructed. He said that it should be composed of two parts, the general theory of planning (microeconomics) and the general theory of development (macroeconomics). The macroeconomic magnitudes could, according to Lindahl, usually be found by summing the microeconomic terms.

Myrdal's dissertation from 1927 and Svennilson's from 1938 approximately constitute the beginning and the end of the life span of the Stockholm School. This means, for example, that Myrdal's analysis from the 1920s was to influence the development of Swedish employment theory whereas Svennilson's contribution was "too late." There were several reasons for this. One was that the research achievements within the framework of the Stockholm School were, for completely different reasons, starting to dwindle (see Siven, 1985). Another was that Svennilson's presentation, in spite of its analytical starting points, did not result in any behavioral equations.

Notes

1 I am very grateful for comments from William Baumol, Leif Björk, Sören Blomquist, Karl-Olof Faxén, and Rolf Henriksson.
2 This terminology was first used by Myrdal (1933).
3 Lundberg abstained from introducing the formation of expectations in his macroanalysis because there was no satisfactory theory of changes of expectations, that is, how the tension between expectations *ex ante* and outcomes

ex post would generate new expectations *ex ante* for the coming periods (see Lundberg, 1937, p. 175). The *ex ante–ex post* analysis was consequently not a common starting point for the macroanalyses of the Stockholm School.

4 Compare, for example, Landgren (1960), Steiger (1971), and Hansson (1982).

5 The microeconomics of the Stockholm School has not been totally neglected, however. The subject is discussed in two dissertations, Björk's from 1942 and Peterson's from 1987.

6 According to Schumpeter (1954, p. 894), J. B. Clark had earlier connected the entrepreneurial income with commercial and organizational advances. Schumpeter (1934) also referred to Clark's *Essentials of Economic Theory* from 1907 as being close to his own theory. Compare also Hawley's book *Enterprise and the Productive Process* from 1907, cited by Knight (1921, p. 41). Hawley argues that profits are due to the risk that the entrepreneur carries (that is a more trivial explanation than Schumpeter's).

7 Here Keynes's discussion of risk and uncertainty should be mentioned. Keynes (1921) is included in the literature references of both Myrdal (1927) and Svennilson (1938). Keynes's argument was that uncertainty (that is, that probabilities cannot be attached to potential events) may arise as a consequence of two reasons. The first is that even if it would in principle be possible to base statements about the probabilities of various events on indirect information (conditional probabilities), limits to human intellectual capacity will in practice make this impossible. The other reason is that the probabilities do not even exist. There is no possible method by which they may be calculated. The latter type of uncertainty may be exemplified by the impossibility of assigning probabilities to future events such as a future war in Europe, the rate of interest in twenty years, or the obsolescence of a new invention (compare Keynes, 1936–7, p. 214).

8 Myrdal referred also to Keynes (1921). Keynes talked about ". . . the degree of belief which is *rational* to entertain in given conditions. . . ." Keynes stressed, however, that what is rational should be interpreted from a logical point of view. According to Keynes, an objective risk assessment does not need to coincide with that which is given by frequency probabilities. This is, on the other hand, Myrdal's position. It should be noted that Myrdal is vague, however. It is thus not certain that his statement is inconsistent with Keynes's logical probabilities. The frequency *may* be interpreted as the probability that would be generated by the true model.

9 The concept of "normal" price is evidently a parallel to Wicksell's concept normal rate of interest (meaning the rate of interest that would be the general equilibrium solution of a stationary economy without money). Analogously, "gaps in pricing" has a parallel in the gap between the natural or real rate of interest and the loan rate of interest in Wicksell's analysis of inflation.

10 The period analysis may be derived from Cournot. The Stockholm School was, on the other hand, first to use the period analysis for macroeconomic purposes (see Faxén, 1957, p. 32).

11 Where it is a matter of maximizing the mathematical expectation of utility.

12 Compare, however, Arvidsson's (1964) discussion on this point.
13 It is interesting to compare Svennilson's account with that of Carlson (1939).
    Carlson's book contains a mathematical treatment of production theory.
    Through its operational form, it gives, in contrast to Svennilson's account, a
    strikingly modern impression. However, Carlson did not analyze the ques-
    tions that were central to the Stockholm School.
14 I have earlier (see Siven, 1985) stated that in Svennilson's dissertation one
    can find attempts at an analysis that started from the maximization of the
    mathematical expectation of utility and dynamic programming, respectively.
    The former is not correct. One should rather say that he developed Myrdal's
    analysis with valuation coefficients. The latter is not correct either. The strat-
    egy concept is, however, hinted at in Svennilson's dissertation in the sense
    that he discusses contingent plans. For further discussion, see Faxén (1957,
    p. 76).
15 Palander (1941, pp. 93–4) has a similar discussion. One could, however, pos-
    sibly talk about surprises in the sense that the probability distribution that
    describes the expectations of the agent will be changed as a result of new
    information. This is discussed by Faxén in his contribution to this volume.
      There is, however, an argument for working with the mathematical expec-
    tation of the outcome, namely, that the stochastic planning for many alter-
    native developments is so demanding in resource terms. Svennilson made
    this an argument for "rolling" planning. Compare also Lindahl's (1939)
    argument for working with period analysis, namely, that people will not have
    sufficient intellectual capacity to manage planning over continuous time.
16 Myrdal (1927) also has a similar discussion of how indivisibilities may cause
    risk aversion. If, for example, wealth will fall short of a certain amount,
    cumulative effects of various sorts will arise. One has to sell assets at a sub-
    normal price (Myrdal has a discussion here that indicates that the price is a
    function of the length of time at disposal for selling), borrow at an exorbitant
    rate of interest, et cetera. Moreover, the future possibilities of borrowing will
    depend on one's wealth as well as whether or not one has been forced into
    bankruptcy.
17 Much of Hansen's (1951) terminology (for example, the twin concepts
    expectation variable–parameter of action) are taken from Svennilson (1938).
    The term parameter of action had, however, been used earlier by Ragnar
    Frisch (1933) (see Faxén, 1957, note 5 on p. 41). In a corresponding way
    Hansen's (1955, Chapter XIII) means–ends analysis has to a great extent
    been influenced by Lindahl (1930, 1939).
18 It is not clear whether Myrdal, like Svennilson, started from the valuation
    coefficient being a function of other variables (for example, as in Svennil-
    son's case the amount of the additional sum or its probability) or whether he
    assumed it to be constant. A constant risk valuation coefficient might, how-
    ever, lead to logical difficulties.
19 In its historical context, the heading is misleading since it was actually not
    until Keynes's *General Theory* that one started to talk about micro and
    macro. The question is also a bit unhistorical since it was not until the 1970s

that it became a conscious ambition to base macro models on a microeconomic analysis of the behavior of the individual agents.

20 This distinction is also clearly accounted for in Myrdal (1927, p. 21).

21 Observe Svennilson's (1938) argument for suboptimal simple plans. This is also a possible reason that individuals *may* be subject to surprises. Another is that, in spite of many-valued expectations, the actual outcome is not included in the set of conceivable outcomes at the time of planning. (Note that this is generally not the same as to say that a surprise presupposes that the probability of an event is zero. The counterexample is continuous probability distributions.)

22 Compare Ohlin's (1937) characteristics of the Stockholm School. Ohlin thought that casuistics (that is, analyzing specific cases) was necessary in order for the discussion to achieve an adequate precision.

23 Already one year after the *General Theory,* Keynes's analysis was translated into a mathematical and diagrammatical analysis in the form of the IS-LM model (see Hicks, 1937). The achievements of Modigliani (1944) and Patinkin (1956) were also important for clarifying the Keynesian system and thus to give it a form that was an easy starting point for further analytical developments.

24 The cyclical change of the market form as a consequence of nonbalanced growth of a market economy with innovations as the main impulse mechanism is a central ingredient of Schumpeter's theory.

25 Ohlin published a review of Lindahl (1939) in *Ekonomisk Tidskrift* in 1941. This started a debate between Lindahl and Ohlin on the principles on which macroeconomics should be based [cf. Lindahl (1941, 1942) and Ohlin (1941a, 1941b]. One of the main questions of their debate was whether one should strive to construct a theory on general principles or whether casuistics was the best approach. See also Jan Petersson's contribution in this volume.

References

Arrow, Kenneth J. (1959), "Toward a Theory of Price Adjustment," in M. Abramovitz, ed., *The Allocation of Economic Resources.* Stanford: Stanford University Press.

Arvidsson, Guy (1964), "Om säkerhetsekvivalenter" (On certainty equivalents), *Ekonomisk Tidskrift,* 66, 39–44.

Barro, Robert J., and Herschel I. Grossman (1971), "A General Disequilibrium Model of Income and Employment," *American Economic Review,* 61, 82–93.

(1976), *Money, Employment and Inflation,* Cambridge, England: Cambridge University Press.

Björk, Leif (1942), *Subjektivismen hos "Stockholmsskolan"* (The subjectivism of the Stockholm School). Uppsala: Licentiatavhandling.

Carlson, Sune (1939). *A Study on the Pure Theory of Production.* New York: Kelley & Millman, Inc., 1956 (first edition 1939).

Cassel, Gustaf (1932), *The Theory of Social Economy.* New York: Harcourt, Brace.

Clark, John (1907), *Essentials of Economic Theory.* New York: The Macmillan Co.

Faxén, Karl-Olof (1957), *Monetary and Fiscal Policy under Uncertainty.* Uppsala: Almqvist & Wiksell.

Frisch, Ragnar (1933), "Propagation Problems and Impulse Problems in Dynamic Economics," *Economic Essays in Honour of Gustav Cassel.* London: George Allen and Unwin, Ltd. Reprinted in *AEA: Readings in Business Cycles,* London: George Allen & Unwin, 1966.

Haavelmo, Trygve (1958), "Hva kan statiske likevektsmodeller fortelle oss?" in *Festskrift till Fredrik Zeuthen,* Supplement to Vol. 96 of *Nationalökonomisk Tidskrift,* Copenhagen. Translated as "What Can Static Equilibrium Models Tell Us?" *Economic Inquiry,* 12, 27–34, 1974.

Hansen, Bent (1951), *A Study in the Theory of Inflation.* London: George Allen & Unwin Ltd.

Finanspolitikens ekonomiska teori (The economic theory of fiscal policy), SOU, 1955:25.

Hansson, Björn (1982), *The Stockholm School and the Development of the Dynamic Method.* London: Croom Helm.

Hicks, John R. (1937), "Mr Keynes and the 'Classics': A Suggested Interpretation," *Econometrica,* 5, 147–59. Reprinted in Hicks, *Critical Essays in Monetary Theory,* Oxford: Oxford University Press, 1967.

Keynes, John M. (1921), *A Treatise on Probability.* London: Macmillan
(1936–7), "The General Theory of Employment," *Quarterly Journal of Economics,* 51, 209–23

Knight, Frank H. (1921), *Risk, Uncertainty, and Profit.* Boston: Houghton Mifflin Company.

Landgren, Karl-Gustav (1960), *Den "nya ekonomien" i Sverige* (The "new economics" in Sweden). Uppsala: Almqvist & Wiksell.

Lindahl, Erik (1919), *Die Gerichtigkeit der Besteuerung. Eine Analyse der Steuerprinzipien auf Grundlage der Grenznutzentheorie.* Lund: Gleerup.
(1930), *Penningpolitikens medel* (The means of monetary policy). Malmö: Förlagsaktiebolaget.
(1939), *Studies in the Theory of Money and Capital,* London: George Allen & Unwin Ltd.
(1941), "Professor Ohlin om dynamisk teori. Ett genmäle" (Professor Ohlin on dynamic theory. A reply), *Ekonomisk Tidskrift,* 43, 236–47.
(1942), "Metodfrågor inom den dynamiska teorien. Ett diskussionsinlägg" (Methodological questions in dynamic theory. A discussion), *Ekonomisk Tidskrift* 44, 41–51.

Lundberg, Erik (1937), *Studies in the Theory of Economic Expansion.* Stockholm: P. S. King & Son, Ltd.

Modigliani, Franco (1944), "Liquidity Preference and the Theory of Interest and Money," *Econometrica,* 12, 45–88. Reprinted in AEA, *Readings in Monetary Theory,* London: George Allen & Unwin, 1952.

Myrdal, Gunnar (1927), *Prisbildningsproblemet och föränderligheten* (Price formation and change). Uppsala: Almqvist & Wiksell.

(1930), *Vetenskap och politik i nationalekonomien*. Stockholm: P. A. Norstedt & Söners Förlag. Translated as *The Political Element in the Development of Economic Theory,* Cambridge, Mass.: Harvard University Press, 1965.

(1931), "Om penningteoretisk jämvikt. En studie över den "normala räntan" i Wicksells penninglära" (On monetary equilibrium. A study of the "normal rate of interest" in Wicksell's monetary theory), *Ekonomisk Tidskrift,* 33, 191–302.

(1933), "Der Gleichgewichtsbegriff als Instrument der geldtheoretischen Analyse," in Hayek, ed., *Beiträge zur Geldtheorie.* Vienna: Julius Springer.

Ohlin, Bertil (1937), "Some Notes on the Stockholm Theory of Saving and Investment I-II," *Economic Journal,* 47, 53–69 (I), 221–40 (II). Reprinted in AER, *Readings in Business Cycle Theory,* London: George Allen & Unwin Ltd., 1950.

(1941a), "Professor Lindahl om dynamisk teori" (Professor Lindahl on dynamic theory), *Ekonomisk Tidskrift,* 43, 170–81.

(1941b), "Metodfrågor inom den dynamiska teorin" (Methodological questions in dynamic theory), *Ekonomisk Tidskrift,* 43, 327–36.

Palander, Tord (1941), "Om 'Stockholmsskolans' begrepp och metoder," *Ekonomisk Tidskrift,* 43, 88–143. Translated as "On the Concepts and Methods of the 'Stockholm School.' Some Methodological Reflections on Myrdal's *Monetary Equilibrium,*" in *International Economic Papers* No. 3, pp. 5–57, 1953.

Patinkin, Don (1956), *Money, Interest, and Prices.* Evanston, Ill.: Row & Peterson.

Petersson, Jan (1987), *Erik Lindahl och stockholmsskolans dynamiska metod* (Erik Lindahl and the dynamic method of the Stockholm School), Lund Economic Studies, Vol. 39, Lund.

Schumpeter, Joseph A. (1912), *Theorie der wirtschaftlichen Entwicklung.* Leipzig: Duncker & Humblot (2nd edition, 1926).

(1934), *The Theory of Economic Development.* Cambridge, Mass.: Harvard University Press (translation of the second German edition).

(1954), *History of Economic Analysis.* New York: Oxford University Press.

Siven, Claes-Henric (1985), "The End of the Stockholm School," *The Scandinavian Journal of Economics,* 87, 577–93.

Steiger, Otto (1971), *Studien zur Entstehung der Neuen Wirtschaftslehre in Schweden.* Berlin: Duncker & Humblot.

Svennilson, Ingvar (1938), *Ekonomisk planering* (Economic planning). Uppsala.

Wicksell, Knut (1898), *Geldzins und Güterpreise,* Jena: G. Fischer. Translated as *Interest and Prices,* London: Macmillan, 1936.

Wicksell, Knut (1906), *Föreläsningar i nationalekonomi,* Part I. Lund: C.W.K. Gleerup, 1937 (first edition, 1906). Translated as *Lectures on Political Economy,* London: George Routledge and Sons, 1934–5.

Comment

WILLIAM J. BAUMOL

Earlier, perhaps somewhat too much was claimed for the achievements of the Stockholm School. The danger now is a reaction that goes much too far the other way. The issue is not whether *all* of of the Keynesian model had been anticipated and laid out clearly before the appearance of the *General Theory*. Of course, the two sets of writing differed in content and in approach, so that while there was overlap, neither can be deemed a replication of the other. And in any event, it seems to me that argument over the proper assignment of priority a half century earlier is not a terribly significant exercise.

Rather, it seems clear that the Stockholm School did make a contribution to ways of thinking about macroproblems that was important and that was uniquely its own. The way of analyzing intertemporal developments that emerged in Sweden in the 1930s made it necessary for the entire discipline to revise its approach to the pertinent subjects. The formal dynamic literature that flourished in the early postwar period and is reemerging now owed little to Sweden in terms of its formal mathematics. But in terms of understanding why the models behaved as they did and how well they did or did not illuminate reality, all of us owe a heavy debt to the earlier Swedish writers, perhaps Erik Lundberg most notably.

The fact that despite its first-rate economists, neither Stockholm nor the remainder of Sweden today provides "a school" with one direct line of continuity to earlier Swedish writings is no discredit to Sweden. It does not mean that Sweden's contribution was an evanescent affair – a transitory manifestation with no lasting power. On the contrary, the vanishing of the separate identity of the earlier Stockholm School is directly attributable to its success in achieving universal acceptance of its approaches, which are now so automatically absorbed by students everywhere that their Swedish origins are effectively obscured.

This, to me, is the central conclusion that emerges from a reconsideration of the body of learning that is our focus here. Siven's fine paper provides valuable insights into the history of the Stockholm School. To me its only shortcoming is that in its pursuit of details, it perhaps unavoidably distracts attention from the central conclusion that has just been enunciated.

CHAPTER 5

Sequence analysis and optimization

KARL O. FAXÉN

Is it possible to give macrosequence analysis in the Stockholm School tradition a micro-foundation, assuming that households and firms are optimizing economic agents? If not, what can be done?

The Wicksellian cumulative process, Schumpeter's innovation-driven growth, and Knight's theory of uncertainty and profit were three starting points for the Stockholm School. In order to give Wicksell's concept of a "natural rate of interest" a strict formulation under the dynamic assumptions, the Stockholm School tried to model how profit maximization determines the volume of investment under the assumption that, because of innovations, *ex ante* yield includes an uncertain component of pure profit. Furthermore, it was an aim of the Stockholm School to model not only the steady-state volume of investment in a stable growth process but also, and in particular, the adjustment path after macroeconomic disturbance, for instance, an increase in the market rate of interest above the natural rate. The time sequence after such a disturbance was the focus of analysis.

The purpose of this paper is to raise the question whether this program led the Stockholm School into a cul-de-sac or whether the necessary analytical tools just were not available in the 1930s. I inherited the problem from my teachers Erik Lundberg and Ingvar Svennilson, and I struggled with it in my dissertation, *Monetary and Fiscal Policy under Uncertainty* (Faxén, 1957). The solution that I arrived at was to combine the ideas of the Stockholm School with those of von Neumann and Morgenstern's *Theory of Games and Economic Behavior* (1944).

1   The period model

To my mind, the Stockholm School adopted a uniform and coherent approach to the problem indicated above. The analysis of inflation and unemployment in different phases of the business cycle required a method for modeling change. Sequences of static equilibria and Cassel's model for steady-state growth were much too limited for that purpose. They just did not catch the essential features of change.

The Walras model is consistent only at the equilibrium point. Therefore, it cannot be a starting point for a dynamic analysis. This was the theme of Erik Lundberg's 1930 article. Even if he did not state his message that bluntly, he was very close to this formulation (in particular, Lundberg, 1930, pp. 136 and 142).

The period model – characterized by the distinction between change that occurs instantaneously at the transition point from one period to the next and developments that take place during the periods – is a skeleton framework to be filled with behavioral assumptions. It constitutes an entirely different logical structure from the Walrasian model. The period model is not an extension of the Walrasian model and does not build upon it. It is intended to model change to facilitate causal analysis. Chains of causes and effects that are muddled in reality become apparent when using the period model.

One central idea of the Stockholm School was that current short-term reactions cannot be explained by current costs, prices, demand levels, and so forth. Expectations over a sequence of future periods are essential. The period model facilitates analysis of how expectations influence decisions.

There were two ways in which assumptions could be formulated with some degree of technical precision concerning the behavior of economic agents. Lundberg (1937, pp. 150–1) used aggregate ad hoc reaction functions that described, for instance, how households distribute income between consumption and saving or between current outlay for housing and other consumer spending. Lindahl (1939, p. 43) and Svennilson (1938, Chapter 5) assumed optimizing behavior by individual households and firms over a sequence of periods. I devote the section "Optimizing behavior" to this approach.

Other Stockholm economists, for instance, Bertil Ohlin, preferred to express the importance of multiperiod prehistory and expectations for current economic behavior in the form of relatively nontechnical verbal reasoning.

2   Reaction functions

Using sequence analysis, Lundberg (1937) wanted to demonstrate how lagged reaction functions in the economy could under appropriate circumstances produce periodic fluctuations similar to business cycles. His reaction functions were introduced ad hoc without any foundation in micro-optimizing behavior. They were selected to correspond to assumptions made in "verbal" models in the literature. The model sequences were intended to add precision to those verbal models.

Lundberg did not believe that reaction functions were constant over time (1937, p. 243). The purpose of the model sequences was not to describe reality but to model interesting aspects of reality. Sequence analysis could be used to criticize the concepts and conclusions of the more static types of analysis and to discard the concept of monetary equilibrium as a tool for analyzing an economic development (Lundberg, 1937, p. 246). Lundberg did not believe that one business cycle was just a repetition of the preceding one. On the contrary, he emphasized that each cycle had its special characteristic, (Lundberg, 1937, appendix, pp. 257–61).

It was not Lundberg's ambition in 1937 to develop a general theory of contracyclical monetary and fiscal policy. For instance, he did not discuss information requirements and decision-making procedures in relation to necessary lead times, lagged reactions, and possible disturbances. The effort to develop contracyclical policies had already been made in 1933–4 by Myrdal, Ohlin, Hammarskjöld, and Johansson. Lundberg (1937) did not develop practical policy advice beyond what was accomplished in 1933–4 and did not intend to do so. In addition to improving precision in verbal models, his intention was to criticize the use of equilibrium methods in the analysis of cycles of inflation and unemployment. For this purpose, it was sufficient to use ad hoc macro-reaction functions with constant coefficients. An attempt at constructing optimizing behavior by households and firms would be an unnecessary complication.

3   Optimizing behavior

It is the strength and beauty of the Walras model that it contains a uniquely determined equilibrium point such that, for each economic agent, this point corresponds to the optimum. It may be inferred from the writings of Lindahl and Svennilson that the ultimate aim of their dynamic multiperiod analysis was to establish a similar uniquely determined equilibrium path for the development of an economy. Along this adjustment or development path, each household and firm would be at an optimum in the same sense as in the Walras equilibrium point.

In his section on "The General Theory of Planning," Erik Lindahl (1939, pp. 40–51) discussed alternative planning, drawing a distinction between uniquely determined plans and plans that determine actions only between certain limits. He also distinguished between unalterable and alterable plans. Furthermore, in a diagram, Lindahl (p. 43) illustrated the "degree of advantageousness" connected with each of a number of alternative plans over three periods of time. In other words, he assumed a preference ordering for alternative plans. Note that this preference ordering did not apply to outcomes but to plans.

Ingvar Svennilson (1938, Chapter 5) presented an attempt to establish preference ordering for multiperiod alternative plans of risk-averse economic agents with time-dependent valuations of outcomes.

Thus, Lindahl and Svennilson studied multiperiod planning for single households or firms, using the concept of "alternative plans." However, they never formulated strategies in the sense of von Neumann and Morgenstern (1944, p. 79), even if they were very close to it.

Svennilson (1938, p. 101) stated that alternative planning means that future actions are not planned absolutely along the time axis, but that plans are made that indicate the functional dependence of future actions upon certain variables, the future values of which are known only in a stochastic sense. To each sequence, up to a particular point of time, corresponds a probability distribution for the continuation of the sequence after that point of time. Later in the same volume, Svennilson (1938, p. 138) expressed alternative planning as the determination of reaction functions that uniquely determine a sequence of future adjustments of parameters of action as functions of past development.

In the macroeconomic comparisons of aggregates, *ex ante* and *ex post,* variables were usually to be single-valued. Deviations between *ex ante* and *ex post* were seen as originating from unexpected events, surprises. This meant that, for alternative planning under risk, the analysis was confronted with a puzzling problem: What is a surprise in alternative planning under risk? Almost anything can happen, even if the probability for that particular event is low (see Siven's contribution in this volume).

The obvious solution to this problem is to assume that, at the end of each period, each household or firm revises its probability distributions for variables in future periods, taking into account the new information obtained during the period just elapsed. This assumption was made by von Neumann and Morgenstern, but not, as far as I have been able to find out, by Lindahl or Svennilson. For instance, Svennilson explains the relationships between the probability distributions of households and firms at the end of three periods that follow upon each other (Svennilson, 1938, diagram 4, p. 47). Yet, he does not develop this into a systematic *ex ante–ex post* analysis, explaining how information obtained during the period transforms probability distributions at the beginning of the period to corresponding distributions at the end of the period.

There is in Lindahl and Svennilson no clear distinction between unexpected events, surprises that arise from deliberate actions by competitors or other economic agents and "normal business risk." In other words, there is no separate treatment of surprises that originate from "game uncertainty." The characteristic of game uncertainty is that the household or firm can conceive of an interval for the variable but not a probability distribution within that interval. These intervals for "game uncertainty" variables are revised at the end of each period in the same way as probability distributions for "risk." In this way, the *ex ante–ex post* analysis can be pursued under uncertainty as well as risk.

One reason Lindahl and Svennilson never saw the need to develop this type of comparison between *ex ante* and *ex post* is that they never took the step from analysis of multiperiod alternative planning of single economic agents to analysis of market interaction among groups of households and firms. Let us see what such a step would have meant.

First, if the strategy of each household and firm as well as of the government is known, the composition of all strategies determines the total development of the economy. The payoff along the adjustment path is thereby determined for each firm or household. Now, the main theorem of game theory is that, in the general case, the solution has a rather complicated structure. It is a set of sets, and to each of those sets there is a specific standard of behavior. In other words, there is a set of standards of behavior, and to each standard of behavior, there is a set of solutions (von Neumann and Morgenstern, 1947, pp. 40–5, and 417–18; see also the analysis of three- and four-person games). Only two-person zero-sum games with transferable cardinal utility have unique solutions.

The solution sets are bounded; that is, adjustment paths move within intervals for prices, wages, quantities, and incomes. What happens within those intervals depends upon what coalitions are formed and what standards of behavior are generally accepted. What standards of behavior will actually emerge cannot be deduced from assumptions of optimizing behavior but have to be observed directly in the economy.

4   Nash equilibria, solution sets, and standards of behavior

No wonder that enthusiasm to apply this theorem has been so limited. Instead, Nash equilibria have been used. I did so myself (Faxén, 1957, p. 104). A Nash equilibrium is a set of strategies for each economic agent such that his strategy is optimal under the condition that the strategies for all other agents are considered given. A Nash equilibrium is not always unique. The difficulties in using the concept of Nash equilibrium for the determination of adjustment paths (and not for static equilibrium points) are obvious. In 1957 I did not realize the extremely abstract nature of the "second-order adjustment paths" leading to a Nash equilibrium between "first-order adjustment paths." The sequences that I described now appear as purely theoretical constructs (see Faxén, 1957, p. 101).

In the example I discussed, two players A and B have five strategies each. The strategies are to be interpreted as jointly determining adjustment paths like the seven macroeconomic processes described on pages 136–40. If A has chosen strategy A-5 and B strategy B-1, the adjustment path has the ordinal utility indicator 4 for A and 1 for B. This is, however, not optimal for A. Strategy A-2 gives 5 to A and is therefore preferred. The resulting adjustment path is not optimal for B, who substitutes strategy B-4 for B-1. In my example, the adjustment path determined by strategies A-2 and B-4 is a Nash equilibrium. In this way, I described a "second-order adjustment path" to a "first-order adjustment path."

I now think that a major reason for rejecting the concept of solution as presented by von Neumann and Morgenstern was my skepticism toward the axiomatic method. The concept of a solution to a game was introduced as as axiom, as something self-evident and natural. This is a dangerous method when conclusions as well as axioms are not supported by examples of actual economic behavior.

It was all right to use this concept for two-person zero-sum games. The demonstration of mixed strategies as solutions to these types of games has proved useful for practical applications. However, the extension to general games with an arbitrary number of players did not lead to any transparent analysis. Complications seemed innumerable. How could this produce any practical advice for monetary and fiscal policy?

Nevertheless, my present view is to prefer the more complicated von Neumann-Morgenstern solutions. One reason for this is that standards of behavior for wage policy, price policy, and so on play an important role for short-term flexibility or rigidity in wage and price formation, in other words, for inflation. Thus, the von Neumann-Morgenstern theory of games with three or more players has an empirical counterpart that makes skepticism toward the axiomatic method unjustified.

In my view, the theory of standards of behavior and solution sets in games can in retrospect be regarded as major missing analytical tools for the Stockholm economists in the 1930s. With that insight, they would have avoided building elaborate models of risk aversion and alternative planning in order to explain behavior under uncertainty as optimizing. Instead, they could have been led to an emphasis on the importance of empirical study of standards of behavior.

5 Risk aversion

As I stated in the introduction, the ambition of the Stockholm School was to model a Schumpeter growth process under Knight uncertainty, assuming optimizing households and firms, in order to create micro foundations for macroeconomic sequences of cyclical variations. We can now see that this would have improved the analysis of profits, liquidity, and the role of equity/debt ratios. Risk aversion is essential for this analysis.

Furthermore, profits, liquidity, and equity/debt ratios link monetary and fiscal policies to decisions by households and firms to save, invest, and employ. This makes reactions to monetary and fiscal policies essentially dependent upon risk aversion among households and firms. It is therefore necessary to explain "risk valuation" in order to understand reactions to policy.

Myrdal and Svennilson assumed "risk valuation" as given. "Risk valuation" was part of an inherent attitude, like preferences for oranges versus bananas. They did not attempt to explain the preference ordering for uncertain prospects. Thus, the compensation for risk and uncertainty to owners of equity, or the rate of profit over and above the market rate of interest, was just a consequence of this assumption and not really explained.

Moreover, Myrdal (1927, p. 11) did not leave the concept of equilibrium prices. He wanted to insert a third deductive step before the infinite field of empiricism: equilibrium prices under growth with structural change, in addition to the stationary-state and steady-state growth. This meant that he treated risk aversion as an equilibrium concept. The assumption of attitudes to risk valuation as part of an inherently given preference ordering made this possible.

Svennilson (1938, p. 116) assumed that "marginal chances" could be treated as independent goods, even if he was aware of the fact that this was not the general case. According to his formula (42) on page 116, the coefficient of risk valuation $v(a,P)$ depends not only upon the probability P but also upon the payoff a. Risk aversion means that for extremely low payoffs, for instance bankruptcy, v is very large. For normal payoffs, v is close to 1.

Difficulties arise with this approach when uncertain prospects are transformed by transactions between risk-averse firms, for instance, through futures contracts and hedging against exchange rate uncertainty. The treatment of this class of problem is facilitated by a theoretical structure that permits the composition of choices during a sequence of periods into one single decision at the beginning of the first period, keeping the function $v(a,P)$ invariant. In the Svennilson approach this is, however, contradictory since the high value of $v(a,P)$ depends upon the situation at the beginning of each period. For risk-averse decision makers, the sequence of decisions cannot be consolidated into a single decision.

For this reason, I prefer, as I did in the section on the Independence Axiom (Faxén, 1957, pp. 70–2), to accept Samuelson's independence axiom, according to which such a consolidation can always be made. Linear utility indicators will then always exist, and the basic structure of game theory can be applied. Profits can be seen as excess in the sense of game theory, and risk aversion as minimax behavior to avoid bankruptcy.

This approach would have led to a much better analysis of monetary and fiscal policy under uncertainty than my use of the Nash equilibrium concept. Naturally, it would also mean the abandonment of any kind of equilibrium growth idea such as Myrdal's "third way." Growth is essentially a disequilibrium process, and monetary and fiscal policies offer a method to make permanent disequilibrium sustainable. "The sequence of changes will continuously upset the given conditions to which adjustments are supposed to take place" according to Lundberg (1937, p. 146).

6   What remains?

The core of Myrdal's, Lindahl's, and Svennilson's efforts was to define – in the Wicksellian tradition – that rate of *ex ante* return on capital under uncertainty that would produce a steadily growing stream of investment, full employment, and a stable price level. In order to compare uncertain yield prospects to the market rate of interest, they modeled risk aversion and alternative planning. However, they never succeeded in formulating criteria for the relationship between the *ex ante* rate of return on new investments and the market rate of interest such that the growth process would have desired properties. In other words, a dynamic formulation similar to the static Walras model was never reached.

As explained earlier, the reason for this can be found in game theory.

No amount of knowledge of preference orderings for households and firms can reduce genuine game uncertainty. Standards of behavior must be observed directly in the economy. Optimization under uncertainty cannot yield a microeconomic foundation for uniquely determined macroeconomic relationships. Hence it is not possible to use this approach to provide a strict formulation of the Wicksellian concept of a "natural rate of interest" for an economy subject to innovation-driven growth and cyclical fluctuations.

On the other hand, the Stockholm School did a great deal of lasting value. The Stockholm economists emphasized that monetary and fiscal policies are not sequences of independent actions. Their effects often depend upon the interaction between the prehistory of the current situation and the expectations held by economic agents regarding future policies. That insight made the Stockholm economists view the monetary and fiscal policies over the cycle as a unit. They emphasized the importance of mutual formation of expectations among households, firms, and policy makers.

Finally, I wish to quote from what I wrote in 1957:

> [T]he analysis shows that, in order to influence the target variables in the desired way, the Government must follow a consistent strategy over a long time-span, so that the expectations of the business firms as to the future Government policy are fulfilled. If the Government shifts its long-term policy too frequently, or does not carry it out consistently, the business firms will be unable to form reliable expectations as to future Government policy, and the effect of this policy will therefore be more or less erratic." (Faxén, 1957, pp. 211–12)

This view corresponds to the current emphasis upon the medium-term horizons for monetary and fiscal policies rather than short-term fine-tuning. Naturally, this shift of emphasis results from practical experience rather than from a reading of the Stockholm School. Yet, it is a source of some satisfaction that theoretical analysis has preceded practical experience in this respect.

References

Faxén, Karl-Olof (1957), *Monetary and Fiscal Policy under Uncertainty,* dissertation, Uppsala.

Lindahl, Erik (1939), *Studies in the Theory of Money and Capital.* London: George Allen & Unwin, Ltd.

Lundberg, Erik (1930), "Om begreppet ekonomisk jämvikt" (On the concept of economic equilibrium), *Ekonomisk Tidskrift,* pp. 133–60.

(1937), *Studies in the Theory of Economic Expansion,* quotations from the London edition (1955).

Myrdal, Gunnar (1927), *Prisbildningsproblemet och föränderligheten.* Uppsala: Almqvist & Wiksell.

Svennilson, Ingvar (1938), *Ekonomisk planering* (Economic planning). Uppsala.

von Neumann, John, and Oskar Morgenstern (1944), *Theory of Games and Economic Behavior,* quotations from the Princeton edition (1947).

CHAPTER 6

There were *two* Stockholm Schools

LARS WERIN

There may be some difficulties in defining *exactly* what constitutes the contribution of the collection of writings Bertil Ohlin christened the "Stockholm School" in his 1937 *Economic Journal* articles (Ohlin, 1937). However, all agree that it consists of the development of macro-economic analysis carried out by, in particular, Erik Lindahl, Gunnar Myrdal, Erik Lundberg, and Bertil Ohlin himself. Most economists agree that this development, even if somewhat incomplete, was impor-tant; and practically everyone seems to be of the opinion that it consti-tutes the crowning achievement of a generation of Swedish economists. But then it seems forgotten that some of the most prominent members of the School had already made another significant contribution in a quite different field of economics: price theory and general-equilibrium analysis. In my opinion, what has been called the Stockholm School should properly be called the "Second Stockholm School," in contra-distinction to the "First Stockholm School" – even if the lists of mem-bers overlap to a large extent.[1] It could easily be argued that the achieve-ments of the First School rank higher. Why, then, is hardly any attention paid to the First School? My answer is simple: mainly because the mem-bers themselves wanted it that way.

The two most important, or at least most characteristic, works of the First School are Erik Lindahl's long and elaborate article "The Place of Capital in the Theory of Price" (Swedish original 1929, in English 1939) and Bertil Ohlin's book *Interregional and International Trade* (1933), preceded by his dissertation with essentially the same message (Ohlin, 1924). Lindahl's study made the Walrasian model intertemporal; Ohl-in's work made it interregional (or "interlocational"). Other important contributions within the First School are the well-known part of Lin-dahl's dissertation (in German 1919, in English 1967), which tried to integrate decisions on taxes and public expenditure in price theory, and Myrdal's dissertation *Prisbildningen och föränderligheten* (1927), which contained an analysis of basic aspects of intertemporal price theory along the lines adopted by Lindahl in his 1929 article. These four works may be regarded as the "Arrow-Debreu theory" of that era.

Thus Lindahl's 1929 article and Ohlin's two books extended the Walrasian general-equilibrium model to cover the full set of future dates and the full set of locations; that is, the model was made strictly intertemporal and strictly interlocational. In doing this, these works started from Cassel's simplified version of the Walrasian system (Cassel, 1918). Both Lindahl and Ohlin considered the verbal analysis that accompanies the extension of the equation system at least as important as the equation system itself.

In a sequence of models, each with its separate assumptions concerning the level of information and dynamic background conditions, Lindahl demonstrated the nature of the resulting general equilibrium, in particular the meaning of the rate of interest and the proper definition of capital. This was a brilliant achievement. But for various reasons, including the delay before the article was translated into English, it did not begin to have an influence for a long time. By then it also had to compete with Irving Fisher's *The Theory of Interest,* published in 1930, and Hicks's *Value and Capital,* published in 1939. Fisher's book was in certain respects a richer work than Lindahl's article, but it did not contain a full intertemporal general-equilibrium model. *Value and Capital* did, although mainly verbally and not by means of a complete equation system. When the Lindahl study eventually exerted its influence, it was right in the mainstream of general-equilibrium analysis, namely, the work of Malinvaud (1953), Koopmans (1957), and Debreu (1959).[2] Recently, members of the rational expectations school have found that the rational expectations equilibrium generated by convergence of expectations had already been specified by Lindahl.

Myrdal's dissertation contained a very rich and profound analysis of expectations and other basic aspects of an intertemporal general-equilibrium model. Cassel's framework was the general starting point, but Myrdal did not apply a formal equation system. The book influenced Lindahl, but the wider impact it could (and should) have had was precluded by the language barrier.

If the influence of Lindahl's 1929 study was delayed and that of Myrdal's dissertation seriously impeded, it may seem as if no such problems burdened Ohlin's 1933 book. *Interregional and International Trade* immediately put its stamp on the research in the field, and its influence has been active ever since. Still, there is a problem in that much of the attention paid to the book has, in fact, been misdirected. This somewhat provocative statement has to be justified.

There is probably general agreement on the following, somewhat stylized scenario: By the 1920s, the marginalist revolution of the 1870s had successfully penetrated economic theory. Prices were now regarded as determined by demand and supply, as described either by a Walrasian general-equilibrium model or a Marshallian partial-equilibrium model. Classical ideas had been subdued – except in one field, the analysis of international trade. There Ricardo's theory, or "doctrine," of comparative cost prevailed as a cost-based preserve within the modern framework. Ohlin wanted to put an end to this compartmentalization of theory, and he did. To quote from the opening sentences of his book, which essentially repeat the corresponding sentences in his dissertation, he set out "to build a theory of international trade in harmony with the mutual-interdependence theory of pricing, – the universally accepted price theory to-day, – and thus independent of the classical theory of value." He did this by strict verbal analysis, by reformulating Cassel's version of the Walrasian system so as to incorporate localization and trade, and by a number of illuminating empirical applications.[3]

However, Ohlin made a pedagogical mistake that should have been innocuous but turned out not to be. Empirical conclusions of practical interest cannot be derived from the general-equilibrium model without specifications appropriate to the problem at hand. Thus, as a general starting point useful for many problems, Ohlin introduced an assumption he had used earlier in his dissertation, taken mainly from an article by Eli Heckscher. With a fair amount of empirical support, he assumed that relative factor supplies usually differ between localities more than technologies and tastes, and hence tend to have a stronger effect on the market equilibrium, that is, on the pattern of trade and localization of production. We now know the result: in the article-producing economic journals industry, Ohlin's grand scheme was transformed into the two-by-two-by-two "Heckscher-Ohlin model." This is certainly a general-equilibrium model, but not the universal, flexible model Ohlin thought he had created. We often envy those economists who have a model or theorem named after them, but in Ohlin's case the satisfaction could not have been unclouded. He may, now and then, have reflected on what his mentor Cassel wrote about him (without much humility) in a volume of memoirs (Cassel, 1941, part II, p. 376): "It came upon him to make my general theory of prices complete by way of a corresponding theory of international trade. ... These achievements represented a large step forward in the theory of international trade. In accomplishing it, Ohlin was, however, hampered to a quite large extent by distorted conceptions conveyed to him by Heckscher."[4]

Even if it was mainly through the simplified Heckscher-Ohlin model, it is obvious that Ohlin's book played a decisive role for the introduction of general-equilibrium methods in the study of international *and* interregional trade. Through its general equilibrium perspective it superseded Haberler's *Theory of International Trade* (1936), which did not emancipate itself fully from the comparative-cost conception. The task of further developing strict interregional general-equilibrium theory was taken on by Mosak (1944).

The oldest work of the First Stockholm School was Lindahl's attempt to extend price (i.e., contract) theory to cover decisions on public expenditure and taxes (Lindahl, 1919, 1928). The framework in this case was partial rather than general equilibrium, although – if successful – the ideas could rather easily be incorporated into a general-equilibrium model. Lindahl's direct purpose seems to have been to interpret the political budget process, analyzed by his inspirer Wicksell, in terms of voluntary contracting. The verdict today probably has to be that he did not succeed. Wicksell's conviction that the process is genuinely political, and thus has to be analyzed on its own terms, has prevailed and generated public choice analysis. But Lindahl's approach *had to* be tried, and the importance of his analysis for public finance during the last decades is considerable.

Now we face a major problem. Erik Lindahl, Gunnar Myrdal, and Bertil Ohlin were responsible for a rather coherent, first-class achievement in price theory and general-equilibrium analysis in the years before they turned their interest toward macroeconomics. Why is hardly any attention paid to their first achievement? Why are these three remembered as founding members of a Stockholm School of macroeconomics but never as a group that constituted a First Stockholm School, which even more firmly made its mark on the future development of economic analysis? Here is a list of possible reasons:

1. The depression caused the group to switch its field of research. Macroeconomics and stabilization policy appeared much more important than "futile" work in price and general-equilibrium theory. The group itself adhered to this view even after the 1930s, and tended to look down on their own microtheoretical work.

2. The group, and its followers, were convinced that they *knew* what Keynes *knew,* and that they had known it before Keynes knew it. They were eager to establish their priority.

3. Lindahl and Ohlin based their general-equilibrium work mainly on Cassel's version of the Walrasian model, while the macroeconomic work of the Second Stockholm School went back to Wicksell. Obviously, Wicksell's work had a much higher scientific standing than the

derivative, although pedagogically influential, work Cassel had done in general-equilibrium theory.[5] Hence, both the group itself, and those who commented on and assessed its achievements later on, favored work based on Wicksell partly for the very reason that it *was* based on Wicksell.

4. Some members of the Second Stockholm School had not belonged to the very small group that composed the First Stockholm School. These members, quite naturally, wanted to emphasize the research program to which they themselves had made significant contributions.

5. Economists often have a journalistic instinct. In their attempts to simplify and clarify, they like to put labels on scientific work and then use them. The very fact that there was something called the Stockholm School made the work covered by the label important, indeed more important than the unlabeled work surrounding it (cf. the label "Heckscher-Ohlin theory"!).

To sum up, what is usually called the Stockholm School – here called the *Second* Stockholm School – made significant although perhaps somewhat secondary achievements in economic research. Prior to that, however, the *First* Stockholm School had carried out first-rate research in general-equilibrium analysis and price theory. It was in fact the "Arrow-Debreu school" of the period before the Keynesian revolution. Why, then, is there so much fuss about the Second School, and so little about the First School? Because the members of the First School played it down for various reasons, because the incoming members of the Second School were naturally most interested in that school, and perhaps to some extent because of the journalistic tendencies of subsequent generations of economists.

Notes

1 Let us, for simplicity, disregard the fact that Lindahl did not live or work in Stockholm. During the period that concerns us here, he was first at the University of Lund and then at the University of Gothenburg.

2 Lindahl probably influenced Hicks, since Hicks was involved in the translation of Lindahl's work (see Lindahl, 1939, p. 12). Hicks does not quote Lindahl in *Value and Capital,* but mentions his influence in *Capital and Growth* (Hicks, 1965, in particular p. 58). See also Hicks's contribution in this volume.

3 Ohlin, rather naturally, seems to have been unaware of the formulation of a mathematical general-equilibrium model of international trade published a year earlier by Yntema (1932). The honor of coming first belongs, of course, to Ohlin since his model is presented already in his dissertation.

4 I once tested the argument presented above on Ohlin himself, who (I think with a sigh) expressed his general sympathy toward it.

5 Note that the group of mainly Austrian and German economists, with Abraham Wald and John von Neumann as leading figures, who led the way toward the formulation of the Arrow-Debreu model in the 1930s also started out from Cassel's framework rather than from Walras himself (see Koopmans, 1951).

References

Cassel, Gustav (1918), *Theoretische Sozialökonomie.* Leipzig: Winter.
   (1941), *I förnuftets tjänst. En ekonomisk självbiografi* (In the service of common sense. An economic autobiography). Parts I–II. Stockholm: Natur och Kultur.
Debreu, Gerard (1959), *Theory of Value.* New York: Wiley.
Fisher, Irving (1930), *The Theory of Interest.* New York: Macmillan.
Haberler, Gottfried (1936), *Theory of International Trade, with Its Application to Commercial Policy.* London: Macmillan.
Hicks, John R. (1939), *Value and Capital.* Oxford: Oxford University Press.
   (1965), *Capital and Growth.* Oxford: Oxford University Press.
Koopmans, Tjalling C. (1951), "Introduction," in T. C. Koopmans, ed., *Activity Analysis of Production and Allocation.* Cowles Commission Monograph No. 13. New York: Wiley.
   (1957), *Three Essays on the State of Economic Science.* New York: McGraw-Hill.
Lindahl, Erik (1919), *Die Gerechtigkeit der Besteuerung. Eine Analyse der Steuerprinzipen auf Grundlage der Grenznutzentheorie.* Lund: Gleerupska universitetsbokhandeln. The principal section translated as "Just Taxation – A Positive Solution" in Richard A. Musgrave and Alan T. Peacock, eds., *Classics in the Theory of Public Finance,* London: Macmillan, 1958.
   (1928), "Eine strittige Fragen der Steuertheorie," in H. Mayer, ed., *Die Wirtschaftstheorie der Gegenwart,* Vol. IV. Vienna: Springer. Translated as "Some Controversial Questions in the Theory of Taxation," in Richard A. Musgrave and Alan T. Peacock, eds., *Classics in the Theory of Public Finance,* London: Macmillan, 1958.
   (1929), "Prisbildningsproblemets uppläggning från kapitalteoretisk synpunkt," *Ekonomisk Tidskrift.* Translated as "The Pricing Problem from the Point of View of Capital Theory," in Lindahl (1939).
   (1939), *Studies in the Theory of Money and Capital.* London: Allen and Unwin.
Malinvaud, Edmond (1953), "Capital Accumulation and Efficient Allocation of Resources," *Econometrica.*
Mosak, Jacob L. (1944), *General-Equilibrium Theory of International Trade.* Cowles Commission Monograph No. 7. Evanston, Ill.: The Principia Press of Illinois.

Myrdal, Gunnar (1927), *Prisbildningen och föränderligheten* (Price formation and change). Uppsala: Almqvist & Wiksell.

Ohlin, Bertil (1924), *Handelns teori* (Trade theory). Stockholm: Central-tryckeriet.

(1933), *Interregional and International Trade*. Cambridge, Mass.: Harvard University Press.

(1937), "Some Notes on the Stockholm Theory of Saving and Investment" I–II, *Economic Journal.*

Yntema, Theodore O. (1932), *A Mathematical Reformulation of the General Theory of International Trade*. Chicago: The University of Chicago Press.

CHAPTER 7

On formal dynamics: From Lundberg to chaos analysis

WILLIAM J. BAUMOL[1]

The Stockholm School and its vital contribution to sequence analysis played a key role in the transition of economic dynamics from the intuitive approaches of earlier business cycle theory to the powerful and rigorous analytics that is the hallmark of theoretical writings in the area since World War II. Erik Lundberg provided a vital contribution to this evolution. Though formal dynamic models had been contributed earlier by Ragnar Frisch, Lundberg's research showed well before Paul Samuelson's profound contributions on the subject how such models could be grounded firmly in the logic of sequence analysis and the pertinent macroeconomic considerations.

Lundberg's basic contribution to the field does not make any use of the now commonplace mathematical tools that sometimes offer general solutions to dynamic relationships; instead, it relies on numerical time sequences generated with the aid of particular illustrative values of the parameters of his dynamic equations. But I will show that this is not as restrictive a procedure as it may appear to be. Rather, there is a trade-off between the abstraction and deemphasis of the details of the underlying economic processes that the more formal procedures engender and the insights offered by the painstaking calculations that are vital for Lundberg's numerical time paths. Indeed, it will be pointed out that the ostensible superiority of the formal approaches in terms of the greater generality of their results is to a considerable degree an illusion, because the mathematical techniques are fully effective in providing analytic solutions for dynamic models only when those models take the most elementary (linear) forms. This fact naturally tempted economists (including myself) to force their models into linear forms, whether or not that was appropriate for the problems under consideration. Such a step itself obviously constitutes a very considerable surrender of generality, one whose consequences turned out to be more serious than was initially realized. Recent work in dynamics, most notably the writings in chaos theory, have had to break decisively with the restrictions of linearity. More than that, parts of the work undertaken recently have been forced to revert to the numerical sorts of procedure that Lundberg's work introduced to economics. There are even significant recent contributions that have reverted directly to the Lundbergian techniques, thereby demonstrating their power to provide profound insights into complex and important issues.

Two avenues of dynamic analysis

A.   *The Lundberg approach*

To understand the methodological issue with which we are dealing, we will, for concreteness, focus on the general nth order difference equation

$$y(t) = f[y(t - 1), \ldots, y(t - n)] \tag{1}$$

where $y(s)$ is the value assumed in period s by the pertinent variable, y. This is the sort of relationship with which Lundberg's writings on dynamics deal. Once formulated explicitly with given parameter values, such a relationship determines the time path of y for all future dates at which the equation continues to hold unchanged. Indeed, it permits a direct calculation of that time path, given as data the initial n values of y, call them $y(0)$, $y(1)$, $\ldots$, $y(n - 1)$. This calculation can be carried out in an obvious way, by substituting the given initial values into equation (1) to obtain the next value of y in the sequence, that is, to obtain $y(n)$. The process can then be replicated over and over again. Thus, after the first round, one can substitute the newly calculated value $y(n)$ along with the initially given values $y(n - 1)$, $\ldots$, $y(1)$ [and dropping $y(0)$ from consideration] to obtain from equation (1) this time

$$y(n + 1) = f[y(n), y(n - 1), \ldots, y(1)]$$

The third round of this sequence of calculations then gives us $y(n + 2)$, the one after that yields $y(n + 3)$, and so on, as far as one wishes to carry the process. From the resulting table of values of y at different dates (and perhaps, of other associated variables) it is possible to study informally the qualitative properties of the time path. Moreover, by changing one or more of the values of the parameters of equation (1), one can study the consequences for the time path, examining whether a given change in some parameter, for example, increases the frequency of cycles or reduces their amplitude.

This is the line of analysis that Professor Lundberg employed. The limitations of the procedure are fairly obvious and are well recognized.

The intertemporal behavior elicited by a given set of parameter values or initial conditions can be atypical and, in any event, may offer no clue about what happens when rather different parameter values are used. But the approach has at least three virtues that are less widely recognized. First, by taking the analysis step by step through the evolution of the time path, it invites direct consideration of the influences that account for the qualitative properties of the move from one step of the time path to the next. This is important if our purpose in the use of formal models is to learn more about the workings of the economy, rather than just the aesthetic pleasures of elegant manipulation of abstract relationships. Second, the approach just described works for *any* sort of difference equation (or system of simultaneous difference equations) and not just for linear relationships with constant coefficients, to which the standard formal methods of analysis are adapted. Third, the Lundberg approach has the enormous advantage (not yet available, of course, when Lundberg's work first appeared) of amenability to calculation by electronic computer. Even a relatively inexpensive desk-top computer can readily be programmed to generate time paths spanning long time periods with ease, to draw graphs of their behavior, and, above all, to recalculate themselves almost instantaneously when one or more parameter values are changed.

It is these last two properties of the Lundberg approach – its ability to deal with cases of nonlinearity and its ready compatibility with computer treatment – that probably account more than anything else for the recent reemergence of the approach. It may be noted also that its amenability to computer treatment also goes far to offset its main limitation. For since computers greatly facilitate exploration of the consequences for the time path of substitution of one set of parameter values for another, one can hope to obtain insights on the qualitative relationships between parameter values and time path over a broad and representative range of values of the former.

B.   *The formal solution approaches and linearity*

The second way of dealing with difference equations like equation (1), as has already been noted, is at its most effective in the case of linearity. As is well known, for such cases there exist analytic expressions for the value of y in the general period t that one may write in the form

$$y(t) = g[t, y(0), y(1), \ldots, y(n - 1)] \tag{2}$$

That is, such a solution expresses the value of y in period t as a function, exclusively, of t and the n initial values $y(0), \ldots, y(n)$. One can study the qualitative properties of the time path and its relationship to the parameter values directly from equation (2). There is no need to review these matters here.

What is worth observing, however, is that the linearity of the models to which this approach was adapted soon proved to be a debilitating restriction and in fact led to a sharp decline in the popularity of the entire line of dynamic analysis. It is shown in the basic writings on the subject that all solutions (2) of linear difference equations systems come down in essence to more complex variants of the solution to the first-order case [the case $n = 1$ in equation (1), i.e., that in which there is a single period lag]. That solution normally takes the form $y_t = ux^t + v$, where u, x, and v are all constants whose values are determined by the parameters of the equation and the initial value $y(0)$. It is clear on a moment's reflection that this solution is compatible with only four types of time path:

Case i. Monotonic explosion: The case where $x > 1$ when y_t will obviously increase monotonically (at an exponential rate) in absolute value.

Case ii. Monotonic stability: The case where $0 < x < 1$ so that x^t approaches zero asymptotically, and therefore $y(t)$ monotonically approaches its equilibrium value, v, as t increases.

Case iii. Oscillatory explosion: The case where $x < -1$ so that x^t also grows exponentially in absolute value, but oscillates from positive to negative as t goes from even to odd values.

Case iv. Stable oscillation: The case where $0 > x > -1$, in which x^t also alternates between positive and negative values, but its absolute value approaches zero with the passage of time.

It is clear that this menu of time paths is far too small to encompass all the significant cases found in reality. For example, for all practical purposes it rules out persistent cycles of more or less constant amplitude that neither peter out nor explode catastrophically as time moves on. Perhaps even more important, it rules out disorderly time paths with complex patterns of fluctuation unless irregularities are imparted to the time path through periodic intervention of exogenous forces or through powerful stochastic influences.

Economists did not take long to show their discomfort under these restrictions. Hicks and Goodwin were among the first to take countermeasures, and they did so by explicit introduction of nonlinearities into their models. But this takes us a bit ahead of our story. First let us review some of the features of the Lundberg approach.

A Lundberg model

In the mathematical chapter of his pathbreaking work Professor Lundberg offers the reader a number of models of cyclical behavior encompassing a variety of consumption and investment relationships. I will describe only one of these constructs, that entailing active investment in working capital. I will first show how the model is constructed, and then I will provide the corresponding sequence analysis table provided by the author. In the mathematics I have taken the liberty of revising the notation to bring it more closely into line with the symbols that have been adopted widely since the book first appeared.

The model involves the following basic relationships.

The consumption (consumer expenditure) function of income derived from consumption goods:

$$D_{ct} = aC_t, \qquad a < 1 \tag{3}$$

where D_{ct} is disposable income derived from the output of consumption goods and C_t is total business expenditure on the production of consumption goods.

The investment-consumption function:

$$D_{It} = aI_t \tag{4}$$

where D_{It} is disposable income derived from investment on working capital, I_t.

The investment demand function:

$$I_t = kC_t - K_{t-1} \tag{5}$$

where K_{t-1} is the stock of working capital inherited from the preceding period and k is the desired ratio of working capital to consumption good output.

The working capital stock expression:

$$K_t = kC_t - (E_t - C_t) \tag{6}$$

where E_t = expenditure on consumers' goods output in period t, so that the difference $E_t - C_t$ represents a drawing-down of working capital below its desired level.

Table 1. *Model sequence determined by investments in working capital*

Period	C_t	D_{ct}	I_t	D_{It}	D_t	K	E_t	K_t
0							1,000	500
1	1,000	800	—	—	800	300	1,020	480
2	1,020	816	30	24	840	300	1,056	474
3	1,056	845	54	43	888	300	1,100	484
4	1,100	880	66	53	933	300	1,140	510
5	1,140	912	60	48	960	300	1,164	546
6	1,164	931	36	29	960	300	1,164	582
7	1,164	931	0	0	931	300	1,138	608
8	1,138	910	0	0	910	300	1,119	627
9	1,119	895	0	0	895	300	1,105	644
⋮								
n	1,071	857	0	0	857	300	1,071	

The output function:

$$C_t = E_{t-1} \tag{7}$$

making desired outlays on production (under perfectly competitive assumptions) equal to business receipts from the sale of consumption goods in the preceding period.

The expenditure function:

$$E_t = c(D_{ct} + D_{It}) + K \tag{8}$$

where c is the marginal propensity to consume and K is autonomous investment in consumers' goods inventory.

We can then solve equations (3)–(8) for D_{ct} and D_{It} to obtain Lundberg's basic difference equation.[2]

$$E_t = acE_{t-1} + ac(1 + k)(E_{t-1} - E_{t-2}) + C \tag{9}$$

From difference equation (9) Lundberg goes on to derive the numerical sequence of values shown in Table 1. Note that the last row in Table 1 shows the equilibrium values for the variables of the model. However, more interesting for the author's purposes were the earlier values of the endogenous variables, which clearly exhibit both an upward and a downward movement; that is, the numerical calculations provide rigorous proof that the assumed relationships are capable of producing a downturn entirely by themselves. This already takes us well beyond what had been achieved by earlier intuitive discussions in business cycle theory, which had at best provided mechanisms that could plausibly be taken to be sufficient to lead to a downturn, but which had generally been incapable of demonstrating rigorously that this is so.

In addition, the Lundberg table permits the author to carry out some experiments in comparative dynamics, changing values of the parameters and studying what happens, for example, to the speed with which the downturn occurs, the magnitude of the fall, and so on. One can, incidentally, imagine how much labor such comparative dynamics calculations cost the author in the 1930s, particularly in contrast to the ease and speed with which a time path hundreds of periods in length can be generated, graphed, and modified by a change in parameter values with the aid of even a relatively small modern computer.

What dynamic models can and cannot be expected to accomplish

In addition to the considerations that have already been adduced there is yet another reason why the lack of generality of the Lundberg approach is not nearly as serious a limitation as it may appear to be. To see why this is so we must first dispel a serious misunderstanding about what one can and cannot hope to achieve with the aid of formal dynamic analysis.

Like all models, those used in dynamics inevitably involve significant oversimplifications of reality. One can hope to improve them, but one cannot expect to produce a tractable model that encompasses all of the complications of reality. These remarks would deserve all the inattention their banality is apt to elicit were it not for the relatively severe sensitivity of the time path generated by a dynamic model to changes in specification of the model or in the values of the parameters. Chaotic behavior is indeed only the case where this phenomenon is carried to an extreme.[3] As a consequence, a slight inaccuracy in the formulation of a dynamic model may yield results dramatically different from those that are really pertinent.

The result is that no dynamic model is likely to serve as a reliable forecasting device or even to permit one to predict with any degree of confidence that if a decision maker changes the value of parameter p from x to $x + \Delta x$ then such and such will happen. Such general statements are denied not only to those who reason from numerical examples such as that laid out in Table 1, but also to those using the most sophisticated mathematical tools available, for no mathematical device can transmute a construct that is highly sensitive to imperfections in its construction into one that is not.

If dynamic models can not be relied upon to either forecast (even conditionally) or to produce dependable comparative dynamic results about the consequences of changes in policy or in other parameters, to what use can they possibly be put? The answer is that they are powerful instruments of proof of what can perhaps be described as "not necessarily" propositions or (what is close to the same thing) propositions which assert that so and so *can* happen.

Professor Maital calls our attention to a Yiddish proverb which asserts that "for example is not a proof." But if what one wishes to prove is that an asserted relationship is *not* necessarily so, dynamic models come into their own. This is so because such models are well suited to generation of the necessary counterexamples (if such counterexamples turn out to exist).

Two such cases will illustrate my point. Some more simplistic disciples of Keynes may well have put forward the proposition that any approximation to a policy that raises government deficits during recessions and reduces them during periods of inflationary pressure can always be relied upon to reduce the frequency and amplitude of business fluctuations. But a simple dynamic model can be used to provide an easy demonstration (see Baumol, 1961) that slight mistiming in such a policy can lead to an increase in both amplitude and frequency. As a second example, consider the proposition (sometimes associated with the Chicago school) that profitable speculation must always stabilize prices because it requires the speculator to buy when prices are relatively low and to sell when they are comparatively high. Once more, a simple model can be used to prove that it isn't *necessarily* so. If the speculator buys when prices are low but rising and sells when they are high but falling, the result can be destabilizing (see Baumol, 1957). In both cases the basic propositions may remain valid *usually,* but dynamic analysis has shown that one should not place too large a bet on the predicted outcome.

Erik Lundberg's pathbreaking proof that his model was sufficient to yield a downturn was a first cousin of the proofs that have just been described. Clearly, he did not show, nor did he claim to show, that all or even most downturns are produced in the manner described by his model. But he did show what others have failed to demonstrate: that his model was *capable* of doing the job of explaining a downturn and here, clearly, an example *is* indeed a proof. But the important point for our purposes is that an example in the form of a numerical display like that in Table 1 is as conclusive a proof of such a proposition as is the most general solution to a formal dynamic model.

Recent developments

Toward an evolutionary theory

Let me conclude my discussion with a brief allusion to two recent developments in economic dynamics that can be taken to have some of their roots in Lundbergian analysis. The first of these, which is to be discussed in this section, is the evolutionary economics associated with the work of Nelson and Winter (1982). The second, considered in the following section, is chaos theory.

The preoccupation of economic theorists with equilibrium analysis has long been an object of criticism. However, few of the critics have been able to offer an operational substitute (or, as I prefer to think of it, an operational and complementary approach). In their valuable book Nelson and Winter have proposed that a fruitful alternative can be found in dynamic models, much of whose interest lies in their ability to provide rigorous descriptions of the process of transition toward an equilibrium target that may in fact never actually be attained. If that target continues to shift, the nature of the transition path may encompass most of what is really of interest in the formal analysis. Formal dynamics provides just the instrument that is needed for an analysis of such a transition, during which disequilibrium prevails. As we have seen, where a formal solution such as equation (2) is available it tells us just how matters can be expected to evolve during the interim periods between the start of the process (or of our observation of that process) and its entry into a narrow neighborhood of the equilibrium toward which it is tending.

Nelson and Winter use such tools to examine a number of crucial topics, among them the processes of investment and innovation. More recently, research along these lines has been carried on in the very stimulating work of Amendola and Gaffard (1987), which sheds considerable new light on the nature of innovation and technical change. Now, there are two reasons driving this approach away from the more formalistic procedures of economic dynamics and toward Lundberg's numerical techniques encapsulated in Table 1. First, as we have seen, formal solution techniques are really powerful only in the linear case, and the assumption that evolutionary processes are inherently linear strains the imagination. As the next section will show, adoption of this premise in circumstances where it does not hold can have consequences that are far from minor.

Perhaps even more important, as it was in Lundberg's case, the concern of formal evolutionary theory is largely not with the nature of the equilibrium itself (if any such exists) but rather with the course of the events that are likely to be encountered along the way. However, to study this, a formal solution may prove to be too compact an instrument, concealing details that from other points of view may be considered to constitute distracting redundancies. A step by step numerical calculation may then be the best means to bring such details back to the surface, where they can readily be observed and discussed. That explains the reversion of Amendola and Gaffard to the procedures Professor Lundberg laid out so effectively some fifty years earlier. And the results fully justify the procedure. It permits enormous enrichment of the discursive comments that accompany the formal analysis, while sacrificing none of the rigor of the discussion.

It is not appropriate here to undertake any sort of summary of the results of the work that has been the subject of this section. This is so because those results consist to a considerable degree of subtle insights rather than any general theorems. The reader is urged, rather, to examine these writings for himself or herself. The point of this section, rather, has been to draw attention to the longevity and continuing fruitfulness of the Lundbergian approach, and this, I trust, it has succeeded in doing.

A few words on chaos theory

Chaos theory is a second line of dynamic analysis that has recently attracted attention in economics (as well as biology, meteorology, and a number of other disciplines). It is of interest to us here primarily because of that fact that, while its literature has employed a good deal of sophisticated and even esoteric mathematics, it has also made effective use of the more direct approach provided by Professor Lundberg's work.

In essence, the technical term "chaos" refers to a nonlinear but perfectly deterministic (nonstochastic) process that generates a time path of its variables which can appear to be beset by randomness of rather extreme proportions. A chaotic time path is, then, deterministic, but it is characterized by behavior that can be sufficiently complex (even bizarre) to enable it nevertheless to pass most of the standard tests of randomness. In addition, chaotic time paths can display extreme sensitivity to changes in initial conditions, or in the values of any of the parameters, with changes, say, in the fifth decimal place of one of these values leading to a modification in the time path that transforms it beyond any resemblance to its former state.

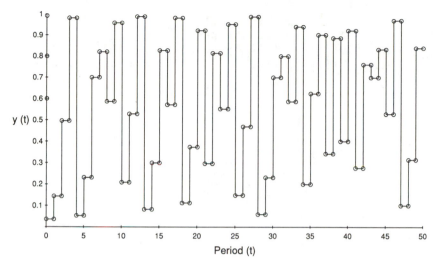

Figure 1. Time path, periods 0–50, $y(t + 1) = 3.935y(t)[1 - y(t)]$, $y(0) = 0.99$.

Yet such complex behavior can be generated by the simplest of non-linear models. For instance the quadratic equation

$$y(t + 1) = ky(t) - K[y(t)]^2 \qquad (11)$$

is a standard example of such a relationship. All of this is illustrated in Figures 1 and 2. Figure 1 is the graph of $y(t)$ given by difference equation (11) when $k = 3.935$ and $y(0) = 0.99$. In contrast, Figure 2 represents the corresponding time path generated by an unchanged initial value and a value of k modified from that in Figure 1 in only the third decimal place, so that now $k = 3.94$ rather than 3.935, as before. Yet we see that the two graphs bear virtually no resemblance to each other.

The main point to be noted so far is that the difference equation that generated the chaotic time path is neither esoteric nor pathological. It involves nonlinearity of the simplest variety, though more complex equations are easily shown to be capable of yielding very similar results. Many plausible economic models satisfying such relationships have already appeared in the literature. Yet, we have been able to generate a time path with the aid of such an equation, which may well preclude any possibility of structural econometric estimation of any degree of reliability. For no one, surely, expects to find economic data sufficiently accurate to permit estimates of parameters whose third decimal place

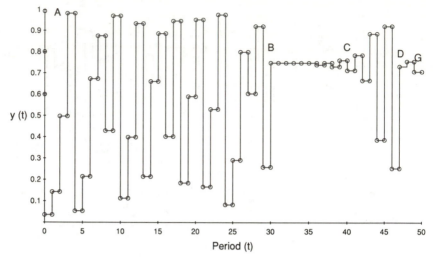

Figure 2. Time path, periods 0–50, $y(t + 1) = 3.94y(t)[1 - y(t)]$, $y(0) = 0.99$.

inspires any degree of confidence. Yet even errors far smaller than that can lead to large qualitative distortions in a chaotic time path.

This same attribute – sensitivity to extremely small changes in parameter values – also means that any economic process characterized by chaotic properties may well be subject to large perturbations elicited by extremely modest changes in the attendant circumstances.

Figure 2 also illustrates a third sort of problem to which chaos can easily give rise: sharp and unforeseeable breaks in the character of the time path. We see from the graph that for about twenty-five periods the time path is characterized by cycles of fairly constant amplitude. Yet this era comes to an abrupt end and is followed by some ten periods of virtually perfect stability. Then, almost as abruptly as before, the interval of near stationary behavior ceases in its turn. The resulting impediment to forecasting by extrapolation hardly needs to be spelled out.

It is appropriate for me here to evade the task of spelling out the reasons why a difference equation model such as (11) can generate complicated time paths like that illustrated in Figure 2. I will only note that such an explanation, while it does require a bit lengthier discussion, is by no means difficult or even beyond intuitive grasp [see, for example, the classic discussion in May (1976); for explanatory material with economic illustrations, see Baumol and Benhabib (1989)].

But how is any of this related to Lundberg's work? The answer is that the complexities of chaos analysis have sometimes forced those who work on the subject to return to more straightforward investigative techniques in order to avoid being overwhelmed by complications from both directions – both in the materials being studied and the means being used to study them. As a result, the Lundberg approach has indeed been invoked in the literature of chaos.

Once again, Figures 1 and 2 provide a direct illustration, for these graphs have been constructed in exactly the same way as Lundberg produced his diagrams and tables in 1937. True, Figures 1 and 2 encompass fifty periods rather than Lundberg's ten, and the graphs here have been drawn by the same computer that so readily carried out the iterative calculations and could with little trouble have extended them for many more periods. Yet other than that, nothing new has been added to the procedure. *Plus ca change, plus c'est la même chose.*

Concluding comment

The discussion of this paper has by necessity confined itself to only a single part of Professor Lundberg's work – indeed, only to a single chapter of one of his books. Yet in even so small a compass it has been possible to show what a major contribution his writings have made. Our profession has ample reason for gratitude to him, and I perhaps even more than most others, for so much of my own work has built upon things that I learned from him. As a matter of fact, the lines of Professor Lundberg's inquiry that I have chosen to emphasize here have been precisely those in which my debt is greatest. In a sense, then, this paper is intended as a small step toward amortization of that heavy obligation.

Notes

1 The author is extremely thankful to the C. V. Starr Center for Applied Economics for its assistance in the preparation of this paper. Above all, I am grateful to the organizers of this conference for giving me the opportunity to acknowledge my tremendous debt to Erik Lundberg.

2 To derive equation (9) we note that it is the same as equation (8) if

$$D_{ct} + D_{It} = aE_{t-1} + a(1 + k)(E_{t-1} - E_{t-2}) \qquad (10)$$

Now by equations (3) and (7), $D_{ct} = aE_{t-1}$. By equations (4), (5), (6), and (7), $D_{It} = aI_t = akE_{t-1} - akE_{t-1} = akE_{t-1} - akE_{t-2} + a(E_{t-1} - E_{t-2})$, or $D_{It} = a(1 + k)(E_{t-1} - E_{t-2})$. From the preceding expressions for D_{ct} and D_{It}, equation (10) and, hence, equation (9) follow at once.

3 This observation may perhaps appear inconsistent with the very limited number of qualitatively different time paths that linear models can generate and

may seem to suggest that there is not much room for an inaccuracy in one's model to make a great deal of difference. However, we cannot limit our concern to linear models. Moreover, it remains true that even the time paths generated by linear models can be extremely sensitive to variations in parameter values and that very small changes in those values, however defined, can transform a time path derived via a linear model from one of the four basic qualitative types to another.

References

Amendola, Mario, and Gaffard, Jean-Luc (1988), *The Innovative Choice.* Oxford and New York: Basil Blackwell.

Baumol, W. J.: (1957), "Speculation, Profitability and Stability," *Review of Economics and Statistics,* 39 (August), 263–71.

(1961), "Pitfalls in Contracyclical Policies: Some Tools and Results," *Review of Economics and Statistics,* 43 (February), 21–6.

Baumol, W. J., and Jess Benhabib (1989), "Chaos: Significance, Mechanism, and Economic Applications," *Journal of Economic Perspectives*, 3, No. 1 (Winter), 77–105.

Frisch, Ragnar (1933), "Propagation Problems and Impulse Problems in Dynamic Economics," in *Economic Essays in Honour of Gustav Cassel.* London: Allen & Unwin, pp. 171–205.

Lundberg, Erik (1964), *Studies in the Theory of Economic Expansion.* Reprints of Economic Classics. New York: A. M. Kelly.

May, Robert (1976), "Simple Mathematical Models with Very Complicated Dynamics," *Nature,* 261 (June), 459–67.

Nelson, R. R., and S. Winter (1982), *An Evolutionary Theory of Economic Change.* Cambridge, Mass.: The Belknap Press.

Samuelson, Paul A. (1947), *Foundations of Economic Analysis.* Cambridge, Mass.: Harvard University Press.

Comment

BJÖRN THALBERG

In his paper, Baumol takes up the cudgels for the method of constructing an analysis based on numerical examples (using relevant values for the parameters of the dynamic equations). Numerical examples played an important role in theoretical economics in the early days, notably in the powerful writings of the classical economists Ricardo, Malthus, and Marx. Graphical and algebraic methods have subsequently dominated the field, permitting more general conclusions. For some time, reasoning from numerical examples has tended to be downgraded by conventional and occasionally arrogant critics who have degraded works in which the author did not deal with his model by analytical methods. However, why should one refrain from the possibility of gaining insight into the workings and results of a model for which we are unable to write down the general analytical solution? The question becomes, as Baumol stresses, all the more important at a time when computers greatly facilitate numerical explorations.

In the first part of his paper, Baumol describes and assesses, in an illuminative way, the "Lundberg approach" to dynamic analysis, that is, reasoning from numerical examples. In the two last sections on recent developments in economic dynamics and chaos theory, we learn how modern researchers revert to the step by step numerical calculation procedure laid out by Lundberg some fifty years ago. I find all this very interesting. My only critical comments concern the section "What Dynamic Models Can and Cannot be Expected to Accomplish."

In this section, Baumol builds strongly on the possibility that the time path generated by a dynamic model can be extremely sensitive to changes in the specification of the model or in the values of the parameters. Because of this possibility, he downgrades the usefulness of dynamic models as a reliable device for forecasting and predictions. Their usefulness, he maintains, rather lies in an ability to generate counterexamples to propositions on the effects of certain policies, or more generally to provide examples which assert that so and so *can* happen.

It is, generally, of course, a fact that time paths generated by a model can be extremely sensitive to variations in parameter values both in the linear and even more so in the nonlinear case. Moreover, stochastic disturbances imposed on the behavior equations may increase the possibilities of "extreme sensitivity" (in Baumol's sense). We do find economic studies where the "extreme sensitivity" possibility plays an essential role per se in the analysis, an example (besides chaos theory) being the study of Haavelmo (1954) of long-term evolutionary dissimilarities between regions. However, in relation to the present discussion it is, I think, pertinent to note that in most short- and medium-term analyses, the economic system in question is assumed to be stable. Only stable equilibria are, we feel, empirically interesting. Schumpeter and Frisch, among others, certainly believed that our economic system is essentially stable. Samuelson's correspondence principle builds on the same idea. One may even recall Marshall's dictum that "in the economic world, Natura non facit saltum" (Marshall 1920, p. 249).

For this reason, our economic models are, it may be argued, very often constructed so as to avoid "extreme sensibility" in Baumol's sense, that is, to make them relatively robust to marginal changes in model specification and parameter values (within the area of plausible values). For example, in the field of business cycle theory, nonlinearities are, as a rule, introduced as a kind of (capacity) "ceiling" or "floor," which assure that the time paths of the variables are kept within certain limits. Thus, instead of increasing the possibilities of "extreme sensibility," such nonlinearities tend to reduce them. Moreover, since we observe that the major economic variables move together over the cycle, a realistic model of the propagation mechanism must "knit" them pretty firmly together (if not, the timepaths of the variables may diverge sharply in the disturbed solutions), another fact that may tend to reduce the possibilities of "extreme sensitivity."

If the outcomes of dynamic models are, as a rule, severely sensitive to marginal changes (in Baumol's sense), analyses by means of numerical examples may after all not be reasonably reliable and efficient. The examples that we happen to have chosen may easily be insufficient to reveal the multiplicity and complexity of the set of (plausible) solutions. However, if our dynamic models are on the whole fairly robust to marginal changes, as I think they very often are, the method of reasoning from numerical examples seems relatively efficient. Consequently, Baumol's claim that their usefulness mainly consists in their ability to provide counterexamples or propositions, which assert that so and so *can* happen, seems exaggerated.

References

Haavelmo, T. (1954), *A Study in the Theory of Economic Evolution.* Amsterdam: North Holland.
Marshall, A. (1920), *Principles of Economics,* 8th edition. London: Macmillan.

Comment

KUMARASWAMY VELUPILLAI

The chaotic attractor of mathematical theory began with Birkhoff in 1916. The chaotic attractor of simulation experiment arrived with Lorenz in 1962. *The identification of these two objects has not yet succeeded,* despite many attempts during the past twenty years. Of course, everyone (including myself) expects this to happen soon. (Abraham, 1985, p. 117; italics added)

Professor Baumol has written a characteristically lucid paper that is both interesting and informative. In the limited space available I can only attempt to comment on a few of the many stimulating points he has taken up on the basis of a thorough study of Lundberg's classic doctoral dissertation.

Baumol's main points seem to be the following: in formal dynamic analysis (especially in economics, but not exclusively so, say, from Frisch and Le Corbeiller up to recent applications of dynamical systems theory) the lessons to be learned are (i) the importance of being nonlinear; (ii) the desirability of inductive generalizations on the basis of numerical simulation "experiments"; (iii) the emptiness – indeed the danger – of formal solutions of the existence-uniqueness variety. Baumol substantiates his case with a variety of useful examples and concepts ranging from structural stability and sensitive dependence on initial conditions in mathematics to evolutionary processes and business cycle models in economics. The canonical examples he has utilized are a version of a Lundbergian model of cyclical behavior and the famous quadratic map.

In the presence of nonlinearities the richness of the lessons that can be learned from numerical investigations of sequential or recursive models is matched only by their extraordinary complexity. This message is clearly brought out in illuminating ways. It must be remembered that a study of difference equations, in the sense advocated here by Baumol, means going from recursive definitions to their corresponding algebraic definitions on the basis of numerical "sequence analysis." That this is often almost impossible can be seen from the classic example of the Fibonacci sequence.[1]

The quadratic map, now a part of the folklore of the mathematics of dynamical systems, is the example chosen by Baumol to drive home his important messages (i.e., i–iii, above). In Baumol's notation the map is given by:

$$y(t + 1) = ky(t)[1 - y(t)] \tag{1}$$

Now a striking feature of the two figures for $k = 3.935$ and $k = 3.94$ seems to be the following:

$$\text{If} \quad y(t + 1) - y(t) < 0$$
$$\text{then} \quad y(t + 2) - y(t + 1) > 0 \tag{2}$$

Phase reversals do not last more than one period! Elementary manipulations of equation (1) leads to the equivalent condition:

$$\{[y(t)]^2 - [y(t + 1)]^2\} - [y(t) - y(t + 1)] > 0 \tag{3}$$

Since phase reversals occur at values of $y(t + 1)$ to the "right" of the nontrivial fix point (and $k > 3$), even a visual inspection of the intersection of the 45° line with the quadratic map would be sufficient as an heuristic "test for randomness"! Even although it would be interesting to work out the analytical ramifications of these heuristic observations, I refrain from doing so on account of space and in view of the spirit in which Baumol has written his paper.

An even more telling point (especially to bolster point iii) can be made against the dangers of naive use of formal analysis by using equation (1) for $k = 4$ in conjunction with Ulam's transformation:

$$y(t) = \sin^2 \pi X(t) \tag{4}$$

(It must be remembered that Baumol implicitly assumes the mapping of the unit interval into itself.) Then, at $k = 4$, we have from equations (1) and (4):

$$X(t + 1) = 2X(t) \quad [\bmod 1] \tag{5}$$

Ostensibly, the analytic solution of equation (5) may be written as:

$$X(t) = 2^t X(0) \quad [\bmod 1] \tag{6}$$

Assuming (especially in view of numerical experiments using digital computers) a representation of the initial condition and the ensuing sequence in terms of binary numbers, it can be seen that each initial condition is of the form, say:

$$X(0) = 0.1110010 \ldots \tag{7}$$

The "future" iterates of equation (7) are given by shifting the binary point to the right and dropping the integer part. Now what would be the meaning of "existence-uniqueness," "analytic solutions," and all the rest of the paraphernalia of formal analysis? These almost metaphysical concepts are meaningful whenever the initial conditions can be specified (accurately). If, however, we regard the digit string [equation (7)] as the representation of coin-tossing sequences where $H = 1$ and $T = 0$, then the set of all $X(0)$ digit strings on the unit interval may be regarded as being identical with the set of all possible random coin tossing sequences!

Quite apart from this paradoxical conflation of "randomness" in a simple deterministic model, there is the even more serious problem of interpreting the usefulness of mathematical concepts like *genericity.*

The examples of the desirability of structural stability given by Baumol (e.g., note 2) have resulted in the need to define "typical behavior" in dynamical systems. Andronov and Pontryagin began this line of research in 1936, and, in the hands of Smale and the disciples of the late Kolmogorov, it has resulted in a study of *generic* behavior.

If, now, *generic* is defined to mean a Baire set, and, as in our example, the possible values of $X(t)$ lie on the unit interval, then the subset of irrationals is the *generic* set. But how does one accurately specify, for a digital computer, an initial $X(0)$ that is irrational? Only the rationals can be precisely specified for digital use [cf. Hirsch (1985) and Jensen (1987) for a lucid discussion of these issues]. The need for models that are not too sensitive to numerical specifications, although almost obvious, is absolutely crucial.

For values of $k > 4$ the iterations given by equation (1) imply that some points $y(t)$ expand out of the unit interval. The finesse in *chaos* analysis is the attempt to study the structure of those points that remain "inside" the unit interval, in the long run. Such residual sets are *Cantor sets,* which also implies *self-similarity* and *fractal* dimension. Therefore I may be permitted to close with some "Swedish Remembrances"!

One of the first, most interesting and, indeed, loveliest fractals is the Koch curve, named after the Swedish mathematician Helge von Koch (the fractal-Hausdorff dimension of the Koch curve is approximately 1.26). It may be a less known fact that Gustav Cassel was the "third opponent" for Koch's dissertation on infinite determinants.[2]

Cassel himself wrote his dissertation on the theory of automorphic functions (Cassel, 1894). The theory of automorphic functions was single-handedly created by Poincaré (who called them *Fuchsian* functions). These concerns were instrumental in Poincaré taking up the challenge offered by the *n*-body problem. King Oscar II of Sweden had instituted, exactly one hundred years ago, in 1887 (at the suggestion of Mittag-Leffler, the teacher of both von Koch and Cassel) a prize for the solution of the *n*-body problem. Poincaré received the prize for his great efforts contributing to an analysis of the special case $n = 3$. It was the near impossibility of a quantitative approach to these problems that made Poincaré define the whole new fields of global analysis and qualitative dynamics – crucial stepping stones towards the dynamics of chaos, strange attractors, and bifurcation theory. His last results on these topics (especially on periodic behavior) were achieved in 1912, the year of his death. These were taken up and studied with great vigor and rigor by the elder Birkhoff, the first student of the mathematics of chaos. We seem to have come full circle in the romance of mathematics and Swedish economics.

Notes

1 The recursive definition is $f(0) = 1; f(1) = 1; f(x + 2) = f(x + 1) + f(x)$. The numerical sequence is $1,1,2,3,5,8,13,21,34, \ldots$. The algebraic definition is

$$f(x) = \frac{\sqrt{5}}{5} \frac{(1 + \sqrt{5})^{x+1}}{2} - \frac{\sqrt{5}}{5} \frac{(1 - \sqrt{5})^{x+1}}{2}$$

(cf. Rogers, 1967).

2 Although it may not be appropriate to mention personal stories in a supposedly scholarly (!) paper, it is interesting to note that Cassel was once engaged to be married to von Koch's sister. Many years later Helge von Koch's son, Fabian, was an important member of the *oral* tradition of the Stockholm School [cf. Giöbel-Lilja (1948) and Myrdal (1956)].

References

Abraham, Ralph (1985), "Is There Chaos without Noise?" in P. Fischer and William R. Smith, eds., *Chaos, Fractals and Dynamics.* Basel: Marcel Dekker.

Cassel, Gustav (1894), *Kritiska studier öfver teorin för de automorfa funktionerna.* Dissertation, Uppsala.

Giöbel-Lilja, Ingrid (1948), *Gustav Cassel: En livsskildring.* Stockholm: Bokförlaget Natur och Kultur.

Hirsch, Morris W. (1985), "The Chaos of Dynamical Systems," in P. Fischer and William R. Smith, eds., *Chaos, Fractals and Dynamics.* Basel: Marcel Dekker.

Jensen, Roderick V. (1987), "Classical Chaos," *The American Scientist,* 75 (No. 2, March–April), 168–81.

Myrdal, Gunnar (1956), *Value in Social Theory: A Selection of Essays on Methodology.* London: Routledge and Kegan Paul.

Rogers, Hartley, Jr. (1967), *Theory of Recursive Functions and Effective Computability.* New York: McGraw-Hill.

CHAPTER 8

Lundberg, Keynes, and the riddles of a general theory

CLAES BERG[1]

One straightforward way for a scientist to achieve fame and immortality is to get his name associated with a concept widely used in his science. The late Erik Lundberg meets this qualification by having given name to the "Lundberg lag," reflecting the time it takes to adjust output to a change in sales. This output lag is found in Lundberg's dissertation, *Studies in the Theory of Economic Expansion* (1937). What is not so well known is that this hardly readable classic work of the Stockholm School also contains at least three important contributions to the dynamics of economics: the multiplier-accelerator, the Harrod-Domar growth model, and the inflationary gap in a multiperiod setting.

Here I will examine the way in which *Studies in the Theory of Economic Expansion* can be seen as a complement to John Maynard Keynes's *General Theory* (1936). The analysis focuses on how Lundberg connects John M. Clark's (1917) investment accelerator with the Keynesian multiplier of efficient demand, using the Lundberg output lag.

William J. Baumol, in a contribution in this volume, is not the first to point to the advantages of Lundberg's dynamic methods. In fact, Joseph Schumpeter (1954, p. 1174), in his *History of Economic Analysis,* gave credit to Lundberg's thesis in the following way: "it displays the micro- and macrodynamic roots of current Keynesianism much better than did Keynes himself." This statement raises two questions: First, what is there to be found in Lundberg's *Studies* but not in the *General Theory?* Second, why did Lundberg's dissertation fail to achieve international attention?

Claes-Henric Siven (1985) has tried to answer the second question, but no one seems to have tried to answer the first one. The reason might be that period analysis of the Stockholm School, in which Lundberg excels, is quite simply hard to read. But, as I will suggest, the reason also might be that Lundberg's main results were absorbed and developed by other economists, for example, Paul Samuelson (1939), J. M. Keynes (1940), Lloyd A. Metzler (1941), Roy F. Harrod (1939), and Evsey Domar (1946).

Lundberg's main contribution was to formalize the equations that characterize the movements of an economic system in a more general way than Keynes had done in his rather static analysis of a recession in the *General Theory*. But Lundberg never tried to find the general solutions of his equations. He was studying specific cases and outcomes of his models, and it is this feature that makes his dissertation so hard to read.

Solving the difference equations of Lundberg's model when equipped with a computer, it becomes possible to reformulate the main chapter (Chapter IX) of his dissertation in two ways. First, I will analyze the general solutions of the models in *Studies* and compare them with the works of Keynes. Second, I will study specific cases and analyze the shortcomings of Lundberg's work. One major finding is the second sequence in Chapter IX where Lundberg allows time to be divided into unit periods, the length of which is determined by the Lundberg output lag. Output decisions are assumed to be guided by the sales experience of the recent past. Hence production for sale in any unit is equal to the amount sold in the preceding period. Any divergence of actual sales from the businessmen's best guesses results in an unplanned positive change in inventories. Lundberg is thereby the first to introduce a formalized dynamic mechanism into Keynes's system, explaining the possibility of the business cycle generated by the multiplier and the accelerator. However, as Lundberg never recognized the possibility of disinvestment in the downward swing, his model is not a complete one. Another important finding is the appearance of the Harrod growth model, worked out in continuous time, and a period analysis version of the Domar model presented in footnotes to Lundberg's Chapter IX.

1   Influences and preludes

1.1   *Wicksell*

In the preface to his *Studies,* Lundberg (1937, p. vi) stated: "Keynes's theories are examined here from the point of view of the traditional methods of approach inaugurated by Wicksell." Clearly, this indicates that Lundberg considered the works of Knut Wicksell [in this case the Wicksell (1898) *Interest and Prices* model of full employment in the presence of a modern banking system] and J. M. Keynes to be complementary to each other. Actually, Wicksell extended the interest theory of Böhm-Bawerk and defined two interest rates: the natural or normal interest rate, determined by the technical productivity of an investment, and the nominal interest rate of the banking system. If the interest rate of the banking system is maintained below the normal rate of interest, entrepreneurs then expect profits and expand their production. They borrow from the banks. However, as Wicksell started out from a situation of full employment, this only results in increasing factor incomes, which in turn bids up prices and leads to the absorption of the expected profits. This process of rising prices will continue as long as the normal interest rate is kept below the interest rate of the bank. Extending the analysis presented in *Interest and Prices,* Lundberg dropped the assumption of full employment. He also tried to explain the actions of the central bank by letting the interest rate of the banking system influence the natural rate of interest and changes in the price level.

1.2   *Hayek*

While Wicksell concentrated on the cumulative development of prices, Friedrich A. Hayek (1931) extended the analysis of how quantities change as the interest rate is maintained below the natural interest rate. As capitalists borrow and expand production, marginal productivity increases more in the capital-intensive industries than in other branches. Rising wages encourage workers to leave the consumer goods industry, and the supply of consumer goods diminishes as prices rise. A continuing upswing in business activity necessitates increasing credits to the capital goods industry, which implies forced saving by consumers. An expansion of production maintained by forced saving cannot go on forever. [This is a main thesis of Hayek (1931, p. 135).] As soon as credit to the capital goods industry stops rising, the process will be reversed. Prices of consumer goods increase relative to prices of capital goods. As the interest rate of the banking system exceeds the natural rate of interest, investments start falling. A crisis due to a lack of savings is a fact when unfinished projects are abandoned and unemployment rises.

Lundberg criticized Hayek on one point. Hayek tried to link changes in income with changes in capital. According to Lundberg (1937, p. 31), it is impossible to include capital as a variable in an equilibrium system. On the other hand, according to Lundberg, Hayek's theory can explain the type of recession in which a lack of saving is the independent variable, in contrast to the Keynesian model in which a lack of demand is causing the slump.

1.3   *Keynes*

I do not intend to analyze in depth the influence of Keynes on Lundberg's *Studies*. First, Lundberg was building on two different books by Keynes, *A Treatise On Money* (1930) and the *General Theory* (1936). Second, Lundberg (1960, p. 198) has shown that the important Chapter IX of his dissertation was written without prior knowledge of the *General Theory*. Third, many Keynesian features of the *Studies* might be the result of the discussions with the neo-Wicksellians of the inner circle of the Stockholm School, such as Gunnar Myrdal, who as early as 1932 gave a concrete example of how the export multiplier works.

Assuming that Keynes's *General Theory* is an equilibrium analysis of an economy with persistent unemployment, Lundberg stressed the absence of an explanation of how the adjustment to unemployment is taking place. As he criticized the Keynesian assumptions of a constant multiplier and a given volume of investment, Lundberg was pursuing the idea that these variables are changing as the process develops in a dynamic setting. Further, Lundberg claimed that in the *General Theory* Keynes mistakingly included windfall profits or losses in gross saving. This means that the propensity to consume is not given a place of its own. Instead, Lundberg prefers Keynes's analysis in the *Treatise,* where saving and investment are separated and windfall profits are excluded from savings. Nor did Lundberg accept the determination of interest rates in the *General Theory.* In the long run, one cannot accept an exogenously given money stock. Lundberg preferred the classical analysis, using the demand for and the supply of bank credit.

1.4   *Other influences*

Gustav Cassel's (1918) model of economic growth is an obvious source of inspiration for one of Lundberg's sequences, but it is almost impossible to trace the influences of the economists of the Stockholm School on Lundberg's *Studies,* as is evident from the following quotation:

> My choice of theories has primarily been governed by the discussions amongst Swedish economists during the last decade on issues raised by Knut Wicksell in his monetary theories. His concepts and methods have since been developed and the problems he investigated brought into closer relation to economic policy. I have profited by these discussions to a much greater extent than is apparent by the bare references made to the works of these economists. (Lundberg, 1937, p. vi)

Here, however, I must confine myself to those authors whose sequence analyses are surveyed by Lundberg in Chapter III: Alf Johansson (1934) and Dag Hammarskjöld (1933). In the same chapter Dennis H. Robertson's condition for an even expansion is analyzed and is given credit:

> Robertson shows how the more microscopic view upon economic events, given by a very short unit-period, makes a greater differentiation of concepts possible: the payments of an income and the use of it are placed in different periods. In this way a differentiation of savings and investment activities appears, which is blurred in Keynes' "macroscopic" analysis. (Lundberg, 1937, p. 67)

Summarizing his views on the credit cycle models of Wicksell, Keynes, Robertson, Johansson, and Hammarskjöld, Lundberg (1937, p. 87) made the following statement:

> The types of sequences vary according to the selection of conditions and variables, as well as time discrepancies. On the other hand, all the theories considered have this in common, that they do not include variations in savings and investment in fixed capital.

2   The period analysis

In Chapter IX, which is the centerpiece of the *Studies*, sequences in five different settings are presented:

1. Expansion of the production of consumer goods at a constant volume of investment
2. Expansion determined by investment in working capital
3. Expansion determined by investment in fixed capital
4. The influence of a variable rate of interest
5. Expansion determined by a rationalization process

For each group the exposition is exemplified by one or more sequences showing the development of savings, investments, total receipts, and so on. As Lundberg never tried to find the general solutions of the systems of equations, his sequences can be regarded as special cases, lacking a discussion of the stability of the general processes. The periods are based on theory, rather than on empirical tests. Lundberg emphasized that it is dangerous to draw conclusions for economic policy from his models. I will present Lundberg's equations and sequences associated with three groups (2–4). Analyzing the general solutions of the systems, it is possible to discuss the stability of the sequences. Equipped with a computer, I also find it worthwhile to reexamine Lundberg's special cases.

Lundberg studies an economic system in an expansion phase. Production, consumption, income, savings, and investment are growing, and the main question posed is whether these variables will continue to rise or whether automatic mechanisms will interrupt the process. The general presumptions are the following. His definition of unit-period was expressed in terms of a reaction interval that measured the average distance between the rise in demand and the subsequent increase in production activity (e.g., the Lundberg output lag). Prices are supposed to be constant.[2] Only part of the costs of production generate income. There are two types of investments: autonomous investments, which are constant, and induced investments, which vary with receipts. The induced investments cannot be negative. This gives rise to important consequences presumably overlooked by Metzler (1941).

2.1   *Expansion of the production of consumer goods at a constant volume of investment*

The period analysis of the first group shows how a Keynesian equilibrium is attained when the volume of investment is constant. On the basis of realized receipts in period t, enterprises determine their production and induced investments in period $t + 1$. They presume that the income in period t will be the same in period $t + 1$. As prices are assumed to be constant, the costs of production in period $t + 1$ are the same as the receipts in period t.

Lundberg established three equations describing the evolution of expenditure on consumer goods output, disposable income, and total business expenditure on the production of consumer goods. He did not solve the system and its difference equation but found that the equilibrium value appears after seventeen iterations.

It is easy to show that the limit of Lundberg's sequence takes the same value as the ordinary Keynesian multiplier. The conclusion is obvious. If the volume of investment is constant, then there is a stable equilibrium, and Lundberg's contribution was to show how this equilibrium is attained.

2.2   *Expansion determined by investment in working capital*

In the second group, Lundberg introduced inventory investments and reached interesting results. I will use the following symbols:

t = period t
E_t = expenditure on output of consumer goods
D_{ct} = disposable income derived from the output of consumption goods

C_t = total business expenditure on the production of consumption goods

S_t = saving

K = autonomous investment in consumer goods inventory

c = marginal propensity to consume

a = ratio of disposable income to C_t (and I_t)

I_t = investment in working capital (inventories)

D_{it} = income generated by investment in working capital

D_t = total disposable income

K_t = stock of working capital

k = desired ratio of working capital to output of consumption goods

The enterprises are supposed to maintain a certain relation between the buildup of inventories and production:

$$kE_{t-1} = kC_t \tag{1}$$

$$I_t = kC_t - K_{t-1} \tag{2}$$

At the same time, inventories at the end of period $t - 1$ equal the planned volume of investment minus the difference between the demand for consumer goods *ex ante* and the demand *ex post*:

$$K_{t-1} = kC_{t-1} - (E_{t-1} - C_{t-1}) \tag{3}$$

The second sequence is given by the following equations:

$$D_{ct} = aC_t \tag{4}$$

$$I_t = kC_t - K_{t-1} \tag{5}$$

$$K_t = (1 + k)C_t - E_t \tag{6}$$

$$D_{it} = aI_t \tag{7}$$

$$E_t = c(D_{ct} + D_{it}) + K \tag{8}$$

$$C_t = E_{t-1} \tag{9}$$

Solving the system one gets

$$E_t = ca[(2 + k)E_{t-1} - (1 + k)E_{t-2}] + K \qquad \text{when } I_t > 0 \tag{10a}$$

The investment can be written as:

$$I_t = (1 + k)(E_{t-1} - E_{t-2}) \tag{11}$$

This means that as soon as the receipts in period $t - 1$ fall below the receipts in period $t - 2$ the investments would become negative. Lund-

Table 1. *Expansion determined by investment in working capital*
$E_0 = 1,000; K = 300; c = 0.9; a = 0.8; k = 0.5$

Period t	Investments I_t	Savings S_t	Expenditures E_t
1	0.0	80.0	1,020.0
2	30.0	84.0	1,056.0
3	54.0	88.8	1,099.2
4	64.8	93.1	1,138.1
5	58.3	95.7	1,161.4
6	35.0	95.7	1,161.4
7	0.0	92.9	1,136.2
8	0.0	90.9	1,118.1
9	0.0	89.4	1,105.0
$\vdots$			
25	0.0	85.7	1,071.6

berg did not allow this to happen. In such cases he set $I_t = 0$. Thus, equation (10a) has to be rewritten for $I_t \leq 0$:

$$E_t = caE_{t-1} + K \tag{10b}$$

Lundberg gave an example of a sequence based on certain assumptions regarding the values of E_0, K, c, a, and k.

A stable equilibrium is attained after twenty-five periods, as shown in Table 1. Metzler (1941, p. 124) pointed out that with Lundberg's assumptions the development of the sequence would instead be an explosive one. I find that this remark is justified. With the values assumed by Lundberg, the solution of equation (10a) turns out to be of a type with imaginary roots and explosive oscillations. Why did Lundberg fail to see this? Was it because he was not able to solve difference equations of a second order as Metzler supposes? No, as far as I can see Metzler did not understand all of Lundberg's assumptions. Specifically, the development of the sequence is determined by the assumption of non-negative inventory investments. Equation (10a) is replaced by (10b) when $E_{t-1} < E_{t-2}$. Equation (10b) is of the same type as the one in the first group, which converges to a stable equilibrium when $0 < ca < 1$.

What then is the significance of Lundberg's second sequence? To my knowledge, we have traced the first example of a formalized combined multiplier-accelerator principle.[3] Assuming variable inventory investments, Lundberg clearly reached further than Keynes did (in the *General Theory*). But there are at least two important deficiencies in Lundberg's inventory model. The first deficiency has already been mentioned; neglect of the possibility of disinvestment in the downward swing. This deficiency is probably not due to the fact that Lundberg did not know how to handle second-order difference equations. The second type of sequence is just one in a row of five increasingly complicated sequences. The central section of Chapter IX seems to be the third and fourth sequences, where Lundberg developed a model with variable investments in the housing sector. In this model, it might be appropriate to allow investment to be non-negative, to avoid the case of demolishing houses (he supposed that only a constant sum goes to replace old houses). Lundberg's main interest was to study the phase of expansion and the causes leading to its termination. He was not really pursuing his investigation to find out everything about what could happen after the peak. The second deficiency is the neglect of considering goods in process (e.g., pipeline inventories), as pointed out by Nurkse.[4]

2.3   *Expansion determined by investment in fixed capital*

In the third group Lundberg studied the expansion of fixed capital. As an example he investigated a special type of capital goods: residential housing. The following symbols will be used:

E_t = expenditure on output of consumer goods

D_{ct} = disposable income derived from the output of consumer goods

I_t = induced investment in housing

D_{ht} = income from owning houses

D_t = total income

G_{ct} = income spent on consumer goods

G_t = total rents

S_t = saving

S_{bt} = gross saving

K = autonomous investment in consumer's goods inventory

$I_{bt} = I_t + K$ = gross investment

c = marginal propensity to consume

a = ratio of disposable income to C_t (and I_t)

b = percentage of total receipts in one period that does not induce income in the next period

m = the quotient between income from building residential houses and the expected rents

s = rents as a percentage of total consumer outlays

h = fixed portion of consumer's expenses for dwellings that does not become income during the following period

According to Lundberg's assumptions, I_{t+1} is determined by the increase in requirements of tenements during the preceding period:

$$I_{t+1} = m(G_t - G_{t-1}) \tag{12}$$

When new building activity attains the volume given by equation (12), the increased demand that appeared during period t will be satisfied at the end of period $t + 1$. But during period $t + 1$, conditions have changed, partly because of the new building investment, and an unsatisfied demand for tenements may again turn up during period $t + 1$. Lundberg analyzed a model sequence where the size of new investments is determined by such a variability in building activity. He took into consideration that a portion of the consumer's total expenses goes to payments for rents, a sum not supposed to be tranformed into income during the next period to the same extent as other receipts (expenses). Building activity is treated separately because of its character of long-term investment. Amortizations on newly built houses become only income by means of new investments. Lundberg assumed that the preceding revival had filled all accumulated replacement demand fairly well and that only a constant sum (included under K) went to replace old houses. Hence a fixed portion of consumer's expenses for dwellings may be assumed not to become income during the following period.

The following equations are established:

$$D_{ct} = (E_{t-1} - sE_{t-1})(1 - b) \tag{13}$$

$$D_{ht} = sE_{t-1}(1 - h) \tag{14}$$

$$I_t = ms(E_{t-1} - E_{t-2}) \tag{15}$$

$$D_t = D_{ct} + D_{ht} + I_t \tag{16}$$

$$S_t = (1 - c)D_t \tag{17}$$

$$E_t = cD_t + K \tag{18}$$

$$G_{ct} = E_t - G_t = (1 - s)E_t \tag{19}$$

$$G_t = sE_t \tag{20}$$

$$S_{bt} = S_t + E_{t-1} - D_{ct} - D_{ht} \tag{21}$$

$$I_{bt} = I_t + K \tag{22}$$

Lundberg did not give the general solution to the system, which is

$$E_t = c[b(s - 1) + s(m - h) + 1]E_{t-1} - cmsE_{t-2} + K \qquad (23)$$

It is straightforward to show that the solution of this second-order difference equation results in three different cases. All these cases cannot be found in Lundberg's model, as he did not allow investment to be negative. When $E_{t-1} < E_{t-2}$ he sets $I_t = 0$. Equation (23) is then replaced by

$$E_t = c[1 - b + s(b - h)]E_{t-1} + K \qquad (24)$$

which is a straightforward first-order difference equation.

Lundberg presented three sequences, with different values for m, the quotient between income from building houses and expected receipts of rents. The higher the value for m, the higher the costs of production in relation to the rents.

Lundberg (1937, pp. 212–13) stated that Keynes's older version of his theory in the *Treatise* can possibly explain the turning point, whereas the *General Theory* cannot:

> Apparently, also, the older theory stressing the importance of the relation between savings and investments contains very little of causal significance and says nothing about the dynamic characteristics of the system. We only learn that the upward movement will go on as long as $(I_{bt} - S_{bt})$ is positive and that the downward swing starts when this difference becomes negative. The table [my Table 2] and diagram, however, show that changes bearing significantly on the ensuing development have occurred, long before the actual "crises" in period (8). New investments have already stopped increasing in period (5) and decline rapidly after period (6); while the difference between investments and savings reaches a maximum one period before investments. A far-reaching analysis may attribute the discrepancy between savings in period (8) to these very changes at an early stage in the development. When the value of investment has stopped increasing, owing to the attainment of a maximum of the series for increment in purchasing power, a decrease must necessarily follow, because savings will continue to rise while total income and receipts are rising.

The third sequence of the third group is interesting. Lundberg chose a value for m that gave rise to a cumulative process. The total receipts rose without limit. Thereafter he observed that a decline must occur due to exogenous causes. Using a computer, I have found the smallest value for m that gives a cumulative development, $m = 24$ (Table 3). (We will return to this sequence in the next section.)

Table 2. *Expansion determined by investment in fixed capital*
$m = 15; c = 0.9; s = 0.1; b = 0.1; h = 0.5$

Period t	Investments I_{bt}	Savings S_{bt}	Expenditures E_t	Investments − savings $I_{bt} - S_{bt}$
1	236.0	226.0	1,010.0	10.0
2	251.0	229.8	1,031.2	21.2
3	267.9	236.2	1,062.9	31.6
4	283.4	244.9	1,101.3	38.5
5	293.7	254.7	1,140.4	39.0
6	294.6	263.6	1,171.3	31.0
7	282.5	269.4	1,184.4	13.1
8	255.6	269.6	1,170.4	−14.0
9	236.0	264.5	1,141.9	−28.5
10	236.0	258.1	1,119.8	−22.1
11	236.0	235.1	1,102.8	−17.1
12	236.0	249.2	1,089.5	−13.2
⋮				
30	236.0	236.1	1,044.7	−0.1

Table 3. *Expansion determined by investment in fixed capital*
$m = 24; c = 0.9; s = 0.1; b = 0.1; h = 0.5$

Period t	Investments I_{bt}	Savings S_{bt}	Expenditures E_t	Investments − savings $I_{bt} - S_{bt}$
1	236.0	226.0	1,010.0	10.0
2	260.0	230.7	1,039.3	29.3
3	306.4	241.9	1,103.8	64.5
4	390.8	264.9	1,229.6	125.8
5	538.0	308.1	1,459.5	229.9
6	787.7	385.0	1,862.2	402.7
7	1,202.4	517.5	2,547.1	684.9
⋮				
15	44,619.8	16,038.7	79,910.1	28,581.0

2.4   *The influence of a variable rate of interest*

In this section Lundberg extended Wicksell's model. He introduced the possibility for the nominal interest rate to influence the development of the sequence and the normal rate of interest. This means that the quotient m that expresses the relation between the cost of producing the investment goods (the income-generating part) and the expected sales value of the corresponding volume of consumer goods (or tenements) will then be a variable, m_t, dependent upon the changes in the rate of interest. One might think of $1/m_t$ as the internal interest rate of the investment. But, as you will see, this part of the dissertation is the least convincing.

The following symbols are used:

$$k = \text{total cost in building a house}$$
$$m_t = \text{the quotient between income from housing pro-}$$
$$\text{duction and expected rents}$$
$$i_t = \text{nominal interest rate}$$
$$d_t = \text{gross receipts of rents (including costs, profits,}$$
$$\text{interest)}$$
$$Ld_t = \text{running costs} + \text{profits of the finished houses}$$
$$a = \text{amortization}$$
$$1 - b = \text{percentage of total receipts that induce income in}$$
$$\text{the next period}$$
$$(1 - b)k = \text{costs paid out as income}$$

First Lundberg determined the first value for m in the following way:

$$d \quad = (i + a)k(1 - b) + Ld$$

gross interest bank loans   running costs
receipts amortization   + profits   (25)
of rents

$$m = (\text{by definition}) = k(1 - b)/d = (1 - L)/(i + a) \quad (26)$$

Analogous with the previous assumptions, Lundberg assumed that the entrepreneur, when devising plans for building new houses during period t, takes the interest rate i_{t-1} as given. In other words, after having built the house he expects this rate to apply to the mortgages. If the interest from period $t - 1$ to t had increased from i_{t-1} to i_t, m_t would have changed in an inverse proportion given by the equation

$$m_t/m_{t-1} = (i_{t-1} + a)/(i_t + a) \quad (27)$$

Lundberg then stated that a given increase in the demand for new dwellings accompanied by an increase in the rate of interest gives rise to a volume of building activity determined through this changed value of m.

The equations are the same as in the previous section, except for the equation that determines the volume of investment. The following system implies a volume of investment that depends on the nominal inter-

Table 4. *The influence of a variable rate of interest*
$m = 30; c = 0.9; s = 0.1; b = 0.1; h = 0.5; i_0 = 5\%; a = 2.5\%$

Period t	Investments I_{bt}	Savings S_{bt}	Expenditures E_t	Interest i
1	236.0	226.0	1,010.0	5.0
2	266.0	231.3	1,044.7	5.1
3	298.0	242.3	1,100.4	5.5
4	243.2	249.4	1,094.2	6.1
5	236.0	247.3	1,082.9	5.4
6	456.7	266.8	1,272.8	5.4
7	780.0	342.1	1,710.7	7.2
8	572.1	420.2	1,862.6	10.0
⋮				
14	236.0	1,080.2	3,935.5	14.9
⋮				
21	236.0	53,567.4	183,692.4	18.8
⋮				
25	61,624,408.6	8,000,072.6	61,755,554.2	0.0

est rate. A rising nominal interest rate will cause increasing rents and a diminishing demand for housing and a decline in the production of residential houses.

If investment in period $t - 1$ exceeds saving in period t, the interest rate is rising. The following equations are added to the system:

$$I_t = m_{t-2}[(i_{t-2} + a)/(i_{t-1} + a)][sE_{t-1}$$
$$- (i_{t-1} + a)sE_{t-2}/(i_{t-2} + a)] \quad (28)$$

$$i_t = i_{t-2}I_{b,t-1}/S_{bt} \quad (29)$$

$$m_t = m_{t-1}(i_{t-1} + a)/(i_t + a) \quad (30)$$

If $m = 30$ the sequence shown in Table 4 is produced. In Lundberg's table, we are given only a sequence showing the development from period one to period five. According to Lundberg, it is the inadequate increase of savings that will interrupt the expansion. Hence the conclusion is more classical than Keynesian. Lundberg stated that this is an example of how the business cycle theory of Hayek can be formulated. However, from my Table 4, we can conclude that, given Lundberg's system of equations, an economic expansion takes off after six periods and economic booms are taking place during periods 8, 14, and 21. After period 22 a cumulative process develops. Therefore we can choose

Table 5. *The influence of a variable rate of interest*
$m = 24; c = 0.9; s = 0.1; b = 0.1; h = 0.5; i_0 = 5\%; a = 2.5\%$

Period t	Investments I_{bt}	Savings S_{bt}	Expenditures E_t	Interest i
1	236.0	226.0	1,010.0	5.0
2	260.0	230.7	1,039.3	5.1
3	268.5	238.1	1,069.7	5.5
4	236.0	241.8	1,063.9	5.7
5	236.0	240.5	1,059.5	5.4
6	322.3	248.1	1,133.7	5.4
7	390.5	271.7	1,252.5	6.4
8	236.0	283.1	1,205.4	7.5
9	236.0	272.4	1,169.0	5.5
10	684.8	309.1	1,544.7	5.7
⋮				
30	38,672,637.5	6,171,978.9	42,698,617.7	4.5

the smallest possible value for $m(m = 24)$ that gave a cumulative response in the preceding section.

Surprisingly, we find that even if the interest rate is variable, a cumulative process develops. From Table 5, it is obvious that the increasing interest rate stops the expansion in period 5. However, as the interest decreases, another expansion takes place with a maximum in period 7. Subsequently the business cycle is in a boom phase during periods 11, 15, and 22. After period 26 a cumulative development occurs. But it is now obvious from the equation that determines I_t that an increasing rate of interest, i_t, will influence not only m_{t-2} but also $(i_{t-2} + a)/(i_{t-1} + a)$ and $(i_{t-1} + a)/i_{t-2} + a)$. Through all these channels the increasing (or decreasing) nominal interest rate will diminish (or increase) the demand for new investments. Lundberg's example has another disadvantage. With the formula that determines m [$m = (1 - L)/(i + a)$], the first value, $m = 30$, is incompatible with the other parameters chosen by Lundberg ($i = 5\%; a = 2.5\%$).[5]

$$30 = (1 - L)/(0.05 + 0.025) \quad \text{which gives} \quad L = -1.25$$

which is an absurd value for the parameter that relates running costs and profits to the total value of the rents. Even if $m = 24$, L takes an absurd value. The value for m should not exceed 10. But in that case there is not a cumulative development that is terminated by the increasing interest rate.

2.5   *Economic growth*

The Domar model: In the last section of Chapter IX Lundberg presented sequences showing how an expansion is created by a process of expansion. This part was written in the spirit of Gustav Cassel rather than Keynes. Siven (1985) points out that Lundberg's growth analysis is a formalization of Cassel's "uniformly progressing economy." In fact, Lundberg also gave us a formalization of the necessary increase of investments to preserve full use of capacity. We find the Domar model on page 240 of *Studies*. The sequence of the third group (see Table 2) is expanded, and the analysis focuses on the propensity to save and the capital-output coefficient. Productivity is increasing at the same time as investment and production. On the other hand, wages are not rising in proportion to production. The profits from newly invested capital are not used for consumption but included in gross savings. Thus, the difference between expected profits and current costs is a windfall profit that is saved. The new sequence will bring about a slower growth than in the third group, and the downturn of the business cycle occurs prematurely. This is a result of the faster growth of gross savings in this case. Lundberg said that the recession is not caused solely by the fact that a part of the gains from rationalization is not paid as wages. Obviously, the sequence of Table 2 reaches its peak as well.

The second example in this section is a sequence that describes what happens when consumer demand is totally directed toward industrial goods. Lundberg then posed the following question. How large is the increase in investment required to bring about a stable equilibrium? In the first period 100 units are invested. Thereafter capital increases from 2,000 to 2,100 units. The equilibrium is stable because expected receipts equal current receipts. In the second period, production must rise at the same rate (5%) to allow production capacity to be utilized in the same proportion as in the first period. Thus the investment needed in period 2 to increase the total income can be calculated. Thereafter the process is repeated with a rapid increment of investments and "in spite of the continued rationalization, creating a rapid growth of 'surplus income' which is saved the development can go on" (Lundberg, 1937, p. 240). Lundberg showed how the time series of new investments in industry displays a rapid growth as a necessary condition to guarantee continuous full use of capacity.

After some tedious but straightforward algebra Lundberg gave us the following equation, showing the necessary increase of investments:

$$I_{t+x} = I_t[1 + 1/m(1 - s)]^x \qquad (31)$$

which is the Domar growth formula with

> m = investments necessary to correspond to a one-unit increase of demand for industrial products
>
> s = propensity to save

The Harrod model: It is also possible to find the Harrod model in Lundberg's *Studies*. It appears at the beginning of Chapter IX on page 185, where "Cassel's simple assumption of a 'gleichförmig fortschreitende wirtschaft' is viewed as a problem to be investigated." Lundberg first assumed that total income and employment increase in time as a straight line and that consumers' outlay and savings are constant proportions of income. Further, he assumed that all costs of production generate income and that no relevant lags exist between costs, income and spending.

The model was then described in the following way: The constant increase in the demand for and production of consumer goods necessitates a certain enlargement of the volume of capital. The expansion for each period requires a constant addition to the volume of capital existing at the beginning of the period. The need for new investment will thus be represented by a straight line parallel to the time axis. If an equilibrium existed at the beginning, saving must necessarily rise progressively above investment during the succeeding periods. The expansion cannot go on, since the increasing output of consumer goods will be sold at declining prices.

On the other hand, according to Lundberg, if investment is brought into line with saving, the total supply of capital will increase in faster progression than is expressed by a constant (equilibrium) relation between capital and output of consumer goods. A surplus capital capacity will appear that will prevent new investment from continuing to increase at the necessary rate.

Lundberg (1937, p. 185) went on:

> Of course the mathematical answer to this dilemma is simply that straight lines do not satisfy the given conditions of the systems. It is easy to show that exponential functions for the growth of income, savings, and capital increase with the same rapidity in accordance with our conditions, although the equilibrium amount of capital is created by the successive cumulation of new investments.

After some exercises in algebra, Lundberg found the growth formula:

$$D(t) = ke^{t(s/m)} \tag{32}$$

where

$D(t)$ = total income
m = investment necessary to correspond to a one-unit increase of demand for industrial products
s = propensity to save

One should observe that Lundberg has worked out the growth formula in continuous time, whereas Harrod (1939) in his famous paper gave only the momentaneous fundamental equation of "warranted growth."

3   Conclusions

First of all I was interested in ascertaining the ways in which Lundberg's *Studies in the Theory of Economic Expansion* (1937) can be seen as a complement to Keynes's *General Theory* (1936). Metzler (1941) pointed out that the difference between the two views might be a question of stressing different matters. If one is interested in the lack of stability, then a study of disequilibria, the dynamics of the economic system, and the turning points becomes necessary. This seems to be the approach adopted by Lundberg. On the other hand, if changes in the system are seen as processes of stabilization in the economy, then a study of the level of the employment becomes important. The multiplier analysis of the *General Theory* was an example of such a static analysis. But in the *General Theory* there is no description of a sequence in which an increase in investments causes an increase in income. Hence, Keynes was not studying how the economic system is moving from one equilibrium to another.

In contrast, Lundberg formalized the equations that characterized the movements of the economic system and used the Lundberg lag to explain the possibility of the business cycle being generated by the multiplier and the accelerator. He also formulated a growth model, later called the Harrod-Domar model, that neglected the lag structure of the economy.

In the Festschrift to Erik Lindahl, Sir John R. Hicks gave us a key to a comparison between the works of Lundberg and Keynes. Hicks proposed four different classes of dynamic methods:

	Flexprice	Fixprice
Ex ante/ex post	1	2
Stocks/flows	3	4

We can conclude that all of Lundberg's sequences are fixprice models, with one exception. In the first sequence of Chapter IX of *Studies* Lundberg analyzed the expansion of the production at a constant volume of investments. Lundberg's sequence took on the same limit value as the Keynesian multiplier. Lundberg was able to show how this equilibrium was attained.

If we study the second type of sequence – expansion determined by investment in working capital – an analysis in terms of stocks and flows seems to be most appropriate. The working capital is the stock variable that is to be held in a certain proportion relative to the volume of production, which is a flow variable, as are the other variables. The investments in working capital will supply the inventories when the demand for goods *ex ante* differs from the demand for good *ex post*. This flow is not supposed to be negative. Therefore, Lundberg's inventory model is incomplete. Another deficiency is the neglect of pipeline investment.[6]

Introducing the accelerator as a determinant of investment, Lundberg, in contrast to Keynes, was connecting the effect of the multiplier to the level of the ratio of profits and total income. Instead of applying a "Robertsonian" lag between income and expenses, the outlays of consumers are influenced directly when income changes. There is instead a one-period Lundberg lag between a change in sales and a change in the volume of production. The increase of receipts in one period does not affect consumer demand in the same period. Only the volume of production and investments in the following period are influenced. Thus, a dynamic mechanism was introduced into Keynes's system. It is important to stress Lundberg's pioneering role in connecting the accelerator to the multiplier. Normally, Samuelson (1939) is given credit for the first formalization of the multiplier-accelerator model.[7]

In a more recent contribution to the history of the theory of business cycles, Victor Zarnowitz (1985) points to the fact that the *General Theory* lacks a dynamic model and that the principle of the accelerator is missing. Further, Zarnowitz gives a description of the development of business cycle models in the 1930s and the 1940s. Five works are mentioned, all contributing to the theory of the multiplier-accelerator: Harrod (1936), Kalecki (1937), Samuelson (1939), Metzler (1941), and Hicks (1950). But Lundberg's *Studies* (1937) is not discussed. Hicks's (1950) book, published thirteen years after Lundberg's dissertation, is not important in this respect. Metzler (1941) and Samuelson (1939) both take Lundberg (1937) as a starting point for their analysis. Consequently, we only need to consider the works of Harrod (1936) and Kalecki (1937), and I can't find that either of them anticipate Lundberg's connection of the accelerator to the multiplier.[8]

In the third group of Chapter IX in *Studies,* Lundberg analyzed an expansion determined by an increased stock of fixed real capital. This was a more elaborate model of the multiplier-accelerator. Lundberg isolated the incentives to investments arising from changes within the economic system. The problem consisted in showing how these incentives change with the development studied, and how the development is partly determined by assumptions as to "rational responses" in investments to these incentives. Lundberg's "simulations" in the precomputer era are indeed impressive. He found the parameter values that resulted in a continuous expansion. Income, savings, and investments tended to follow exponential growth rates. Another finding was that a higher capital-output ratio implied a faster expansion during the upturn but also a greater downturn when the expansion was broken.

In the fourth section, Lundberg extended Wicksell's model, by including the nominal interest rate in the model of the third section. According to Lundberg, he tried to formalize the business cycle theory of Hayek. However, I find this part of *Studies* dubious. If one studies the movements of Lundberg's system of equations during more periods than Lundberg did, it is obvious that a cumulative process develops. Therefore Lundberg's conclusion of an expansion interrupted by an inadequate increase of savings is not justified. Second, the parameter values chosen by Lundberg in this section are incompatible with one another. Third, as pointed out by Siven (1985), it is difficult to see why Lundberg did not use the Keynesian liquidity preference theory to determine the interest rate.

In contrast, when it comes to the growth analysis of Chapter IX of *Studies,* one has to point to another pioneering role played by Lundberg. Obviously, he anticipated the complete Harrod-Domar growth model.[9] First, Lundberg was able to formalize the necessary increase in investments required to preserve full use of capacity in a uniformly progressing economy. This is the Domar model. Second, Lundberg showed that exponential functions for the growth of income, savings, and capital increase with the same rapidity, although the equilibrium amount of capital is created by the cumulation of new investments. The analysis showed that the growth path of real income that maintains equilibrium in the goods market requires the economy to grow at a steady exponential rate. This is the rate of growth that allows desired savings to be equal to desired investment while maintaining full-capacity output at every moment in time. Thus, he worked out Harrod's fundamental equation of "warranted growth" two years before it appeared in Harrod (1939).

As pointed out earlier in this paper, Schumpeter (1954, p. 1174) stated that Lundberg displays the "micro- and macrodynamic roots of current Keynesianism much better than Keynes himself did." Lundberg's (1960, p. 197) comment on this is well known: "My own hypothesis is that Schumpeter's, in my view, exaggerated appreciation of my dissertation is due to some kind of rivalry with Keynes for being the most influential economist of the time." But why would Schumpeter jeopardize his reputation by giving estimates that could easily be shown to be false? Further, is it necessarily true that the rivalry with Keynes must lead to an exaggerated homage to Lundberg?

In conclusion, I hope I have substantiated Schumpeter's claim: There are parts of Lundberg's *Studies* that go well beyond the central message of Keynes's *General Theory*.[10]

Notes

1 In preparing this paper I am indebted to the late Erik Lundberg and to Rolf Henriksson and Claes-Henric Siven for constructive advice. I am particularly grateful to Rolf Henriksson for suggesting a study of the differences between the models of Lundberg and Keynes. I would also like to thank Lars Jonung for important editorial assistance.
2 Actually, there is one example of a model with flexible prices in Lundberg's *Studies* (1937, p. 196): "In a special case, the model may be used for this reaction type, namely, for a pure price and income inflation. The supply of production factors is assumed to be completely inelastic." Lundberg then gave a formalized example of an inflationary gap. This was more than two years before Keynes published *How to Pay for the War* (1940); see Berg (1987) for a full discussion of this issue.
3 Ohlin (1934) seems to be the first to have connected them verbally; see Brems's contribution in this volume and Blomquist and Siven (1988).
4 "But the more or less automatic changes in pipeline stocks that result from changes in the flow of finished output for sale and for stock cannot be left out of account. For they, too, contribute to changes in income and hence consumer expenditure, reacting on business stocks of finished goods. They must be counted as part of active inventory investment, in addition to output of finished goods for stock" (Nurkse, 1961, p. 111).
5 Dargent (1953, p. 129).
6 By considering changes in the pipeline separately from changes in stocks of finished goods, one would revert, in a way, to the distinction between working capital and liquid stocks that Keynes made in the *Treatise* (see Nurkse, 1961, p. 115).
7 Evans (1969, p. 362), for example, says: "Samuelson's article marked the first step to integrate Keynesian theory with older business theory, particularly the accelerator."

8 Harrod's *The Trade Cycle* (1936) is the only work I know of that attempts
   to integrate the multiplier with the accelerator and that was published before
   Studies. Harrod calls the accelerator "the relation." His theory, though, is
   not a complete one. To imitate the business cycle, the accelerator and the
   multiplier have to be integrated with a lag or a nonlinear function. This is
   lacking in Harrod's work. In fact, one cannot find a formalized theory in
   Harrod (1936).

   Let us now turn to Kalecki (1937). *"A Theory of the Business Cycle"*
   appeared at almost the same time as Lundberg's *Studies*. According to
   Patinkin (1982), Kalecki had better success than the economists of the Stockholm school in *almost* anticipating the *General Theory*. In Kalecki (1937)
   we are shown how the process of investment by necessity produces a business
   cycle. Kalecki introduced a lag between the decision to invest and the
   accomplishment of the investment. But, as far as I can see, Kalecki is not
   anticipating Lundberg's integration of the multiplier with the accelerator.
   First, Kalecki reduced the role played by the multiplier (Kalecki, 1937, p.
   85). Second, savings equal investments in each period (Kalecki, 1937, p. 85).
   Third, the business cycle of Kalecki is generated as follows: "The rate of
   investment decisions is an increasing function of the gap between the prospective rate of profit and the rate of interest" (Kalecki, 1937, p. 85). The
   central message of Kalecki is applicable to the investment cycle. He is pursuing a theory of the accelerator, without integrating it, as Lundberg did,
   with the analysis of how a change in aggregate demand influences total
   income.

   The contribution of Lundberg is productive, as he separates savings and
   investments in his model of the multiplier-accelerator and at the same time
   introduces a lag between the change in receipts and a change in the volume
   of production. According to Metzler (1948, p. 25), the Lundberg lag was
   consistent with empirical tests.

9 According to Göran Ohlin (1970, p. 201): "During the earliest post-war
   experience the most important tool in development planning was based on
   the model of economic growth presented by Erik Lundberg in the thirties
   and later taken up as the Harrod-Domar growth-model." Lundberg (1984,
   p. 59) himself pointed to the fact that the Harrod-Domar model was anticipated by Cassel as early as 1918. This is not the whole truth. Marx was the
   first economist to develop a formalized model of economic growth (see
   Wicksell, 1935, p. 13, and Gustafsson, 1971, p. 70). This growth model
   appears in the second volume of *Das Kapital*. The Marxian model probably
   influenced Cassel through the writings of Tugan Baranovskij (Gustafsson,
   1971, p. 70). A more adequate name for this growth model might therefore
   be the Marx-Tugan Baranovskij-Cassel-Lundberg-Harrod-Domar growth
   model!

10 Indeed, it was possible to trace the "macrodynamic roots of current Keynesianism" in *Studies*. In contrast, we have not found evidence of any "microdynamic roots" in the dissertation. This was pointed out to me by the late

Erik Lundberg after he read an earlier version of this contribution. Lundberg also expressed his gratitude for the interest shown in his earlier work, especially as he found the lack of references to his dissertation in the international literature surprising.

References

Berg, Claes (1987), "Utvecklingen av de svenska bidragen till inflationsgapsanalysen," in R. Henriksson, ed., *Konjunkturinstitutet under Erik Lundbergs tid.* Stockholm: Konjunkturinstitutet, Norstedts. ("The Development of the Swedish Contributions to the Inflationary Gap Analysis," forthcoming in L. Jonung, ed., *Swedish Economic Thought: Explorations and Advances,* Routledge).

Blomquist, Sören, and Claes-Henric Siven (1988), "Bertil Ohlin," *Ekonomisk Debatt,* 4, 307–15.

Cassel, Gustav (1918), *Theory of Social Economy.* Translated by Joseph McCabe (1923), London: T. Fisher Unwin. Translated by S. L. Barron (1932), New York.

Clark, John M. (1917), "Business Acceleration and the Law of Demand: A Technical Factor in Economic Cycles," *Journal of Political Economy,* 25, 217–35.

Dargent, E. (1953), *Les Modéles Macroeconomic de Sequence.* Paris: Imprimerie National.

Domar, Evsey (1946), "Capital Expansion, Rate of Growth and Employment," *Econometrica,* 14, 137–47.

Evans, Michael K. (1969), *Macroeconomic Activity.* New York: Harper & Row.

Gustafsson, Bo (1971), "Ekonomisk tillväxtteori och ekonomisk historia," *Ur ekonomisk-historisk synvinkel, festskrift till Hildebrand.* Stockholm: Läromedelsförlaget.

Hammarskjöld, Dag (1933), *Konjunkturspridningen: en teoretisk och historisk undersökning.* Stockholm.

Hansen, Alvin (1951), *Business Cycles and National Income.* New York: Norton.

Harrod, Roy F. (1936), *The Trade Cycle.* Oxford: Oxford University Press.
(1939), "An Essay in Dynamic Theory," *Economic Journal,* 49, 14–33.

Hayek, Friedrich A. (1931), *Prices and Production.* London: Routledge.

Hicks, John R. (1950), *A Contribution to the Theory of the Trade Cycle.* Oxford.

Johansson, Alf (1934), *Löneutvecklingen och arbetslösheten,* Stockholm.

Kalecki, Michal (1937), "A Theory of the Business Cycle," *Review of Economic Studies,* 4, 77–97.

Keynes, John M. (1930), *A Treatise On Money,* Collected Writings Vol. V and VI (1971). London: Macmillan.
(1936), *The General Theory of Employment, Interest and Money.* London: Macmillan.

228   Comment by Mats Persson

(1940), *How To Pay For The War,* Collected Writings Vol. XII (1973). London: Macmillan.

Lundberg, Erik (1937), *Studies in the Theory of Economic Expansion.* London: P. S. King & Son (Stockholm Economic Studies No. 6).

(1960), "Om att begripa Keynes och förstå andra," *Ekonomisk Tidskrift,* pp. 195–205.

(1984), *Kriserna och ekonomerna.* Stockholm: Liber.

Metzler, Lloyd A. (1941), "The Nature and Stability of Inventory Cycles," *Review of Economic Statistics,* 23, 113–29.

(1948), "Three Lags in the Circular Flow of Income," in *Income, Employment and Public Policy,* Essays in honor of Alvin Hansen. New York: Norton.

Nurkse, Ragnar (1961), "Periods Analysis and Inventory Cycles," in R. Nurkse, *Equilibrium and Growth in the World Economy.* Harvard Economic Studies 11 (G. Haberler and R. Stern, eds.), Cambridge Mass.

Ohlin, Bertil (1934), *Penningpolitik, offentliga arbeten, subventioner och tullar som medel mot arbetslöshet,* SOU, 1934:12.

Ohlin, Göran (1970), "Den ekonomiska teorin inför u-ländernas problem," in *Ekonomisk politik i förvandling.* Stockholm: EFI, Norstedts.

Patinkin, Don (1982), *Anticipations of the General Theory?* Chicago: University of Chicago Press.

Samuelson, Paul (1939), "Interactions Between the Multiplier Analysis and the Principle of Acceleration," *Review of Economic Statistics,* 21, 75–78.

Schumpeter, Joseph (1954), *History of Economic Analysis.* New York.

Siven, Claes-Henric (1985), "The End of the Stockholm School," *Scandinavian Journal of Economics,* 87, 577–93.

Wicksell, Knut (1899), *Geldzins und Güterpreise.* Jena: Gustav Fischer.

Wicksell, Knut (1935), *Lectures on Political Economy,* Vol. 2. London: Routledge & Kegan.

Zarnowitz, Victor (1985), "Recent Work on Business Cycles in Historical Perspective: A Review of Theories and Evidence," *Journal of Economic Literature,* 23, 523–80.

Comment

MATS PERSSON

The main contribution of Claes Berg's paper is to disentangle the various models in the ninth chapter of Lundberg's 1937 dissertation and to provide an explicit formulation of the equations underlying his calculations. By doing this, Berg can, in a pedagogical and convincing manner, compare Lundberg's models to those of Samuelson, Metzler, Harrod, and Domar.

It is interesting to note that this explicit spelling out of the equations also provides a clue to the explanation of why the models of the latter authors were quickly accepted in the standard economics literature, whereas those of Lundberg never found their way into the textbooks. By imposing non-negativity constraints (i.e., investment can never turn negative), the mathematical structure – which was in principle quite simple – became in practice so complicated that it only lent itself to numerical solutions. Thus the simple analytical solutions, which are necessary for models to be useful in textbooks, were lacking in Lundberg's work, although the economic insights were not.

It is refreshing to note that Berg does not argue that Lundberg "discovered" the Samuelson model of the interaction between the accelerator and the multiplier, or the Harrod-Domar model of economic growth, or the Metzler model of the inventory cycle. This seems to be a very reasonable attitude; the question of scientific priority is an intricate, and in most cases even meaningless, enterprise. Most ideas have been more or less vaguely perceived, pursued, and expressed by a long line of researchers reaching far back in the history of economic doctrines.

We have the early pioneer, who mentions a new idea *en passant*, who expresses it in an obscure and perhaps incorrect fashion, and who does not emphasize it or in any way give an indication that he is aware of its significance. At the other end of the spectrum we have the pedagogical interpreter, who picks up an idea that already exists in one form or another, who presents it in a simple and striking way, and who manages to persuade the academic community that the matter is of importance. Then there are all the intermediate cases.

What Samuelson did in this 1939 paper undoubtedly falls in the "pedagogical interpreter" category, and an interesting question is why Lundberg did not assume that role himself. Samuelson's contribution was to pick out one set of equations, to make some strategic simplifications to obtain a second-order difference equation in national income, and to analyze its stability properties. This is a fairly straightforward matter – once you have come up with the idea – and Lundberg had enough mathematical knowledge to do it himself. Furthermore, his father, Filip Lundberg, had a Ph.D. in statistics, and his brother, Ove Lundberg, completed the equivalent of an M.Sc. ("filosofie licentiat") in statistics in 1937. Both of these individuals (as well as Erik himself, who had taken undergraduate math courses at the university) were very well able to solve second-order difference equations.

The difference in approach between Lundberg and Samuelson might illuminate a difference in scientific attitude. Samuelson was obviously driven by the zeal to find the fundamental mechanism; behind the multitude of dynamic patterns that emerged from the numerical examples in the ninth chapter of Lundberg's book, there must be a simple, fundamental principle that could perhaps be captured in the form of a pedagogical formula. Lundberg, on the other hand, wanted to illustrate various possible sequences; if there were any principle behind the dynamic patterns of the numerical exercises, it would probably be so complicated that it would be useless to search for it.

On the other side of the spectrum, we have the pioneers who fail to give their more or less vaguely perceived ideas the striking form that finds its way into the textbooks. Harrod's 1936 book *The Trade Cycle* is an example of this case.

There is, however, another pioneer who has not been mentioned at this conference but who might have been a common source for both Harrod and Lundberg in their view of the business cycle. I am referring to Wesley C. Mitchell, whom Lundberg met during his visit to the United States in 1931–3. Lundberg was very familiar with the work of the founder of the NBER (National Bureau of Economic Research) and, in fact, referred to Mitchell's *Business Cycles* (1913) and *Business Cycles, The Problem and Its Setting* (1927) in his 1937 dissertation. Now, one can argue that Mitchell's view of the business cycle is that of an interaction between the multiplier and the accelerator, which results in a second-order difference equation in national income (see Friedman, 1950, pp. 490 ff.).

I do not think it really matters whether Harrod got his ideas from Lundberg or vice versa, or whether both got their ideas simultaneously from a common pool of ideas that was available to the academic community of the 1930s (and Mitchell's works could then be a part of that pool). But I may be wrong. If the history of doctrines is an important part of economics, and if the search for scientific priority is an important part of the historiography of doctrines, then I think Wesley C. Mitchell's role in the development of macrodynamics has been somewhat neglected.

References

Friedman, Milton (1950), "Wesley C. Mitchell as an Economic Theorist," *Journal of Political Economy,* Vol. 58, No. 6.
Mitchell, Wesley C. (1913), *Business Cycles.* Berkeley.
(1927), *Business Cycles, The Problem and Its Setting.* New York.

CHAPTER 9

Macrodynamics and the Stockholm School

HANS BREMS[1]

The Stockholm School and its dynamics

A fifty-year perspective

The Stockholm School is identified with economic dynamics, microeconomic as well as macroeconomic. Its founding fathers were Knut Wicksell and Gustav Cassel. Wicksell's macrodynamic accomplishment was his cumulative process of inflation at frozen physical output (Wicksell, 1898). Cassel's microdynamic accomplishment was his dynamization of a Walrasian general economic equilibrium into a model of a "uniformly progressing state" growing in its physical quantities at frozen prices (Cassel, 1918, 1932, pp. 32–41 and 137–55). His macrodynamic accomplishment was his aggregation of such a model (Cassel, 1918, 1932, pp. 61–2).

The Stockholm School climaxed in the 1930s. As Petersson (1987) does, one might distinguish between an earlier Stockholm School, typified by Myrdal (1927, 1931), Lindahl (1930), Ohlin (1934, 1937), and Lundberg (1937), that laid the groundwork and a later Stockholm School, typified by Svennilson (1938) and Lindahl (1939), that provided the methodology. What, then, was the Stockholm School?

Ever since the days of Wicksell and Cassel the Swedish method had been dynamic: Economic variables were functions of time. But dynamics has two intersecting dimensions shown in Table 1 and exemplified by some of the authors mentioned in the present paper.

Equilibrium versus disequilibrium dynamics

The first dimension of dynamics is equilibrium versus disequilibrium dynamics. In equilibrium dynamics expectations come true; in disequilibrium dynamics they do not come true. The key to Swedish dynamic

Table 1. *Four categories of dynamics*

	EQUILIBRIUM	DISEQUILIBRIUM
CONTINUOUS	Cassel	Phillips
DISCONTINUOUS	von Neumann	Lindahl Lundberg Ohlin Samuelson Wicksell

theory was the tripod of plan, period, and expectation: The motive force of a cumulative process was the revision of the plan at the end of the period caused by the disappointed expectation – disappointed by what Lindahl called "unforeseen events." To Lindahl, indeed to the entire Stockholm School, dynamics was always such disequilibrium dynamics. But Lindahl used it in two forms.

In the first form, called the "temporary-equilibrium" method by Lindahl (1930) and called the flexprice method by Hicks (1965), markets always cleared within the period, but the price that cleared them might not be the expected one. The expectations that were disappointed, then, were price expectations. In the second form, called the "disequilibrium" method by Lindahl (1939) and called the fixprice method by Hicks (1965), a price was announced at the beginning of the period and adhered to throughout the period. At this price markets might not clear within the period, so sales might not be the expected ones, and inventory might pile up or be depleted. The expectations that were disappointed, then, were sales expectations. In either form of disequilibrium dynamics the motive force of the cumulative process was a lagged response to disappointed expectations.

Continuous versus discontinuous dynamics

The second dimension of dynamics is continuous versus discontinuous dynamics. Continuous dynamics uses differential equations expressing relationships between variables and their simultaneous derivatives with respect to time. It follows from the definition of a derivative that differential equations must use periods of vanishing length.

Discontinuous dynamics uses difference equations expressing relationships between variables belonging to different times. For such times to differ, difference equations must use periods of finite length. Without writing his difference equations explicitly, Wicksell (1898) used such discontinuous dynamics, and so did Robertson (1926, p. 59), who defined his "days" as "finite but indivisible atoms of time." To Lindahl, indeed to the entire Stockholm School, dynamics was always such discontinuous dynamics. To Lindahl (1929a, 1929b, 1930), his "unforeseen events" occurred at discrete intervals and were banished to the transition points between periods of finite length. Later, Lindahl (1939) softened such banishment: The unforeseen events were now allowed to occur within periods but would remain unregistered until the next transition point between periods. Either way, unforeseen events were registered and expectations disappointed in the transition points between periods of finite length.

Discontinuous disequilibrium dynamics

Multiplier-accelerator interaction: Words (Ohlin)

Wicksell had given the Swedes a macrodynamic discontinuous disequilibrium model to work with, but he had frozen his physical output and let price be his only variable. Keynes had done the opposite; he had frozen his price and let physical output be his only variable.

Using Wicksell's method and inspired by Lindahl's (1930) refinement of it, Ohlin (1933, 1934) added physical output as an additional variable. Two years ahead of Keynes, Ohlin used three Keynesian tools – the propensity to consume, liquidity preference, and the multiplier – and one as yet non-Keynesian tool, the accelerator. The four tools would interact as follows in a feedback mechanism. Let consumption demand be stimulated. As a result physical output would rise, generating new income. The propensity to consume would link physical consumption to the *level* of physical output and thus establish a consumption feedback. The accelerator would link physical investment to the *growth* of physical output and thus establish an investment feedback. As did the Wicksellian one, Ohlin's two feedbacks unfolded in a cumulative process along a time axis as a succession of disequilibria: Expectations and plans were forever being revised in the light of new experience.

Ohlin and Keynes

Who had the richer model? Keynes used only the consumption feedback and telescoped it into an instant static equilibrium along an output axis. Clearly, Ohlin had the richer model: He went Keynes one better by using the accelerator, which gave him a feedback and cumulative process, both missing in Keynes's macrostatics. Still Keynes won and the Swedes lost.

Richness isn't everything; operational significance also matters. And sometimes richness may stand in the way of operational significance. Keynes won on his operational significance: There was so much you could *do* with his model, and you could do it so sure-footedly! Ironically, precisely because Ohlin's model was richer, he was facing a multitude of possible sequences of his cumulative process.

Ohlin used nothing but words. His conscientious, accurate, cautious, and honest words certainly made no attempt to hide his multitude of possibilities. Worse, his words did not, and perhaps could not, sort out the possibilities and specify the exact circumstances under which each would materialize. As a result, his readers came away with the impression that anything could happen. And away they went – to Keynes! To sum up, the instrument Ohlin had chosen for communicating with his readers was too blunt.

Multiplier-accelerator interactions: Recursive solution (Lundberg)

Would a keener instrument have served better? A big step forward was Lundberg's (1937) period analysis. Lundberg wrote the difference equations and solved them recursively for five cases: (1) a pure Keynesian multiplier with autonomous investment; (2) the interaction between the multiplier and an accelerator based on a constant working-capital coefficient equaling one-half and applying to inventory of raw materials and goods in process; (3) the interaction between the multiplier and an accelerator based on a constant fixed-capital coefficient equaling 15, 20, or 30 and applying to residential housing; (4) the interaction between the multiplier and an accelerator based on a variable capital coefficient that was a function of an endogenously determined rate of interest; and (5) the interaction between the multiplier and an accelerator based on a constant fixed-capital coefficient equaling four and applying to new labor-saving machinery.

With his recursive solutions Lundberg achieved a high degree of operational significance. But his answers remained case studies, as Siven (1985) observed. What remained to be done was to recover the primitive that gave rise to such difference equations. That was done before the end of the 1930s. What prompted it was the accelerator.

The accelerator

For his accelerator Lundberg credited Clark (1917) and Frisch (1931) and could have credited Cassel (1918, 1932, pp. 61–2), who used it and estimated it empirically. Kalecki (1935, 1936) used no accelerator but made investment a function of profits.

Containing a derivative with respect to time, the accelerator is inherently dynamic and will dynamize any system including it, Keynesian or non-Keynesian. Neither Keynes himself nor his disciples would remain confined to the statics of the *General Theory*. In the very year of the *General Theory*, Harrod (1936, 1939, 1948) brought in the accelerator, calling it "the relation." The next year Keynes (1937) himself for once considered a secular problem, estimated a secular propensity to save of between 8 and 15 percent, estimated a secular capital coefficient of four years, divided the former by the latter, and found capital stock growing at a rate between 2 and 4 percent per annum. For the period 1860–1913 Keynes estimated that half of that growth had been required to serve an increasing population. When population became stationary, as Keynes expected, that source of demand would dry up – which was the secular problem.

Harrod's accelerator was noticed by Hansen, who in 1927 had surveyed business-cycle theories and later (1951, p. ix) always emphasized "the vast importance of the Continental development of the theory of investment demand and the role of investment in income formation – the work of Wicksell, Tugan-Baranowsky, Spiethoff, Schumpeter, and Cassel – a development largely overlooked by English-speaking economists." According to Samuelson (1976, pp. 29–30), a "Minnesota visit of Frisch in 1931 was important for Hansen's quick integration of the acceleration principle into the Keynesian system." By the time Hansen came to Harvard in 1937 he liked to see physical investment as the change in desired physical capital stock and, in turn, see desired physical capital stock in direct proportion to physical output of consumer goods. Like Lundberg at the same time, Hansen tried to work out the arithmetic of an interaction between the multiplier and the accelerator. Surprised by the resulting multitude of possibilities, Hansen turned to his brightest student for help.

Multiplier-accelerator interaction: Primitive recovered (Samuelson)

That student was Samuelson (1939), who wrote Hansen's system as follows:

Variables

$C \equiv$ physical consumption

$I \equiv$ physical net investment
$X \equiv$ physical net output

Parameters

$b \equiv$ capital coefficient, the accelerator
$c \equiv$ propensity to consume
$G \equiv$ physical government purchase of goods and services

The system had only three equations. First, the lagged consumption function

$$C(t) = cX(t - 1) \tag{1}$$

Second, the lagged investment function

$$I(t) = b[C(t) - C(t - 1)] \tag{2}$$

Third, the goods-market equilibrium condition

$$X(t) = C(t) + I(t) + G \tag{3}$$

For our purposes we may ignore Samuelson's government purchase G, insert equations (1) and (2) into equation (3) thus collapsed, and write his reduced system as the linear homogeneous second-order difference equation

$$X(t) + AX(t - 1) + BX(t - 2) = 0 \tag{4}$$

where $A \equiv -(1 + b)c$ and $B \equiv bc$.

Try a solution of the form $X(t) = x^t$ and find the "characteristic" or "auxiliary" quadratic

$$x^2 + Ax + B = 0 \tag{5}$$

Our tentative solution $X(t) = x^t$ is then a solution if and only if x is a root of equation (5). A weighted sum of such roots will be the primitive. As we know, if the roots of equation (5) were complex, physical output would display oscillations. If they were not, physical output would converge to a stationary state or be growing smoothly.

Here Hansen's brightest disciple had recovered the primitive underlying an Ohlin-Lundberg–type cumulative process and thus had given the latter more operational significance than it ever had in Sweden. At twenty-four, had Samuelson heard of the Swedes? He had and concluded (Samuelson, 1939) by mentioning "in passing that the formal structure of our problem is identical with the model sequences of Lundberg. . ."

Rigorous macrodynamics soon found its way into curricula and had textbooks of its own. The first was Baumol's (1951). Had Baumol heard of the Swedes? He had. His text was based on London lectures in 1947–9 and paid tribute to Ralph Turvey, who knew Swedish, contributed a chapter and an appendix, and (Baumol, 1951, p. ix) "made his influence felt throughout the volume."

Continuous disequilibrium dynamics

Multiplier-accelerator interactions: Primitive recovered (Phillips)

Could what Lundberg and Samuelson did with their difference equations also have been done with differential equations? Phillips (1954) almost did it [see Allen's (1956, pp. 72–4) straightforward summary].

Differential equations can handle lags but require them to be continuously distributed, and Phillips used a continuously distributed investment lag corresponding to Samuelson's rigid lag [equation (2)]. But Phillips used a lagless consumption function. Instead he had a continuously distributed supply lag. For comparability with Samuelson we must modify Phillips as follows. Samuelson's notation will do except for two new parameters:

$\alpha \equiv$ speed of response of consumption to output
$\beta \equiv$ speed of response of investment to change in output

First, let there be a continuously distributed lag in the response of consumption to output. Specifically, let the response dC/dt of consumption be in proportion to the gap between desired and current consumption. Desired consumption, in turn, is the propensity to consume c times current output. Consequently:

$$\frac{dC}{dt} = \alpha(cX - C) \qquad (6)$$

Next, let there be a continuously distributed lag in the response of investment to the change in output. Specifically, let the response dI/dt of investment be in proportion to the gap between desired and current investment. Desired investment, in turn, is the accelerator b times current change in output. Consequently

$$\frac{dI}{dt} = \beta\left(b\frac{dX}{dt} - I\right) \qquad (7)$$

As in Samuelson, ignore the supply lag and let goods-market equilibrium be

$$X = C + I \tag{8}$$

To solve the system, differentiate equation (8) with respect to time and insert equations (6) and (7) into the derivative. Then write equation (8) as $C = X - I$, insert that, rearrange, and arrive at I expressed in X alone:

$$I = \frac{1 - b\beta}{\alpha - \beta} \frac{dX}{dt} + \frac{\alpha(1 - c)}{\alpha - \beta} X \tag{9}$$

Notice that equation (9) would be meaningless if the speeds of response α and β were equal. Assuming they are not, differentiate equation (9) with respect to time and arrive at dI/dt expressed in X alone:

$$\frac{dI}{dt} = \frac{1 - b\beta}{\alpha - \beta} \frac{d^2X}{dt^2} + \frac{\alpha(1 - c)}{\alpha - \beta} \frac{dX}{dt} \tag{10}$$

Inserting equations (9) and (10) into the right-hand and left-hand sides, respectively, of equation (7) will finally give us the linear homogeneous second-order differential equation

$$\frac{d^2X}{dt^2} + A \frac{dX}{dt} + BX = 0 \tag{11}$$

where

$$A \equiv \frac{\alpha(1 - c) + (1 - \alpha b)\beta}{1 - b\beta}$$

$$B \equiv \frac{\alpha\beta(1 - c)}{1 - b\beta}$$

Try a solution of the form $X = e^{xt}$ and find the very same form of the characteristic of auxiliary quadratic as in the case of difference equations:

$$x^2 + Ax + B = 0 \tag{12}$$

Our tentative solution $X = e^{xt}$ is then a solution if and only if x is a root of equation (12). Again, a weighted sum of such roots will be the primitive.

Comparison

The Swedes always insisted that lags were important. Samuelson's interaction had two rigid one-period lags in it, that is, equations (1) and (2), generating the second-order difference equation (4). Our Phillips-like interaction had the same two lags but in continuously distributed forms, that is, equations (6) and (7), generating the second-order differential equation (11). Our Phillips-like interaction may look less Swedish but has a very Swedish substance: At finite speeds of response α and β disequilibrium will take the form of gaps $cX - C$ or $bdX/dt - I$ between desired and current consumption or investment, respectively. Current consumption C or investment I will be trying to catch up in the form of the responses dC/dt or dI/dt, respectively, constituting the motive force of a cumulative process.

So what Lundberg and Samuelson did with their difference equations can indeed also be done with differential equations. As a matter of fact, with their freedom of choice of the speeds of response α and β, continuously distributed lags are more flexible, hence more efficient and more realistic than rigid one-period lags.

Continuous equilibrium dynamics

Indeed our Phillips-like continuously distributed lags are flexible enough to include equilibrium as the special case of speeds of response α and β rising beyond bounds. To see how, merely insert A and B into equation (12), multiply both sides by $1 - b\beta$, divide them by $\alpha\beta$, and write the characteristic equation

$$\left(\frac{1}{\alpha\beta} - \frac{b}{\alpha}\right) x^2 + \left(\frac{1-c}{\beta} + \frac{1}{\alpha} - b\right) x + 1 - c = 0 \qquad (13)$$

whose limit for $\alpha \to \infty$ and $\beta \to \infty$ is $-bx + 1 - c = 0$ or $x = (1 - c)/b$, which is Cassel's (1918, 1932, pp. 61–2) steady-state equilibrium growth at a rate equaling the propensity to save divided by the capital coefficient (accelerator). Here is the equilibrium dynamics always ignored by Lindahl: Growth materializes as expected. No expectations are disappointed and no plans are revised, yet variables keep growing over time.

Like the Keynesian model, the Stockholm model had been closely tailored to the fundamental disequilibrium of mass unemployment of its time. In the new reality of the steady-state equilibrium growth of the 1950s and 1960s, the Swedes and Keynes alike were becoming obsolescent. By contrast, a much older Swedish tradition was having a remarkable comeback: Cassel's (1918, 1932, pp. 289–97) long-run optimal depletion of mines came back with Hotelling (1931); Cassel's (1918, 1932, pp. 32–41 and 137–55) microeconomic growth came back in a much refined form with von Neumann (1937); Cassel's (1899, 1918, 1932) revealed preference came back with Samuelson (1938); Cassel's

(1918, 1932, pp. 61–2) macroeconomic growth came back in identical algebra, except for notation, with Harrod (1939, 1948); and Cassel's (1918, 1932, pp. 154–5) dichotomy between nominal and real variables came back with Friedman (1968).[2]

Conclusion

If differential equations can handle lags at least as well as difference equations do, then the length of the period does not matter and may easily vanish. In that case the lasting contribution of the Stockholm School cannot have been its adamant insistence on the use of a period of finite length or, mathematically, the use of difference equations.

Rather, the lasting contribution of the Stockholm School was its early insistence on the use of lags. Stockholm School lags were the rigid lags of difference equations. Differential equations can handle lags in the more efficient and more elegant form of continuously distributed lags. In such modern forms a Stockholm heritage may be traced, as the present paper has tried to do.

Notes

1 For careful reading and several suggestions the writer is indebted to Paul A. Samuelson.
2 More on Cassel in Brems (1989).

References

Allen, Sir Roy George Douglas (1956), *Mathematical Economics,* London: Macmillan.
Baumol, William J. (1951), *Economic Dynamics – With a Contribution by Ralph Turvey,* 1st ed. New York: Macmillan.
Brems, Hans (1989), "Gustav Cassel Revisited," *History of Political Economy,* vol. 21.
Cassel, Karl Gustav (1899), "Grundriss einer elementaren Preislehre," *Zeitschrift für die gesamte Staatswissenschaft,* 55, 395–458.
   (1918), *Theoretische Sozialökonomie.* Leipzig: Wintersche Verlagshandlung.
   (1932), *The Theory of Social Economy,* translated by S. L. Barron. New York: Harcourt, Brace.
Clark, John M. (1917), "Business Acceleration and the Law of Demand: A Technical Factor in Economic Cycles," *Journal of Political Economy,* 25 (March), 217–35. Reprinted in G. Haberler, ed., *Readings in Business Cycle Theory,* Philadelphia: Blakiston, 1951, pp. 235–60.

Friedman, Milton (1968), "The Role of Monetary Policy," *American Economic Review,* 58 (March), 1–17.

Frisch, Ragnar (1931), "The Interrelation Between Capital Production and Consumer-Taking," *Journal of Political Economy,* 39 (October), 646–54.

Hansen, Alvin H. (1927), *Business-Cycle Theory.* Boston: Ginn.

(1951), *Business Cycles and National Income.* New York: Norton.

Harrod, Sir Roy F. (1936), *The Trade Cycle: An Essay.* Oxford: Clarendon.

(1939), "An Essay in Dynamic Theory," *Economic Journal,* 49 (March), 14–33.

(1948), *Towards a Dynamic Economics.* London: Macmillan.

Hicks, Sir John (1965), *Capital and Growth.* Oxford: Oxford University Press.

Hotelling, Harold (1931), "The Economics of Exhaustible Resources," *Journal of Political Economy,* 39 (April), 137–75.

Kalecki, Michael (1935), "A Macrodynamic Theory of Business Cycles," *Econometrica,* 3 (July), 327–44.

(1936), "Comments on the Macrodynamic Theory of Business Cycles," *Econometrica,* 4 (October), 356–60.

Keynes, John Maynard (1937), "Some Economic Consequences of a Declining Population," *Eugenics Review,* April, pp. 13–17. Reprinted in Moggridge, ed., *The Collected Writings of John Maynard Keynes,* vol. XIV, Part II, London: Macmillan, St. Martin's Press, 1973, pp. 124–33.

Lindahl, Erik (1929a), *Penningpolitikens mål.* Malmö: Förlagsaktiebolagets i Malmö boktryckeri.

(1929b), Prisbildningsproblemets uppläggning från kapitalteoretisk synpunkt," *Ekonomisk Tidskrift,* 31, 31–81. Translated as "The Place of Capital in the Theory of Price," in Erik Lindahl, *Studies in the Theory of Money and Capital,* Part III, London: Allen & Unwin, 1939.

(1930), *Penningpolitikens medel.* Lund: Gleerup. Partially translated as "The Rate of Interest and the Price Level," in Erik Lindahl, *Studies in the Theory of Money and Capital,* Part II, London: Allen & Unwin, 1939.

(1939), "The Dynamic Aspect to Economic Theory," in Erik Lindahl, *Studies in the Theory of Money and Capital,* Part I. London: Allen & Unwin.

Lundberg, Erik (1937), *Studies in the Theory of Economic Expansion.* London: King.

Myrdal, Gunnar (1927), *Prisbildningsproblemet och föränderligheten.* Uppsala: Almqvist & Wiksell.

(1931), "Om penningteoretisk jämvikt," *Ekonomisk Tidskrift,* vol. 33. Translated as "Der Gleichgewichtsbegriff als Instrument der geldtheoretischen Analyse," in Friedrich A. Hayek, ed., *Beiträge zur Geldtheorie,* Vienna: Springer, 1933, and as *Monetary Equilibrium,* London: Hodge, 1939.

Ohlin, Bertil (1933), "Till frågan om penningteoriens uppläggning," *Ekonomisk Tidskrift,* 35, 45–81. Translated by Hans Brems as "On the Formulation of Monetary Theory," *History of Political Economy,* 10, 353–88, 1978.

(1934), *Penningpolitik, offentliga arbeten, subventioner och tullar som medel mot arbetslöshet – bidrag till expansionens teori.* Stockholm: P. A. Norstedt & Söner.

(1937), "Some Notes on the Stockholm Theory of Savings and Investment," *Economic Journal,* 47 (March), 53–69, and 47 (June), 221–40.

Petersson, Jan (1987), *Erik Lindahl och Stockholmsskolans dynamiska metod.* Lund: Dialogos.

Phillips, Alban Williams (1954), "Stabilisation Policy in a Closed Economy," *Economic Journal,* 64 (June), 290–323.

Robertson, Dennis (1926), *Banking Policy and the Price Level.* London: Staples Press.

Samuelson, Paul A. (1938), "A Note on the Pure Theory of Consumer's Behavior," *Economica,* 5 (February), 61–71.

——— (1939), "Interactions Between the Multiplier Analysis and the Principle of Acceleration," *Review of Economics and Statistics,* 21 (May) 75–8.

——— (1976), "Alvin Hansen As A Creative Economic Theorist," *Quarterly Journal of Economics,* 90 (February), 24–31.

Siven, Claes-Henric (1985), "The End of the Stockholm School," *Scandinavian Journal of Economics,* 87, 577–93.

Svennilson, Sven Ingvar (1938), *Ekonomisk plannering.* Uppsala: Almqvist & Wiksell.

von Neumann, John (1937), "Über ein ökonomisches Gleichungssystem und eine Verallgemeinerung des Brouwerschen Fixpunktsatzes," *Ergebnisse eines mathematischen Kolloquiums,* 8, 73–83. Translated by G. Morgenstern (Morton) in William J. Baumol and Stephen M. Goldfield, eds., *Precursors in Mathematical Economics: An Anthology,* London: London School of Economics, 1968, pp. 296–306.

Wicksell, Knut (1898), *Geldzins und Güterpreise.* Jena: G. Fischer. Translated by R. F. Kahn with an introduction by Bertil Ohlin as *Interest and Prices,* London: Macmillan, 1936.

Comment

BJÖRN HANSSON

Professor Brems gives a very articulate analysis of the Stockholm School and Keynes from the point of view "of the new reality of the steady-state equilibrium growth of the 1950s and 1960s" and he finds them, not unexpectedly, to be "obsolescent." The only lasting contribution of the Stockholm School, from this perspective, is their "early insistence on the use of lags." However, that was certainly not very original since Dennis Robertson excelled everybody in this respect with all types of lags in *Banking Policy and the Price Level* of 1926, which had a seminal influence on Keynes in his *Treatise on Money* of 1930.

From the perspective of the 1970s and 1980s, steady-state equilibrium growth has become obsolescent. Interest has focused on the role of information, for or against rational expectations, and disequilibrium dynamics. In this development, there has been a new interest in temporary equilibrium and sequential economics, both of which were central contributions of the Stockholm School.

CHAPTER 10

Ohlin and the *General Theory*[1]

ROBERT W. CLOWER

> "'Tis a pitiful tale," said the Bellman, whose face
>   Had grown longer at every word:
> "But now that you've stated the whole of your case,
>   More debate would be simply absurd."
> Lewis Carroll, *The Hunting of the Snark*

In a 1972 volume of economic essays, Gunnar Myrdal describes the Keynesian Revolution as "mainly an Anglo-American occurrence. In Sweden, where we grew up in the tradition of Knut Wicksell, Keynes' works were read as interesting and important contributions along a familiar line of thought, but not in any sense as a revolutionary break-through" (Myrdal, 1972, pp. 4–5). This description applies with particular force to Bertil Ohlin, as indicated by the concluding paragraph of his 1937 "Notes on the Stockholm Theory of Savings and Investment":

> In his attempt to bring about a coordination of economic theory Keynes does not – at least from the Stockholm horizon – appear to have been radical or revolutionary enough. The equilibrium method instead of process analysis in which not more of the equilibrium idea is left than consideration of more or less stable positions, the insufficient distinction between "realisations" and "expectations," the retaining of physical marginal productivity, the disutility analysis of labour supply, in a way also the aggregate supply function, are all evidence of an exaggerated conservatism in *method* which has hampered his work.[2]

The inference is plain: Ohlin acknowledges the novelty of Keynes's application of equilibrium analysis to the theory of output as a whole, but he questions the probable scientific fruitfulness of such a conventional approach to unconventional problems.

If my interpretation of Ohlin is valid, what sense can one make of recent discussions of the question whether the Stockholm School and, more particularly, Bertil Ohlin can be credited with the simultaneous "discovery" of the *General Theory*?[3] To be sure, no one before Keynes appears to have thought of applying equilibrium analysis to the demand and supply of output as a whole. A book that adopted such a perspective, particularly as a basis for interpreting the depression of the 1930s, surely would not have attracted so much professional attention had its author not already been an acknowledged economic genius (cf. Patinkin, 1982, p. 88). And there is no doubt that the *General Theory* produced a revolution in economics. But was there anything revolutionary in the analytical content of the *General Theory*?[4]

1   The Patinkin interpretation

How Keynes would have answered this question is indicated in Chapter 3 of the *General Theory* where, following a preliminary account of the determination of "effective demand" by aggregate supply and demand, Keynes remarks: "Since this is the substance of the General Theory of Employment, which it will be our object to expound, the succeeding chapters will be largely occupied with examining the various factors upon which these two functions depend" (JMK, VII, p. 25). In itself, of course, this passage settles nothing, since it leaves open the question whether Keynes's "central message"[5] lies in his theory of effective demand or in "succeeding chapters." Any doubts one might otherwise have had on this score, however, surely have been put to rest by Don Patinkin's analysis of this question (Patinkin, 1982, pp. 5–11), which definitively[6] rules out the "necessary originality"[7] of material found in succeeding chapters, thereby leaving Keynes's theory of effective demand as the sole contender for that title.

But here another issue arises, for as Patinkin himself acknowledges and emphasizes (1982, p. 9, fn. 7), what *he* means by "Keynes's" theory of effective demand "does not exactly accord with the presentation in Chapter 3 of the *General Theory*." That is surely an understatement, for what Patinkin puts forward as an account of the "central message of the *General Theory*" is the familiar Keynesian cross analysis that has dominated textbook expositions of elementary macroeconomics since it appeared in the first (1948) edition of Paul Samuelson's *Economics*. Let me be clear on this point. I do not doubt the formal or economic validity of Patinkin's interpretation of the theory of effective demand; a coherent conceptual basis for Patinkin's interpretation is, in fact, adumbrated in Chapter XIII of Patinkin's *Money, Interest, and Prices* (pp. 214–21 of the 1956 edition, pp. 316–24 of the 1965 edition).[8] But that is not the issue; the issue is whether Patinkin's interpretation of Keynes's theory of effective demand, like his identification of Keynes's "central message," can be regarded as definitive? As matters presently stand, the answer is problematic.

So we come to the point of this discussion: If Patinkin's interpretation of Keynes is accepted, the Swedes cannot validly claim to have anticipated the distinctive analytical contribution of the *General Theory,* for they surely did not anticipate Samuelson's Keynesian cross analysis; but if Patinkin's interpretation is rejected, then the central issue in the controversy about the relation between Keynes's *General Theory* and the earlier writings of Ohlin and the Stockholm School remains to be resolved.

My purpose in this paper is to bring the controversy to a head. Specifically, I shall suggest an interpretation of the theory of effective demand that is both more general than Patinkin's and more consistent with the conceptual framework of Keynes's *General Theory,* and I shall show that – on this more general view – Patinkin's unfavorable assessment of the claims of the Stockholm School has no force. Indeed, I shall argue for a stronger result: Patinkin to the contrary notwithstanding, there is merit in Ohlin's contention that "the Keynesian reasoning about underemployment equilibrium is . . . chiefly a simplified demonstration of some of the results of the sequence analysis in Stockholm"[9] (Ohlin, 1981b, p. 222).

2   An alternative interpretation[10]

My point of departure is a provocative remark that appears in Ohlin's posthumously published essay on "Pre-War Keynesian and Stockholm Theories of Employment" (Ohlin, 1981b, p. 223): "Keynes' theory of effective demand is based on [Marshallian] supply and demand curves [that refer to] aggregate income and output in the whole country."[11] Evidently, Ohlin is suggesting that Keynes's supposedly novel apparatus of aggregate demand and supply, as presented in Chapter 3 of the *General Theory,* is actually a disguised version of Marshall's short-period theory of demand and supply.

Following this lead, let us consider the supply and demand diagram in Figure 1 where, in keeping with Marshall's practice, we assume that the D and S curves[12] relate demand and supply prices to "the aggregate volume of production" rather than quantities demanded and supplied to "market price" (cf. Marshall, 1920, pp. 342 ff.). Suppose initially that the short-period "output of the economy as a whole" – here presumed to be a meaningful concept – is at the level q_0 so that the demand price p_0^d as given by the demand curve $D(Z_0)$ is greater than the supply price p_0^s as given by the supply curve $S(w_0)$. If we assume that the current

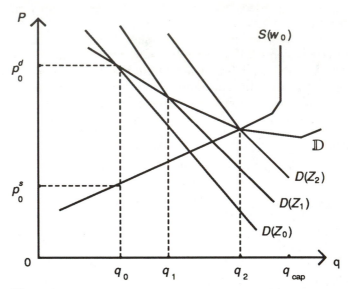

Figure 1.

market price lies generally in the neighborhood of the demand price,[13] then on standard Marshallian reasoning, producers will have an incentive to increase output and employment.

Here we run into a complication: Unless unemployed workers are available at the going wage rate, producers can increase output only by bidding up the prevailing money wage rate, in which case the supply curve will shift. To avoid this problem, let us assume that, at the existing money wage rate, w_0, unemployed workers are available at all values of output less than q_{cap} so that the aggregate level of output and employment may be presumed to depend solely upon the hiring decisions of business firms. A second complication then arises: Unless the demand curve is independent of "aggregate producer outlay" (defined as $Z = p^s q$),[14] changes in output will produce shifts in the demand curve, the amount of such shifts depending on the responsiveness of aggregate producer outlay to changes in output and on the responsiveness of demand to changes in aggregate producer outlay. This problem can be handled, at least in principle, by defining a *mutatis mutandis* demand curve (illustrated by curve $\mathbb{D}$ in Figure 1) that shows demand price as a function of aggregate output, due allowance being made for the effect of changes in output on aggregate producer outlay and for the resultant effect of changes in aggregate outlay on the *ceteris paribus* demand curves $D(Z_i)$.[15]

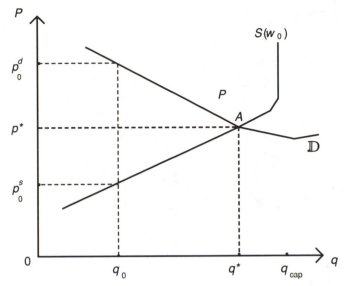

Figure 2.

Working now with the demand curve $\mathbb{D}$ and the supply curve S, we identify short-period equilibrium of aggregate output and price with the point A in Figure 2, where $q = q^*$, $p^s = p^d = p^*$, and aggregate expenditure, $E = p^d q = p^* q^* = E^*$, is equal to aggregate producer outlay, $Z = p^s q = p^* q^* = Z^*$ [i.e., $q(p^d - p^s) = 0$]. Applying the usual Marshallian "stability" condition, we may then describe the equilibrium as "stable" if the demand curve $\mathbb{D}$ lies above the supply curve S to the left of the equilibrium point A.[16]

The meaning of this stability condition for the theory of output as a whole may be brought out more clearly by translating the relations shown in Figure 2 into a "Marshallian Cross" diagram as shown in Figure 3. Here, distances along the horizontal axis measure alternative (notional) levels of aggregate producer outlay, Z, as determined by the S curve in Figure 2 (i.e., distances along OZ in Figure 3 correspond to *areas* such as $Z_0 = p_0^s q_0$ in Figure 2). Similarly, distances along the vertical axis in Figure 3 measure alternative (notional) levels of aggregate consumer outlay, E, as defined by the $\mathbb{D}$ curve in Figure 2 (i.e., distances along OE in Figure 3 correspond to *areas* such as $E_0 = p_0^d q_0$ in Figure 2). Treating the output variable as a parameter, we first define the *aggregate spending function* by writing $E(q) = f(Z\{q\})$. The equilibrium level of aggregate producer outlay, Z^*, is then defined by the requirement $E = Z$ [i.e., $q(p^d - p^s) = 0$], at which level the aggregate spending func-

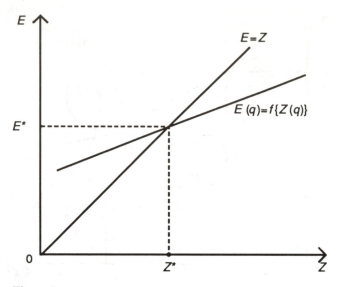

Figure 3.

tion must intersect the 45° line. On this interpretation, the Marshallian stability condition is that, in the neighborhood of the intersection point, the slope of the spending function, which we may call the *marginal propensity to spend,* must be less than one. Thus, through straightforward development of an analysis that is now more than a century old,[17] we have "discovered" the "fundamental psychological law" (JMK VII, p. 96) that Keynes, pursuing an independent route, took perhaps two years to find![18]

If the marginal propensity to spend is equal to one, then the D and S curves in Figure 2 – hence the aggregate spending function and the 45° line in Figure 3 – coincide in the neighborhood of the equilibrium point and we have what Marshall called "neutral" equilibrium (see Whitaker, 1975, p. 153). This corresponds, of course, to what Keynes later defined as "Say's Law" (JMK, VII, pp. 25–6). Needless to say, this "Law" formed no part of the thinking of Marshall or any other "orthodox" economist. Keynes's confusion on this matter is just one aspect of a more general confusion about the foundations of his theory of effective demand to which Patinkin has drawn attention (Patinkin, 1982, Chapter 5, particularly pp. 149–53). These same confusions are, of course, strong evidence of the "subjective originality" of Keynes's version of the theory.

The present line of argument might be extended in several directions, but to carry it further would serve no useful purpose here. Already it will be evident that our Marshallian "theory of effective demand" is what Keynes himself probably would have arrived at[19] had he been less concerned to "raise a dust" (JMK, XIII, p. 548). Considered in this context, there is nothing "revolutionary" about Keynes's theory as such; it is just the "classical" equilibrium economics of Marshall, Walras, Pigou, and Wicksell, applied to the determination of the general price level and aggregate output and employment on the assumption that there exist unemployed resources (the last condition being rationalized by supposing that wages and prices are rigid or sticky).[20]

3 Alternative theories of short-period supply

I turn now to the task of showing that Patinkin's version of the theory of effective demand inaccurately characterizes Keynes's analysis. This task might be approached directly through detailed exegesis of textual evidence, but the heart of my argument can be reached more effectively by another route. Specifically, I shall begin by sketching two alternative models of short-period competitive output and price determination. Though the two models have a common source in the writings of Alfred Marshall, and though the models differ conceptually only in that one deals with trading in "thick" markets while the other deals with trading in "thin" markets, we shall discover that their behavioral implications are unambiguously distinguishable. It will then be a simple matter to show that one model is substantially equivalent to the theory of short-period supply that underlies Keynes's analysis in the *General Theory*, while the other is substantially equivalent to the different conception of short-period supply that underlies Patinkin's version of Keynes's theory of effective demand.

Taking our cue from Marshall, let us imagine a money economy in which the typical market is one where traders are so numerous and the physical volume of trading so large and continuous that, even in the very short run, no seller or buyer either imagines himself or is, in fact, capable of significantly influencing the terms of trade by his own actions. More succinctly, assume that every trader can buy or sell any desired quantity of any traded commodity on short notice at the "going" price (for future reference, let us call this assumption the *thick market hypothesis*).[21] Suppose, further, that the typical producer independently chooses both his asking price and his output. On the thick market hypothesis, we may assume that the producer feels free to choose his current output without regard to his present level of sales, for he can be presumed to know that "undesired" inventory holdings produced by unanticipated differences between output and sales can quickly be eliminated by moderate adjustments in asking price. Assuming that the producer seeks to maximize profits, therefore, it is plausible to define short-period equilibrium output by the requirement that marginal cost equal current asking price, and to define short-period equilibrium asking price by the requirement that inventories be at some desired level (possibly zero).

There is little point in carrying this sketch further. Except that the model makes individual producers responsible for setting asking prices, it is simply an alternative (Marshallian) version of the familiar textbook theory of short-period demand and supply. Though asking prices are "administered," the "going" price is governed by impersonal market forces that tend always to drive individual asking prices toward equality; so short-period market equilibrium is defined by the usual requirement that the "going" price equate aggregate quantity demanded with aggregate quantity supplied (the latter magnitude being defined, of course, as the sum of the profit-maximizing outputs of individual producers).[22]

The simplicity and analytical tautness of the thick market model depends crucially on the fact that, because of high volume and continuous trading, individual producers can reliably predict the qualitative effect of changes in asking price on individual sales. In these circumstances, rational behavior implies that individual producers treat asking prices as short-period instruments of inventory control. Thin markets are different. Here, by hypothesis, trading volume per unit of time is too slight and too erratic to permit individual producers to gauge even the qualitative effect of changes in asking price on short-period sales (call this the *thin market hypothesis*). Thus, asking prices are neither efficient nor reliable short-period instruments of inventory control. Just what kind of behavior would be "rational" in these circumstances is problematic,[23] but to vary asking price in response to short-run variations in sales plainly would be "irrational."[24]

There is a vast literature on thin markets,[25] for in every actual economy such markets account for the bulk of all trade in retailing, food processing, wholesaling, manufacturing, transportation, and service; so we have a surfeit of "seat-of-the-pants" knowledge about the way these markets work in practice. The stylized fact that stands out from all others is that short-period output in such markets is demand-determined. Another well-confirmed fact is that asking prices are governed more by past and prospective costs and by actual and potential competition than by short-run demand conditions. Let us suppose, then, that rational behavior in thin markets requires the typical producer to: (1) set short-period asking price at a level that ensures average total costs will be cov-

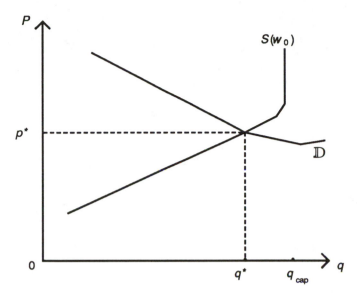

Figure 4.

ered for a range of sales significantly less than capacity output; (2) adjust output passively within the period to match the average volume of sales; (3) hold buffer stocks of inventories to avoid frequent transient adjustments in output. In situations of significant unused capacity, producers can be expected to engage in competitive selling activities (temporary discounts, rebates, prize contests, etc.) in an effort to boost short-period sales, so average transaction prices will tend to fall. Similarly, in situations involving little unused capacity, producers can be expected to compete for factors in ways that increase both variable and fixed costs, and some of these increases will be passed on in the form of higher asking prices. By and large, however, we may suppose that in thin markets an individual producer's short-period asking and transaction prices are inflexible and that short-period output is determined by short-period sales (subject, of course, to the proviso that marginal cost be no greater than price).

So much for the microeconomics of thick and thin markets. Proceeding once more on the assumption that aggregate output, aggregate sales, and so on are heuristically meaningful concepts, we may illustrate the macroeconomic implications of the two models by considering the corresponding aggregate demand and supply diagrams as shown in Figures 4 and 5. On the *thick market hypothesis* the relevant relations are those shown in Figure 4, which are, of course, replicas of those shown earlier

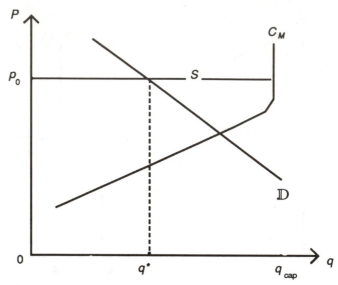

Figure 5.

in Figure 2. On the *thin market hypothesis,* however, the relevant relations are those shown in Figure 5. Here the short-period aggregate supply curve, S, appears as a horizontal line segment, situated at the (given)
aggregate asking price p_0 and terminating at the "capacity" level of output q_{cap}. In keeping with earlier discussion, S in Figure 5 is assumed to
lie everywhere above the aggregate marginal cost curve C_M (C_M is, of
course, a replica of the S curve shown in Figure 4). Because the form of
the *mutatis mutandis* demand curve depends in part on the form of the
aggregate supply curve, the *mutatis mutandis* demand curve $\mathbb{D}$ in Figure 5 also differs from its analogue in Figure 4.

   Obviously the short-period comparative statics of these two macromodels differ in just one important respect: In a world of thick markets,
shifts in aggregate demand produce equilibrating shifts in both output
and price; but in a world of thin markets, shifts in aggregate demand
produce equilibrating shifts in output alone.

   No serious argument is required to establish that the thin-market
hypothesis underlies Patinkin's interpretation of Keynes's theory of
effective demand; Patinkin himself effectively affirms this in his 1978
assessment of Ohlin's 1933 essay on monetary theory (Patinkin, 1978;
see also Patinkin, 1982, especially pp. 52–6).[26] Indeed, Patinkin's
implicit rejection of the thick market hypothesis was a recurrent target
of wrath for Ohlin in his posthumously published reply to Patinkin

(Ohlin, 1981b, pp. 206–12, especially the comment on p. 211: "[Keynes] left to Patinkin the role to regard it as a *deathly sin* to give a more complicated picture than his own exceedingly simplified one.").

There remains the question whether the thick market hypothesis underlies Keynes's *General Theory*. On that issue, Patinkin has the dubious distinction of being perhaps the only Keynes scholar who seems to have any serious doubts. He expressed these doubts most forcefully in his 1982 "Critique of Keynes' Theory of Effective Demand," where he concludes:

> [T]he obscurity with which the aggregate supply curve is presented in the *General Theory* is a sign not of profundity, but of obscurity: not, as some would have us believe, of a deep underlying analytical framework in which everything falls into place, but of the same confusions and imprecisions which manifested themselves in the 1933 drafts of the book and which continued to live on in Keynes' mind furtively, below the surface, through the final version as well.

The truth of these observations may be granted. Keynes undoubtedly was confused in his handling of aggregative concepts that were new to him and, in his mind at least, not directly derivable from conventional theory because (as he put it): "the community's output of goods and services is a non-homogeneous complex which cannot be measured, strictly speaking, except in certain special cases. . . ." But does this mean that Keynes also repudiated Marshall's theory of short-period competitive supply? That is the crux of the matter, for as our earlier argument makes clear (see especially the concluding paragraph of section 2), acceptance of the conventional theory of short-period supply is logically equivalent to acceptance of the thick market macromodel.

Did Keynes in the *General Theory* mean to repudiate the conventional profit-maximization theory of short-period competitive supply? Surely, had Keynes intended anything so radical, we should find better evidence of it in the *General Theory* than the indirect indications of "obscurity and confusion" on which Patinkin relies. But to clinch the matter, let me cite three pieces of evidence that, when considered together, seem to me to remove "all reasonable doubt."

In Chapter 3 of the last 1933 draft table of contents of the *General Theory*, Keynes writes:

> The process which decides the volume of employment is as follows. Each firm calculates the prospective selling price of its output and its variable cost in respect of output on various possible scales of production. Its variable cost per unit is not, as a rule, constant for all volumes of output but increases as output increases. Output is then pushed to

the point at which the prospective selling price no longer exceeds the marginal variable cost. In this way the volume of output, and hence the volume of employment, is determined. (JMK, XXIX, p. 98)

In mid-1935, some months before the *General Theory* was finally published, we find further evidence of Keynes's commitment to standard analysis in a letter from Keynes to R. F. Kahn:

I have been making rather extensive changes in the early chapters of my book, to a considerable extent consequential on a simple and obvious, but beautiful and important (I think) precise definition of what is meant by effective demand: –
Let W be the marginal price cost of production when output is O.
Let P be the expected selling price of this output.
Then OP is effective demand.
The fundamental assumption of the classical theory, "supply creates its own demand," is that OW = OP *whatever* the level of O, so that effective demand is incapable of setting a limit to employment.... On *my* theory OW [is not equal to] OP for *all* values of O and entrepreneurs have to choose a value of O for which it *is* equal; – *otherwise the equality of price and marginal prime cost is infringed.* This is the real starting point of everything. (JMK XIII, pp. 422–3; my italics in the penultimate sentence)

Finally, we have evidence from Keynes's 1937 personal correspondence with Ohlin over publication of Ohlin's "Notes." In the third instalment of the "Notes," Ohlin put forward a criticism of Keynes's *General Theory* based explicitly on dissatisfaction with the conventional theory of short-period competitive supply or, as Ohlin calls it, "the old reasoning." At one point he even chides Keynes for apparently having "never discussed imperfect competition with Mrs Robinson."[27] Keynes's response (JMK, XIV, p. 190) was blunt: "I have not been able to make out here what you are driving at. The reference to imperfect competition is very perplexing. I cannot see how on earth it comes in." There is an obvious irony here: Patinkin's assessment of Ohlin implicitly rests on his attribution to Keynes of a conception of the theory of short-period supply for which Ohlin expressed support and Keynes expressed disdain![28]

4   The anticipation issue once more

As intimated earlier, I side with Ohlin in feeling that Keynes's theory of effective demand contained nothing essentially new; that Keynes's analysis, though subjectively original, was ". . . chiefly a simplified demonstration of some of the results of the sequence analysis in Stockholm."

In light of my subsequent elaboration of the Mashallian foundations of Keynes's theory, this conclusion may well appear disingenuous, for what I am effectively arguing is that neither Keynes nor the Swedish economists of the 1930s discovered anything essentially new: *The analytical substance of Keynes's* General Theory *and of the "Stockholm Theory" is already contained in earlier work by Marshall and Wicksell.*

Patinkin reaches a different conclusion – or so I conjecture – because he starts from the presumption that "a book on economic theory which . . . revolutionize[d] the way the world thinks about economic problems" (JMK, XIII, p. 492) must have contained at least one great analytical "discovery." I believe this presumption reflects an erroneous standard for evaluating scientific achievement. What most impresses me about the work of so-called "great scientists" is not the originality of their analytical ideas but the catalytic quality of their conceptual perspectives. It is this aspect of scientific thought that leads us unhesitatingly to put Copernicus, Galileo, Newton, Darwin, Einstein and a handful of other seminal thinkers in a class by themselves. It is for similar reasons that, in economics, only a few people such as Smith, Ricardo, Marshall, Wicksell, and Keynes are universally thought to merit the encomium "great."

Two further observations are in order before I conclude. First, I find it hard to imagine that anyone could read Ohlin's "Notes on the Stockholm Theory" carefully and doubt that Ohlin understood Keynes's *General Theory* perhaps better than its author. Ohlin's detailed critical remarks – about the consumption function, the multiplier, the liquidity preference theory of the rate of interest, the relation between movements in output and real wage rates, user cost, the definition of savings and investment, the aggregate supply function, and a host of other contentious topics – were generally "right on target," as subsequent professional discussion has revealed. Such acuteness, such prescience, is hardly likely to be found except in a critic who independently has already "discovered" the essential ideas of the theory under review. Second, I should like to draw attention to a passage in Ohlin's 1933 essay on monetary theory where he effectively enunciates what I would call "the Marshall-Keynes condition" for the stability of macroeconomic equilibrium:

> Neo-Wicksellian theory habitually expresses as follows the conditions for an interruption of [a] price decline. Since investment is too low relative to saving, either more must be invested or less saved. But such reasoning is conclusive only if income is thought of as given and independent of what is happening within the period. In that case, the alternatives laid down simply imply an increase of either investment demand or consumption demand. But if income is falling, aggregate

demand and prices may fall. *A correct formulation would quite simply be that the price fall will tend to be ending whenever aggregate demand is growing relative to supply.* (Ohlin, 1978, p. 379)

V   Conclusion

The Stockholm School is alive and well, but the new one seems to draw its inspiration more from Samuelson than from Wicksell. The "old" Stockholm School is gone, but the spirit that moved it still flourishes in Sweden and elsewhere: the urge to maintain close links between economic theory and its applications. Who can say that the theoretical insights of Ohlin and other Swedish economists of the 1930s will not bear fruit in the decade of the 1990s? Who, more particularly, can say that the future of Keynesian economics does not lie in the direction suggested by Ohlin in the passage of his "Notes" quoted at the outset of this paper: "process analysis in which not more of the equilibrium idea is left than consideration of more or less stable positions"?[29] My own conjecture is that the last and most significant chapter in the Ohlin-Keynes story has yet to be written.

Notes

1 I have received valuable comments from participants at the Stockholm School conference.

2 These remarks are from the posthumously published third instalment of Ohlin's "Notes" (Ohlin, 1981a, p. 249), but similar – indeed, much more sharply worded – critical observations are a prominent feature of the two installments published in the 1937 volume of the *Economic Journal* (Ohlin, 1937).

3 See Patinkin (1982, Chapter 2) for discussion and references.

4 Cf. T. S. Kuhn's comment on Copernicus: "The significance of the *De Revolutionibus* lies ... less in what it says itself than in what it caused others to say. The book gave rise to a revolution that it had scarcely enunciated. It is a revolution-making rather than a revolutionary text" (Kuhn, 1957, p. 135).

5 This is Patinkin's term. For a characteristically erudite discussion of its meaning, see Patinkin (1982, Chapter 4).

6 The word "definitively" is perhaps a bit strong; after all, Marx reached his labor theory of value by a similar elimination process.

7 *Pace* Gunnar Myrdal, who is perhaps best known among modern-day economists as the Nobel Laureate who described Keynes's *Treatise* as "unnecessarily original."

8 I say "adumbrated" because the argument presented there is so clear an example of "seat-of-the-pants" analysis. As Patinkin remarks in a final footnote (fn. 9, both editions): "There is ... a basic analytical problem here

whose full solution is still not clear to me. [...] It may be that, as Mr. [Nissan] Liviatan has suggested, *a complete answer to this question depends on the development of a theory of the firm operating under conditions of uncertainty with respect to the size of its market"* (italics mine).

9 Cf. Myrdal, 1982 (as cited in Jonung, 1987, fn. 7): "we in the Stockholm School were not only far ahead of Keynes and his colleagues in breaking away from the conventional view on monetary and stabilization policy but our approach was superior to that of Keynes in a number of respects."

10 This section draws freely from a paper on "Keynes's *General Theory:* The Marshall Connection" that I presented at the June 1978 meetings of the History of Economics Society in Boston.

11 This is not a continuous quotation, but it accurately expresses the sense of Ohlin's remark. For a similar view of Keynes's theory, see my "The Keynesian Perplex" (Clower, 1975, as reprinted in Walker, ed., 1984, 189–90).

12 For convenience in working with my computer, I have shown the "curves" in Figure 1, and also in later graphs, as linear or piecewise-linear relations. needless to say, this aspect of the geometry of the diagrams plays no essential role in the subsequent theoretical argument.

13 This is eminently plausible in the context of Marshall's thinking, for to Marshall the typical market was one in which ". . . the forces of demand and supply have free play; . . . there is no close combination among dealers on either side, but each acts for himself, and there is much free competition; that is, buyers generally compete freely with buyers, and sellers compete freely with sellers. But though everyone acts for himself, his knowledge of what others are doing is supposed to be generally sufficient to prevent him from taking a lower or paying a higher price than others are doing. This is assumed provisionally to be true both of finished goods and of their factors of production, of the hire of labor and of the hiring of capital" (Marshall, 1920, p. 341).

14 Marshall described the same notion on page 420 (fn. 2) of the first edition of his *Principles* but omits it from later editions. The magnitude in question corresponds precisely to what Keynes later called "Aggregate Supply Price," so I follow Keynes and denote it by the letter Z.

15 The derivation of the *mutatis mutandis* demand curve is straightforward: It is the locus of intersections of alternative *ceteris paribus* demand curves, $D(Z_0)$, $D(Z_1)$, $D(Z_2)$, and so on, with perpendiculars erected from alternative values of aggregate output, q_0, q_1, q_2, and so on, that enter into the determination of corresponding values of aggregate producer outlay Z_0, Z_1, Z_2, and so on. Cf. Parinello (1980, p. 72) and Kregel (1985, pp. 544–5).

16 I put quotation marks here because the "stability" in question is purely virtual. Marshall's analysis, like all exercises of its kind, is concerned with *tendencies* that are assumed to be operative in alternative initial situations, not with real-time adjustment processes (cf. Samuelson, 1947, pp. 273 ff.).

17 Marshall's ideas, in virtually modern form, are set out in work that Marshall completed before 1875 (on this, see Whitaker, 1975, Vol. 1, pp. 37 ff.).

18 This time estimate is based on the careful analysis of Patinkin in Chapter 2

of Patinkin and Leith (1977), and on a fascinating paper by Ingo Berens entitled "From the 'Banana Parable' to the Principle of Effective Demand" that was presented at the annual conference of the History of Economics Society in Boston, June 1987.

19 Just such a development was suggested in the "manifesto" that Joan and Austin Robinson and Richard Kahn sent to Keynes in May 1932 (JMK, XXIX, pp. 43 ff.) and was later urged upon him by Joan Robinson as a "method more general than yours" (JMK, XXIX, p. 47). In his reply, Keynes treated the issue as a "question of which is the best of two alternative exegetical methods. Here I am open to conviction [but] I lack at present sufficient evidence to the contrary to induce me to scrap all my present half-forged weapons" (JMK, XIII, p. 378).

20 Axel Leijonhufvud has disputed the "rigid-wage-rate" interpretation of Keynes in various publications over the past twenty years (see especially Leijonhufvud, 1969, section IV, and his comments as reported in the volume on Cambridge University Keynes Centenary celebration of July, 1983 (Worswick and Trevithick, 1983). Whether he would still dispute it, given the Marshall connection established here, I do not know.

21 Notice that, on this definition of thick markets, all non-purely competitive models in which demand *as seen by the individual seller* is assumed acurately to reflect demand *as it actually is* would be classified as "thick" (this includes all "large group" models of monopolistic competition as well as the conventional theory of monopoly). The now-standard textbook distinction between "price takers" and "price searchers" is clearly misleading: If an individual seller "knows" his demand curve, he has no need to "search" for the price at which alternative levels of output can be sold.

22 The model incidentally provides a simple answer to Arrow's query about who determines competitive price if there is no "auctioneer" (Arrow, 1959, pp. 42–3, 1986, p. 387). The mere posing of that query should have suggested the inappropriateness of the Walrasian model for considering such issues.

23 Cf. the similar remark by Patinkin (note 8) that precedes his summary of Liviatan's prescient suggestion about the need for a "theory of the firm operating under conditions of uncertainty with respect to the size of its market."

24 Cf. JMK, VII, p. 407; Arrow, 1986, p. 386.

25 An account of some particularly instructive items in this literature is given in Okun (1981, pp. 178 – 81). (Okun's "customer market" is, of course, a particular instance of my "thin market.")

26 In this same connection it is also pertinent to recall Patinkin's earlier analysis of "Keynesian" unemployment in Chapter 13 of his *Money, Interest, and Prices* (see note 8).

27 Ohlin might have conveyed his true meaning more effectively had he expressed wonder that Keynes apparently had never read Chamberlin's book on *monopolistic* competition which, unlike Joan Robinson's *imperfect* competition, contains numerous insightful remarks about the economics of thin markets (cf. note 20).

28 As is well known, Keynes changes his mind later in response to criticism by

Dunlop and Tarshis that mirrored precisely the criticisms advanced earlier by Ohlin (see section v of Keynes's response to Dunlop and Tarshis, reprinted as Appendix 3 of JMK, VII).

29 Compare the argument in the penultimate section of my "Keynes's *General Theory:* A Contemporary Perspective" (forthcoming in a volume of the Oxford Money Study Group containing papers from the September 1986 conference in honor of Sir John Hicks's contributions to monetary economics).

References

Arrow, K. J. (1959), "Toward a Theory of Price Adjustment," in Moses Abramovitz and others, *The Allocation of Economic Resources: Essays in Honor Of Bernard Haley,* Stanford Studies in History, Economics, and Political Science, 12. Stanford: Stanford University Press.

(1986), "Rationality of Self and Others in an Economic System," *Journal of Business,* 59 (No. 4, Pt. 2), 385–98.

Berens, Ingo (1987), "From the 'Banana Parable' to the Principle of Effective Demand: On the Origin, Development and Structure of Keynes' Thought," paper presented at the Fourteenth Annual meeting of the History of Economics Society, Boston, June 19–22.

Clower, Robert W. (1975), "Reflections on the Keynesian Perplex," as reprinted in Walker, *Money and Markets,* Cambridge, England: Cambridge University Press, 1984.

(1987a), "Keynes's General Theory: The Marshall Connection," draft of paper presented at the History of Economics Society meeting in Boston, June 1987.

(1987b), "Keynes's *General Theory:* A Contemporary Perspective," forthcoming.

Jonung, Lars (1987), "The Stockholm School After 50 Years," paper presented at the June meeting of the History of Economics Society, Boston.

Keynes, John Maynard (1930), *A Treatise on Money,* as reprinted in Keynes, *Collected Writings* (cited as JMK), Vols. V and VI.

(1936), *The General Theory of Employment, Interest and Money,* JMK, Vol. VII.

Kregel, Jan (1985), "Sidney Weintraub's Macrofoundations of Microeconomics and the Theory of Distribution," *Journal of Post-Keynesian Economics,* 7 (Summer), 540–58.

Kuhn, Thomas S. (1957), *The Copernican Revolution.* New York: Vintage Books.

Leijonhufvud, Axel (1969), "Keynes and the Classics," published by The Institute of Economics Affairs, Westminster, July.

Marshall, Alfred (1920), *Principles of Economics,* 8th ed. London: Macmillan.

Myrdal, Gunnar (1972), *Against the Stream: Critical Essays in Economics.* New York: Pantheon.

Ohlin, Bertil (1937), "Some Notes on the Stockholm Theory of Saving and Investment," *Economic Journal,* 47 (March), 53–69; 47 (June), 221–40.

(1978), "On the Formulation of Monetary Theory," 1933 essay translated by Hans Brems and William Yohe, *History of Political Economy,* 10 (Fall), 353–88.

(1981a), "Some Notes on the Stockholm Theory of Saving and Investment, (1937)," Appendix III, *History of Political Economy,* 13 (Summer), 239–55.

(1981b), "Stockholm and Cambridge: Four Papers on the Monetary and Employment Theory of the 1930s," *History of Political Economy,* 13 (Summer), 189–238.

Okun, Arthur (1981), *Prices and Quantities,* Oxford: Basil Blackwell.

Parrinello, Sergio (1980), "The Price Level Implicit in Keynes' Effective Demand," *Journal of Post-Keynesian Economics,* 3 (Fall), 63–78.

Patinkin, Don (1956, 1965), *Money, Interest and Prices,* 1st ed., Evanston: Row Peterson, 1956; 2nd ed., New York: Harper & Row, 1965.

(1978), "Some Observations on Ohlin's 1933 Article," *History of Political Economy,* (Fall), 413–18.

(1982), *Anticipations of the General Theory?* Chicago: University of Chicago Press.

Patinkin, Don, and Clark Leith, eds. (1977), *Keynes, Cambridge and the General Theory.* Toronto: University of Toronto Press.

Samuelson, Paul A. (1974), *Foundations of Economic Analysis.* Cambridge, Mass.: Harvard University Press.

Walker, Donald A., ed. (1984), *Money and Markets: Essays by Robert W. Clower.* New York: Cambridge University Press.

Whitaker, J. K. (1975). *The Early Economic Writings of Alfred Marshall, 1867–1890.* New York: Free Press.

Worswick, David, and James Trevithick, eds. (1983), *Keynes and the Modern World,* Proceedings of the Keynes Centenary Conference, King's College, Cambridge. Cambridge, England: Cambridge University Press.

Comment

ASSAR LINDBECK

Exactly how should we formulate alternative interpretations of Keynes's theory of aggregate demand and employment? This is, it seems to me, the main issue that is raised by Clower's paper. (I leave out the question of what Keynes actually meant himself, on the ground that I have nothing to contribute to that exegetic issue.)

Let the term "Keynes I" refer to a macromodel in which the aggregate product market is in (Marshallian or Walrasian) equilibrium, while the labor market is in disequilibrium in the sense that at least some households (those that are involuntarily unemployed) are *inside* their (notional) supply curves for labor as a result of sticky nominal wages. Let the term "Keynes II" refer to a macromodel in which there is simultaneously excess supply in *both* the labor market *and* the product market as a result of stickiness of both nominal wages and nominal prices; this model corresponds, of course, to the Barro-Grossman interpretation of Keynes, and it is the foundation for the simple multiplier model and the 45° cross diagram.

Whereas the "Keynes I" model implies that changes in employment are depicted as movements along a notional demand curve for labor, the "Keynes II" model implies that an (vertical) "effective" labor demand curve *shifts* in response to changes in product demand. With either of these interpretations, Keynes certainly made an important contribution to macroeconomics by suggesting mechanisms both for the determination of the actual level of aggregate output and employment and for influencing the labor market by way of variations in aggregate product demand. In neither of these models, is it reasonable to say, as Clower does, that Keynes just repeated Marshall's short-term equilibrium analysis, though for output as a whole rather than for output in some specific sector of the economy. After all, Keynes analyzed unemployment as a disequilibrium phenomenon in the labor market, providing transmission mechanisms that worked from aggregate product demand to aggregate employment. However, he did fail (along with subsequent Keynesian economists) to provide reasonable microfoundations for the asserted macroeconomic mechanisms.

It seems to me that the Stockholm School of the 1930s had neither a macrotheory for the determination of aggregate production and employment nor a transmission mechanism from the product to the labor market. Thus Patinkin seems to be correct in his view that the Stockholm School did not really anticipate Keynes's theory of aggregate demand and employment determination, regardless of whether we interpret Keynes as Keynes I or Keynes II.

Clower, challenging Patinkin's interpretation, chooses a different classification of Keynesian models than the one used above; he builds his interpretation of Keynes on the distinction between "thick" and "thin" markets. The reason that Keynes, according to Clower, did not come with anything fundamentally new, as compared to an aggregate version of Marshall's analysis of short-term equilibrium, was that Keynes accepted the idea of thick markets. Unfortunately, Clower's distinction between thick and thin markets is not clear to me. At some places in

Clower's paper, it sounds as if a thick market is a market with perfect competition in the sense of "price-taking" firms, while a thin market would be a market with imperfect competition.

However, these different market forms do *not* produce fundamentally different roles for aggregate demand management in the product market. Both imply a downward-sloping relation between the real wage and employment, and hence both are subject to "the tyranny of the downward-sloping" marginal product curve of labor. The main differences for the labor market of imperfect, as compared to perfect, competition is really that this relation in the case of imperfect competition is a reduced-form equilibrium relation, rather than a "proper" labor demand curve, and that the marginal product is premultiplied by a coefficient that depends on the elasticity of the demand for products (see A. Lindbeck and Dennis Snower in *American Economic Review, Papers and Proceedings,* May 1988). As long as this elasticity is not a (sufficiently strong) positive function of aggregate demand in the product market, there is, qualitatively speaking, the same negative relation between the real wage and the employment level as in the case of perfect competition, and aggregate demand management may influence aggregate employment only by way of movements *along* that negatively sloped labor market relation. A macrotheory built on asserted *systematic* changes in this elasticity in response to aggregate demand management is not a strong theory.

However, in other passages of Clower's paper it sounds as if the distinction between thick and thin markets is instead that there are different degrees of *uncertainty* for firms in these two types of markets – in particular regarding the consequences for the profit level of a firm when it changes its price. But Clower hardly provides any explanation *why* a thick market, with many agents and large volumes, would necessarily be characterized by less uncertainty in this respect than will a thin market.

However, assume that it is actually true that a thick market is characterized by less uncertainty than a thin market. Would it necessarily follow that firms in thin markets, because of the asserted difference in uncertainty, would react to demand fluctuations by *quantity adjustments* rather than by price adjustment? In other words, how do we know that the effects on profits in a thin market are more predictable if the firm changes its output than if it instead responds by changing its price? The impact of a discretionary change in *output* must inevitably also create a degree of uncertainty regarding profits, through its effect on both the product price and production costs.

Thus, the predictive powers of using the distinction between thick and thin markets, as described by Clower, do not seem to be very strong. I am therefore not convinced that Clower has succeeded in showing that a classification of markets into thin and thick markets – regardless of how we interpret this distinction – is of much help in distinguishing between alternative interpretations of Keynes. Nor does this classification make it possible to show, as Clower asserts, that Keynes was simply an "aggregate Marshallian" and that the Stockholm School of economists had basically developed the same framework for macroeconomic analysis as Keynes.

Comment

DON PATINKIN

I am going to restrict myself to the doctrinal aspects of Clower's paper, and from that viewpoint I can be very brief. In this paper Clower says that the question of the interpretation of Keynes and Ohlin "might be approached directly through detailed exegesis of textual evidence" – but chooses not to do so, and accordingly presents an interpretation that is practically devoid of references to their writings. I, on the other hand, do not understand how doctrinal history can be approached in any other way. In any event, I can find no textual evidence either in Keynes or in Ohlin to support Clower's interpretations of their respective positions.

Insofar as Keynes is concerned, I have elsewhere and at length presented my documented interpretation of the *General Theory* (Patinkin, 1976, 1982), and it would not be feasible to repeat all that here. Let me note, however, that Clower misrepresents my exposition when he quotes me as saying that my presentation of Keynes's theory of effective demand in terms of the 45°-cross diagram "does not exactly accord with the presentation in Chapter 3 of the *General Theory*" – and ends the quotation at that point. For that sentence goes on to say that this diagram nevertheless "captures its essence" (Patinkin, 1982, p. 9, fn. 7).

It is, of course, true that this diagram does not appear in the *General Theory*. But little significance can be attached to this fact per se for the simple reason that, with one exception, Keynes did not use analytical diagrams in any of his writings. The one exception is the diagram that appears on page 180 of the *General Theory*—a diagram that, in the accompanying footnote, Keynes attributes to Harrod (cf. Patinkin, 1976, pp. 21 and 87). Furthermore, in his *How to Pay for the War* (1940), Keynes essentially made use of the $C + I + G = Y$ analytical framework for which the 45°-cross diagram is the geometrical counterpart. In particular, he estimated the reduction in consumption expenditures necessary to avoid the generation of inflationary pressure in the

British war economy by comparing estimated total real expenditures of the economy on consumption, investment, and the war effort with the estimated real value of its output (Keynes, 1940, pp. 416–17). This is clearly the arithmetical counterpart of the graphic analysis of the "inflationary gap" that was subsequently carried out by means of the 45°-cross diagram.

Clower attempts to interpret Keynes within the framework of Marshallian price theory, and it is true that in the *General Theory* – especially in its Chapter 3 – we find references to the Marshallian notion of "demand price" and "supply price." But first of all there is the question of whether Keynes applied these notions correctly, and I have shown elsewhere that he had a confused and incorrect notion of his "aggregate supply curve" (Patinkin, 1982, Chap. 5). Second, and in the present context far more important, the central message of the *General Theory* had to do with output and employment, not prices. In Keynes's words: "the theory of prices falls into its proper place as a matter which is subsidiary to our general theory" (Keynes, 1936, p. 32).

Insofar as Ohlin is concerned, I can only repeat that his writings contain no basis for Clower's interpretation (see my detailed examination of these writings in Patinkin, 1982, Chap. 2). Furthermore, in connection with my own work on the Stockholm School, I at the time carried on a long and detailed correspondence with Ohlin, and that too is devoid of anything that would support Clower's interpretation.

Let me conclude with a technical point: I do not understand why Clower's aggregate demand curves in his Figures 1 and 2 slope downwards. The downward slope of the traditional Marshallian demand curve is due to the substitution effect, but there is obviously no such effect in the case of demand for total output. The only possible reason for a downward slope in this case is the positive real-balance effect generated by a price decline, but there is no such effect in the *General Theory* (Patinkin, 1976, pp. 110–11).

References

Keynes, John Maynard (1936). *The General Theory of Employment, Interest and Money.* London: Macmillan.

    (1940). *How to Pay for the War.* As reprinted in Keynes, *Collected Writings,* Vol. IX, pp. 367–439.

Patinkin, Don (1976). *Keynes' Monetary Thought: A Study of Its Development.* Durham, N.C.: Duke University Press.

    (1982). *Anticipations of the General Theory? And Other Essays on Keynes.* Chicago: University of Chicago Press.

CHAPTER 11

The monetary economics of the Stockholm School

JOHAN MYHRMAN[1]

The Stockholm School was christened by Bertil Ohlin in *Economic Journal* in 1937. He used this name to refer to the scientific work by Alf Johansson, Dag Hammarskjöld, Erik Lindahl, Erik Lundberg, Gunnar Myrdal, and himself that was published between 1927 and 1937, mostly in Swedish. Ohlin wanted to challenge Keynes's claim of having conceived a new theory about macroeconomic developments. According to Ohlin, the Stockholm School had worked with similar tools and problems for many years and had successfully reached similar conclusions. Schumpeter (1954) picked up this thread, although without any far-reaching analysis of the subject. Later Landgren (1960) questioned Ohlin's conclusion. In more recent years Steiger (1971, 1978) and Brems (1978) have praised Ohlin's articles (1933, 1934) as clear forerunners of Keynes's *General Theory*. Patinkin (1982), however, has remained skeptical about this interpretation.

It is the purpose of this article to reopen the case. My starting point in this endeavor is the following interpretation of what was new in the *General Theory*. In my opinion, the first important building block in Keynes's theory is the idea that output adjustment instead of price adjustment equilibrates the output market. This is emphasized by Patinkin (1982). The second significant building block is Keynes's monetary theory. In it we see the continuation from Marshall (1975) and Pigou (1917) in focusing on the supply of money and the demand for money. But by setting the interest elasticity at the center of liquidity preference, Keynes moved a long way toward a portfolio theory.[2]

In my reexamination of the Stockholm School, I concentrate on these issues and particularly on the content of the monetary theory formulated by the Stockholm School. The result of my study is a riddle, which I have not been able to solve. The riddle is why such prominent economists and scholars, brought up in the excellent monetary tradition handed down from Wicksell, Davidson, and Cassel, landed in a monetary theory where money was almost completely passive and without an explicit and convincing explanation.

My ambition is to examine the monetary economics of the Stockholm School in a broader framework, that is, to set the monetary economics of these scientists in the context of earlier work and later developments.[3] Using this approach, I hope to provide a better understanding of their place in the history of monetary theory.

For this reason I begin, in section 1, with a review of Knut Wicksell's monetary theory. Then I present the writings of the Stockholm School with some comments along the way. Section 2 is about Lindahl, 3 about Myrdal, and 4 about Ohlin. Section 5 introduces an evaluation of the Stockholm School that is continued in Section 6. Section 7 contains the main conclusions.

1   Knut Wicksell

For the classical economists as represented by, for example, Bagehot (1873), Jevons (1875), Marshall (1975), or Mill (1865), the major problem for monetary theory was to explain the role of money and credit in determining the general price level or, as they frequently wrote, in determining the value of money. In their analysis of this problem, the starting point was always the Quantity Theory of Money. They concentrated on the mechanism of exchange, which they found to be of central importance for the problem, and they used the equation of exchange as their tool.[4]

The classical economists were used to analyzing price determination in terms of supply and demand. And so they went about analyzing the determination of the value of money with the help of the supply and demand for money. The problem with their approach was, first of all, that they tended to see this market as a flow market rather than a market for a stock of money to be held. Related to this confusion was the tendency toward the invalid dichotomy, as pointed out by Patinkin (1956). This also involved the problem of the nature of the transmission mechanism, that is, how an excess supply of money is transmitted to an increase in the general price level. Furthermore, the interest rate was treated as a real variable. Their approach led to a common interpretation of the (neo)classical model as a general equilibrium system of markets to determine relative prices, a quantity theory to determine the general price level, and a loanable funds theory to determine the real rate of interest.

The use of the quantity theory in the case of a pure commodity (gold) standard did not raise much objection. The problem arose with the spread of commercial banks and the increasing use of private bank notes, which resulted in the famous Currency versus Banking School controversy. The Currency School insisted that the issue of bank notes had to be regulated in a rigid manner; otherwise the result would be an overissue of bank notes leading to increased inflation and/or an outflow of gold from the country. The major proponent of the Banking School, Thomas Tooke (1840), argued that an overissue of bank notes could not occur because the banks would not issue more bank notes than the public needed and that this need was determined by the level of prices, in turn determined by the cost of production. Tooke also argued strongly against the proposition that a low rate of interest will lead to higher prices. He rested his argument on his empirical observation that low interest rates tend to appear along with low prices. He explained this fact, the Gibson paradox, with a cost of production theory of price determination. Since the interest rate is a cost of production, a lower interest rate will lead to lower prices.

The issues that were not solved in a satisfactory way were thus the problem of causation and the role of the interest rate in the monetary process. These are problems to which Knut Wicksell turned his attention. In Wicksell's view, a bank note could be said to be a "means of payment," but it was *not* money. He used the latter concept only for hard currency. He then stated that there is a close relationship between money and credit, in which credit is the foremost leverage for increasing the velocity of money and thereby reducing the need for money. Credit, or bank notes, is thus a perfect substitute for money in the form of currency. An increase in credit is equivalent to an increase in money.

Wicksell introduced the banking system as the major producer of credit and presented his highly original idea of the "ideal bank." This bank is able to extend credit without limit and can therefore eliminate the use of money. It is a complete giro system of the type discussed today by, for example, Fama (1980).[5] Wicksell cleverly used this example as a frame of reference to illustrate the importance of bank credit to the demand for money. He mentioned three obstacles to the realization of the "ideal bank": (1) the need for small payments, (2) international payments, and (3) industrial use of precious metals.

Wicksell's next task was to explain the process through which an increase in the quantity of money, which, as we recall, consists of hard currency (in this example gold), leads to an increase in the price level in countries belonging to the gold standard. Wicksell explained how a gold discovery leads to huge and almost immediate price increases in the geographical neighborhood of the gold mines. This will not spread evenly to all other countries on the gold standard, as many would describe the process. Instead, according to Wicksell, it will cause a flow of commodities to the gold-producing areas and this will dampen price increases. However, if increased gold production continues, higher prices will sooner or later reach the other countries through their traded goods. Now Wicksell makes the important statement:

> Experience shows, however – and the opponents of the Quantity Theory have not been slow to point it out – that the position is rather the reverse: periods of rising prices are usually characterized by high interest rates, while falling prices and low interest rates usually coincide. In what follows, when we come to speak of the influence of credit on prices, we shall find what I believe to be a fully satisfactory explanation of this fact. It will be sufficient to say here that even if price fluctuations were caused exclusively by changes in the production of gold – which is certainly not the case – then the contradiction would perhaps not be as great as it appears at first sight. A rise in prices may be conceived as due to increased demand even before the cases of gold have been received in payment for exported goods, perhaps even long before, since even the preparations for gold mining require large amounts of labour and capital, i.e. of goods which will only be paid for in the future by the newly mined gold, and the capital perhaps may only be partly created by actual savings (and thus by a diminished demand for goods) the rest being brought into being by claims on bank credit. Meanwhile a rise in prices becomes possible and may perhaps be caused in the first instance by a freer use of credit, and interest rates will have a tendency to rise rather than fall. The increasing gold stocks would then act as a kind of buttress to the price movement, preventing it from falling back, as it would otherwise sooner or later have to do in consequence of the contraction of credit, i.e. as a prop introduced *later* for a rise in prices which has already started, rather than as its prime cause. (Wicksell, 1935, pp. 164–5)

This is a clear statement of the small open economy in the *Monetary Approach to the Balance of Payments.* This novel formulation of the process was introduced by Wicksell in the first Swedish edition of the *Lectures;* it did not appear in *Interest and Prices.* To his surprise, he found that it was not necessarily the case that the rate of interest had to fall during the process. In the traditional explanation, gold arrives in the industrial countries and leads to excess reserves in the banks, which lowers interest rates and ultimately raises prices.

Next Wicksell considered notes issued by the government and concluded that they could be analyzed in a rather similar way.

> We might explain the heavy fall in the value of money which is usually the consequence of successive issues of paper money in very much the same way. (Wicksell, 1935, pp. 165–6)

> Thus here also the rise in prices is, strictly speaking, primary and the
> increase of credit media secondary, and it is at least conceivable that
> under such circumstances any real superfluity of paper money, with a
> resulting fall in interest rates, will never occur. (Wicksell, 1935, p. 168)

Here, Wicksell has brought forward the direct transmission mechanism,
the real balance effect, which was neglected in *Interest and Prices,* where
he concentrated on the indirect mechanism.

Wicksell continued his treatment of monetary problems by turning
his attention to the role of credit. To him, a change in velocity is equivalent to a change in the quantity of money and a change in velocity is
brought about by a change in credit.

> We have hitherto only concerned ourselves with the influence exercised
> by a change in the actual amount of money – principally, but not
> exclusively, metallic money – on the value of money or commodity
> prices. Every change in the normal velocity of circulation of money
> must, however, be regarded as acting in essentially the same way. The
> best proof of this is the fact that the different kinds of credit used in the
> course of business, bills of exchange, cheques, banknotes, may be
> regarded either as real money, competing with or replacing hard cash,
> or as merely a means of increasing the velocity of circulation of money
> in the real sense, in so far as we extend the term to include what we
> have called the virtual velocity of circulation. (Wicksell, 1935, pp. 168–
> 9)

Wicksell's starting point was the treatment of the importance of bank
credit by the Currency School and the Banking School and by Mill,
whom he accused of trying to accept both views at the same time.
According to Wicksell, the missing link in both of these Schools was the
role of the rate of interest in the process whereby an increase in bank
credit led to an increase in the price level. He began with the remark
that the level of the money rate of interest is ultimately governed by the
supply of and demand for real capital. He then stated that a loan rate
that is an immediate expression of the real capital interest rate is the
normal rate of interest. His next observation, in *Lectures,* was that this
normal rate is an abstraction and that therefore

> The rate of interest at which *the demand for loan capital and the supply
> of savings* exactly agree, and which more or less corresponds to the
> expected yield or newly created capital, will then be the normal or nat-
> ural real rate. (Wicksell, 1935, p. 193)

If the loan rate is lower than the normal rate of interest, there will be
a reduction in savings, which means an increased demand for consumption goods and, at the same time, an increased demand for capital goods.

This will lead to an increase in the price level, and this increase will continue as long as the loan rate is below the normal rate. It is, accordingly, a *cumulative* process.

In this way, Wicksell had shown the direct mechanism of an increase in the supply of money under a commodity standard. For the small open economy he noted, somewhat to his own surprise it seems, that there is not necessarily any link through increased gold reserves, reduction in the rate of interest, increased demand for goods, and finally price increases. Instead, price increases may come first, inducing an increased demand for money that leads to an inflow of gold. The interest rate may be unchanged.

Next, he showed that government-supplied paper currency is likely to work in the same way. Finally, he had constructed an indirect mechanism that explained the role of credit, or inside money, and the rate of interest in the transmission of monetary impulses to the price level.

With these mechanisms the causation runs from the monetary system to the price level. Wicksell considered Tooke's theory to have been refuted.

2   Erik Lindahl

Wicksell never questioned the validity of the quantity theory in *Interest and Prices* or in *Lectures,* but all the members of the Stockholm School regarded it as a major subject for attack. Within this group, Erik Lindahl dealt most thoroughly with monetary theory. In an article about the relationship between the quantity of money and the price level, Lindahl (1929) thoroughly investigated the quantity theory in the transactions version. He began with two propositions, that (1) *ceteris paribus,* the price level will vary in proportion to the quantity of money in comparative static experiments and (2) under "really dynamic conditions," when even the total volume of transactions can change, the price level will vary in proportion to the relationship between the quantity of money and the volume of transactions. According to Lindahl, the controversy focused on the nature of these relationships and whether any laws had been established about deviations from strict proportionality.

The article contains a detailed discussion of alternative definitions of M, V, P, and T, followed by a comment on actual or potential empirical cicumstances. Lindahl's conclusion was that it is both conceptually difficult to find definitions consistent with a suitable definition of the price level and empirically questionable whether there is any proportionality.

Lindahl presented a mechanical treatment of the quantity equation. There is no hint about the possibility and consequences of turning it into a supply of and demand for money framework. This is surprising since he commented on both Pigou (1917) and Keynes (1923) in footnotes.

In an extensive manuscript entitled *Penningpolitikens medel* (The Means of Monetary Policy)[6] Lindahl stated that the goal of monetary policy should be to reduce the risks that imperfectly expected events imply for economic activity. Since monetary policy of this type means that people are exposed to as few surprises as possible, a norm for the value of money should be laid down once and for all, and then be fulfilled unyieldingly.

Lindahl (1939, pp. 139–41) began with the following assumptions:

> (1) The monetary system operates in a *closed economy*. . . .
>
> (2) A *free currency* is assumed to be established. The factors determining the general price level are most easily brought out if it is assumed that the Monetary Authority can follow a completely autonomous policy. . . .
>
> (3) All granting of bank credits is *centralized* under the Monetary Authority or the Central Bank – which has also the sole right of creating legal tender. . . .
>
> (4) The credit system is assumed to be so developed that there are *no cash holdings*. We accordingly assume that short-term credits are freely granted between individuals and that any other direct payments which still require to be made are financed by book transfers between banking accounts, on which full interest is paid. . . .

These assumptions are essentially a slightly different way of describing Wicksell's ideal bank by assuming a pure credit economy. Although the Quantity Theory will always be an important part of the theory of money, according to Lindahl, this theory does not reach a sufficiently general explanation of changes in the value of money because it fails under the assumptions made above. This is really not surprising since he had assumed that there is no quantity of money (in Wicksell's definition)!

Lindahl concluded that a more *general* explanation was required. He therefore presented the following equation:

$$E(1 - S) = P \cdot Q \tag{1}$$

where

E = total nominal income
S = savings ratio
P = price of consumer goods
Q = quantity of consumer goods

Solving for P

$$P = \frac{E(1 - S)}{Q} \tag{2}$$

The price level of consumer goods depends on the relationship between the part of income going to consumption and the quantity (supply) of consumer goods. It is then, according to Lindahl, a matter of finding out the primary causes of changes in the price level. Starting with the case where a certain price change is perfectly expected, he concluded that the "other factors in the equation adjust themselves to this anticipated development of the price level" (Lindahl, 1939, p. 147).

The price level can change in any way because a fully expected change does not have any effects:

> ... anticipated changes in the price level have no economic relevance, since they neither influence the relative prices of factors of production and consumption goods, nor the extent and direction of production. (Lindahl, 1939, p. 148)

It is interesting to note this explicit treatment of the role of expectations, although the crucial question is how expectations are determined. Why is a certain price change and not another expected?

> From this it follows that under the assumption just made, the Monetary Authority must follow a purely passive interest policy. For the price development is the primary factor, unequivocally determined by general anticipations, and the rate of interest must adjust itself to this anticipated price development, if the system is not to break down. The Monetary Authority, therefore, cannot directly regulate the price level through its interest policy, but it can do so indirectly by influencing the primary determining factor, i.e. general anticipations. For if it starts by laying down a definite norm for the price level as an end to be realized, and if the members of the community become assured that the price level will actually follow this norm, because the Monetary Authority would oppose any other programme, then expectations concerning the future will give rise to exactly the price development desired by the Central Bank. The only active measure of monetary policy in this case will thus be to establish a norm for the value of money. (Lindahl, 1939, pp. 149–50)

This comes close to a rational expectations *cum* credibility point of view, but Lindahl did not explain explicitly how the central bank is going to convince the public about what is the "right" price development to expect, when the public knows that whatever price development it chooses to expect will be accommodated, since – according to the earlier assumption – "the Monetary Authority must follow a purely passive interest policy." One possible interpretation is that the central bank has stated its aim as price stability, that this policy is credible, and that given a certain natural rate, the central bank sets the bank rate accordingly, all of which is correctly anticipated by the public. Interest policy is passive in the sense that given the desired price level and given the natural rate, there is only one bank rate to select. In terms of this interpretation, the quantity of money is also passive. (We note here the methodological difficulty of determining causality.)

Next Lindahl considered monetary policy that is a change in interest rates. Here it is important to note that he defined income as the rate of return on wealth. If interest rates on all maturities fall, capital values rise, but the present value is discounted by a smaller factor than previously.[7] It is therefore not certain that income, demand for consumer goods, and the price level will rise. Lindahl criticized Wicksell for not having been precise enough in stating the conditions for such a result to appear.

When Lindahl finally relaxed the assumption of the absence of cash balances or money, he argued that even in this case the price level is determined primarily by the supply of and demand for commodities and that the central bank may determine the price level through its influence on commodity supply and demand. At the price level ruling on every occasion, firms and households will adjust their cash holdings so that the central bank does not need to take measures to regulate the size of the stock of money.

According to Lindahl, the common assertion that the central bank influences the price level *through* regulation of the quantity of money and that changes in the quantity of money are therefore a *cause* of the change in the price level is not generally valid. Under the assumptions just made we have the opposite case. The change in the price level is the primary factor in relation to the change in the quantity of money. The former causes the latter. It is a case of reverse causation.

In the 1930s Lindahl became a staunch defender of, not to say a propagandist for, a monetary norm as the ultimate goal for stabilization policy.[8] This recommendation implied an active monetary policy in strict control of the development of the monetary aggregates. However, to my knowledge, Lindahl did not discuss the problem of monetary control. He was apparently satisfied with the general Wicksellian principle of "setting the interest rate right," without further discussing the operationality of such a scheme.

In the 1950s Lindahl returned to issues of stabilization policy. In an important essay, Lindahl (1957) summarized his views on this subject. A most impressive feature of this article is the clarity with which Lindahl stated that there is no trade-off between inflation and unemployment, once inflation is fully expected. Lindahl attacked the idea that it would be justified to give up price stability in order to achieve higher employment. Lindahl (1957, p. 24) continued:

> This conception is here rejected above all for the reason that inflation has to come as a surprise to have favorable effects in these respects, and that it therefore cannot be part of an open program for economic policy. If government through its declarations or actions would give the public the idea that it would tolerate a continuing increase of the price level, implying for example a yearly increase in the cost of living of 3–4 percent, this fact will be taken into consideration in all settlements concerning the future. At wage negotiations these percentages will be at the bottom of all demands for wage increases, and lending agreements will be provided with index clauses, unless the interest rate can be increased to such an extent that compensation is received for the expected fall in the value of money. Though this inflation will no longer have any positive effect, but it will on the whole be fairly meaningless. For a policy that does not have the intention of misleading the public but is designed according to rational principles, there is in reality no choice about the value of money: a stabilization of one form or another stands out as the only possibility.

3   Gunnar Myrdal

In *Ekonomisk Tidskrift* of 1931 (published in the spring of 1932), Gunnar Myrdal published a long article, "Om penningteoretisk jämvikt" (On Monetary Equilibrium). A revised version of this article appeared in German (Myrdal, 1933). Another revised version was published in English entitled *Monetary Equilibrium* (Myrdal, 1939). According to Myrdal, this study is an "immanent" cirtique of Wicksell's theory; that is, Myrdal wanted to criticize Wicksell without changing his basic theoretical structure. The object of his critique is to investigate Wicksell's determination of the equilibrium interest rate in relation to conditions in three different areas of price formation: (1) productivity of real capital, (2) conditions in the capital market, and (3) conditions in the commodity market. Myrdal's analysis aimed at clarifying the meaning of these concepts and their relationship. In his own words:

> Wicksell assumes that these three criteria for the normal rate of interest are equivalent – i.e. never mutually inconsistent; but he cannot prove it. His formulations are, indeed, too loose and contradictory for this purpose. In the following I will prove that they cannot be identical: Only the first and the second of the equilibrium conditions are even consistent; they are interrelated in such a way that the first is condi-

tioned by the second and otherwise not determined. They both correspond to the main argument which is implicit in the whole theory. But this is so only after they have been corrected in essential points and more precisely formulated. With respect to the commodity market, however, the fulfilment of these two monetary equilibrium relations means something quite different from an unchanged price level. (Myrdal, 1939, p. 38)

Myrdal's work was mainly a methodological study. He wanted to make an inquiry into the circumstances under which Wicksell's three conditions were consitent. [To a large extent the work of Lindahl (1929) and Ohlin (1933) is also a variation on the Wicksellian theme. However, all three contributed important insights of their own to macroeconomic theory.] One of Myrdal's major contributions was to introduce the concepts of *ex ante* and *ex post* and in general his treatment of uncertainty, anticipations, and plans. This reflects the analysis in Myrdal's (1927) dissertation.

What about Myrdal's monetary system? Well, there was very little of it. Whereas Wicksell had been anxious to state that his theory was an elaboration and an extension of the quantity theory, Myrdal was very scornful of it. Moreover, he was also uninterested in applying his analysis to the monetary aspects of his work. He called it "monetary theoretic equilibrium" in the Swedish publication, but there is no explanation (or even consideration) of the demand for and supply of money.

4 Bertil Ohlin

One year after Myrdal's article appeared in *Ekonomisk Tidskrift,* Bertil Ohlin published an article in the same journal, "Till frågan om penningteorins uppläggning" (see Ohlin, 1978).

> Among these notions, the path-breaking concept which left its mark on postwar monetary theory is the lack of equality between saving and new investment as the 'cause' of general price movements. . . . Such a formulation of the theory directs its attention to the output of and the demand for capital goods, including change in the inventory of consumers' goods. If demand for consumers' goods is added on the demand side and the output of consumers' goods plus or minus inventory change is added on the supply side, then the equilibrium condition will be that aggregate income (spent on consumption plus saved) equals the value of aggregate output (consumers' goods plus capital goods), i.e., that all income is 'spent'. (p. 353–4)

Ohlin's article is to a large extent a discussion of the definition and classification of various aggregate macroeconomic concepts. In the course of this discussion, he criticized Lindahl and Myrdal for their methods. The problem for Ohlin himself was to switch from saving and investment to aggregate demand and aggregate supply as the proper framework for explaining movements of the price level. This interpretation was strengthened by Ohlin's statement that "The problem is to describe price changes over time, i.e., during a period . . ." (p. 359).

It is very clear that what Ohlin wanted to do in this article was to use his new approach involving total demand and supply and his new concepts and definitions to explain changes in the price level, thereby using a period analysis instead of Myrdal's method of studying the tendencies at a point in time.

After stating the problem, Ohlin went on to analyze the timing of price changes. He did this by taking several examples of events and following them in some detail. First, he considered a decrease in savings. He pointed out that the first effect on goods for which there are inventories is not an increase in their prices but increased sales at unchanged prices. The next effect is an increased demand for new production of these goods. Whether or not prices at the factory level will increase immediately then depends on the stock of orders and the degree of capacity utilization. In any case there will be increased orders and investment demand goes up. For some firms the situation is such that prices will rise immediately. Even if it takes some time, most prices of wholesale goods will increase before the prices of retail goods.

If the decision to reduce savings does not lead to tightening of credit conditions so that investment demand continues as before, then the increased demand for investment in the consumer goods industry will lead to an increase in total investments. Net savings will therefore not decrease but will, on the contrary, increase in spite of the increase in consumption. This is made possible by the increase in production.

The last part of the argument seems to be similar to Keynes's *General Theory,* and this is how Brems (1978) interprets the story. But it is really clear from the context that what Ohlin is describing is *not* how total demand and output adjust to a new "temporary equilibrium" without price adjustment, but the dynamics of price change. It is true that he allows production and saving to change in this process, but they do not substitute for price change as the equilibrating mechanism.

In his conclusions, Ohlin stated that he tried to achieve five things in his article: (1) substitute a better income concept for the one used by Lindahl and Myrdal, (2) give a hint of a more general description of price movements, (3) touch upon how the result of Austrian capital theory about the time structure of price formation could be fitted into monetary theory, (4) make clear that the exchange structure of price movements belongs to central monetary theory, and (5) show that the idea of the static theory of price formation about a normal or equilibrium interest rate is misleading in an analysis of dynamic price movements. Ohlin did not mention unemployment or output equilibrating mechanisms in his conclusions.

In 1934 Ohlin published a book entitled *Penningpolitik, offentliga arbeten, subventioner och tullar som medel mot arbetslöshet* or, in English, *Monetary Policy, Public Works, Subsidies and Tariffs as Means against Unemployment.* This was a report for the Committee on Unemployment. Since the explicit purpose was to analyze unemployment, one would expect a clear statement that variations in the level of aggregate demand led to variations in the level of output and employment rather than to variations in the price level if Ohlin had "anticipated" the *General Theory.* However, this is exactly what is excluded. Instead Ohlin's treatment of the problem is rather similar to the analysis in his 1933 paper. In Chapter II, "The Characteristic of Expansionary and Contractionary Processes," Ohlin analyzed what happens during such processes. His starting point is a "more or less deep depression or a mediocre business cycle," which means that the quantity produced is below 80 to 90 percent of potential production.

Next, he investigated the effects of a reduction in the discount rate. The result is that investment in durable capital goods appears to be more profitable, in spite of the fact that all existing capital is not fully used. The reason is that many new capital goods have a more "economic technical form" and that they are bought with respect to an expected future increase in production; ". . . demand for capital goods grows from people and firms, who have means of payment and credit possibilities, and prices for these goods tend to rise" (p. 25).

Ohlin went on to describe the whole process of expansion. Next incomes rise, which leads to an increased demand for consumption goods. "An increase in the volume of production takes place, often before a price increase takes place. Retail prices usually go up only still later on" (p. 26).

One difference from Lindahl and Myrdal that Ohlin emphasized is that he defined monetary equilibrium as an absence of price change and the necessary condition for this is that total demand is equal to total supply, not that saving is equal to investment.

> Observe, however, that a similar expansion and price development can equally well be evoked if planned savings is in accordance with planned investment. The presumption is then that income expectations and planned demand for consumption – the demand curve – increases. (p. 27)

Ohlin generally treated expansion in volume and prices as taking place at roughly the same time and also regarded this as true for contraction in volume and prices. *He did not include an explicit analysis of the causes of the distinction between volume and price effects.* However, being a careful scholar, Ohlin also inserted frequent qualifications to his general case.

Ohlin's book is mostly about the concepts and dynamics of the macroeconomic process. There *are* insights about quantity relations, although it is more a description and analysis of the typical variations in production, employment, and prices that take place during a business cycle, of which many pre-Keynesian (1936) writers were well aware.

In his 1933 paper, Ohlin was for the most part not very explicit about the monetary sector. However, the basic assumption about aggregate demand is already spelled out clearly in this article. Demand is determined by the *willingness* to consume and the *ability* to consume. The former depends on income expectations, price expectations, and expected future credit market conditions. The latter, for the individual, depends on holdings of means of payment and the availabilty of credit. Monetary conditions become a constraint on the maximum demand for consumption.

Ohlin also noted that the time interval between payments varies over the business cycle. "An assumption about the constancy of the 'habits of payments' is accordingly unreasonable for the analysis of the course of the business cycle" (p. 22).

> The relationship between the volumes of the different transactions is subject to considerable variation from one month to another and even more from one year to the next. On these grounds something decisive and for different phases of the business cycle valid connection between the amount of the means of payment and the sum of the 'productive' transactions could not be concluded. . . . It is, among other things, for these reasons that the amount of the means of payments in the following will be very little mentioned. (p. 23)

Here, Ohlin's monetary assumptions are more explicit than Myrdal's – or Ohlin's own in 1933 – but many obscurities remain. One problem that runs through both of the publications by Ohlin is an ambition to be very rigourous and theoretical, while at the same time realistic. This means, for example, that in several places the amount of credit is demand determined because monetary policy only sets the interest rate. In other places, however, Ohlin talked about restrictions on the availability of credit and unwillingness to lend. These issues were probably not yet quite clear to Ohlin, but he devoted much more time to these problems subsequently.

In 1941 he published a textbook on money and in 1943 an article in *Ekonomisk Tidskrift* called "Stockholmsskolan kontra kvantitetsteorien" ("The Stockholm School versus the Quantity Theory"). At the beginning of this article Ohlin stated:

> What is the characteristic of the Swedish analysis of monetary processes of the 1930s and in what way is this method different from the Quantity Theory? Well, in my opinion it is that the attention is focused primarily on the acting individuals and their motives, not on money and its "velocity." It is not money that buys, but *people* that buy with the help of money or credit. Neither is it the speed in money's movement from one individual to another that determines the speed of reactions that takes place when, for example, the purchase for one reason or another is increased on one or more points in business. These reactions depend rather on how fast the expectations of the future and thereby the willingness to buy indirectly are influenced. (p. 28)

This is a relevant criticism of mechanical use of the Quantity Theory. But what did Ohlin have to offer instead? After a lengthy discussion of definitions of the monetary base (public liquid debt), he used some examples to show that the means of payments, or money, has only a passive or indirect effect on the rate of price increase.

Ohlin's central position in this article was that control of the monetary base is in the hands of the central bank. (He wrote without considering a fixed exchange rate.) Next, he asserted that "The quantity of such privately held means of payments is changed through the credit policy of the banking system" (p. 32). By this he meant that the quantity of money is determined by the choice of reserve ratio made by the banking system, given the monetary base, which is determined by the central bank. (He forgot to discuss determination and stability of the currency ratio.)

He defined an individual's purchasing power as his money holdings plus his possible net credits or new loans. He then stated that purchasing power in this sense cannot be used up for society as a whole; it can only be transferred.

> Money is not used up but move around and is always available for new purchases. From this it is possible to draw an important conclusion. It is not the total purchasing power or ability to purchase, which create the effective restriction for the purchases that are made within a certain period. *There is always "unused purchasing power."*

Ohlin did not seem to be aware that he was assuming an infinite velocity of money. He did not discuss, let alone explain, how individuals, but not society, can be constrained by lack of money, and he reasoned in the context of the real world and not the ideal bank of Wicksell and Lindahl.

Ohlin continued with some examples to show the loose connection between the quantity of money and the price level. First he considered the case

> ... when *the public* for one reason or another, for example political unrest, *wishes to strengthen its liquidity* and therefore withdraw bank-notes from the commercial banks. Such a *hoarding* reduces to the same extent the amount of base money in the banking system. If its liquidity earlier was not good, the effect of this will primarily be a tendency to an increase of the rate of interest and to a reduced willingness from the banks to give credit. If, however, the liquidity of the banks is so strong, that the withdrawals by the public does not essentially change it, then the effect on the money and capital markets will be small or zero. Are the purchases by the public directly affected? The decisive factor is in this case to what extent the willingness to buy and the ability to buy are influenced in the productive sphere. A desire for strengthened liquidity can, of course, lead to a reduction of the public's purchases, but this reduction is not an *effect* of the reduced liquidity. (p. 41)

This is a case of an unstable reserve ratio.

Next, he considered a case of scarcity of commodities, for example, in war time. There is now an excess demand for commodities and prices go up.

> The increase in the value of the turnover of goods, however, presup-poses an increase of either the quantity of money or of velocity. In a situation like the present one, when the total quantity of base money is far larger than the need, with the banks having large deposits in the central bank the need by the public is automatically satisfied by the public withdrawing money from the banks and these from the central bank without any influence on the credit policy. (p. 45)

Once more an unstable reserve ratio!

The next example is technical change. This leads to an increased quantity of goods,

> and the quantity of money is adjusted upwards. It is probably difficult and peculiar to press such sequences into a scheme such as that the "normal rate of interest" has gone up and that the expansion of income and the rest of the sequence depends on the failure of the banking sys-tem to adjust the credit policy to this. ... One could accordingly not say that what prevents processes of price increase is that the central bank creates the necessary scarcity of money, which seems to be the inner kernel of the quantity theory. ... Monetary theory must as well as the rest of economic theory be made to an analysis of a process in time, where the changes in incomes are accounted for and a much

larger amount of monetary concepts are needed than those that are included in the formulas of the quantity theory. (pp. 45–6)

Ohlin did not regard the quantity theory as the supply of and demand for money. Furthermore, he was not aware of the possibility of constructing a money supply process that is consistent with the quantity theory.

5   Interest rate pegging, endogenous money, and reverse causation

A characteristic feature of the monetary economics of the Stockholm School, which is the oral tradition in which I was trained in the 1960s, is the dictum that money matters almost not at all, in spite of its central position in Wicksell's work. It is difficult to find the reason for this attitude, but it was almost the only thing on which they could all agree. How then could they explain the minor role of money in their theories?

In the case of Erik Lindahl, it is clear that in the main part of his analysis he used Wicksell's idea of the ideal bank to get the problem out of the way in order to concentrate on other aspects of the problem of macroeconomic equilibrium and dynamic methods. *But,* if you have arrived at the conclusion that the most important goal for macroeconomic policy is the behavior of the general price level, and this was Lindahl's position, and if you live in an economy where some 80 to 90 percent of the means of payment is money in the form of coins and government-issued bank notes, then you cannot avoid including a serious analysis of the role of money in the determination of the price level.

Wicksell was well aware of this problem and was careful in discussing both the demand for money and the limitations of the ideal bank, even if he was not quite successful in integrating the role of money and the role of velocity. Lindahl was also consistent on this issue because he introduced cash holdings and commercial banks later on in his analysis. But he did it reluctantly and as an afterthought and he did not really seem very interested.

When introducing cash holdings he was anxious to emphasize that, in spite of the existence of cash, the price level is still determined primarily by the demand for and supply of consumer goods and that the central bank can regulate the price level *through these, according to the previously mentioned methods* (which were the rate of interest and declarations by the central bank). Firms and private persons adjust their cash holdings at each point in time to the prevailing price level, so that "the central bank does not have to take any specific actions to regulate the size of the cash holdings." It is quite clear from this and subsequent passages that Lindahl wanted to treat the quantity of money as demand determined.

Later, however, he discussed the possibility that the policy of the central bank is not smoothly adjusted to the needs of the economy. His conclusion was that if there is too much money it does not matter very much for regulation of the price level, but if there is too little money there can be disastrous consequences for the price level, which will start to fall, causing considerable trouble for business.

Through these remarks Lindahl admitted that the central bank *can* regulate the price level, at least in the downward direction, by controlling the money stock. The question than becomes whether it is better, in the sense of higher efficiency in reaching the goal, to regulate the price level by setting interest rates or by a more direct control of the money supply. This is an important question, but Lindahl left us here without any explicit discussion of the problem formulated in this way.

In the case of Ohlin (1934), his views are relatively similar to those of Lindahl even if they were expressed in a different way. He was less explicit about the set of assumptions that he used for the monetary sector, but it is clear that he regarded the monetary factors as mainly an upper limit, a constraint on the individual's purchasing plans, on his ability to buy. But from this, as well as from many of his examples, it is evident that he had no stable demand for money, or that there is no individual who optimizes his demand for consumption and cash holdings simultaneously, making the opportunity cost of holding money explicit.

Bertil Ohlin went to great lengths to avoid the concept of the quantity of money and to deny its usefulness. When describing an open market purchase, he concluded that during times of depression, this method of increasing the assets of the central bank and "thereby influencing the interest rate level and the availability of credit is as a rule far more important than the discount policy."

Given that there is an economy with a monetary base of "outside money," let us examine the different possibilities.

1. First of all, the central bank can aim at controlling the money supply in order to stabilize the price level (or nominal income). The problems here are well known and concern stability of the monetary multiplier and monetary velocity.
2. Second, the empirical problem just mentioned is not the major difference from the alternative, which is interest rate setting policy introduced by Wicksell and followed by Lindahl, Myrdal,

and Ohlin. Of course, such an assumption is close at hand since most central banks have usually worked by fixing one or more interest rates. The question for the analysis is the way in which they do it.

At one extreme, this is merely another method for control of the money supply. If the central bank knows all the behavior functions and, in particular, the demand for money function, setting an interest rate is equivalent to choosing a certain money supply. The two policies are wholly equivalent.[9] This was shown by Poole (1970) for a Keynesian IS-LM model. If the central bank has only partial information about the economy, the choice of policy depends on the nature of shocks to the economic system.

In rational expectations models with flexible prices, some of the implications of Poole's policy alternatives are drastically different, but one equivalence result is strengthened. The distribution of real activity is invariant to the sort of contemporaneous policy response discussed by Poole if the policy rule is known to the public.[10]

At another extreme, the central bank simply pegs the interest rate as under a "low interest rate policy." This leads to a completely demand-determined money stock. It has been emphasized by Patinkin that under such a policy the price level will become indeterminate. To prevent this, the central bank has to determine at least some money variable, for example, nominal reserves.

It is fairly obvious that the ideal bank will have this property, if the interest rate is not at the natural equilibrium level. The ideal bank is the same as an economy with purely inside money. But a similar argument holds for an economy with purely outside money or a mixed system, where the central bank issues paper money. If the central bank lends money at a lending rate (discount rate) that is "too low," the result will be cumulative price increases. The only escape would be if the real bills doctrine were true.

It is not surprising that the Stockholm School did not work out the solutions to these problems in monetary theory. However, it is surprising that with Wicksell and his ideal bank as a background – for Lindahl even the starting point – they could go on arguing that in a world with tangible money, the actual money stock was demand determined, that is, the causality went from prices to money and not the other way around, without asking about the consequences for the price level. The goal of stability of the price level was nearly as sacred to Lindahl as to Wicksell. I now think that the solution to the mystery has been revealed through some formulations by Lindahl. One solution is to interpret the situation as implying that the central bank achieves price stability by its choice of the level of the interest rate that it sets. Then the public chooses the demand for money that is consistent with this price level.

But if this interpretation is correct, the whole problem boils down to a matter of semantics because the central bank determines the actual money stock but does so through the technique of setting the interest rate (at the right level). In this case there is little defense for all their programmatic criticisms of the quantity theory.

Lindahl and Ohlin were right when they claimed that there may be other causes of a change in the price level than a change in the supply of money, for example, a change in the savings ratio. But they were wrong when they thought that this implied a passive supply of money.

6   Money and output

Writers prior to the *General Theory* did not always proceed on the presumption of full employment. The more careful they were in their examples from reality, the greater the variations in output and employment there would be in their stories. But the dividing line in monetary theory is that Keynes, after having finished his *Treatise* at the age of forty-seven, consciously decided that he had to construct a theory, the purpose of which was to explain variations in employment. The result was a theory in which the major ingredient was that if wages are not capable of clearing the labor market, variations in spending will determine variations in unemployment and the economy may settle down at an unemployment equilibrium.

To what extent did the Stockholm School anticipate Keynes? In Myrdal (1931) and Ohlin (1933) there is no clear vision that the problem was to focus on unemployment and to explain why there is persistence in unemployment instead of price adjustment. In both articles, the major concentration and emphasis was on the conditions for monetary equilibrium and on the consequences for price increases and price decreases in the absence of monetary equilibrium.

It is true that they both mentioned unemployment and output fluctuations but solely as one realistic detail in the contractionary process. The major focus was on price behavior and monetary disequilibrium. The depression phase of the trade cycle involved increased unemployment and it would disappear as the cycle proceeded into the boom period. Automatic forces were set in motion to counteract and finally overcome the depressive forces.

Keynes was interested in the case where the automatic forces were too weak, when the economy got stuck in an unemployment equilibrium and when there was presistent unemployment. This is not the scene in Myrdal (1931) and Ohlin (1933). Anybody who reads them and is asked about the theory of unemployment in these studies would not have much to say. This was also Joan Robinson's (1939) impression in her review of Myrdal's book. She wrote:

> His treatment of unemployment is less satisfactory. He regards a certain amount of unemployment as necessary and desirable in order to prevent the continuous rise of money wages and prices which comes about when the "monopoly position" of the workers is too strong. But this is not at all the same thing as to say that a rise in money wages directly causes unemployment, and he appears to hold both that a rise in money wages which is not expected to be reversed will not reduce employment and that a fall in money wages will increase it.

The problem of anticipation of the *General Theory* becomes more complicated in Ohlin (1934). This was written during the worst year of the depression and at the request of a government committee on unemployment. One would therefore expect to find a clear statement of a general theory of unemployment. This is not the case. What we find is a description of cases or processes of expansion and contraction of the economy, but these processes are characterized by increases and decreases in the price level, as in Myrdal (1931) and Ohlin (1933). The difference is that there is more emphasis on unemployment, but it is still not the case that variations in output take the place of variations in prices as the equilibrating mechanism and there is no unemployment equilibrium.

There is, of course, considerable discussion of economic policy against unemployment in this report as well as in newspaper articles and other publications by members of the Stockholm School. But this does not provide any evidence of anticipation of the *General Theory* because the whole debate in Sweden regarding this question was influenced very early by the *White Paper* and different publications in Britain by Keynes and others. Ernst Wigforss, the Swedish Social Democrat who was Minister of Finance from September 1932, had advocated public works and fiscal stimulation to combat unemployment. He got his inspiration from Keynes's public writings.

7   Conclusions

The conclusion from this examination of the monetary theory of the Stockholm School is rather negative. The quantity theory was dismissed and monetary factors were assigned only passive effects.

The public gets the money that it needs. There was no careful analysis of the implications of such an assumption for the behavior of the price level. This lack of analysis of the monetary mechanism is not justified against the background of Pigou, (Marshall), Cannan, Lavington and, in particular, the German language products of Menger and Mises, which should have been well known to German-oriented Swedes. There seems to be a self-sufficient isolationism in relying only on Wicksell.

A weak point of the Stockholm School economists is that they merely stated their views on monetary factors without analyzing why they chose their assumptions instead of the assumptions of their predecessors. There is, for example, no analysis and articulated criticism of Pigou and Mises. If the assumption was that these scholars were wrong, the basis for this was not shown.

Finally, there is very little evidence that there was any anticipation of the *General Theory* before its publication in 1936. There are discussions about unemployment, in particular in Ohlin (1934), but a close reading does not reveal any similarity to Keynes's idea about output adjustment instead of price adjustment. Had the author had any intentions in this direction, one would expect to find it mentioned in the conclusions. There is no trace of such ideas.

Notes

1 I am grateful to David Laidler, Axel Leijonhufvud, and Allan Meltzer for helpful discussion of some of the issues dealt with here, but they are not responsible for any opinions in the paper.
2 See Meltzer (1988) for a recent reinterpretation of Keynes.
3 For a comprehensive review of the role of money in macroeconomic theory, see Brunner–Meltzer (1989).
4 For an excellent review of this subject, see Laidler (1986).
5 For a pentrating review of this literature, see McCallum (1985).
6 Published in English in 1939 as Part II in *Studies in the Theory of Money and Capital.*
7 Lindahl (1939, p. 146) defines income in the following way:

$$E = r_1\left(\frac{a_1}{1 + r_1} + \frac{a_2}{(1 + r_1)(1 + r_2)} + \frac{a_3}{(1 + r_1)(1 + r_2)(1 + r_3)} + \cdots\right)$$

8 While Wicksell's norm was a stable price level, Lindahl followed Davidson and argued for a level that changes in inverted proportion to productivity. See Jonung (1979).
9 This seems to have been Cassel's view.
10 See Dotsey and King (1986) and McCallum (1986b).

References

Bagehot, Walter (1873), *Lombard Street – A Description of the Money Market.* London: Kegan Paul, Trench, Trübner, Ltd.

Brems, Hans (1978), "What Was New in Ohlin's 1933–34 Macroeconomics?" *History of Political Economy,* 10, 398–412.

Brunner, Karl, and Allan H. Meltzer (1989), *Monetary Economics.* Oxford: Basil Blackwell.

Dotsey, Michael, and Robert King (1986), "Informational Implications of Interest Rate Rules," *American Economic Review,* 76, 33–42.

Fama, Eugene (1980), "Banking in the Theory of Finance," *Journal of Monetary Economics,* 6, 39–57.

Jevons, William Stanley (1875), *Money and the Mechanism of Exchange,* London: Kegan Paul, Trench, Trübner, Ltd.

Jonung, Lars (1979), "Knut Wicksell's Norm of Price Stabilization and Swedish Monetary Policy in the 1930's," *Journal of Monetary Economics,* 5, 459–96.

Keynes, John M. (1923), *A Tract on Monetary Reform.* London: Macmillan.

Laidler, David (1986), *Classical Monetary Economics in the 1870s,* manuscript.

Landgren, Karl-Gustav (1960), *Den 'nya ekonomien' i Sverige.* Stockholm: Almqvist & Wiksell.

Lindahl, Erik (1929), *Om förhållandet mellan penningmängd och prisnivå.* Uppsala: Juridiska Fakulteten.

(1939), *Studies in the Theory of Money and Capital.* London: Allen and Unwin.

(1957), *Spelet om penningvärdet.* Stockholm.

Marshall, Alfred (1975), "Money," in J. Whitaker, ed., *Early Economic Writings of Alfred Marshall.* London: Macmillan.

McCallum, Bennett (1985), "Bank Deregulation, Accounting Systems of Exchange, and the Unit of Account: A Critical Review," *Carnegie-Rochester Conference Series on Public Policy,* 23, 13–45.

(1986a), "On 'Real' and 'Sticky – Price' Theories of the Business Cycle," *Journal of Money, Credit, and Banking,* 18, 397–414.

(1986b), "Some Issues Concerning Interest Pegging, Price Level Determinacy, and the Real Bills Doctrine," *Journal of Monetary Economics,* 17, 135–60.

Mill, John Stuart (1865), *Principles of Political Economy,* 6th ed. London.

Myrdal, Gunnar (1927), *Prisbildningsproblemet och föränderligheten,* Uppsala.

(1931), "Om penningteoretisk jämvikt," *Ekonomisk Tidskrift,* 33, 191–302.

(1933), "Der Gleichgewichtsbegriff als Instrument der geldtheoretischen Analyse," in Friedrich v. Hayek, ed., *Beiträge zur Geldtheorie.* Vienna: Julius Springer Verlag.

(1939), *Monetary Equilibrium.* London.

Ohlin, Bertil, (1933), "Till frågan om penningteoriens uppläggning," *Ekonomisk Tidskrift,* 35, 45–81.

(1934), *Penningpolitik, offentliga arbeten, subventioner och tullar som medel mot arbetslöshet.* Stockholm.

(1943), "Stockholmsskolan kontra kvantitetsteorien," *Ekonomisk Tidskrift,* 45, 27–46.

(1978), "On the Formulation of Monetary Theory," *History of Political Economy,* 10, 353–88.

Patinkin, Don (1956), *Money, Interest and Prices.* New York: Harper and Row.

(1982), *Anticipations of the General Theory?* Oxford: Blackwell.

Pigou, A. C. (1917), "The Value of Money," *The Quarterly Journal of Economics,* 32, 38–65.

Poole, William (1970), "Optimal Choice of Monetary Instruments in a Simple Stochastic Macro Model," *Quarterly Journal of Economics,* 84, 197–216.

Robinson, Joan (1939), "Review of Myrdal, G. 'Monetary Equilibrium,'" *Economic Journal,* 10, 493–5.

Schumpeter, Joseph (1954), *History of Economic Analysis.* New York.

Steiger, Otto (1971), *Studien zur Entstehung der neuen Wirtschaftslehre in Schweden. Eine Anti-Kritik.* Berlin.

(1978), Prelude to the Theory of a Monetary Economy: Origins and Significance of Ohlin's 1933 approach," *History of Political Economy,* 10, 389–446.

Tooke, Thomas (1840), *An Inquiry into the Currency Principles.* London.

Wicksell, Knut (1935), *Lectures on Political Economy.* London: Routledge & Kegan Paul.

Comments

DAVID LAIDLER

Johan Myhrman is rather critical of the Stockholm School considered as a group of monetary economists, and with one partial exception that I shall note below, I share his qualms. Let it be clear, though, that our doubts arise because we have a particular view about what constitutes "good" monetary economics and a particular view about the historical development of the ideas we find particularly attractive. This view is not one that is universally shared by respectable monetary economists even today, let alone in the 1930s, and so the position Myhrman takes, though eminently defensible, is nevertheless bound to be controversial. It will help to place his work in context if I briefly and explicitly describe the vision of "good" monetary economics that underlies it. Myhrman and I would both, I think, loosely characterise overselves as "quantity theorists," and by that we would mean the following: that the critical (though not the only) variable to be explained by monetary economics is the general price level, and that pride of place should be given to the quantity of money (suitably defined, and I shall return to this point in a moment) as an explanatory variable here. Moreover, we would both deploy a stock supply and demand apparatus in constructing any explanation of the connection between money and prices. Thus our conception of "good" monetary economics involves some kind of an amalgamation of the best insights of Wicksell and Marshall as developed by, among others, Keynes and Friedman.

Now it is well known that Wicksell was a self-styled quantity theorist, who regarded his "cumulative process" analysis as supplementing rather than replacing the classical quantity theory. Moreover, much of the work of the Stockholm School in the 1920s and 1930s had deep roots in Wicksell's analysis, not least, as Myhrman notes, in its shared emphasis on price level as opposed to output behavior. To this extent, their work should, and indeed does, appeal to modern quantity theorists. However, Wicksell often discussed his process in the context of what he termed a "pure credit economy," and he also used the word "money" to refer to currency alone; hence he seemed to many to have developed a theory of price level behavior that could do without money. His successors, who based so much of their work on the assumption of a "pure credit economy," thus tended to present their work as superseding, rather than supplementing, the quantity theory. For them, the centerpiece of monetary policy became the interest rate, bank credit became the critical monetary aggregate variable, and the quantity of money, if it was mentioned at all, became a passive variable. These views are, of course quite antithetical to those Myhrman and I espouse, which is why we do not rate the contributions of the Stockholm School to monetary economics very highly.

Nevertheless, it should be noted explicitly that, even if we confine ourselves to the literature of the 1920s and 1930s, the above characterization of the monetary economics of the Stockholm School is a more accurate account of the views of Myrdal, Ohlin, and Lundberg, than it is of Lindahl, and I hope that, in a subsequent draft of his paper, Myhrman will pay more attention to this distinction. Lindahl was, in 1930 (1939, pp. 236 et seq.), careful to draw attention to the complications that would arise for his analysis of various cumulative processes if the economy used currency and if the demand for currency varied systematically with nominal income. He also noted that the assumption of a gold standard would lead to results very different from those to be derived on the assumption of what he called a "free curency." In these matters, of course, Lindahl echoed Wicksell's insights into the very factors that linked cumulative process analysis to the traditional quantity theory.

However, at least in his writings during the 1930s (I cannot speak for later), Lindahl did not analyze the interrelationship between the credit market activities of banks and their consequences for the volume of their deposit liabilities. Closely related is his failure to expand the idea of "money" to encompass those liabilities in a way that would open up the possibility of applying the tools of the quantity theory to analyzing their role in conditioning the expenditure behavior of the private sector. The view of the quantity theory that came to dominate Swedish monetary economics in the 1930s was Ohlin's characterization of it as a mechanical theory, unrelated to the analysis of individual behavior and superseded by his own and his associates' analysis of the role of nominal expenditure flows in the process of price formation. Hence, as Myhrman notes, the monetary economics of the Stockholm School looks, from a modern perspective, to be a contribution to the development of the type of analysis, of which the *Radcliffe Report* (1959) is the most noteworthy example, whose most memorable characteristic is a systematic tendency to underestimate the importance of the quantity of money (however defined) as an active influence on the economy.

Having said all that, though, it is as well to remember that the ideas that the Stockholm School would have had to integrate in order to place themselves firmly on what Myhrman and I would both regard as the right track, though available, were scattered through the literature and rather controversial in the 1920s and early 1930s: the capacity of the banking system to create deposit money was understood by some, but the idea in question was by no means universally accepted; the Marshall-Pigou reformulation of the quantity theory in stock supply and demand terms did not find its way into that standard exposition of Cambridge monetary economics, Sir Dennis Robertson's *Money*, until its 1929 edition; a portfolio theoretic treatment of the demand for money is certainly present in the *Treatise on Money* (1930), but it plays at best a peripheral role in the Wicksellian process analysis that is that book's most notable feature; and so on. The necessary integration of ideas was accomplished in the course of the debates that followed the publication of the *General Theory;* but those who accept Patinkin's judgement that, considerable though the contributions of the Stockholm School were, they did not anticipate the central insights of that book, should hesitate to censor them too harshly for having failed to anticipate one line of monetary theory that grew out of the literature it generated.

References

Committee on the Working of the Monetary System (The Radcliffe Committee) (1959), Report. London: HMSO.
Keynes J. M. (1930), *A Treatise on Money,* 2 vols. London: Macmillan
Lindahl E. (1930), *The Rate of Interest and the Price Level.* Translated and reprinted (in part) in *Studies in the Theory of Money and Capital,* London: Allen and Unwin, 1939.
Robertson D. H. (1929), *Money,* 3rd ed. London: Nisbet.

CHAPTER 12

The Austrians and the Stockholm School: Two failures in the development of modern macroeconomics?

DAVID LAIDLER[1]

Nowadays Keynesian economics is the most visible legacy of the debates about macroeconomic issues that marked the 1920s and 1930s. That is because Keynes and his associates were successful, in the well-defined sense of laying down an agenda for research, a syllabus for instruction, and a program for the conduct of policy that dominated the subject for three decades. In the 1920s and 1930s, however, Cambridge was but one of a number of centers where potentially important developments in what we would now call macroeconomics took place. Austrian business cycle theory, developed in Vienna and at the London School of Economics, and the work of the Stockholm School on problems of "monetary equilibrium," attracted just as much attention as the efforts of Keynes and his associates, and no sign in the pre-1936 literature warned how quickly and completely Keynesian economics would come to dominate the discipline.

That two bodies of work could fail as completely as those produced by the Austrians and the Stockholm School are now commonly judged to have done presents an interesting problem in and of itself, and one of the aims of this paper is to investigate the nature of these failures.[2] It has a second purpose though. Both the Austrians and the Stockholm School were self-consciously working on problems that grew out of the work of Knut Wicksell, indeed the very same problems. Even so, by about 1936 the Stockholm School had arrived at a set of ideas that some commentators (e.g., Shackle, 1967) claim anticipated to an important extent those of Keynes's *General Theory,* and that at the very least enabled them readily to understand and assimilate Keynes's thought. The Austrians, on the other hand, created a theory and derived from it a set of policy proposals that were quite antithetical to what was to become Keynesian economics. The question of how two groups, in at least sporadic contact with one another and starting in the same place, could so quickly move so far apart provides the second theme of this study.

295

Wicksell

Knut Wicksell's work provides a crucial link between the quantity theory of money, as it was understood in the later years of the nineteenth century, and modern macroeconomics.[3] Wicksell himself was a quantity theorist, but he was dissatisfied with the analytic apparatus he had inherited from his classical predecessors. In particular, he saw that Say's Law, as they understood it, precluded the existence of a supply and demand mechanism capable of moving the general price level toward whatever equilibrium value the quantity theory might require after a monetary disturbance. In seeking to repair this defect in the logical structure of classical economics, he became a pioneer of the integration of monetary theory with neoclassical value theory that has been one of the principal items on the research agenda of twentieth-century economics. Wicksell applied the concepts of supply and demand to the economy's output as a whole and argued that the general price level would move in response to a discrepancy between them. In postulating the existence of such a discrepancy, of course, he both abandoned Say's Law, as the classical economists had usually understood it, and made use (albeit in embryo form, and to deal with the determination of prices rather than output) of the concept of aggregate demand that was to play a central role in the Keynesian revolution.

Wicksell's celebrated "cumulative process" was, for its creator, a supplement to the quantity theory, meant to elucidate the processes whereby the price level moved from one equilibrium level to another in the presence of a modern banking system. As is well known, it postulated that the existence of a shortfall of the banks' lending rate of interest, the "money rate," from the "natural interest rate" (to be defined in a moment) would induce entrepreneurs to increase their borrowing from the banks and to bid up the prices of factors of production. The increase in factor incomes, thus induced, in turn ensured that the price level of output would also increase. Given the assumption about entrepreneurs' expectations usually made by Wicksell, namely, that this period's prices were expected to prevail next period, this mechanism would work to raise prices period after period, until the discrepancy between the two interest rates was removed. It would be removed eventually, though, because a commodity currency usually lay in the background of Wicksell's analysis. Rising prices would cause an increasing demand for currency on the part of the public, the banks would lose reserves, and in response the banks would increase their lending rate. Hence the price level would settle down at a new and, according to Wicksell, meta-stable equilibrium value.

Though this process was conceived by Wicksell as a supplement to the quantity theory, the quantity of money itself, which he, in common with most of his contemporaries thought of as consisting solely of what we would now call currency, played no role in the actual process of price formation. Credit granted by the banking system was the active element here. Furthermore, in some expositions of the cumulative process (e.g., 1905, 1935, p. 194 ff.) Wicksell found it convenient to analyze the operation of what was usually called a "pure credit economy" in which currency did not exist. Thus a body of analysis designed to supplement the quantity theory had the potential to supersede it, for the conditions of "monetary equilibrium" had to do with the credit market operations of the banking system, and not, except indirectly in the particular case of a currency-using economy whose banks also held currency as a reserve, with the quantity of "money" and its velocity of circulation. In order fully to realize the potential of Wicksell's contribution, though, his successors had first of all to clarify the notion of "monetary equilibrium," and this proved problematic. Wicksell had attributed to it no less than three distinct characteristics. First, treating the "natural rate of interest" as the marginal product of the economy's capital stock, Wicksell had argued that monetary equilibrium would rule when the money rate of interest was equal to that natural (or, in the vocabulary of the *Lectures,* "normal") rate; second, he had suggested that equality between the economy's rates of saving and investment was a property of that same equilibrium; and third, he had argued that monetary equilibrium would be characterized by constancy of the general price level.

In his first and most careful exposition of the cumulative process, that of his 1898 book *Interest and Prices* (Wicksell, 1936, Chap. 9), Wicksell had worked with a model whose properties ensured that the above-mentioned conditions were indeed simultaneously attainable. No fixed capital accumulation took place, and land and labor were available in given quantities to be hired by entrepreneurs, in order to produce, over a uniform production period, a homogeneous "corn" output, which also functioned as the wage good. Hence, with output and capital consisting of the same physical units, the natural interest rate was well defined as the marginal product per unit of variable capital of the aggregate stock of variable capital. Moreover, with aggregate savings and investment always zero, output remained constant, and zero net credit creation by the banking system resulted in stable prices. Perhaps to add realism to his analysis of the cumulative process, in later expositions (e.g., 1907, 1935) Wicksell placed it in the context of a growing economy with fixed capital accumulation and potentially heterogeneous output, without facing up to the following questions: Would the marginal product of capital per unit of capital then remain well defined? Would positive saving and investment be equilibrated by a rate of interest equal to it if it was? And would the amount of bank credit creation taking place at whatever turned out to be this critical value of the money interest rate indeed be such as to produce price stability in a growing economy?[4]

Some theoretical muddles mark the end of a line of research, and others mark the beginning. Wicksell's muddle was seminal, for it defined the theoretical starting point for the research of both the Austrians and the Stockholm School. Both groups, though, were motivated by more than a desire to sort out a theoretical difficulty. The economic instability that plagued Europe in the wake of World War I, and would come to plague the United States after 1929, gave their research a strong practical impetus; and though "monetary equilibrium" was first and foremost a theoretical concept, it appeared to be of considerable policy significance as well. If the conditions producing monetary equilibrium could be clarified and defined in terms of variables with readily observable real world counterparts, then so it seemed, a successful formula for ridding the real world of economic fluctuations might be at hand. Both groups, in short, took up this concept, which in Wicksell's hands had been a tool for analyzing secular movements in the price level, and transformed it into the central idea of business cycle analysis, both theoretical and policy oriented. How the two groups in question tackled the questions involved here, why their answers to them came to diverge so greatly, and how those answers failed to attain a lasting, well-identified place in the body of macroeconomic knowledge will form the subject matter of the remainder of this essay.

The Austrians

The adjective "Austrian" is used in a very narrow sense here to refer to that body of business cycle theory developed during the later 1920s and early 1930s from certain insight of Ludwig von Mises, particularly by Friedrich von Hayek but also by Lionel Robbins. Thus, I am not here concerned with the contributions to mathematical economics that were made in Vienna in the 1920s and early 1930s, with Schumpeterian business cycle analysis, or indeed with that vision of economics as dealing with an ongoing and essentially creative process of competition that marks current work in the "Austrian" tradition, work which also owes much to Mises and Hayek. The business cycle theory in question, whose *locus classicus* is Hayek's famous lectures in 1931–2 on *Prices and Production* (Hayek, 1936), was, for a short time before the publication of the *General Theory,* the most fully developed theoretical account available of economic fluctuations, and it seemed to some contemporary observers to represent a line of inquiry at least as likely to come to dominate the discipline as anything being developed at Cambridge.

The Wicksellian origins of this work were quite explicitly recognized by the Austrians, not least by Mises in his 1924 analysis of "the gratuitous nature of credit" (Mises, 1953, p. 352), by which he meant the problem of what the forces are that compel the rate of interest charged by the banking system to move toward "the level determined by the circumstances of the capital market, i.e. the market in which present goods and future goods are exchanged for one another" (p. 352). Though Mises found Wicksell's analysis of the interaction of the money and natural (or normal) interest rates inadequate, he nevertheless conceded to him" the merit of having stated the problem clearly" (p. 355). As we have seen above, the mechanism in Wicksell's analysis linking the money and normal interest rates was the effect that any discrepancy between them would have on the price level, hence on the public's demand for commodity money, and therefore on the credit terms the banking system offered its customers. He thus created, as has already been stressed, a theory of the role of interest rates in the transition from one equilibrium price level to another. Mises, noting the crucial role played by a commodity money in restoring equilibrium between Wicksell's money and natural interest rates, and noting that this particular institution, though highly desirable, did not seem essential to the economic system, sought a deeper and more general analysis, and in so doing began the process of converting a theory of price level change into one of real economic fluctuations.

Wicksell's work was not the only starting point for the Austrians. Böhm-Bawerk's capital theory, which had deeply influenced Wicksell's first, and in many respects most thorough, exposition of the cumulative process, that of *Interest and Prices,* provided a vital component of their model, as we shall see, while the influence of Walrasian general equilibrium analysis is also much in evidence, particulary in Hayek's work. Moreover, and crucially, Austrian business cycle theory was a self-conscious application of a particular methodology of economics, one whose most accessible account is to be found in Lionel Robbins's *Nature and Significance of Economic Science* (Robbins, 1935) but which under the influence of Carl Menger had marked Austrian work from the very outset. This method was, as is well known, individualistic, but above all rigorously deductive. Economic theory was thought of as being exclusively a matter of deriving conclusions from premises that, being self-evidently true, could yield only true implications. Empirical evidence might have its uses to illustrate the truth of conclusions gained by deductive methods, or to provide a quantitative foundation for their practical implementation, but it had no role to play in establishing their validity:

> If . . . the theory is logically sound . . . the best that statistical investigation can do is show that there still remains an unexplained residue of processes. It could never prove that the determining relationships are of a different character from those maintained by the theory. (Hayek, 1932a, p. 33)

For the Austrians, only conclusions rigorously derived from what we would nowadays term "maximizing premises" had scientific validity, and Robbins (1935, p. 115) was surely referring to Austrian business cycle theory when he wound up his attack on "quantitative economics" with the remark that

> a few isolated thinkers, using the despised apparatus of deductive theory, have brought our knowledge of the theory of fluctuations to a point from which the fateful events of the last few years can be explained in general terms, and a complete solution of the riddle of depressions within the next few years does not seem outside the bounds of probability.

It has sometimes been suggested that the revolution in deductive microeconomic theorizing, which Robbins and his associates at the London School of Economics had so much to do with creating in the 1930s, brought about a change in the discipline almost as important as that brought about by Keynes (and some modern commentators would, I am confident, replace "almost" with "more"). It is worth noting, therefore, that to at least one of the architects of that revolution, Austrian business cycle theory appeared to be part and parcel of it.

What then was Austrian business cycle theory? It began, as I have already remarked, with Mises's attempts to find a more general explanation than Wicksell had provided of the tendency of the money rate of interest to converge upon a normal value determined on the real side of the economy. In his hands, and those of Hayek, Austrian business cycle theory became an explicit attempt to explain the occurrence of depressions in real income and employment. As far as Hayek was concerned the starting point of such an explanation had to be a state of general equilibrium characterized by full employment. He put it in the following terms in *Prices and Production* (Hayek, 1936, p. 3):

> [i]f we want to explain economic phenomena at all, we have no means available but to build on foundations given by the concept of a tendency towards equilibrium. . . . If we are to proceed systematically, therefore, we must start with a situation which is already sufficiently explained by the general body of economic theory. And the only situ-

ation which satisfies this criterion is the situation in which all available resources are employed. The existence of unused resources must be one of the main objects of our explanation.

Or again (p. 95):

[w]e can gain a theoretically unexceptionable explanation of complex phenomena only by first assuming the full activity of the elementary economic interconnections as shown by the equilibrium theory, and then introducing consciously and successively, just those elements which are capable of relaxing those rigid inter-relationships. (passage originally in italics)

But though by "equilibrium theory" Hayek explicitly meant the work of "the Lausanne School of theoretical economics" (Hayek, 1932, p. 42, fn.), the interrelationships that for him, as for Mises, needed to be relaxed if the cycle was to be explained were those that Böhm-Bawerk, rather than Walras, had particularly stressed, namely, those involved in allocating resources over time.[5] The role of the rate of interest was, according to the Austrians, to coordinate intertemporal choices. The act of saving involved the sacrifice of current consumption in the future. The act of investment involved devoting currently available resources to the production over time of those future goods. Moreover, in a modern economy, these two acts were usually undertaken by different sets of agents:

Only in comparitively few cases will the people who have saved money and the people who want to use it in production be identical. In the majority of cases, therefore, the money which is directed to new uses will first have to pass into other hands. The question *who* is going to use the additional funds available for investment in producers' goods will be decided on the loan market. (Hayek, 1936, p. 84)

If the loan market worked as it should, an increase in the attractiveness of saving for the sake of future consumption would lower the rate of interest, thus providing the necessary incentive to producers to adopt a more roundabout, and therefore in Austrian eyes necessarily more productive, method of production. Unfortunately, in a monetary economy, the loan market could not be relied on always to work in this way.

Like Wicksell, the Austrians took the quantity theory as the starting point for their monetary analysis, but they were particularly critical of the central place that theory accorded the idea of the "general price level": The latter was a statistical artifact that corresponded to no economic variable of importance for individual maximizing behavior.[6] Here the critical prices were relative prices, and the quantity theory, in focusing on the effects of monetary changes on an aggregate statistical artifact, overlooked their all-important non-neutral influence on relative prices.

> Those who hold the mechanical version of the Quantity Theory . . . believe that the increase in the quantity of money must eventually lead to a uniform increase in the prices of all economic goods. . . . Thorough comprehension of the mechanism by means of which the quantity of money affects the prices of commodities makes their point of view untenable. Since the increased quantity of money is received in the first place by a limited number of economic agents only and not by all, the increase in prices at first embraces only those goods that are demanded by these persons. . . . (Mises, 1953, p. 140)

The rate of interest was a particular relative price, and to the extent that monetary changes influenced it, they were capable of dislocating the mechanisms coordinating the intertemporal allocation of resources. This was the central insight upon which Austrian business cycle theory was built.

In Austrian analysis the equilibrium value of the rate of interest is that which equates the supply of voluntary saving in the economy to the demand for resources for investment. *Any* credit creation on the part of the banking system involving an increase in the money supply will be associated with a lower than equilibrium value for the rate of interest and, *to the extent that the newly created funds come first into the hands of firms,* will lead to a demand for investment goods in excess of voluntary saving. The newly created money in question will, however, enable firms to realize their demands and to obtain resources by bidding them away from consumers. Such "forced saving," however, is the first step toward economic crisis, because "incomes of wage earners will be rising in consequence of the increased amount of money available for investment by entrepreneurs" while at the same time "these decisions will not change the amount of consumers' goods immediately available . . ." (Hayek, 1936, p. 87). Indeed, in due course the supply of consumer goods will shrink, because a curtailment of their current production (albeit with a view to an increase in their production at some time in the future) is of the very essence of the forced saving process.[7]

Wage earners, however, will wish to divide their incomes between consumption and saving in the same proportion as before, and once money passes into their hands, it will underpin an undiminished real, but increased nominal, demand for consumption goods. The first consequence of the excess demand for consumer goods implicit here will be a rise in their relative price. This may, in turn, influence profit expectations and for a while encourage firms to persist in borrowing from the banks. The latter, however, "for obvious reasons . . . cannot continue indefinitely to extend credits. . . ." (Hayek, 1936, p. 89). Eventually, then, the economy's underlying savings rate reasserts itself as a constraint on investment, but in the interim resources have been devoted to initiating investments that can no longer be seen through to fruition. Producers working on "a process where the transition to longer roundabout processes is not yet completed when the amount of money ceases to increase . . . will have to abandon the attempt to change over to more capitalistic methods of production." (p. 60).

Resources will now have to be shifted away from more, toward less, roundabout methods of production, but unlike the preceding shift in the opposite direction, this movement cannot be smoothly accomplished. On the contrary, this "transition to shorter processes . . . will regularly be accompanied by a crisis" (p. 93): Capital equipment embodied in roundabout processes, and perhaps still under construction, being durable and specific in nature, cannot immediately be transferred to other uses. Thus "a loss of capital and reduction of income [are] inevitable" (p. 93). How severe the crisis is depends upon how much forced saving has preceded it. The more prolonged and vigorous the boom, the more prolonged and severe the slump, for the latter will come to an end only when redundant capital has at last been amortized and a time structure restored to production compatible with the economy's underlying saving rate.[8]

That capital should necessarily be idle in the slump is clear, but it is less obvious why labor could not be redeployed to the short production period industries from which it had been withdrawn in the first place. This problem was certainly evident to Hayek and Robbins, and they invoked at various points downwardly rigid wages, and fixed (or nearly so) proportions in production, in order to explain why redundancy of capital would be accompanied by redundancy of labor. The explanations in question, though, are not integral to the Austrian model and have something of an ad hoc air to them. In Haberler's words, "This . . . explanation of the depression is . . . incomplete and unsatisfactory" (1964, p. 58). To modern students of macroeconomics, whether brought up on conventional Keynesian wisdom or on more recent "new-Classical" analysis, this failure of Austrian business cycle theory to provide a properly integrated account of unemployment must seem a grave one, but before passing judgment, the reader should recall that until 1936, no one provided a satisfactory account of this phenomenon. Even so, the absence of a theory of unemployment did not prevent Austrian analysis from being used to derive policy proposals of a sort, proposals that, despite the novelty of the theoretical analysis upon which they were based, bore more than a passing resemblance to the time-honored wisdom of English classical economics.[9]

For most classical economists, not least the proponents of the 1844 Bank Charter Act, the essence of the problem of preventing slumps was seen to lie in preventing the preceding boom, or if that was impossible, in ensuring that it was as mild as possible. Hayek stated the Austrian position in the following words in *Prices and Production:* " . . . we arrive at results which only confirm the old truth that we may perhaps prevent a crisis by checking expansion in time, but that we can do nothing to get out of it before its natural end, once it has come" (Hayek, 1936, p. 99). In principle the boom could be prolonged by credit expansion that permitted firms to continue to outbid consumers for resources, but Lionel Robbins's warning on this matter is quite representative of Austrian views.

> Once costs have begun to rise it would require a continuous increase in the rate of increase of credit to prevent the thing coming to disaster. But that itself, as we have seen in the great post-war inflations would eventually generate panic. Sooner or later the initial errors are discovered. And then starts a reverse rush for liquidity. The Stock Exchange collapses. There is a stoppage of new issues. Production in the industries producing capital-goods slows down. The boom is at an end. (Robbins, 1934, pp. 41–2)

Accelerating inflation, followed by collapse, was thus the predicted consequence of attempting to prolong the boom by prolonging the monetary impulse that had started it (or permitted it to begin) in the first place.[10] Nor could the expansion of credit to finance consumer demand be expected to mitigate a crisis already characterized by an excess demand for consumer goods. On the contrary, as Hayek noted, "a relative increase in the demand for consumers' goods could only make matters worse" (Hayek, 1936, p. 97). As to public works, their implementation would have consequences similar to policies designed to maintain private sector investment. Robbins, discussing contemporary American experiments along such lines, warned that

> The unbalancing of the budget and the vast expenditures on public works have an inflationary tendency which may well . . . engender an inflationary boom – a boom which . . . would be likely to be followed by a deflationary collapse. (Robbins, 1934, p. 125)

Once in a crisis, then, there was nothing to be done but await "its natural end." Better by far to avoid it by maintaining monetary equilibrium in the first place, but this would be well nigh impossible.

> The rate of interest at which, in an expanding economy, the amount of new money entering circulation is just sufficient to keep the price-level stable, is always lower than the rate which would keep the amount

of available loan-capital equal to the amount simultaneously saved by the public. (Hayek, 1932a, p. 114; original in italics)

For the Austrians, price level constancy was not a characteristic of monetary equilibrium. What was needed was a rate of interest that would equate saving and investment; this in turn required a constant money supply and, therefore, in a growing economy with no change in the technology of exchange, a *falling* price level.[11] But to maintain a constant money supply in the presence of a modern banking system was essentially impossible. Though Mises tended to regard the behavior of the banking system as initiating the cycle, Hayek, who in this respect followed Wicksell, did not. For him "an improvement in the expectations of profit or . . . a diminution in the rate of saving" (Hayek, 1932a, p. 147) could just as well initiate discrepancy between the money and natural interest rates (my use of the Wicksellian vocabulary here reflects Hayek's, or his translators', choice), because in the face of such changes the banks would be bound, for a while at least, to continue to lend at the preexisting interest rate. They could do so even under a gold standard by means of the "often-disputed 'creation' of deposits" (p. 148) because "the ratio of reserves to deposits does not represent a constant magnitude, but, as experience shows, is itself variable" (p. 163).[12]

The practical implication of all this was that "So long as we make use of bank credit as a means of furthering economic development we shall have to put up with the resulting trade cycles" (Hayek, 1932a, p. 189), not least because any effort to do better "could only be attempted by a central monetary authority for the whole world . . ." (Hayek, 1936, p. 125). To have individual central banks attempt to maintain a constant supply of money would – at least under a gold standard – interfere with world wide allocative efficiency. He stated:

> It is probably an illusion to suppose that we shall ever be able entirely to eliminate industrial fluctuations by means of monetary policy. The most we may hope for is that the growing information of the public may make it easier for central banks both to follow a cautious policy during the upward swing of the cycle, and so to mitigate the following depression, and to resist the well-meaning but dangerous proposals to fight depression by "a little inflation." (p. 125)

The Stockholm School

Long before there was Austrian business cycle theory, there existed a well established "Austrian (or Vienna) School" of economics, working out a research program whose outlines are clearly discernible in the writings of its acknowledged founder, Carl Menger; in the previous section of this paper I drew attention to aspects of the relationship that the cycle theory of Mises, Hayek, and Robbins bore to that broader tradition. The Stockholm School is altogether less well defined. There is no figure in the history of Swedish economics comparable to Menger, and though Wicksell, Cassel, Davidson, and their contemporaries did much to advance our subject, their contributions grew out of what sometimes seems to be a propensity to argue about almost everything, rather than from any collective attempt to seek the answers to a common set of problems using mutually agreed methods to derive the implications of an acceptable set of assumptions. Even the Swedish contemporaries of Hayek were not defined as belonging to a definite "school" until Bertil Ohlin (1937) did so in his well-known commentary on the relationship between their work and the central ideas of the *General Theory.*

The casual reader of Ohlin can easily gain the impression that there had emerged in Stockholm by the mid-1930s a consensus about the theory of macroeconomic fluctuations as coherent as that to be found among any group of Keynesians or Austrians, a consensus that had in certain crucial respects anticipated Keynes's central insights into the problem of unemployment. However, matters are not quite so clearcut. A reading of the important Swedish contributions of the period reveals far less of a consensus than marks contemporary Austrian writings. If Lindahl, Lundberg, Myrdal, and indeed Ohlin himself really did think of themselves as belonging to a "school" before (or even after) 1937, it was a school with rather lax rules. Moreover, as Patinkin (1982) has shown, the key Keynesian insight that output changes themselves can act as an equilibrating mechanism did not play a central role in Swedish economics before 1936. Even so, the label "Stockholm School" has stuck, and it is hard to see that it would have done so if those to whom it was affixed had not held some important ideas in common. Furthermore, the speed with which Keynesian analysis was assimilated by Swedish economists, notably by Lundberg (1937, Chaps. 5, 8, and 9), after the publication of the *General Theory* also suggests a strong affinity between those commonly held ideas and those out of which the *General Theory* developed.

Now no one would take seriously a suggestion that Mises, Hayek, and Robbins were prototype Keynesians. But, as was stressed at the outset of this paper, their macroeconomic analysis started from the same point as that of the Stockholm School, namely, the incompatible concepts of "monetary equilibrium" that Wicksell had bequeathed to his successors. As was also noted earlier, these two facts surely present something of a puzzle. How could two groups of economists, starting in essentially the same place, and dealing with essentially the same problem, move so far apart so quickly? What was it about the economics of the Stockholm School that makes their work appear so Keynesian and so antithetical to that of the Austrians?

Gunnar Myrdal remarked in 1932 that

> It is not surprising that it was the Austrians who found the connexions with Wicksell: Wicksell himself was a pupil of Böhm-Bawerk and he put his thoughts into forms and constructions based directly on Austrian habits of thought. (1939, p. 7)

Myrdal and his colleagues did share Austrian views on the inadequacy of the quantity theory, on the grounds that "credit is a causal factor for the price *level*, but also for price *relations* [i.e., relative prices]" so that "the problem of credit requires a monetary theory which is really integrated with the central economic theory" (Myrdal, 1939, p. 16), but otherwise their notions of what constituted a valid body of "central economic theory" were far removed from "Austrian habits of thought."[13]

Wicksell's natural interest rate was, as Myrdal correctly noted, "the physical marginal productivity of the roundabout process of production" (Myrdal, 1939, p. 24). This concept derived directly from Böhm-Bawerk and became completely central to Austrian cycle theory, where the key mechanism giving rise to economic fluctuations was precisely a departure of the money interest rate from this natural level. But the relation between Wicksell and Böhm-Bawerk is most noticeable in *Interest and Prices*. As his thought developed to encompass a growing economy with heterogeneous output, the concept of the "natural" or "normal" rate of interest became less well defined as "the physical marginal productivity of the roundabout process of production." The Austrian solution to clarifying the rather confused concept of monetary equilibrium with which Wicksell had ended up involved restoring to it a much stronger element of Böhm-Bawerk's ideas about capital than he himself had utilized in his later expositions of it. Wicksell's Swedish successors, on the other hand, took it as one of their first tasks to rid his monetary theory of any reliance that remained in his later work on just these ideas.

As early as his 1929 essay on "The Place of Capital in the Theory of Price," Eric Lindahl had explicitly dealt with problems of measuring capital (cf. Lindahl, 1939a, pp. 313 ff.), noting the arbitrary elements inevitably present in any treatment of such an aggregate, and by 1930 he had come to understand that

> Only under very special assumptions is it possible to conceive of a natural or real rate of interest determined purely by technical considerations, and thus independent of the price level. For this to be true it must be supposed that the productive process consists only in investing

> units of goods or services of the same type as the final product, the
> latter increasing with the passage of time alone without the co-opera-
> tion of other scarce factors. . . . Under more realistic assumptions . . .
> the real rate of interest does not depend only on technical conditions,
> but also on the price situation, and cannot be regarded as existing inde-
> pendently on the loan rate of interest. (1939b, pp. 247–8)

Myrdal too understood the point (cf. 1939, pp. 50 ff.) and devoted a
large part of the early sections of his "immanent criticism" of Wicksell
to purging the latter's monetary theory of the concept of a natural interest rate determined independently of monetary conditions.

Myrdal's approach here was, in essence, the Fisherian one, which even
today dominates monetary economics, namely, to recognize "capital
value [as] nothing else than the discounted sum of all future gross
incomes minus operating costs" (p. 62) and to state as an aggregate
approximation to the condition for monetary equilibrium (at this point
in a static economy) "the condition of *equality between the capital value
and the cost of reproduction of existing real capital*" (p. 69, Myrdal's
italics). As to the case of a growing economy, a discrepancy between the
value of existing capital and the cost of producing new equipment had
to exist so as to create "a complex of profit margins in different firms
which stimulates just the amount of total investment which can be taken
care of by the available capital disposal" (p. 82, original in italics). For
the Austrians the conditions of "monetary equilibrium" involved the
relationship between bank lending rates and what they treated as a technically determined natural rate of interest.[14] For Myrdal and the other
Swedes, bank lending rates were important for monetary equilibrium
too, but they replaced what for the Austrians seemed to be the *objective
and stable* technical characteristics of the production function with a
subjective and volatile factor, namely, firms' expectations about future
net revenue, as the other element to be considered. For those interpret-
ers of Keynes (1936) (e.g., Shackle) for whom his stress on expectations
marks an essential contribution, this characteristic of the work of the
Stockholm School is, for obvious reasons, of particular significance.

The Stockholm School took it for granted that the analysis of a monetary economy should be based on variables measured in nominal
terms, and indeed slowness to adopt such a mode of analysis was, for
Ohlin (1937, p. 230), a fault of English economics in the Marshallian
tradition. To anyone reasoning in terms of nominal variables, it was
obvious that both relative price and price level expectations must under-
lie expectations about future net revenue. It was but a small step from
this point to the view that price level fluctuations, *provided they were*

fully anticipated, were irrelevant to other aspects of the economy's performance. Hence the behavior of the quantity of money, which was so important for the Austrians, was reduced to a matter of no theoretical significance for the Stockholm School.

Lindahl (1939b) treats the matter of price level expectations more thoroughly than anyone else among the Stockholm School, though there is ample textual evidence that Myrdal too had a firm grasp of the issues involved (cf., e.g., Myrdal, 1939, p. 121). Here, as with the problems of giving content to the concept of a natural interest rate, Lindahl develops ideas first noted in his 1929 essay (cf., e.g., 1939c, p. 330). To begin with, he is clear that the irrelevance of perfectly foreseen price level fluctuations arises from the fact that "[a] shift in the price level that is foreseen by everybody early enough can be taken into account in all contracts for the future" (Lindahl, 1939b, p. 148). Such an insight, though it has obvious enough roots in the work of Marshall (1890) and Fisher (1896), was nevertheless something of a rarity in the early 1930s; however, Lindahl not only stated it, but went on to point out several crucial implications that it yielded, namely: that "The monetary authority . . . cannot directly regulate the price level through its interest policy, but it can do so indirectly by influencing the primary determining factor, i.e. general anticipations" (1939b, p. 149); that "A neutral rate of interest does not necessarily imply an unchanged price level, but rather such a development of prices as is in accordance with the expectations of the public" (1939b, p. 252); and that, because

> [i]n a community with perfect foresight, the height of the loan rate of interest depends upon the anticipated course of prices . . . [a] rate of interest that is normal in relation to a certain foreseen course of prices would . . . be abnormal in relation to other anticipated developments, even if in other respects the conditions in which it influenced the demand for and supply of saving are unaltered. (1939b, p. 252)

Now the Stockholm economists did not, of course, regard the perfect foresight assumption as being of immediate practical relevance. Rather, the device was used heuristically to enable them to bring out the crucial role of expectations in influencing the conditions of monetary equilibrium. They understood well enough that, if one was willing to assume perfect foresight, the social problem of coordinating intertemporal choices posed no special analytic difficulties. In Lindahl's words,

> Under the assumption that the future is perfectly foreseen, all prices in all the periods included in the dynamic process thus become linked

> together in a uniform system. The equilibrium of this sytem is main-
> tained by the same laws as under stationary conditions.(1939a, p. 330)

Lindahl and his fellow Swedes, like the Austrians, saw that the really interesting problems arose when the activities of agents, *lacking perfect foresight,* had to be coordinated over time.

For the Austrians prices conveyed information and incentives to agents, and, for intertemporal choices the money interest rate was the relevant price. In their theory, agents extracted the information and acted on the incentives contained therein, on the crucial but usually implicit assumption of expected price level constancy. If that exercise resulted in attempts to execute incompatible plans for saving and invest-ment, then crisis was the inevitable result. The Stockholm School under-stood that a given interest rate, or term structure of interest rates (cf. particularly Lindahl, 1939, Part II, Chap. 3), would convey very differ-ent information and incentives depending upon the expectations in whose light it was interpreted. They also believed that expectations could differ among agents and vary over time in response to both exog-enous and endogenous variables. Hence they went on to consider a bewilderingly varied menu of possibilities, and the stress on the impor-tance of expectations and their maleability, which is one of the great strengths of the economics of the Stockholm School, also became one of its great weaknesses. It prevented them from developing a simple ana-lytic model that could yield unambiguous predictions. As Bjorn Hans-son (1982) has shown, their main theoretical contribution was a method of analysis capable of dealing with alternative possible "dynamic sequences" as the term came to be used, rather than any core theoretical model.

There is not space here to give an account of the efforts of the Stock-holm School to create a satisfactory method of dynamic analysis, and in any event Hansson's valuable study deals with just this issue. Suffice it to sketch the main outlines of their contributions here. Starting with a notion of equilibrium every bit as Walrasian as Hayek's, they noted first, as did he, the importance of expectations about the future values of eco-nomic variables as parameters determining their current values. In the absence of perfect foresight, they [and in particular Lindahl (1939a, 1939b)] went on to consider a series of Walrasian equilibria evolving over time in response to new information, but rejected this approach as unsatisfactory because it led to the explanation of the evolution of the values of endogenous variables solely in terms of the evolution of exog-enous factors. What we would now call "intrinsic dynamics" seemed to the Stockholm School to be essential ingredients of any satisfactory model of economic fluctuations. The key analytic concepts that they developed to deal with them were "the unit period," and the distinction between "ex ante" and "ex post" values of variables.

> It is . . . essential for the very concept of monetary equilibrium . . . that the analysis be restricted to a particular *point* of time. . . . [T]he dynamic problem proper concerns the development from the point of time to a second and a third and so on . . . [*P*]*eriods* of time are defined as the interval between two points of time. (Myrdal, 1939, p. 43; Myrdal's italics)

At the beginning of the unit period, variables take their *ex ante* values, and "[i]n the ex ante calculus it is a question not of realised results but of the anticipations, calculations and plans driving the dynamic process forward." *Ex post* values are observed when "[l]ooking backward on a period which is finished," they are the values "actually realised" (p. 46).

In due course it became apparent that the problem of analyzing the economy's evolution over time could be divided into two subproblems: how an *ex ante* "tendency to disparity" in variables might, within the unit period, "develop into an ex post balance" (Myrdal, 1939, p. 46), and how the *ex ante* "plans and expectations" with which any particular period began related to the "'realisations' of earlier periods" (Ohlin, 1937, p. 222). Thus the fully developed "sequence" analysis of the Stockholm School dealt with both the evolution of economic variables *within* the unit period and the development of plans and expectations *between* such periods.[15] The voluntary savings-investment disparity and resulting crisis studied by the Austrians is analogous in a rough and ready way to a particular treatment of the first of these problems, but, as we have seen, the Austrians never systematically integrated into their analysis the notion that the expectations and plans of agents might evolve over time as a result of the economy's behavior. The capacity of Swedish analysis to yield unidirectional cumulative movements in economic variables of an essentially Wicksellian nature, as well as booms truncated by a crisis, stems in large measure from its treatment of the plans and expectations of agents as endogenous to an ongoing dynamic process. Different conclusions followed from different assumptions about expectations.

Lindahl's work yields an early and readily accessible illustration of this characteristic of Swedish analysis. In 1930 (1939b, pp. 169 ff.) he considered the effects of a fall in the money rate of interest from an initial equilibrium value. He noted that, as a result, "[f]actors of production will be transferred from the direct production of consumption goods to the production of capital goods." This effect would, in due course, render "a rise in the prices of consumption goods . . . unavoidable" (p. 170). Up to this point in the analysis he told a completely Austrian story, but he then went on to show that *"[u]nder the assumption that existing prices of consumption goods are expected to continue in the future"* (which was, of course, Wicksell's usual assumption about expectations) this would involve a rise in capital values too, and therefore a cumulative inflation "since capital values are partly determined by the anticipated prices of consumption goods" (Lindahl's italics). Moreover, because the increased money incomes arising from such a process would be concentrated in the hands of entrepreneurs rather than workers or capitalists, "[t]he saving required to enable production to be more capitalistic" would be forthcoming and "from the point of view of the individual . . . in large part quite voluntary" (Lindahl, 1939b, p. 173).

Thus, an experiment with an Austrian beginning need not, according to Lindahl, end in crisis at all, but ultimately in a new equilibrium with a more capital intensive mode of production in place (cf. Lindahl, 1939b, p. 181). The particular assumption made about expectations here was, however, understood to be crucial, for Lindahl went on to warn his readers that:

> If we now assume alternatively that individuals, and especially entrepreneurs, expect the rising price movement to continue, the anticipation of higher prices will make longer investments . . . appear still more profitable. This will accelerate the transfer of factors from the consumers' goods industries, with the result that the rise in prices of consumption goods will proceed at an ever increasing pace. . . . [T]he rise in the price level . . . will be cumulative, until the process is brought to an end by a crisis. (1939b, p. 182)

Thus, he concluded:

> The objection made by Cassel . . . to Wicksell that a new equilibrium with a higher price level must always eventually be achieved when the rate of interest has been lowered, therefore holds good only under very special conditions. (p. 186)

This capacity of the analysis of the Stockholm School to generate a variety of conclusions about the economy's time path when out of equilibrium, depending upon the specific assumptions made about the nature of the disequilibrium processes driving that time path, was to become increasingly prominent as it developed during the 1930s.[16] Although the foregoing example depends upon alternative assumptions about price expectations to generate differing conclusions, the Stockholm School did not become overdependent upon the analysis of expectations to generate alternative dynamic sequences. The degree of price and wage stickiness, the availability of unemployed resources, their distribution between the capital goods and consumption goods industries, their mobility between sectors, the extent to which the behavior of agents vis-à-vis cash holding might intrude on the functioning of the "pure credit" system upon which their monetary analysis was usually based, the length of the "unit period" – all of these could vary.[17] In doing so they could radically alter the outcome of any experiment that began with a specific departure of the economy from a situation of monetary equilibrium. The following passage of Myrdal's forms the core of the case for treating him as having anticipated the central theoretical contribution of the *General Theory:*

> Let us assume the case of a downward process. The decrease of income will diminish savings less, the more consumption decreases. A shift in the distribution of incomes, however, in favour of classes which save less at the expense of those which save more, which takes place during such a process, counteracts this decrease of consumption. In the degree to which consumption is maintained by such a shift, losses need not become as big as they must otherwise be in order to bring about the bookkeeping correspondence between capital disposal and the value of real investments which is subsequently necessary. This means that the intensity of the depressive process is then not as great as it would otherwise be. (1939, p. 119)

When read in context, this passage is seen to present one possible outcome of the consequences of an initial discrepancy between the *ex ante* plans of savers and investors, not an attempt to state a uniquely important insight into the equilibrating mechanisms at work in an economy sinking into a depression.

Though I have referred to the absence of a core model, yielding definite predictions, as a weakness in the economics of the Stockholm School, the Stockholm economists regarded the open-endedness of their analysis as something of a virtue. Certainly it had a well-articulated methodological basis that seems to this commentator to be closely related to the Marshallian view of economic theory as "an engine for the discovery of concrete truth." Their method was deductive, but they did not, in contrast to the Austrians, expect deductive reasoning alone to produce empirically valid and useful results. Myrdal's justification of "a priori procedure . . . at present particularly in need of being emphasised in the social sciences" was that "[the] first requirement for receiving sensible answers is to have raised sensible questions" (Myrdal, 1939, p. 209), not that such procedure would in and of itself yield such answers. Lundberg's attitude was similar. His *Studies in the Theory of Economic Expansion* was intended to show how "we may introduce time elements in order to carry . . . static theory further" but he recognized "an infinite number of possibilities for dynamising the static relations" as a result of which "[t]heories of the business cycle tend . . . to follow as many lines of explanation as there are possibilities of disrupting static relations" (Lundberg, 1937, p. 51).

Lundberg (1937) made no claim to have made "a complete, or even an "unbiased" selection among the numerous theories of money and business cycles." With respect to the theories he did choose to discuss, a "choice . . . primarily . . . governed by discussions among Swedish economists during the last decade" (p. 5), he claimed no more than that:

> We have tried to state the underlying assumptions as clearly as possible in order to make the limitations of the conclusions evident. Against the objection to the abstract nature of these assumptions the fact should be taken into account that we have not directly aimed at explaining the actual course of events in a business cycle. (p. 244)

He was willing to go no further than Myrdal in justifying theoretical work:

> [T]o be able to discuss the effects of . . . [economic policy] . . . our reasoning must always be based upon the conception of a simplified economic system . . . Any statistical investigation of business cycles, however extensive, cannot diminish our need of such a general conception of economic processes if . . . fundamental questions are to be answered. (p. 245)

Deductive reasoning, that is to say, was a means of asking relevant questions, not of answering them, as far as the Stockholm School economists were concerned, and it is hard to quarrel with such a defense of their work. The trouble is, though, that economists seem to prefer economic theory to yield answers, even wrong answers, rather than questions, even interesting ones. If, for a modern reader, the central contribution of the Stockholm School economists is hard to pin down, that is surely because their work yielded so many more questions than answers.

Be that as it may, abstract and (for its time) mathematical though the theorizing of the Stockholm School was, it derived its purposes from the practical policy problems facing the Swedish economy during the interwar depression, and that analysis was indeed used to underpin policy advice. As with their theoretical work, so too with their comments on policy, the Stockholm School economists were a good deal more eclectic than their Austrian contemporaries, although here too they started from very much the same place, namely, "the *value premise* that cyclical movements should be made less severe and the *factual premise* that this requires primarily the maintenance of the conditions of monetary equilibrium" (Myrdal, 1939, p. 181). The Swedes, though, were suspicious, and Myrdal in particular was downright scornful, of an approach to business cycle and monetary theory that represented "a rationalisation of economic liberalism, which erects its own fatalistic, negative attitude toward planned economic control into a doctrine."[18] Myrdal cited with approval a remark he attributed to Cassel, to the effect that

> perhaps the whole attitude was ultimately based upon a primitive puritanism; happiness is somehow evil, something immoral, which should be accompanied by a purifying misery now and then in order that those who have experienced it may be redeemed; and so it is only proper, right and natural that after the upswing, with all its sad mistakes, bad times should follow. (Myrdal, 1939, p. 201)

The policy pragmatism of the Stockholm School was nevertheless far from being devoid of theoretical discipline. To begin with, the members agreed that, because of the key role played by expectations in determining the economy's time path, the aim of monetary policy, which was conceived of in terms the manipulation of interest rates, "should be determined and announced, and in each case the reason for the measures taken should be explained" (Lindahl,1939b, p. 232). More specifically, Myrdal urged that the aims of monetary policy be defined in terms of the behavior of prices, not, though, because economic theory dictated that prices had to behave in a particular way to preserve monetary equilibrium, for we have seen that it did not. Rather, he took this position on the practical grounds that "[a] publicly declared monetary policy can hardly serve its purpose if it is not stated in simple terms and in terms which are of direct importance to the anticipations of entrepreneurs" (Myrdal, 1939, p. 193). He explicitly rejected the idea that "monetary policy should attempt to maintain the employment of the means of production at a maximum" on the grounds that "a monetary policy with this aim as the only standard would either lead to certain and general cumulative price movements . . . or require extensive public regulation of markets" (p. 196).

The affinity of this statement to similar propositions of Hayek and Robbins is not so close as it looks at first sight. It must be read in the context of Myrdal's view that:

> Maintaining a monetary equilibrium [is] a question not only of monetary policy but of economic policy as a whole, social policy and the institutions which rule the labour market, cartel legislations and all related factors. Various combinations of these heterogeneous things, more or less under political control, together with appropriate values of the standard combination of credit conditions, produce stable monetary equilibrium relations. (1939, p. 184)

Hence, the open-ended economic theory of the Stockholm School yielded a large "field of indifference," in the choice for the setting of policy instruments. The assignment of monetary policy to the maintenance of equilibrium between saving and investment in the context of a stated policy goal of price stability was just that, an assignment of a particular instrument to a particular target.[19] It did not imply any ranking on theoretical grounds of price stability above other policy goals.

Nor is "price stability" here to be interpreted as constancy of consumer prices or some other convenient index. The members of Stockholm School were well aware that not all prices were equally flexible, singling out money wages, particularly in the unionized sector, as likely to be sticky. In this they were early exponents of the idea, later associated with Hicks (1955), of a "labour standard" for the determination of the price level, and for Myrdal, at least, "a monetary policy aimed to preserve the equilibrium relations, must, therefore, *adapt the flexible prices to the absolute level of the sticky ones*" (Myrdal, 1939, p. 133; Myrdal's italics). Though the Stockholm economists stressed the role of inflation expectations when discussing nominal interest rates, they did not discuss the possibility that money wages might be influenced by expectations. Even so, they did see scope for other policy tools (cartel policy and such) to affect the behavior of sticky prices. Hence this injunction of Myrdal's implied no uniquely appropriate behavior for the monetary authorities.

The "failures" of the Austrians and the Stockholm School

The "failures" of the ideas of the Stockholm School and their Austrian counterparts are as distinct in nature as the two bodies of analysis themselves, and as we shall see, the differences between the "failures" are intimately related to the differences between the doctrines. Both were superseded by what came to be known as Keynesian economics. However, though after 1936 the major works of the Stockholm School were not to become staples of university reading lists, their principal ideas were nevertheless absorbed into what was in the following three decades the mainstream of macroeconomics. In contrast, over the same period, the contributions of their Austrian counterparts simply fell into neglect, to the point of being abandoned even by many of their own most enthusiastic exponents.

Why the Swedish literature rather than that originating in Cambridge was not chosen by economists at large as the foundation for the macroeconomics of the 1940s and subsequent decades must inevitably be a matter of conjecture.[20] Suffice it here to list a few possible reasons: the relative isolation of the Swedish economists from their American and British colleagues during the war; the inability of most English and American economists to read Swedish and German, combined with their overwhelming numbers in the profession; the closely related inability of the Swedish profession to generate a textbook through which identifiably Swedish ideas about macroeconomics could be instilled into anyone studying economics; and also, perhaps most important of all, a factor intrinsic to the economics of the Stockholm School, its already noted reluctance (or inability) to come to sharp, easily grasped, and definite conclusions about specific problems. The contrast between the simplicity of the Keynesian message that movements in output and employment were themselves equilibrating mechanisms, a message readily summarized in a diagram that could be embossed on the cover of a textbook, and the complexity of the exercises whereby Lundberg, say, demonstrated that almost anything could be the outcome of a dynamic sequence, is a telling one. Simple and definite messages are, for good or ill, the ones that catch on in our subject, almost regardless, it sometimes seems, of whether or not they are misleading.

In drawing the above-mentioned contrast betwen the open-minded complexity of the economics of the Stockholm School and the straightforward simplicity of Keynesian economics, though, we should not lose sight of two facts. Keynesian economics did not long retain its simplicity; and much of the clarity of the Keynesian message as it was transmitted to students of economics derived from its being cast in terms of the *ex ante-ex post* distinction that was one of the principal conceptual contributions, indeed according to Shackle (1967) the all important contribution, of the Stockholm School. It will be convenient to elaborate on the latter point first of all. In the *General Theory* Keynes *did* argue that saving always equaled investment, and as a result he *did* leave it unclear whether what we would now term the static multiplier summarized the equilibrium relationship between output and autonomous expenditure or a mere accounting identity.[21] As Ohlin (1937, p. 237) put it, discussing Keynes's insistence on the equality of savings and investment as a basis for deriving the multiplier relationship:

> either Keynes' reasoning is *ex-post,* and it explains nothing, or it is *ex-ante,* and then it is entirely wrong. There is no reason why the planned investment plus the planned consumption should be equal to the expected total income for society as a whole. . . . planned investment will differ from planned saving.

For Ohlin, applying conventional Stockholm reasoning, it was precisely the inequality between planned saving and investment that "sets in motion a process which makes realised income differ from expected income, realised savings from planned savings and realised new investments differ from the corresponding plan" (Ohlin, 1937, p. 64). Nevertheless, Ohlin had little time for the simple multiplier, even correctly analyzed, as an account of the outcome of that process. To begin with, "planned consumption" depended

> not on . . . expected income during the first coming period only, but on what [the consumer] expects to earn over a long period in the future. If a man gets a temporary, well-paid job which gives him a much higher salary than he is used to and more than he can expect to earn later on, his standards of consumption will obviously be much affected by consideration of this latter fact. . . . Keynes' analysis on this point seems a little superficial. (p. 62)

Furthermore:

> The chief reason why the multiplier theory can tell us but a little about the effects of a certain increase in investment is not its fluctuation, but the fact that it leaves out of account the reaction of a certain change in the volume of output . . . on profit expectations and the willingness to invest. (p. 240)

The Stockholm School's longstanding stress on the importance of expectations thus led to immediate doubts about the stability of the Keynesian consumption function, for reasons that, much elaborated, were later to underpin the work of Friedman (1957) as well as Modigliani and his associates (e.g., Modigliani and Brumberg, 1954) on this relationship; and also to a proposal that Keynesian analysis needed extending by treating the willingness to invest as an endogenous variable. In the latter respect, as Lundberg was later to note in his introduction to the postwar reprint of his *Studies,* the Stockholm School were among the leading precursors of the "dynamic economics" of Harrod (1949) and Hicks (1950), and of much pioneering econometric work on macroeconomic issues too.[22]

By the late 1950s there had emerged a consensus body of macroeconomic analysis, both theoretical and empirical, known as Keynesian economics, of which the *General Theory* was but one important source. The best analytic ideas of the Stockholm School were simply absorbed into that framework along with a host of other influences. The Swedes' policy analysis too became part of a similar consensus that viewed monetary policy as but one not particularly important tool among several available for achieving a variety of economic and social goals. What Lundberg (1985) has recently called the "Swedish Model" of economic and social policy was by no means a unique experiment. Rather it provides an example, albeit a rather extreme one, of a pervasive interventionism in economic and social affairs that characterized policy throughout the western world down to the beginning of the 1970s. The "failure" of the Stockholm School, that is to say, did not lie in any inability on their part to gain acceptance for a significant proportion of their ideas. Rather it lay in the fact that the discipline at large lost sight of the Swedish element in those ideas as it adopted them.[23]

If the distinctive contributions of the Stockholm School were absorbed by the mainstream of macroeconomics, those of the Austrians seemed to meet a less happy fate. In the political climate of the 1930s, a body of theory that taught that the depression simply had to be waited out could hardly be expected to withstand the arrival of Keynesian analysis. The latter provided an almost irresistible justification for the ad hoc interventionist policies that the majority of economists had long advocated. Robbins was soon converted to Keynesian ideas, while Hayek, with his (1937) *Economica* essay on "Economics and Knowledge" began to move away from equilibrium theorizing deriving from Walras and Böhm-Bawerk toward that vision of economic life as a perpetually evolving set of disequilibrium processes that nowadays is regarded as the hallmark of Austrian economics. One characteristic insight of Austrian analysis of the 1930s, into the relationship between what we now call the capital-output ratio and the rate of interest, did, as Hicks (1967b) noted, survive in the growth models that were so popular in the 1950s and 1960s, but those models too are out of favor now. Only Mises and a few disciples (e.g., Murray Rothbart, 1975) remained faithful to the Austrian business cycle theory discussed in this paper, and their work now lies on the fringes of the subject as far as the majority of practitioners are concerned.

A judgment that the failure of Austrian theory involved the wholesale and permanent rejection of its ideas would have commanded widespread assent among economists as recently as fifteen years ago. Since then, though, "new-classical" business cycle theory has laid a strong (though still disputed) claim to be the mainstream doctrine of a new macroeconomics that asserts the desirability of basing all economic analysis, including macroeconomic analysis, on explicitly maximizing premises; proclaims the primacy of deductive reasoning in a Walrasian framework as the most fruitful path to knowledge of the workings of the economy; treats the response of individuals to misleading relative price signals about the terms of certain crucial intertemporal choices (albeit real wage signals concerning labor-leisure substitution opportunities, rather than interest rate signals about consumption-investment choices) as the key mechanism driving the business cycle; rejects the endogenously adjusting backward-looking expectations of the macroeconometric dynamic systems descended from Stockholm style sequence analysis and substitutes forward looking rational expectations; and provides the basis of policy doctrines every bit as anti-activist as those of the Austrians.

As should be apparent from a comparison of this brief summary of the business cycle analysis of Lucas, Barro, Sargent, and Wallace with that of Mises, Hayek, and Robbins, though the doctrines are by no means identical, they have several features in common. Nor is this an accident. I have already noted that Austrian business cycle theory represented part of a much more broadly based attempt to establish economics as a deductive science based on individualistic maximizing premises, and I have also drawn attention to the success of that attempt outside of what we now call macroeconomics. The exponents of new-classical economics have from the outset been conscious of the tensions in the subject arising from the coexistence of "Keynesian" macroeconomics with essentially Walrasian microeconomics, and have seen their task as being to extend the microeconomics they inherited to a point at which it could supersede Keynesian economics in dealing with macroproblems. The purpose of the new-classicals, that is to say, has been precisely to succeed where the Austrian business cycle theorists of the 1920s and 1930s apparently failed.

New-classical analysis differs in certain respects, sometimes important ones to be sure, from the work of the Austrians, not least in its ability to produce a coherent account of employment fluctuations as a consequence of maximizing choices. But, and for good reasons just sketched out, its overall flavor has been very similar to that of the earlier doctrine. Indeed, this commentator has elsewhere (Laidler, 1982) suggested that "neo-Austrian" is a more accurate label for it than "new-classical."[24] At this point in the development of our subject, it is hard to say how much of this work will prove to be of lasting value. If the claims of its proponents about its inherent superiority are justified, though, and if the demise of the postwar Keynesian consensus about macroeconomics proves permanent, then far from having been rejected, Austrian notions will after all have survived to be absorbed into the mainstream of the discipline, and it will be the ideas of the Stockholm School that will be seen to have suffered wholesale abandoment.

Perhaps, however, on a longer view, the "hunted hare" (to borrow from an apt metaphor from Sir Dennis Robertson) of analytic fashion will continue to run in circles. If it does, then the "failure" of the economic ideas discussed in this essay will turn out to be, like treason, merely a matter of dates.

Notes

1 I am grateful to Lars Jonung, Johan Myhrman, and Erik Lundberg for helpful discussion of some of the issues dealt with here, and to Hans Brems, Karl-Olof Faxén, Herbert Giersch, Peter Howitt, Lars Jonung, Axel Leijonhufvud, Johan Myhrman, and Paul Samuleson for helpful comments on an earlier draft of this paper. None of them is responsible for the opinions I express, though. I also gratefully acknowledge the financial support of the Social Science and Humanities Research Council of Canada.

2 Both Siven (1985), in describing the outcome of the Stockholm School's efforts, and Hicks (1967b), in describing the disappearance of Austrian business cycle theory from the scene, without using the word "failure" nevertheless tell stories to which it surely could be applied. In the case of Austrian theory it might also be noted that Shackle's (1967) *Years of High Theory,* which deals with "Invention and Tradition in Economic Thought 1926–39," mentions Mises not at all, Robbins once (as an opponent of the Marshallian idea of the "representative firm"), and Hayek twice (in his capacity as the editor of the German version of Myrdal's *Monetary Equilibrium).*

3 Indeed, Leijonhufvud (1981) has aptly referred to a "Wicksell connection" in the development of macroeconomics, for his influence on Keynes, though perhaps indirect, is marked. The influence is most notable in the *Treatise,* but is clearly present in the *General Theory* too, as Leijonhuvfud (1967) has shown. Nor, I think, can it be argued that the influence is just a matter of appearances. Richard Kahn was translating *Interest and Prices* while commenting on Keynes's drafts of the *General Theory,* and Keynes himself refereed Claassen's translation of the *Lectures* for Macmillan in 1932. See Keynes (1983, pp. 862–5).

4 Wicksell's work is analyzed in detail by Patinkin (1965), Laidler (1972), and Hansson (1985), who pays particular attention to the problematic nature of Wicksell's monetary equilibrium concept and its relationship to the relative vagueness of his later expositions of the "cumulative process."

5 The extension of the Walrasian vision to an intertemporal choice framework was accomplished by Hayek in his 1928 article "Intertemporal Price Equilibrium and Movements in the Value of Money" (Hayek, 1984), a piece much cited by the Stockholm School as well as the Austrians.

6 Indeed, Mises would have no truck with the concept at all, regarding it as essentially meaningless. He nevertheless frequently discussed the influence of the quantity of money on the "value of money," thus creating considerable confusion for modern readers. However, by "value of money" Mises meant something akin to the marginal utility of the services of a unit of nominal balances, not the inverse of a price index. That marginal utility, in turn, was, to use a phrase from Hicks's 1935 essay, "the ghost" of the marginal

utility of whatever commodity had served as money at some time in the past (Hicks, 1967a).

7 The concept of forced saving has a long history in monetary economics, going all the way back to Cantillon (1734). Hayek (1932b) is still the definitive study of the history of this idea.

8 See Hayek (1939, pp. 62 ff.) for an example of such discussions.

9 And the Austrians were very conscious of the historical origins of their ideas. Hayek's work on the history of forced saving has already been alluded to, and his introductory essay to Henry Thornton's *Paper Credit,* still the standard reference, was also a product of the 1930s. Lionel Robbins's prowess as a teacher of the history of economic thought verges on the legendary. Nor were Hayek and Robbins alone in finding support for Austrian analysis in earlier work. One of their colleagues at the London School of Economics, T. E. (later Sir Theodore) Gregory (1928) went so far in his introduction to Tooke and Newmarch's *History of Prices* as to refer to the Currency School as "the elect." The use of Calvinist vocabulary to characterize favorably the originators of an economic doctrine is of some interest in the light of Myrdal's comments quoted later.

10 It should be noted explicitly that the "accelerationism" of the foregoing passage, and the many others like it that occur in Austrian writings, in no way anticipates the accelerationism of Friedman (1968) or Phelps (1967). It stems from the argument that, to enable forced saving to continue at its original rate, the price of producers' goods must remain at a constant level *relative* to consumer goods. With the price level of the latter rising, this will require a steady increase in the size of the injection of nominal bank credit to sustain the relative price distortion in question. Austrian analysis paid no formal attention to the effects of inflation expectations on the time path of money wages and prices, which lie at the heart of modern theories of accelerating inflation. However, in less formal analysis, something more akin to modern accelerationism driven by expectations effects, indeed rational expectations effects, does appear. Consider the following quotation from Mises (1932): "A nation which has experienced inflation till its final breakdown will not submit to a second experiment . . . until the memory of the previous one faded. . . . Made overcautious by what they suffered, at the very outset of the inflation they would start a panic. The rise of prices would be out of all proportion to the increase in the quantity of paper money; it would anticipate the expected increase of notes" (p. 233)

11 A modern reader would argue that the rate of growth of the nominal money supply should make no difference here, provided that inflation expectations adjusted so that real variables' values would be independent of the time path of the nominal money supply. He would be right to raise this point, though a latter day Austrian could perhaps counter by arguing that anticipated deflation would distribute new real balances in the community in proportion to existing holdings and hence would be neutral, whereas adding to real balances by creating nominal balances at a constant price level would lead to

their initial distribution being determined by the pattern of bank lending, and hence being non-neutral. Hayek does at one point (1936, p. 97) entertain the possibility of avoiding a crisis, at least in principle, by engineering a time path for bank credit that would maintain the "right" ratio of prices between producers' and consumers' goods, but dismisses the theoretical possibility as impractical. However, anticipations about the behavior of prices play no role in conditioning the behavior of agents in the formal Austrian model, as has already been noted (note 10). This is one of its great weaknesses, both in comparison with modern work and, as we shall see and more to the point, with the work of the Stockholm School too.

Underlying the "non-neutrality" of monetary injections discussed here was a very mechanical vision of the price formation process, in which prices are determined so as to equate the value of a flow supply of output to the flow of money expenditures directed at it. The considerable attention that Hayek pays in *Prices and Production* to the effects of vertical integration of industries on the interaction of money and prices is also related to this vision, which the Austrians seem to have inherited from English classical economics. See Laider (1988) for a discussion of this process of price formation as it was viewed in the 1870s.

12 To hinge a theory of the business cycle on a variable reserve-deposit ratio, on the proclivity of banks to make loans to firms but not consumers, and on the short-run non-neutralities arising therefrom will strike the modern reader as rendering it heavily dependent on particular institutional assumptions, but that is what Hayek did.

13 Though not all members of the Stockholm School shared Myrdal's contempt for marginal utility theory. [See Myrdal (1939, p. 4) for an expression of this attitude.]

14 I do not mean to imply here that the Austrians were innocent of the difficulties involved in the concept of an aggregate capital stock. Hayek (1941) provides ample evidence to the contrary. However, when it mattered, in the early 1930s, the Austrians did anchor their vision of monetary equilibrium to a technically determined natural rate of interest and their vision was, therefore, deeply flawed. The Stockholm School avoided this particular trap.

15 Hansson (1982) credits Hammarskjöld with producing the first sequence analysis in 1933 and Lindahl with having ironed out certain remaining problems with Hammarskjöld's work in 1934. In the early 1930s, Myrdal and Ohlin concentrated on developing the within period *ex ante-ex post* distinction and Lindahl on developing the links between period in terms of his influential "temporary equilibrium" concept.

16 It is also worth noting that the formal analysis that underlies Lindahl's conclusions involved linking a series of temporary static equilibria with changing expectations. He did not analyze the convergence of variables from their *ex ante* to *ex post* values within the period for which the equilibrium was determined. Hence his conclusions did not come from a full "sequence analysis." Lindahl comments explicitly that applying a more elaborate dynamic

method to these particular cases did not seem to change any conclusions (1939c, pp. 261 ff.).

17 For examples of some of these variations, see Myrdal (1939, pp. 150–6) and Lindahl (1939c, pp. 164–70, 236–9). Note that Lundberg (1937, Chap. 3) provides a valuable survey of the various dynamic sequences that some of his predecessors and contemporaries, not all members of the Stockholm School, had analyzed.

18 Myrdal was, though, something of a methodological extremist in his own right, being particularly anxious to stress the ethical and downplay the scientific element in discussions of economic policy. For a comparison of Myrdal's and Robbins's views on this and related issues, see Hicks (1983).

19 It is also worth noting explicitly that the Stockholm School's policy pragmatism permitted its members to offer concrete advice to the government of a particular open economy about economic policy. The contrast between this characteristic of their work and Hayek's view that policy to maintain monetary equilibrium had to be conducted on a worldwide basis is, to say the least, striking. Jonung (1981) gives an account of the practical application of economic ideas in the conduct of Swedish economic policy during the depression.

20 This problem is specifically addressed by Siven (1985), and the reader familiar with his essay will recognize its influence on the arguments advanced here. The reader is warned that I do not intend here to give the impression that influences between Sweden and the rest of the world ran in only one direction during the 1930s. If Keynes did not read the Swedes in the 1920s and early 1930s, they certainly read him, and they also read Dennis Robertson, whose development of business cycle theory ran parallel to Swedish work in many important respects, though he himself was unaware of this until the 1930s. Moreover, the Swedish economists paid careful attention to American, German, and Austrian literature too.

21 And, it might be pointed out, Roy Harrod, who of all British economists remained most faithful to the *General Theory* as the source of knowledge about short-run macroeconomics, left just this matter equally unclear in the textbook he based on his undergraduate lectures on monetary topics. See Harrod (1969, pp. 166 ff.).

22 In denying the stability of the consumption function, and the usefulness of the multiplier concept, Ohlin provides powerful evidence against the claim that the Stockholm School anticipated the central analytic contributions of the *General Theory*, which hinge on just these two matters. I hasten to add that there is no implication here that that Keynes was right on these matters and Ohlin wrong. Indeed, with benefit of the last fifty years of economics, it would be easier to defend the contrary argument.

23 It is worth pointing out that Sir John Hicks, whose work has left such a deep mark on macroeconomics, was, from the very outset of his own work, a careful reader of the output of the Stockholm School and that his writings, including those dating from before the publication of the *General Theory*,

have provided an important source of information about Swedish ideas for English-speaking economists. See his contribution in this volume.
24 And since my commentary (Laidler, 1982) was written, there has emerged a new variation in new-classical theory, namely, "real" business cycle theory, stemming from the work of Kydland and Prescott (1982). The fundamental building block of their work is an aggregate production function, exogenous shocks to which are thought of as being the prime cause of the business cycle. The affinity to Austrian work of a model that puts the physical conditions of production at the center of an explanation of the cycle is obvious enough. So too ought to be the flimsiness of its microeconomic foundations, given the long understood difficulties in defining an aggregate production function discussed earlier. On this matter, see also Blaug (1985, Chap. 12).

References

Blaug, M. (1985), *Economic Theory in Retrospect,* 4th ed. Cambridge, England: Cambridge University Press.

Cantillon, R. (1734), *Essai sur la nature du commerce en général,* trans. and ed., H. Higgs, London, 1931). Reissued for the Royal Economic Society, F. Cass (1959).

Fisher, I. (1896), "Appreciation and Interest," *Publications of the American Economic Association,* 3rd Series, II (August) 331–442.

Friedman, M. (1957), *A Theory of the Consumption Function* Princeton: Princeton University Press for the National Bureau of Economic Research.

   (1968), "The Role of Monetary Policy," *American Economic Review,* 58 (March), 1–17.

Gregory, T. E. (1928), *An Introduction to T. Tooke and W. Newmarch's 'A History of Prices.'* London: P. S. King.

Haberler G. (1964), *Prosperity and Depression,* 5th ed. London: Allen and Unwin. (Originally published, 1937; revised and enlarged, 1939; and reprinted with additions, various dates.)

Hansson, B. (1982), *The Stockholm School and the Development of Dynamic Method.* London: Croom Helm.

   (1985), "Wicksell's Cumulative Process as a Critique and Development of Dynamic Theory," University of Lund (mimeo).

Harrod, R. (1949), *Towards a Dynamic Economics.* London: Macmillan.

   (1969), *Money.* London: Macmillan.

Hayek, F. A. von (1932a), *Monetary Theory and the Trade Cycle,* trans., N. Kaldor and H. Croome. London: Routledge and Kegan Paul.

   (1932b), "A Note on the Development of the Doctrine of Forced Saving," *Quarterly Journal of Economics,* 47 (November), 123–33.

   (1936), *Prices and Production,* 2nd ed. London: Routledge and Kegan Paul.

   (1937), "Economics and Knowledge," *Economica* N.S., 4 (Feburary), 33–54.

   (1939), *Profits, Interest and Investment.* London: Routledge and Kegan Paul.

(1941), *The Pure Theory of Capital.* Chicago: University of Chicago Press (reprinted 1975).

(1984), "Intertemporal Price Equilibrium and Movements in the Value of Money," translated and reprinted in *Money, Capital and Fluctuations, Early Essays.* London: Routledge and Kegan Paul. (Originally published in 1928).

Hicks, J. R. (1950), *A Contribution to the Theory of the Trade Cycle.* Oxford: Clarendon Press.

(1955), "Economic Foundations of Wage Policy," *Economic Journal,* 65 (September), 389–404.

Hicks, J. R. (1967a), "A Suggestion for Simplifying the Theory of Money," in *Critical Essays in Monetary Theory.* London: Oxford University Press.

(1967b), "The Hayek Story," in *Critical Essays in Monetary Theory,* London: Oxford University Press.

(1983), "Myrdal," in *Classics and Moderns: Collected Essays on Economic Theory,* vol. III. London: Oxford University Press.

Jonung, L. (1981), "The Depression in Sweden and the United States: A Comparison of Causes and Policies," in K. Brunner, ed., *The Great Depression Revisited.* The Hague; Martinus Nijhoff.

Keynes, J. M. (1936), *The General Theory of Employment, Interest and Money.* London: Macmillan.

(1983) *Collected Writings,* Vol. XII (D. Moggridge, ed.). London and Cambridge: Macmillan and Cambridge University Press, for the Royal Economic Society.

Kydland, F., and E. Prescott (1982), "Time to Build and Aggregate Fluctuations," *Econometrica,* 50 (September), 1345–70.

Laidler, D. (1972) "On Wicksell's Theory of Price Level Dynamics," *Manchester School* 40 (June), 125–44.

(1982), *Monetarist Perspectives.* Deddington, Philip Allan. Cambridge, Mass.: Harvard University Press.

(1988), "British Monetary Orthodoxy in the 1870s," *Oxford Economic Papers,* March, 74–109.

Leijonhufvud, A. (1967), *On Keynesian Economics and the Economics of Keynes.* London: Oxford University Press.

(1981), "The Wicksell Connection: Variations on a Theme," in *Information and Co-ordination.* London: Oxford University Press.

Lindahl, E. (1939a), "The Place of Capital in the Theory of Price," in *Studies in the Theory of Money and Capital.* (Published in Swedish in 1929.)

(1939b), "The Rate of Interest and the Price Level," in *Studies in the Theory of Economic Expansion.* (Published in Swedish in 1930.)

(1939c), *Studies in the Theory of Money and Capital.* London: Allen and Unwin.

Lundberg, E. (1937), *Studies in the Theory of Economic Expansion.* London: P. S. King and Son.

(1985), "The Rise and Fall of the Swedish Model," *Journal of Economic Literature*, 23 (March), 1–36.

Marshall, A. (1890), *Principles of Economics*. London: Macmillan.

Mises, L. von (1932), "The Great German Inflation," *Economica*, 12 (May), 227–34.

(1953), *The Theory of Money and Credit* (2nd German edition, trans. H. E. Batson, London, 1934). New Haven: Yale University Press.

Modigliani, F., and R. Brumberg. (1954), "Utility Analysis and the Consumption Function," in K. Kurihara, ed., *Post Keynesian Economics*. New Brunswick, N.J.: Rutgers University Press.

Myrdal, G. (1939), *Monetary Equilibrium*, translated with minor emendations. London: W. Hodge.

Ohlin, B. (1938), "Some Notes on the Stockholm Theory of Saving and Investment, *Economic Journal* 47 (March), 54–69 and 47 (June), 221–40.

Patinkin, D. (1965) "Wicksell's Monetary Theory," in *Money, Interest and Prices*, 2nd ed. New York: Harper & Row.

(1982), "The Stockholm School," in *Anticipations of the General Theory?* Chicago: University of Chicago Press.

Phelps, E. (1967), "Phillips Curves, Expectations of Inflation and Optimal Unemployment over Time," *Economica* NS, 34 (August), 254–81.

Robbins, L. C. (1934), *The Great Depression*. London: Macmillan.

(1935), *The Nature and Significance of Economic Science*, London: Macmillan.

Rothbart, M. (1975), *America's Great Depression*. Kansas City: Sheed and Ward.

Shackle, G. L. S. (1967), *The Years of High Theory*, Cambridge: Cambridge University Press.

Siven, C-H. (1985), "The End of the Stockholm School," *Scandinavian Journal of Economics*, 87 (4), 577–93.

Wicksell, K. (1907), "The Influence of the Rate of Interest on Prices," *Economic Journal*, 17 (June), 213–20.

(1936), *Interest and Prices* trans. by R. F. Kahn for the Royal Economic Society, London.

(1935), *Lectures on Political Economy*, Vol. II, trans. E. Claassen. London: Routledge and Kegal Paul.

Comment

AXEL LEIJONHUFVUD[1]

Laidler makes it hard on a discussant. It is such a good paper – very insightful, very balanced; there is much in it to admire. The idea of doing the Austrians and the Swedes together is a good one. The juxta-position of the two helps put both in perspective at the same time. In macroeconomics, both start from Knut Wicksell. It is curious that from this common point of departure they would diverge so fast.

My first comment is a bit speculative and has to do with the concepts of "natural values" and "neutrality of money." I wonder if there might not be a missing strain here. It may not be crucial to Laidler's story about the Austrians and the Swedes, but it might help to explain what they were about and to explain, moreover, why what they tried to do had its limitations in certain directions.

But I am not quite sure about doctrine history on the point I want to make. I tried to bring this up with Don Patinkin when he spoke on the neutrality of money (cf. his article in the *New Palgrave*) at UCLA in the fall of 1986, but I do not think he saw it my way. So I should stress that this is speculative. I want to point out a connection between old doc-trines about natural values on the one hand and neutrality of money (in a particular sense) on the other. It seems to me that there is this line running through nineteenth-century monetary theory. What everybody is trying to accomplish is to figure out how to manage fractional reserve banking under a commodity standard so that it would not be a source of instability. So in the background there is always a gold standard (or a bimetallic standard), and of course gold money was never neutral in the Patinkin sense. Increasing the quantity of gold money would have to change relative values since gold was itself a commodity. Nineteenth-century authors would not have thought of gold as being neutral in the (fiat) quantity theory sense.

These authors were concerned with how to manage bank money in such a way that it would not distort the equilibrium of natural values that would have prevailed if there had been no "paper credit" (to use Henry Thornton's term). In this context, bank money would be "neu-tral" (or monetary policy would be "neutral") when natural values pre-vailed, that is, when it leaves relative values unaffected. For Patinkin-neutrality, we require relative prices to be constant when the absolute price level changes in response to changes in the stock of *outside* (fiat) money. The concept of neutrality that I am after is different. It is a cri-terion for the "neutrality" of *inside* money. It requires both relative val-ues *and* the price level to behave as they would in the absence of "paper credit."

Now, this reference motion – the conceptual experiment of what the world would be like without banks – was probably not all that well defined. (In considering a world without circulating bank liabilities, should we imagine that it is also without financial intermediation services? How do we correct for the effects of bank money on the monetary demand for gold?) Nonetheless, Wicksell was in the tradition of posing this kind of question. His language reveals it. True, he sometimes uses "normal" rate in place of *natural* rate but, surely, the latter term is to be preferred on grounds of its rich resonance in the older literature. When Wicksell refers to the natural rate, he is referring to what the real equilibrium would be like if it evolved undisturbed by movements in bank credit.

Laidler discusses the problems with Wicksell's three conditions. Wicksell did not succeed in stating the conditions of monetary equilibrium clearly and with generality. He *couldn't* very well have succeeded – the groundwork for specifying precisely the conditions of dynamic intertemporal general equilibrium for an economy on a commodity standard had simply not been laid. (Turn of the century Austrian capital theory was not the most promising starting point for the production possibilities side of that problem and had nothing to say on the intertemporal consumption allocation side.) David Davidson's critique and, later, Gunnar Myrdal's *Monetary Equilibrium* (and Tord Palander's critique of Myrdal) are among the Swedish attempts to clear matters up. The discussion, around 1930, involving several of the Austrians and D. H. Robertson on neutral money – which had nothing to do with Patinkin-neutrality – again circled around trying to clarify the same set of issues.

It helps us understand what Wicksell was about, I think, if we take note of the fact that, in the original version, his first condition was that the interest rate should be the one that would have prevailed if capital was lent and borrowed *in kind.* The natural rate emerges when intertemporal transactions are made *in natura!* Here again, the reference system is a world without bank credit. In that world without banks, saving and investment would be equal – at least, if we allow ourselves to assume no hoarding. And with no banks and no hoarding and with generally stationary conditions, the price level (in terms of commodity money) would be constant.

Davidson's problem, which was then taken up again in the discussion around 1930, was how Wicksell's stationary case should be generalized to a growing economy. In an economy where labor productivity increases over time, did "neutral money" require a constant money price level and rising money wage rates or did it require constant money wages and falling prices? Put in a context of Patinkin-neutral outside fiat money, the question hardly makes sense: it should not matter. Writers who offered a definite opinion usually did so, therefore, on the suspicion that Patinkin-neutrality might fail to hold. In particular, if money prices might be "rigid downwards," it would be better to obtain the rising real wage through rising money wages. If Davidson's question is put back in the context of "natural values", on the other hand, we do get a less arbitrary answer. What it will be depends on whether or not labor productivity in the production of the monetary commodity behaves as it does for all the other goods. If it does (and if the income elasticity of the demand for gold is approximately one), the natural values of other goods in terms of gold could be expected to stay constant, and bank money is "neutral" in the growing economy if it leaves the money price level constant.

When the background to Wicksell's work is seen in this way, its limitations become clearer. Business cycle hypotheses that, for example, see "bubbles" in bank credit as a source of aggregative fluctuations have a natural starting point in Wicksell. But other important cycle hypotheses that do not stress problems of intertemporal coordination are not conveniently approached from this direction.

Toward the end of Laidler's paper, the New Classicals are brought in and the question raised whether in Robert Lucas et al. we see the Austrians riding again. Laidler has argued this matter before, but I do not see the parallells as all that striking. I am not particularly concerned to dispute the similarities that Laidler adduces but would like to stress at least one distinction.

The Austrian theory assumes a unique real equilibrium time-path. The economy can very easily be propelled away from this path (by mistakes of the central bank, or whatever), but it is nonetheless a stable and unique long-run equilibrium path, so that eventually it has to reassert itself – with a vengeance. One can see, particularly in Hayek, that this is an underlying belief, because he did not orginally have a good account of why, after a period of overinvestment, it had to reassert itself with a vengeance, and he kept coming back to it, trying to find a convincing argument for why what he believed to be so had to be so.

The Swedes started from the same Wicksellian point of departure. But they were not at all sure that the system would have to return to any unique equilibrium path. So in the Stockholm School, as Laidler rightly stresses, disturbances to the system produce these analytical sequences wandering off in almost any direction. Path-dependent history leaves equilibrium theory submerged. Laidler has put his finger on the main reason that was so, namely, that the Stockholm School did not have an analytical discipline to constrain what was said about the evolution of expectations and, consequently, they got all kinds of hysteresis phenomena in expectations formation.

The New Classicals, of course, are constraining the formation of expectations – they have to be rational in the sense of Muth. This gets us back to equilibrium theory. Now, much has been made recently of rational expectations models with multiple equilibria and various types of indeterminacy. But in the spirit of New Classical theory, the real equilibrium path really should be unique. (Think of the policy ineffectiveness results!) The difference from the Austrians – and this is where I would modify Laidler's account – is that the New Classical equilibrium is not at all easily distorted in any significant way by mistakes of the monetary authorities. It is not clear that even the most bumbling government can twist this system off its course for more than five minutes – well, maybe five days (from Monday until the Friday money supply announcement). A major reason for this, of course, is that the New Classicals operate with Patinkin-neutral outside money and never worry, as the Austrians did, about the possibly "non-neutral" (and thus "unnatural") behavior of inside money.

In the more recent real business cycle branch of New Classical theory, as Laidler also pointed out in his presentation, the equilibrium is never distorted even for a moment. There the task of the theorist, rather, is to explain why, whatever the observed time-path is, that path is an equilibrium. So, while the Austrians and the New Classicals may both be ideological non-interventionists, the difference between the two belief systems is that in the Austrian one things can very easily go wrong.

Finally, this matter of the "Two Failures." In brief, Laidler concludes that the best Swedish ideas merged into the mainstream and lost their distinctiveness, whereas the distinctive Austrian business cycle hypothesis failed. I think that is roughly right.

Two minor comments, however. If we widen the perspective on the Austrians a bit, can it be said that Hayek (in particular) failed? For some thirty-odd years, from his early forties to his late seventies, maybe the profession at large considered him a failure of sorts. But in recent years, his reputation has soared again.

Hayek's *Prices and Production* failed, I agree, as a general theory of business fluctuations. But if we consider the work he did in his repeated attempts to explain and reexplain what he was about to an uncomprehending British audience – that is, the work that led to the famous essays on "The Role of Knowledge in Society" and "The Meaning of Competition," and so on – there he surely did not fail. Instead, on those themes, his influence has become pervasive. Moreover, if we take a 1930s perspective on what macroeconomics is about, we would have to include the socialist calculation debate. And there he did not fail either. He won.

One final note on the distinction between the two kinds of "failures," the Swedish and the Austrian. It hinges, really on our perception that the Austrians refused to merge into the mainstream, insisted on their distinctiveness, and so lost out. But how accurate is that perception? In the course of interviewing all these distinguished Austrians for the project on the intellectual immigration in economics that my wife, Earlene Craver, is doing, I remember talking to them – Hayek, in particular, but also Machlup and Morgenstern, for instance – about this. Did they see themselves at that time in Vienna as participants in a distinctive Austrian School?

The answers we received to this question were very similar to those given by the Stockholm group – they refuse to say that there was a school but then go on to talk about all the things they had in common. Hayek's recollection was that the best young economists in Vienna in the 1920s were looking forward to seeing the characteristic Austrian ideas merge into an international neoclassical economics and that there was no attempt then on their part to maintain a distinct body of doctrine. Several of them, moreover, had a most ambivalent attitude to the Mises seminar that was reformed in New York, and from which stems this determined attempt to put an Austrian brand name on certain ideas, the insistence on their basic incompatibility with mainstream neoclassicism – and even, on occasion, the labeling of those who did merge as "not truly Austrian." In their younger days, I believe, they were conscious of working in a period of the development of our subject when national traditions or schools were, for natural reasons, merging and losing their distinctiveness in the process.

Notes

1 I am grateful to my colleague Seongwhan Oh for helpful comments.

CHAPTER 13

The political arithmetics of the Stockholm School

KUMARASWAMY VELUPILLAI

Outside Britain the most interesting development in the analysis of fiscal policy was in Sweden, where a group of young economists (especially E. Lindahl and G. Myrdal) brought up in *the general or macroeconomic approach* by their teacher, Knut Wicksell, were groping for a comprehensive and rational policy of compensatory finance. The Swedish contribution was notable for emphasizing from an early stage ... the need to gear the system of public accounting and the arrangement of the budget so as to make it appropriate for the additional responsibilities of fiscal policy....

The *first country* to manifest any interest in the economic classification of the budget was Sweden, which established a fairly comprehensive reorganization of the budgetary structure on a current/capital basis in 1938. (Ursula Hicks, 1947, pp. 272 and 339; italics added).

Bertil Ohlin's celebrated article in the *Economic Journal* (Ohlin, 1937) ushered into the Anglo-Saxon world the now familiar concepts by which all and sundry refer to the Stockholm School: dynamic method, disequilibrium dynamics, temporary equilibrium, *ex ante* versus *ex post,* process analysis, liquidity preference versus loanable funds, and so on. Section B of part I of Ohlin's paper, where the above much-maligned concepts were elegantly introduced, has attained the status of a classic: much quoted, seldom read. Ohlin, in one respect at least, presented the fundamental, unifying theme of Swedish economics extending from Davidson, Wicksell, and Cassel to Lindahl and Myrdal: the necessity of starting from feasible and useful accounting conventions.

To analyse and explain what happens or what will happen in certain circumstances it is necessary to register the relevant events. One needs a system of book-keeping which is relative to time. ... It is therefore practical to use periods of time as a basis for book-keeping. At the end of each period one can survey the registrations which refer to that period. This answers the question what has happened during a passed period. It is an account Ex-post. (Ohlin, 1937, p. 58)

333

Public finance, as Sargent and Wallace (1981) and Lucas (1981a, 1981b) have, in recent years, forcefully reminded us, is accounting theory par excellence. The essential ingredient of accounting theory is double entry bookkeeping, and the object of such a theory is the "application of economic principles to . . . book keeping . . . [and] to find the philosophical basis of accounting" (Fisher, 1906, p. 140). This "philosophical basis," for the nation state, can be found in banking, trade, war finance, and justice via taxation. These determined one strand in the development of Swedish economic thought in the hands of Davidson, Heckscher, Cassel, Wicksell, Lindahl, Myrdal, and Ohlin over the half century from the end of the 1880s to the end of the 1930s.

It is my contention that there were two other seeds from which the tradition of Swedish economics sprouted: demographic statistics and actuarial practice; the two were linked, in the field of political philosophy and economic policy, by the development of social insurance.

I will propose that the foundation and development of Swedish economic theory and policy can, or should, be sought in the tripod formed by *accounting theory, demographic statistics, and actuarial practice.* A tradition[1] of theoretical concept formation based on this trinity cannot but be *dynamic* in scope; could not avoid dealing with *risk and uncertainty;* had, almost unwillingly, to consider the distinctions between *individual and collective risk* and, hence, social insurance; and, above all, had to integrate social and economic policy at all stages and levels of theorizing. It is in this sense that I claim a justification for the implicit assertion that the Swedes are descendants of the early political arithmeticians.

Political arithmetics – "the art of reasoning by figures upon things relating to government"[2] – became, in time, political economy and, after Wicksell, Hayek, Lindahl, and Keynes, eventually macroeconomics. Somewhere between Petty and Keynes, that which had been monetary economics and public finance on the one hand and capital and trade theory on the other, with business cycle theory as the cementing force, became today's macroeconomics. And, in that same two and one-half centuries – between the death of Petty and the publication of the macroeconomic masterpieces of the 1930s – to *justice* and *dynamics,* the major concerns of the political arithmeticians, was added *rationality.*

The triple trinity of:

1. (a) Accounting theory
   (b) Demographic statistics
   (c) Actuarial practice
2. (a) Monetary economics and public finance

  (b) Capital and trade theory
  (c) Business cycle theory
  3. (a) Justice
  (b) Dynamics
  (c) Rationality

form the basis of the Swedish codification and development of the political arithmetics of Petty and his early followers.[3]

In the ensuing pages I will try to substantiate the above thesis, at least
as a plausible story, with some evidence.[4]

The political arithmetics of the "Stockholm School"

> The study of the principles of taxation, which used to occupy an houn-
> oured place in the theory of public finance, seems in recent years to
> have fallen into dispute. This is also true of the early Swedish contri-
> bution on this subject – Knut Wicksell's *A New Principle of Just Tax-
> ation* published in 1896, and my own doctor's thesis of 1919 entitled
> *Just Taxation.* Both these works are attempts to explain the relation-
> ship between the concepts of just distribution of property, on the basis
> of an analysis of the motivating forces in the fiscal process. (Lindahl,
> 1959, p. 7)

The theme I wish to develop here, that the Swedes are the descendants
of political arithmeticians in the sense of Petty (1894) and Malthus
(1798, 1820),[5] is best introduced by asking, first, the following questions:

  1. Had Wicksell written nothing after *Über Wert, Kapital und
      Rente,* would he have any place in the history of the subject
      different from, say, Wicksteed?
  2. How many people even – or especially – in Sweden know that
      Cassel's first forays into economics were articles on "Progressive
      Taxation" and "Proportional Representations"?
  3. Wicksell embraced utilitarianism; Lindahl followed him; Myr-
      dal was fiercely critical. But all this was irrelevant in their "mac-
      roeconomic" works. Why?
  4. Davidson, Wicksell, Cassel, and Lindahl remain the fountain-
      head – or were that – for the development of the macroeconom-
      ics of the "Stockholm" School. What was the common thread
      that linked them together?
  5. How and where does Myrdal enter the scene?

The answers to these five questions provide, I think, some hints on the
distinctive nature of the development of Swedish economics in the fifty
years from Davidson (1889) to Lindahl (1939).

The answer to the first question is probably in the affirmative, that is, Wicksell would receive respectful nods in appropriate footnotes in books and articles on marginal productivity theory. Not even that would appear for his earlier neo-Malthusian speculations on population dynamics and social welfare.

The answer to the second question, on Cassel, is an even more definite one – except, of course, for "Cassel specialists": almost none.

The answer to the third question is important. A short answer would be the following: simply because precisely here they were following in the great traditon of Petty and Malthus: social dynamics, social account-ing, and social insurance.

In the case of question 4, I suggest that the common link is the initial condition: All of them, at the "initial point" in their subsequent sus-tained works in economics, were concerned with the issue of justice in taxation and its political implications and conceptual difficulties.

As for question 5, Myrdal's importance lies in inspiring Lindahl to be much more explicit about the treatment of risk and uncertainty in the theory of monetary policy.[6]

If we gather the threads together, it is possible to weave the following tentative piece of summary.[7] Taxation, in any form, required a reason-ably rigorous and useful definition of income and wealth; once such a definition was conceptually available, it related to taxation, deficit finance, distributive justice, and, hence, to economic and social policy. Some of the elements were tackled, to some extent, normatively, espe-cially in the now famous (Wicksell-)Lindahl equilibrium in the theory of public goods; but the main impetus was toward the thorny problem of defining income, estimating it, and analyzing it within the framework of a system of national accounts. Thus, *from public finance to national (income) accounts was a natural step for the fundamental question of justice in taxation.* The explicit political link was, of course, the conten-tion that the structure of taxes reflects the balance of political forces (in the legislature).

Thus it was that a clear scheme of national (income) accounting, monetary (dis-)equilibrium, and taxation for social justice was a corol-lary of the analysis of the accounts for the state budget, the balance of trade, and the balance of international payments. The link with the state budget gave the Swedes a head start in dynamics, for there was always the concept of a forward account in such a budget (Hicks, 1956; Lin-dahl, 1950).

From taxation for social justice, and hence from a search for a defi-nition of the concepts of income and wealth in a scheme of social accounting, to social justice per se was only a small step. Thus the social consequences of inflation and deflation set the tone and theme for the sustained discussion between Wicksell, Davidson, Lindahl, and Myrdal on the appropriate norms for monetary policy.

This latter discussion and theme, more than any other topic, lies at the base of what subsequently came to be known as the Stockholm School – although there is very little "Stockholm" in it at the origins: Davidson was in Uppsala, Wicksell in Lund, and Lindahl successively in Gothenburg, Lund, and Uppsala.

Lindahl, in lectures in the University of Lund, almost immediately after the submission of his justly famous doctoral dissertation (Lindahl, 1919), had set down two fundamental postulates for the overall implementation of monetary policy. (1) Monetary policy must aim for a stable "monetary regime" to induce confidence in economic life – independent from political vicissitudes. (2) The desirable norm for monetary policy with respect to prices, practically is an inverse variation of the price level with respect to changes in productivity. The theoretical side of their practical postulate was couched in terms of the stability of monetary contracts.

The basic theme of the desirability of a stable monetary regime as the prerequisite for the efficiency of the economic system was the unifying thread in Lindahl's writings from 1919 to 1959. This was set forth with great clarity, forcefulness, and persuasiveness when the early post–World War I lectures were published in 1924 as *Penningpolitikens mål och medel* (Lindahl, 1924). But between this and Lindahl's 1929 masterpiece *Penningpolitikens medel* there was Myrdal's own doctoral dissertation.

Myrdal's much neglected classic brought to the forefront the tools and concepts of insurance markets in the analysis of dynamic factors in pricing (Myrdal, 1927): risk, uncertainty, and expectations. Although Lindahl had tried to incorporate intelligent expectation formation in the consideration of the repercussions of monetary policy in economic life in his earlier work, it remained unsatisfactory and incomplete.

As Hammarskjöld points out very clearly (cf. note 6), Myrdal's influence "left clear traces in Lindahl's second work on monetary policy," and he goes on to state:

> Thus the second postulate of 1924 was reformulated in terms of diminishing the risk which imperfectly forseen events involve for economic activity. This clearly implies that Lindahl put the requirement of agreement between the actual and intended content of monetary contracts within the framework of the broader requirement of agreement between the actual and *anticipated course of events. . . .* [and] *Lindahl followed up his basic examination of the issues in* EX ANTE *terms by a*

> *discussion on* EX POST lines of the means of putting various norms of monetary policy into effect. (Hammarskjöld, 1944, p. 151; italics added)

Thus was born *"Ex ante, Ex post,* and *Ex* whatever": the sequence is much more complicated than the Ohlin-Keynes discussions may suggest. Above all, it is an outcome of an analysis of the design of stable monetary regimes and norms for monetary policy – not simply exotic excursions into terminological calisthenics to equate savings and investment.

Dynamics as a *Method* – a way of reasoning about events or cases – was the result of these exciting controversies centered around the aims and means of monetary policy. *Phenomenological dynamics* was quite another thing. There were two sources for this internal to the works of the triumvirate of Davidson, Wicksell, and Cassel, particularly the latter two:(1) Wicksell's cumulative process and his "enigma of the business cycle" (Wicksell, 1907), in addition to his important review of Petander (Wicksell, 1918), and (2) Cassel's "uniformly progressive economy" and his work on business cycles (Cassel, 1934).

I shall call it phenomenological dynamics in analogy with phenomenological thermodynamics. The reasons are obvious. The cumulative process, business cycles, and steady-state dynamics were about change and fluctuations at a phenomenological level, and the path of analysis was characteristically Malthusian in the sense in which I earlier framed the latter's method (Velupillai, 1987): induction rather than deduction. Cassel, uncharacteristically, was quite explicit about this:

> In the first two books of this work we have ignored, as far as we could, the possiblity of change in the economy. To show as clearly as possible the simplest theoretical principles, we first of all considered the stationary state and then introduced the concept of the uniformly progressive economy, which allowed us to study the simplest and most important kind of change. In all these inquiries a strictly deductive procedure was necessary, for we were dealing with imaginary pictures having no exact counterpart in reality. If we wish to approach a step nearer to reality, the deductive method must be replaced by an inductive one. So we have to see how far the actual economic development diverges from the previously assumed uniformity of progress. Such divergencies can, of course, only be established by a study of the actual facts. (Cassel, 1967, p. 533).

Of course, any careful reading of "Interest and Prices" substantiates this methodological pinciple. Indeed, I would venture to go even further and put forward the suggestion that the phenomenological dynamics of the cumulative process was, for Wicksell, largely a Malthusian inspiration: the inconsistency between the constraints of nature (the arithmetic growth rate of the means of subsistence) and the controllable growth of population (geometric growth in the demand for subsistence). To translate this, having mastered Böhm-Bawerk's capital theory, into an incompatibility between a "natural" rate and a "money" rate of interest was, of course, a leap of the imagination and a mark of genius. The crucial question, however, is (again), had Wicksell been only " a Wicksteed" and not also a neo-Malthusian, would he have managed the crucial leap? I think not and I put forward this suggestion as yet another example of the role – the crucial role – of analogies in scientific discoveries.

It is, therefore, important to keep in mind the distinction between the dynamic method and the dynamics of phenomena. It is possible, indeed almost inevitable, to apply static method to dynamic phenomena: Most of equilibrium business cycle theory is about such a strategy. The correspondence principle is a clear illustration of the need to keep this distinction in mind. Above all, the point of the distinction is that the dynamics of phenomena lend themselves, almost naturally, to the inductive method. In this sense again the Swedes, and now even Cassel, were the true descendants of the political arithmeticians and Malthus.

One final point must be faced: What about the utilitarian foundations of the works of Wicksell and Lindahl? How does that square up with the claims of political arithmetics and phenomenological dynamics? In other words, the compatibility of justice and dynamics with rationality. I think there is both a simple and an interesting answer to this puzzle.

First the former. In a relatively unknown work, Sidney D. Merlin made the acute observation that:

> By and large the Swedish economists are elastic in their use of value theory and argue for certain empirically observed (value) relations such as the desire to maximize profits, *irrespective of the utilitarian justification of such behaviour in traditional theory.* (Merlin, 1949, p. 79; italics added).

This is most clearly the case with Myrdal (cf. Myrdal, 1939, p. 207). It is a simple – almost simplistic – answer, but it is both plausible as an explanation and feasible analytically. However, it does not come to grips with the fact of Wicksell's (1896, 1898) work in capital theory and taxation and Lindahl's on "Just Taxation." The plausible interesting answer to this is almost an exploration in cultural history. Wicksell's path to utilitarianism has been elegantly described by Gårdlund (1958).

Indeed Wicksell's problem had been the search to fill the gap left by abandoning the comforts of faith in Christianity:

> A problem that they [Öhrvall and Wicksell] continually discussed was how Christian morality might be replaced by an ethical code that could be combined with the demands of truthfulness and utility. *They were*

> *eventually to find a doctrine answering their needs in John Stuart Mill's utilitarianism.* Their introduction to these ideas came through an anonymous neo-Malthusian work. THE ELEMENT OF SOCIAL SCIENCE.... "The great importance of this doctrine was clear to us at once" wrote Knut Wicksell later about their encounter with neo-Malthusianism, "it was, as it were, the *password for which we were both waiting before taking up a firm stand on social questions."* (Gårdlund, 1958, p. 45; italics added).

It is perhaps interesting to compare Keynes and Wicksell in this repsect. Mill was to Wicksell what Moore was to Keynes. Mill's (1891) *Utilitarianism* was to Wicksell what Moore's *Principia Ethica* was to Keynes – and, years later, the scene was reenacted when Myrdal was struggling to escape from the conservative idealism of Boström to embrace the philosophy of Axel Hägerström.

It was the search, for nonbelievers, for the Good, the True, and the Beautiful, that led them to Moore and Russell. In an earlier era, in the search for the Just and the True and the Useful, one was led to Mill. Russell's great scheme of deductivism – the fountainhead for the formalists and the latter-day Platonists in mathematics – did not hinder Keynes the inductivist, who proceeded "to accept his religion but discard the morals" – to accept the technique but discard the method.[8]

So it was with Wicksell and Lindahl with utilitarianism, and there is nothing more to it than that. They were, first and last, political arithmeticians in the sense of Petty and Malthus. They were also graced by the touch of Mill's utilitarianism – not the untrammeled hedonism of the Benthamite calculus.

The innovation in budgetary technique and its relation to business cycle theory and political arthmetics is another chapter, another episode, in the Swedish story. It is, in a sense, the afterglow. That connection I have tried to discuss in a companion piece to this one (cf. Velupillai, 1988a).

Concluding notes

> Thus according to this view (of unrestricted liberty and free trade), the fundamental principle of political economy was that its subject matter, the national household, did not exist.
>
> In our day, it is true, there has been a reaction against this ultraliberal principle, but nevertheless, it is still in reality the individualistic, purely private, system which predominates. For this reason *many modern writers have desired to reject the qualifying adjective "political" or "national" and to speak merely of economics....* In accordance with the modern outlook, *the subject matter of political economy* is becom-

ing more and more the doctrine of economic phenomena, in their interrelations, seen AS A WHOLE: i.e. *in so far as they uniformly affect whole classes of the community,* or whole people, or the totality of all peoples. (Wicksell, 1934, pp. 1–2; italics added)

The most interesting recent developments in macroeconomic theory seem to me describable as the reincorporation of aggregative problems such as inflation and the business cycle within the general framework of "microeconomic" theory. If these developments succeed, the term "macroeconomic" will simply disappear from use and the modifier "micro" will become superfluous. We will simply speak, as did Smith, Ricardo, Marshall and Walras, of ECONOMIC theory." (Lucas, 1987, pp. 107–8)

Evidently Lucas has not been scrupulous with his reading of the "classics," at least not Smith and Ricardo. Indeed the titles of their best known works were: "An Inquiry into the Nature and Causes of the Wealth of Nations" and "The Principles of Political Economy and Taxation," respectively. The subject matter of "political economy" was, as Wicksell so clearly observes, the "national household" – or the nation as a whole. Hence "nationalekonomi" and finally, in the hands of Lindahl: "The processes studied in economics, however, are generally MACRO-ECONOMIC in character . . ." (Lindahl, 1939, p. 52).

From the "art of reasoning upon figures relating to government" to the "economics of the nation as a whole" was the path from political arithmetics to political economics. Social accounting is, after all, merely the economic arithmetics of the Nation as a whole. Whether this is best studied within the framework of "microeconomic" theory is a moot question. Even if the answer is in the affirmative, not even the Lucasians can will away the need to account the transactions of the nation as a whole – at least not so long as nation states with unique political and social traditions exist. And the transactions of the nation as a whole are, of course, figures relating to government. Again, even the Lucasians cannot object to the application of the art of reasoning upon figures reflecting the transactions of the nation as a whole. They, however, would like us to confine the art of reasoning to those that are exclusively applied in microeconomic theory. Why? Are such arts of reasoning superior to other possibilities or distinct from those that are applied in other branches of the arts and sciences? Or is it only because of the superiority of the subject matter of microeconomic theory.

What, however, are "the most interesting recent developments in macroeconomic theory"? In these developments the Lucasians have played a crucial role: *neutrality, credibility, policy ineffectiveness, monetary regimes, equilibrium business cycle theories, public finance, and taxation.* All this in a theorectical setting of rational expectations, asymmetric information, and equilibrium values. It is to their lasting credit that they have resurrected these great issues of political arithmetics and political economy. It cannot be denied that:

> *It* [i.e., that the taking of a dynamic point of view involves thinking of private agents as choosing contingency plans for the current and future variables under their control, taking as given their EXPECTATIONS about the way other economic actors – including the government – are going to behave] *also reflects a traditional view that long predates modern theoretical formulation, to the effect that the most useful way to think about government policy is as a choice of* RULES OF THE GAME *to which government is committed for some length of time."* (Lucas, 1987, pp. 103–4; italics added)

This was the theme of Lindahl's macroecnomic framework from his earliest writings on "The Aims and Means of Monetary Policy" to "The Game of Inflation" – from 1919 to 1959. The very same issues the New Classicals now discuss at the frontiers of research in macroeconomic theory had been the subject of analytical and policy deliberations by the Swedes from Davidson to Lindahl, but not within a theorectical framework based on the sort of microeconomic theory the Lucasians advocate. Theirs was within the framework and concepts of political arithmetics. The implicit Lucasian claim that the only way or, perhaps, the only desirable way to study the great issues of political economy is in the setting of microeconomic theory – and that a very special microeconomic theory – cannot be substantiated analytically or historically. The Swedes, from Davidson to Lindahl, are a counterexample on both counts.

Notes

1 "If we are not to be led astray by our wandering whims, if our personal intuitions are to be guided by the accumulated wisdom of the race, only tradition can help us. It takes centuries of life to make a little history, and it takes centuries of history to produce a little tradition, and we cannot lightly set it aside" (Radhakrishnan, 1937, p. 61).

2 Charles Davenant in "Of the Use of Political Arithmetick," Works, 1, p. 128; quoted by Schumpeter (1954, p. 210).

3 I have tried to develop the interlinkages between these trinities in a series of related works (cf. Velupillai, 1987, 1988a, 1988b). Professor Carl G. Uhr's summary of the earlier version of the present paper encapsulates accurately the theme I wish to develop: "What emerges from your survey of the works of Davidson, Wicksell, Cassel, Lindahl, Hecksher, Myrdal, Ohlin and others is the doctrinal evolution that is the underpinning of the Swedish Welfare

State, or Child's, *Sweden the Middle Way*. In one way or another both Davidson and Wicksell were concerned about public finance and justice in taxation,
to reason about which national income accounts and fiscal analysis in terms
of such is necessary, and then, when account is taken of available economic
resources, population growth and its age-sex composition, this leads eventually to considerations of general social welfare and social insurance, and along
that line, I believe both Sismondi and later on Bismarck have to be given
recognition" (Letter from Carl Uhr to the author, January 25, 1988).

4 "The tight proofs are missing" – as one generous discussant, Jan Petersson,
pointed out. Dr. Petersson is quite correct. In his remarkable recent reconstruction of "The Afroasiatic Roots of Classical Civilization," Martin Bernal
points out: "Proof or certainty is difficult enough to achieve, even in the
experimental sciences or documented history. In the fields with which this
work is concerned it is out of the question: all one can hope to find is more
or less plausibility" (Bernal, 1987, p. 8)

5 This background is developed in greater detail in Velupillai (1987, 1988b).

6 "Between 1924 and 1929 [i.e., between *Penningpolitikens mål och medel* and
Penningpolitikens medel], Myrdal's *The Pricing Problem and Change*
appeared and its treatment of risk and expectations left clear traces in Lindahl's second work on monetary policy" (Hammarskjöld, 1944, p. 150).

7 The ensuing is a reworking of the "reconstruction" in Velupillai (1988a).

8 Paraphrasing Keynes on Moore: "We accepted Moore's religion, so to speak,
and discarded his morals" (Keynes, 1972, p. 436).

References

Bernal, M. (1987), *Black Athena: The Afroasciatic Roots of Classical Civilization*. London, Free Association Books.

Cassel, G. (1934), *Teoretisk socialekonomi*. Stockholm: Kooperativa Förbun-
dets Bokförlag.

(1967), *The Theory of Social Economy*. New York: Augustus M. Kelly.

Davidson, D. (1889), *Om beskattningsnormen vid inkomstskatten*. Uppsala:
Lundequistska Bokhandeln.

Fisher, I. (1906), *The Nature of Capital and Income*. New York: The Macmillan
Co.

Gårdlund, T. (1958), *The Life of Knut Wiksell*. Stockholm: Almqvist och
Wiksell.

Hammarskjöld, D. (1944), "Den svenska diskussionen om penningspolitikens
mål" in *Studier i ekonomi och historia tillägnade Eli F. Heckscher*,
24.11.1944. Uppsala: Almqvist och Wiksell.

Hicks, Sir John (1956), "Methods of Dynamic Analysis," in *25 Economic
Essays in Honour of Erik Lindahl*. Stockholm.

Hicks, Ursula K. (1947), *Public Finance*. London: James Nisbet and Co., Ltd.

Keynes, J. M. (1972), Essays in Biography: *The Collected Writings of John Maynard Keynes*, Vol. 10, London: Macmillan.

Lindahl, E. (1919), *Die Gerechtigkeit der Besteuerung: Eine Analyse der Steuerprinzipien auf Grundlage der Grenznutzentheorie.* Lund. Gleerupska Universitetsbokhandeln.

(1924), *Penningpolitikens mål och medel.* Malmö: Förlagsaktiebolaget i Malmö Boktryckeri.

(1930), *Penningpolitikens medel.* Skrifter utgivna av Fahlbeckska Stiftelsen. Malmö: Förlagsaktiebolaget i Malmö Boktryckeri.

(1939), *Studies in the Theory of Money and Capital,* London: Allan & Unwin.

(1950), "The Swedish Experiences in Planning." *American Economic Review,* 40 (2 May), 11–20.

(1959), "Tax Principles and Tax Policy," *International Economic Papers,* No. 10, pp. 7–23.

Lucas, R. E. Jr. (1981a), "Deficit Finance and Inflation," *New York Times,* August 28, p. 30.

(1981b), "Inconsistency in Fiscal Aims," *New York Times,* August 30, p. 30.

(1987), *Models of Business Cycles.* Oxford: Basil Blackwell.

Malthus, T. R. (1798), *Essays on Population.* London.

(1820), *Principles of Political Economy Considered with a View to Their Practical Application.* London.

Merlin, S. D. (1949), *The Theory of Fluctuations in Contemporary Economic Thought.* New York: Columbia University Press.

Mill, John Stuart (1891), *Utilitarianism,* 11th ed. London: Longmans Green and Co.

Myrdal, G. (1927), *Prisbildningsproblemet och föränderligheten.* Uppsala: Almqvist och Wiksell.

(1939), *Monetary Equilibrium.* London: Hodge.

Ohlin, B. (1937), "Some Notes on the Stockholm Theory of Savings and Investment," *Economic Journal,* 47 pt. I (March) 53–69, pt. II (June) 221–40.

Petty, Sir William (1894), *Essays on Mankind and Political Arithmetic.* London: Cassel and Co., Ltd.

Radhakrishnan, S. (1937), *An Idealist View of Life.* London: Unwin books.

Sargent, T. J., and N. Wallace (1981), "Some Unpleasant Monetarist Arithmetic," *Federal Reserve Bank of Minneapolis Quarterly Review,* Fall, pp. 1–17.

Schumpeter, J. A. (1954), *History of Economic Analysis.* London: George Allen and Unwin, Ltd.

Velupillai, K. (1987), "The Political Arithmetics of the Stockholm School." Mimeo, August, Aalborg.

(1988a), "Some Swedish Stepping Stones to Modern Macroeconomics," *Eastern Economic Journal,* March.

(1988b), *Some Swedish Stepping Stones to Modern Macroeconomics.* In preparation, Hampshire: Gower Publishing Co., Ltd.

Wicksell, K. (1896), *Finanztheoretische Untersuchungen nebst Darstellung und Kritik des Steuerwesens Schwedens.* Jena: Verlag von Gustav Fischer.

(1898), *Geldzins und Güterpreise.* Jena: Gustav Fischer.

(1907), "Krisernas gåta," *Statsekonomisk Tidskrift,* 21, 225–84.

(1918), Review of Karl Petander: "Goda och dåliga tider," *Ekonomisk Tidskrift.*

(1934), *Lectures on Political Economy,* Vol. 1. London: Routledge and Kegan Paul.

Comment

JAN PETERSSON

My first reflection will be methodological. I have devoted some time to reading the social philosopher Michel Foucault because some social scientist friends of mine insisted on his relevance for an understanding of social history. Foucault left me with a feeling that different aspects of an epoch are linked together and that a change of epochs has many causal dimensions that are best understood together. I felt that I was looking at patterns in history from a new perspective.

In a way, Kumara Velupillai's article reminds me of this reading of Foucault. Scientific discoveries have historic roots that linger on and develop, as well as appearing as urgent questions for a particular period. Roots from Petty and Malthus together with questions of "justice in taxation" form a picture "painted" by Velupillai. It takes a supreme intellect to propose these grand links and thereby present his reader with a broad understanding.

However, there exists a problem for me as a reader. As with Foucault, the closely argued proofs are missing. They are not part of the method. I only intuitively feel that Velupillai is right. One has to rely on the author's judgment. However, I do believe that Velupillai is far more accurate than wrong in his reconstruction of developments in economics.

I will now proceed to a more detailed remark that ends up, as I see it, at a "transcendent" level. Velupillai quotes Sir John Hicks saying that Lindahl was the founder of social accounting theory. The important concepts of *ex ante-ex post* used by the Stockholm School naturally provide an example of a link to accounting. This idea of a connection is put forward by Velupillai. It makes sense and seems obvious. At the same time a contrary opinion is upheld by Ingvar Ohlsson (1953) and directly stated by Gunnar Myrdal (see Carlson, 1982). They argued that the empirical "national income" studies and the development of theory were far apart. The two represented different approaches with little reconciliation between them. It is hard to sidestep these arguments. Can Velupillai's theme be upheld at the same time? Must not either opinion be wrong? The answer to the latter question is: I don't think so. While Myrdal's view is hard to question, it could be interpreted as relating to a clearcut divison of labor. However, what went on within the brains of the Swedes was hardly in the same way divided up, that is, schizophrenic. As mental conditioning, the two belong together. At a "transcendent" level what seems obvious makes sense, so to speak. Velupillai is, in other words, justified by his own method.

References

Carlson, Benny (1982), *Bagge, Lindahl och nationalinkomsten. On National Income of Sweden 1861–1930.* Lund.
Ohlsson, Ingvar (1953), *On National Accounting.* Stockholm.

CHAPTER 14

After the Stockholm School

BJÖRN HANSSON

This essay analyzes the late development of the Stockholm School, that is, the progress *after* the founding years of 1927–37, which have been dealt with in my work *The Stockholm School and the Development of Dynamic Method* (Hansson, 1982). That work defined the Stockholm School by the interrelated development of different dynamic methods among its members, and this process was, for the period 1927–37, an internal Swedish affair.

The analysis of the development after 1937 is still concentrated on contributions that deal with the dynamic method, but these contributions are no longer isolated from foreign influences. It is therefore not possible to speak of a school in the same strict sense as for the initial period. This paper includes contributions that relate to the ideas of the Stockholm School. However, the works must contain something original concerning the dynamic method. Hence, I look at a sequel to the Stockholm School from this limited point of view, and it is not at all excluded that the School might have had an important influence in other areas. Both Bertil Ohlin and Erik Lundberg, for example, wrote long tracts on economic policy that are obviously based on the old approach.

This essay starts with a brief recapitulation of the contribution of the Stockholm School during 1927–37. Then Erik Lindahl's reaction to Keynes's *General Theory* is considered, showing that his critique of Keynes's static method is based on his own period analysis. Section 3 analyzes the notion of quasi-equilibrium developed by Bent Hansen in his 1951 dissertation. Recursive and interdependent models are the subjects of section 4. These notions were used by Ragnar Bentzel and Bent Hansen in their analysis of recursive system, which might be considered to characterize the fully developed sequence analysis of the Stockholm School. Section 5 deals with Karl-Olof Faxén's idea of strategic equilibrium, which is an application of sequence analysis under oligopolistic

347

conditions. In the final section, I try to assess the contribution of the Stockholm School and to respond to the argument that the Keynesian revolution wiped out any traces of the Swedish message.

1   The Stockholm School, 1927–37

Equilibrium approaches

The first contribution to the development of dynamic method is Gunnar Myrdal's 1927 dissertation, *Prisbildningsproblemet och föränderligheten* (Price Formation and Change). His method includes anticipations at the same methodological level as resources, preferences, and techniques, that is, among the data or the immediate determinants of relative prices. This method has been called "the method of expectation," which means the inclusion of expectations as explicit variables in a formal equilibrium theory (see Hicks, 1973, p. 143, n. 11).

Lindahl's aim in the article "The Place of Capital in the Theory of Price" (Lindahl, 1929) was to analyze the effects of including capital goods in the determination of a static equilibrium. In *The Rate of Interest and the Price Level,* Lindahl (1930) was interested in explaining changes in the price level. He constructed intertemporal equilibrium and temporary equilibrium, respectively, to solve these problems. These methods are both examples of an *equilibrium approach,* which means that for each individual and commodity, the anticipated price achieves a balance of demand and supply and all expectations are therefore fulfilled.

Intertemporal equilibrium is a simultaneous determination of prices, quantities, and interest rates for all periods under the assumption of equilibrium within each period. Temporary equilibrium was supposed to avoid the problem of simultaneity. However, temporary equilibrium implies that for each period, prices are in equilibrium states in the sense that there will be equality between supply and demand during the period. The dynamic process is analyzed as a series of temporary equilibria. The missing element is an analysis of the link between consecutive periods.

Disequilibrium approaches

In *Monetary Equilibrium,* Myrdal (1939) attemtped a critical reconstruction of Wicksell's normal rate of interest. The most important contribution to the School is the construction of the famous *ex ante-ex post* calculus. *Ex ante* is a business calculation based on an estimation of what will happen in the future, and *ex post* is bookkeeping about what has actually happened during the previous period.

There is always an *ex post* balance, but it is more interesting to analyze the changes during the period that are required to bring about the *ex post* balance. These changes must be the result of inconsistent anticipations or exogenous changes during the period. Lindahl's insufficient analysis of the balancing changes was criticized by Myrdal and by Lundberg: The intervening changes could not be explained in Lindahl's framework because time is divided into a number of short equilibrium periods during which no changes occur. However, with the application of *ex ante* and *ex post,* which makes a proper analysis of the intervening changes, it is possible to be released from the straitjacket of the equilibrium approach implied by temporary equilibrium.

Sequence analysis

Lindahl's "A Note on the Dynamic Pricing Problem," a short (four pages) and privately circulated paper (Lindahl, 1934), lays the foundation of sequence analysis. To develop his general dynamic approach, Lindahl had to postulate that individual actions represent the fulfillment of certain plans. As far as changes in plans are concerned, Lindahl assumed that these take place at the transition point between two consecutive periods. It is implied that a period is defined by unchanged plans, which was already hinted at by Dag Hammarskjöld (1932).

To develop sequence analysis, Lindahl assumed the following. At an arbitrary point in time (t), the plans for production and consumption are given for a certain period of time (t to $t + 1$), which means that if prices are known, then the individual actions are determined for the period. However, to determine the *ex post* results from the given *ex ante* plans at time t, which show what is going to happen during one single period, does not imply that the ongoing process after time $t + 1$ can be determined at t without further assumptions. The crucial assumption of the continuation analysis concerns the relation between *ex ante* plans for the forthcoming period and the *ex post* results for the current period. Lindahl then made the following assumption: If the plans are fulfilled and there are no changes in the exterior events, it is then possible to postulate a simple functional relation between the *ex ante* plans for the next period and the *ex post* results of the current period.

Erik Lundberg's development of sequence analysis, in his *Studies in the Theory of Economic Expansion* (1937), employed a disequilibrium approach but at the same time made use of an equilibrium process. For the continuation analysis, Lundberg assumed given response funtions, which means that, for example, current investment is functionally related to the profit for the outgoing period and the function will have the same form independent of whether or not expectations are fulfilled. This is an important difference from Lindahl's version of sequence analysis, which assumed that expectations were fulfilled. Lundberg's version is therefore a *disequilibrium sequence analysis,* whereas Lindahl in 1934 pursued an *equilibrium sequence analysis.* In Lundberg's analysis, the equilibrium notion is represented by the fixed response function – an expectation function of a constant form – which is presupposed for the existence of equilibrium through time (see Hahn, 1952, p. 804). Sequence analysis therefore belongs to the class of equilibrium processes, since constant expectation functions imply that behavior is invariant over a certain period of time, which is a crucial aspect of a general notion of equilibrium.

2   Lindahl's comments on Keynes's *General Theory*

This section takes a look at Lindahl's somewhat belated reaction to the *General Theory;* Lindahl's first response to Keynes's book came in 1953 in the form of a long article in *Ekonomisk Tidskrift,* which was later published in *Economic Record* in 1954 with the title "On Keynes' Economic System." It has to be emphasized that I limit myself to an analysis of his critique of Keynes's dynamic method. I am not concerned with his views on Keynes's theory of effective demand.

It was obvious to Lindahl that Keynes put a lot of emphasis on the causal connections in his theory, but it is difficult to maintain this interpretation since Keynes at the same time discussed "an equilibrium with simultaneous interdependence of the various magnitudes" (Lindahl, 1954, p. 25). Our problem is therefore to study Lindahl's interpretation of the nature of a Keynesian equilibrium; this will at the same time show that Lindahl's dynamic method has developed compared with the earlier methods from the 1930s.

The interdependent relation between different variables in a system of simultaneous equations might easily be applied to stationary conditions, that is to say, "when the development during one period is repeated without changes during the following periods"(Lindahl, 1954, p. 27). The same system may as well be used for "the case concerning the determination of the conditions for *correctly anticipated* processes" (ibid.), and the fundamental assumptions for such situations are the following:

> that the individuals have such expectations of the future that they act in ways which are necessary for their expectations to be fulfilled. It fol-

lows that the interdependence between present and future magnitudes is conditioned in this case by the fact that the latter, via correct anticipations, influence the former.

If the assumption is valid, then anticipated processes might be characterized as equilibrium processes, but they differ in their mathematical formulation from a stationary equilibrium since the variables in an anticipated process have to be dated. According to Lindahl, it is impossible to understand Keynes's constructions unless they are interpreted as explanations of correctly anticipated processes. Lindahl is critical of Keynes's system since it includes a mixture of *static long-run functions* (e.g., the consumption function) and *static short-run functions* (e.g., the liquidity preference function) (Lindahl, 1954, p. 32). The former functions are used to determine the equilibrium conditions and may be used for applications of comparative statics. Static short-run functions, which are defined in the relation to the equilibrium determined by the static long-run functions, can, on the other hand, only be used "in a study of the directions of the movements initiated by an assumed change of the parameters or functions in the equilibrium situation to which the system [of static short-run functions] refers" (Lindahl, 1954, p. 31). Both types of functions can coincide in the sense that the system of long-run functions and short-run functions have the same equilibrium situation; that is to say, "they [the functions] have the same value at the point of equilibrium (in other words, the forms of the functions are different but the solution is the same)" (Lindahl, 1954, p. 168). This distinction between two types of function is an innovation in relation to Lindahl's earlier treatment of dynamic methods.

Keynes analyzes the conditions for different equilibrium situations, which presumes a system of only static long-run functions, at the same time as the tendencies to move in a given situation, which presumes a system of short-run functions (Lindahl, 1954, p. 32). However, Keynes's system should only consist of static short-run functions for the following reason:

> With regard to *substance* and *purpose* the system is ... dynamic: it clarifies the actual tendencies in a certain equilibrium and can, consequently, be used for an investigation of how a movement is generated when the equilibrium is broken; furthermore, it gives material for a building of dynamic processes and for an examination of the transition from one equilibrium to another. (Lindahl, 1954, p. 167)

At first Lindahl assumes correctly that in anticipated processes, expectations do not have to be completely certain, which permits the existence of liquidity preference since there is "some uncertainty in as much as a rise in the interest level is not considered impossible" (Lindahl, 1954, p. 29, n. 12 and p. 164). However, later in the article Lindahl shifts to the assumption that "the conditions are assumed to be permanent or correctly anticipated" (p. 164), and the basis for liquidity preference disappears. If Lindahl had maintained that anticipated processes are not necessarily based on complete foresight, then he might have seen the possibility of determining a Keynesian long-run equilibrium (see Hansson, 1985, pp. 334f.).

The system of static short-run functions only "gives material" to the analysis of a transition between two different equilibria, since the system must "also contain connecting parts of a dynamic character" (Lindahl, 1954, p. 32; and Hansson, 1982, pp. 211–13). However, Lindahl never gives a more specific definition of the "connecting parts." Thus, the static short-run functions of the system only give the *tendencies* for a few periods ahead:

> one can hardly assume that a real process can carry on for any longer period of time based on underlying conditions which are unchanged [these "underlying conditions" explain why the functions are static]. (Lindahl, 1953, p. 221)

It is therefore necessary "to modify successively the premises and thereby the models" (ibid.), which seems to imply that the parameters have to change in at least some of the static short-run functions. This short-run system is akin to Lindahl's dynamic method of 1935, and in particular Lundberg's sequence analysis of 1937 where it is emphasized that the method is only valid for an analysis over a few periods (see Hansson 1982, Chap. 9, sect. 4; Chap. 10, sect. 2).

3   Bent Hansen's quasi-equilibrium

I have not included Bent Hansen in the original Stockholm School since it is obvious that his contribution, *A Study in the Theory of Inflation,* which is his 1951 dissertation, has been influenced by foreign sources (see Hansson, 1982, pp. 9–10). Hansen describes these influences in the following way:

> The analytical equipment used is not new, but neither is it out-moded. It employs the terminology of the Stockholm School, as presented by Erik Lindahl, and some of the lines of reasoning of that school of thought whose pioneer is J. R. Hicks. (Hansen, 1951, p. viii)

The empirical problem of Hansen's analysis is so-called *suppressed inflation,* which was a common fact during and after World War II. Hansen does not assume monopoly, but the agent's buying plans nevertheless take into consideration that their spending at existing prices might be limited, (Hansen, 1951, pp. 23–4), which is reminiscent of the development during the 1970s of price theory with rationing.

From the Stockholm School and Lindahl in particular, who was Hansen's supervisor, Hansen has taken notions such as plans and periods, which together with the assumption of fixed prices *during* the period are fundamental notions of their disequilibrium method. In this method, prices do not equilibrate demand and supply, which, of course, is a suitable assumption for the analysis of suppressed inflation, since the latter is usually characterized by some type of price regulation (Hansen, 1951, p. 28). It is obvious that Hansen deviates from the usual assumption of the Stockholm School, namely, that all spending plans can be realized.

Bent Hansen takes a step beyond what the Stockholm School had hitherto accomplished, since he shows how prices change between periods and offers a stricter exposition than Lundberg's model sequences. He uses excess demand functions: The excess demand for goods – only one good is supposed to be produced – determines the rate of inflation for the consumption good, and the excess demand for labor – which is the only variable factor – determines the rate of wage increases (Hansen, 1951, pp. 159–63). It seems likely that this construction was influenced by Hicks's *Value and Capital* (see the quotation above), but Hansen also refers to Samuelson's *Foundation of Economic Analysis* and Lange's *Price Flexibility and Employment* (ibid., p. 163, n. 1). Bent Hansen has thus added to the Stockholm School what he considered their main drawback, namely, "laws of motion" that show how plans and anticipations are revised (Hansen, 1966, pp. 2–3).

In the above analysis, Hansen applies the notion of *quasi-equilibrium,* which is characterized by prices and wages rising at the same speed (Hansen, 1951, p. 164). This situation is an equilibrium in the sense that the relative price, the relation between the price of the consumer good and the wage, and excess demand in both markets are constant. But it is not a traditional static equilibrium since prices and wages are rising all the time, and excess demand is different from zero. Hence, it is denominated as a *quasi*-equilibrium (Hansen, 1951, p. 164, and 1966, pp. 92–5). Bent Hansen extends his model to include several markets. Quasi-equilibrium then signifies that all relative prices are unchanged over time and the general price level is increasing continuously (Hansen, 1966, p. 198). If it is assumed that the goods are gross substitutes, then it can be proved that the quasi-equilibrium is stable (ibid., p. 205).

From the point of view of the Stockholm School, Bent Hansen's contribution is of great interest since he constructs a new equilibrium notion. Furthermore, he combines the methods of the Stockholm School with the development of dynamic theory outside Sweden. The foreign influence gives his contribution a formal mathematical touch that was far above anything else presented by the original members of the Stockholm School.

4   On recursive and interdependent models

Ragnar Bentzel's and Bent Hansen's 1954 article "On Recursiveness and Interdependency in Economic Models" intervened in the debate among econometricians on whether recursive/consecutive or interdependent/simultaneous models should be the basis for econometric research. Herman Wold and Trygve Haavelmo represented the two different conceptions (Bentzel and Hansen, 1954, pp. 153–4). This debate sheds light on the dynamic methods of the Stockholm School. In this way it is possible to consider Wold's idea on recursive system – a term promoted by Wold in his 1952 book *Demand Analysis* – which to a great extent is influenced by the dynamic methods of the Stockholm School.

A *recursive* system consists solely of unidirectional relations between the variables of the model, which allows for a causal interpretation (Wold, 1952, pp. 50–1). A *simultaneous* system, on the other hand, is also made up of mutual relations among the variables. Wold holds that the sequence analysis of the Stockholm School, where there is not equilibrium in each period, was thought of as a recursive system (ibid., pp. 66–7). Bentzel and Hansen now add the following complementary distinction to the one between recursiveness and simultaneity:

> When we talk about a *basic* model, we mean a model in which complete and explicit regard is taken of each single economic subject and each single good in the society considered. It is obvious that such models can only be discussed in a very abstract way. The economic subjects are the millions of households, firms, organisations and public authorities, and from a practical point of view it is not possible to write down on the paper the enormous number of equations necessary for the description of *all* actions of *all* subjects. But still it is possible to discuss some general properties of such "perfectionistic," basic models, and this will turn out to be useful in this context. If, on the other hand, a basic model is simplified so that not all the variables and relations of the basic model are shown explicitly, we talk about a *derived* model. (Bentzel, 1954, pp. 155–6)

By constructing a basic model that builds on the disequilibrium method of the Stockholm School it should be possible, if a sufficiently short period is assumed, to have a model that contains only recursive relations (Bentzel, 1954, pp. 159–60).

Basic or recursive models are mostly suited for applications at an abstract and theoretical level, and it is not necessary that all economic theory should consist of basic models that are rooted in sequence analysis. As a matter of fact, most dynamic models are derived models and therefore they contain simultaneous relations. There are three practical reasons, all of which are due to deficiencies in the statistical material, for using derived models. First, information about plans, that is, the *ex ante* magnitudes, is generally lacking, and it is therefore necessary to work with *ex post* magnitudes. Second, it is mostly impossible to get information about each single agent and commodity, and it is necessary to use aggregates. The third reason is also related to the problem with aggregation: The statistical material relates to longer time periods than the unit period of sequence analysis according to the Stockholm School (Bentzel, 1954, p. 163).

Bentzel and Hansen have shown that, from a theoretical point of view, sequence analysis can be considered as an analysis of recursive relations, since the analysis is built on a basic model. This problem is analogous with the movement from micro to macro, which the Stockholm School generally thought of as a simple summation over the micromagnitudes. However, it is obvious that in their *empirical* work recursive models were applied to macromagnitudes without ever having used a basic model as a foundation. Lundberg was from the beginning aware of this problem, and he suggested that the length of the unit period had to be chosen with respect to the aggregate magnitudes that were the variables of the model (Lundberg, 1937, pp. 47–50). That was one of the reasons Lundberg restricted his analysis to one single period, which only expressed whether, for example, the government budget increased or decreased the tendency to inflation (Lundberg, 1953, p. 336; Hansson, 1982, pp. 233–5).

5   Faxén's equilibrium between strategies

Faxén's dissertation *Monetary and Fiscal Policy under Uncertainty* was the first to use the ideas of the Stockholm School for performing a general analysis of cases with imperfect competition (Faxén, 1957, pp. 12–13). His interest was concentrated on the analysis of monetary and fiscal policy in a situation with oligopolistic relations among firms and between firms and trade unions. Despite Faxén's general use of game theory Ragnar Bentzel considered, in his review for *Ekonomisk Tidskrift*, the dissertation as a continuation of the Stockholm School:

> What he has taken from game theory is mainly the dualistic view, certain technical methods and the terminology. For the rest the disserta-

tion builds to such an extent on the earlier generation of Swedish economists that the work despite its gametheoretical dress could almost be
considered as a continuation of the research tradition of the Stockholm
School. (Bentzel, 1957, p. 221)

It has to be noted that Lundberg and Svennilson are both mentioned in
Faxén's preface; therefore, there is also a direct personal relationship
with the Stockholm School.

The main problem is to study the manner in which uncertainty concerning the furture is reflected in the agent's plans, which is akin to Myrdal's dissertation from 1927. Faxén has taken his views on uncertainty
from Knight's well-known distinction between risk and uncertainty;
that is, the latter notion cannot be described by objective probabilities
(Faxén, 1957, pp. 42–4). The real existence of uncertainty may, for
example, manifest itself in the attempts by firms to maintain a certain
flexibility via assurances of a certain amount of liquidity (Faxén, 1957,
pp. 14 and 58–9).

The purpose is to construct a dynamic analysis in which from the
beginning incomplete anticipations have been explicitly incorporated
(Faxén, 1957, p. 10). It should also study how the formation of anticipations may influence the rate of change of the economic variables
(Faxén, 1957, p. 24). This problem is close to the interest of the Stockholm School in the adjustment process between two equilibrium situations, where the process itself may influence the final equilibrium and is
different from the propositions of comparative statics (Faxén, 1957, p.
27; Hansson, 1982, p. 50). Faxén's opposite pole, within dynamic theory, is the approach that takes changes in prices and quantities as given,
that is, models based on difference and differential equations.

Faxén takes the period analysis of the Stockholm School as a basis for
the investigation of his own problem, because this method allows for an
analysis of the changes in anticipations and plans between consecutive
periods. At the same time, it is obvious that the Stockholm School in its
initial stage almost never discussed the formation of anticipations,
which was the object of Ingvar Svennilson's 1938 dissertation *Ekonomisk Planering* (Economic Planning) (see Hansson, 1982, p. 9). This
fact is more of an advantage to Faxén, since it facilitates the linkage
between his own problem and the analytical methods of the Stockholm
School:

> the framework of the model – period, plan, expectation, decision to act
> – which is the characteristic feature of the Stockholm School, can *per
> se* be combined with any theory of the origin of the expectations and
> any theory of motivation whatsoever. (Faxén, 1957, p. 31)

The game theoretical formulations are introduced via the concept of "game uncertainty," which characterizes the uncertainty for oligopolistic relations. *Game uncertainty* is defined as follows:

> The characteristic feature of "game uncertainty" as distinct from "uncertainty" is that the acting person must use his knowledge of the objectives of the other acting persons in his immediate environment, of their ways of thinking when making decisions, etc., when he makes a rational analysis of his own situation in order to reduce the game uncertainty. He must also assume that the other persons are analysing his own objectives and decisions in the same way. (Faxén, 1957, p. 45)

Faxén (1957) relates directly to the notion of "strategy," as it had been developed by von Neumann and Morgenstern, to analyze choices over several periods (p. 76). Then it is necessary for an individual's rational choice between the alternatives for the present period that he also chooses between furture possible situations. The latter are also dependent on the original choice. A strategy, which is chosen at the transition to the first period, contains then a determinate choice for several periods:

> that an agent, in a situation with several successive opportunities to choose, does not look upon the choice at the first opportunity as a choice between the actual alternatives at that point of time, but as a choice between different combinations of decisions – *strategies* – at the present point of time and in the future. (Bentzel, 1957, p. 226)

Thus, the agents choose at the initial point of time between different strategies. Equilibrium in a multiperiod analysis with uncertainty can then be determined with the help of the following notion of *strategy:* "each economic unit has a strategy, which is optimal for that unit, if it regards all the others' strategies as fixed" (Faxén, 1957, p. 100). This definition, which is taken from Nash, implies that in equilibrium there is no tendency to change strategy, and the equilibrium may be described as a point on the contract curve in an Edgeworth box.

Faxén's contribution to the Stockholm School is an application of period analysis to oligopolistic conditions, which used game theory and then constructed the notion of strategy equilibrium.

6 Assessment

According to Hicks it is possible to speak of two different revolutions in the 1930s:

> To pass from one *pure* method to the other [flexprice to fixprice] is quite a revolution. It is a revolution that is mixed up with the so-called

> "Keynesian Revolution"; but I do not think that it is accurate to iden-
> tify them. Though the "methods" that are used in the *Treatise on
> Money* and in the *General Theory* are different, neither of them is a
> *pure* method. . . . There is, however, no question that, as between his
> two works, Keynes was moving in the direction of the new method;
> and it is in the work of his interpreters and successors that the clearest
> examples of the new method are to be found. In their hands the
> method is often presented as a Keynesian method; but it is wiser, in
> my view, to avoid committing ourselves to taking it as such. It is better
> to recognize that the direction of movement is one that is very wide-
> spread in contemporary economics, both through the influence of
> Keynes and otherwise. . . . A corresponding change was occurring in
> Sweden. The original (1929–30) form of Lindahl's theory, which we
> have been discussing, was pure Temporary Equilibrium. But in Myr-
> dal's *Monetary Equilibrium* (1933), in spite of its title, the change is
> beginning. In Lundberg's *Economic Expansion* (1937) it is fairly com-
> plete. In Lindahl's later work . . . he also moved in the same direction.
> (Hicks, 1965, p. 77)

Hence, one revolution was concerned with dynamic methods, and in
this field the Stockholm School played a major role, while the other one
was the Keynesian revolution in a narrow sense, that is, the principle of
effective demand. In this perspective, Keynes's contribution in the *General Theory* and the contribution of the Stockholm School are complementary rather than contradictory.

This view differs from Siven's and Jonung's opinion of the death of
the Stockholm School:

> Why were the Stockholm School and, specifically, its original contri-
> bution – the dynamic method – never able to reach an international
> breakthrough? The production of the Stockholm School culminated in,
> and was ended by, the dissertations of Erik Lundberg and Ingvar Sven-
> nilson in 1937 and 1938, respectively. . . . Why was the Stockholm
> School unable to make an international breakthrough, either on its
> own merit or by means of complementary analysis to Keynesian
> unemployment theory? (Sivén, 1985, pp. 578–9; see also Jonung, 1987)

It is true that the Stockholm School culminated around 1937–8, but this
paper has shown that in Sweden there was also an afterglow to the early
most productive period. Moreover, the Stockholm School did not complement Keynesian unemployment theory, if the latter is supposed to
be the principle of effective demand. However, there is a great deficiency
in this view of the complete defeat of the Stockholm School, since it does
not give a precise definition of the content and form in which the
Keynesian revolution conquered the minds of professional economists,
students, and politicians. It is my opinion that the Keynesian revolution

as the dominating theory took the form of Hicks's IS-LM model, Hicks-Hansen's income-expenditure diagram, and Samuelson's model of the multiplier-accelerator. The IS-LM approach uses temporary equilibrium with fixed prices in the markets for goods and labor, which is an obvious link back to Lindahl. The income-expenditure model analyzes accommodations in stocks and quantities via the notions of *ex ante* and *ex post*. Samuelson's development is more related to Frisch, Tinbergen, and Kalecki, and there is only a tenuous relation to Lundberg.

It is true that disequilibrium sequence analysis, the most advanced notion of the Stockholm School, has hardly been used at all in either the Swedish or foreign contributions. The role of this notion is discussed by Lundberg in his evaluation of the dynamic methods developed by the Stockholm School:

> It is clearly an advantage to have theories of expansion and of the possible course of expansionist processes in the back of the mind and to use concepts that can be fitted into a dynamic sequence. But we have to be aware of the extremely limited applicability of our more involved models to an ever changing economic reality, where it is precisely the *changes* in the assumed coefficients that will often be more important than the fixed relations. My experience shows that the more modest approach to dynamics by way of the *disequilibrium method* – that is, *ex ante* discrepancies between plans made and measures taken by different groups and countries – in nearly all cases gives the necessary starting point for dynamic analysis. (Lundberg, 1937, p. iv; see the preface to the 1953 edition of *Economic Expansion)*

On the basis of his "experience in practical research" Lundberg thus advocated a single period analysis for practical purposes. Sequence analysis had a restricted practical value and it should not be carried to far ahead in time, since the assumption of given response functions was only accidentally valid over a short period of time. In fact, during the 1940s most of the empirical works done by the Swedes belonged to the category of single period analysis, for example, their analyses of the inflationary gap that was initiated by Keynes in his 1940 pamphlet *How to Pay for the War*. The construction of "probable sequences of economic development," that is, a full-blown sequence analysis, functioned more as a tool that could be used for analytical purposes rather than something directly applicable to an empirical analysis. Nowadays, theoreticians are struggling to make a formal development of sequence analysis, or the analysis of *sequence economies* where there is trading at every date and which goes beyond an Arrow-Debreu economy (i.e., intertemporal equilibrium), in an attempt to construct a theory of a monetary economy (Hahn, 1982, p. 2).

Here, I have argued that the Stockholm School was still influential in Sweden in the 1950s and that there was even a sequel to the original development of dynamic methods. However, we cannot speak of a School in the same limited sense as was possible for the 1930s since the foreign impulses were important for the later development. But at least some of the material of the Stockholm School was flexible enough either to be included in other methods or to incorporate extraneous ideas. In this sense there is no reason to say that the Stockholm School was killed by the Keynesian revolution, since some of the dynamic methods developed by the Swedes became part and parcel of the presentation of the Keynesian message.

References

Bentzel, Ragnar (1957), "Review of Faxén," *Ekonomisk Tidskrift.*

Bentzel, Ragnar, and Bent Hansen (1954), "On Recursiveness and Interdependency in Economic Models," *The Review of Economic Studies.*

Faxén, Karl-Olof (1957), *Monetary and Fiscal Policy under Uncertainty.* Uppsala: Almquist & Wiksell.

Hahn, Frank H. (1952), "Expectations and Equilibrium," *Economic Journal.*

(1982), *Money and Inflation.* Oxford: Basil Blackwell.

Hammarskjöld, Dag (1932), "Utkast till en algebraisk metod för dynamisk prisanalys," *Ekonomisk Tidskrift.*

Hansen, Bent (1951), *A Study in the Theory of Inflation.* London: George Allen & Unwin.

(1966), *Lectures in Economic Theory.* Part I. Lund: Studentlitteratur.

Hansson, Björn A. (1982), *The Stockholm School and the Development of Dynamic Method.* London: Croom & Helm.

(1985), "Keynes's Notion of Equilibrium in the General Theory," *Journal of Post-Keynesian Economics.*

Hicks, John R. (1965), *Capital and Growth.* Oxford: Clarendon Press.

(1973), "Recollections and Documents," *Economica.* As reprinted in Hicks, *Economic Perspectives,* Oxford: Clarendon Press.

Jonung, Lars (1987), "The Stockholm School after 50 Years: An Attempt at Appraisal." Paper presented at *History of Economic Society Annual Meeting* in Boston, 1987.

Lindahl, Erik (1929), "Prisbildningsproblemet från kapitalteoretisk synpunkt." *Ekonomisk Tidskrift.* Translated as "The Place of Capital in the Theory of Price" and published in Lindahl, *Studies in the Theory of Money and Capital,* London: George Allen & Unwin, 1939.

(1930), *Penningpolitikens medel.* Malmö: Förlagsaktiebolaget. Translated as "The Rate of Interest and the Price Level" and published in Lindahl, *Studies in the Theory of Money and Capital,* London: George Allen & Unwin, 1939.

(1934), "A Note on the Dynamic Pricing Problem." Mimeo, Gothenburg 23 October 1934. As reprinted in Otto Steiger, *Studien zur Entstehung der Neuen Wirtschaftslehre in Schweden,* Berlin: Duncker & Humblot, 1971.

(1939), "The Dynamic Approach to Economic Theory," Part one of *Studies in the Theory of Money and Capital.* London: George Allen & Unwin.

(1953), "Om Keynes ekonomiska system," *Ekonomisk Tidskrift.*

(1954), "On Keynes' Economic System," *Economic Record.*

Lundberg, Erik (1937), *Studies in the Theory of Economic Expansion,* 1st ed. Reprinted New York: Kelly & Millman, 1955.

(1953), *Konjunkturer och ekonomisk politik.* Stockholm: P. A. Norstedt & Söner.

Myrdal, Gunnar (1927), *Prisbildningsproblemet och föränderligheten.* Uppsala and Stockholm: Almquist & Wiksell.

(1939), *Monetary Equilibrium,* 1st English edition. A translation and extended version of the 1933 German edition, which is a translation and an extension of an article in *Ekonomisk Tidskrift* (1931), reprinted New York: Kelley, 1965.

Ohlin, Bertil (1937), "Some Notes on the Stockholm Theory of Savings and Investments," *Economic Journal.*

Siven, Claes-Henric (1985), "The End of the Stockholm School," *Scandinavian Journal of Economics.*

Wold, Herman (1952), *Demand Analysis.* Uppsala: Almquist & Wiksell.

Comment

DAVID LAIDLER

I learned a good deal from Björn Hansson's paper, as I did from his book (Hansson, 1982), and I agree with his main conclusion, namely, that the ideas of the Stockholm School did not so much disappear from economics as lose their national identity when they became absorbed into the discipline's mainstream. Thus I have nothing in the way of adversely critical comments to offer, and of the three points I would like to make, two come in to the category of "suggestions for further work," rather than bearing directly on the substance of Hansson's contribution.

Let me first deal with a matter that arises from the paper, however. Hansson suggests, at the very outset of his argument, that "after 1937 . . . the contributions [of the Stockholm School] are no longer isolated from foreign influences," and he returns to this same theme later, for example, when discussing the work of Bent Hansen. One must be very careful when one speaks of the isolation of the Stockholm School, because throughout the first three decades of this century, it would be hard to find a group more aware of work going on elsewhere than the Swedes. A glance at Wicksell's *Lectures* will readily confirm that he was both one of the best read of his contemporaries, and also, particularly by the standards of his time, extremely conscientious about drawing his readers' attention to the work of others. The comparison here with Marshall, shall we say, is hardly to the credit of the latter.

And it is not only Wicksell who was open to foreign ideas. Lindahl and Lundberg both make frequent explicit references to non-Swedish sources, and they, along with Myrdal, make extensive use of such identifiably foreign ideas as Irving Fisher's "rate of return over cost" (later to be renamed the "marginal efficiency of capital" by Keynes) and the Marshall-Fisher analysis of the influence of inflation expectations on nominal interst rates. What differentiates the work of the Stockholm School before 1937 from that coming afterwards is not that before 1937 its analysis was immune to foreign influence. Rather it is that before 1937 the Stockholm economists wrote in Swedish, in order to communicate with one another about analytic ideas that seemed particularly relevant to contemporary Swedish policy problems. After 1937 they were more likely to publish their ideas in English in an attempt to secure for them a place in a then emerging internationally recognized body of knowledge. What we are seeing here is not a change unique to the Stockholm School, but one aspect of the internationalization of economics that gathered momentum so rapidly in the 1930s.

My first "suggestion for further work" arises naturally from the foregoing considerations. Hansson has done all of us a service in providing a guide to the more important contributions of Swedish economists to the international literature of economics after 1937, and has skillfully documented the way in which, with the passage of time, the work in question became less and less Swedish in character. There is, though, a complementary aspect to the absorption of the Stockholm School into mainstream economics, namely, the extent to which ideas of identifiably Swedish origin came to permeate the work of foreign economists after about 1937. Let me give but one illustration of what I have in mind here. Even today, virtually every introductory textbook contains a discussion of elementary national income accounting and an account of the real income determination process built around the famous "45-degree line" diagram. When one recalls the confusion that surrounded the question of the equality of savings and investment in the debates of the late 1930s, and compares it with the completely routine treatment of this issue, invariably based on the *ex ante-ex post* distinction, in elementary teaching nowadays, one immediately recognizes that one important Swedish idea has become the common property of everyone with the slightest acquaintance with economics. It would make an interesting, albeit taxing, study to trace the absorption of this idea, and others like it, by non-Swedish economists.

Finally, let me turn to a comment that is as much on Hansson's book as it is on this paper. His identification of the development of a method of analysis as the central contribution of the Stockholm School enables us to think more clearly about a host of questions concerning that group's cohesiveness. I suspect, though, that we might get an even clearer view of their place in the history of our subject if we paid explicit attention to what seems to me to be the essentially Marshallian nature of their view of economic analysis. By this I do not mean that the Swedish economists were simply developing tools originated by Marshall. Rather, I mean that their approach to economic theory conforms to the Marshallian type of "an engine of analysis for the discovery of concrete truth." Much has been made at this conference of the absence of a "central theoretical message" in the work of the Stockholm School, about their tendency to proliferate examples of dynamic sequences in which anything can happen. It is worth noting that Marshallian supply and demand analysis is open to exactly the same critique. This "theory" makes no predictions about the world. It is a tool that enables one to deduce the consequences of differing assumptions, a device for framing questions clearly and then answering them; but it gives no help in distinguishing the interesting questions from the uninteresting, the socially relevant answers from the irrelevant.

Historians of economic thought who are inclined to praise Marshallian methodology as a contribution to microeconomics ought perhaps to think twice about criticizing the Stockholm School for deploying a similar methodolgy in the macrosphere and for having developed a conceptual framework, based on concepts such as *ex ante-ex post* and the unit period, which has contributed so much to macroeconomists' ability to frame their questions, and state their disagreements, clearly. At the very least the similarity in view of the role of theory that seems to underly the work of Marshall and the Stockholm School is surely worth a more systematic investigation than I can give it here, as is the closely related question of the extent to which the Swedish economists were self-conscious about the Marshallian character of their work on economic theory. Perhaps the ability of the Stockholm School to come to terms so quickly with the *General Theory* owes something to a common Marshallian heritage. I hope that I can provoke Dr. Hansson into taking up these questions in his future work.

Reference

Hansson, B. A. (1982), *The Stockholm School and the Development of Dynamic Method.* London: Croom Helm.

Comment

LARS E. O. SVENSSON

The Stockholm School set out to perform a very ambitious dynamic macroanalysis, their so-called sequence analysis. However, the school was faced with a number of problems since it lacked the necessary tools for such analysis. Let me mention some of these problems.

Expectations and expectations formation were crucial for the dynamic method, but the Stockholm School did not have a theory of expectations. The participants of the School instead assumed arbitrarily given expectations. The exception was that of Lindahl's self-fulfilled expectations in a deterministic framework, that is, the assumption of perfect foresight in an intertemporal general equilibrium setup.

The Stockholm School also suffered from having insufficient micro-foundations for its behavioral assumptions. They either lacked the capacity or the desire to provide such microfoundations. Instead they assumed rather arbitrarily given response functions. Lindahl assumed, for instance, that when expectations were fulfilled, *ex ante* plans for the next period were a function of *ex post* realizations of the current period. Lundberg assumed, for instance, that investment was a given function of current profits, regardless of whether or not expectations were fulfilled. These arbitrary assumptions led to arbitrary conclusions, what David Laidler calls a bewildering variety of possible outcomes depending upon the specific set of assumptions made.

The Stockholm School also faced a purely technical problem, in that they could not solve or manipulate the systems of simultaneous difference or differential equations that would be unavoidably generated by the proper specification of dynamic economic models. Alternatively, they failed to see the benefits of such technical analysis since at least part of the knowledge certainly did exist at that time, as William Baumol's paper and Mats Persson's comment make clear. Consequently, the Stockholm School did not reach any clear-cut conclusions, and their theories never became operational.

The Keynesian School handled the problems faced by the Stockholm

School by sweeping them under the rug. It did not have a theory for expectations, nor did it provide any microfoundations. The main characteristic of the Keynesian School is instead the strategic and drastic simplification, most powerfully demonstrated in the Keynesian cross and in the few simultaneous static equations of the IS-LM model, or in Paul Samuelson's formulation of Lundberg's multiplier-accelerator model.

In this way, the Keynesian School reached clear-cut conclusions and became extremely operational, no doubt at the cost of oversimplification.

These days, the simple Keynesian School is in the process of becoming history. In current macroeconomics, its sweeping under the rug has been replaced by new and powerful methods of handling and solving the difficulties faced by the Stockholm School. With regard to expectations formation, the rational expectations hypothesis is now dominant, in its basic idea that economic agents show the same rationality in collecting and using information as they are assumed to show in other activities. This can be seen as a natural extension of the neoclassical principle of rationality into the realm of uncertainty, imperfect information, and dynamics. With regard to microfoundations, the dominant modeling of behavior is that of rational optimizing under constraints, the latter including the information available (or the technology through which information can be obtained). The techniques of solving (analytically or numerically) simultaneous systems of dynamic equations has also been much improved. Although the conclusions reached in current macroeconomics may be less clear-cut than those of the Keynesian School, their precise validity is certainly much better understood.

The ambitious dynamic analysis that the Stockholm School aimed at but never reached is now being pursued in current macroeconomics. From this point of view, the Stockholm School is not dead, but has rather been absorbed into mainstream macroeconomics.

PART III

The impact of the Stockholm School

CHAPTER 15

The Swedish influence on *Value and Capital*

SIR JOHN HICKS

My *Value and Capital* was published in 1939 – in January 1939, for in that year it is best to be precise about dates. My first visit to Sweden was in the June that followed, getting close to the September when England would be at war. I have never learned Swedish, so Swedish influence on my book can have come in only two ways: from the works of Swedish economists written in other languages or translated into other languages, or alternatively from meetings with Swedish economists, in England or at international conferences. There were not many of the latter in the 1930s; the Econometric Society was a pioneer. I attended some of its meetings, but I do not recollect any contact at them with Swedish economists.

The first Swedish economist, some of whose writings were early available in English, was, of course, Cassel; but though I had read some of his productions before my story starts, the impact they had made on me was not deep. (Perhaps, I now think, it should have been deeper, but that was how it was.) So I begin, not with him, but with Wicksell.

I was introduced to the work of Wicksell by Hayek. During these years (1926–35 to be exact) I was teaching, at first in a very junior capacity, at the London School of Economics (LSE). Hayek gave his famous (or dare I now say infamous?) *Prices and Production* lectures as a visitor to LSE in February 1931; he came back in the following September as professor, a regular member of the department to which I was attached. But already by the February – or perhaps even earlier, in anticipation of his arrival – we were reading the Austrians, Böhm-Bawerk in particular. I read them in German, for I could (more or less) read German (though not Swedish). So I could also read Wicksell, in the German version.

It was the monetary theory of Wicksell to which Hayek had mainly directed our attention; but that is in Volume II of the *Lectures,* and I never like to read Volume II of anything without having at least a look at Volume I. And I found, at that date, that Volume I had more of what

I wanted. For Wicksell was linking Böhm-Bawerk with Walras, on whom I was already lecturing; so his version was easier than that of Böhm, or even of Hayek, for me to understand. There is quite a lot of Wicksell Volume I in my *Theory of Wages* (to be published in late 1932).

I may remark, in passing, that I had a good deal to do with the English translation of that volume of Wicksell (1934). I had to correct a version in very imperfect English taken directly from the Swedish, with nothing to help me except the German translation I had been using, which I have been told by better linguists does not give a good repute. But it was possible to work out from these what the author was trying to say and to put it in my own English words. The result, surprisingly, appears to have been quite acceptable.

The most Wicksellian part of my *Wages* book is the concluding chapters, in which I discuss the effect of "too high wages" in a closed economy – distinguishing, as it was useful to distinguish, what I later called the income and the substitution effect. But since my "equilibrium" was the stationary state of Wicksell, my income effect, on profits and saving, was described, on Hayekian lines, as "capital consumption"; and this, as I remember being told by Dennis Robertson, was just wrong. "There is some excuse for Hayek," he told me, "having lived in mouldering Vienna, but none for the rest of you, having lived in London and the Home Counties." (One should remember that in that dreadful year 1932 the southeast of England was the most prosperous place to the world.) I should have started with the "equilibrium" of a progressive economy, when the effect under discussion would have shown up as a retardation of growth.

I think I may reckon that letter, which was sent to me while *Wages* was in the press but before it was published, as the stimulus that set me off in a new direction. It was the direction that led to the "dynamic" parts of *Value and Capital* (III and IV). There is evidence that I had started on that track before the end of 1932 – almost at once after *Wages* had come out.

Thus I think I may count the turn of 1932–3 to date the beginning of the work that was to lead to *Value and Capital,* which applies to the "static" parts (I had II) as well to the "dynamic." But I need not here attend to those static parts, for there is nothing Swedish in them. The only influences in them are Pareto (and Marshall). They carry on from Pareto; they seek to make his General Equilibrium theory more usable by incorporating the work I did with Allen on demand theory (published in *Economica* early 1934).

The six years from that start in 1932–3 to completion in 1938–9 fall, in my personal biography, into two nearly equal parts. There are three things that happened very near to the midpoint by which they are divided. The first was my move from LSE to Cambridge; the second was my marriage to Ursula; the third was the publication of Keynes's *General Theory*. Each of these, I shall be showing, is relevant.

The actual writing of *Value and Capital* must have been largely done at Cambridge, though there was some of the static part that must have been written in 1934 (year II of my six). And quite six months out of year IV, my first at Cambridge, were occupied in writing two papers on Keynes's theory, one of which is very well known. I would say that these papers had little to do with *Value and Capital;* they come in as extras. The book could have been completed, with its main lines much the same, if I had never been asked to write those papers on Keynes but had been able to put his book aside until I had finished my own job.

I want to emphasize that *Value and Capital* is in essence an LSE book, not at all a Cambridge book. The ideas that went into it were fairly fully formed before I left LSE. So it is years I–III of my six that are relevant to my present subject. It is in years II and III that a (contemporary) Swedish influence comes in, but something must be said about year I, to serve as background.

Theory of Wages was off my hands, so I was free to start thinking seriously about the theory of Hayek – in particular, about the Wicksell monetary construction on which he thought he was building. Wicksell had just looked at monetary consequences of his disequilibrium (between market rate and natural rate); Hayek thought there were *real* consequences also. But that made it more necessary for Hayek than it had been for Wicksell to define what he meant by equilibrium – though, as Myrdal was to show (I come to him later), there was a lot to be said about that without going off on Hayek's tack. Nevertheless, as was natural, it was from the Hayek form of the problem that I began.

There does happen to be on record a statement of where I had got to, in my worries about "equilibrium," before I knew anything of Myrdal (or of Lindahl). It is an article that was published in a German translation in the Vienna *Zeitschrift* before the end of 1933, my year I. (It has had to be retranslated into English to appear in the second volume of my *Collected Essays*.) I am not very proud of that paper – it is very much an interim report – but I need to refer to it here, as background.

Hayek's disequilibrium was to be a *real* disequilibrium, a distortion of the "structure of production"; so it was incumbent on him to provide a criterion for non-distortion, non-distortion in real (non-monetary) terms. In his London lectures, with which I and my friends at LSE were wrestling, he had not offered any such criterion. A Wicksellian stationary state would be non-distorted, but for Hayek, as he himself accepted, that would not do. When I put my trouble to him, he showed me a paper he had written and published, in German, in 1928; here he had given a non-stationary definition – disequilibrium was disappointment of expectations. Thus an economy would be in equilibrium when what happened was what was expected to happen – "perfect foresight." Now a perfect foresight model is a possible economic model, having some sort of use in theoretical discussions, but it cannot be claimed that it is a realistic model; no actual economy could ever be "in equilibrium" in that sense. It must always in that sense be in disequilibrium.

Hayek could only make use of this construction, as he did, by saying that he was going to concentrate attention on disequilibria that are due to monetary causes. But how does one distinguish them from other disequilibria?

Besides, on this line of thought, what happens if one admits, as one surely ought to admit, that expectations are uncertain? I found that one had to introduce uncertainty before one could introduce money.

That led, still in my Year I paper, to a first consideration of the effect of uncertainty on the demand for money at a point of time – the "spectrum of assets." This was much better put, a year later, toward the end of year II, in my "Suggestion for Simplifying the Theory of Money," on which the greater part of my later work on monetary theory has been based. But though at that time I was already in touch with Sweden, there is not much that I can recognize as "Swedish" in it, nor is it at all well represented in *Value and Capital.*

The beginning of my contact with contemporary Sweden was my reading (for review) Myrdal's *Monetary Equilibrium* (in the German version) some time in the first half of 1934. This was immensely clarifying on the old Wicksell doctrine; as criticism of Wicksell it has hardly even now been superseded. But it was not exactly what, at that stage, I wanted. I was already clear (or was on the way to getting clear) about substitution between money and interest-bearing securities, the basis of a "point of time" or balance-sheet equilibrium, one element in a theory of economic change, to be an analysis of process. It was the flow aspect, the analysis of change over a period, that was holding me up. Myrdal on that was tantalizing; he seemed often to be just on the point of helping me, but it did not quite come off.

I could see that he must have been drawing upon discussions that had been taking place in Sweden and had been written down in that language, which was closed to me. The name that was most often quoted in connection with it was that of Lindahl. I was just wondering whether I could venture to write to Lindahl when I met him. He came into tea at LSE and Robbins introduced us. (There were other important visitors to LSE whom one met that way.) I was so excited that I ventured to ask him out to dinner.

He explained that his purpose in visiting England was to find someone who could help him with an English translation of his writings; could I help him to find someone? The helper I found was a lady who had taken part in the discussions at LSE that I have been describing. She was herself a public finance specialist, so that in all that side of Lindahl's work she was particularly interested, and she was prepared to take the trouble to get a reading knowledge of Swedish. So it was that we went on working together, up to my marriage with the lady, at the end of 1935, and after until all our books came out in 1938–9: his *Studies in the Theory of Money and Capital*, her *Finance of British Government*, my *Value and Capital*.

The most obviously Lindahlian chapter in *Value and Capital* is the chapter on Income. This in substance follows Lindahl's well-known paper "The Concept of Income," which had appeared in English in 1933. I ought to have read it before I met him, but I don't think I had done so. It restates his argument in a less paradoxical manner; and it seems to have been acceptable to national income people and suchlike, who (I have been told) regard it as rather standard. It is, however, remarkable that it would be possible to cross out that chapter without making much difference to the rest of the book. That was designed to proceed without any reference to income, or to the savings and investment that go with it.

Why did I do that? It was itself a consequence of what I had got from Lindahl. The curious "week" and "Monday" assumptions that are employed throughout almost the whole of the latter parts of *Value and Capital* were designed to get the analysis as far as possible while avoiding the "*ex ante-ex post*" trouble on which he and Myrdal had thrown so bright a light.

Their basic point was simply that no one can decide *now* what *shall* happen at some future date. He can only decide what he intends to happen, taking steps to facilitate the execution of his decision, the steps that he can take now. He can enter into contracts, which hand over the execution of the decision (or a part of it) to someone else; the contract is a promise, but no contract can offer perfect certainty that the promise will be kept. There is a vital distinction between promising that a thing shall be done and actually doing it.

My device was based on this distinction. I was trying to find a way of bringing the behavior of an economy, over a period, into a formal model. Many older economists had thought that this could easily be done; but in the light of what I had learned from Lindahl, I could see that it was terribly hard. Could one find a device (it would have to be an artificial device) that would help one to do it? A device that would recognize the distinction I have just been making, but that would still allow one to construct a usable model? My device, which must have arisen in conversations with Lindahl (I wish that I could check with him or with the other witness), was to think of decisions – and contracts to embody those decisions – all being made at the beginning of the "week" (my "Monday"); execution of those decisions, and of the contracts embodying them, continuing during the week, but no new decisions being taken until the following Monday. This made it possible for me to use "point of time" theory, which I thought I understood, to determine a *temporary equilibrium* – of decision makers and between decision makers – on the Monday, in the light of information available on that Monday, while recognizing that on the next Monday there would be new information.

So what follows in *Value and Capital* is just temporary equilibrium theory, in this narrow sense. It is solely concerned with what happens on the "Monday," so the methods of "point of time" theory can be used, and are used. But since the decisions concern not only the distribution of assets on the Monday, but also the flows of inputs and outputs that are planned for the week (and after), the distinction between stocks and flows is not at that stage of much importance. I got as far as I could then see my way to go in that direction; I know that I ought to have tried to go a bit further. I have been trying ever since to find ways of going further, and there are several that I have explored.

One thing that has become clear to me, rather recently, in these explorations is so much to the point that I must mention it. The problem is to get a theory of behavior over a period (week or longer). Such a period has a start and a finish. All I had done, by 1939, was concerned with the start. There ought to be a corresponding theory of the finish. It also would be a "point of time" theory, so one might think, and for a long time I did think, that it would be just like the theory of the start. But that is not correct. For there are two things that will have happened between start and finish: (1) informational things, the moving-on of expectations – I have nothing fresh to say about that – and (2) the actual things that have happened during the period. The things that happened before the start are bygones; for any analysis *of* the period they are data. But the things that happened during the period, though they have a similar place with regard to the finish of the period, do not have a similar place in the analysis of the period as a whole. They are part of what, in analysis of the period, has to be explained.

One major subject that this change in point of view affects is the determination of the rate of interest, discussed in a well-known chapter of *Value and Capital,* Part III. The argument of that chapter runs, of course, in temporary equilibrium terms; that is to say, it is just looking at the Monday, say the first Monday, in isolation. The Walrasian proof there given, that either the demand-supply for bonds or that for money may be eliminated, is in those terms perfectly valid. But if one looks at the period as a whole, comparing the end-equilibrium with the start-equilibrium, this is misleading. For suppose that there are no significant informational, or expectational, changes between start and finish; but there has been new borrowing, an increase, we may say, in the supply of bonds. If the bonds are held as money substitutes, as Keynes (and myself in 1939) must have been supposing them to be, the effect on the rate of interest must be a matter of liquidity preference (the LM curve of that old diagram). But, over the period, there is time for them to be taken up by additional saving; that is a possibility that should also be taken into account.

It could be that on some occasions the one might be more important, on other occasions the other. Thus it could be that Marshall, who was surely on this matter the "classical" theorist whom Keynes had most in mind, was mainly right in his day, while Keynes was mostly right in his. In ours, we should not commit ourselves to either view without looking around. (I don't think that the empirical "research" that would be required need be very arduous!)

I have just one more thing to say. I am firmly of the opinion that the use of Lindahl's approach to the theory of the income concept is by no means exhausted. It was not exhausted by what I said in *Value and Capital.* Only a few years ago (see Hicks, 1979) I managed to write a paper about capital gains (or capital profits) that I think went far toward clearing up that elusive concept. I showed that there are two (in principle) quite different meanings that have got superimposed: "external" and "exceptional" gains I called them. The former is an accountant's concept that economists find uninteresting; the latter is an economist's concept that does not appeal to the accountant since he cannot find a way of measuring it. I believe I showed (1) that there are significant business purposes for which the accountant's definition is appropriate, (2) that practical business, though it is unable to avoid doing its accounts in the accountant's manner, nevertheless shows, when it sets aside reserves, that it cannot altogether get away from the economist's concepts, and (3) that it is the latter which is properly relevant to questions of taxation, though since the taxing authority finds accounts presented to it in the other manner, it is faced with a problem of translation that is bound to be difficult. Incidentally, in terms of this analysis, Friedman's *permanent income,* Keynes's *user cost,* and Lindahl's own paradoxical *income as interest* all fit into their places. It was Lindahl himself who had provided the key. I could not have got the matter clear except by using what I got from him.

I am sure that there are many other ways in which new insights can still be drawn from that "old" Swedish economics. I hope that this meeting will be a stimulus to people to find them.

References

Hayek, Friedrich A. von (1928), "Das Intertemporale Gleichgewichtssystem der Preise und die Bewegungen des Geldwertes," *Weltwirtschaftliches Archiv,* 32.

Hicks, John (1932), *Theory of Wages.* London: Macmillan.

(1939), *Value and Capital.* London: Oxford University Press.

(1979), "The Concept of Business Income," in Hicks, *Classics and Moderns,* Vol. 3 of Collected Essays, Oxford: Blackwell, pp. 189–203. Original version in *Greek Economic Review,* December 1979, with the title "The Concept of Income in Relation to Taxation and Business Management."

Hicks, Ursula (1938), *The Finance of the British Government 1920–1936.* Oxford: Clarendon Press. Reprinted 1970 with a new introduction.

Lindahl, Erik (1933), "The Concept of Income," pp. 399–407, in *Economic Essays in Honour of Gustav Cassel.* London: Allen and Unwin.

(1939), *Studies in the Theory of Money and Capital.* London: Allen and Unwin.

Myrdal, Gunnar (1939), *Monetary Equilibrium.* London: William Hodge & Company, Ltd. German version "Der Gleichgewichtsbegriff als Instrument der Geldtheoretischen Analyse" in Friedrich A. von Hayek, ed., *Beiträge zur Geldtheorie,* Vienna, 1933.

Wicksell, Knut (1934), *Lectures on Political Economy,* Vol. I. London: Routledge and Sons. Translated by E. Classen from the Swedish original *Föreläsningar i nationalekonomi,* 3rd ed., Lund, 1928 (1st edition 1901).

CHAPTER 16

The London School of Economics and the Stockholm School in the 1930s

NADIM SHEHADI

Whereas the Stockholm School has been defined as a "school," it is not so easy to define the London School of Economics (LSE) as such. If one were to attribute such a definition to the LSE, it would not be in the field we are concerned with here – that of analytical deductive economics. The story of the Stockholm School and the LSE is best treated on the level of the interaction of individual members. However, the role played by Swedish ideas can best be demonstrated in the context of the battle of ideas that was going on in the 1930s and led to the establishment of Keynesian economics as the principal economic doctrine of the post–World War II era.

The material is rich and deserves a fuller account than can be accorded to it here. There is the influence on Hayek, which is treated in this volume by David Laidler; the influence on John Hicks, of which we also have a more direct account in this volume; and the relations between Gunnar Myrdal and Friedrich Hayek that culminated in their obtaining a joint Nobel Prize. The most interesting story, as far as our subject is concerned, is that of Brinley Thomas, who also gives a personal account of it himself (see Thomas, 1988). Brinley Thomas's lectures on Swedish economics at the LSE in the interwar period had an influence on George L. S. Shackle, who, as a result, changed the subject of his thesis. Lord Kaldor also figures in the story, but much later.

But first let us examine the historical and institutional background of the LSE and say a few words about the atmosphere in the 1930s. This is essential for understanding many of the episodes mentioned. The issues include the foundation of the school and its character, and the general question of economics in England and the place LSE took in that context.

The 1930s and the battle of ideas

As an economist F. A. von Hayek became world famous at the age of thirty-two; he was almost forgotten by the age of forty-one. In 1967 it is significant that Sir John Hicks (1967) sees it necessary in his article "The Hayek Story" to introduce Hayek to his readers as having been an economist of standing comparable to Keynes. This gives an indication of the "battle of ideas" that occurred in the 1930s. And it is in this context that the Stockholm–LSE interactions are best understood.

The LSE was founded mainly as an alternative center of economic learning to Alfred Marshall's Cambridge. The main currents that converged at the School upon its creation were opposed to analytical deductive economics and favored an historical inductive method.

In the 1930s, in addition to the external battle with Keynes, there was, at the LSE, an internal one being waged inside the School and on many fronts. One of these fronts was the difficult task of establishing a center for theoretical economics in an atmosphere that was essentially hostile to theory. Then there was the task of establishing the department vis-à-vis Cambridge and Keynes. A third front was within the department itself, where members of the junior faculty and graduate students were gradually shifting in allegiance to the other side. In this context Swedish ideas were the (not so) innocent bystanders.

Here, I want to investigate the interaction of personalities and ideas in an institutional setting, taking into account historical trends and forces at play (see Coats, 1982). This approach, while not leading to definite conclusions, provides us with an insight into the process of the rise and fall of ideas, with the many implications they have. For ideas are held by men, and the study of the propagation and establishment of ideas must therefore have a sociological dimension.

The Stockholm School is relevant here because it preceded Keynes but did not have the same impact: it was considered as "anticipant." In fact, very little is new in monetary theory, and the essence of the Keynes–Hayek differences were present in classical economics where Thornton is also regarded as an anticipant of Keynes. According to G. L. S. Shackle (1968, p. xv), Myrdal's essay that later became his *Monetary Equilibrium* "has been perhaps the most undervalued work of economic theory ever written"; what it lacked was "Keynes's personal charisma, the mind-seducing style of his thought and expression, and the vatic power and assurance of his attack." I might also add that there were institutional considerations such as Keynes being in Cambridge and writing in English. The atmosphere at Cambridge and in English economics in general was traditionally insular. This was even more so with Marshall and his disciples;[1] the motto was, "It's all in Marshall."

The LSE in the 1920s and 1930s was the main center of economic learning where continental economists were read in their original language and translations were initiated.[2] Economists of the LSE read and were influenced by the Austrians, the Swedes, Pareto, and Walras before some of these were translated into English. One of the forgotten influences here is Sir Theodore Gregory, who was the professor of banking and currency and introduced his students, of whom Robbins was one, to works in continental languages.[3] The teaching of Edwin Cannan planted irreverence toward Marshall in the students, and the continentals were an interesting alternative.

Many continental and American economists were frequent visitors to the School. "We had personal relations with most of the more interesting economists of the day and special lectures from a good many – Gottfried Haberler and Fritz Machlup from Vienna, Bresciani Turoni from Rome, Erik Lindahl, Bertil Ohlin and Ragnar Frisch from Scandinavia, Arthur W. Marget, Frank H. Knight, and Jacob Viner from the United States" (Robbins, 1971, p. 132). Joseph A. Schumpeter was also a frequent visitor and had senior common room rights.

Students were encouraged to take up a foreign language since the early days (Robbins got a distinction in German as an undergraduate), and many translations were initiated, of which Wicksell's *Lectures* is one. The LSE series of reprints is the best indication of this.

Economics at the School

The LSE was founded to promote a descriptive inductive method in the study of economics, what we now recognize more as economic history. This was the view of the Webbs and many of the early faculty at the School. Economics, or the analytical deductive brand of it that concerns us, had no real place in the ideas that were behind the creation of the School. When Lionel Robbins founded the department as we now know it, he was acting against the main currents present in the School. He had an internal battle to establish analytical economics in a school where most of the funds were allocated to a different sort of program. He also had the task of establishing a new center of economics – a discipline dominated by the Cambridge department. A quick review of the main figures in the development of economics at the School in the interwar period will give a clearer picture of the atmosphere.

Edwin Cannan

It is significant that Edwin Cannan was only part-time at the School, commuting from Oxford for his lectures. He joined LSE in 1895 at the School's foundation and until his retirement in 1926 taught the only courses in theoretical economics offered. Many of his students were to occupy prominent positions in the teaching of economics at the School, among whom we will mention people such as T. E. Gregory, Lionel Robbins, Arnold Plant, W. H. Hutt, Frederick Benham, and others.

Cannan's main preoccupation and lifelong obsession was to contradict Marshall and the Classics (see Kadish, 1983). He also advocated a simpler economics, accessible to everybody and hence a practical subject. He was against high theory and mathematical economics (see Cannan, 1933). What was most significant about Edwin Cannan is that he was all there was in terms of economics at the School at the time. His influence on his students was great and he "gave one a sense of the sweep and the power of the subject and its relevance to human happiness" (Robbins, 1971, pp. 86 ff.).

Allyn Young

Although a brilliant economic theorist and supervisor of Frank Knight and Edward Chamberlain, Allyn Young's period at the School was too short to have an impact. Young was not very efficient as an administrator (Robbins, 1971, pp. 119–21), but he had an influence on Nicholas Kaldor and wrote his most important article while he was at the LSE.[4] His appointment, however, was a turning point at the School because it was an important full-time chair in analytical economics instead of the part-time one Cannan had.

Sir William Beveridge

Another figure who had a major impact in the interwar period was Sir William Beveridge, who was director of the School from 1919 to 1937. His conception of economics, which he thought was in line with that of the Webbs, consisted of a vision to provide the natural basis of the social sciences. He thus introduced subjects such as social psychology and social biology and encouraged empirical inductive work. He was hostile to analytical economics.[5]

During the directorship of Beveridge the School grew considerably in size and importance. The main push for that was from the Laura Spelman Rockfeller Foundation. It is significant that the main negotiations between LSE and the Foundation happened in the mid-1920s when Beveridge had an almost completely free hand at the School and the money was given according to his program.

Lionel Robbins

When Lionel Robbins became professor in 1929 with the clear intention of promoting analytical, theoretical economics,[6] he was then working against the general trends in the School. He had been exposed to continental ideas of the Austrians, Pareto, the Lausanne School, and others.[7] Robbins imported Hayek from Austria to give lectures, and together they formed a team that was the nucleus of the economics department at the School.[8]

Many other forces were acting on Robbins when he took the chair. He was young and was founding a center for economic theory in a country that had been chiefly dominated by Cambridge. At the same time he was working against trends inside the School and in a setting where the major part of the finances had been designed for Beveridge-style research.

Lord Kaldor (1986, p. 4) gives us an account of Robbins at the time:

> young, flamboyant and enthusiastic (he was only thirty at the time of his appointment) and extremely devoted both to teaching and to economics as a subject. He lavished his energies and vitality on his pupils. . . .
>
> It was inevitable that those of us who were fortunate to have been among his first pupils . . . shoud fall completely under his spell. . . . For students of the present generation it is difficult to convey the atmosphere of creative tension and excitement which prevailed at LSE in the early years of the 1930s. Much of it was due to the youthful leadership of Robbins.

One can find similar statements about the atmosphere that give credit to Robbins.

Hayek

When F. A. von Hayek came to England looking for a place where English classical liberalism was still alive, and where he could pursue his analytical work in economics, he obviously came to the wrong institution. The major movements in the country that were opposed to liberalism and to analytical economics had themselves converged at the School.

Hayek succeeded, with Robbins, in forming a group of young theorists who were more or less like-minded about economics and could have all been called Hayekians at the time. Included in that group were people such as Hicks, Kaldor, Lerner, Lachman, and Ursula Webb; even Paul Sweezy was a passionate Hayekian at the time. In the words of Sir John Hicks (1982, p. 3):

> We seemed, at the start, to share a common viewpoint, or even, one might say, a common faith. . . . The faith in question was a belief in the free market, or "price-mechanism" – that a competitive system, free of all "interferences," by government or by monopolistic combinations, of capital or of labour, would easily find an "equilibrium." . . . Hayek, when he joined us, was to introduce into this doctrine an important qualification – that money (somehow) must be kept "neutral," in order that the mechanism should work smoothly. That . . . was to cause us quite a lot of trouble.

The two men were different. "While Hayek was the very model of a patient, courteous man of learning in pursuit of truth, Robbins was a much more emotional and passionate man, who could exude great warmth and enthusiasm but who could also flare up in towering rage."[9]

Although Hayek was not a militant and argumentative figure by temperament, he had come to Britain from a different atmosphere where the method of discourse was much more polemical. At Cambridge there was still the Marshallian tradition of avoiding public controversey to preserve the unity and reputation of the discipline.

The difference in style is well illustrated in the way Hayek reviewed Keynes's *Treatise on Money,* which led to a fruitless exchange involving Sraffa, and to some other incidents such as exchanges of letters in *The Times.* The LSE group begged to differ with Cambridge as a way of asserting themselves.

The story of Hayek and the Stockholm School is linked to the Austrian School's Wicksellian tradition. In the 1930s Hayek got interested in the ideas of Erik Lindahl, and he asked Lindahl to contribute to a book he was editing in German, *Beiträge zur Geldtheorie* (Hayek, 1933). Lindahl, who is well known for never meeting deadlines, excused himself and offered Myrdal instead. This resulted in Myrdal's famous article, *Der Gleichgewichtsbegriff als Instrument der Geldtheoretischen Analyse.* Although Hayek did not like the article and its policy conclusions, he felt honor bound to accept it but resented the fact. It is ironic that Hayek should have felt compelled to publish the article that made Myrdal famous outside Sweden. Although they had not much personal contact, the rivalry continued throughout both their careers. Hayek recalls not agreeing to allow Myrdal to give a lecture at LSE on the suggestion of

Brinley Thomas. Nicholas Kaldor was refused leave of absence by Hayek to join the Economic Commission for Europe under the direction of Myrdal in 1946. The relationship culminated in their obtaining a joint Nobel Prize.

Brinley Thomas

Returning from a two-year traveling scholarship, one year of which he spent in Germany and the other in Sweden, Brinley Thomas gave lectures on his experience in which he put forward Myrdal's ideas and at the same time criticized the neoclassical policies of Brüning in Germany.

The impressions he brought back with him, which he no doubt expounded in his lectures, were bound to displease Hayek and Robbins, and there is significant evidence that this had something to do with his not being promoted to a permanent position at the School for some time.

An indication of the lectures can be obtained from his writings at the time. While discussing his German experience, Thomas (1934, pp. 212–13) comments on the neoclassical deflationary measures adopted by Brüning:

> It was no coincidence that the phenomenal advance of the Nazi Party was contemporaneous with Dr. Brüning's "Heroic" emergency decrees and that its electoral strength began to ebb ... when the policy of extreme deflation had been followed by mild expansion! ... Brüning staked everything on the chance that a prompt application of the surgeon's knife would enable the patient to recover in a short space of time. He overestimated both the efficiency of the operation and the resisting power of the patient. If he could have foreseen what has subsequently happened to himself and to the unfortunate patient, it is doubtful whether he would have insisted on the necessity of such a serious operation.

As if that was not enough, there is a reference to Myrdal at this stage also:

> One or two authors have taken the other approach and have discussed the effect of various governmental measures on the course of the trade cycle [and here there is a footnote to Myrdal]. The fruitfulness of this latter type of theoretical enquiry depends on a satisfactory interpretation of industrial fluctuations ... when this has been done it will be profitable to pronounce the merits of various specimens of state policy applied at different phases of the cycle. (Thomas, 1934, pp. 211–12)

Monetary Policy and Crises is the book that resulted from Thomas's Swedish experience.

> It is only the accident of language which has prevented Swedish economic thought from exercising a greater influence on other countries. In the last few years, economic analysis in England has been enriched by the absorption of ideas from another small country – Austria. There is, however, a northern shrine where the English-speaking pilgrim may also derive inspiration, if he is prepared to take upon himself the burden of a difficult language. (Thomas, 1936, p. xx)

He proceeds to outline the theories of Lindahl and Myrdal and contrasts them with those of the Austrians and Mises and Hayek in particular. He recommended the theoretical and policy implications of the Swedes and in some places openly condemns the Hayekian framework (Thomas, 1936, pp. 97–101).

The lectures of Brinley Thomas played a major part in the conversion of the junior members in the LSE group to Keynesian ideas and the *General Theory*. Hicks, Kaldor, and Shackle have spoken of that impact.

John Hicks

Hicks is himself contributing his experience with the Stockholm School in this volume. It is important to note that although *Value and Capital* was published in 1939, it is largely a product of the LSE in the early 1930s. Following Hicks's career in the 1920s and 1930s is a fascinating exercise and reflects the major developments in the profession.

Hicks came to the LSE in 1926 from an Oxford PPE (philosophy, politics, and economics) degree where very little economics is acquired. He was introduced to Pareto, Walras, Wicksell, and the Austrians at the LSE chiefly through the influence of Robbins. "We were such good Europeans in London that it was Cambridge that seemed foreign" (Hicks, 1963, p. 306). He left the LSE in 1935 "owing to Beveridge's insensate hostility to pure theory" (Robbins, 1971, p. 129) and moved to Cambridge where he was associated with D. H. Robertson on the internal front. Both he and Robertson left Cambridge in 1938: Hicks for Manchester and Robertson to the LSE.

G. L. S. Shackle

An enthusiastic student of economics in the early 1930s, although not a student of LSE at the time, Shackle followed some of the lectures there. He later joined the School and started work with Hayek on Austrian capital theory until his encounter with the Swedish ideas through Brinley Thomas. He then changed his thesis to work on what became his *Expectations, Investment and Income.* In the introduction to the second edition of this work he describes the intellectual circumstances of writing the original text:

> To me, having no German, Myrdal's ideas became known only through a lecture course given by Mr Brinley Thomas in 1935 on his return to the London School of Economics from a year in Sweden. His class was a mere half-dozen, or less, but he had one deeply excited hearer. I emerged with only an inkling of what Myrdal had said, but the idea of *ex ante* and *ex post,* of the vital role of expecations, had struck fire into my thoughts. The excitement that I found in this perspective was doubtless enhanced by the lecturer's charismatic spell; to have joined his class in the first place, I must have had some notion of what was afoot; but the argument itself plainly found in me some natural and instinctive echo and response. When in October of that year, in Cambridge (on a visit which a number of London and Oxford research students had organised for that purpose) I heard from Mrs Joan Robinson and Mr Kahn an exposition of what was in the forthcoming *General Theory,* the two elements of this present book came into contact. I tore up a year's work on the Austrian theory of capital (retaining a life long feeling for its essential beauty and a profound admiration for its modern recreator, professor Hayek) and began to study the new Keynesianism in the light of the new Wicksellianism. (Shackle, 1968)

When Shackle (1967) wrote his retrospective assessment of the period in *The Years of High Theory,* there was barely any reference to Hayek.

The reaction of the "Old Guard" of the department, that is, of Hayek and Robbins, was to try to restrict the divulgence of these ideas. On the other hand, no plausible theoretical framework was put forward at the time. Hugh Dalton, on a visit to Germany in the spring of 1933, noted, "Geistige Gluchschaltung (intellectual co-ordination) is the Nazi ideal in education. There is something of this too in the economics department of the school of economics."[10] This statement is, of course, much too serious to be quoted now. What was going on at the LSE then is not an uncommon occurrence in academic departments.

Robbins and Hayek were true liberals and believers in academic freedom, but they were carried away with trying to establish an analytical free-market department in a world moving away from those ideas. Ideological factors were important, no doubt, but the internal politics of the School sometimes transcended ideological boundaries. Robbins and Laski had no problems cooperating when a confrontation with Beveridge over the chair in social biology was at hand.

Disintegration of the LSE group

In the period between the *Treatise on Money* and the *General Theory* there were the beginnings of the disintegration of the LSE group. Young members of the faculty started getting interested in the goings on at Cambridge and made contacts with people there. Abba Lerner was the main link. There was a joint London and Cambridge Seminar that was a gathering in a pub between junior members of both faculties.[11] The *Review of Economic Studies* was formed at that time.

By the time the *General Theory* appeared there were noted differences between the older members of the faculty and the junior faculty, which reflected themselves in promotions within the department. Abba Lerner left for the United States. When Hayek and Robbins were confronted with the choice of keeping either Lerner or Kaldor, Hayek favored Lerner and Robbins favored Kaldor. Although Kaldor stayed, he was never promoted to senior status as befitted his then international reputation.

The LSE at the time was described as a court where the favorites were the ones who adhered to the Neo-Classical principles and the non-favorites were those who had affinities to Keynesian ideas. The former got promotion; the latter were weeded out gradually. Brinley Thomas left in the late 1930s to work on population; Hicks left in 1935 to go to Cambridge; Lerner went to the United States.

Kaldor was the most resilient and stayed on until after the war. He had become an ardent critic of Hayek, and this was apparent through seminars and later through his article on the "Concertina Effect." But he had to resign when Hayek refused to grant him leave to go to Geneva and join the Economic Commission for Europe under Myrdal. Kaldor was introduced to Myrdal by Hicks, who had read him in German:

> and it was owing to him [Hicks] that I was put on the track (among others) of the younger Swedish economists, particularly Myrdal, who first made me realise the shortcomings of the "monetarist" approach of the Austrian School of von Mises and von Hayek and made me such an easy convert to Keynes after the appearance of the *General Theory* three years later. (Kaldor, 1986, p. 7)

The reaction of Hayek and Robbins to the behavior of their juniors is interesting. There was a kind of censorship of their ideas either through not promoting them in their posts or even directly preventing them from lecturing on certain topics. Robbins asked Kaldor not to lecture his students on Keynes because it would confuse them, and even attended his class to make sure he did not. Myrdal was invited to give a talk and was prevented from coming. Even Keynes was prevented from giving a talk in the lecture room and had to give it in the graduate student common room, which was packed to the stairs.

By the late 1930s the rift was greater, and even students felt it. Hayek was almost isolated by then. Lachman says that the only two Austrians left in the department were himself and Hayek.[12] Robbins' shift away from Hayek came later during the war.

One of the students in the second half of the 1930s, Tibor Scitovsky, describes how he had to strike a balance between his integrity and his objective of passing his exams. He had fears that if he used Keynesian terms, he would fail.[13]

The role of the Stockholm School

What I have been trying to outline in this paper are events and circumstances that might help us understand the process through which ideas get established and are accepted. This is one of the phases of the battle of ideas. There is no doubt that ideas are in themselves very important. But important ideas can be bypassed and history shows that false ideas can become established.

The theories of the Stockholm School have not received the recognition they deserve. The postwar world has been described as the Keynesian era and not as the Stockholm era. As far as the LSE is concerned, the Stockholm School played a major role in the conversion of people to the *General Theory*. It would be interesting to speculate what would have happened had the LSE been more "liberal" in its acceptance of these ideas. The geographical and linguistic handicap of the Stockholm School would have been overcompensated for in the English-speaking world had the LSE become a platform for its propagation. Apart from being theoretically more refined, the ideas of the Stockholm School had the experience of their application in their favor, and the circumstances at the time made the world of economics receptive to such ideas.

Notes

1 See T. W. Hutchinson (1955, pp. 1–16): "from the 1890s down to 1914, contemporary with the predominance of Marshall and his school, the flow of economic ideas into Britain from abroad and their acceptance and appreciation dries up considerably."

2 A good indication of this is given by browsing through H. E. Batson (1983) (with an introduction by Lionel Robbins).

3 Obituary of Gregory by Robbins in *LSE Magazine* (1973). Gregory seems to have been out of favor at the School in the 1930s; this is indicated in correspondence with Cannan.

4 See Young (1928). See also *Journal of Post Keynesian Economics* (1985) on the occasion of Kaldor's seventy-fifth birthday.
5 See Robbins (1971, pp. 129 and 158), Jose Harris (1977), and Beveridge's own account of the period in Beveridge (1960).
6 See his inaugural lecture (Robbins, 1930).
7 See Robbins (1971), especially Chapters 4 and 5.
8 There is no evidence that Robbins had met Hayek before he came to the School. Hayek seems to have been in contact with Gregory.
9 Durbin (1985, p. 102). On an intellectual level Hayek had himself and Robbins in mind in his essay "Two Types of Mind": one is the innovator and the other the master of his subject. (Author's interview with Hayek.)
10 Quoted in Durbin (1985, p. 103).
11 There is an account of this in Robinson (1978, p. xv).
12 Interview with professor Lachman by professor W. W. Bartley III.
13 Interview with professor Scitovsky.

References

Batson, H. E. (1930), *A Select Bibliography of Modern Economic Theory, 1870–1929*. London: George Routledge and Sons.

Beveridge, William (1960), *The London School of Economics and its Problems: 1919–1937*. London: Allen & Unwin.

Cannan, Edwin (1933), "The Need for Simpler Economics," *Economic Journal,* 44 (September), 367–78.

Coats, A. W. (1982), "The Distinctive LSE Ethos in the Interwar Years," *Atlantic Economic Journal,* 10.1 (March), 18–34.

Durbin, Elizabeth (1985), *The New Jerusalems: The Labour Party and the Economics of Democratic Socialism*. London: Routledge and Kegan Paul.

Harris, Jose (1977), *William Beveridge: A Biography*. Oxford: Clarendon Press.

Hayek, F. A. von (1933), *Beiträge zur Geldtheorie*. Vienna: Springer.

Hicks, J. R. (1963), *The Theory of Wages,* London: Macmillan.

    (1967), "The Hayek Story," in *Critical Essays in Monetary Theory*. Oxford: Clarendon, pp. 203–15.

    (1982), *Money, Interest, and Wages*. Oxford: Blackwell.

Hutchinson, T. W. (1955), "Insularity and Cosmopolitanism in Economic Ideas, 1870–1914," *American Economic Review. Papers and Proceedings,* pp. 1–16.

Kadish, Alon (1983), "Cannan vs Marshall and the History of Economic Thought," in *Research in the History of Economic Thought and Methodology: A Research Annual,* vol. 1, pp 61–77. London: JAI Press.

Kaldor, Lord (1986), "Recollections of an Economist," *Banca Nazionale del Lavoro Quarterly Review,* March, pp. 3–26.

Robbins, Lionel (1930), "The Present Position of Economic Science," *Economica,* pp. 14–24.

    (1971), *Autobiography of an Economist*. London: Macmillan.

Robinson, Joan (1978), *Contributions to Modern Economics*. Oxford: Blackwell.
Shackle, G. L. S. (1967), *The Years of High Theory*. London: Cambridge University Press.
  (1968), *Expectations, Investment and Income,* 2nd ed. Oxford: Clarendon Press.
Thomas, Brinley (1934), "Germany," in H. Dalton, ed., *Unbalanced Budgets.* London: Routledge, pp. 19–216.
  (1936), *Monetary Policy and Crises: A Study of the Swedish Experience.* London: George Routledge.
  (1988), "Memories of the Stockholm School and the London School of Economics," forthcoming in L. Jonung, ed., *The Stockholm School of Economics Remembered.*
Young, Allyn (1928), "Increasing Returns and Economic Progress," *Economic Journal,* December, pp. 527–42.

Comment

BRINLEY THOMAS

Shehadi succeeds in capturing an important aspect of the spirit of LSE in the 1930s. Those who had the good fortune to start their careers there will agree that it was a place of unique intellectual excitement. I remember the day I was appointed Assistant Lecturer. Lionel Robbins took me to the Senior Common Room, saying "You are now entering a republic – we're all equal here. Make yourself at home." I was warmly greeted by the assembled company – Beveridge, Bowley, Tawney, Dalton, Postan, Laski, Eileen Power, Hogben. There would never be a dull moment in that Common Room.

Inside the Economics Department there was plenty of excitement. Robbins had become Chairman at the age of thirty and, with energy and enthusiasm, he was determined to make LSE a leading center of economic theory. It is important to recall that there were two battles going on. The director of LSE, Sir William Beveridge, was strongly opposed to Robbins's emphasis on pure theory against empirical work. As Shehadi points out, it was ". . . Beveridge's insensate hostility to pure theory" that caused John Hicks to leave LSE for Cambridge in 1935. On this front Robbins had the support of his colleagues and was bound to win. This was not true of his other ambition – to hitch LSE's wagon to the Viennese star. Even before 1936 it was evident that this battle he was bound to lose. The following list of lecture courses for graduates at LSE in 1935–6 speaks for itself.

Hayek	Capital and Interest
	Selected Problems of Advanced Economics II
	Problems of a Collectivist Economy
	Development of English Classical Economy
Robbins	Selected Problems of Advanced Economics I
Hayek, Robbins, and Plant	Economic Aspects of Social Institutions
Allen	Econometrics and Mathematical Economics
Kaldor	Theory and Practice of Tariff-making
Ursula Hicks	The Italian Contribution to Economic Theory
Thomas	Recent Economic Thought in Sweden

The Department was split between those who accepted and those who rejected the Hayek-Robbins line – favorites and the nonfavorites, respectively. In 1935 most of the young economists – Durbin, Hicks, Kaldor, Lerner, and Shackle – welcomed the ideas of the Stockholm School, and this helped to intensify the interest in the epoch-making book that Keynes was expected to publish soon. Supporting the orthodox line were the "old guard" – Paish, Schwartz, Benham, and Coase. The ruling powers were passionate believers in freedom, and this included freedom to adjust the constraints within which freedom was exercised by the nonfavorites. The main type of adjustment was the postponement of tenure. In my own case I did not receive tenure until, on the advice of Sir Alexander Carr-Saunders, I moved from monetary theory to migration and economic growth.

Shehadi has given a valuable account of the "battle of ideas" at LSE in the 1930s.

CHAPTER 17

Thoughts on the Stockholm School and on Scandinavian economics

PAUL A. SAMUELSON[1]

We are gathered to celebrate the fiftieth anniversary of something, that something being what Bertil Ohlin defined in 1937 as the Stockholm School. At the same time we could be said to be celebrating the fiftieth birthday of Erik Lundberg's 1937 book, *Studies in the Theory of Economic Expansion*. Or, becoming more personal, we are celebrating also the fiftieth anniversary of Erik Lundberg's thirtieth birthday and thereby acknowledging his three score and twenty milestone.

On this occasion I do not want to focus primarily on the single big question: Did that collective called the Stockholm School independently generate the same paradigm that Keynes published in his 1936 *General Theory of Employment, Money and Interest?* Bertil Ohlin certainly claimed that to be the case in his famous *Economic Journal* articles of 1937. Abba Lerner (1940) and Don Patinkin (1978, 1982) have documented their disagreements with this Ohlin claim, and I must record a measure of agreement with their objective discountings.

I find it useful to broaden my discussion. Stockholm is one city in Sweden, and Sweden is one country in Scandinavia, a region whose scholars understand each others' languages. I believe that Scandinavian economics is a useful category to survey and analyze. At the least, it was that prior to the mid-twentieth century when English became the lingua franca for economic science pretty much everywhere in the world.

Teleologists postulate that if our coat sleeves contain buttons, they must have been put there by the Darwinian gods for a purpose. Separation of the species must, by similar reasoning, perform an ecological function. Differentiation of languages has since the time of the Tower of Babel permitted different places to have somewhat different scientific and scholarly traditions.

This has disadvantages and advantages. During World War II in the U.S. scientific defense establishment, there was sometimes a deliberate design to set independent research parties working on the same task.

391

They might even be prohibited from communicating with each other, lest the chance originality of a fresh approach be inhibited. Working against this Balkanization was of course any economy of scale in research. Ideally, the best of both worlds might perhaps be attained by use of a referee, who learns all that each source discovers but only selectively communicates to any what is deemed best for them to know. F. Y. Edgeworth at the turn of the century was just such an economist referee.

The separate languages of English, French, German, Dutch, Russian, and Swedish-Danish-Norwegian willy-nilly used to occasion something of such a mixed pattern of decentralization and centralization in economics. Educated scholars knew their own language and one or more universal tongues, such as Latin, French, or English. But knowing a foreign language and being really comfortable in it are different things. Clifford Truesdell, editor of Euler's works and a rational mechanist, has regretted that science abandoned the easy renaissance Latin that was the Esperanto for Newton and Euler.

Spatial localization, even within one language, can produce and sustain some differentiations of emphasis: The Austrian deductive school begun by Carl Menger, so different from the German Historical Schools, provides a case in point. The universities of northernmost Europe gained in unity of viewpoint from their unity of language. And yet, with the possible unimportant exception of Finland, the German and English tongues were sufficiently similar to those of Scandinavia to keep the various subcultures interconnected.

As far as the world of scholarship is concerned, the fifty years just gone by have tipped the previous pattern of differentiation in the direction of an all-encompassing English. A Maurice Allais who writes only in French may risk his right to a fair hearing, and involved here is the language of Voltaire and Benjamin Franklin. Once upon a time a young scholar published his less-than-best articles in the local-language journal. Or she might have two reputations: the one first earned at home, and the same one earned abroad.

Much that once upon a time was now no longer obtains. We have added some geographically dispersed academic journals in English and lost some native-language journals. The process is a self-perpetuating, self-aggravating one. The less modern students know non-English languages, the less they need to know them. More gets translated into English. More gets originally published in English. If a generation of scholars go off on a tangent, or stagnate, they tend to do so everywhere together. The flame of civilization does not burn on in Timbuktu or Copenhagen when it is flickering away in Cambridge or Rome. When one species dominates all of nature, the risk of extinction when the environment rolls new dice is hardly reduced.

The broad view

For almost a century Swedish economics has been first rate. The quartet of Knut Wicksell, Gustav Cassel, Eli Heckscher, and David Davidson compares well with Britain's Francis Edgeworth, Maynard Keynes, Alfred Marshall, and A. C. Pigou; with America's Irving Fisher, John Bates Clark, Frank Taussig, and Frank Knight; with Austria's Carl Menger, Eugen von Böhm-Bawerk, Josef Schumpeter, and Friedrich von Wieser; with Italy's Vilfredo Pareto, Enrico Barone, and Maffeo Pantaleoni; and with France's Leon Walras, A. A. Cournot, and Jules Dupuit.

The first Swedish giants begot new Scandinavian stars: Bertil Ohlin, Erik Lindahl, Gunnar Myrdal, Ragnar Frisch (of Norway), and Erik Lundberg, to name just a few.

Moreover, Sweden after 1930 was moving into the stage of State Interventionism. The prescriptions of economists were in demand. Nature abhors a vacuum. And if academic economists will not fill that demand, a kind of Gresham's Law will operate to call forth a requisite supply from elsewhere. Swedish academic economists were only too eager in the first half of this century to supply political advice and activism. After Britain was forced to devalue the pound in September of 1931, Scandinavia detached from the old gold parities with her. And this gave Swedish economists the opportunity to prescribe internal macroeconomic stimulation. In the end, as Seymour Harris (1936) was one of the first to discern, the 1931 devaluation was not so much a beggar-my-neighbor tort by Britain and the Sterling Bloc against France, Belgium, and the United States as it was the liberating device that permitted the Sterling Bloc to engineer internally their early autonomous recovery: What importing they ceased to do by virtue of the depreciation-induced dearness of imports was largely offset by the incremental demand for imports occasioned by their incremental level of aggregate income. In Sweden even the conservative Cassel and Heckscher were money activists in the depression, to the nation's benefit.

The four economists who were commissioned in late 1931 by the Committee on Unemployment – Ohlin, Myrdal, Hammarskjöld, and Johansson – and who published their separate results in the 1933–5 period, were all de facto effective-demand economists. I only wish I knew Swedish so that I could compare their intuitions with those of heterodox contemporaries in Europe and North America. Nor should we make too much of the testimony of Ernst Wigforss, the laborite finance minister after 1932, that he was little affected by Sweden's domestic economists. That is standard drill. Roosevelt's Secretary of the Treasury, Henry Morgenthau, Jr., was if anything anti-Keynesian. And most 1933–6 New Deal policies relied little on respectable macroeconomic analysis. Nonetheless, the influence of Lauchlin Currie, Alvin Hansen, and Keynesianism was important for 1936–80 American fiscal policy. Live, as well as dead, economists have influence that those influenced are not always fully aware of.

A formal theory of output as a whole

Bertil Ohlin was not a shrinking violet when it came to making claims for the originality of either his international trade innovations or his macroeconomic innovations. I judge Bertil to be less diffident in this regard than Knut Wicksell was. Knut valued himself, I am sure, but at this moment the only explicit claim for originality that I can recall his making was in connection with his 1923 assertion concerning the detection of alleged logical error in Ricardo in his third edition's chapter on machinery where David contended that a viable invention could depress a society's real gross equilibrium product. Wicksell (1923 and 1981, p. 201) remarks, "I may be mistaken but as far as I know I am myself the first who has pointed out that Ricardo's conclusion as to a possible diminution of the gross product is *wrong*." [It is ironical that Knut happens to be incorrect on this point, as is argued in Samuelson (1988, 1989)!]

Gustav Cassel by contrast was notorious for his excessive immodesties and his unannounced borrowings from others. Fate has taken a cruel revenge. Both in Scandinavia and abroad Cassel is, I believe, valued below his true worth, which certainly puts him in the first ten of the turn-of-the-century scholars. If we devise a coefficient for blowing one's own horn, and put Gustav at 100 and Knut at 5, I fear Bertil must be placed around 30. That means his contentions do need careful auditings. Prior to refreshing my impressions from Lerner and Patinkin, on rereading Ohlin (1937) I was struck by the following thoughts.

Wicksell's price-level preoccupation

Ohlin exaggerated, I believe, when he wrote (1937, p. 53) that Wicksell's 1898 classic and his later writings contained "the embryo of a 'theory of output as whole.'" If we write nominal output as PQ, my recent rereadings of Wicksell surprised me by his preoccupation with the P factor to the neglect of the Q. Wicksell rashly advocated restoration of exchange parities after World War I, playing down the toll on Q to be expected from an overvalued currency. His polemics with Ricardo espouse curing unemployment by having wage rates float downward to clear markets – in simple Say's Law fashion. Wicksell's business cycle theory was concerned with Spiethoff-like exogenous technical shocks, resonating with the system's endogenous natural periodicities (like a child's rocking horse, as he put it). Wicksell's well-known cumulative processes, which Ohlin and his generation are so concerned with, primarily involve long-time trends in dP/dt that will result from discrepancies between Wicksell's natural interest rate and the market interest rate. Those few passages in Wicksell's writings that go beyond this are to me remarkable for their rarity.

Wicksell was a *quantity theory* economist. He says so and Ohlin's generation would be wrong to deny this. Wicksell does go beyond those who regard M as purely exogenous and V as constant in a $PQ = MV$ tautology. Systematic discrepancies between the natural and market interest rates drive M upward (or downward); and any resulting trend for the right-hand side of the tautology, Wicksell regards as working its effects chiefly on the trend in P and not primarily or systematically on Q.

When Wicksell emphasized alterations in "credit," engineered by the banks even when the total of metal M was little changing, he does seem to have in the back of his mind a theory of augmentable V velocity. In terms of Irving Fisher's 1911 identity

$$PQ = MV + M'V'$$

where these velocities are altered to be "income" rather than "transaction" velocities, and where M' is some kind of *bank* money. Wicksell did seem to believe that the PQ/M ratio was manipulatable by engineering *market* interest rates above or below *real interest rates in natura.* But it is fatal to Ohlin's claims concerning pre–*General Theory* innovations that Wicksell regarded contrived variations in the right-hand side of either tautology as having its effects almost exclusively on the P factor alone. What Wicksell liked about Irving Fisher's macroeconomics was not his suggestive debt-deflation theory of depressions or his money-illusion preoccupation. Rather it was primarily to improve Fisher's gimmicks for stabilizing P that Wicksell concerned himself in writing for the *Quarterly Journal of Economics* an article that F. W. Taussig refused just prior to World War I.

Ohlin tries to make something of the fact that Wicksell, and later his protégé Erik Lindahl, speak of PQ as being determined by a flow of spending out of "income." Arthur Marget, I seem to recall, found similar turns of phrase in Ralph Hawtrey, Josef Schumpeter, and Leon Walras. This is thought to be a move away from having the stock of M or of (M,M'), generating the spending that constituted PQ with the help of some V or (V,V') concept of velocity. Be that as it may, why is such a paradigm a necessary departure from a doctrine of neutrality-of-the-absolute-price level? The left-hand expression PQ can involve primarily trends in P alone even when the right-hand side is varied in its formulation.

The tyranny of a doctrine of neutral money in the short run, which clouded the mind of Lloyd Mints, my first teacher of macroeconomics at Chicago, is coming somewhat back into fashion. The most that I can concede to Ohlin is that scholars with an income-stream approach to PQ are less likely to reify short-run velocity of M if their expositions skirt around the mentioning of V symbols.

Other Swedish macrotheorists

The original title suggested for this piece was something like "Influence Abroad of the Stockholm School." Had I not broken away from that label, this might have been an embarrassingly short lecture. Using myself and my many friends as guinea pigs, I might have summed up tersely as follows:

1. Erik Lundberg's numerical sequences (linear difference equations) were widely read in 1937 and thereafter.

2. Ohlin's 1937 claims for a Stockholm School were widely read. We gave him the benefit of the doubt but had no way to confirm his contentions.

3. Ragnar Frisch's work in Oslo and in the 1933 Cassel Festschrift were well known. So was his 1931 work on the acceleration principle, which benefited from his 1931 American sojourn with Alvin Hansen in Minneapolis.

4. Save for John Hicks, few of us knew Lindahl's work – except his thesis carrying forward the public-goods concepts of Wicksell. Late in the 1930s Lindahl's work to clarify time-phased concepts of income *was* well thought of but not carefully studied outside of Hicksian circles.

Lindahl did publish in 1939, and perhaps even as early as 1930 in Swedish, a definitional equation that I can write as

Total spending $=$ consumption spending $+$ investment spending
$$= E = P_c Q_c + P_I Q_I$$

$P_c Q_c/E = 1 - s$, a hypothetical parameter that is constant. But this system leaves us shy of the equations needed to have a determinate theory of (E, Q_c, Q_I, P_c, P_I). Someone should check whether he stipulated something about P_tQ_t as an exogenous creature of animal spirits or otherwise. Unless he did that, Lindahl would seem not to have reached as far as Kahn (1931), and those who know Swedish should tell us just when Lindahl first did what he did do.

5. Having caught echoes of Gunnar Myrdal's *ex ante* and *ex post* terminology, we expected great things from translation of his 1933 *Monetary Equilibrium*. Using myself as typical, we found the book anticlimactic. My first reading of it discerned even less on systematic variation of Q in PQ than even such austere critics as Abba Lerner and Don Patinkin have been able to unearth.

6. After World War II, I heard Bertil Ohlin at Harvard say new and exciting things about the economics of over-full-employment. When I early tried out in Stockholm my notions of a liberal pro-investment policy based on austere fiscal programs fully compensated by easy-money programs, I learned this was old hat there – called by critics of Gunnar Myrdal, "the socialization of thrift."

7. Scandinavia's second golden age in economics – say from 1930 to 1950 – seemed to regress back eventually toward the mean. The diagnosis I heard about most on my visits to Northern Europe was to the effect that temptations of public service and consultancies to banks, corporations, and international agencies caused the wine of talent to be consumed too green. I added on my own, diplomatically only in my own boudoir, that the cynicism toward mathematics in economics and econometrics expressed by most of Sweden's wise academics conduced to her falling behind in the treasure hunt of recent science. (I had to admit that Frisch's capture of Norwegian academic economics, which certainly was not anti-mathematics in ideology, did not forestall that country's retrogression as a place for sabbatical visits by leading young economists. And the Netherlands, after a longer-lasting time in the sun, also seemed to lose ground relative to the colossus of America with its affluent resources for research support.)

Tracing origins

Although I do not focus here on the degree to which a Stockholm School anticipated Keynes's *General Theory,* independently formulated it, or influenced non-Scandinavian economists in developing such macroeconomics, let me say a few words on this subject. Reversing Axel Leijonhufvud's thesis by 180 degrees and disagreeing gently with Robert Clower, I identify what was scientifically important in Keynes as the macroeconomic paradigm that the advanced and elementary texts dub to be Keynesian. (This does not belittle Keynes's personal wisdoms, nor his never fully articulate perceptions and hypotheses. It puts them in their proper place within the history of the living science of economics.)

The single most important core of the Keynesian revolution was its theory of output as a whole as determined by effective demand, which is a sea change from Walrasian market-clearing equilibrium. In baldest form this can be written as

$$
\begin{aligned}
&\text{Income} = \text{consumption} + \text{investment} \\
&Y = C + I \qquad \text{definition} \\
&C = f(Y), 0 < f'(Y) < 1 \qquad \text{propensity to consume} \\
&I = \bar{I} \text{ or } \bar{I}(t) \qquad \text{autonomous investment}
\end{aligned} \tag{1}
$$

This is the "multiplier" doctrine.[2] Its formulation, in my view, ante-dates the early 1936 publication of Keynes's book. As an example, there is Richard Kahn's 1931 *Economic Journal* paper. J. M. Clark quasi-independently arrived at similar notions when studying for the Carnegie Foundation the economics of World War I, and how belligerents' demand for U.S. exports induced a positive (but *limited*) rise in our output. J. M. Clark's *Economics of Planning Public Works* was published in 1935, before the *General Theory* but with knowledge by then of Kahn's work and Keynes's 1933 *Means to Prosperity*. I shall show that Clark's dynamic sequences, which resemble some in Erik Lundberg (1937), D. H. Robertson (1939), and Fritz Machlup (1939), are *logically isomorphic* with my equation (1) and thus spell out the essential identity between Kahn of 1931 and Keynes of 1936. I do not expect Don Patinkin will agree with this, but on the present occasion I am under oath to give my opinion.

Many writers other than Clark presented, in the years 1932–5, analyses much like his in their essential content. I pick these dates because my own study of economics begins with the New Year of 1932 and I am staying with my own impressions. Sumner Slichter, I recall, in his published lectures given in Utah, stressed that consumption is passive and driven by active investment. (Slichter regarded himself as anti-Keynesian. When I mentioned to Alvin Hansen years after Slichter's death how implicitly Keynesian Slichter had often been, suggesting he had never realized it, the gentle Hansen said uncharacteristically: "I always thought of Sumner as a closet Keynesian.")

I concede that the historian of thought wishes to distinguish between writers who self-consciously utilize what they perceive to be a new paradigm and those who are driven by the new data to depart, without always realizing it, from accepted paradigms. Don Patinkin thus does have a point. But so do I. And in connection with this conference, I have to judge that the Swedish economists of the 1931–4 period coherently analyzed the increase in real and nominal income that would be generated by unconventional fiscal stimuli. In those years of the great depression, those Swedes would have regarded as a crank a John the Baptist (to Robert Lucas) who insisted on Say's Law, market-clearing mechanisms, and neutral-money responses of the price level to continued programs of fiscal and central-bank stimulus. Unlike Patinkin, I would not so curtly dismiss Frisch's models of circulation planning as not being pre-Keynes stepping stones.

In my reading, Maynard Keynes at the 1931 Harris Foundation conference already showed signs of postulating equation (1)'s $f(Y)$ propensity-to-consume function.[3] Although Michal Kalecki almost missed having equation (1)'s system for Y because of his extreme preoccupation with the profit-investment nexus, I believe Patinkin strains at a gnat when he seems to deny as a consumption function Kalecki's 1939 form of $f(Y)$, in which $f'(Y)$ is the constant fraction of income that workers receive in a world where capitalists save *all* of their extra income and workers save *none* of theirs. That constitutes a well-defined propensity-to-consume function. I regard the claims on behalf of Kalecki's originality by Joan Robinson and Lawrence Klein as overblown, and I regard Kalecki's polar case of worker's and capitalists' saving propensities as empirically bizarre. But once Kalecki at whatever date came to stipulate an equation relating the share and magnitude of profits to each level of income, Kalecki's investment-profit multiplier model did become logically isomorphic with my system in equation (1).

The wider Keynesian system involves, along with Y, the variables for interest rates and for endogenous investment – all as being affectable by the exogenous stock of money M. A dozen reviewers of the *General Theory,* most of whom were in constant contact with Keynes, discerned in that book the following amplification of equation (1):

$$Y = C + I \tag{2a}$$
$$= f(Y) + g(r,Y) \qquad g_r < 0, 0 < g_y < 1 - f' < 1$$
$$M = m(Y,r) \qquad m_y > 0, m_r < 0 \tag{2b}$$
$$= Y/V(r) \qquad \text{say, } V'(r) > 0$$

Relations between output, Y, and employment, E, were also specified in Keynes (1936).

Once deep-depression conditions were left behind, endogenous changes in the price level, P, became a concern. By 1940 relations like $PY = y$ were studied; M in the equation (2b) $m(Y,r)$ relation was replaced by M/P; and relations determining (P, nominal wage rate) were beginning to be investigated.

Where equation (2) differs from equation (1), I believe the pre-1936 anticipations of Keynes are harder to identify. Thus, the Chicago tradition that I knew so well in 1932–5 involved (a little but) precious little of equation (2). Nor were Irving Fisher's formalisms much better, despite his perceptive fears of debt deflation. What I would have to add to Patinkin's excellent debunking of a mythical subtle oral tradition at Chicago is that Patinkin exaggerates the degree to which the Chicago of 1925–40 differed from the universal $MV = PQ$ orthodoxy. As an example, all ten of the Big Ten universities subscribed to Fisher-Marshall-Pigou-1923 Keynes paradigms.

Let me analyze the 1935 Clark dynamics to show that it and Kahn (1931) are indeed predecessors to the equation (1) 1936 multiplier doctrine, in quite the same sense as historians of science have properly regarded Galileo's falling-body analysis as a predecessor of Newton's gravitational laws and a breakthrough away from Aristotelian physics.

Clark (1935, pp. 91–2) contemplated the difference equation

$$Y_t = C_t + I_t \qquad t = \ldots, -1, 0, 1, 2, \ldots \tag{2}$$
$$= \tfrac{2}{3} Y_{t-1} + I_t \qquad I_t \equiv 0, t < 0; \ I_t \equiv \overline{I} > 0, t \geqq 0$$

He graphs its solution

$$Y_t = (1 + \tfrac{2}{3} + \ldots + \tfrac{2}{3}^t)\overline{I} \tag{3}$$
$$= \frac{\overline{I}}{1 - \tfrac{2}{3}}(1 - \tfrac{2}{3}^{t+1})$$

$$\lim_{t \to \infty} Y_t = Y_\infty = \frac{\overline{I}}{1 - \tfrac{2}{3}} \tag{4}$$

where Y_∞ is seen by any reader to be definable precisely as in my equation (1), namely, by

$$Y_\infty = C_\infty + I_\infty = (MPC)Y + \overline{I} \qquad Y = \frac{\overline{I}}{1 - MPC}, \tag{5}$$
$$0 < MPC < 1$$

Clark's graph of the asymptotic steady states makes clear equation (1)'s paradigm for "output as a whole" as determined by the response to autonomous investment of income so as to achieve the level of induced saving that matches postulated investment. QED.

If we grant the logical isomorphism to Keynes's equation (1) in Clark (1935), can we logically refuse it to Kahn of 1931 and Keynes of 1933? Not by my canons of hair splitting.

History-of-science precedent

A word about Galileo. Using hymn singing as his clock, he could observe that a ball released a short distance above the earth will display short-period downward ("average") velocities proportional to the odd digits: 1, 3, 5, ... Not knowing calculus, Galileo still had the perception of an *instantaneous* velocity – which would be 2 at the time just between the time intervals with adjacent average velocities 1 and 3, and likewise for 4 between 3 and 5, and so forth – a serendipitous simplification provided by the quadratic case. The total distances fallen by the end of the time intervals (1, 2, 3, . . .) were seen by him to be 1, 1 + 3 = 4, 1 + 3 + 5 = 9, . . . ; these were perceived to obey the quadratic formula (1, $2^2, 3^2, 4^2, \ldots, t^2$), or

$$\text{distance} - (\text{velocity})^2 \equiv \text{constant} = 0 \tag{6}$$

The above formula[4] was later generalized by Leibniz and others to the law of conservation of (mechanical) energy.

Now for Newton. He regarded the ball as being attracted (or "accelerated") toward the earth's center by a force proportional to 1/(radius of earth + altitude of ball)$^2 \approx$ 1/(radius of earth)^2, an approximate constant.

Therefore, Newton can write in terms of second and first time derivatives

$$\ddot{x} = -g, \dot{x} = 0 - gt, x = x^0 - \tfrac{1}{2}gt^2 \tag{7}$$
$$\dot{x}^2 + g(x_0 - x) = \text{kinetic energy} + \text{potential energy}$$
$$= \text{constant} = 0$$

I say we are using hindsight, not to *read into* Galileo what was never there but rather to perceive what was genuinely there [even though he did not *always* correctly understand it perfectly – as, for example, when in earlier decades he made $x - x^0$ proportional to velocity rather than (velocity)^2, an error he later came to recognize clearly].

Discussion

Let me sum up. I do agree with Lerner (1940) and Patinkin (1982) that Ohlin exaggerated (1) the sense in which Wicksell ever had a theory of "output as a whole" or a theory of effective demand or a theory of *systematically unneutral* money; (2) the sense in which Myrdal's 1933 *Monetary Equilibrium* had a *formal* model for endogenous *real* GNP; or (3) the sense in which Lindahl and Ohlin ever had such an articulated model. But Ohlin and the other economists commissioned by the government to write about the depression of the early 1930s did not have to have such an explicit model to take for granted that measures which expand the total of $PQ = \Sigma p_j q_j$ can be expected *systematically* to increase Q.

This is not saying a lot. Every village crank, including those who could not reason clearly, believed as much. But in the groves of academe that I first entered, particularly in the solemn hours devoted to theory and methodology, this was never explicitly accepted – even by those who in less solemn hours lapsed into good sense and signed petitions for fiscal deficits and Fed expansionisms. Where was Robert Lucas when the Great Depression raged? He was everywhere, and an agnostic like Harvard's John Williams, who confessed to not knowing how to refute conclusively Foster and Catchings, was an object of some pity and condescension.

I need to make another point. When a Patinkin or a Samuelson takes notice in the 1970s of a passage written in the 1930s that refers explicitly to price level stabilization, or to reflation to restore, say, a 1925 price level, there is a danger that this will be misinterpreted to be evidence for that earlier writer's being preoccupied with P in PQ and *not* at all with Q. Having lived as an economist in those earlier times, I can affirm boldly that this would be a gross mistake. All of us acutely desired a rise in Q, and our espousal of a rise in PQ was in the hope that Q would be raised – especially since, during those years of the Great Depression, we were for once relieved of the usual concern about P rises because defending the slump's trough of the price index was not deemed something worth sacrificing for. (To their shame many Fed officials and some civil servants did worry about the bogey man of inflation even in 1931 and 1932!) Only after 1936 did inflation loom up for sensible humanitarians again as an evil in its own right. When one reads Myrdal, Lindahl, Cassel, and Ohlin, one must keep this in mind, realizing that they did correlate rises in P with desired rises in Q; and the same was then true of Seymour Harris, Henry Simons, and the writer of my various term papers. This imprecision of speaking did little harm until, during World War II, an occasional naive Congressman objected to needing controls and limitations on prices on the ground that "the price level was still not back to 100."

Today we have a new reason to accord more value to pre-Keynes pioneers who thought in terms of effective demand even before their thoughts had firm foundations in explicit economic theory. (Here I make a point like that in Bob Clower's paper.) Our new reason is that modern critics of Keynes have rediscovered what we early converts to Keynes well knew but chose to conveniently forget: The system (1), as well as the system (2a) and (2b), does lack firm "foundations," micro or otherwise. Better no foundations than bad ones! As a reduced form description, (1) served us better than any Lucas-Sargent rationalization could have done. As Oliver Heaviside said in exasperated reply to the critics of his pioneering but intuitive electrical engineering operators, "Shall I refuse my dinner because I do not know the laws of digestion?"

Don Patinkin has raised to new levels the history of science as applied to economics. I applaud his insistence on written documentation to validate remembrances and vague claims by interested witnesses. But sometimes, looking into a microscope, we lose the *gestalt* apparent to the naked eye or perhaps perceivable only in the aperture of a telescope.

When one puts the microscope on Galileo, one fails to find in him so simple a Newton concept as a second-order differential equation

$$d^2/dt^2 = f(x, dx/dt)$$

much less an inverse-square law of acceleration. Although Galileo fails this Patinkin-like test for anticipation of Newton, commentators are right to stress Galileo's recognition that the burden of proof is on the assertion that a velocity will change: A new force is needed to produce an acceleration, not to continue a velocity – which is a tremendous emancipation from Aristotle's basic notion.

Or consider the famous 1744 incident at the Court of Frederic the Great, where Maupertuis enunciated the principle of least action and Euler magnanimously made sense out of the sounds Maupertuis was perpetrating. A Patinkin could rightly demonstrate that Maupertuis never discovered Euler's principle that a cannonball's path in a vacuum provides a minimum of the *difference* between its kinetic and potential energy, as compared to all other paths that conserve the same *total* of those energies. So what credit ought Maupertuis to get for his bombastic claim? I would say he deserves a lot of credit for conjecturing a basic minimum principle in nature (but only if the jury determines that what he intuitively had in mind was not already old hat, was not, for, example already tacitly contained in Hero's ancient writings on light as following a path of least time of arrival or in Fermat's similar speculations about optics).

Patinkin's colleague Yehuda Elkana must surely be right that the different discoveries of the nineteenth-century first law of conservation of energy were not identical in their expositions and findings. That does not mean Tom Kuhn is wrong in enumerating twelve quasi-independent discoverers of that law. When I have made a discovery in economics, my second paper on the subject might well dominate the first paper. Still, it is usually the first one, rough as it is and incomplete as it may be, that most represents the incremental innovation to knowledge. As Littlewood said to Hardy – or was it the other way? – most famous first proofs of important theorems are crude. Later the elegant undertakers and tailors take over. If the proofs could be easy and slick, their dates of discovery would have been earlier ones.

What strikes me as I review Mertonian stories about doubletons and multiple discoveries in science – Darwin and Wallace, Newton and Leibniz, Joule and Mayer, Jevons, Menger, and Walras – is not how genuinely different their versions are, but rather how oddly similar they may be. The laws of probability are defied when it is Malthus's population theory that led Darwin to the notion of natural selection as he climbed a country stile and that also led Wallace in a Malayan fever to the same apprehension. Jevons and Walras even made the same mistake about the necessity for utility to be cardinally measurable! The contemporaneous discoveries of the so-called balanced-budget theorem – earlier by Jörgen Gelting, Keynes, William Salant, Samuelson, Harold Somers, Hansen-Perloff, and Kaldor, and later by Henry Wallich, Richard Goodwin, Trygve Haavelmo, Gottfried Haberler, Everett Hagen, Richard Musgrave, Tom Schelling, and Arthur Smithies – differed in expositions and emphases but agreed in the essentials of the phenomenon.

There were many Molière characters speaking Keynesian prose in the depression years before 1936. What Keynes's *General Theory* gave us, which Ohlin's inspired journalisms could not at all offer, was a new manageable paradigm that we could explicitly express – and test, and criticize, and improve, . . . , and be bewitched by.

Long before Kuhn, Schumpeter used to insist that old theories are not killed by simple facts: It takes a new theory to kill an old one. The mind cannot operate in terms of a melange of sensations. It needs a road map to perceive patterns of regularity and persistence.

So pervasive is the Keynes version that in the same year that a Martin Feldstein or Arthur Burns is castigating the model, his journal papers are utilizing it. To dig the Keynes paradigm's grave, I must use the shovel that it was the first to provide. That, I suppose, after half a century is true fame in science.

If we are candid, we must say that Ohlin's Stockholm School is now part of history – occupying an honorable niche to be sure, but not in 1987 at the cutting edge of economic science.

Notes

1 I owe thanks for partial support to my MIT Sloan School of Management's postdoctoral fellowship and for editorial assistance to Aase Huggins and Ruth Pelizzon.

2 Equation (1) becomes more elaborate once disposable income, which equals $Y - $ Taxes, becomes the argument in $f(\ )$; and when we have to add to $\bar{I}$ a term $\bar{G}$ for governemnt expenditure; and when Taxes is postulated to be a stipulated function $T(Y)$, $0 < T'(Y) < 1$. Similarly, an open economy requires the further variables of the Harrod-Keynes-Metzler type.

I see from Robert Clower's contribution to this volume that he regards the system (1) here, and my later (2a) and (2b), not as the essential Keynes *General Theory* but rather as a "Samuelson" fabrication. I protest the great honor. Harrod, Hicks, Lange, Reddaway, Meade, J. Robinson, Lerner, and many others wrote down *exactly* this system. I did invent the 45° Keynesian cross as a device for classroom exposition.

3 Patinkin may magnify the probability that Myrdal read the Harris Foundation proceedings and forgot about it. The circulation of that item was minuscule. I never saw it until years after my own Chicago sojourn, and a citation count would show how little was its ripple.

4 To avoid calculus, in equation (6) Galileo can replace (velocity)^2 by (centered-average-velocity)^2.

References

Clark, J. M. (1935), *Economics of Planning Public Works.* Washington, D.C.: U.S. Government Printing Office.

Committee on Unemployment (1931–5), Commissioned reports by Hammar-skjöld, Johansson, Myrdal, and Ohlin; and Final Report on *Remedies for Unemployment* (all in Swedish).

Frisch, Ragnar (1933), "Propagation Problems and Impulse Problems in Dynamic Economics," in *Economic Essays in Honour of Gustav Cassel.* London: George Allen and Unwin.

(1934) "Circulation Planning: Proposal for a National Organization of a Commodity and Service Exchange," Parts I–II, *Econometrica* 2 (July), 258–336; 2 (October), 422–35.

Harris Memorial Foundation (1931), *Unemployment as a World Problem,* Q. Wright, ed., Chicago: University of Chicago Press.

Harris, Seymour (1936), *Exchange Depreciation.* Cambridge, Mass.: Harvard University Press.

Kahn, R. F. (1931), "The Relation of Home Investment to Unemployment," *Economic Journal,* 41 (June), 173–98.

Kalecki, M. (1971), *Selected Essays on the Dynamics of the Capitalist Economy 1933–1970.* Cambridge: Cambridge University Press.

Keynes, J. M. (1923), *A Tract on Monetary Reform.* London: Macmillan.
    (1933), *The Means to Prosperity.* London: Macmillan.
    (1936), *The General Theory of Employment, Interest and Money.* London: Macmillan.
Leijonhufvud, Axel (1968), *On Keynesian Economics and the Economics of Keynes.* New York: Oxford University Press.
Lerner, Abba P. (1940), "Some Swedish Stepping Stones in Economic Theory," *Canadian Journal of Economics and Political Science,* 6 (November), 574–91.
Lindahl, Erik (1939), *Studies in the Theory of Money and Capital.* London: Allan and Unwin.
Lundberg, Erik (1937), *Studies in the Theory of Economic Expansion.* London: P. S. King & Son.
Machlup, Fritz (1939), "Period Analysis and Multiplier Theory," *Quarterly Journal of Economics,* 54 (November), 1–27.
Myrdal, Gunnar (1939), *Monetary Equilibrium.* London: W. Hodge (English translation and revision of 1932 Swedish and 1933 German versions).
Ohlin, Bertil (1937), "Some Notes on the Stockholm Theory of Saving and Investment," *Economic Journal,* 47, 53–69, 221–40.
    (1978), "Keynesian Economics and the Stockholm School, A Comment on Patinkin's Paper," *Scandinavian Journal of Economics,* 80 (No. 2), 144–7.
    (1981), "Stockholm and Cambridge: Four Papers on the Monetary and Employment Theory of the 1930s." Posthumously edited by O. Steiger. *History of Political Economy,* 13 (Summer), 189–255.
Patinkin, Don (1978), "On the Relation between Keynesian Economics and 'The Stockholm School,'" *Scandinavian Journal of Economics,* 80 (No. 2), 135–43. Reprinted in 1982 book below.
    (1981), *Essays on and in the Chicago Tradition.* Durham, N.C.: Duke University Press, Chapters 10–12.
    (1982), *Anticipations of the General Theory? And Other Essays on Keynes.* Chicago: University of Chicago Press.
Robertson, D. H. (1939), "Mr. Clark and the Foreign Trade Multiplier," *Economic Journal,* 49, 354–6.
Samuelson, P. A. (1988), "Mathematical Vindication of Ricardo on Machinery," *Journal of Political Economy,* 96, 274–82.
    (1989), "Ricardo Was Right!" *Scandinavian Journal of Economics,* 91, 47–62.
Slichter, S. H. (1934), *Towards Stability – The Problems of Economic Balance.* New York: Henry Holt and Co.
Wicksell, Knut (1934), *Interest and Prices,* English translation of 1898 German edition.
    (1923 and 1981), "Ricardo on Machinery and the Present Unemployment," *Economic Journal,* 91, 200–5, a paper rejected by Keynes in 1923–4 and reproduced with commentary by L. Jonung in *Economic Journal,* pp. 195–

205, under the above title plus the subtitle "An Unpublished Manuscript by Knut Wicksell."

Comment

DON PATINKIN

Paul Samuelson has listed three fiftieth anniversaries that are marked by this conference; let me add that it also marks the delayed tenth anniversary of a similar argument between Paul and myself about the relation between Kahn's 1931 multiplier article and the *General Theory,* which took place at a 1975 conference at the University of Western Ontario. But before turning to that issue – which is the main one that will concern me in this discussion – let me make a few remarks about some other points in Paul's paper.

First, I am glad that Paul and I are essentially in agreement about the relation of the Stockholm School to the *General Theory* (see my *Anticipations of the General Theory?,* Chapter 2).

Second, Paul seems to regard the *gestalt* approach to the history of thought as being in contrast to my emphasis on the importance of textual evidence. I see no such contrast. On the contrary, I consider my principle of identifying the contribution of an economist with the central message of his writings, and disregarding things he said in passing and to which he clearly did not attach much importance at the time, as being precisely an application of the *gestalt* approach. Ohlin's 1933 article is a good example of this: for as I point out in my *Anticipations of the General Theory?* (Patinkin, 1982, p. 54), in the concluding section of this article Ohlin lists five major objectives that he has attempted to accomplish in it, and none of them have to do with Keynes's central message of the theory of effective demand *cum* equilibrating role of changes in output. That is my *gestalt* view of Ohlin's contribution, which despite one or two suggestive passages in his article has led me to reject Ohlin's claim to have anticipated the *General Theory.*

Two further points, of a minor nature: First, I do not know why Paul says that I deny that Kalecki had a consumption function. It is clear from my discussion in *Anticipations* (pp. 70–1) that I attribute to Kalecki a consumption function for capitalists and even speak of his assumption about "the marginal propensity to consume of capitalists." Second, in note 3 of his paper Samuelson forcefully rejects my contention that Myrdal had read Keynes's Harris Foundation lecture (*Antici-*

pations, p. 51). I suggest, however, that he compare the wording in the respective passages that I cite from Myrdal and Keynes on which I base my contention. I might also mention that this possibility has also been noted by Otto Steiger in his monograph on the Stockholm School (referred to in *Anticipations,* p. 51, footnote 31).

I come now to my main point, and that is Samuelson's contention that Kahn's 1931 multiplier article is "logically isomorphic" with Keynes's 1936 *General Theory,* and that there is accordingly an "essential identity" between these two writings. In this context I can only repeat what I said at the aforementioned 1975 conference (Patinkin and Leith, 1977, pp. 18–20, 84–7) and in my *Anticipations* (pp. 26–31). In particular, logical equivalence does not imply chronological equivalence: The fact that A implies B does not in turn imply that at the time scholars understood A they also understood B. This is a commonplace of the history of ideas. Indeed – as has frequently been noted – if this principle were not true, then mathematicians would have nothing to discover, for their theorems are implicit in their assumptions.

The fact that at the time he wrote the multiplier article Kahn did not have an understanding of what was to be the central message of the *General Theory* is clear from a *gestalt* view of his article – a view of his article that places it in its historical context. Specifically, in support of the Liberal Party in the 1929 elections, Keynes (together with Hubert Henderson) has written *Can Lloyd George Do It? An Examination of the Liberal Pledge.* In this pamphlet Keynes had shown that besides the "primary employment" created by the initial public-works expenditures, there would be additional "indirect employment" created by the subsequent chain of increased expenditures that would be generated. He also contended that, contrary to the so-called Treasury view, the increase in government investment would not be entirely at the expense of private investment but, by virtue of the increased employment that it would create, would itself generate an increase in savings that would enable a net increase in investment. But in connection with the "indirect employment" so created, Keynes went on to say, "it is not possible to measure effects of this character with any sort of precision" (Keynes and Henderson, 1929, p. 107). A year later, in an unpublished memorandum, Colin Clark also addressed himself to this subject. Clark spoke of the "infinite series of beneficial repercussions" that would be generated by public works expenditure, but concluded that "the limiting factors, however, are obscure and economic theory cannot state the possibilities with precision" (cited in *Anticipations,* p. 196). And now the stage was set for Kahn's 1931 article, whose major purpose was to prove (by means of the multiplier formula he developed) that not only would there be an increase in savings, but this increase would exactly equal the initial increase in investment. That was the central message of Kahn's article, not the development of a theory of effective demand.

Further evidence in support of this interpretation is provided by three additional facts. First, Kahn develops his multiplier analysis within the analytical framework of the *Treatise,* so different from that of the *General Theory.* Second, and perhaps most revealing of all, in his article, Kahn refers to the initial government investment as the "aggravation" and the additional savings generated by the multiplier process as the "alleviation" – hardly a terminology that reflects the attitude of the *General Theory* toward these respective activities! Third, and last, Paul is claiming more for Kahn's 1931 article than Kahn himself! For in correspondence about his multiplier aritcle that I had with him about fifteen years ago, Kahn enumerated what he regarded as the three objectives of his article, and he does not include among them Keynes's theory of effective demand (see the letter as reproduced in Patinkin and Leith, 1977, pp. 146–8).

This is not the first such disagreement that Paul Samuelson and I have had on doctrinal mattters. About twenty years ago we disagreed on whether or not neoclassical monetary theory had been guilty of the "invalid dichotomy," with Paul rejecting my conclusion that they had been (Samuelson, 1968, 1972; Patinkin, 1972). I have frequently asked myself why we have such disagreements, and I think I know the reason. The history of doctrines is the history of the false starts, errors, and faltering manner in which a new theory is developed and its implications fully understood; and Paul's extraordinarily quick and encompassing mind makes him less inclined to believe that others did not understand what seems so obvious to him.

And so I turn to my good friend Paul Samuelson and bluntly say to him that his brilliance, his instantaneous and pentrating grasp, his phenomenal intellect – these qualities are a comparative *dis*advantage in the study of the history of the development of thought.[1]

Note

1 And if any further evidence is needed on the lightning speed with which the mind of Paul Samuelson works, let me simply note that his immediate, on-the-spot reaction to this gibe was to say, "Just like judo: using your opponent's strength to throw him."

References

Kahn, R. F. (1931), "The Relation of Home Investment to Unemployment." *Economic Journal,* 41 (June), 173–98.

Keynes, J. M. (1936), *The General Theory of Employment, Interest and Money.* London: Macmillan.

Keynes, J. M., and H. Henderson (1929), *Can Lloyd George Do It?: An Examination of the Liberal Pledge.* As reprinted in Keynes, *Collected Writings,* Vol. IX, pp. 86–125.

Ohlin, B. (1933), "Till frågan om penningteoriens uppläggning," *Ekonomisk Tidskrift,* 35 (No. 2), 45–81. Translated under the title "On the Formulation of Monetary Theory" by Hans J. Brems and William P. Yohe, *History of Political Economy,* 10 (Fall 1978), 353–88.

Patinkin, D. (1972), "Samuelson on the Neoclassical Dichotomy: A Comment," *Canadian Journal of Economics,* 5 (May), 279–83. As reprinted in Patinkin, *Essays On and In the Chicago Tradition,* Durham, N.C.: Duke University Press, 1981, pp. 149–53.

(1982), *Anticipations of the General Theory? And Other Essays on Keynes.* Chicago: University of Chicago Press.

(1983), "Paul Samuelson's Contribution to Monetary Economics," in E. Cary Brown and Robert M. Solow, ed., *Paul Samuelson and Modern Economic Theory.* New York: McGraw-Hill, pp. 157–68.

Patinkin, D., and J. C. Leith, ed., (1977), *Keynes, Cambridge and the General Theory: The Process of Criticism and Discussion Connected with the Development of the General Theory.* London: Macmillan.

Samuelson, P. A. (1968), "What Classical and Neoclassical Monetary Theory Really Was," *Canadian Journal of Economics,* 1 (Feb.), 1–15. As reprinted in Samuleson, *Collected Scientific Papers,* Vol. III, Chap. 176.

(1972), "Samuelson on the Neoclassical Dichotomy. A Reply," *Canadian Journal of Economics,* 5 (May), 284–92. As reprinted in Samuelson, *Collected Scientific Papers,* Vol. IV, Chap. 265.

CHAPTER 18

Ragnar Frisch and the Stockholm School

JENS CHRISTOPHER ANDVIG[1]

Whatever their differences in interests, outlook, and scientific style, Ragnar Frisch and the Stockholm School had one thing in common: Their main scientific interests and scientific contributions were of a methodological kind. They were more interested in changing the ways in which economists tried to understand the "world" than in supplying new explanations of how it actually worked.

To compare all aspects of their work would require roaming through the whole field of interwar economics. Rather than try to do that, I will narrow the field and compare only the macroeconomic thinking of Erik Lindahl and Gunnar Myrdal with that of Frisch. I have little to say about Frisch's influence on the Stockholm School, but will discuss his response to the work of the Swedes in detail.

1   Frisch and the Swedish tradition

Like the Swedish economists, Frisch was strongly influenced by Knut Wicksell. However, he read him differently. Although Frisch stood outside the Swedes' theoretical approach, observing it from the sideline, he discussed their approach systematically in a series of lectures on monetary theory held during 1934–5. In these lectures he voiced the skepticism that has inspired one major argument of the present paper: The problems that the theoretically oriented macroeconomists from this period attacked were too complex to be handled by the analytical methods actually applied. By theoretical macroeconomists, I mean economists who tried to explain phenomena like unemployment and inflation by relating them to some kind of neoclassical general equilibrium framework. In addition to the Stockholm School, the Cambridge School and economists like Friedrich von Hayek clearly belonged to this group. All of them tried to deal with this complexity in various ways.

One thing that most of these theoretically inclined economists did, in parts of their work, was some more or less systematic storytelling without making any pretensions that they could reach conclusive results; that is, the models were *explicitly indeterminate*. Sometimes they tried to simplify the structure of endogenous variables to such an extent that it was possible to handle the model logically by verbal methods. This was basically what Keynes succeeded in doing in his *General Theory*. If one could build a recursive model structure, one could, of course, handle larger structures verbally.

Another way to simplify the structure was to apply what I shall call the *casuistic* method, that is, one started out by listing a large number of variables and a few equations. Some variables were assumed to be exogenous, and the interaction between the few remaining endogenous variables was then studied and constituted a first case. The next step was to assume a different set of variables to be exogenous. The resulting different set of endogenous variables would then constitute a new case. Erik Lindahl used this method consciously to achieve simplification in both his temporary equilibrium and disequilibrium models. Gunnar Myrdal also sometimes used it, but he applied another simplification, which I shall call the *definitional* method. Put briefly, the definitional method consisted in formulating accounting relations between variables and, sometimes, reasoning as if such relations were sufficient to formulate a determinate model.

Frisch, however, argued in favor of mathematical methods of simplification. With one partial exception, his model of circulation planning (Frisch, 1934), he did not try to develop models for the problems that most interested the Swedish economists. He was too preoccupied with the mechanical properties of cycles to deal seriously with the underlying theoretical question of how to explain them as a logical outcome of the workings of complex market systems.

2   Macroeconomics should be dynamic

Both Frisch and the Stockholm School claimed that macroeconomic phenomena demanded dynamic explanations. However, this similarity was more linguistic than real. Frisch considered dynamics as a way of thinking – a property of the models used. Models that comprised relations where certain variables may undergo fundamental change over time were dynamic. In practice, he was thinking of models that had to be formulated mathematically as systems of functional equations. In his view, macroeconomics was essentially a dynamics-oriented field of economics, where the essential problem was to explain the exact time-path of the variables and why they followed cyclical trajectories.

On the other hand, when Lindahl and Myrdal were thinking about macroeconomics as a field of economic dynamics, they were concerned with the characteristics of the economic phenomena themselves. Although their conception of what dynamics was about became more complex through the 1930s (cf. Björn Hansson, 1982), their basic idea here can be seen as rather simple. Dynamics was about the forward-looking aspect of economic behavior. As economic behavior in general, and macroeconomic phenomena in particular, could in principle be largely explained in terms of economic plans and expectations and their eventual disappointments, economic dynamics was essential.

In order to illustrate the two different definitions of dynamics we should note that according to Frisch's classification, intertemporal, temporary equilibrium and most disequilibrium models would be static, whereas to the Stockholm School they would be clearly dynamic. On the other hand, models that contained functional equations but represented only blind behavior patterns would be static according to the latter's terminology; that is, most of Frisch's macrodynamic models would be static. In economic theory after World War II, Frisch's classification of statics versus dynamics became known through Paul A. Samuelson (1947) while the Lindahl-Myrdal position was advocated by John R. Hicks (1946). The important thing here is, of course, not the different terminology, but the fact that it reflected different approaches to macroeconomic problems.

Here we should note that while the Stockholm School's conception of macroeconomic phenomena as dynamic implied that one needed to go into basic microeconomic theory in order to look for explanations, Frisch's focus on dynamics as a set of mathematical tools did not. His way of looking at the basic macroeconomic problem as one of explaining eventual cyclical time-paths was linked historically to the more empirically oriented, but theoretically ad hoc, business cycle research that was so prominent in this period. This points to the greatest difficulty when comparing Frisch and the Stockholm School: the lack of common ground.

However, they shared an important intellectual starting point in Knut Wicksell, and the different ways that they looked upon and developed his work tell us much about their own thinking. Our discussion of the Stockholm School will mainly be confined to two works, one by Erik Lindahl (1930), *Penningpolitikens medel* (The Means of Monetary Policy),[2] and the other by Gunnar Myrdal, "Om penningteoretisk jämvikt" (On Monetary Equilibrium).[3] Both works were closely linked to Wicksell's discussion of the cumulative process, and their thinking here can be directly compared to Frisch's. These two works were among those described and evaluated by Frisch in his 1934–5 lectures on monetary economics. The confrontation between the two approaches is thus not a hypothetical *ex post* reconstruction.[4]

3   Lindahl and Myrdal on Wicksell's major theoretical problem

While Frisch brought out the logic of Wicksell's explanation of the cumulative process in order to show that he had created a proper dynamic model, Lindahl and Myrdal were mainly interested in Wicksell's main economic theoretical problem: How can one explain macroeconomic disturbances, such as a positive inflation rate, by the combination of general equilibrium theory and the idea that all interesting economic behavior is forward looking?

On a very general level, this problem was behind their development of "methods" for deriving interesting macroeconomic propositions on the basis of some kind of microeconomic behavior. The ideal case was Lindahl's famous *temporary equilibrium method,* developed in the late 1920s. By linking a set of static models in which neither differential nor difference equations were necessary, this method allowed one to make plausible propositions about possible developments of the variables through time. Strictly applied, temporary equilibrium methods presupposed use of market clearing assumptions for all markets, and hence should deal only with full employment situations. In *Penningpolitikens medel* Lindahl tried to apply it also to unemployment. That experience was frustrating, and in 1934 he suggested a new method, his so-called *disequilibrium method.*[5] Prices were no longer flexible in the short run, and not all plans reconciled, which meant that macroeconomic propositions could not be derived by means of a simple summation of all the individuals' plans. Lindahl suggested instead that one should distinguish between those agents whose plans would become effective (those on the short side) and those who would become frustrated (those on the long side). The effective plans were decisive for the aggregate result, and thus one should be able to go directly from these effective individual plans and deduce the macroeconomic results.

Myrdal considered Lindahl's method of specifying a chain of temporary equilibrium states as too ambitious, demanding too many specific and unrealistic assumptions. Instead he suggested an *equilibrium method.* He considered it sufficient to study the plans and expectaions in the savings and investment "market" at a given point of time. If they were consistent, it was difficult to tell what would happen – that demanded a closer study of the situation – but if they were not, a cumulative process would be triggered. In fact, Myrdal's equilibrium method was based upon implicitly stated and strong assumptions of the dynamic instability of the savings and investment market. Although one could not derive exactly the aggregate outcome on the basis of the knowledge of the individuals' plans and expecations, Myrdal claimed that one could at least use them to predict the basic direction in cases where violent changes were expected.

Frisch by contrast was uninterested in the problems of microeconomic roots, regarding them either as trivial or intractable.[6]

4   Lindahl's indeterminate models and Frisch's criticism

Wicksell's analysis of the cumulative process in *Interest and Prices,* which supplied the main inspiration for Lindahl's *Penningpolitikens medel,* is a convenient starting point for dealing with the question of analytical complexity.

While Frisch could argue with good reason that Wicksell had constructed a determinate model of a cumulative process in his *Lectures II,* it is a more open question whether he had created a complete logical structure for discussing the more complex problems raised in *Interest and Prices.* Here Wicksell had studied both labor and goods markets, and the interaction of four analytically different groups of agents: banks, capitalists/storeowners, workers/landowners, and entrepreneurs. It is clear that WIcksell needed some peculiar behaviorist assumptions in order to generate a cumulative rise in prices from an exogenous increase in the real rate of interest in that setting. In particular he assumed that the whole increase in production would be consumed by the entrepreneurs and thus not cause any increase in the aggregate net supply.[7] If the net supply increased, no cumulative price increase seemed plausible, given Wicksell's setup. Such a peculiar assumption about entrepreneurs' behavior worried Lindahl a great deal. Another worry was Wicksell's use of a stationary state assumption for what Lindahl considered to be a short-run macroeconomic problem.

Lindahl's major problem was how to replace the unrealistic assumption of the entrepreneurs' behavior and the restrictive stationary state assumption with more realistic ones, and still demonstrate the possibilty of cumulative processes under some circumstances.

In order to specify those assumptions, the theory had to be more explicitly dynamic; that is, plans and expectations had to be better specified than Wicksell had done. In addition, the consumer goods- and capital goods-producing industries had to be sharply differentiated, and the degree of factor mobility between them specified.[8]

The difference between the consumer goods and capital goods industries was analytically important, mainly because changes in interest rates had a different impact on the two sectors. Whereas the effects of the changes in interest rates on the price level of consumer goods were indirect and took a long time to develop, the impact on the price level of capital goods was immediate and direct. Producers in the two sectors also behaved differently in other important respects. For example, while the price level of consumer goods had (for unstated reasons) a direct impact on the price and income expectations of the entrepreneurs in the capital goods industries, the prices of capital goods had no such effect on expectations prevailing in the consumer goods industries.

Lindahl sketched a great number of initial states (not a single stationary one as Wicksell had done) that differed with respect to the degree of factor mobility, the kind of price expectations held by the entrepreneurs, the degree of unemployment and its allocation between the two industries, and so on, and then studied the effects of a decline in the nominal rate of interest, the nominal rate of interest being controlled by a central Wicksellian bank. The question explored was whether the economy was likely to return to an equilibrium position or would plunge into a cumulative process.

The answer clearly depended on the characteristics of the initial situation. For instance, if full employment, static price expectations, and no factor mobility existed, an exogenous drop in the interest rate would simply result in a once-and-for-all increase in the prices of capital goods, while the prices of consumer goods would remain approximately constant. If, however, factors could move towards the capital goods sector, a cumulative price increase would result and would continue until an increased amount of capital goods reached the market. What then happened depended on price expectations: Did producers expect that the previous price level would continue, or did they believe that the inflation rate would be constant? If the latter possibility occurred, the cumulative price increases woud continue even in the long run.

What Lindahl outlined was not implausible, but it was hardly a precise model. Variables were picked out at certain points in the succession of various temporary equilibria, discussed in some detail, and then allowed to recede into the background. In particular, Lindahl was vague about the characteristics of the final equilibrium, although the different temporary equilibria had been described in more detail.

This was not surprising. Lindahl had sketched a model of an even more complex economy than the one described by Wicksell in *Interest and Prices,* with more markets, more periods, and more types of agents. He operated with at least three periods, two producing sectors, and five types of agents. In addition, stocks of goods were held, and all agents had expectations and made plans for future periods. How could he ensure a logical structure without the help of mathematical formulations? The number of variables implied certainly exceeded the number that even the most conscientious researcher could control when relying on verbal analysis. Frequently the result was indeterminate models.

Frisch pointed to the lack of completely specified models in Lindahl's analyses. Noting Lindahl's proposition that whether or not a decline in the interest rates would give rise to a lasting cumulative process depended on the entrepreneurs' expectations of future prices, Frisch (*Pengeteori,* p. 8312.19) commented:

> This surely contains a kernel of truth, but one should perhaps not express oneself as categorically as Lindahl does. The form of the development will depend on the further assumptions one makes about the citizens' reaction pattern. In order to reach a definite answer one would need to specify these assumptions in definite equations and then solve them, as we did in our discussion of Wicksell's theory.

Lindahl was certainly aware of the problem of handling large models, and he attempted to maintain control of their logical structure. However, in the absence of explicit mathematical formulation, he had to maintain control by the primitive method of constructing examples in which most variables were assumed exogenous and only a few were endogenous at the same time.[9] Therefore Lindahl's analyses became less general than necessary, and occasionally he lost control of the logic of some of the simplified examples. In both these respects, when considered from Frisch's point of view, Wicksell's discussions of the cumulative process were superior to Lindahl's.

Lindahl, of course, considered his analyses to be an improvement on Wicksell's; in particular, he was very critical of Wicksell's concepts of a "normal" equilibrium and a "normal" rate of interest that could simultaneously equilibrate saving and investment and keep the price level constant. Lindahl criticized Wicksell's analysis of the "normal" rate for being confined to long-run general equilibrium situations; such analysis, he thought, could hardly be applied directly to the study of short-run effects of macroeconomic disturbances, which was Lindahl's major problem.[10] Although Lindahl accepted the idea that a theoretical study of macroeconomic disturbances demanded notions of (temporary) equilibria, he claimed that one could not expect any unique normal rate of interest. Since the number of possible equilibria – including ones of unemployment – was large, that was too much to expect.

In this comparison of the macroeconomic research methodology used by Frisch and Lindahl, two major areas of difference have been discovered. The first issue pertained to the use of mathematical formulations. Frisch claimed that Lindahl's and the other Swedish economists' sparse use of mathematical methods frequently made their models indeterminate.[11] Furthermore, it sometimes led to serious restrictions in the number of endogenous variables. Accordingly, problems that should have been and were intended to be studied in a general equilibrium framework were in fact discussed as a partial equilibrium problem. This latter property also tended to multiply the number of "cases" studied and obscure the logical interconnections between them. That problem was confounded by the usual ambiguities of verbal analysis.

The second issue concerned the microeconomic foundation of macroeconomics, which Frisch considered unimportant while Lindahl placed it at the center of his research. Related to this issue was the question of the role of expectations in macroeconomics. The search by the Stockholm economists for microeconomic foundations can perhaps best be explained by the importance that they gave to expectations and plans. The contrast between Frisch's and the Stockholm School's thinking in this matter may, however, be brought into sharper focus by looking at Gunnar Myrdal.

5   Numbers versus equations: Myrdal's macroeconomics and Frisch's response

Although the Stockholm School considered expectations to be extremely important, for analytical purposes, they were usually held to be exogenous. Since their results were strongly influenced by the expectations assumed, their work frequently left the impression that everything was possible in their models. It is difficult to tell how far this mode of analysis was simply due to the analytical convenience of keeping variables exogenous or was due to beliefs about the workings of the real world: that the economy was considered so unstable and outcomes so influenced by volatile shifts in the moods of the entrepreneurs and the public that it was almost useless to postulate functions between variables.

Like Lindahl, Myrdal used Wicksell's description of the cumulative process as a framework for his macroeconomic analysis. While Wicksell had neglected the role of expectations and Lindahl's conclusions rested at least as much on assumptions about factor mobility, the systematic part of Myrdal's explanation of cumulative processes was almost wholly about expectations: how cumulative processes were brought about by changing or inconsistent expectations.

The essential idea of Wicksell's study of a natural rate–market rate difference was, according to Myrdal, to predict whether the economy was heading for a general expansion or contraction, or whether the change was likely to be of a less drastic character. Myrdal accepted that approach as fruitful, but interpreted Wicksell's natural rate not as the value of the interest rate in a hypothetical general equilibrium situation, defined by a set of equations (as Frisch had done), but more as a "real" rate, a figure that reflected the average productivity of real investment.[12] However, Wicksell's analysis needed to be improved for various reasons.

First of all, Wicksell's concept of the real rate was deficient because it was insufficiently forward looking. Myrdal suggested instead that the real natural rate of interest, y_1, should be defined as

$$y_1 = e/K \tag{1}$$

where e was defined as expected net income of the first period, that is, the income that if it occurred was expected to keep the value of the stock of capital, K, intact. The value of the capital stock was defined as the discounted value of future income streams of all periods. Hence, human capital was included. Let i be the market rate of interest; the major problem with this definition was that, given Myrdal's method of defining expected (net) income, it had to equal the expected interest income of the capital stock pertaining to that period, hence $e = iK$ and, accordingly, $i = y_1$. The market rate would be equal to the real rate whatever the sentiments of entrepreneurs and the general public. Hence, the second major problem with Wicksell's approach, according to Myrdal, was a logical one: How could one base an analysis of macroeconomic disturbances on a study of a difference that by definition had to equal zero?

At this point, Myrdal asked whether it was possible to construct another pair of numbers instead that could signal the same kind of general expansion or contraction as the one Wicksell had looked for. Finally, Myrdal discovered an answer he was satisfied with, a new "natural" rate of interest, y_2, defined by

$$y_2 = e/F \tag{2}$$

where e was expected income as before and F was defined as the expected replacement cost of the stock of capital. By studying the relationship between the value of that variable and the market rate of interest, one could proceed along Wicksellian lines in a fairly straightforward manner.

If an investor considered investing an additional unit of capital, he could expect to gain that rate of return above costs, and if that rate was above the market rate of interest, entrepreneurs would make larger returns by investing in real rather than financial capital and consequently would invest in the former. Let us define $q = K/F$[13] and note that this implied $q = y_1/i$; q is not a well-specified variable, however, but an amalgam of expected interest rates, anticipated future earnings, and expected, short-run supply conditions in the capital goods industries.

If $q = 1$, equilibrium conditions would prevail. But there was nothing to ensure that $q = 1$; and if q happened to equal one, what would then be the rate of investment? Myrdal claimed that Wicksell's condition of the natural rate equal to the market rate of interest was in general not sufficient to define any meaningful equilibrium rate of investment.

To define such a rate, it was necessary to look at the savings mechanism. According to Myrdal, this had been overlooked by Wicksell because of his concentration on stationary states where net savings were, by assumption, equal to zero. One should note that savings decisions were made independently of investment decisions and could be considered here to be exogenous. Savings, S, were defined as equal to expected income, e, minus consumption, c, hence $S = e - c$. In the German verison of his work he tried to show that $S = I$ implied $q = 1$, but his proof was flawed.[14]

Myrdal wanted $S > I$ to indicate a contraction. The problem with his definition in this context can be illustrated by his following "use" of it: Consider an equilibrium situation where $S = I$. Then aggregate, planned savings suddenly increase. In his subsequent verbal discussion, Myrdal claimed that this would trigger off a downwards cumulative process, even though the initial shock was not directed toward consumption. The decline in consumption was brought about as a consequence of the disruption of the savings–investment equilibrium. The only way savings could increase, however, would then be through an increase in expected income, e. But then it would also be plausible that q would increase rather than decline (an increase in e is likely to increase the dicounted value of future income streams more than the expected replacement costs of the existing capital stock). An increase in q would signal expansion rather than contraction.[15] Thus Myrdal seemed unable to formulate his vision of cumulative processes in a consistent way. It is likely that the savings–investment (dis)equilibrium states could have been more satisfactorily linked to a q-theory of investment within his framework, but Myrdal's own intuition was led astray by the complex semiverbal exposition.

Neglecting the possible logical defects and considering the capital market in isolation, the basic idea was to look at two pairs of variables, first the q-ratio and then the savings–investment realtionship. The value of each variable was determined by a complex amalgam of expectations and plans made by the agents. At each point of time, the variables were given as fixed numbers, but were also liable to shift as expectations and moods changed. The numbers were then compared with each other. When the period for which they pertained ended, these so-called *ex ante* numbers were then compared to the numbers actually recorded for the period, the *ex post* magnitudes. These *ex post* values, however, were also strongly influenced by expectations and plans formulated at the end of the period or at the beginning of the next. On the basis of the two sets of comparisons Myrdal would suggest verbally how a new set of *ex ante* savings and investment numbers could differ from the preceding set. That was Myrdal's *ex ante–ex post* analysis.

The initial savings and investment magnitudes were unrelated in the short run. No kind of equilibrating mechanism was proposed; and they would be equal only by coincidence. How did Frisch respond to Myrdal's way of doing macroeconomics? Frisch was both attracted and repelled by it. On the one hand, he was quite fascinated by all the conceptual complexities suggested by Myrdal and he spent the largest section of his first theoretical study of national accounting on clearing up the depreciation concepts used by his Swedish colleague.[16]

He also noted that Myrdal had discussed the implications of fixed prices and had also raised several original points of interest from an economic policy point of view. Nevertheless, his overall evaluation of Myrdal's contributions was more negative. He told his students (Frisch, *Pengeteori,* pp. 8314 2.1–2.2):

> We will at once formulate our main results regarding Myrdal's monetary theory:
> Firstly, Wicksell's theory does not need any thorough revision like the one Myrdal has started. The only thing needed is to distinguish sharply between the three concepts [r, n, and i]. These concepts are evidently contained in Wicksell's own thinking. The only thing one could reproach Wicksell for is that he, on a few occasions, has been incomplete and unclear in his method of expression. To make these concepts precise does not imply any "repairing" of Wicksell's thought, but only an improvement of language. When one clearly distinguishes between these three concepts, Wicksell's theory becomes logically unassailable.
> Secondly, the "revision" of Wicksell's theory that Myrdal has performed is . . . not in the spirit of Wicksell; it introduces foreign elements that, moreover, do not plough as deeply into the chains of causation as the ones that Wicksell emphasized.

When Frisch claimed that Myrdal was not "ploughing as deeply" as Wicksell, he emphasized Myrdal's study of isolated numbers instead of

Wicksell's use of mathematical functions connected into equation systems. Frisch complained (p. 8316.7):

> Myrdal perceived the equilibrium analysis of investment and saving as an analysis of the relationship between the natural rate, y_2, and the loan rate of interest, i. y_2 is in principle an observable magnitude, while i is, of course, observable in fact. This procedure Myrdal believes is the same as comparing the productivity rate, r, with the loan rate. According to Myrdal, this is what Wicksell has done. In other words, he believes his own magnitude, y_2, is the same as Wicksell's r, and that r and n are the same in Wicksell. As our analysis of Wicksell's theory shows, this interpretation of Wicksell is completely wrong. Wicksell's construction ploughs much deeper. Wicksell understood that in order to really construct a theory of an equilibrium, one has to compare the number i with a theoretical level of the loan rate at the equilibrium point, namely n, and then discuss their relationship over time.

Frisch was also skeptical about the way Lindahl and, more particularly, Myrdal had based their analyses on anticipations. He criticized both for defining income as the interest on the capitalized value of future income streams, a concept he believed to be non-operational. It was confusing to add human and real capital in macroeconomic analyses. In the case of Myrdal it had serious consequences, since he had based his final analysis on a study of the difference between the value of capital and its expected reproduction costs, or, as Frisch (p. 8315.14) stated:

> For example, we have now to calculate the expected reproduction costs of human beings. . . . In this way monetary theory certainly is transgressing all bounds. It then becomes not monetary theory, but social philosophy.

A further consequence of having formulated his macroeconomic theory in terms of a comparison of magnitudes, was that Myrdal had not understood the marginal character of Wicksell's investment function. Accordingly, his own "natural" rate of interest was defined as an average yield:

> The concept of interest with which Myrdal is operating is a *total* concept, an average defined by relating income to the capital stock. This is very much counter to the spirit of Wicksell. Wicksell's considerations here are typically marginal: When the entrepreneurs deduce their demand for capital, it is a question of which productivity rate they may gain by a *small increase* in capital.[17]

Myrdal's and Frisch's concepts of dynamics

We have seen that Frisch considered the statics–dynamics distinction as a question of modeling procedures. He had once shown how Wicksell could be interpreted as having constructed a determinate, dynamic model of the cumulative process that was exemplary from an analytical point of view (see Andvig, 1985, pp. 158–173). In addition, it had the advantage that it could be easily modified to handle the important questions posed by business cycle theory: It could explain the cyclical time-paths of the variables in question.

Seen from Myrdal's perspective, one of the main defects of Wicksell's analysis was its static character. It neglected the dynamic problem that agents were forward looking and that anticipations determined current actions. The cumulative process itself consisted of shifting plans based upon shifting or inconsistent expectations. Wicksell's analysis had to be completed at this point, and Myrdal's task was *"to include anticipations in the monetary system"* (Myrdal, 1939, p. 32).

This did not imply that Myrdal made no use of dynamics in Frisch's sense. However, the basic dynamic assumptions that he used were rather simple in Frisch's terms. They were based upon Myrdal's studies of Lindahl's temporary equilibrium approach where the properties of short-run responses to interest rate changes could be shown to be basically different from the medium-term response, a result Myrdal considered to yield predictions that were much too ambitious and complex. Although he hardly ever mentioned Frisch's macrodynamics, he must have, by implication, considered Frisch's attempts to construct mathematical cycle theories in a similar fashion: that is, they were too ambitious. One could only predict the major direction of change. More precisely, one had an area of monetary equilibrium where savings were roughly equal to investment. Inside this area one could even experience complete minor business cycles. Myrdal believed that it was difficult to tell, on the basis of monetary theory, which one of the many equilibrium states was likely to be realized. Outside this "indifference field" one could only tell the direction of change: falling prices and production levels in the case when $S > I$, increasing prices and production levels when $I > S$. Once classification systems of expectations had been improved and there was a better knowledge of expectations formation, it might be possible to deal with more complex trajectories such as cyclical ones. However, that was a task for the future.

6   Myrdal and Frisch and empirical issues

Although Lindahl participated in a large empirical project that studied the national income of Sweden, and Ohlin made several empirical studies of the economic depression of the 1930s, they did not apply their theoretical work to empirical problems. The only serious attempt to do so that I have found was made by Gunnar Myrdal. It was a failure.

Myrdal's basic question was to ask how one could judge, on the basis of observations, whether or not the economy was moving into a cumulative process. The answer hinged upon the state of the capital market: Was it in equilibrium or not? Only the capital market had to be observed; the problem was, however, to predict, on the basis of empirical observations, whether or not it would move into a basic disequilibrium process.

In principle, Myrdal's solution was simple and was based on the idea that analysis could proceed by comparing magnitudes rather than specifying functions. First, he suggested that it was possible to construct two independent indices of the *ex ante* values of the two complexes of variables that would have the same value *ex post,* one for each side of the capital market. These indices would either be based on direct observations of the relevant *ex ante* variables or determined indirectly, by using the realized values of other variables that were strongly influenced by plans and expectations for the coming period. The value of the two indices would then be compared. If the numerical discrepancy was great, it would indicate a basic disequilibrium in the market.

Thus, while Frisch and other econometricians had to estimate parameters on the assumption of an assumed constancy of behaviorist patterns, apply methods requiring many observations per variable whether they were time-series or cross-section observations, and use explanations that in most cases needed many variables, the only requirement Myrdal had to meet in order to generate "good" predictions was simply to construct two indices for one time period, compare them, and record their differences.[18] Myrdal's construction of "disequilibrium" indices might best be understood through an example. The most ambitious of his attempts to develop an operational discrepancy index was to derive a theoretical measure of the difference between the "normal" and the market rate of interest.

We should note that Myrdal had already discarded the expected yield (y_1) of the expected value of the existing stock of real capital (c_1) as an appropriate measure of the "real" rate because y_1 would by definition equal the market rate of interest. Instead he defined the real rate of interest as the expected yield (y_2) in relation to the expected reproduction costs of real capital (r_1). Myrdal was not satisfied by studying the ($y_2 - i$) difference, however, since the measurement of both variables raised considerable problems. Although it is evident that y_2 was a difficult concept to make operational, it is harder to see that it was exceptionally difficult to construct an index of interest rates, i. Nevertheless, Myrdal insisted that this was the case and argued that it was much easier to determine the ($c_1 - r_1$) discrepancy than the ($y_2 - i$) one from empirical observations.

So far, Myrdal's abstract reasoning followed approximately the same path as the one actually taken by economists who have tried to make Tobin's q-theory of investment operational. It was when Myrdal tried to construct an index for the whole economy that his way of "defining" himself out of any difficulty led him astray.

In brief, in order to construct the indices he made certain assumptions about the agents' behavior that one was unlikely to know beforehand and that these same indices were intended to reveal. For example, in order to aggregate the disequilibrium index of the capital market by means of the differences $(c_i - r_i)$ for each subsector, the value of each such difference had to be weighted by the strength of the investment response to a given discrepancy between the natural and market rates of interest. A subsector with a strong investment response would hence count more heavily in the aggregate index than a subsector with a weak response.[19]

Wicksell believed that it was sufficient to look at observations of an ordinary price index during a certain period to verify whether or not the economy had moved into a cumulative process. Cassel and then Lindahl had severed this cord to the empirical world by denying that there were any strong reasons to believe that the rate of price change reflected the state of disequilibrium in the capital market. The links between theory and empirical obserations were further weakened by Myrdal's use of increasingly more complex and non-observable concepts. The development and actual use of appropriate mathematical tools were now essential. Myrdal was unable to handle and develop these mathematical tools.

7   Conclusions

At a superficial level, Frisch and the Stockholm School had much in common. Frisch, Ohlin, and Myrdal demanded a greater integration between theoretical and empirical work in macroeconomics and asked for operational concepts. They all said that the problems of macroeconomics were essentially dynamic and deplored the statics of Keynes's *General Theory*. They all stressed the importance of the development of proper methodology.

The similarity was to a large extent of a purely verbal nature. In the view of the Stockholm School, the concept of dynamics was concerned with the way in which current economic actions are strongly influenced by future plans and expectations. On the other hand, Frisch treated dynamics as a way of thinking that in practice would demand a set of mathematical techniques, for example, differential equations, difference equations, variational analysis, and so on. Since he felt that macroeconomics dealt with the problem of time configurations of the central macroeconomic variables, it had to be essentially dynamic. Expectations and plans were not so essential, and he appears to have considered it futile to base macroeconomics on strict microeconomic considerations. Hence Frisch's models were considered static in the eyes of the Stockholm School, since economic agents, if they existed at all in his models, acted in a somewhat blind manner. The view that dynamics was more fruitful for macroeconomics than statics was thus not necessarily a shared view.

In order to make economics a progressive science, Frisch considered that the development of proper analytical methods for empirical investigations and for more purely theoretical work was the most urgent methodological task. In practice, it meant the application of mathematical techniques to new economic problems, and the development and application of proper statistical analysis.

In my view, the scientific intentions behind the methodological discussions of the Stockholm School seem very mixed. Hence it is difficult to tell what they meant by methodology. On the one hand, it was about how to carry out the very ambitious attempts to construct general logical methods for linking economic events over time periods. More implicitly, it was concerned with trying to determine the macro-outcome of all individual actions, plans, and expectations. It is not clear whether the idea was to develop such groups of models as aids to the construction of specific, determinate models in Frisch's sense, or something else. On the other hand, their ambition sometimes appears to take on more modest proportions, for instance, in outlining schemes for the interpretation of economic policy situations, where these schemes would only point out a few of the systematic relations and leave the rest behind in a fog of intuition. The development of methodological rules would then assist in the choice of which scheme of thought to apply to a given situation, for example, by indicating which scheme should be considered as a subclass of another.

Among the Swedish economists, Myrdal was most strongly struck by the importance of expectations and, by implication, their volatility. This made it unreasonable to go far in the direction of mathematical specification. Furthermore, it became natural to regard theories as instruments for the interpretation of specific situations rather than as a means of identifying set patterns of behavior. Accordingly, economics may be regarded as idiographic, not as the nomothetic science that was evidently Frisch's ambition.

Although Frisch certainly expressed his dislike for the expectational flavor of the Stockholm School's thinking in general and Myrdal's in particular, we should have expected him to be even more critical. The approach of the Stockholm School had implications that went directly against his ambitious ideas of developing economics into a rigorous science based on many of the same principles that were applied in the natural sciences. If Myrdal was right, what sense would it make to specify functions and estimate parameters empirically? Why use mathematical formulations if one could not believe that the functions were invariant with respect to time, and that not only the functional forms but also their arguments would be liable to shift as a consequence of circumstances that were impossible to specify?

Another point of contention lay in the real world behavior and role of commercial banks. While Myrdal/Lindahl and Frisch in his Wicksell interpretations had used models in which the banks endogenously supplied money to the economy at given interest rates, the Swedes had considered that assumption to be an analytical fiction, useful in order not to worry about the impact of money stocks. Frisch, on the other hand, felt deeply that it was this money-creating power of the commercial banks that was at the bottom of the cumulative process in the economy. It was money creation and money destruction that disrupted the savings–investment equilibrium and made the independent decision-making power of savers and investors so dangerous. It was that power that made *ex ante* saving so frequently differ from *ex ante* investment and, given a proper accounting system, even made great *ex post* discrepancies possible.

To the Stockholm School, and to Myrdal in particular, banks were unimportant. What mattered was that the current behavior of agents on both sides of the capital market was heavily influenced by moods dependent on uncertain expectations regarding the future consequences of today's behavior.[20]

In this context we should note that, like Ohlin, Frisch put greater emphasis on the active role of consumer behavior during cycles than did Myrdal and Lindahl. His perception of the economic depression was more dramatic, and his policy recommendations were frequently more drastic and unrealistic. However, they were all Keynesian. That was not a matter of dispute between Frisch and the Stockholm School.

Despite the strong disagreement about what the problems in macroeconomics really were, and how they should be studied, the agreement between the two and the "modernity" of their views was more striking than their differences. This reflected a common attitude to social problems among Nordic intellectuals at the time, not a shared macroeconomic model.

Jens Christopher Andvig

Notes

1 I am indebeted to Lars Jonung, Mary Morgan, and Björn Thalberg for their informed criticism, Eilert Struksnes for linguistic advice and corrections, and the Norwegian Council for Science and Humanities and the Norwegian Institute of International Affairs for financial assistance.

2 Lindahl (1930) is translated with a few corrections to English as "part Two" in Lindahl (1939).

3 "Om penningteoretisk jämvikt" was actually first printed in 1932 and then appeared in German. Frisch had access to both the Swedish and German editions when he discussed Myrdal. The English version was published in 1939. The three editions were all different, but for our purposes significantly so at only one point.

4 Frisch's lectures on Lindahl and Myrdal were planned as a part of the same series of lectures as the ones held on Wicksell. They too were called *83. Pengeteori* (Monetary Economics), which I shall use as a shorthand reference. The lectures on Lindahl and Myrdal, probably held during the autumn of 1935, were also reported and paginated, but not typed.

The reports were made by Trygve Haavelmo and were fairly long (more than 50 handwritten pages on Myrdal and over 100 pages on Lindahl). Frisch looked through the reports, but they were left rather unfinished and have not been mimeographed or published in any form. They were not officially approved by him. Nevertheless, I consider the reports on the whole to give an accurate account of Frisch's response to Myrdal's and Lindahl's theories. Thus I find it valid to use them in the following. They are filed in Ragnar Frisch's papers, box no. 38, "The Frisch Room," at the Department of Economics, University of Oslo.

5 His first formulation of the method was later published in Steiger (1971, pp. 204–11).

6 Cf. his remark in Frisch (1933, pp. 172–3): "The macro-dynamic analysis . . . tries to give an account of the fluctuations of the whole economic system taken in its entirety. Obviously in this case it is impossible to carry through the analysis in great detail. Of course, it is always possible to give even a macrodynamic analysis in detail if we confine ourselves to a purely *formal* theory. Indeed, it is always possible by a suitable system of subscripts and superscripts, etc., to introduce practically all factors imaginable. . . . Such a theory, however, would only have a rather limited interest. In such a theory it would hardly be possible to study such fundamental problems as the *exact time configuration* of solutions. . . ."

7 For a discussion on this weak link in Wicksell's theory, see Uhr (1960, pp. 241–6).

8 Frisch (*Pengeteori,* pp. 8311.3–6) noted these two major directions in which Lindahl developed Wicksell: "Lindahl's mode of analysis is mainly built on Wicksell's but has become more refined, especially in the following two respects: Firstly, Lindahl explicitly introduces the distinction *ex ante* and *ex*

post. . . . Secondly, . . . Lindahl considers production in the various stages. . . . The upper stage is represented by consumer goods production, the second stage by production which makes first order means of production, . . . and so on.

9 Bent Hansen (1981) made a similar observation on the Stockholm School. Frisch was not completely negative to the method as a preliminary exploration of the field, and told his students so: "Lindahl's method is really casuistic. He works through certain examples. Such a method has much to say for it in this case where the problem is so complicated. By appropriately chosen simplified assumptions one may then often succeed in elucidating essential features of the interconnections" (Frisch, *Pengeteori,* p. 8312.4). He even used the same method himself when he was asked to analyze the effects of open market operations for the Norwegian government in 1935 (see Frisch, 1935).

10 From a historical point of view, one may doubt whether Wicksell really intended to use his analysis of the "normal" rate for the study of short-run macroeconomic problems, as both Lindahl and Frisch presupposed. See Jonung (1979).

11 Frisch once asked Ohlin to publish his "Till frågan om penningteoriens uppläggning" for *Econometrica,* if he could elaborate it "a little bit" further, and then said that he by elaboration meant, first, "that the main lines of the argument could be expressed in an exact mathematical way, so it might be possible to see whether the problem was determinate or not. . . . [O]nly that way will it be possible to really explore whether the piece of reasoning really may yield a complete explanation of the economic system in question. . . . [I]t would also be interesting if it would be possible to make available certain numerical information that may specify the forms of the relation the theory consists of. . . . Do you recall when we took a long walk in the outskirts of Copenhagen and you told me about how difficult it was to choose between scientific and journalist-type work. I understood that you longed to return to the scientific work. Here is an excellent occasion" (letter from Frisch to Ohlin, September 26, 1933).

12 That is, it corresponded to Frisch's productivity rate in his Wicksell interpretation. See Andvig (1985, p. 161). As will be pointed out in the following, there were also other important dissimilarities: Frisch's productivity rate was a marginal concept while Myrdal's real rate was an average rate. Given the lack of explicit functions, marginal values of variables were difficult to discuss in Myrdal's construction.

13. Myrdal did not use the q symbol himself. I have chosen q because of the affinity of Myrdal's theory to Tobin's q-theory of investment (see Tobin, 1969). Like Keynes's investment demand schedule, this was not a pure demand function, but included the supply reactions of capital producers as well.

14 The mistake was pointed out by Frisch in a letter to Myrdal, February 7, 1935. (The letter is filed in the middle of Frisch's lectures on Myrdal, between p. 8310.1 and p. 8310.2.) I have been unable to discover Myrdal's

answer. It was later noted by Tord Palander (1941, p. 124). Palander was probably not quite aware of the importance of Myrdal's mistake here, since he did not emphasize it, and the mistake was crucial to the whole logical structure of Myrdal's macroeconomic reconstruction of Wicksell. It is difficult to see whether Myrdal actually responded to Frisch's criticism in the later English edition, since his discussion of this matter was less than precise.

15 Myrdal (1939) discussed this case on pages 106–9. He might have meant increased *rate* of savings out of a given income, but then his comments on consumption would have been trivial. I have simplified Myrdal's definition of savings by disregarding his discussion of gross savings, which in addition to net savings included an extremely complicated and obscure depreciation variable.

16 Ragnar Frisch "Et generelt monetært begrep- og symbol-system. Del av professor Frisch's forelesninger over Moderne Pengeteorier/Vårsem. og Høstsem. 1935" (A General System of Monetary Concepts and Terms. Part of Lectures Held on Monetary Theory/Spring term and Autumn term 1935). Mimeographed, but not published. It was reported by Trygve Haavelmo.

17 Frisch, Pengeteori, p. 8315.16. The same criticism of Myrdal was later made by Tord Palander (1941, pp. 112–13). The weakness of Myrdal's analysis on this point is obvious.

18 This does not imply that Myrdal would have no use for statistical regression techniques when eventually constructing his indices, but the statistical techniques were then used at a lower level of the analysis. They were not to be used in a direct way to confront his theory with empirical observations. This was done through the comparison of the indices. Myrdal's idea of index comparisons was probably partly inspired by the then influential business cycle research tradition. See Andvig (1981).

19 A more detailed exposition and criticism is found in Andvig (1985, pp. 265–70).

20 Here we may note the fact that the Norwegian banking system was very decentralized compared to the Swedish one and had behaved in a very disorderly way several times during the interwar period. In this respect it was more like the U.S. system than the Swedish system.

References

Andvig, Jens Christopher (1981), "Ragnar Frisch and Business Cycle Research During the Interwar Years," *History of Political Economy,* No. 4.

(1985), *Ragnar Frisch and the Great Depression: A Study in the Interwar History of Macroeconomic Theory and Policy.* Oslo: Norwegian Institute of International Affairs.

Frisch, Ragnar (1933), "Propagation Problems and Impulse Problems in Dynamic Economics," in Karin Koch, ed., *Economic Essays in Honour of Gustav Cassel.* London: George Allen and Unwin Ltd.

(1934), "Circulation Planning. Proposal for a National Organization of a Commodity and Service Exchange," *Econometrica*.

(1934-5), "Pengeteori. En gjennomgåelse av hovedpunktene i de moderne penge- og kreditt-teorier" (partly mimeographed, partly handwritten manuscripts), Oslo.

(1935), "Open Market Operations og deres virkninger på banksystemet," in Finans- og Tolldepartementet, "Innstilling om Markedsoperasjoner" (Open Market Operations), avgitt av Komitéen til utredning av økonomiske og pengepolitiske spørsmål. Oslo: Det Mallingske Bogtrykkeri.

Hansen, Bent (1981), "Unemployment, Keynes and the Stockholm School," *History of Political Economy*, No. 2.

Hansson, Björn (1982), *The Stockholm School and the Development of Dynamic Method.* London: Croom Helm.

Hayek, Friedrich A. von, ed. (1933), *Beiträge zur Geldtheorie.* Vienna: Verlag von Julius Springer.

Hicks, John (1946), *Value and Capital.* Oxford: Oxford University Press.

Jonung, Lars (1979), "Knut Wicksell and Gustav Cassel on Secular Movements in Prices," *Journal of Money, Credit and Banking,* no. 2.

Keynes, John Maynard (1936), *The General Theory of Employment, Interest and Money.* London: Macmillan. Reprint ed. London: Macmillan, 1967.

(1930), *A Treatise on Money,* Vol. I: *The Pure Theory of Money.* As reprinted in J. M. Keynes, *Collected Writings,* Vol. V, London: Macmillan, for the Royal Economic Society, 1971.

Lindahl, Erik (1929), "Prisbildningsproblemet från kapitalteoretisk synpunkt," *Ekonomisk Tidskrift.*

(1930), *Penningpolitikens medel.* Lund: C. W. K. Gleerup.

(1939), *Studies in the Theory of Money and Capital.* London: George Allen & Unwin.

(1971), "A Note on the Dynamic Pricing Problem," Anhang II in Otto Steiger, *Studien zur Entstehung der neuen Wirtschaftslehre in Schweden.*

Lundberg, Erik (1937), *Studies in the Theory of Economic Expansion.* London: R. S. King and Son.

Myrdal, Gunnar (1927), *Prisbildningen och föränderligheten.* Uppsala: Almquist & Wiksell.

(1930), "Om penningteoretisk jämvikt," *Ekonomisk Tidskrift,* No. 5-6.

(1933), "Der Gleichgewichtsbegriff als Instrument in der geldtheoretischen Analyse," in Friedrich A. von Hayek, ed., *Beiträge zur Geldtheorie.*

(1934), *Finanspolitikens ekonomiska verkningar* (SOU, 1934:1), Stockholm: Kungliga Boktryckeriet P. A. Nordstedt & Söner.

(1939), *Monetary Equilibrium.* London: W. Hodge.

Palander, Tord (1941), "Om Stockholmsskolans begrepp och metoder. Metodologiska reflexioner kring Myrdals 'Monetary Equilibrium,'" *Ekonomisk Tidskrift,* No. 3.

Petersson, Jan (1987), *Erik Lindahl och Stockholmsskolans dynamiska metod,* Lund: Universitetsförlaget Dialogos AB.

Schumpeter, Joseph A. (1965), *History of Economic Analysis.* New York: Oxford University Press.

Tobin, James (1969), "A General Equilibrium Approach to Monetary Theory," *Journal of Money, Credit and Banking,* February.

Uhr, Carl G. (1960), *The Economic Doctrines of Knut Wicksell.* Berkeley: University of California Press.

Comment

BJÖRN THALBERG

The mutual influence between the Stockholm School and Ragnar Frisch of Oslo was, as is evident from Andvig's paper, very limited. The Stockholm School may be described as a group of Swedish economists who, between 1927 and 1937, worked together to develop a dynamic method, a development that was, once under way, almost completely isolated from outside influences (Hansson, 1982). Frisch, on the other side, was obviously very interested in and well acquainted with the ideas and thoughts of the Stockholm School. He lectured on Lindahl and Myrdal in the mid-1930s, and he considered, as did most members of the Stockholm School, Wicksell his most important teacher. However, he as a rule opposed the Stockholm School's ideas.

Andvig's paper gives an illuminative and fairly detailed account of Frisch's view of the writings of the Stockholm School. I shall limit my comments on it to giving, partly as a supplement to Andvig's exposition, a brief perspective of the differences in methods and outlook between Frisch and the Stockholm School that I find particularly interesting.

1. Frisch had early [in an explicitly stated program (Andvig, 1985)] devoted himself to the task of making economics a more precise and quantitative science. For this reason he wanted to continue the work of Cournot, Jevons, et al., to develop static and dynamic mathematical analyses, and moreover to develop econometrics. His program and efforts also included a crusade against "verbalism," more precisely "unsound verbalism," that is, the typical verbal and loose writings at the time, with very often unclear or imprecise assumptions, invalid conclusions, and speculations without reliable empirical foundation.

The members of the Stockholm School would, I think, wholeheartedly endorse only one part of the Frisch program: his attempt to improve the empirical foundation of economic theory. They were themselves often engaged in empirical research. Still, they did not take part in the development of econometrics. (In fact, econometrics became for a long time a neglected subject in Stockholm.) They met Frisch's enthusiasm for formalization and more mathematical methods in economics with a great deal of skepticism. While Frisch did not hesitate to use complicated mathematics whenever he found it necessary, the Stockholm School members expressed themselves in formal terms only occasionally, and then as a rule in a simple way. In contrast to Frisch, they were not trained, and did not train their students, in formal methods. They generally emphasized that their writings should be readable also for the interested layman, and did not take any great interest in Frisch's crusade against verbalism.

2. In order to construct a manageable macroeconomic model, Frisch often used very crude simplifications and ad hoc assumptions. He wrote (Frisch, 1933) that in order to analyze an economy in its entirety, we may disregard a considerable amount of details in the picture, throw all kinds of production into one variable, all consumption into another, and so on. In fact, he was willing, at least as a first approximation, to neglect the question of microeconomic underpinning of macroeconomic theory.

The Stockholm School members, on the other hand, strived to construct dynamic macromodels that were comparatively less aggregated and simplified, and that built directly on assumptions of the behavior of the acting economic agents. Thus, they were relatively strong as to the question of underpinning, but on the other hand, their analyses tended to be overly complicated and thus they often ended up with more partial models than they originally intended or with application of a casuistic method discussing through certain examples.

3. The Stockholm School members strongly emphasized the need to apply dynamic methods. Typically, they criticized the model of Keynes's *General Theory* as being too static. They were inclined, I think, to consider the usual IS-LM comparative statics exercises as oversimplified.

Frisch too was eager to develop dynamic theory. However, he certainly also acknowledged the comparative advantages of the method of comparative statics, and he did not refrain from simple comparative statics analysis when he found it instructive. [I disagree with Andvig's assertion that Frisch also "deplored the statics of Keynes's *General Theory*." Cf. his favorable assessment of Keynes's book (Frisch, 1947).]

4. As to the question of the degree of permanence of economic laws, Frisch was probably more optimistic than most other economists. When formulated in an appropriate way, laws that express economic behavior or phenomena were, he believed, as a rule reasonably stable. He used to

demonstrate to his students how (for large groups) the average behavior could be fairly stable even when the individual behavior was highly volatile and unpredictable.

The Swedes obviously did not share Frisch's optimism in this respect. They emphasized, to the contrary, volatile expectations and other factors that tend to make economic relationships not very time invariant.

5. Both Frisch and the members of the Stockholm School were strongly engaged in guidance of economic policy, but their approaches differed. Frisch stuck to an econometric model-building approach, working first with macroeconomic "decision models" and later with planning models of the programming type. He even attempted, by interviews and other methods, to establish preference functions of leading politicians so as to be able to approach the policy-decision problem on the basis of an optimization procedure.

The approach of the Stockholm School members was surely more modest. They did not have the same confidence in explicit use of large macroeconomic models, but instead built their advice on their insight based partly on economic theory and partly on practical experience.

References

Andvig, J. C. (1985), *Ragnar Frisch and the Great Depression: A Study in the Interwar History of Macroeconomic Theory and Policy.* Oslo: NUPI.

Hansson, B. A. (1982), *The Stockholm School and the Development of Dynamic Method.* London: Croom Helm.

Frisch, R. (1933), "Propagation Problems and Impulse Problems in Dynamic Economics," in *Essays in Honour of Gustav Cassel.* London: George Allen & Unwin.

Frisch, R. (1947), *Noen trekk av konjunkturlären.* Oslo: Aschehoug.

CHAPTER 19

The late development of the Stockholm School and the criticism from Johan Åkerman[1]

JAN PETERSSON

For many economists, the Stockholm School came to an end around 1937 when Bertil Ohlin gave it a name and based it on earlier contributions by Swedish economists. The "battle" was then lost to John Maynard Keynes, whose method, while less genuinely dynamic, was easier to handle. A discussion of the macroeconomics of the Stockholm School up to 1937 still appears to be of interest and underlines the role of Bertil Ohlin, Erik Lindahl, and Erik Lundberg as prominent members of the School.

To restate the critique of the Stockholm School by Johan Åkerman implies focusing on a very special part of the work carried out within the School. To understand his critique, we cannot restrict ourselves to the years before 1937 and to merely the macroeconomics of those years. When Åkerman is critical toward the Stockholm School, he is critical toward a method and a microeconomic construction.

During the years following 1937 the Stockholm School came to be associated with a method within Sweden. The cornerstones of that method were *plans, periods,* and *expectations.* They were microeconomic concepts and were fully elaborated *after* 1937. Maybe it would be wise to talk about a "late Stockholm School" in this context (see Petersson, 1987). The idea of change within the Stockholm School is not a new one. Otto Steiger (1971) suggested such a division and Björn A. Hansson (1982) made the development of dynamic method the main theme of his thesis on the School.

There was a lively discussion of these issues in the 1950s. To understand Åkerman's criticism, we need to elaborate the methodological standpoint and the microeconomic construction of Erik Lindahl. This paper does that and brings Lindahl into a more prominent position within the School than is generally recognized.

435

1   Lindahl's methodology

In the newly written first part of his *Studies,* Lindahl (1939) argued for the construction of a general dynamic theory. By that time, he was convinced that the relationship between actual macroeconomic developments and microeconomic behavior needed to be worked out. This would provide the 1937 "School" with a *stålskelett* (blueprint) and strengthen its position. Scattered theoretical approaches, more or less based on Wicksell, could be made coherent if they could be founded on *one* common microeconomic theory.

Lindahl in particular had arrived at the conclusion that the theoretical starting point for an explanation of inflation must be a microeconomic theory of price movements. This was a central idea when he started to think of writing a new book in the early 1930s. For a while, he planned to write an extensive book, moving from micro to macro as the main thread, to be published in English with Allen & Unwin as publisher. Although he produced an outline of this grand idea, it nevertheless collapsed into a dense and somewhat fragmentary first part in *Studies.* The remaining parts were by and large translations into English of his earlier main writings (Lindahl, 1929b, 1930).

In the first part of *Studies,* Lindahl tells us that a *general* theory must be constructed before special theories are elaborated. "Theory comes before evidence" for Lindahl. Besides being general, he thought that his theory had to be *dynamic.* A microeconomic theory that would help to provide the right connection to Swedish macroeconomics had further to be dynamic in a proper sense to Lindahl, that is, built on time lags, many decision makers, and incomplete information.

In a way, Lindahl was the right person to try to construct a dynamic theory. He had extensive experience of static methods. Gustav Cassel's and Gunnar Myrdal's writings were available, and Lindahl (1929a) had himself worked on the inclusion of capital theory on Austrian/Wicksellian lines in the Walras/Cassel general equilibrium construction. At the same time he seems to have made a mistake, not rare in the 1930s; he identified the Walrasian construction as the theory for a stationary state and thereby underestimated its usefulness.

2   Lindahl's microeconomics

Lindahl worked with what he called "one basic assumption," namely, that economic acts "represent merely the fulfillment of certain plans given at the beginning of the period and determined by certain principles which it is possible to state in one way or another" (*Studies,* p. 36).

Lindahl gave the planning concept a central position. In his view, the acts of *all* decision makers could be characterized as acts of planning, achieving the generalization he aimed at. Harald Dickson (1957d) later called this planning in "a wide sense."

Plans, however, point to the preliminary character of a decision. In "a strict sense" plans disclose that acts are only expected to be brought about. Unforeseen events make future acts only preliminary, that is, open to modification or elimination. By focusing on expectations, planning in "a strict sense" paved the way for the dynamic approach.

Plans and expectations became two cornerstones in the microeconomic construction of the Stockholm School. Lindahl probably was quite satisfied with this development, something he had not been a few years earlier. In correspondence with Albert Gailord Hart in 1934 Lindahl regretted that he had not been working himself on a more formal microeconomic representation, using the word plan. He needed help from outside, and it would soon materialize.

Previously, Gunnar Myrdal (1927) had thoroughly penetrated the problem of uncertainty in his dissertation. All components of uncertainty were examined by him, aiming at *Verstehen*. By gaining a total understanding, the problem of uncertainty could be worked into a static theory of price formation. Nothing but the time factor itself should be left out, as Myrdal saw it. The first step toward a theory of "planning at a certain point" was, if we look upon it in this way, worked out by Myrdal. To become useful to Lindahl, it had to be developed further. This was done by Ingvar Svennilson, who extended Myrdal's approach by making explicit intertemporal connections that had to be considered if one was to talk more accurately about decisions as plans. Moreover, in contrast to Myrdal, Svennilson (1938) made planning the centerpiece of his dissertation and not just an element in understanding and describing price formation.

A plausible conclusion is that Svennilson, drawing on Myrdal, provided Lindahl with a tighter description of "planning at a certain point." This planning recurred at certain intervals. "Periods of fixed relevant plans" succeeded one another, according to Svennilson. Lindahl was encouraged. However, he was in need of one more element to get a more fully dynamic treatment. The *ex ante–ex post* elements had to be brought in. Only then could the new microeconomics correspond to earlier Swedish macroeconomics. Lindahl himself outlined the "revision of plans." While Myrdal and Svennilson had worked on the *ex ante* problem, Lindahl studied the *ex post* side by addressing this problem of revising plans.

The need for revision comes out of disappointments caused by

incomplete information. Unforeseen events, altered "valuation attitudes," and rigid prices caused problems and the need for revision. Lindahl presented the "period of registration" as an element of a formal
solution. Its existence was due to "the general deficiency of human
knowledge" (*Studies,* p. 49). Period analysis completed the dynamic
approach that Lindahl (1930) and Dag Hammarskjöld (1933) had outlined on general lines earlier.

There is nothing new about period analysis. Actual economic life
abounds with periods. The identification of time lags means denoting a
period. Periods had been part of theories and models for a long time.
Business cycles, for example, are built on periodic recurrences. Explicit
theoretical treatment of periods, however, is complicated if these theories are not very partial since there are so many periods. Lindahl
touched upon a usable idea. The period analysis could be based on general problems in decision making. The two periods presented above
were fundamental in decision making.

John Hicks (1979), Lindahl's and Myrdal's dialectical partner in chis-
eling out the "temporary equilibrium" concept, later devised a prior and
a posterior step as essentials in decision making. These reflections come
close to Lindahl's interpretation of the problem. There is, however, one
main problem left. If the two periods were to be used in one and the
same period analysis, they had to be theoretical concepts. They could
indeed be based on essential empirical properties. However, in trying to
cope with many different aspects affecting decision making and many
actors, the analysis lost contact with an empirically defined unifying
period that had overall validity.

Åkerman's repeated attacks on the Stockholm School are principally
connected with the questions of methodology and of microeconomics
raised here.

3   Johan Åkerman as an economist

Johan Åkerman was not impressed by the method devised by Lindahl
that characterized the Stockholm School. To underline his dissatisfaction with the School and, it should be pointed out, with most economic
theories as well, Åkerman presented an alternative. He accepted the
name of the Lund School for it, alluding to the university where he was
professor, when he debated the Stockholm School in *Ekonomisk Tidskrift* in the 1950s (see Åkerman, 1953, 1954, 1956a, 1956b, 1957a,
1957b, 1957c). To understand his criticism, we must first take a closer
look at Johan Åkerman as an economist.

Åkerman had two great interests in his work in economics. One was the study of economic fluctuation – business cycles, structural changes, and long-term changes. The other was methodology. These two interests combined to form the background and starting point of his criticism of the Stockholm School. Åkerman had a marked tendency to express strong opinions and to use rather personal concepts and language. Sometimes it is difficult to understand exactly what he meant, and it is easy to misinterpret him. What is presented here should be considered as one interpretation of his ideas.

Åkerman's (1928) doctoral dissertation was a study of the business cycle, using a large amount of statistical data. It is accurate to regard his dissertation as the first econometric study of any importance in Sweden.[2] Some years later (Åkerman, 1939, 1944), he published a large methodological, theoretical, and empirical study, including an analysis of every business cycle from 1815. His idea was that the total economic activity, and therefore the business cycle, was the result of the actions of different social groups with different goals, different means, and different planning periods. He singled out eight such groups, estimating an index for each of them to denote its influence during the upswings and the downswings of the cycles.

The existence of social groups and the complicated interplay among them give rise to what Åkerman called the summation problem, a problem of relating the actions of separate groups to total activity, that is, a sort of aggregation problem. In his opinion, it was necessary to start every study of a business cycle, or of other developments in the economy, by an identification not only of the important social groups but also of the social structure in which they were acting. The latter point involved, among other things, the relative size of the public sector. One cannot expect, he held, the same theory to be relevant in an economy where the public sector takes 10 percent of the national income and also in an economy where that sector takes a 50 percent share. However, the summation problem in all its details could not be solved once and for all since the social structure, the relative influence of various groups, and the behavior of these groups will change from one situation to another.

Åkerman was interested in making economic theory more "realistic." Neoclassical economics relied on simplifications like economic man and perfect competition that represented, he thought, an "ordre naturel" long bypassed. Åkerman (1956b) even dared to believe that Knut Wicksell, if brought back to life, would agree. It is not wrong to call Åkerman an institutionalist. At least he praised Veblen and Myrdal's scientific style. When he characterized his own method, Åkerman (1942, p. 51) argued that it was a synthesis between "rationalism and empiricism."

4   Åkerman's criticism of the Stockholm School

Åkerman's arguments against the Stockholm School were centered around three main points.

First, he disliked the idea of a general theory. He explicitly stated that this was the "most extraneous idea among those of the Stockholm School" (Åkerman, 1957c, p. 216). Åkerman opposed the idea that one could start with a general theory and make this more special when studying concrete cases. Empirical considerations could not be made secondary, in Åkerman's opinion. In consequence, he disliked Lindahl's idea of a general theory of planning, where specific actors were not singled out.

There is no doubt that Åkerman, though not a "positivist," on this point criticized the Stockholm School from the positivist side. As scientific styles changed with the passage of time, the Stockholm School's insistence on starting out from general theory rather than partial evidence made their approach outmoded.

The aim of the microeconomics Lindahl developed was to build a bridge to the more elaborated macroeconomics of the School. Its macroeconomics was developed with a good insight into accounting problems and national income categories. Åkerman, however, was dissatisfied with the School's failure to examine problems of aggregation. He related this criticism to his own summation problem.

A second major point of criticism against the Stockholm School was initiated by the summation problem. From a methodological point of view, Åkerman meant that the School underestimated the importance of the aggregation problem and did not show any interest in its solution. He also held that the problem could not be solved in the general setting of the School. It was inadequately treated in the general scheme of Lindahl and in the sequence analysis of Lundberg (1937), where general concepts like total consumption, saving, and investment were used without going back to the relevant actors behind the concepts. This concealed the difficulties of the summation problem.

Åkerman also held that the summation problem had consequences for the central concepts of period, plan, and expectations in the Stockholm School. The fundamental reason was that the planning horizon will change not only between different actors, but also for a certain actor between different time points because of changes in the social and structural setting. During a crisis the planning period will be very short, and during a period of prosperity and stability it will be relatively long. In his study of political cycles in the United States, he expressed the idea that the planning period tended to be short before an election and to increase when the new president had been elected and his program was known. When Åkerman discussed the summation problem, his criticism of Lindahl's general concepts become more detailed.

There is little doubt that Åkerman was of the opinion that he was revealing a major weakness of the Stockholm School when he pointed out that they neglected the summation problem. Åkerman's and Lindahl's different approaches are, however, due to differences in methodology. Åkerman stressed the importance of different social groups and the problem of how the interaction of these groups generated factual developments. Lindahl, on the other hand, tried to handle this complex situation with an abstract, general theory and a general idea of periods, expectations, and plans without an explicit treatment of special groups of actors. Åkerman's summation problem was not overtly relevant to Lindahl; maybe it was even nonexistent to him.

A third point of criticism of the School concerned its treatment of expectations. Lindahl in *Studies* and Lundberg in his dissertation of 1937 played down the complications of the formation of expectations. Åkerman pointed this out and considered it to be a deficiency. Lundberg's model sequences, which Åkerman saw as too mechanical, became the target of recurring criticism.

Åkerman disliked the way expectations were treated in economic theory in general. The Stockholm School obviously became the object of Åkerman's critical arguments because it was close at hand. And I think that he was most unjust toward the School on this point. Particularly Myrdal and Lindahl in the 1920s thoroughly discussed the problems involved, as stressed above. When Lindahl later tried to build a general theory, he found the formation of expectations too complicated to deal with it extensively. The more "subjective" elements as well as noneconomic unforeseen events must be left to the special theories, where "differentiations" should be considered, he argued. When in *Studies* he presented a general setting and focused on short-sighted, recurring decisions, he could further ignore the formation of expectations to some extent. However, to a critic like Åkerman the general theory was outlined in a "stereotyped" way. We should note that Lundberg, too, deliberately disregarded behavioral equations in his dissertation since an inquiry into microeconomics did not serve his purpose. The decision process was thus left out.

The critique by Johan Åkerman, mainly in the early 1950s, and the defending arguments by Harald Dickson (1957a, 1957b, 1957c, 1957d, 1958) and Ragnar Bentzel and Bent Hansen (1953, 1954a, 1954b) on behalf of the Stockholm School represent somewhat of an end in looking at the School as a topic of current interest. Some shortcomings of the Stockholm School were clearly brought out in that debate – a debate that Lindahl himself did not enter – and should not be regarded as recent findings. I will mention two that are important in understanding why the Stockholm School failed to attract the interest of young economists in the post–World War II period.

First, the Stockholm School had a hard time finding the proper degree of generality. They had, like the Austrians, a problem in balancing accurate and complete descriptions of reality with workable, manageable models. Second, from the 1930s and onwards the idea of general theory as a starting point lost out to partial empirically oriented theories as the common methodology in economics.

Notes

1 This chapter contains ideas which are more fully elaborated in my dissertation (see Petersson, 1987). The comments made at the conference by Bengt Höglund are incorporated into the sections on Johan Åkerman.
2 Three famous names in the Scandinavian history of economics appeared at the *disputation* in Lund. The first was Ragnar Frisch, who was the opponent selected by the university. The second was Fredrik Zeuthen, selected by Åkerman himself. The third was Wicksell, not Knut of course but Sven, a son of Knut, at that time professor of statistics in Lund.

References

Åkerman, Johan (1928), *Om det ekonomiska livets rytmik.* Stockholm: Nordiska bokhandeln.
   (1939), *Ekonomisk teori I.* Lund: Gleerup.
   (1942), "Ekonomisk kalkyl och kausalanalys," *Ekonomisk Tidskrift,* 3–22.
   (1944), *Ekonomisk teori II.* Lund: Gleerup.
   (1953), "Summeringsproblemet, modellförlopp och konjunkturproblem," *Ekonomisk Tidskrift,* 247–64.
   (1954), "Genmäle till Ragnar Bentzel och Bent Hansen," *Ekonomisk Tidskrift,* 55–65.
   (1956a), "Recension av F. Zeuthen, *Economic Theory and Method,*" *Ekonomisk Tidskrift,* 180–2.
   (1956b), "De ekonomiska beslutens katalysatorer," *Ekonomisk Tidskrift,* 201–8.
   (1957a), "Genmäle," *Ekonomisk Tidskrift,* 62–3.
   (1957b), "Genmäle till Dickson," *Ekonomisk Tidskrift,* 161–5.
   (1957c), "Replik till Harald Dickson," *Ekonomisk Tidskrift,* 213–18.
Bentzel, Ragnar, and Bent Hansen, (1953), "Om simultanitet i ekonomiska modeller," *Ekonomisk Tidskrift,* 81–99.

(1954a), "Summeringsproblemet, modellförlopp och konjunkturpolitik. Replik till Johan Åkerman," *Ekonomisk Tidskrift*, 48–55.

(1954b), "Summeringsproblemet, modellförlopp och konjunkturpolitik, Slutreplik till Johan Åkerman," *Ekonomisk Tidskrift*, 139–47.

Dickson, Harald (1957a), "Orden 'plan' och 'beslut' hos Johan Åkerman och hos Stockholmsskolan," *Ekonomisk Tidskrift*, 60–2.

(1957b), "Om orden 'kausalanalys' och 'kalkylmodell' i Johan Åkermans kritik av Stockholmsskolan m m.," *Ekonomisk Tidskrift*, 251–72.

(1957c), "Om Stockholmsskolans teoribildning," *Ekonomisk Tidskrift*, 158–61.

(1957d), "Plan och period," *Ekonomisk Tidskrift*, 251–72.

Dickson, Harald, and Johan Åkerman (1958), "Om Stockholmsskolans metod. En ekonomisk-teoretisk diskussion," *Statsvetenskaplig Tidskrift*, 117–40.

Hammarskjöld, Dag (1933), *Konjunkturspridningen. En teoretisk och historisk undersökning*. SOU, 1933:29.

Hansson, Björn (1982), *The Stockholm School and the Development of Dynamic Method*. London: Croom Helm.

Hicks, John R. (1979), *Causality in Economics*. Oxford: Blackwell.

Lindahl, Erik (1929a), "Prisbildningsproblemets uppläggning från kapitalteoretisk synpunkt," *Ekonomisk Tidskrift*, 31–81.

(1929b), *Penningpolitikens mål*. Lund: Gleerup.

(1930), *Penningpolitikens medel*. Lund: Gleerup.

(1939), *Studies in the Theory of Money and Capital*. London: Allen & Unwin.

Lundberg, Erik (1937), *Studies in the Theory of Economic Expansion*. Stockholm.

Myrdal, Gunnar (1927), *Prisbildningsproblemet och föränderligheten*. Uppsala: Almqvist & Wiksell.

Petersson, Jan (1987), *Erik Lindahl och Stockholmsskolans dynamiska metod*. Lund: Dialogos.

Steiger, Otto (1971), *Studien zur Entstehung der Neuen Wirtschaftslehre in Schweden. Eine Anti-Kritik*. Berlin.

Svennilson, Ingvar (1938), *Ekonomisk planering. Teoretiska studier*. Uppsala.

Comment

ROLF G. H. HENRIKSSON

In his dissertation, Jan Petersson (1987) discusses the microfoundations of the Stockholm School as set out by Erik Lindahl (1939) in his *Studies in the Theory of Money and Capital*. Here Lindahl attempted to meet the Keynesian challenge and give the Stockholm School a new lease on life by clarifying how its research program was a quest for a general dynamic theory. In providing the background to Lindahl's work, Petersson also sheds new light on the development of the Stockholm School during the 1930s. However, the major thrust of his dissertation is forward in time, rendering an account of the debate in Sweden that followed Lindahl's study. Petersson argues that this debate and the continued theoretical discussion in Sweden justifies calling it "the late Stockholm School," or at least "the late phase" of the Stockholm School.

Since Petersson's interesting dissertation is available only in Swedish, it is regrettable that the brevity of his paper does not fully satisfy the need for an English exposition. It only whets the appetite for a more elaborate presentation and offers little scope for criticism. However, Erik Lindahl's and Johan Åkerman's contributions concern the central issues in present-day controversy on the Stockholm School approach. Fairness to the author as well as to the theme invites at least a small transgression of the tight page constraint that might otherwise be appropriate for a commentary on such a brief paper. Building on research of my own into Lindahl's writings, I would like to offer a few complementary notes. However, since I have in addition benefited from a close reading of Petersson's dissertation, they should also be viewed as complimentary.

The most striking point in Petersson's account of Åkerman's criticism of the Stockholm School is perhaps Åkerman's view that two of its leading members, Erik Lundberg and Erik Lindahl, played down the role of expectations. It is true that this was the way expectations were formally treated in Lundberg's (1937) dissertation and by Lindahl in his *Studies* of 1939. However, Lundberg never held the view that they were of only minor importance from a causal point of view. The main reason he played them down in his formal numerical sequence models was that they could not be operationalized and measured as objective behavior relations. The reason they played such a small role in Lindahl's account was, as Petersson points out, that they were to receive their due attention in the various special theories Lindahl had in mind but never spelled out in his *Studies.*

I agree with Petersson that Åkerman's failure to recognize this fact led to his grossly unjust criticism of the School, whose very banner was the notion of *ex ante.* However, Petersson does not explain why Åkerman adopted this view. He says that Åkerman "disliked the way expectations were treated in economic theory in general" and that "the Stockholm School obviously became the object of Åkerman's criticism because it was close at hand." However, his research suggests that the main reason for Åkerman's adverse view of the work of other economists on expectations was that he thought he had a theory of his own contained in the notion of planning horizon. Furthermore, the reason he did not pay closer attention to the way the Stockholm School members treated expectations is that, "being close at hand," their treatment was not that far from Åkerman's own approach. There seems to have been a psychological defense mechanism at work that might have prevented Åkerman from admitting that he too was simply spurred on by the seminal work of Myrdal. However, this hypothesis is not the only one possible. Petersson's account of Åkerman's criticism of the Stockholm School approach to expectations brings attention to the fact that a major difficulty for Åkerman was the inherent awkwardness of Lindahl's planning concept combined with the intricacies of all the other microtheoretical base concepts used by Lindahl. However, it should of course be added that on this point Lindahl is a marvel of lucid reasoning in comparison with Åkerman himself.

Despite the difficulties, Petersson generally succeeds in giving a fairly good account of Åkerman's position. Åkerman's criticism of the way in which his so-called summation problem was treated seems quite well stated, although one suspects that the criticism was directed more at the Keynesian school than at the Stockholm School. However, Petersson's contrasting of Lindahl and Åkerman seems a bit overdrawn. Lindahl (1941, pp. 238 and 246) yielded to Åkerman on this point, as Åkerman himself later recognized (see Åkerman, 1953, p. 252). In fact, Lindahl actually endorsed Åkerman's concern for "the institutional fit" already in 1939 (see Lindahl, 1939, p. 28).

However, Petersson is certainly correct in stressing the difference between their approaches as an account of how Åkerman viewed them. We might again want to invoke Åkerman's particular personality characteristics. Unlike Lindahl he was prone to enhancing the differences rather than the similarities between their approaches.

The charges directed at the Stockholm School by Åkerman emanated from a deep methodological disagreement with the School. This was revealed by Åkerman's declamatory denouncement of the general approach of Lindahl, as is well spelled out in Petersson's quotation. However, his account only touches upon, but quite understandably never mentions by name, the two key terms in Åkerman's "dualistic'" position: *kausal* analysis and *kalkyl* analysis. Admittedly, they are very difficult to render into English. Certainly, using the translation "causal" for *kausal* is formally correct, but this can invite misunderstandings. The term *kalkyl* stands for subjective evaluations and appraisals but should not be equated with the notion of planning. Although both concepts seem close to the respective Stockholm School notions, *ex ante* and *ex post*, Åkerman never admitted that the difference between himself and the Stockholm School was mainly one of terminology. As Petersson accepts Åkerman's position after his close reading of the texts, we would have welcomed his expert elaboration of this very inaccessible heartland of Åkerman's thinking.

The undertaking of *kausal* and *kalkyl* analysis is, according to Åkerman, a necessary prerequisite before the summation problem can be solved. Furthermore, his vehement attacks on both the Keynesian and the Stockholm School theories on this score are, as Petersson notes, backed up by the somewhat baffling claim that Wicksell seems to have taken "precursory" notice of Åkerman's methodological norm. According to Åkerman, Wicksell performed such an analysis in setting forth his famous amendment to the quantity theory (see Wicksell, 1898, 1936). This claim cannot withstand closer scrutiny, although Åkerman has touched on an aspect of Wicksell's work that has been neglected. Wicksell strongly advocated historical and empirical testing of theories in a quite modern manner (see Wicksell, 1958).

According to Petersson, Lindahl made the mistake of identifying the Walrasian construction as the theory for the stationary state and thereby also underestimated the usefulness of the Walrasian construction. However, in my view Lindahl's argument against the Walrasian approach had less to do with its lack of time dimension and was more a reaction against its "atomistic" premise. Here Lindahl seems actually to have joined forces with Åkerman in a criticism of Ohlin.

In concluding, Petersson explains why the Stockholm School failed despite the resuscitation attempt by Lindahl; in his view, Lindahl's approach was too general. Lindahl never worked out any of the special theories that would have been required to hold on to a leading place in the international scientific advance of the profession. Yet, did the Stockholm School fail? Ohlin said in 1941, while lauding Lindahl's study, that if the School could produce another work of that quality within a decade, the School would be saved. Of course, many would argue that the work of Bent Hansen (1951) was such a work.

Petersson also says that Lindahl never joined the debate in the 1950s about his proposed microfoundations for the Stockholm School. It may be true that he never himself answered Åkerman, but he was at that time the grand old man of the School, leading the work in Uppsala where both Hansen and Bentzel, who had criticized Åkerman, were his disciples. Furthermore, Lindahl continued to work on the issues raised in *Studies*. He would no doubt have come out with a formal statement in reply to the Åkerman criticism in due time if his life had not been cut short somewhat prematurely. He did, however, publish his final thoughts on Keynes (see Lindahl, 1954). In this profound paper, Lindahl presented a Stockholm School interpretation using his microfoundation concepts to explain why Keynes's equilibrium method could win the day in relation to policy concerns by using a long-run static approach while failing to solve the real analytical problem, that is, the short-run dynamic one. This could only be tackled by the disequilibrium method Lindahl dealt with in his *Studies*. Here Lindahl presented an interpretation of Keynes that seems not to have been understood by those on the Keynesian bandwagon until Clower and Leijonhufvud opened the Pandora's box of disequilibrium interpretations of Keynes first provided by Patinkin.

We have today come full circle via the Lucasian revolution to a somewhat pre-Keynesian position in the New Classical Economics, reminiscent of the embryonic Stockholm School in the late 1920s. We may now at last be ready to understand what Lindahl wanted to say.

References

Åkerman, Johan (1953), "Summeringsproblemet, modellförlopp och konjunkturproblem" (The summation problem, model sequences and business cycle problems), *Ekonomisk Tidskrift*, 55, 247–64.

Hansen, Bent (1951), *A Study in the Theory of Inflation*. London: Allen & Unwin.

Lindahl, Erik (1939), *Studies in the Theory of Money and Capital*. London: Allen & Unwin.

(1941), "Professor Ohlin om dynamisk teori. Ett genmäle" (Professor Ohlin on dynamic theory. A reply), *Ekonomisk Tidskrift*, 43, 236–47.

(1954), "On Keynes' Economic System," *Economic Record*, 30, 19–32 and 159–71.

Lundberg, Erik, (1937), *Studies in the Theory of Economic Expansion*, Stockholm Economic Studies, No. 6. London: P. S. King and Son.

Petersson, Jan (1987), *Erik Lindahl och Stockholmsskolans dynamiska metod* (Erik Lindahl and the dynamic method of the Stockholm School), Lund Economic Studies, No. 39. Lund: Dialogos.

Wicksell, Knut (1898), *Geldzins und Güterpreise*. Jena: Gustav Fischer.

(1936), *Interest and Prices*. London: Macmillan.

(1958), "Ends and Means in Economics," in E. Lindahl, ed., *Selected Papers in Economic Theory by Knut Wicksell*. London: Allen & Unwin.

PART IV

What Remains of the Stockholm School?

Roundtable discussion

Assar Lindbeck

It is important to emphasize the obvious distinction between the Stockholm *economists* of the 1930s and the Stockholm *School* of Keynesian-oriented macroeconomics. The former was a brilliant group of individuals who, except for Erik Lundberg, made their main contributions in fields outside of Keynesian-oriented macroeconomics. I refer, for instance, to Erik Lindahl's contributions to the theory of public finance, intertemporal allocation of resources, and the theory of interest rates and prices; Bertil Ohlin's achievements in the theory of international trade; Gunnar Myrdal's creative discussion of uncertainty and his reinterpretation of Wicksell's monetary theory (as well as his later monumental work on the race problem in the United States); and Ingvar Svennilson's microeconomic theory of the firm (as well as his subsequent empirical analysis of economic growth and structural change in Europe). I make this obvious point simply to emphasize that our judgment of the contributions to economics of this brilliant group of people should not be made solely on the claims, emanating mainly from Myrdal and Ohlin, that they anticipated Keynes's *General Theory,* but also on their achievements in other branches of economic analysis.

I basically agree with the judgment of Don Patinkin and Paul Samuelson that the contribution of the Stockholm School to "the Keynesian Revolution" was rather modest. First, the Stockholm economists of the 1930s did not really have a full-fledged theory of the determination of aggregate output and employment and of "transmission mechanisms" from product to labor markets. Second, although their policy recommendations were concerned with employment and unemployment, their *theories* placed a greater emphasis, in the manner of Knut Wicksell, on the determination of the price level.

451

Did the Swedish economists in the 1930s make any contributions at all to macroeconomic theory? Yes, they did. Erik Lindahl conducted a sophisticated discussion on the role of monetary policy, in particular in explaining the importance of interest rate expectations. He also emphasized the distinction between expected and unexpected policy changes and discussed the importance of *policy rules,* including monetary targets. But these contributions were more a "bridge" between the old classical and the "new classical" macrotheory than a forerunner to Keynes. Gunnar Myrdal's distinction between *ex ante* and *ex post* has, of course, clarified why the difference between saving and investment in the Keynesian model has explanatory power in macroeconomic analysis. Moreover, it is clear that discussion of macroeconomic problems by the Stockholm economists of the 1930s was conducted at a sophisticated level and had an undoubted Keynesian flavor.

The Stockholm School of the 1930s could perhaps be characterized as a sophisticated, on-going *seminar* in Keynesian macroeconomics and macroeconomic policy. In general, we may say that their contributions to policy issues were more profound than their achievements in pure theory. For instance, Gunnar Myrdal pursued an interesting policy discussion of various problems related to budget deficits and balance of payment problems for countries that tried to pursue an expansionary fiscal policy, and Bertil Ohlin conducted an interesting discussion of the role of public works programs and trade restrictions as tools of stabilization policy.

The main theoretical contribution to macroeconomics among Swedish economists in the 1930s was probably Erik Lundberg's *The Theory of Economic Expansion.* However, this achievement was *not* to anticipate Keynes, and Lundberg never asserted that it was. Instead he transformed a static Keynesian-type macrotheory into a business cycle model, emphasizing the interaction between multipliers and accelerators, in the context of a system of difference equations. Lundberg also embedded his theory into a growth context with productivity growth and capacity-enhancing effects of new investment. Thus, instead of being a forerunner to Keynes, Lundberg was rather a forerunner to Harrod's theory of economic growth and Samuelson's multiplier-accelerator model. What prevented Lundberg's contribution from becoming a standard element of macroeconomics was probably his unwillingness, or inability, to strip his model of "unnecessary complications," and to work out explicit solutions for the model, as was done later by Harrod-Domar and Samuelson, respectively.

The myth that the Swedes anticipated Keynes has probably been boosted by a second myth, namely, that Keynesian economics was *applied* by the Swedish government in the 1930s and that this policy pulled the Swedish economy out of the Great Depression. We know today (or should know) that the fiscal stimulus in Sweden during the 1930s was negligible. In an economy with unemployment rates of between 15 and 20 percent in 1933, the size of the fiscal expansion was about 0.5 percent of GDP. Indeed, this was more or less the same level of fiscal stimulus as undertaken by the Liberal-Conservative government in 1930–1, which was supposed to have acted according to "old-fashioned" non-Keynesian macrotheories.

What pulled the Swedish economy out of the depression was instead increased international demand for raw materials and semimanufactures, mainly from the forest industry. This expansion was further enhanced by the heavy devaluation of the Swedish crown in the first half of the 1930s, after Sweden abandoned the gold standard. Was it, then, a "clever" central bank, rather than Keynesian fiscal policy, that helped Sweden out of the depression? That is difficult to say. However, the generally accepted interpretation by Swedish economists of exchange rate policy at that time is that the determination of the exchange rate in 1931 was "accidental." The central bank just accepted the fall in the crown, dictated by market forces, of some 30 percent against currencies remaining on the gold standard in 1931. The lack of criteria for an "appropriate exchange rate," as the story goes, made the Central Bank fix the exchange rate at the level where the market happened to have put it.

Thus it would seem that *both* the claim that Swedish economists, all by themselves, developed Keynesian-type macroeconomic theories *and* the assertion that a Keynesian-type fiscal policy pulled Sweden out of the depression are based more on myths than realities. However, as emphasized at the beginning of my discussion, this does not contradict the view that there was an exceptionally brilliant group of economists in Sweden in the 1930s and that they made important contributions to various fields of economic analysis and economic policy discussions.

Don Patinkin

My answer to the question posed in this panel discussion is that the central message of the Stockholm School – its emphasis on expectations, its related basic distinction between *ex ante* and *ex post,* its corresponding emphasis on the dynamic adjustment process – was rapidly incorporated into Keynesian economics and continues to be an essential part of present-day macroeconomics.

Needless to say, the *General Theory* also assigns great importance to expectations, but it does not make use of the disappointment of expectations as the motive force of a dynamic process. Thus in Chapter 3 of the *General Theory,* Keynes (1936) defines the equilibrium level of employment (and hence national income) as that level which equates aggregate demand and supply. But nowhere in this chapter – nor indeed at any other point in the *General Theory* – does he explain the dynamic process that brings the economy to this position. Nor was such an explanation forthcoming in any of the major review articles that appeared in the years immediately following the book's publication [cf., e.g., Hicks's (1937) famous IS-LM interpretation]. In brief, the *General Theory* lacks a short-run stability analysis.

Though Ohlin's famous two-part 1937 article on the Stockholm School did not spell out the details of such an analysis, it did emphasize the lack of dynamic analysis in this book. Indeed, this was the last of the three points with which Ohlin summarized his criticism of the *General Theory* in the third and unpublished part of his article (Ohlin, 1981, p. 249). The dynamic analysis with which Ohlin then filled this lacuna was, of course, based on Myrdal's distinction between *ex ante* planning and *ex post* realization, applied (inter alia) to investment in inventories. Within a short time (and I do not know when it first appeared in the literature), these unplanned changes in inventories became the standard explanation of the market force that caused output to increase (or decrease) until aggregate supply was brought into equilibrium with aggregate demand. And this dynamic stability analysis was so thoroughly integrated into Keynesian economics that it lost its Swedish identity.

I might note that there were additional things that could have been learned from Ohlin's 1937 article. I have in mind particularly his emphasis on the fact that an individual's "planned consumption depend[s] . . . not [on] his expected income during the first coming period only, but on what he expects to earn over a long period in the future. . . . The consideration of income expectations for many future periods is, of course, the principal reason why people during depressions often consume much more than the income they expect or actually earn during the periods at the bottom of the depression" (Ohlin, 1937, pp. 98–9). Here is the notion that Friedman (1957) was twenty years later to develop – in a precise and operational manner – into the permanent-income hypothesis.

Why did the Stockholm School not have a more distinctive impact on the profession? I think that the main reason was that it did not provide a precise theory of how expectations were formed. [It is particularly appropriate at this conference in honor of Erik Lundberg to note that he pointed out this deficiency in his classic work (Lundberg, 1937, pp. 143, 172, 175–6).] Thus, the theoretical framework of the Stockholm School was one in which anything could happen, depending on the assumptions that were made about expectations. Correspondingly, it was not too useful a framework for policy purposes.

A corollary deficiency of the Stockholm School (which further decreased its policy usefulness) was that its basic analytical concept of *ex ante* decisions based on expectations did not readily lend itself to quantification. In any event, the Stockholm School itself did not attempt to quantify them. Indeed, I think that the first empirical estimate of expectations was not made until Phillip Cagan's (1956) use of what came to be known as the assumption of adaptive expectations to estimate the expected rate of inflation in his classic study of hyperinflation. This was in sharp contrast to the immediate use of the concurrent development of national-income estimation in the 1930s to quantify the basic analytical variables of Keynes's *General Theory*. This fruitful interaction between theory and measurement was undoubtedly a major factor in explaining the rapid and widespread acceptance of Keynesian economics, its practical application to policy problems, and its corresponding overshadowing of the teachings of the Stockholm School (cf. Patinkin, 1982, Chaps. 4 and 9).

David Laidler

One could discuss the relevance of the Stockholm School's work to modern economics from many viewpoints. In these remarks I shall concentrate on the importance for current macroeconomic research of two ideas that figured prominently in its contribution. I shall argue that a propensity to ignore one of them is leading to the uncritical acceptance, as macroeconomics rigorously derived from sound microfoundations, of some very shaky arguments; and that our overconfidence in having solved all the problems inherent in the other is leading to unwarranted smugness about the superior quality of much current work. The ideas in question concern, respectively, the measurability of capital and the rationality of expectations.

As I noted in my own contribution to this conference, Erik Lindahl and Gunnar Myrdal both understood quite clearly that, in a world of heterogeneous goods, it was, in general, impossible to define aggregate variables such as the capital stock and its rate of return independently of the structure of relative prices. That is why the Swedish economists gave up Austrian capital theory as a foundation for business cycle analysis. The problem here is an old one, descending as it does from Ricardo's (1821) discovery of the impossibility of explaining relative prices solely by the ratio of labor inputs in the presence of differing organic compositions of capital and a positive rate of profit; but it has also surfaced more recently in the so-called Cambridge Controversies about the existence of an aggregate production function. There is no need to rehearse this tortuous literature here.[1] It established rigorously only a little more than Lindahl and Myrdal knew in 1930, namely, that with heterogeneous goods and a positive interest rate, there is no way of defining an aggregate production function whose properties are independent of the structure of relative prices, except in the special case in which all the underlying micro-production functions display a common capital–labor ratio (organic composition of capital) for every possible structure of relative input prices.

The implication of this result is that the aggregate production function had better be used with great care in macroeconomic analysis. If the object of the exercise is to demonstrate, shall we say, the fragility of the "super-neutrality" of money, a growth model based on an aggregate production function may serve the purpose admirably. If super-neutrality breaks down easily (as it does) in so simple a theoretical case, it is unlikely to become suddenly robust in a more complicated environment. If instead, to carry on with the example, the purpose is to investigate and theoretically explain the extent of departures from super-neutrality in any actual economy, such a model emphatically will not do. It is of the essence of the absence of the super-neutrality that changes in the expected rate of monetary expansion change the real rate of interest, but such a change in any real-world economy must also involve changes in relative prices that destroy the stability of the weights used to aggregate capital and output. These effects in turn cause the observed relationships among aggregate output, capital, and labor to vary, not because of any techological change but simply because relative prices have altered, and feed back to our measure of the real rate of interest into the bargain.

Now this does not imply that super-neutrality cannot be investigated in a disaggregated framework; or that, when the rate of monetary expansion changes, the resulting structure of relative prices generated by the system will not include an intertemporal relative price that may be called the real rate of interest; or that, at the new set of relative prices, it is impossible to compute an index of the aggregate capital stock. It does imply, though, that to compare the new estimate of the capital stock with the initial one "as if" it represented simply a different quantity of the same durable input, and to compare the new real interest rate with the intitial one "as if" both measured ratios of a rate of flow to a stock of the same homogeneous product, are dubious excercises. Aggregation in empirical work requiring study of production functions does not lead to useful simplification but to results that have no theoretical interpretation. The problem here is not just that aggregate data are measured with error. The issue is at heart theoretical, not empirical, because *economic theory tells us that a well-defined aggregate production function cannot, except in extremely special cases, be derived from properly specified microfoundations.*

Now no one, as far as I know, is using neoclassical growth theory to study the super-neutrality, or otherwise, of money, but Kydland, Prescott, and their disciples are using just such a framework with an aggregate production function at its heart to investigate business cycle phenomena.[2] The arguments of the preceding paragraphs apply just as much to this work as to any other. So long as "real business cycle theory" confines itself to purely abstract excercises showing that shocks to technology can lead to cyclical phenomena, and to warning us that such phenomena might well represent a Pareto optimal response to such shocks, so that their stabilization by a well-meaning government would reduce economic welfare, it is making a useful contribution to macroeconomic thought. The moment it deploys an aggregate production function as the starting point of an empirical investigation of real-world business cycle behavior, it begins to deal with relationships among aggregate data that cannot be interpreted meaningfully with the aid of such a device.

Prescott (1986) has recently produced a paper whose principal finding is described as follows in his own abstract:

> ... the [Solow] growth model, which was developed to account for the secular patterns in important economic aggregates, displays the business cycle phenomena once it incorporates the observed randomness in the rate of technological advance. The amplitudes and serial correlation properties of fluctuations in output and employment that the growth model predicts match those historically experienced in the United States. Further, the model continues to display the growth facts it was developed to explain.

The title he has given that paper, "Theory Ahead of Business Cycle Measurement," suggests that he and his associates have lost sight of the difficulties involved in deriving the aggregate production function from microfoundations. This is a harsh criticism to make of a body of work whose basic methodological thrust is to ensure that all of its predictions are properly grounded in defensible microassumptions about tastes and technology, but it surely implies that at least one idea that played an important role in the analysis of the Stockholm School has retained its relevance over the years, and indeed needs to attract renewed attention.

As I also noted in my own paper for this conference, when the Stockholm School set aside Austrian capital theory, it also began to pay particular attention to expectational phenomena as important factors in the business cycle. Indeed, in Myrdal's work, and particularly in Lindahl's, notions to which we would nowadays give such labels as "rational expectations" and "the credibility of policy" play an important role. But though the Stockholm School developed such ideas, it did not know how to use them in business cycle modeling. The formal dynamic structures it developed, particularly those of Lundberg, no matter how great an analytic achievement they represented by contemporary standards (and the achievement was considerable), nowadays look "mechanical" and "ad hoc" to use two terms of abuse much favored by modern macroeconomists. The reason for this, of course, is that the technical apparatus developed in the 1970s by Robert Lucas and his associates has enabled the "rational expectations" idea to be incorporated into what amounts to the same dynamic general equilibrium framework from which the Stockholm School (and for that matter the Austrians too) started. The resulting formal model generates fluctuations that, in some respects, mimic those real-world fluctuations we term "the business cycle."

I do not wish for an instant to deny the importance of Lucas's intellectual achievement, but I would caution against treating a solution to the problem of incorporating rational expectations into business cycle theory as *the* solution. As McCallum (1986) in particular has noted, Lucas-style models have not stood up well to empirical evidence – that is one reason for the growth of interest in "real business cycle theory" among some of Lucas's erstwhile disciples. When one considers the technology surrounding the formation of expectations in those models, that is perhaps not surprising. Lucas's agents know the history of the economies they inhabit, and they understand their structure. What they lack are data on the current pattern of relative prices, but they have ready access to the technology needed to extract optimal estimates of that pattern from available data. In short, for Lucas, the marginal costs of information are either zero or the data simply are not available. To put it bluntly, though modern New-Classical business cycle theory has made a considerable advance by incorporating rational expectations, formed even in so simple an environment, into a formal general equilibrium model, we are not entitled to conclude that the problem of dealing with the role of expectations in the business cycle has been solved in any general sense.

Suppose information came at rising marginal cost and produced benefits of declining marginal value: how much of it would be utilized in decision making, relative to the amount that New-Classical theory assumes is used? Would this amount change over time, even given a constant technology for data gathering and processing? It might do so either because agents have memories, so that once they have learned something they have no need to do so again, or because they have finite lives and imperfect techniques for passing on what they know to their successors. But are these factors important? And if information is scarce, might not social institutions such as monetary exchange and fixed price contracts evolve to economize on its use? And what effects might their operation have on the course of the business cycle relative to that charted by Lucas's model? Such questions, and many others of the same genre, have been raised time and time again by critics of New-Classical economics.

The trouble is that, valuable and sensible though the insights underlying such questions might be, no one has succeeded in systematically putting them to work to produce a better model of cyclical fluctuations. This conclusion has an obvious moral: We have many more insights into questions about expectations than we know how to make use of. But so did the Stockholm School. Have we really moved as far beyond the intellectual frontiers they bequeathed us as we sometimes like to think?

Kumaraswamy Vellupillai

Not very recently Tord Palander, in his "methodological reflections on Myrdal's *Monetary Equilibrium*," observed perceptively (and almost timelessly!) that:

> A good deal has been written of recent years in England and America about "the Swedish Monetary School," or, as Ohlin prefers to call it, "The Stockholm School." The flattering attention which this school has drawn to itself seems, however, hardly to stand in any reasonable proportion to the degree of acquaintance with its characteristic features. The factual basis for judgement has been hidden in what are, for most of the English-speaking world, the somewhat mysterious depths of Swedish and German writing. (Palander, 1941, p. 5)

My own view has been that Palander's remarks apply even more forcefully now, almost a century after David Davidson's early work on "Taxation Norms," although *some* of the "mysterious depth of Swedish and German writing" have, in the past fifty years, surfaced in English translations. However, apart from Wicksell's *Interest and Prices* the major works have not been properly translated in their entirety or have not been translated at all (Lundberg's dissertation is an exception – indeed, it is not a translation).[3] To discuss, therefore, the relevance of the work of the Stockholm School for modern macro is not a fair game.

An urgent agenda, assuming its relevance, would be a plan for the systematic and complete translations of the interchange between Wicksell and Davidson on norms for price stabilization, Lindahl's famous monographs on "Ends and Means in Monetary Policy," Myrdal's dissertation and his memorandum on the "Economic Effects of Fiscal Policy," the dissertations by Dag Hammarskjöld, Alf Johansson, and Ingvar Svennilson, and even the early capital theoretic monographs by Gustav Åkerman. It is not fair to expect those afflicted with that peculiar and "attractive Anglo-Saxon kind of unnecessary originality" (Myrdal, 1939, pp. 8–9) to understand the relevance of works they are unable (perhaps unwilling) to read. I make this almost banal point simply because (not being an Anglo-Saxon!) I myself have been astonished, to say the least, at the topicality, freshness, and depth, in relation to modern macro, of the works by these Swedish masters.

To discuss, even in a cursory way, the relevance to modern macro of Swedish contributions means that there is an identifiable core of issues that span the broad spectrum of macroeconomics. I think it will be agreed that the following issues delineate some, if not most, of the frontiers of modern macroeconomics:

1. Neutrality propositions
2. Policy ineffectiveness
3. Dynamic inconsistency
4. Credibility in policy models
5. Business cycle theories
6. Ethical norms in taxation and the theory of the public finances
7. Monetary regimes
8. Methodology in economic theory

Macroeconomics in its classical connotations had been about the issues of justice, rationality, and dynamics. The macroeconomic framework that Wicksell pioneered was based precisely on this trinity of issues – just taxation, utilitarian underpinnings for rational behavior, and the demographic foundations of dynamics. These are the issues that the Lucasians have revitalized, although their dynamics is formal rather than the phenomenological dynamics of Wicksell. On the basis of the drive to study the intertwining relationships between justice, rationality, and dynamics, the New-Classical economists have been forced to reopen discussions about 1–8, and it is to their lasting credit that they have done so. These were precisely the issues that occupied the Swedes in the fifty years from David Davidson (1889) to Lindahl (1939).

The question, however, is whether there is anything to be learned in the Swedish approach – say, methodologically, theoretically, or empirically – given that the Lucasians tackle the same issues with a "theoretical technology" that is advanced by half a century!

I do not think an unequivocal answer is possible or even desirable. My own feeling is that there is much to be distilled from the vintage Swedish works. The Swedish approach to the eternal trinity of justice, rationality, and dynamics was within the framework of political arithmetics (cf. my contribution to this conference) and used a judicious mixture of induction and deduction. The Lucasians seem to claim that the only possible way to tackle the impossible triangle of justice, rationality, and dynamics is in the setting of a very special microeconomic theory.

At least in this important sense there is much of great relevance in what should be the "Swedish approach to modern macro."

Axel Leijonhufvud

By now other people have taken all the best bits, so let me run through a few things I had intended to say very rapidly.

First, a question that has come up repeatedly: Was there really a school? If the participants disputed it, how can we allege that there was? We can all agree that there was a group of extremely talented individuals, and it is always possible for us to go back and judge them all individually for their contributions and get a picture of their importance in that way. But, whether they wanted to emphasize it or not, it is also true that they had some things in common – some practical concerns in common, some intellectual influences in common – and that what they had in common was important enough for outsiders to be justified in treating them as a school. I think we can take that for granted.

Second, two questions have been raised here over and over again: Was the School successful? What remains of the Stockholm School? My overall feeling about the conference is that we have discussed these questions too much. I do not think we should be so concerned to decide whether the Stockholm School deserves a B, a B+, or an A−, or whatever. The point is not to grade people in this way. What remains? Well, the School appeared at a particular historical stage when there were schools here and there – in Austria, in Lausanne, at LSE, and so on–but they were all in the process of merging in what might loosely be called the "mainstream." Most of the participants were aware of that and aware of being part of this process and not really resistant to it. So it should not be surprising if the Stockholm School contributions have merged into that mainstream and are no longer so distinctly perceivable today.

But let me return to this concern with "success." There is one major issue that was touched on by Baumol that I would like to develop a bit further. Two months ago, at the History of Economics Society meetings at Harvard, Paul Samuelson referred to the "Whig" approach to history. I have serious reservations about it. Samuelson, I think, made himself rather a spokesman for it at the time, but the context was such that I did not know quite how seriously to take it. Today, however, he also said in passing, "Who cares what was in Keynes that was not in Keynesianism?" – which I take to be the sentiment of a Whig historian. It is a short step to "Who cares what was in the Stockholm School that was not in Keynes?" and next to "Who cares what was in Wicksell that was not in the later Stockholmians?" The line can be pursued until you end up with some similar rhetorical question about Adam Smith or, perhaps, Aristotle in an ongoing regress of trying to grade people as anticipators of later developments.

We obviously have different perceptions of what you are doing when you are doing intellectual history. And these preconceptions also differ depending on whether we are considering doing the history of economics or the history of a field like physics. In Paul Samuelson's session this afternoon, he brought up James Watson's book on the double helix and referred to Watson as "Honest Jim" because Watson owned up to his own feelings in the race to explain the structure of DNA. This reminds me that Peter Medawar put the title "Lucky Jim" on his review of *The Double Helix,* referring to the feeling on the part of many of Watson's competitors that he had been tremendously lucky in getting there first when so many other people were close. Medawar then went on to discuss the complaints that Watson had not given enough credit to his forerunners and other people who had come close. Medawar offered an interesting defense for Watson, arguing that it is natural for scientists not to be aware of the history of their field. In a passage that I have already quoted elsewhere, he wrote:

> A scientist's present thoughts and actions are of necessity shaped by what others have done and thought before him; they are the wave-front of a continuous secular process in which The Past does not have a dignified independent existence of its own. Scientific understanding is the integral of a curve of learning; science therefore in some sense comprehends its history within itself.

So that is a natural scientist's view. What does the "integral of a curve of learning . . ." and so on mean? It means, I take it, that if you understand the present state of the subject, you understand what was worth understanding of its past – so its history is of no interest except as a matter of idle curiosity. Now, should we look at economics as Medawar looks at the natural sciences or is economics different? Should we perhaps accord The Past a somewhat more dignified independence in economics?

Permit me to change Medawar's metaphor of the wave of knowledge to one that I like better for my purposes. I think of the history of economics as a decision tree. Economists make decisions. They choose assumptions, they choose approaches, they choose, in the end, what to believe about the real world, and so on. These choices are the forks of the decision tree. Now, if you are in a subject that possesses tremendously effective methods for always eliminating the false alternatives, then you get a tree with a very tall trunk – a California redwood or something like that – where all the false branches have fallen off and there are only a few green alternatives up there a tremendous distance from the ground. This is the way you would view a discipline in which, whenever you have a good question, you finally get an answer that kills the question, that is, kills it in the sense that all the alternative possibilities that once seemed plausible have become impossible so that the question is no longer interesting. Well, my conception of economics is that, rather than a redwood, it is some sort of untidy, ill-pruned bush with a lot of branches and with the sap still running in some rather unlikely places. This, I think, is of some importance for how you look at the past of a subject and for what you think you are doing when you go into the past.

For example, if you go back to Keynes, let us say, you are aware that between you and Keynes there are a lot of important names in macroeconomics that are important because they made significant decisions subsequent to Keynes, decisions not made by Keynes. There is Hicks and there is Samuelson and there is Tobin and so on – all of them marking forks in the decision tree between the big Keynesian Revolution fork and the twigs on which we little birds of today are twittering. And you should not imagine that Keynes anticipated all these later choices (and here I am echoing Patinkin's comment) when, for instance, he wrote a letter to John Hicks saying that he thought IS-LM really did fit what he had intended to convey, that he understood all the logical implications that were to be drawn from versions of that model.

The great works of economics are open, in a sense. If you want to learn something from reading the *General Theory* or from reading the Stockholm School, you should *not* read them in the light of subsequent choices made by other people, or grade them for being in accord or not being in accord with the state of economics at some later date. You are much more likely to get some benefit from it if you realize that the major works of the past had *alternative futures* at the time, alternatives that were later closed by the decisions of other writers or by the collective decisions of subsequent generations of theorists. This is particularly worth doing if you have come to conclude that some recent development has led into a cul-de-sac. Laidler argued during the conference, for example, that we now know what micro-founded macromodels with rational expectations look like and it is clear that they are too restrictive for many of the problems and phenomena we want to deal with. Well, we might then go back to the Stockholm School and, instead of being condescending about how loose and imprecise they were in their treatment of expectations, see the force in what they were trying to do.

I think there is lots of work left to be done on the Stockholm School. It is a measure of the success of this conference that, rather than closing the book on the School, it leaves us with more work to do on the Stockholm School. I, at least, have become aware of how much serious work remains to be done on the subject. We should hope that capable people take it on and that, when they do, they do not do the Whig history of the subject but instead try to unearth those alternative futures.

They are there to be found in the works of these Swedes. Some months ago, my friend Velupillai made me take a look at some of Lindahl's work in monetary theory from the 1920s. It looks tremendously modern in the light of rational expectations theory: The credibility problems are all there, the time inconsistency issue is there, the reputation of the central banks is there, the concept of monetary regime is there, and the rationale for having the regime clearly understood by the public is there. Moreover, it is forcefully put, as clearly written as anybody could ask, and perfectly modern in conception. My point is not that Lindahl, therefore, should be given a "good grade" by what happens to be today's standard. He should, but that is a Whig point to make. My point is that Lindahl's work was there for us to read ten, twenty, thirty, or forty years ago – before Lucas and Sargent–and could have been read with great profit by anyone wise enough to look for the alternative futures at the time.

Notes

1 Seminal contributions to these controversies include Robinson (1956), Sraffa (1960), and Samuelson (1962). Harcourt (1972) is the definitive survey, and

Sen (1974) covers the essential analysis with a welcome streak of good humor. Note also that Fisher (1969) deals with essentially the same set of issues.
2 The seminal article here is Kydland and Prescott (1982). See also Prescott (1986).
3 The other exception is Myrdal (1939).

References

Cagan, P. (1956), "The Monetary Dynamics of Hyperinflation," in Milton Friedman, ed., *Studies in the Quantity Theory of Money.* Chicago: University of Chicago Press, pp. 25–117.

Davidson, D. (1889), *Om beskattningsnormen vid inkomstskatten.* Uppsala: Lundequistska Bokhandel.

Fisher, F. M. (1969), "The Existence of Aggregate Production Functions," *Econometrica,* 37 (October), 553–77.

Friedman, M. (1957), *A Theory of the Consumption Function.* Princeton: Princeton University Press, for the National Bureau of Economic Research.

Harcourt, G. C. (1972), *Some Cambridge Controversies in the Theory of Capital.* Cambridge: Cambridge University Press.

Hicks, J. R. (1937), "Mr. Keynes and the 'Classics'; A Suggested Interpretation," *Econometrica,* 5 (April), 147–59.

Keynes, J. M. (1936), *The General Theory of Employment, Interest and Money.* London: Macmillan.

Kydland, F. E., and E. C. Prescott (1982), "Time to Build and Aggregate Fluctuations," *Econometrica,* 50 (September), 1345–70.

Lindahl, E. (1939), *Studies in the Theory of Money and Capital.* London: Allen and Unwin.

Lundberg, E. (1937), *Studies in the Theory of Economic Expansion.* London: P. S. King and Son.

McCallum, B. T. (1986), "On 'Real' and 'Sticky Price' Theories of the Business Cycle," *Journal of Money, Credit and Banking,* 18 (November), 397–414.

Myrdal, G. (1939), *Monetary Equilibrium.* London: Hodge.

Ohlin, B. (1937), "Some Notes on the Stockholm Theory of Saving and Investment," *Economic Journal* 47, Part I (March), 43–69, Part II (June), 221–40.

(1981), "Some Notes on the Stockholm Theory of Saving and Investment," posthumously edited by Otto Steiger, *History of Political Economy,* 13 (Summer), 239–59.

Palander, T. (1941), "Om 'Stockholmskolans' begrepp och metoder," *Ekonomisk Tidskrift,* No. 1. Translated as "On the Concepts and Methods of the 'Stockholm School,'" in *International Economic Papers,* No. 3, 1953, pp. 5–57.

Patinkin, D. (1982), *Anticipations of the General Theory? And Other Essays on Keynes.* Chicago: University of Chicago Press.

Prescott, E. C. (1986), "Theory ahead of Business Cycle Measurement," Federal Reserve Bank of Minneapolis, Research Department Staff Report 102 (mimeo).

Ricardo, D. (1821), *On the Principles of Political Economy and Taxation* (3rd ed.), London. (Reprinted as Vol. I of the *Works and Correspondence of David Ricardo* (ed. P. Sraffa), Cambridge: Cambridge University Press, for the Royal Economic Society, 1951.)

Robinson, J. V. (1956), *The Accumulation of Capital.* London: Macmillan.

Samuelson, P. A. (1962), "Parable and Realism in Capital Theory: the Surrogate Production Function," *Review of Economic Studies,* 29 (April), 193–206.

Sen, A. R. (1974), "On Some Debates in Capital Theory," *Economica,* 41 (August), 328–35.

Sraffa, P. (1960), *Production of Commodities by Means of Commodities.* Cambridge: Cambridge University Press.

The Stockholm School: A non-Swedish bibliography

compiled by KLAS FREGERT

Asimakopulos, A. (1983), "Anticipations of Keynes's *General Theory*," *Canadian Journal of Economics,* 16(3), August, 517–30.

Brems, Hans J. (1956), "Current Economic Thought in Europe: the Scandinavian Countries," *American Economic Review,* 46(2), May, 352–9.

(1978), "What Was New in Ohlin's 1933–34 Macroeconomics," *History of Political Economy,* 10(3), Fall, 398–412.

Bryce, R. B. (1938), Review of *Studies in the Theory of Economic Expansion* by Erik Lundberg, *Canadian Journal of Economics and Political Science,* 4(1), February, 118–22.

Caplan, Benjamin (1941), "Some Swedish Stepping Stones in Economic Theory: A Comment," *Canadian Journal of Economics and Political Science,* 7(4), November, 559–62.

Carlsson, Benny (1988), "Lindahl, Dynamics and Death," *Scandinavian Economic History Review,* 36(1), 76–86.

Ebeling, Richard M. (1981), "The Stockholm School of Economics: An Annotated Bibliography," *Austrian Economics Newsletter,* 3(2), Winter, 1–12.

Ellis, Howard (1940), Review of *Monetary Equilibrium* by Gunnar Myrdal, *Journal of Political Economy,* 48(3), June, 434–6.

Faxén, Karl-Olof (1957), *Monetary and Fiscal Policy under Uncertainty.* Uppsala: Almqvist & Wiksell.

Gustafsson, Bo (1973), "A Perennial of Doctrinal History – Keynes and the 'Stockholm School,'" *Economy and History,* 16, 114–28.

Hamilton, Carl (1979), "Expectations and the Stockholm School," *Scandinavian Journal of Economics,* 81(3), 434–9.

Hansen, Bent (1951), *A Study in the Theory of Inflation.* London: George Allen & Unwin.

(1981), "Unemployment, Keynes and the Stockholm School," *History of Political Economy,* 13(2), Summer, 256–77.

Hansson, Björn A. (1982), *The Stockholm School and the Development of the Dynamic Method.* London: Croom Helm.

Harrod, Roy F. (1950), Review of *The Problem of Employment Stabilization* by Bertil Ohlin, *Economic Journal,* 60(239), September, 552–6.

Hart, Albert (1940), Review of *Studies in the Theory of Money and Capital* by Erik Lindahl, *American Economic Review,* 30(3), September, 584–5.

Hawtrey, R. G. (1937), "Alternative Theories of the Rate of Interest III," *Economic Journal,* 47(187), September, 436–43.

Hayek, Friedrich (1940), Review of *Studies in the Theory of Money and Capital* by Erik Lindahl, *Economica,* 7(27) n.s., August, 332–3.

Heckscher, Eli (1953), "A Survey of Economic Thought in Sweden, 1875–1950," *Scandinavian Economic History Review,* 1(2), 105–26.

Hicks, John (1934), Review of *Monetary Equilibrium* by Gunnar Myrdal, *Economica,* 1(4) n.s., November, 479–83. Reprinted in J. Hicks, *Collected Essays on Economic Theory,* Vol. 2: *Money, Interest and Wages.* Oxford: Basil Blackwell, 1982, pp. 42–5.

  (1956), "Methods in Dynamic Analysis," in *25 Economic Essays in Honour of Erik Lindahl.* Stockholm: Svenska Tryckeriaktiebolaget. Reprinted in J. Hicks, *Collected Essays on Economic Theory,* Vol. 2: *Money, Interest and Wages.* Oxford: Basil Blackwell, 1982, 217–35.

  (1973), "Recollections and Documents," *Economica,* 40(157) n.s., February, 2–11.

Iwai, Katsuhito (1981), *Disequilibrium Dynamics. A Theoretical Analysis of Inflation and Unemployment.* New Haven and London: Yale University Press.

Jonung, Lars (1987), "The Stockholm School after Fifty Years: A Conversation with Lars Jonung," *Eastern Economic Journal,* 13(2), June, 93–7.

Kahn, Richard (1938), Review of *Studies in the Theory of Economic Expansion* by Erik Lundberg, *Economic Journal,* 48(190), June, 265–8.

Keynes, John M. (1937), "Alternative Theories of the Rate of Interest," *Economic Journal,* 47(186), September, 241–52.

  (1937), "The 'Ex-Ante' Theory of the Rate of Interest," *Economic Journal,* 47(188), December, 663–9.

Kregel, J. A. (1977), "On the Existence of Expectations in English Neoclassical Economics," *Journal of Economic Literature,* 15(2), June, 495–500.

Landgren, Karl-Gustav (1957), *Economics in Sweden.* Washington, D.C.: Library of Congress.

Lange, Oskar (1938), Review of *Studies in the Theory of Economic Expansion* by Erik Lundberg, *Economica,* 5(18) n.s., May, 243–7.

Lerner, Abba (1939), "Ex-ante Analysis and Wage Theory," *Economica,* 6(24) n.s., November, 436–49.

  (1940), "Some Swedish Stepping Stones in Economic Theory." Review of *Monetary Equilibrium* by Gunnar Myrdal, and *Studies in the Theory of Money and Capital by* Erik Lindahl, *Canadian Journal of Economics and Political Science,* 6(4), November, 574–91.

Lindahl, Erik (1929), Review of *Prisbildningsproblemet och föränderligheten* (The problem of price formation and change) by Gunnar Myrdal, Almqvist & Wiksell, 1927, *Economic Journal,* 39(153), March, 89–91.

  (1934), "A Note on the Dynamic Pricing Problem." Reprinted in Steiger (1971) and in Keynes, *Collected Works,* Vol. 29, London: Macmillan, 1979.

(1939), *Studies in the Theory of Money and Capital.* London: George Allen & Unwin.

(1954), "On Keynes' Economic System – Part One," *Economic Record,* 30(58), May, 19–32.

(1954), "On Keynes' Economic System – Part Two," *Economic Record,* 30(59), November, 159–71.

Lundberg, Erik (1937), *Studies in the Theory of Economic Expansion.* Stockholm Economic Studies, No. 6. Reprinted by Kelley & Millman, New York, 1955.

(1985), "The Rise and Fall of the Swedish Model," *Journal of Economic Literature,* 23(1), March, 1–36.

Marschak, Jacob (1941), Review of *Monetary Equilibrium* by Gunnar Myrdal, *Social Research,* 8(3), November, 469–78.

Meade, James E. (1950), Review of *The Problem of Employment Stabilization* by Bertil Ohlin, *Economica,* 17(67), August, 328–30.

Merlin, Sidney D. (1949), *The Theory of Economic Fluctuations in Current Economic Thought.* New York: Columbia University Press.

Milgate, Murray (1979), "On the Origin of the Notion of Intertemporal Equilibrium," *Economica,* 46(181) n.s., February, 1–10.

Myrdal, Gunnar (1933), "Der Gleichgewichtsbegriff als Instrument in der geldtheoretischen Analyse," in F. Hayek, ed., *Beiträge zur Geldtheorie.* Vienna: Julius Springer.

(1939), *Monetary Equilibrium.* London: William Hodge & Co. Reprinted by Kelley, New York, 1965.

(1958), "Postscript," in Myrdal, *Value in Social Theory.* London: Routledge & Kegan Paul.

Neisser, Hans (1938), Review of *Studies in the Theory of Economic Expansion* by Erik Lundberg, *Journal of Political Economy,* 46(2), April, 253–6.

(1941), Review of *Studies in the Theory of Money and Capital* by Erik Lindahl, *Journal of Political Economy,* 49(3), June, 451–3.

(1941), Review of *Monetary Equilibrium* by Gunnar Myrdal, *Social Research,* 8(3), November, 454–68.

Ohlin, Bertil (1931), *The Course and Phases of World Depression.* Geneva: League of Nations

(1932), "Ungelöste Probleme der gegenwärtigen Krises." *Weltwirtschaftliches Archiv,* 36, Band(1932 II), 1–23.

(1932), "Now or Never. Action to Combat World Depression," *Svenska Handelsbankens Index,* 77(7), May.

(1933), "A Note on Price Theory with Special Reference to Interdependence and Time," in *Economic Essays in Honour of Gustav Cassel.* London: George Allen & Unwin.

(1933), "On the Formulation of Monetary Theory." A translation by Hans J. Brems and William P. Yohe, *History of Political Economy,* 10(3), Fall, 1978, 353–88.

(1937), "Some Notes on the Stockholm Theory of Savings and Investment – I," *Economic Journal,* 47(185), March, 53–69.

(1937), "Some Notes on the Stockholm Theory of Savings and Investment – II," *Economic Journal,* 47(186), June, 221–40.

(1937), "Alternative Theories of the Rate of Interest I," *Economic Journal* 47(187), September, 423–27.

(1937), "Employment Stabilization and Price Stabilization," in A. D. Gayer, ed., *The Lessons of Monetary Experience. Essays in Honor of Irving Fisher.* London: George Allen & Unwin Ltd., pp. 318–38.

(1949), *The Problem of Employment Stabilization.* New York: Columbia University Press.

(1960), "The Stockholm School versus the Quantity Theory," *International Economic Papers,* No. 10, 132–46. A translation from *Ekonomisk Tidskrift,* 45(1), 1943.

(1974), "On the Slow Development of the 'Total Demand Idea' in Economic Theory – Reflections in Connection with Dr. Oppenheimer's Note," *Journal of Economic Literature,* 12(3), September, 888–96.

(1977), "Some Comments on Keynesianism and the Swedish School before 1935," in Don Patinkin and J. C. Leith, eds., *Keynes, Cambridge and "The General Theory."* London: Macmillan.

(1978), "Keynesian Economics and the Stockholm School – Comment on Don Patinkin's Paper," *Scandinavian Journal of Economics,* 80(2), 144–7.

(1981), "Stockholm and Cambridge – Four Papers on the Monetary and Employment Theory of the 1930s." Edited with introduction and comments by O. Steiger, *History of Political Economy,* 13(2), Summer, 189–255.

Palander, Tord (1953), "On the Concepts and Methods of the 'Stockholm School.' Some Methodological Reflections on Myrdal's *Monetary Equilibrium,*" *International Economic Papers,* No. 3, 1953, 5–57. A translation from *Ekonomisk Tidskrift,* 43(1), 1941.

Patinkin, Don (1978), "Some Observations on Ohlin's 1933 Article," *History of Political Economy,* 10(3), Fall, 413–19.

(1978), "The Relation between Keynesian Economics and the Stockholm School," *Scandinavian Journal of Economics,* 80(2), 135–43.

(1982), *Anticipations of the General Theory? And Other Essays on Keynes.* Chicago: The University of Chicago Press.

(1983), "Multiple Discoveries and the Central Message," *American Journal of Sociology,* 89(2), September, 306–23.

Robertson, Dennis H. (1937), "Alternative Theories of the Rate of Interest II," *Economic Journal,* 47(187), September, 428–36.

Robinson, Joan (1939), Review of *Monetary Equilibrium* by Gunnar Myrdal, *Economic Journal,* 49(195), September, 493–5.

Saffran, B. (1983), Review of *The Stockholm School and the Development of the Dynamic Method* by Björn A. Hansson, *Journal of Economic Literature,* 21(4), December, 1502–4.

Samuelson, Paul (1940), Review of *Monetary Equilibrium* by Gunnar Myrdal, *American Economic Review,* 30(1), March, 129–30.

Shackle, G. L. S. (1940), Review of *Studies in the Theory of Money and Capital* by Erik Lindahl, *Economic Journal*, 50(197), March, 103–5.

(1945), Review of *Monetary Equilibrium* by Gunnar Myrdal, *Oxford Economic Papers*, No. 7, March, 47–66.

(1967), *The Years of High Theory: Invention and Tradition in Economic Thought*. Cambridge: Cambridge University Press.

Siven, Claes-Henrik (1985), "The End of the Stockholm School," *Scandinavian Journal of Economics*, 87(4), 577–93.

Steiger, Otto (1971), *Studien zur Entstehung der Neuen Wirtschaftslehre in Schweden. Eine Anti-Kritik*. Berlin: Duncker & Humblot.

(1976), "Bertil Ohlin and the Origins of the Keynesian Revolution," *History of Political Economy*, 8(3), Fall, 341–66.

(1978), "Substantive Changes in the Final Version of Ohlin's 1933 Paper," *History of Political Economy*, 10(3), Fall, 389–97.

(1978), "Prelude to the Theory of a Monetary Economy: Origins and Significance of Ohlin's 1933 Approach to Monetary Theory," *History of Political Economy*, 10(3), Fall, 420–46.

(1981), "Bertil Ohlin, 1899–1979," *History of Political Economy*, 13(2), Summer, 179–88.

(1984), Review of *The Stockholm School and the Development of the Dynamic Method* by Björn A. Hansson, *Economic Journal*, 94, March, 196–8.

Tarshis, Lorie (1950), Review of *The Problem of Employment Stabilization* by Bertil Ohlin, *Journal of Political Economy*, 58(4), August, 359–60.

Thomas, Brinley (1936), *Monetary Policy and Crises: A Study of Swedish Experience*. London: George Routledge and Sons.

Uhr, Carl G. (1973), "The Emergence of the New Economics in Sweden – Review of a Study by O. Steiger," *History of Political Economy*, 5(1), Spring, 243–60.

(1977), "Economists and Policy Making 1930–1936, Sweden's Experience," *History of Political Economy*, 9(1), Spring, 89–121.

(1983), Review of *The Stockholm School and the Development of the Dynamic Method* by Björn A. Hansson, *Southern Economic Journal*, 50(1), July, 309–12.

Velupillai, K. (1988), "Some Swedish Stepping Stones to Modern Macroeconomics," *Eastern Economic Journal*, 14(1), January, 87–98.

Winch, Donald (1966), "The Keynesian Revolution in Sweden," *Journal of Political Economy*, 74(2), April, 168–76.

Yohe, William P. (1959), "An Analysis of Professor Lindahl's Sequence Model," *L'industria*, No. 2, 3–12.

(1962), "A Note on Some Lesser-Known Works of Erik Lindahl," *Canadian Journal of Economics and Political Science*, 28(2), May, 274–80.

(1978), "Ohlin's 1933 Reformation of Monetary Theory," *History of Political Economy*, 10(3), Fall, 447–53.